AUTOCOURSE

The World's Leading Grand Prix Annual

HAZLETON PUBLISHING

SUDDENLY

WEEKENDS

ARE A BLUR

AGAIN.

Ah, the excitement, the thrill,
the uninhibited freedom of yesterday.
(Not to mention tomorrow, the day after,
and the day after that.)

Call 0800 70 80 60 for details of your nearest dealer or visit www.jaguar.com

JAGUAR

THE ART *of* PERFORMANCE

1220

contents

AUTOCOURSE 1999-2000

is published by
Hazleton Publishing Ltd,
3 Richmond Hill,
Richmond, Surrey
TW10 6RE.

Colour reproduction by
Barrett Berkeley Ltd, London.

Printed in England by
Butler and Tanner Ltd,
Frome, Somerset.

ISBN: 1-874557-34-9

DISTRIBUTORS

UNITED KINGDOM
Biblios Ltd
Star Road
Partridge Green
West Sussex RH13 8LD
Telephone: 01403 710971
Fax: 01403 711143

NORTH AMERICA
Motorbooks International
PO Box 1
729 Prospect Ave.
Osceola
Wisconsin 54020, USA
Telephone: (1) 715 294 3345
Fax: (1) 715 294 4448

NEW ZEALAND
David Bateman Ltd
PO Box 100-242
North Shore Mail Centre
Auckland 1330
Telephone: (64) 9 415 7664
Fax: (64) 9 415 8892

REST OF THE WORLD
Menoshire Ltd
Unit 13
Wadsworth Road
Perivale
Middlesex UB6 7LQ
Telephone: 020 8566 7344
Fax: 020 8991 2439

Dust-jacket photograph:
World Champion Mika Häkkinen

Title page photograph:
Mika Salo
Both photographs by Paul-Henri Cahier

acknowledgements

The Editor of AUTOCOURSE wishes to thank the following for their assistance in compiling the 1999–2000 edition: **France:** ACO, Fédération Française du Sport Automobile, FIA (Bernie Ecclestone, Max Mosley, Francesco Longanesi-Cattani, Claus E. Kramer, Charlie Whiting, Herbie Blash and Pat Behar); Peugeot Sport (Jean-Claude Lefebvre), Prost F1 (Alain Prost, Alan Jenkins, Sophie Sicot and Marie-Pierre Dupasquier), Supertec; **Germany:** Formul 3 Vereinigung, Mercedes-Benz (Norbert Haug, Wolfgang Schattling and Xander Heijnen); **Great Britain:** Arrows (Tom Walkinshaw, Daniele Audetto, Ann Bradshaw, Christine Goreham and Mike Coughlan); *Autocar*, John Barnard; British American Racing (Craig Pollock, Adrian Reynard, Rick Gorne, Malcolm Oastler and Robert Synge), Martin Brundle, Timothy Collings, Bob Constanduros, Cosworth Engineering, Steve Cropley, Ford (Neil Ressler, Martin Whitaker and Ellen Kolby), Peter Foubster, Mike Greasley, Maurice Hamilton, Brian Hart, Jane Brace, Nick Henry, Ian Hutchinson, Ilmor Engineering (Mario Illien), Jordan Grand Prix (Eddie Jordan, Ian Phillips, Giselle Davies, Mike Gascoyne and Lindsay Haylett), McLaren International (Ron Dennis, Adrian Newey, Martin Whitmarsh, Justine Blake, Anna Guerrier, Neil Oatley, Steve Hallam, Peter Stayner and Stuart Wingham), Stan Piecha, Silverstone Circuits, Eric Silberman, Stewart Grand Prix (Jackie and Paul Stewart, Gary Anderson and Cameron Kellaher); Simon Taylor; Murray Walker; Professor Sid Watkins; Williams Grand Prix Engineering (Patrick Head, James Robinson, Dickie Stanford, Lindsay Morle, Silvia Frangipani and Frank Williams); **Italy:** Benetton Formula (Rocco Benetton, Pat Symonds, Nick Wirth, David Warren, Andrea Ficarelli and Julia Horden); Commissione Sportiva Automobilistica Italiana; Scuderia Ferrari (Ross Brawn, Claudio Berro, Antonio Ghini, Stefania Bocci, Jean Todt and Tim Watson); Minardi Team (Giancarlo Minardi and Stefania Torelli); **Japan:** Bridgestone (Hirode Hamashima and Jane Parisi de Lima); **Switzerland:** Peter Sauber; **USA:** CART, Daytona International Speedway; Indianapolis Motor Speedway, Indy Lights, NASCAR, Roger Penske, SportsCar.

photographs published in AUTOCOURSE 1999–2000 have been contributed by:

Allsport UK/Michael Cooper/Clive Mason/Dave Rogers/Mark Thompson, *BMW*, Bothwell Photographic, Michael C. Brown, Diana Burnett, Paul-Henri Cahier, Dave Cundy, Steve Etherington/*EPI*, Bruce Grant-Braham, Lukas Gorys, *GP Photo*/Peter Nygaard, Nigel Kinrade, *LAT Photographic*/Lorenzo Bellanca, Gary Hawkins, Gavin Lawrence, Pamela Lauesen/*FOSA*, Brandon Malone/*Action Images*, Michael Roberts, Matthias Schneider, *Shutterspeed Photografik*, Nigel Snowdon, *Sporting Pictures (UK) Ltd*, Bryn Williams, Kaz Winiemko.

publisher
RICHARD POULTER

editor
ALAN HENRY

managing editor
ROBERT YARHAM

art editor
STEVE SMALL

production manager
STEVEN PALMER

publishing development manager
SIMON MAURICE

business development manager
SIMON SANDERSON

sales promotion
CLARE KRISTENSEN

results and statistics
DAVID HAYHOE
NICK HENRY

f1 illustrations
IAN HUTCHINSON
NICOLA FOX

chief contributing photographers
ALLSPORT
PAUL-HENRI CAHIER
MICHAEL ROBERTS
MATTHIAS SCHNEIDER
BRYN WILLIAMS

Nigel Snowdon

foreword
by Mika Häkkinen

IT was with a huge sense of relief, both for myself and the West McLaren Mercedes team, that I clinched my second straight World Championship title with that memorable victory in the Japanese Grand Prix at Suzuka. All race victories are important, and I am always reminded by my friend Ron Dennis that World Championships are achieved by the sum total of results from a full season's races, but this win was particularly sweet because we were coming from behind in the points table and got the job done.

In many ways, the strains and stresses of attempting to win a second World Championship are more intense than doing it first time round. We certainly had our ups and downs this season but I would like to thank everybody in the team and, once again, my wife Erja for her unstinting enthusiasm and support.

Twelve months ago when I wrote this foreword for AUTOCOURSE I speculated that I might be back again this year to do it again. So it has turned out. I won't be bold enough to make any predictions for next season, but you can rest assured that I will be giving it 100 per cent as usual!

GRAND Prix racing moved from the sports to the financial pages of the daily newspapers for much of the 1999 season as its commercial dimension changed up yet one more gear on the back of seemingly insatiable growth in global television coverage.

As F1 Commercial Rights Holder Bernie Ecclestone spent much of the season streamlining his F1 Holdings empire in preparation for an eventual sale of 50 per cent of its value to Morgan Grenfell Private Equity, so the racing team owners and shareholders benefited from similar boosts to their wealth.

Arrows had already struck a deal with Morgan Grenfell, while Jordan followed their example by selling a stake to Warburg Pincus and Jackie and Paul Stewart trumped them both by selling their team lock, stock and barrel to the Ford Motor Company for a figure variously speculated as being between 60 and 90 million dollars.

Over at McLaren, the TAG McLaren group negotiated a sale of 40 per cent of its equity to DaimlerChrysler, owners of its F1 engine supplier Mercedes-Benz. Meanwhile BMW, while stopping short of taking a stake in Williams, slipped into the British team's commercial driving seat with a deal which will see the team entered as BMW-Williams when the famous Munich company formally commences its five-year partnership with the team at the start of next season.

Of course, even before the start of the year, British American Tobacco had already bought a share in the all-new British American Racing team which began the year with lavish equipment and high hopes. Yet if ever there was a demonstration of the truism that success in Grand Prix racing cannot be hurried – and that all the finance in the world cannot speed up the process of making an F1 organisational infrastructure gel ahead of its time – then it was the Brackley-based team which failed to score a single point during its freshman year.

Despite this, the good times were rolling in F1 during the 1999 season. The sport was simply awash with cash and conspicuous consumption was the hallmark, with as much effort and expense being directed towards one-upmanship in the paddock motorhome stakes as success out on the circuit.

Yet this was an absolutely crucial factor within the sport's continued development. The sort of people bankrolling F1's ambitious future were not the sort who would have taken to the muddy spectator areas and gravel-strewn paddocks which were *de rigeur* barely a decade ago. If you are a Prime Minister or President of global corporation, investing in a Grand Prix race or racing team respectively, the last thing you want to do is get a speck of mud on your hand-made shoes.

To the reader, the foregoing paragraphs may seem, at first glance, as a classic case of putting the cart before the horse. So the rich got richer, I hear you say. But what about the racing?

Ah yes, I was coming to that. The answer would have to be that, taken over the year as a whole, it was of an encouragingly good standard. Even if all the old caveats applied.

Overtaking remained difficult away from the strategy of refuelling stops, the drivers initially moaned incessantly that the new four-groove front tyres made the cars almost impossible to drive and there is no doubt that a major aerodynamic re-think is required to

Sepang circuit at Kuala Lumpur. The original exclusion was for a dimensional infringement relating to the Ferrari F399 bargeboards, possibly the most controversial single decision of the year.

The reinstatement hung on an interpretation within the technical regulations on which Ferrari and the governing body remained in a small minority in the pit lane. On the one hand it was hard to believe that such a miniscule deviation from the rules could have offered any discernible performance increment, but on the other it seemed as though Ferrari acknowledged its inadvertent rule breach in Malaysia, only to pursue the appeal the following week.

It was an episode which fuelled the well-established mutual sense of antipathy which exists between McLaren and Ferrari, as well as casting a worrying shadow over how certain of the technical regulations may be interpreted in the future.

Elsewhere on the F1 landscape, Jordan came of age with a magnificent run to third place in the constructors' championship followed by the Stewart-Ford squad which beat Williams to fourth place. It was also a season which saw Damon Hill shuffle off the F1 stage after a depressing slump in his personal performances, while double CART champion Alex Zanardi failed to come to terms with an F1 return for Williams, a bewildering development which must necessarily cast reservations on the quality of the US series as a training ground for future F1 stars.

That said, the CART series produced another season rich in variety and close racing. Colombian Juan Montoya just won the championship for the Ganassi team – its fourth on the trot – but Britain's Dario Franchitti equalled him on points with his Team KOOL Green Reynard-Honda.

Tragically, the season was overshadowed by the deaths of rookie Gonzalo Rodriguez at Laguna Seca and established star Greg Moore, the latter in a horrifying high-speed accident in the final race of the season at the Fontana speedway in California, a disaster which left many observers wondering uncomfortably if high-banked superspeedways were really the sort of facility that promoters should be building in the 1990s.

The prospect of a rapprochement between CART and IRL seems as far away as ever, Indianapolis now looking forward to hosting the first US Grand Prix in a decade as a major consolation prize which more than compensates for the reduced status of the Indy 500. Talking of the US scene, it is well worth noting that NASCAR stock saloon racing continues to flourish as never before and is now the sole major preserve of Goodyear tyre support now that Akron has followed up its withdrawal from F1 with a similar hurried retreat from CART and the IRL.

As far as sports cars were concerned, BMW came away with the jewel in the crown by winning Le Mans, Audi produced an encouraging performance and Mercedes-Benz had a disastrous time it would undoubtedly prefer to forget with no fewer than three of its CLRs doing backward flips during the course of the weekend. One doubts if Mercedes will ever return to the Sarthe circuit in the foreseeable future.

For all this, the most worrying aspect implicit in the 1999 FIA Formula 1 World Championship season is 'what happens after Bernie?' The man whose vision and commercial perspicacity has taken Grand Prix racing to its current stratospheric levels of wealth and popularity showed the first intimations of mortality.

Despite his 69th birthday looming with all the inevitability of a McLaren lapping a Minardi, Bernie sailed through a heart-bypass operation during the summer. Even so, by all accounts, he ought to be taking things a little easier. With his companies now poised for that possible full stock exchange flotation over the next couple of years, Mr E. may soon choose to take a back seat and leave us with a corporate entity in place of an iron dictatorship.

Many believe that this will work better, but I frankly doubt it. F1 has traditionally been a sport which responds quite well to a firm hand, a view which has been reflected in the upper echelons of its governing body by successive FIA Presidents Jean-Marie Balestre and Max Mosley, albeit in different styles. Many insiders feel that nothing would ever get done or decided if the level of debate required to finalise the text of the current Concorde agreement was applied to the sport's day-to-day administration.

Making a smooth transition to Life After Bernie remains Grand Prix motor racing's single most challenging task over the next few years. How well it manages that sea change will largely determine how long it can sustain its position bestriding the global horizon as the sporting goose which continues to lay the commercially irresistible golden egg.

Alan Henry,
Tillingham, Essex
November, 1999

enable F1 machinery to run as close as Champ cars regularly manage to do, although a combination of stubbornness and the 'not-invented-here' syndrome prevents the FIA and teams agreeing to take a wider overview of what is necessary to make the changes.

More than ever, the 1999 season again emphasised that there are two drivers and two teams at the very pinnacle of F1 achievement. These are of course, Michael Schumacher with Ferrari and Mika Häkkinen with McLaren-Mercedes. Schumacher missed seven races after breaking his leg at Silverstone but returned, better than ever, before the end of the season.

You might have been forgiven for thinking that the absence of the German ace would leave Häkkinen facing a cakewalk towards his second straight title. Not a bit of it. A combination of mechanical malfunctions, driver errors and questionable strategies saw McLaren drop the constructors' title into Ferrari's waiting arms before Häkkinen reversed a distinctly uncertain spell of results to clinch the drivers' title with a brilliant end of season win in Japan.

Bullet-proof mechanical reliability on the part of the Ferrari team enabled Eddie Irvine to consolidate his own personal challenge for the championship during Schumacher's absence. By any standards, his was a game effort which showed the Ulsterman to have higher standards of focus and consistency than several of his key rivals. In the end, he was a gallant loser by just two points.

In amassing those points, Irvine was the beneficiary of an FIA Court of Appeal decision to reinstate him and Michael Schumacher to their 1–2 victory in the first Malaysian Grand Prix to be held on the impressive new

Is it possible to build cars without seeking direct competition? Not for us: Almost immediately after the first BMW on four wheels saw the light of day, we started racing. And we came out on top right from the start, winning the 1929 Alpine Trophy. Competition has always been an incentive in car production for innovations in technology, new concepts and new solutions. This has created benefits for cars the world over – and for BMW cars in particular. For we see participation in motorsport as a driving force for development. Nowhere else do we learn as much about dynamic, high-performance cars as on the race track.

This is where we meet competitors and make comparisons time and again – as here in France on the Paul Ricard Circuit in 1971. Many of these comparisons have turned out in our favour. This not only makes us feel good, but also confirms that through experiences we seem to get things right.

Progress is our objective. This is why, in returning to Formula 1, we will focus consistently on our own know-how and experience. The engines for the BMW WilliamsF1 team are being developed and built in Munich. So that while we are probably taking a more difficult path to success than other teams, we are definitely showing a greater commitment. And this, we believe, is what really counts.

We tend to meet from time to time.

And the next time will be in Melbourne – on 12 March 2000.

AUTOCOURSE
50 YEARS OF WORLD CHAMPIONSHIP
GRAND PRIX MOTOR RACING

ALAN HENRY

AUTOCOURSE – The definitive book of Formula 1 Grand Prix racing brings you the definitive history of 50 years of the FIA Drivers' World Championship.

The 1999 Formula 1 season was the fiftieth since the creation of the FIA Drivers' World Championship in 1950. Since the first race was held on a former wartime airfield at Silverstone in 1950, Grand Prix motor racing has evolved in spectacular fashion, developing from a minority sport followed by a small number of dedicated enthusiasts into the biggest sporting spectacular in the world.

Although the book will be broadly chronological, it will not attempt to give a blow-by-blow account of the races of the last 50 years. Instead our aim is to capture the flavour of each period and identify the trends and technical developments that characterise it.

There will be plenty of feature material, in the form of sidebars, profiling the leading figures (team owners, drivers, designers, etc.) and the leading marques, as well as the most famous circuits. There will also be discussion of technical trends, as it has generally been technical innovations that have determined the outcome of the races, and an examination of the way the organisation and finances of Grand Prix racing have evolved.

AUTOCOURSE was founded in 1951 but this history will not attempt to condense the contents of 49 editions of the annual into a single volume. It will, however, draw on AUTOCOURSE to help create a feel for the period, with extracts from features and interviews.

A comprehensive section of results and statistics covering the last 50 years complete this eagerly-awaited volume making it a valuable source of reference.

Specifications:
● ●
336 pages • 312 x 232 mm upright • over 280 photos • Hardback with dust-jacket • Available Mid-February 2000 • Order Code: H780
Retail Price: £40.00 Post & Packing Free on UK deliveries

To reserve your copy or for more information, please contact: Hazleton Publishing Ltd, 3 Richmond Hill, Richmond, Surrey TW10 6RE England. Tel: +44 020 8948 5151 ~ Fax: +44 020 8948 4111. The standard edition will be available from bookshops and specialist motoring outlets from February 2000.

LEATHER-BOUND LIMITED EDITIONS

We are creating 250 leather-bound editions, dyed to British Racing Green, presented in their own high-quality board slip-case covered in cloth of the same colour. Both the leather bound edition and the slip case will have the title of the book and author embossed in gold leaf.

Each edition will have an additional page bound-in which will be individually numbered from 1 to 250.

Although the contents will not differ from the standard book, the leather-bound edition will have superior endpapers to further distinguish the craftsmanship involved.

We aim to have the leather-bound editions completed by the end of March 2000.

Price: £195.00 each plus £10.00 delivery.

To request an order form please call Hazleton Publishing direct on +44 020 8948 5151.

FIA FORMULA ONE
WORLD CHAMPIONSHIP 1999

top ten
drivers

Chosen by the
Editor, taking into
account their racing
performances and
the equipment at
their disposal

photography by
Matthias Schneider

heinz-harald
frentzen

1

Date of birth: 18 May 1967

Team: B&H Jordan Mugen Honda

Grand Prix starts in 1999: 16

World Championship placing: 3rd

Wins: 2; Poles: 1; Points: 54

ONE of the few front-line drivers who did not make a mistake under pressure during the course of a race in 1999, Heinz-Harald successfully reinvented himself in much the same way as Damon Hill managed at Williams three years before. Ironically, Williams had hired Frentzen to replace the British driver at the end of that title-winning campaign, yet two years later he would be summarily ejected from Sir Frank's famous F1 squad.

As a parting shot, Williams technical director Patrick Head admitted that there was no shortage of talent lurking within Heinz-Harald's persona, merely a problem with its application. It was a perceptive remark from a senior figure in a team not renowned for throwing psychological lifelines to drivers whose confidence is wobbling.

The Williams team verdict was both right and wrong. A change of teams proved that Eddie Jordan's judgement that there were still a good few races left in Frentzen proved to be something of a masterly understatement. Once installed at the wheel of a Jordan-Mugen Honda 199, he proved the revelation of the year, blending a cool approach to the task in hand with an increasing capacity to remain unflustered under the most intense pressure his rivals could offer.

Frentzen is outwardly mild-mannered and easy-going. Yet he is also perceptive, strong-willed and prepared to be stubborn in order to get his way. At Nürburgring, during qualifying for the European Grand Prix, he argued strenuously with his pit crew in favour of not going out early in the session.

In his view, the track surface was going to dry out quickly. Voices were raised in a frank exchange of views. But Heinz would not budge from his plan of campaign. Later, after confidently taking pole position, he apologised sweetly for getting a little excited about the whole affair.

Frentzen's drive in the opening stages at Nürburgring was possibly his best performance of the year as he fended off both McLaren drivers right up to his refuelling stop, only to retire with electrical problems as he accelerated back into the race ahead of Coulthard.

It was a huge disappointment, coming as it did only a fortnight after he'd added his Monza victory to his win early in the year at Magny-Cours. But for the intervention of the FIA Court of Appeal, Frentzen would have gone to Suzuka aiming to take second place in the championship. Many reckoned the pleasant Jordan driver deserved that and more.

Date of birth: 28 September 1968

Team: West McLaren Mercedes

Grand Prix starts in 1999: 16

World Championship placing: 1st

Wins: 5; Poles: 11; Points: 76

MIKA Häkkinen claimed de facto Number One status in the McLaren Mercedes team by virtue of the fact that he was the reigning World Champion and his sheer speed was underlined by the fact that he qualified on pole position in no fewer than 11 out of 16 races of the season.

Having won the Championship in 1998, the pleasant Finnish driver picked up at the start of the new season as he meant to go on. In command. He won three out of the first six races, but punctuated this early section of the season with a rare error which saw him crash out of the San Marino Grand Prix at Imola. This was followed by a very disappointing run to third place at Monaco followed by commanding performances at both Barcelona and Montreal.

Then came McLaren's mid-season slump and a succession of irritating problems, by far the most tiresome of which occurred on the opening lap of the Austrian Grand Prix when David Coulthard tapped him into a spin on the second corner of the race. You could argue that Mika came off lightly in the sense that he was able to gather everything together again and resume his chase from the tail of the field. Yet it was an episode which produced distinctly delineated opinions from the touchlines. Some said that Coulthard made a major misjudgement, others that the Scot had gone for a legitimate gap which Mika had made the mistake of leaving wide open.

Third place was, in the circumstances, a worthy reward for an inspired recovery and he then cemented his apparent status and superiority by dominating the Hungarian race at Budapest. Yet after he'd been beaten into second place at Spa-Francorchamps by Coulthard, Mika began to look like a man who had lost the thread and his spin into retirement while leading the Italian Grand Prix sent a very firm message to title rival Eddie Irvine that he was feeling the pressure.

From that point onwards the Finn was fighting against the prevailing tide and showed flashes of vulnerability which were not finally erased until he and McLaren scored that brilliant victory in the final race of the year at Suzuka.

2

mika
häkkinen

ralf

schumacher

3

Date of birth: 30 June 1975

Team: Winfield Williams

Grand Prix starts in 1999: 16

World Championship placing: 6th

Wins: 0; Poles: 0; Points: 35

EVEN before he had left Jordan for Williams, Ralf Schumacher had already shrugged aside his image as an impetuous kid with a somewhat abrasive manner. His first season at Williams saw that march towards maturity continue both on and off the circuit. Not only did Ralf develop quickly into a formidable talent, but away from the cockpit he increasingly projected a charmingly convivial and business-like manner.

With hindsight, swapping a Jordan-Mugen Honda for a Williams-Supertec might not have looked the ideal career move. Yet Schumacher was thinking long-term, determined to position himself to best effect in preparation for the British team's forthcoming alliance with BMW. In the meantime, he would do his best to raise Williams morale by helping them through another transitional season with a customer engine.

Ralf opened the year with a tidy drive to third place at Melbourne behind Irvine's Ferrari and Frentzen's Jordan. He kept more or less in play during the first half of the season but really began to come alive after Williams successfully revamped the FW21's aerodynamics mid-season, further enhancing its performance on low-downforce circuits.

A strong third at Silverstone followed by a hard-driving fourth in front of his home crowd at Hockenheim, where he climbed through the field from a lowly grid position, helped confirm Ralf's position as one of the most improved drivers of the year. At Monza, the Williams team's reluctance to instruct his team-mate Alex Zanardi to give way in the opening stages of the race may have cost Ralf the chance of his maiden Grand Prix victory.

In the European Grand Prix he was the undoubted star of the show, demonstrating no inhibitions about getting off-line onto the wet on dry tyres in an audacious effort to outbrake David Coulthard's McLaren. Later in that same race he should have trusted his own judgement and pitted earlier when he suspected a slow puncture in a rear tyre, the ensuing deflation costing him another chance of a win. The price, perhaps, paid by a talent which is still on an upward learning curve.

That Ralf's ability and straightforward approach to his motor racing were appreciated by the Williams team was reflected by the fact that Sir Frank re-negotiated his contract before the end of the season to ensure that baby 'Schu' will be driving a Williams-BMW at least until the end of 2002. By then, he may well have even eclipsed his elder brother.

WHEN Eddie Irvine won the Australian Grand Prix to open the 1999 season everybody in the pit lane applauded what was seen as the long overdue achievement of a strong Number Two driver. Michael Schumacher, reasoned the pundits, was the man who would really take on the McLarens as the season unfolded. Cometh the hour, cometh the man. When Schumacher's title challenge ended prematurely amidst the debris of his wrecked Ferrari F399 at Silverstone's Stowe corner, so Irvine moved forward to fill the breach. Thanks to a combination of opportunism, consistent driving and a refusal to be ruffled by the apparent enormity of the task ahead of him, Eddie rose to the occasion and capitalised brilliantly on the situation in which he suddenly found himself.

Far from being over-awed by the responsibility thrust onto his shoulders, Irvine continued being himself and played the game from week to week. There was no grand strategy here, just an outward resilience which reflected the man's personality. Irvine was best at being himself and needed to play no other role. If he came over as slightly laid-back and over-relaxed about the situation this was because he inwardly realised that the rival McLaren-Mercedes package was technically better and that all he could do was to plug away and hope that Häkkinen and Coulthard proved vulnerable. That frequently proved to be the case.

Irvine was also good at mind games. Not only did he drive superbly to beat Coulthard in Austria – his best race of the season – but he also nettled the Scot with his throw-away lines out of the cockpit referring to the pressure his rival seemed to be under. None of this was contrived. Again, it was simply Eddie being himself and speaking his mind.

Much was made during 1999 of how difficult the latest breed of F1 car was to drive on its four-grooved front tyres. In that respect, Irvine was out of step with many of his rivals. In his view, so he explained, the Ferrari F399 was one of the nicest-to-drive Grand Prix cars he had ever experienced.

At the height of his summer of achievement, Irvine was courted by McLaren before finally inking a multi-million dollar deal to drive for the newly branded Jaguar F1 operation. He certainly made the most of what was clearly a massive opportunity. Which just about summed up his year.

Date of birth: 10 November 1965

Team: Scuderia Ferrari Marlboro

Grand Prix starts in 1999: 16

World Championship placing: 2nd

Wins: 4; Poles: 0; Points: 74

4

eddie
irvine

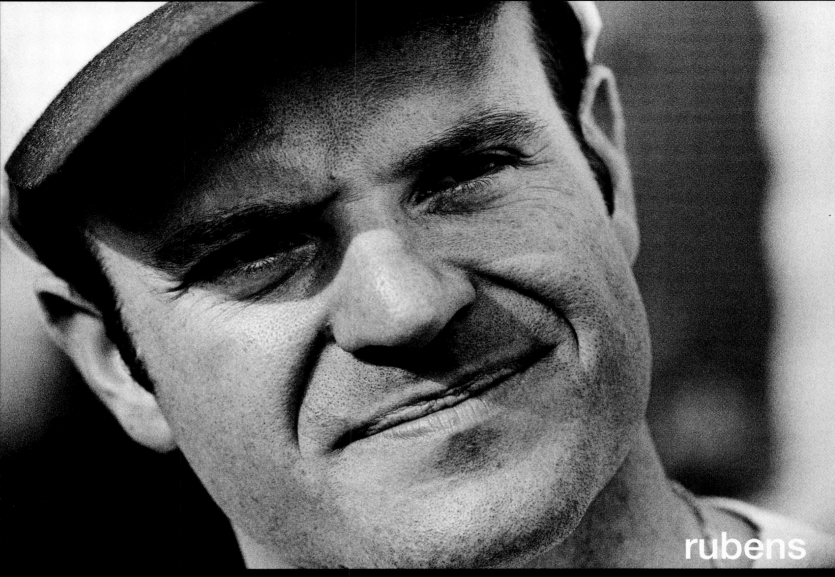

rubens
barrichello

5

IT was his seventh season in F1 and one might objectively wonder what long-term future there might be for a driver who has yet to win his first Grand Prix by this stage in his career. Yet 1999 saw Rubens Barrichello emerge as an assured and confident performer who had really come on in leaps and bounds since switching from Jordan to the Stewart-Ford squad at the start of 1997.

His car control and underlying skill had never been in doubt since his superb second place at Monaco in the rain during Stewart's first season, but he had seemed to struggle too much perhaps when the car was against him. Yet in 1999 he at last had the equipment to run near the front of the field and utilised it to excellent effect.

His fifth place in Melbourne set the tone of what Stewart might conceivably achieve and he also attained celebrity status in his own land by running for many laps at the head of the field during the Brazilian Grand Prix at Interlagos. Yet if this was a high-profile showing, some of Barrichello's other races were in fact more impressive. A strong third place at Imola, a well-judged pole at Magny-Cours and a beautifully mature drive at the head of the French Grand Prix field for many laps in extremely tricky conditions all helped flag Rubens's increasing maturity.

He also made a one-stop strategy work respectably in Hungary where he took fifth place and drove an immaculate race to fourth place at Monza, highlighted by an audacious overtaking manoeuvre on David Coulthard's McLaren. He also drove well to finish third at Nürburgring on a day when team-mate Johnny Herbert scored the team's maiden victory.

Barrichello felt comfortable and at home in the Stewart-Ford environment, yet felt that an offer from Ferrari for the 2000 season was just too good to pass up. Whether this gentle Brazilian has the temperament to flourish in the political hot house which is Maranello is set to be one of the most tantalising facets of the season to come.

Date of birth: 23 May 1972

Team: Stewart Ford

Grand Prix starts in 1999: 16

World Championship placing: 7th

Wins: 0; Poles: 1; Points: 21

DAVID Coulthard believes that, technically, he drove better than ever in 1999, even if a cursory examination of the season's results fail to bear that out. In reality, it was a bruising year for the ever-popular Scot who suffered more than his fair share of mechanical unreliability, on two occasions when he was poised to deliver a first-rate result.

There were two races in particular where David looked set for a win only for his car to wilt beneath him. He was storming away from the French GP pack at Magny-Cours before electrical failure intervened and held the inaugural Malaysian race in the palm of his hand only for the fuel pump to fail. He also drove a beautiful race at Spa-Francorchamps to score a flawless victory in the Belgian Grand Prix.

Yet the fact remains that David was invariably outqualified by team-mate Mika Häkkinen and there were days on which he could look quite average. His British Grand Prix win was fortuitous, coming at the end of an afternoon when Häkkinen had the legs on the opposition. He allowed himself to get badly tangled up in traffic at Imola where he should have been able to press Michael Schumacher's winning Ferrari much harder, and blotted his copybook by ramming Häkkinen at the A1-Ring as well as spinning off while leading the European Grand Prix.

There is no shortage of skill and ambition here, merely a lack of consistency. Coulthard makes no secret of the fact that he relishes the privacy of the F1 cockpit and is only really happy at work when he is out on the circuit driving his car. Despite his easy charm, he has often appeared over-defensive about his status and his performance at press conferences is generally so cautious as to be almost non-committal.

David rightly points out that it is his performance at the wheel which counts and this is a basically correct contention. Yet he was probably slightly fortunate to keep his McLaren drive for next season, but being prized as an excellent team player compensated for the fact that he all too rarely got the best out of the best equipment.

Date of birth: 27 March 1971

Team: West McLaren Mercedes

Grand Prix starts in 1999: 16

World Championship placing: 4th

Wins: 2; Poles: 0; Points: 48

6

david
coulthard

jacques
villeneuve

Date of birth: 9 April 1971

Team: British American Racing

Grand Prix starts in 1999: 16

World Championship placing: unplaced

Wins: 0; Poles: 0; Points: 0

UNDER the circumstances, it was a huge career gamble for Jacques Villeneuve when he turned his back on the Williams team to throw in his lot with British American Racing. It was a move which was certainly buttressed by financial compensation; Villeneuve's retainer reputedly placed him second only to Michael Schumacher in the F1 earning league, but you could argue that the independent-minded Canadian driver was worth every penny.

What British American needed most crucially from the start of the year was a baseline by which they could judge their progress. Villeneuve provided that and more. If the team had experienced its catalogue of misfortunes without a driver of his calibre on the books, its morale might have evaporated. But Jacques was always there or thereabouts; although seldom managing to get to the finishing line, he proved that, although the BAR 01 might have had more than its fair share of teething troubles, it was fundamentally no bad car.

Qualifying fifth at Imola represented a really worthwhile boost for the team's fortunes, even though the car failed to get off the starting line. He then followed that up with a strong run in third place during the opening stages of the Spanish Grand Prix at Barcelona, confidently fending off Schumacher's Ferrari until the first round of refuelling stops.

Prior to the Japanese Grand Prix Villeneuve had qualified eight times in the top ten in a season punctuated by ten mechanical retirements and not a single World Championship point. At Spa, Nürburgring and Sepang he was knocking on the door of a top-six finish before the car let him down, by which time in the season the car was working pretty well.

Villeneuve's biggest plus point is that he never, ever stops trying. In qualifying at Spa he fell foul of the tricky Eau Rouge turn for the second successive season, walking away unhurt from a massive high-speed accident in which he actually rolled his machine. Prior to the start of the season there had been speculation that Villeneuve had received an approach from McLaren. One can only imagine how different the 1999 season would have been had such a move come off.

J~~ohnny~~ ~~was~~ ~~originally~~ ~~hired~~ ~~by~~ ~~the~~ ~~Stewart~~ ~~Ford~~ ~~team~~ ~~for~~ ~~his~~ ~~dependable~~ qualities rather than any expectation of out-and-out speed. This was the season in which he celebrated the tenth anniversary of his Grand Prix debut at the wheel of a Benetton at Rio de Janeiro, a decade marked largely by flashes of promise rather than any consistent demonstrations of virtuoso brilliance.

From the outset the easy-going Englishman seemed to be shaded by Barrichello's presence in the other car, and continued unreliability on Herbert's car during the first part of the season gave rise to suggestions that the Brazilian was being overtly favoured. This was hard to believe and this line of speculation gradually faded as the season unfolded and Herbert duly picked up the pace.

Fifth place after an energetic tussle with Eddie Irvine's Ferrari at Montreal gave a hint of what could be expected from Herbert once he was satisfied with the car. He should have been in the points at Hockenheim only to retire in the closing stages of the race, but the incorporation of a more user-friendly hydraulic differential from Austria onwards made the car easier for Johnny to handle.

Eventually Johnny's persistence and dedication were rewarded when he scored the Stewart team's maiden Grand Prix victory at the Nürburgring. It was a success achieved through canny foresight, consistent driving and a dash of the good fortune which all-too-frequently has tended to desert this 35-year old F1 veteran.

As if buoyed by public confirmation of his winning potential, Herbert again rose to the occasion in the Malaysian Grand Prix where he struggled to battle Mika Häkkinen's McLaren-Mercedes for third, only being overtaken by the Finn in the closing stages of the chase when he made a slight error. Herbert did a good job restoring his credibility and status during the 1999 season, preparing the way for a fighting partnership with Eddie Irvine in the Jaguar squad into the 2000 season. How this all-British partnership will unfold is anybody's guess.

Date of birth: 25 June 1964

Team: Stewart Ford

Grand Prix starts in 1999: 16

World Championship placing: 8th

Wins: 1; Poles: 0; Points: 15

johnny
herbert

giancarlo
fisichella

9

Date of birth: 14 January 1973

Team: Mild Seven Benetton Playlife

Grand Prix starts in 1999: 16

World Championship placing: 9th

Wins: 0; Poles: 0; Points: 13

GIANCARLO Fisichella enjoys considerable status in his native Italy where he is perceived as one of the brightest of F1 rising stars. Even so, the 26-year old from Rome really needs to start delivering results on a more impressive and consistent basis if he is not to be prematurely lost to the contemporary F1 scene.

Handsomely rewarded for his position in the Benetton team on a rising financial scale which will reputedly receive a 10 million-dollar fee for the 2001 World Championship season. Yet the verdict is still out on this pleasant young man who is not afraid to have a glass or two of red wine with an evening meal, followed up by the occasional digestivo.

Fisichella can be quick when the conditions are with him but has yet to develop the skill and assurance which enables a driver to grab a team by the scruff of its neck and inspire it into a winning position. Ironically, his two best drives were in Canada and Budapest – respectively low- and high-downforce circuits – where his Benetton seemed ideally suited to the conditions, even though Fisichella and his partner Alexander Wurz never quite managed to impose a consistent track record on a car which at best was unpredictable, at worst ineffective.

An artistic and stylish performer who can fight his corner when called upon to do so, Fisichella qualified fourth at Budapest and was running strongly in that position in the race when his engine mysteriously cut out coming in for a refuelling stop. It was a bitter blow on a day which should have seen him on the rostrum for the first time since Montreal where he scrambled home second to Mika Häkkinen's winning McLaren-Mercedes. Truth be told, Fisichella was almost good enough to get the job done on a consistent basis. He tried hard, but there were also moments where he seemed to be taking his time.

JARNO Trulli is another promising young Italian ace for whom time in F1 could be running out if he does not make an excellent job of his new contract to drive alongside Heinz-Harald Frentzen at Jordan during the coming season.

A great karting ace and F3 exponent, Trulli came into F1 at the relatively early age of 23 three years ago and has managed to sustain just enough images of promise and moments of success to maintain his currency on the driver transfer market. In 1997 his early season soirée with Minardi came to an abrupt end when he was asked to transfer to the Prost team which was making heavy weather of his efforts after Olivier Panis had sustained two broken legs in the Canadian Grand Prix.

Initially Trulli saw off a class of F1 aspirants with an apparently assured confidence. Eight times this season prior to Suzuka the Prost driver qualified in the top ten, but his race performances could vary alarmingly. Eventually he managed to string everything together to finish a strong second at Nürburging, expertly handling ever-increasing pressure from Rubens Barrichello's Stewart which loomed large in his mirrors throughout.

By the end of the season, Prost was beginning to conclude that Trulli was taking things easier than he should have been, given that by then he had a lucrative Jordan contract in his pocket. Much is expected from the Italian driver next season. As team-mate to Heinz-Harald Frentzen, he certainly has a hard act to follow.

Date of birth: 13 July 1974

Team: Gauloises Prost Peugeot

Grand Prix starts in 1999: 15

World Championship placing: 11th=

Wins: 0; Poles: 0; Points: 7

10

jarno
trulli

T HE most glaringly obvious omission from the AUTOCOURSE Top Ten driver rating is Michael Schumacher, the man who had dominated the number one slot over recent years, but who forfeited his position in line with established tradition following his Silverstone accident.

It has always been AUTOCOURSE editorial policy not to include drivers who have failed to compete in all, or nearly all, the rounds of the World Championship, but we must admit that this decision certainly creates an anomalous situation. Michael is an absolutely outstanding competitor and his brilliant victories in the San Marino and Monaco Grands Prix remind us that he would have quite likely taken the top slot – and indeed the drivers' World Championship – had he not sustained that broken right leg.

Michael made an absolutely remarkable return in Malaysia where he qualified on pole position and led commandingly, eventually finishing second on a one-stop strategy behind Irvine. It was a dazzling return and although it was followed up by a slightly less convincing run to second place at Suzuka – where the sceptics suggested he was none-too-disappointed to see Häkkinen emerge with the drivers' crown – there was no doubt that he had fully recovered from the accident.

Schumacher's stand-in Mika Salo is another who deserves an honourable mention. The 'other Finn' shone at Hockenheim and Monza, but was unaccountably off the pace at both Hungary and Nürburgring. He did a good job keeping Michael's seat warm in the second Ferrari F399, a performance which probably earned him a Sauber drive for next season where he will have to accept being midfield fodder at the very most.

While the lead drivers at both Jordan and Williams were both stars of the season, their Number Twos were, to put it politely, embarrassingly subdued. Damon Hill set his heart on retirement mid-season and should have gone long before the end of the year. Twice he pulled out of races through lack of motivation; his obvious anguish with his dilemma seemed desperate and painful to behold.

Alex Zanardi's inability to get to grips with an F1 return was one of the most baffling aspects of the entire season. He had a brief flourish at Spa and Monza which raised everybody's hopes, before lapsing back into his previous form. At the time of writing the future at Williams for this immensely pleasant man seems very shaky indeed.

At Benetton, Alexander Wurz seldom produced the sort of performances many had expected from him. Jean Alesi continued to drive with his heart rather than his head at Sauber and produced several storming drives. Sadly, they seldom lasted as far as the chequered flag. His team-mate Pedro Diniz was a respectable midfield performer, something that could also be said for Prost's Olivier Panis when he managed to get his head together for a complete race weekend.

In the Arrows squad Toranosuke Takagi and Pedro de la Rosa were unquantifiable talents; Ricardo Zonta took some time to get his nerve back in the second BAR after a massive practice crash in Brazil caused him to miss three more races. At Minardi, Luca Badoer was not as quick as one might have expected him to be while newcomer Marc Gene was one of the more cheerful finds of the season and netted a good sixth place at Nürburgring to keep the little Italian team in business for another year.

damon
hill

michael
schumacher

top ten drivers

photography by

Matthias Schneider

DETERMINED TO SUCCEED

Opposite page: British American Racing's first season was certainly a character-building exercise for the team, and bringing the cars to the grid was just the start of a huge learning curve for the Grand Prix newcomers.

Left: The distinctive livery of the BAR on its race debut at Melbourne.

Centre left: Mika Salo substituted for Ricardo Zonta in three races.

Below left: Jacques Villeneuve with his mentor Craig Pollock.

Below left, middle: Villeneuve ran in third place in the Spanish Grand Prix.

Bottom left: Malcolm Oastler, the designer of the BAR 01.

BRITISH AMERICAN RACING: THE FIRST SEASON

IN the Spring of 1999 Honda announced a major assault on Grand Prix racing which is intended to revive the front-running form which saw them power Williams and McLaren to six constructors' world championships between 1986 and 1991.

The Japanese car giant signed a three-year technical partnership with F1's newest team, British American Racing, to supply works engines and chassis technology from the start of the 2000 season.

That Honda had chosen to take this step was seen as a major endorsement of the potential offered by Grand Prix racing's most ambitious new team, British American Racing, which had made its debut at the start of the 1999 season.

Independent-minded and audacious, this newcomer to the Grand Prix fraternity aimed high from the word go. It broke new ground with British American Tobacco deciding to become involved by taking a shareholding in the operation from the outset, setting a trend for the F1 future which set the tone for similarly direct involvement in the sport's most prestigious category on the part of Ford, BMW and Mercedes-Benz.

British American Racing was the brainchild of Craig Pollock, the long-time manager of Canadian driver Jacques Villeneuve, the son of the famous Ferrari F1 star Gilles Villeneuve. Pollock had steered and guided Jacques Villeneuve's career through much of the 1990s, culminating in his victories in the 1995 Indianapolis 500 race and the CART championship title in that same season.

On the back of that success, Pollock negotiated for Villeneuve to move to the Williams F1 team at the wheel of whose cars he would win the 1997 World Championship.

The first seeds from which British American Racing would grow had been sown on the morning after Villeneuve's first Indy car win at Elkhart Lake in 1994 when Craig Pollock, then Villeneuve's business manager, had invited car constructor Adrian Reynard and his co-director Rick Gorne to his home at Indianapolis.

Pollock persuaded the Reynard directors to enter a partnership to establish a new Grand Prix team which would aim to take on the very best in this highly competitive business.

Yet, in the final analysis it was Tom Moser at British American Tobacco who threw the giant tobacco group's commercial support behind Craig Pollock's ambitions. Moser had been impressed from the outset with the way in which Pollock had steered and cared for Jacques Villeneuve's career from their first encounter back in Canada.

Pollock's 'clean sheet' approach turned out to be the element of the proposed F1 partnership which most intrigued British American Tobacco.

For their part, British American Tobacco had carried out a huge amount of research into brand awareness. They probed in detail what made Formula 1 tick and how the images of their various competing teams might affect the individual brands within their control. It was a painstaking and meticulous process.

In the end, British American Tobacco concluded that the most advantageous route would be to back the outsider. With the Reynard group becoming technology partners with both Pollock and British American Tobacco, the new team would be founded on a secure three-pronged base.

'British American Tobacco had now merged with Rothmans and we have 80,000 employees in over 180 countries,' explained Moser. 'The F1 programme was one thing that offered a very strong unity of purpose, something that all the employees around the world could believe in and support at a time of changing strategies, different brands and so on. It was one thing that we could all rally behind and support.'

Not until late November, 1998, was British American Racing's new headquarters at Brackley, near Silverstone, fully operational. It had taken less than a year to transform the Brackley site from a muddy field into a striking glass and steel structure which would become home to the newest contender on the Formula 1 starting grid.

Design work was carried out under the direction of Malcolm Oastler with a team of around a dozen engineers. He finalised the design of the British American Racing 01 which made its debut in the Australian Grand Prix at Melbourne on 7th March 1999.

The decision to opt for a Supertec engine was essentially pragmatic, but also bold in the sense that British American Racing immediately pitched itself into a direct confrontation with fellow Supertec users Williams and Benetton.

Villeneuve would be partnered by the young Brazilian Ricardo Zonta who had won the 1997 International Formula 3000 Championship and the FIA GT title in 1998 for Mercedes-Benz. Unfortunately a crash during practice for his home Grand Prix at Interlagos left Zonta with leg injuries which sidelined him for three races during which Finn Mika Salo undertook a stand-in role.

It turned out to be a demanding season by any standards, serving to prove that there are no short cuts to success in a pastime as demanding as Grand Prix racing. In the early races of the season the team looked as if it was paying the penalty for its sheer inexperience and the magnitude of the task it had chosen to take on. Yet gradually the whole concept began to gel.

The first sign of genuine promise came at the third round of the title chase, the San Marino Grand Prix at Imola. It was not simply the fact that Villeneuve qualified the British American 01 in fifth place on the starting grid, but the fact that its best lap time was less than a second away from reigning World Champion Mika Häkkinen's McLaren-Mercedes which had started from pole position.

It was proof that Oastler and his colleagues had certainly produced a good-handling chassis on their first attempt at the F1 business. It was all the more frustrating, therefore, when Jacques found himself stranded on the starting grid due to an electric glitch with the car's gearchange mechanism. Another salutary reminder as to just what complex and unpredictable thoroughbreds these Grand Prix cars can be.

Two races later, at Barcelona's Circuit de Catalunya, Villeneuve qualified in sixth place – just six-tenths of a second away from Häkkinen's best – and ran superbly in third place ahead of Michael Schumacher's Ferrari F399 during the opening laps.

Schumacher finally got his break on lap 24 when he and Villeneuve both came in for their first refuelling stop, the Ferrari driver vaulting ahead to take third while Villeneuve resumed fifth behind Irvine.

Villeneuve was slightly disappointed at this. 'I made a great start, which surprised me as all my practice starts this weekend hadn't been so good, but that was a lucky one,' he grinned. 'The car was really good and I was running strongly, easily able to hold off Michael until the first pit stop. But in spite of a great effort by my crew, he managed to pass me in the pit lane.'

Jacques eventually retired after 40 laps with gearbox problems, but this had certainly been a highly convincing performance and one in which the British American Racing 01 had proved more competitive than any of the other Supertec-engined machines.

However, for all this early promise, it would take until the Belgian Grand Prix at Spa-Francorchamps in late August before Jacques posted his first finish for the team, albeit out of the championship points.

However at both the European Grand Prix at Nürburgring and the inaugural Malaysian Grand Prix at Kuala Lumpur's spectacular new Sepang circuit, Jacques took the British American 01 briefly into the top six before being sidelined by frustrating technical failures.

'This has been a character-building season,' said Craig Pollock, 'but we have learned quickly when it comes to establishing an improved infrastructure. We have addressed many problems including component manufacturing difficulties at the factory.

'We are confident that everybody will see British American Racing making a much more significant mark on the F1 landscape in its new partnership with Honda.'

PLAYING CATCH-UP

by Alan Henry

THERE was an uncomfortable sub-text to the 1999 F1 World Championship season. After a 16-race series which saw Jordan and Stewart vault ahead of Williams in the constructors' championship stakes, many insiders were left wondering whether the technical complexity of Grand Prix racing has now been raised to such a frenzied level that nobody can muster the firepower required to traverse the daunting chasm which separates these two super teams from the rest of the field.

The truth is, of course, that nothing lasts for ever. McLaren has been strong in the past with Honda, then fought back from a disastrous mid-1990s slump to achieve their present level of pre-eminence in partnership with Mercedes. Moreover, it is all too easy to forget that only two years ago Williams won a then-record ninth constructors' title.

Williams technical director Patrick Head firmly rejects the contention that McLaren and Ferrari have now effectively moved into a league which makes them uncatchable. He believes that Jordan – and, of course, Williams – can reach that exclusive enclave.

'I think Jordan did a good job this year,' he said. 'They fairly, if not entirely genuinely, won two Grands Prix. At Magny-Cours you could say that

they perhaps thought out a better refuelling strategy than the rest of us, and while Frentzen was lucky to win at Monza after Häkkinen spun off, it wasn't as if Mika was half a minute ahead when he did so.

'Similarly for ourselves at Williams, I think it is possible to get back to operating at that level, provided we get a better engine – which we hope we will from BMW – and raise our game in terms of chassis development, but we have got to become generally more competitive.

'That said, it is very difficult to sustain the sort of effort that is required to compete at the highest level. Usually some crucial trigger such as losing an engine deal – as faced McLaren when they lost Honda in 1992 and when we ourselves lost Renault in 1997 – precipitates a dip in form. The nature of this business is such that you need to know three years ahead if you need to arrange a change in engine supplier which has minimal adverse effect on your competitive level.'

However, Head admits that if one asked him a subtly different question, namely 'has F1 become too money-orientated as far as technical development is concerned?' then he would probably have to reply 'yes.'

'Don't get me wrong, I personally love all the scope for technical

development offered by the F1 regulations,' he admitted. 'But does massive expenditure on exotic materials and huge outlay on research and development make the racing any better? I don't really think so.

'On the other hand, one finds oneself considering, should we impose F3000-type rules on F1. Standard engines, transmissions, suspension uprights and so-on. I suspect the answer to that is no. Things have developed too far to go back to that.

'It's not like back in the 1950s, when most engineers knew so little about what made a car better or worse. It's the old Garden of Eden syndrome. We've bitten the apple and there is probably no going back. You cannot uninvent technology!'

In 1998, F1 racing continued that trend. More money was spent on trying to eke out ever-more marginal performance gains within the strictures of technical regulations – in this case, the requirement for an additional, fourth circumferential groove on the front tyres – which are increasingly restrictive on car performance.

Benetton technical director Pat Symonds gives a dramatic illustration of just what investment is required. 'We committed twelve and a half million pounds on our new wind tunnel which took two and a half years to

Above: Hope springs eternal as Jordan's 1999 challenger sits on the grid at Melbourne. For Mike Gascoyne of Jordan *(right)*, the first race of the season is always the acid test of a car's true level of competitiveness.

Below and far right: Alex Zanardi moved from the all-conquering Ganassi Champ Car team to a Williams team in a transitional phase. Bewilderingly, the talented Italian struggled to adapt to the current breed of F1 car.

All photographs: Paul-Henri Cahier

Below: Still the benchmark. McLaren-Mercedes are currently the team to beat, despite Ferrari taking the constructors' championship.

Paul-Henri Cahier

build,' he explained. 'Gone are the days when we were looking for perhaps three or four per cent performance increments. Today we need equipment like our new wind tunnel in order to chase benefits of somewhere in the region of 0.3 per cent. That gives you an indication of the depth of the challenge involved.'

Mike Gascoyne, Jordan's chief designer feels exactly the same way about the challenge ahead. 'We run six days a week in the wind tunnel, on average trying around 30 different configurations each day for about 50 weeks of the year,' he reflects. 'This is what we have had to do in order to reach our current level. But we are still aiming higher.'

The end result of these endeavours in 1999 was to produce a generation of Grand Prix cars which most of the men behind the wheel criticised as unpleasant, difficult and non-progressive to drive. There were a few exceptions to this rule, of course, but the majority certainly did not subscribe to the view – expressed by many designers in years gone by – that if a car is handling well, the chances are that you're not driving it quickly enough.

It is an anomalous situation that aspiring Grand Prix hopefuls are trained in F3 and F3000, both categories which use slick tyres and manual gearchanges, before finally gaining access to F1 machines on grooved tyres with semi-automatic transmissions.

The issue over manual gearboxes versus automatics is non-contentious and very much a matter of personal preference. In terms of pure driving skill, completing a Grand Prix distance without a single missed gearchange was once the hallmark of a truly competent driver. Yet today the use of sophisticated electro-hydraulic systems is defended on the grounds that engine failure rates would prove prohibitively expensive if manual shifts were readopted. For a business which has transformed conspicuous consumption into something approaching an art form, this is a far from compelling argument.

If there was one driver who seemed sunk by the change of technique required by a switch from a slick to grooved tyre environment, it was twice CART champion Alex Zanardi. The Italian's failure to get to grips with this situation was one of the most bewildering, some would say inexplicable, aspects of the season. Yet characteristically, the eloquent Italian seemed able to explain the problem, if not offer a solution to his uncomfortable dilemma.

'Previously you could simply seek out a chassis set-up which would suit your driving style, but on the grooved tyres it was not as simple as that,' he said. 'With these cars you have a level of downforce which will achieve a certain level of suspension movement through fast corners, but when you get into the slow corners, you can't get enough grip in the tyres to create sufficient load which will produce the necessary suspension movement.

'To just describe the car's behaviour in these situations as "understeer" is too simple. If you could transform the car's grip into a graph, as you go over the slip angle of the tyre, the grip drops away dramatically. Not progressively. The idea was that it would bring the best out of the driver, but I'm not sure that is the case. That said, while I think that it is much more difficult to get a good lap out of the car than it used to be, I can't deny that Ralf [Schumacher] had a technique which clearly got more out of the car than I did.'

David Coulthard agreed with the basic premise that these new tyres were much more difficult to handle. 'There is quite a marked difference in terms of reduced front-end grip,' he said. 'You have less front-end bite from the moment you hit the brakes and the grip falls away very suddenly, a situation which is heightened by the amount of camber we [at McLaren] were running on the front wheels in order to help the turn-in.'

For all this, the intensely competitive nature of Grand Prix racing is such that there is far from universal agreement as to how the technical rules should be amended in the future, if at all. Once a top team has mastered the art of getting the best performance out of the rules as they are, they are unlikely to sit by and watch that advantage become dissipated, as TAG McLaren Managing Director Ron Dennis is quick to remind us.

'I am not a cynic in these areas,' he grinned. 'I try to be a professional, but in the back of my mind there is always the need to look for the hidden agenda [when it comes to proposed rule changes].'

'We have strengths in the McLaren organisation, one of which is a sound understanding of automotive aerodynamics, and there are some people, let's say, amongst those who influence the F1 rule-making process, who appreciate that if there is a reversion to a slick tyre in F1, then a door of change opens which could see efforts being made to dampen or reverse some of the advantage we have from this level of aerodynamic understanding.

'So what I am saying is that any changes in the technical rules have to be a complete package, not an apparently minor one followed by "oh, and by the way, we're going to ban this and that as well."

'If the hidden agenda is an attempt to level the playing field, then we would obviously resist it, because where we are in terms of technical knowledge we have worked hard to achieve and we don't like the idea of being brought back to a common denominator just because of the inability of some Grand Prix teams to cope with the technology which is needed.'

Firm words indeed. Yet Dennis's rivals know him well enough to understand that McLaren would always push to the outer limits of the envelope as they strive to excel, whatever the prevailing regulations. Nobody underestimates McLaren. Least of all Williams or Patrick Head. Nothing lasts for ever, but toppling them and Ferrari from their current technical domination will certainly not be the work of a moment.

Formula won.

▶ It couldn't have been more exciting. Congratulations on winning the world title, Mika.
Thanks to David and the entire West McLaren Mercedes team for your tireless support.
We're already looking forward to the 2000 season and hope it's just as action-packed.

Mercedes-Benz

STEADY EDDIE

by Maurice Hamilton

All Photographs: Paul-Henri Cahier

FOUR hours after the Malaysian Grand Prix had finished, Edmund and Kathleen Irvine relaxed on plastic garden chairs arranged outside the Ferrari office. They were slowly decanting chilled white wine into several glasses and offering cheerful sustenance to passers-by.

News of their son's exclusion from first place had been circulating the paddock for a couple of hours. After a thrilling race and a wonderful weekend, this was a kick in the crutch which suddenly made the day seem long and the humidity a debilitating factor. The Irvines had won and yet they had lost. Never mind. There's always tomorrow. Come and have a drink.

That summed up the Irvine attitude to life just as surely as the absence of Eddie himself, long gone on his Falcon 10 jet en route to private social engagements in Macau and Hong Kong.

How was the boy taking this news? Mum and Dad didn't know for sure

because they hadn't spoken to him since the morning. But their daughter, Sonia, had caught him on his mobile shortly before take-off with the brief message that something was afoot. Apparently he hadn't said much. That, too, was very Eddie Irvine, his sister tidying up the loose ends and getting no thanks for it as he went full pelt into the rest of his life.

Sonia, a qualified physiotherapist, looked worn out, her job having long since gone beyond the mere massaging of aching limbs. Ever since her brother's arrival at Ferrari in 1996, she had also become his personal assistant. Given the whirl of Eddie's bachelor existence and the demands on his time by females, the team, the media and sponsors, Sonia had discovered that the avoidance of personal collisions and anti-social remarks required the point-switching skills of a signalman at Clapham Junction in the rush hour. It was always going to be like that, of course.

Eddie Irvine had never really cared for anyone but himself.

Actually, that's not quite true. Irvine likes to create the impression of selfish insouciance yet there are probably few F1 drivers who are as quietly loyal to friends from the past. He keeps in touch with those he raced for in Formula Ford and Formula Three; formative days in England when he lived in a freezing cold house (he and his fellow racers could just about pay the rent, never mind the heating bill) and lived off Fray Bentos corned beef and pies. Every day. They got them from a friend who worked at the meat factory. Never mind the tedium on the taste buds. This food was free.

A keen appreciation of money is the product of a no-nonsense upbringing. His family ran a scrap yard and Eddie bought his first racing car – a Crossle Formula Ford – with the proceeds of a profitable deal on a Ford Capri which he had restored to mint condition.

Irvine has a physical peculiarity in that his comparatively short legs are out of proportion with a long upper body. It may have caused him back problems while trying to get comfortable in F1 cars but it's no excuse for claiming he can't reach the bottom of his pockets.

Irvine's tightfistedness is legendary. He'll do anything to have others pay for a meal. Yet he won't tell you about the financial help he has given to impoverished but promising racers from his home country. And he'll say nothing about the gifts of cars to his parents. On top of that, Eddie and Sonia bought 'Big Ed' and Kathleen a Fiat Ducato motorhome to tour the European Grands Prix and then paid for the round-the-world trip which took them to Malaysia and Japan – hopefully to see their boy become the first World Champion from Northern Ireland.

Suzuka was a big event, and no mistake. The *Belfast Telegraph* carried nightly back-page lead stories on

32

Below: Irvine's four seasons at Ferrari have been the making of the man from Ulster, who moves on to Jaguar for 2000, and the chance to step from Michael Schumacher's shadow.

Irvine's progress. BBC Radio Ulster mentioned him at the head of news bulletins. Public houses and hotels in and around County Down received extensions to their licences as bars remained open through the night – as if they needed an excuse! John Watson and Kenny Acheson, two former F1 drivers from Ulster, flew on their own coin to Suzuka. Just to be there in case the boy from the village of Conlig pulled it off.

The fact that he didn't was received with equanimity. What was the point in getting upset? The one certainty was that the man himself wasn't at the back of the paddock crying in the bushes. He was on his way to Tokyo and a return to the night life he had enjoyed so much when racing Japanese F3000 in the early nineties. That's when he earned more than the back half the F1 field put together.

When he made his F1 debut at Suzuka for Jordan in 1993, he said he could take it or leave it. Up to a point. Just as he gave the impression of smiling acceptance as he left Suzuka for the last time as a Ferrari driver who had failed to win the title, so his couldn't-care-less attitude on arrival at Jordan six years before had covered a stubborn determination and colossal belief in his own ability.

When Irvine ran round the outside of the front runners in the wet at the first corner in 1993, it wasn't bravado or a risk-all strategy just to get noticed. He did it simply because he knew that he could. What, he wanted to know afterwards, was the big deal? And why the fuss when he tried to unlap himself by overtaking Ayrton Senna? As he said when confronted by the outraged Brazilian: 'I was racing and you were too slow.' Senna went into orbit and struck the Irishman a now infamous blow.

Ayrton could count himself lucky that Irvine didn't retaliate. We never did get to discover whether or not Senna's cultured ways could have coped with a head butt – or worse –from a street-wise 27-year-old who had learned through necessity to look after himself. As it was, the name Eddie Irvine was splashed across the British national dailies for the first time. And it wouldn't be the last.

His natural resilience would carry him through the toughest test of all; tougher, even, than the pressures associated with leading the World Championship. Becoming a serious contender, more or less overnight, was something of a bonus thanks to Michael Schumacher removing himself from the equation by crashing at Silverstone.

Irvine would give it his best shot. His destiny would largely be in his hands.

That was not the case in early 1994 when the FIA, the same governing body which accommodated Ferrari in the appeal court last October, produced the most callous response to Jordan's appeal against Irvine's one-race ban for his part in a multiple shunt during the Brazilian Grand Prix. They extended the ban to three races and Irvine was immediately branded a mad man and a crasher. He is anything but.

Irvine's record during the past few seasons shows remarkably few shunts, his progress governed by a sharp mind which calculates the odds and out-psyches the opposition before they hit the track, never mind when they are on it. But, when he returned to the cockpit in 1994, the odds were stacked against him. He went racing in the knowledge that the slightest incident, no matter how innocent his involvement, would automatically be seen as his fault. The opposition could show him a wheel knowing he could not afford a vigorous response. It was the equivalent of fighting with one hand behind his back. But he survived. In fact, the FIA probably did him a favour since he was seen as someone not to be trifled with.

The newspaper headlines in 1999 were more sympathetic, if only because

sports writers enjoyed the presence of a driver with a mind of his own. Not for Irvine the numbing F1 correctness of thinking what the team would want him to say. This, plus his energetic lifestyle, earned recent profiles in the likes of *The Sunday Times*, *Arena* and *GQ*. Alongside the Tommy Hilfiger ads of a rakish Irvine in a leather jacket would be words which would strip the grey paint off the wall at McLaren.

'If you think you are going to lose or don't stand a chance, you might as well not be out there,' he told *GQ*. 'You need to make sure your car is ready for you, which is why we have testing, but a lot of it is down to natural ability – which is why I'm so good at it. I want to stay alive long enough to spend all my money.'

And, just in case you missed the point, he concluded the interview with this when asked if he was completely satisfied with his jet, helicopter and yacht: 'No. I'm grateful and I appreciate what I have, but I don't think there's anything wrong with wanting to better your lot. I'm not always going to be a Number Two.'

So, now you know. 1999 is history already. Watch him as the main man at Jaguar in 2000. You may like him or loathe him. But you sure as hell can't ignore him.

The all new Suzuki GSX-R750.

This might be the only time you'll see one from the front!

The all new Suzuki GSX-R750

Most manufacturer's would be more than satisfied with a machine as good as the current GSX-R750. It is, after all, the motorcycle that established the race replica class. It has always been the choice of those who demand outrageous performance and exceptional handling. For two years' running, it's won the gruelling 24 hour Bol d'Or and now the best just got even better. Lighter, more powerful, more advanced and now even more desirable. The all new Suzuki GSX-R750, if you want to see it you better be fast, or you'll be furious.

24 hour hotline: 01892 707001
Suzuki Information Department, PO Box 56, Tunbridge Wells, Kent TN1 2XY or visit our website at www.suzuki.co.uk

$ SUZUKI
Ride the winds of change

DAMON HILL
FAREWELL TO A CHAMPION

by Alan Henry

DAMON Hill retired from Formula 1 after the Japanese Grand Prix at Suzuka, living up to a promise he had originally voiced in the middle of the season after crashing out of the Canadian race at Montreal.

Truth be told, everybody in the pit lane was keeping their fingers crossed for the 1996 World Champion. In his heart of hearts he would have liked to have stopped earlier, but the process of disentangling himself from his Jordan team contract was not as straightforward as perhaps either party would have liked.

Hill's reservoir of motivation may not have dried up completely, but the warning light was ominously flickering towards the end of his career. Particularly in the second half of the season, his mood seemed to alternate between a light-headed elation that he was approaching retirement and a certain nervousness over whether perhaps he'd lingered too long.

From the very start of the 1999 season many F1 insiders suspected that Hill was already toying with the idea of retirement. On many occasions, he expressed his distaste for the current breed of F1 car, with its acute lack of grip and over-sensitivity to side-winds. At the same time it seemed that he was wrong-footed over the speed of his new Jordan team-mate Heinz-Harald Frentzen, ironically the man who replaced him in the Williams team when he was dropped at the end of his 1996 World Championship season.

In reality, Damon's record in the Grand Prix history books looks pretty impressive. He won 22 of his 115 races and became the only second-generation family member to win a title crown, duplicating the achievements of his late father Graham who won the Championship in 1962 and 1968.

It is therefore beyond question that Damon Hill's departure will leave a certain void in the F1 community. It has always been popular to categorise Grand Prix drivers as either great natural talents or workers. Using this yardstick, Hill probably falls into the second category. Yet he was a great career opportunist who, seeing a crucial door ajar, burst it wide open with his shoulder.

Ironically, as a teenager, Damon was far more interested in motor cycling, and simply regarded father Graham's job as 'winning the Monaco Grand Prix.'

He competed on motor cycles with some success at club level in the early 1980s before his mother paid for him to attend a car racing school in France. Then he raced Formula Ford and graduated to Formula 3 with some success, winning the 1988 British Grand Prix supporting race at Silverstone.

After that, Hill moved into Formula 3000 where he showed considerable speed but was blighted by a succession of mechanical failures. For 1992, he accepted an offer from Williams to succeed Mark Blundell as the official test driver. It was also understood that if regular drivers Nigel Mansell or Riccardo Patrese were sidelined for any reason, Hill would take over as their deputy. But it never happened.

Nevertheless, Damon relished the contribution he was making to the development of the superbly competitive Williams FW14B, but realised that he was not being given the chance of driving the machine for his own benefit.

'I am not asked to drive the best car in Formula 1 today for my own personal pleasure,' he once said. 'A test session has nothing like the excitement or glamour of a Grand Prix. Even so, it can be immensely fulfilling. Each time a Williams-Renault wins, it's my win in a way as well.' He would receive his pay-back sooner than he could have imagined.

In the absence of anything else to race, Damon also drove an uncompetitive Brabham-Judd BT60 in the early races of 1992 but the team ran into dire financial trouble and could not complete the season.

In 1993 he got his big break when Mansell fell out with Williams and stormed off to drive in the US Indy car series. Alain Prost took over as team leader and Hill found himself promoted to number two. He was always fractionally slower than the Frenchman, but mopped up every morsel of information he could learn from Prost's technique.

In 1994 Hill stood to be eclipsed by the arrival of the brilliant Ayrton Senna as Prost's successor at Williams. Instead, he was Williams's saviour. Just as his father Graham had restored the Lotus team's morale after Jim Clark's death in 1968, so now he did the same for Williams 26 years later.

In 1995 Hill seemed to struggle slightly, but he still won four races, and the following year bounced back to win the title with eight wins from 16 races. Controversially dropped by Williams in favour of Heinz-Harald Frentzen for 1997, he had a largely fruitless year with Arrows before signing for Jordan in 1998 and posting the team's first Grand Prix triumph at Spa-Francorchamps.

Perhaps curiously, there has always been something slightly ambivalent about Hill's attitude towards his father, bordering on a crisis of identity. On the one hand he was happy for his helmet to carry the same distinctive markings of the London Rowing Club, yet at the same time he always emphasised that his father's career was something totally separate from his own. He seemed to like the dynastic touch it brought to the F1 grids, yet felt resentful that his father's death in an air crash had left the family in straitened circumstances.

Yet Damon could display Graham's steely resolve. Never more so did he show his bravery than at Imola when he climbed back into his Williams FW14 for the Grand Prix restart after team-mate Senna's accident, not really sure if a mechanical failure had caused the tragedy.

Later that season his rivalry with Michael Schumacher ended in tears when the two drivers collided in the Australian Grand Prix. Many believe that Michael deliberately rammed his rival to save his own title hopes. Whatever the truth of the matter, the German driver never quite lived down the episode.

That rivalry with Schumacher was the making of Hill. He came off second-best during the 1995 championship struggle, and always seemed to be on the wrong end of Schumacher's tongue, but the collisions, back-biting and traded insults all contributed to the legend. Schumacher may have been the better driver – something Damon never acknowledged – but Damon was quicker off the mark with the verbal put-down. Just like his Old Man.

THE WORKS

*Why buy hundreds of books
when one official work answers
all your questions ?*

Teams, Drivers, Cars, Key people, Mechanics, Engineers, Sponsors, Suppliers,
Engine manufacturers, Media, Tracks, Officials, Addresses, Fan clubs, Web sites, E-mail...

Who they are   What they do   How to reach them

www.who-works-in.com
Phone: +44 7000 WHO WORKS, or +44 1304 214494 Fax: +44 1304 212030

F1 REVIEW

CONTRIBUTORS

Bob Constanduros

Maurice Hamilton

Alan Henry

F1 ILLUSTRATIONS

Ian Hutchinson

Nicola Fox

1 McLAREN
2

MIKA HÄKKINEN

DAVID COULTHARD

DEFENDING World Champions McLaren-Mercedes took a bold step in developing the new MP4/14, one of their most ambitious F1 designs ever, and the team made plans to keep the previous year's MP4/13s in reserve just in case it was judged that they might be a more reliable bet for the first few races of the season.

In the event, such a fall-back strategy was deemed unnecessary. In any event, many of McLaren's problems would turn out to be self-inflicted and what should have been a dominant season with a superior car gradually fell apart thanks to a succession of irritating mechanical failures, driver errors and, on occasion, questionable race strategies.

At the end of the day, however, Mika Häkkinen retained his drivers' championship by the narrow margin of two points although the team lost the constructors' crown to arch-rivals Ferrari.

'This car does not carry with it the word "evolutionary," said TAG Mc-Laren Group managing director Ron Dennis as the wraps came off the new

machine. 'It represents the biggest single step we felt we could take for 1999 and has perhaps the smallest ever percentage of carry-over components from last year's car.'

Powered by a lighter and lower 72-degree Mercedes F0110H V10 engine developing around 785 bhp at 16,700 rpm, the new car represented McLaren technical director Adrian Newey's formula to claw back some of the grip lost by the extra fourth groove now required in the front tyres by the revised 1999 technical rules.

The MP4/14 had a 'medium height' nose configuration and notably high-mounted bargeboards on either side of the cockpit while the rear bodywork features distinctive deflectors ahead of the rear wheels.

'We have changed the packaging quite a bit,' said Newey, 'which was actually something I'd wanted to do on last year's car but arrived with the team too late to make those changes. We've re-packaged the oil tank and the hydraulic system which I think should be an improvement.'

'The gearbox is all new, slightly shorter, but still a six-speed longitudinal configuration. We've also fitted torsion bar rear suspension, which is another thing we didn't have time to do last year, and the front suspension is very similar to the 1998 chassis.'

With extra weight trimmed off the entire chassis/engine package, the new car had even more scope for strategic placement of ballast around the chassis. The new car was also more complex than its predecessor in terms of packaging many of the car's ancillary components within the monocoque walls.

'It was not a car like MP4/13, when you all smile at each other on the first day that it ran,' said Martin Whitmarsh, McLaren International's managing director.

'Perhaps in terms or riding the bumps, stability on the straight and sheer chuckability it did not instil quite the same initial confidence in the driver in the way that MP4/13 did. But operating on the limit, MP4/14 was a step forward.'

McLaren thought seriously enough about running MP4/13 in some early

season races that the car new frontal crash structures were designed for the 1998 car, even though eventually they were not needed.

One of the main issues which particularly affected the new McLaren's design (and indeed every other F1 car) was the reduction in the front tyre contact patch consequent on the introduction of a fourth circumferential groove. This was expected, but what came as something of a surprise was the reduction in rear grip produced by the latest generation of Bridgestone rubber.

This only became apparent during the early development of the MP4/14 after various fixed parameters of its design were established. This resulted in the need to alter the deployment of ballast around the car, but eventually everything was satisfactorily resolved in time for the opening race of the year.

Even so, assimilating all the lessons from the 1998 car and incorporating them into a ground-up redesign which ended up with too many inherent risks. It was a more complex design which needed honing in the interests

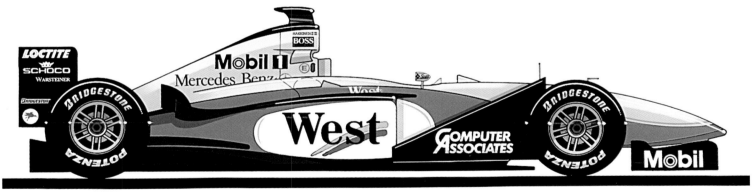

McLAREN MP4/14-MERCEDES

Sponsors: West, Mobil, Loctite, Schuco, Warsteiner, Computer Associates, Sun, Boss, Schweppes

Team principal: Ron Dennis **Technical director:** Adrian Newey. **Team manager:** Dave Ryan. **Chief mechanic:** Mike Negline.

ENGINE **Type:** Mercedes-Benz F0110H **No. of cylinders (vee angle):** V10 (72°) **Sparking plugs:** NGK **Electronics:** TAG **Fuel:** Mobil **Oil:** Mobil

TRANSMISSION **Gearbox:** McLaren six-speed longitudinal semi-automatic **Driveshafts:** McLaren **Clutch:** AP (hand-operated)

CHASSIS: **Front suspension:** double wishbones, pushrod **Rear suspension:** double wishbones, pushrod **Suspension dampers:** McLaren/Penske **Wheel diameter:** front: 13in.

rear: 13in. **Wheels:** Enkei **Tyres:** Bridgestone **Brake pads:** AP/Hitco **Brake discs:** AP/Hitco **Brake calipers:** AP **Steering:** McLaren **Radiators:** not given

Fuel tanks: ATL **Battery:** GS **Instruments:** TAG

DIMENSIONS **Wheelbase:** not given **Track:** front: not given rear: not given **Formula weight:** 1322.8 lb/600 kg including driver **Fuel capacity:** not given

There is only one car in Formula 1 that will never be overtaken.

▶ The racetrack is the home of the AMG sports car. Even in Formula 1, the jewel in the crown of motor racing, you will regularly see an AMG car leading the way. We're talking about the CLK 55 AMG, a vehicle that focuses heavily on designs from AMG's motor racing division. A vehicle that offers enhanced performance, superb endurance and a chassis that is even quicker than the engine. Add to that a braking system that keeps this powerhouse in check at all times, and the CLK 55 AMG picture is complete: supreme dynamism and control – both on and off the track.

▶ For more information on AMG please contact: Mercedes-AMG GmbH, Daimlerstraße 1, D-71563 Affalterbach, telephone +49(0)7144/302-0.

AMG. Sportswear for your Mercedes.

Mercedes-Benz

Top left: Dave Ryan, Norbert Haug and Ron Dennis in light mood.
Paul-Henri Cahier

Top right: Mario Ilien kept McLaren on pole in the horsepower department.
Nigel Snowdon

Above: Nose-cones at the ready... Every eventuality must be catered for.
Paul-Henri Cahier

Right: Man at work. Mika Häkkinen at the wheel of the McLaren MP4/14 Mercedes-Benz.
Paul-Henri Cahier

of reliability. And that process ate into too much of the season.

The partnership of Häkkinen and Coulthard continued for its fourth straight season, both drivers operating on identical contractual terms which meant that they were free to race for the World Championship until the management decided it was appropriate to call time and ask one to help the other. In this case it would be Coul-

thard being asked to help the reigning title holder, but by the time the McLaren management decided to intervene the team was starting to look boxed into a mathematical corner.

'New car' mechanical problems stopped both cars in the Australian Grand Prix and while Häkkinen triumphed in Brazil, it was only after a peculiar gearchange glitch dropped him to third place in the opening stages. Coulthard

again stopped with gearbox problems and did not get his points score off the deck until Imola where he was roundly beaten into second place in San Marino.

On that occasion David still believes that his one-stop strategy would have been good enough to get the job done had it not been for the unfortunate intervention of many uncooperative backmarkers. It was a disappointment, but not as much as the outcome of the

race for Häkkinen who fell off in the early stages pressing too hard to prove in vain that his two-stop strategy would leave him with the upper hand.

Monaco was a disaster for McLaren, possibly Häkkinen's worst race of the season. Beaten off pole, he eventually had to settle for a distant third place, unsettled and uncomfortable with the feel of his MP4/14. The car was subsequently checked over from end to end

SIEMENS

MIKA HAKKINEN:
"It takes more than speed to win the championship."

"You have to become a leader in every field."

"With Siemens at our side, we are confident that we will continue to lead the race with cutting-edge technology."

"The best teamwork comes from having confidence in your partners."

"Information and communications technology are essential to Formula One racing success."

Mika Hakkinen, 1999 Formula One World Champion, demands the best – in every situation. That's why Siemens, Technology Partner to West McLaren Mercedes, is providing a state-of-the-art communications solution for the team. In a mere 20 minutes, a full-scale mobile transmission system can be installed to link the pit crews at any circuit in the world to the team back at McLaren's headquarters in England. Equipped with Siemens convergence technology for voice, data and video transmission, both teams can evaluate all telemetry data, such as vehicle dynamics and engine performance. With this kind of support, the race team can make tactical and strategic decisions to help Mika give his best. To learn more, email us: info.ic@siemens.com

Siemens Convergence Advantage – Creating a Universe of One.

www.siemens.convergence-advantage.com

 **Information and Communications**

Above: One of David Coulthard's best races of the year was at Spa-Francorchamps when he took an immediate lead over team-mate Mika Häkkinen and stormed off to a convincing victory.
Paul-Henri Cahier

Overleaf: Häkkinen prepares to dominate another qualifying session. The Finn took pole for 11 out of 16 races.
Paul-Henri Cahier

and no tangible mechanical defect was located.

Häkkinen then won in Spain and Canada before everything started to unravel for the Finn. He should have won at Magny-Cours had it not been for the team's surprising decision not to allow him out early in the rain-drenched qualifying session. He finally qualified 14th and finished second, despite an equally crucial spin.

That race saw Coulthard drive brilliantly in the opening stages, seizing the lead and pulling away strongly before electrical problems shut down his Merc V10. It was a performance which set the pleasant Scot for a fine win on his home turf at Silverstone, this being a happy consolation prize after Häkkinen's car was withdrawn from the race after problems with the left rear wheel securing mechanism had earlier seen him shed a wheel out on the track.

Now came the sequence of bitter disappointment which could have cost Häkkinen his run at the title. The Austrian GP produced the lowest moment when Coulthard tapped the Finn into a second corner spin. David then didn't get sufficient assistance from the pits to evolve a winning strategy and the McLarens finished 2–3 behind Irvine's Ferrari with a furious Häkkinen storming through to take the final place on the podium.

Tyre problems at Hockenheim saw Mika crash out of the German Grand Prix, allowing Irvine to win again. Precise details of the cause of the failure were never released and although McLaren denied operating the tyres at pressures outside the recommended range, it certainly seemed that a patch of tread had detached from the tyre carcass.

McLaren reasserted itself with a fine 1–2 at Hungaroring, Coulthard following Häkkinen home after the Scot pressed Irvine into a mistake during the closing stages.

Then came another controversy. At Spa Coulthard beat Häkkinen off the line and the two cars rubbed wheels at the first corner, David staying ahead. Mika settled for second place and was hardly the happiest man in town, his discomfort heightened by the fact that Ron Dennis said that he'd been in the wrong as far as that first-corner incident was concerned.

Dennis was technically right, but one could also understand Häkkinen's private belief that team orders should have been invoked in his favour on this day when the McLarens had a huge performance advantage. Coulthard might have deserved a fair crack at the title, but he hadn't been as quick as his team-mate over much of the season and McLaren seemed increasingly inclined to ignore the fact that it was battling for the crown with a rival who was prepared to put all its eggs in Eddie Irvine's basket.

Thereafter it seemed to be downhill all the way. Häkkinen, now frazzled, threw away a dominant victory at Monza, dodgy team strategy scrambled his chances at Nürburgring and the inaugural Malaysian Grand Prix saw him stitched up into third place by F1 returnee Michael Schumacher who pushed gamesmanship to the outer limits of acceptability with his blocking tactics.

For his part, Coulthard was off the pace at Monza, threw it off the road at Nürburgring and then had potential for a brilliant result in Malaysia thwarted by a fuel pump failure. This was a rare malfunction indeed, for the Mercedes

V10s, built by the German company's Ilmor subsidiary, had demonstrated enviable mechanical reliability for much of the season. It was just a shame that the rest of the MP4/14 package did not reflect those standards.

Aerodynamic excellence was the key to the McLaren design with a wide range of front and rear wings used during the course of the season, plus revised bargeboards in time for the European Grand Prix at Nürburgring.

McLaren also paid a lot of attention to their detailed suspension development, balancing springing, damping and anti-roll qualities to optimum effect which helped MP4/14 continue its predecessor's impressive ability to ride kerbs while maintaining its handling composure.

Development on the MP4/14 continued right up to the final race with a revised front aerodynamic package being prepared for Suzuka. By then, of course, the Championship contest was stiflingly close and, surveying the debris of their troubled summer, it was no consolation for Häkkinen and McLaren to reflect that the championship should have been sewn up by late August. Yet although they should never have drifted into a position where they were vulnerable to Ferrari's challenge in the first place, the team produced a vintage performance at the Japanese Grand Prix with Häkkinen dominating the race throughout.

In 2000 the team should remain the one to beat at the head of the pack, aiming to improve on the record of seven wins out of 16 races which represented its modest 1999 tally.

Alan Henry

www.finlandia-vodka.com

NEXT STOP : 21ST CENTURY

FINLANDIA
VODKA

West McLaren Mercedes
FORMULA ONE WORLD CHAMPIONS 1998
ASSOCIATE PARTNER

3
FERRARI
4

MICHAEL SCHUMACHER   **EDDIE IRVINE**

Both photographs: Paul-Henri Cahier

ROSS Brawn describes 1999 as a very unusual year. Ferrari's technical director should know because, one way or another, his team has been at the centre of it. Race wins, crashes, exclusions, reinstatements, mediocre performances, brilliant tactics, bungled pit stops; you name it and Ferrari has been there.

All of this was played out against a theatrical backdrop as the team from Maranello attempted to secure the drivers' championship for the first time in 20 years, having twice let the cup slip through their fingers at the eleventh hour in recent years. Oh, and one last thing. The wrong driver was in the running for the title. It doesn't get more unusual than that. Not even at Ferrari.

When Eddie Irvine won the first race of the season, there was no question that Ferrari's championship momentum would remain with Michael Schumacher. Various problems meant the Number One did not create much of an impression in Melbourne as he limped home in eighth place, but Schumacher was back on song in Brazil, where he chased after the fleeing McLarens and eventually finished second.

At Imola, he moved to the head of the championship table after a victory brought about by a brilliant mid-race stint. Schumacher then consolidated that with a powerful performance two weeks later in Monte Carlo.

Despite these visits to the podium, there was concern within Ferrari. McLaren had an edge and the chances of overcoming it depended on the reigning champions messing up. Which they duly did from time to time.

'McLaren had the advantage of having worked with Bridgestone in 1998,' says Brawn. 'For sure, that was a help because there are some things – suspension geometry, weight distribution, and so on – which are difficult to change during the season. Having said that, teams such as Jordan and Williams were in the same boat as Ferrari and, at the beginning of the season, I think they weren't quite on top of the tyre situation whereas we got there a bit sooner than they did.

'Melbourne was a disappointment because we thought we were where we wanted to be [compared with McLaren] but that didn't turn out to be the case. I was a little bit surprised by that. In Brazil, we ran out of suspension travel at the rear and the car was very bad for quite a long time until we got that sorted. We were a bit more competitive at Imola and, at Monaco, we actually got a bit complacent.

'We were first and second near the end of the qualifying in Monte Carlo and then, suddenly, we were second and fourth on the grid when McLaren pipped us at the end. There had been a reluctance by the drivers to go out because they thought they had it nicely sewn up! It turned out to be a blessing in disguise because, from the side of the grid they were on, they both made tremendous starts and finished first and second. It really was a great performance from everyone; one of the highlights of the season, for sure.'

The low points were about to come in quick succession. Schumacher crashed into the wall while leading in Canada and rain turned Ferrari's race on its head in France as Schumacher struggled into fifth. Irvine, after a misunderstanding during a pit stop, was relegated to sixth.

As they went to Silverstone, Häkkinen was back in charge of the championship. Then came lap one, a poor start from the front row by Schumacher and a risky move to pass Irvine going into Stowe corner which ended with the Ferrari in the wall (due to an hydraulic fluid leak to the rear brakes) and Schumacher in hospital with a broken leg. Ferrari thought their championship chances had been blown even though the season had just reached the halfway mark. Then Irvine was allowed his head.

Two wins in succession, the second victory in Germany, helped greatly by new recruit Mika Salo, put Irvine into the championship frame after a consistent run of finishes. But, as the season ground on, it appeared that Ferrari's momentum was wilting, particularly in Belgium and Italy.

'Michael's accident at Silverstone was the core event of the season for us,'

FERRARI F399

Sponsors: Marlboro, Shell, Fiat, Bridgestone, Tictac, TIM, FedEx, Magneti Marelli, Tommy Hilfiger, GE, Arexons, Brembo, PPG, SKF

Team principal: Jean Todt **Technical director:** Ross Brawn **Team manager:** Stefano Domenicali **Chief mechanic:** Nigel Stepney

ENGINE   Type: Ferrari 048/B/C **No. of cylinders/vee angle:** V10 (75°) **Sparking Plugs:** Champion **Electronics:** Magneti Marelli **Fuel:** Shell **Oil:** Shell

TRANSMISSION   Gearbox: Ferrari seven-speed longitudinal semi–automatic **Driveshafts:** Ferrari **Clutch:** AP (hand-operated)

CHASSIS   Front suspension: double wishbones, pushrod **Rear suspension:** double wishbones, pushrod **Suspension dampers:** Koni **Wheel diameter:** front: 13 in. rear: 13in.

Wheels: BBS **Tyres:** Bridgestone **Brake pads:** Brembo **Brake discs:** Brembo **Brake calipers:** Brembo **Steering:** Ferrari **Radiators:** Secan **Fuel tanks:** ATL

Battery: Magneti Marelli **Instruments:** Magneti Marelli

DIMENSIONS   Wheelbase: not given **Track:** front: not given rear: not given **Formula weight:** 1322.8 lb/600 kg including driver **Fuel capacity:** not given

MIKA SALO

says Brawn. 'It affected the team quite a lot, both directly and indirectly. Eddie did a great job considering but we were fighting with one arm behind our back because two drivers such as Michael and Eddie as a collective are much stronger that Eddie alone.

'Despite a very good effort by Mika, you couldn't get away from the fact that he had not been in the team long enough. He was not at the same level we'd experienced with Michael. The team had developed and evolved around Michael and Eddie for almost four years. Take Michael away from that and it leaves a fairly big hole.

'Overall, though, Eddie did a great job. He saw the championship as a possibility but he didn't have a reference to

compare himself to. Until Michael came back in Malaysia, it had started to hurt Eddie not having a good partner. And, to be fair, all of us got a bit wobbly leading up to the last two races.'

Having said that, Brawn refutes the suggestion that there was a drop-off in effort and development during Schumacher's absence.

'It was not through a lack of effort,' says Brawn. 'It's true that we didn't make as much progress as we had in previous years but, it was quite a complex set of circumstances and conditions that didn't help in that respect. Everything – testing, feedback, and so on – suffered a little bit because Michael was not here. That led to a lot of inconsistency, particularly in the second

half of the season.

'People pointed to Spa and Monza. The truth is we've never been particularly strong at Spa for the last two or three years even though we tended to look good there. That was mainly because of wet conditions. In the dry we weren't particularly good and that's been something we've spent quite a lot of time thinking about.

'We took some stick at Monza because people compared that performance with Hockenheim, where we finished first and second. But what happened at Monza was that our drivers were in similar relative positions [compared to McLaren] to where they had [been] at Hockenheim. But, at Monza, you threw Williams and Jordan into the

Above: Michael Schumacher was the focus of Ferrari's championship challenge, but ended up having to support team-mate Eddie Irvine's bid.

Top, centre: Team manager Jean Todt offered to resign after the debacle at Malaysia.

Top right: Ross Brawn certainly gained satisfaction with Ferrari winning the constructors' title.

All photographs: Paul-Henri Cahier

Top left: Mika Salo takes the applause of the crowd after his third place at Monza.

Top, right: The Ferrari enjoyed an enviable reliability record.

Above: Eddie Irvine locks his brakes in an attempt to hold off the McLaren of Mika Häkkinen during the European Grand Prix. This was the race in which the Finn scrambled two points, which in retrospect terminally damaged the Ulsterman's title challenge.

All photographs: Paul-Henri Cahier

plot and that's what made it look a lot worse. We weren't particularly special at Monza but we weren't that bad either. It didn't look great, I admit, but it wasn't disastrous. We didn't quite have an edge.

'I know Eddie was very unhappy about the variation between the test and the race; he thought we had a very good car at the test and didn't have a good car at the race but, equally, if you look at the testing times for all the teams, the track wasn't as good for the race weekend at Monza as it had been for the test.'

The F399, an evolution of the 1998 car, was described by Irvine as one of the best he had driven – but only when it was working properly. That was not always the case, as Brawn admits.

'It was basically a very nice car. It's just that sometimes we fell off the edge a little bit. One of the areas we concentrated on was having a car that was more effective in the lower downforce range. Previous years we had a car that was quite good with middle to high downforce but maybe not so strong at low downforce. We did make some reasonable progress in that respect.'

While every effort was made to keep the team ahead in the technical stakes, Ferrari – like McLaren – were occasionally caught out by the most elementary

detail, particularly during unscheduled pit stops at Magny-Cours and the Nürburgring where, each time, Irvine was the hapless victim.

'In France, Eddie was coming in and he radioed the guy on the pit wall. He, in turn, tried to radio the crew to tell them to get ready but they didn't hear it; something went wrong. It was as simple as that. It was chaos because the guys weren't ready. That made us realise a few weaknesses in the system, particularly when we have the unexpected arrival of a car.

'At the Nürburgring, because of the changing conditions, we were still debating on the radio whether to fit wets

360 MODENA CHALLENGE – 8 CYLINDERS – 400BHP – 1170KG

Maranello Sales Ltd.
The Home of Ferrari.

MARANELLO
Financial Services
Ask for details of finance
plans over £15,000

| SALES | SERVICE | PARTS | BODY REPAIRS | FINANCE |

Maranello Sales Ltd. Tower Garage, The By Pass (A30), Egham, Surrey TW20 0AX Telephone 01784 436431
Web Site:- www.maranellosales.com

email:owen@maranellosales.com

An Inchcape
Company

Top left: More adjustments are made to the car.

Top, right: Michael Schumacher in last-minute discussions on the grid at Interlagos.

Above: Mika Salo sits quietly in his Ferrari before practice at the German Grand Prix. The Finnish driver gave up a Grand Prix win to bolster team-mate Irvine's title chances.

All photographs: Paul-Henri Cahier

or dries. Both sets were ready for Eddie so that he could call it at the last minute coming into the pits.

'Then Mika broke his nose wing and came in and we had to swap to Mika's tyres and change the nose. That didn't cause a huge drama but Eddie was then coming in 30 or 40 seconds later and he wanted dries. Someone on the team had mistakenly picked up those tyres that were ready for the right-hand side, wrapped them back up and put them at the back of the garage. So the poor guys on the right-hand side turned round and the tyres weren't there! Someone had used a bit of initiative but

as I explained to them all later, we don't need initiative in pit stops; just do what you've got to do!

'It was really unfortunate because we have a very good team. There were a few races this year when the crew won it for us and there is no way they could go from heroes to incompetents overnight.

'Ferrari is still a relatively new team. By that I mean that the F399 is only the second car from the new design group. We've got some excellent people, but they're still establishing themselves as a team. I can see things starting to happen now which are real-

ly pleasing in the way they are coming together. We have a good R&D group and a strong vehicle dynamics group. All these things are coming together and you don't get the benefit overnight. I think the best times for Ferrari are still to come.'

In the end it was good enough to clinch Ferrari's first constructors' championship since 1983. Yet the drivers' crown still proved as elusive as ever.

Maurice Hamilton

automotive
mmannesmann
Sachs

THE 24 h
CHALLENGE

SACHS RACE ENGINEERING

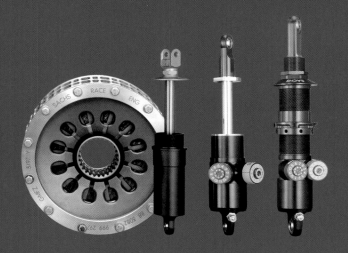

SACHS RACE ENGINEERING – is a German-based company specializing in the design, development, manufacture and world-wide service support of racing clutches and shock absorbers. It is an official supplier of Scuderia Ferrari (shock absorbers) and Sauber (clutch and shock absorbers). Sachs Race Engineering is also one of the leading manufacturers of performance dampers and clutches, servicing especially the international performance car and tuning industry.

Sachs Race Engineering GmbH · A Mannesmann Sachs company
Ernst-Sachs-Str. 62 · D-97424 Schweinfurt · Phone +49 9721 98 43 00 · Fax +49 9721 98 42 99
e-mail olaf.schwaier@sachs-ag.de · www.sachs-race-engineering.de

SACHS
RACE ENGINEERING

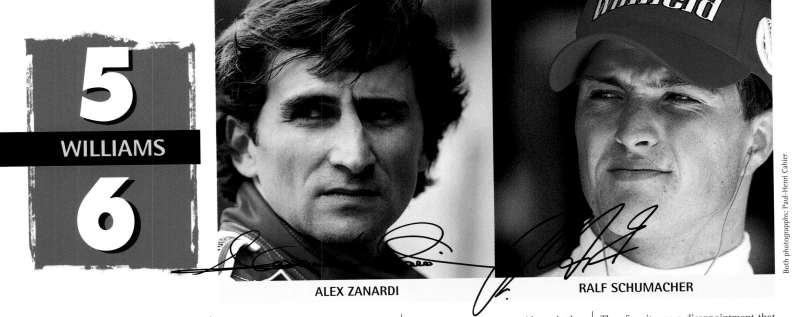

5 6 WILLIAMS

ALEX ZANARDI

RALF SCHUMACHER

IF they thought 1998 was bad, then Williams might well have been even more depressed by the results of 1999. At least they finished third in the constructors' title in 1998 but in 1999 they were pushed another two places down the pit lane, principally by Jordan, most of whose points were scored by 1998 Williams reject Heinz-Harald Frentzen.

Whether one blames this on a clean sweep of drivers, the ex-Renault V10 being a year older, or the after-effects of the loss of Adrian Newey doesn't really matter. The fact is that no team is more aware of its fall from grace than Williams, and no team more aware that there is no quick fix, in spite of the imminent arrival of BMW.

The year began with two new drivers, and a switch from Goodyears to the ubiquitous Bridgestones. On the driver front, gone were Jacques Villeneuve and Frentzen; enter reigning Indy Car champion Alex Zanardi returning from a four-year Formula One absence, and Ralf Schumacher after his two-year apprenticeship with Jordan.

Elsewhere, there was no change: same designers and technicians, and the same engine.

Williams's first contact with two of their novelties came a day or two after the last Grand Prix of 1998, at the post-Suzuka test. 'The Bridgestones,' said technical director Patrick Head, 'have been the same for everybody, but generally speaking they are not very happy about taking side load when they are taking longitudinal load, more so than the Goodyears. So when you're braking into a corner, the rear tends not to be very happy.' The tyres made it hard to set up a car that could brake deep into a corner, continued Head, while acknowledging it was the same for everyone.

Ralf Schumacher was instantly a hit, Williams's kind of driver. 'He's been very good from the moment he stepped into the car at Suzuka,' said Head. 'He's very precise, doesn't waste our time, is very focused on what characteristic of the car is going to allow him to go faster. He goes out in the car and the first lap he's on it straight away so

you immediately get an idea whether you've made an improvement or not. He's definitely been a good find and you only have to look at the number of points he's got and where he is in the championship considering the equipment to know that he's very good.'

The equipment, all in all, did not come up to expectations. 'The car was generally a bit of a disappointment in that we definitely had taken some pretty big steps relative to the FW20,' said Head. 'The car was a lot lighter than the FW20, it had a lot lower centre of gravity, there were quite a few things about it that were new and we thought were a lot better and I was expecting it to be considerably faster than the FW20.

'But in truth, at the beginning of the year, it wasn't and from that point of view, it was a big disappointment. The reason why we'd thought we'd made a good step forward was that we had pushed hard during the winter to lower the centre of gravity and we had succeeded by some considerable way.

Therefore it was a disappointment that the car didn't respond by producing considerably better lap times.

'Mainly, the problem was the stability. In common with most other teams we've had a problem with the stability of the car under braking and corner entry and we've been working to try and improve that.'

Changes to the bodywork and the diffuser just before the British Grand Prix, halfway through the season, certainly improved the car, and its performance, particularly on fast circuits, improved. 'It helped,' added Head, 'but it wasn't a cure.'

The fast circuit performance was, in a way, surprising, given the use of a customer engine that was designed in 1996 and which had seen precious little development in 1998 in spite of promises to the contrary.

Head acknowledges that it is a very well engineered unit but with no budget from Renault for development, any changes had to come out of the fees paid by the three teams that were using it. The reliability was excellent but

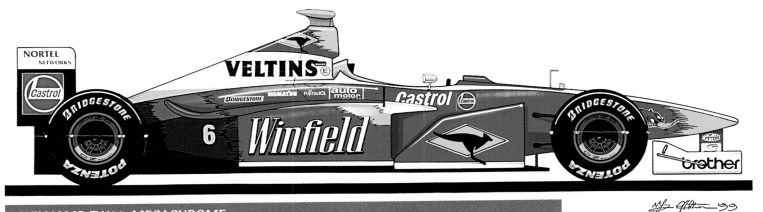

WILLIAMS FW21-MECACHROME

Sponsors: Winfield, Castrol, Champion, Sonax, Nortel, Petrobras, Anderson Consulting, Fujitsu, Brother, Auto Motorsport

Team principal: Frank Williams **Technical director:** Patrick Head **Team manager:** Dickie Stanford **Chief mechanic:** Carl Gaden

ENGINE **Type:** Supertec FB01 **No. of cylinders/vee angle:** V10 (71°) **Sparking plugs:** Champion **Electronics:** Magneti Marelli **Fuel:** Petrobras **Oil:** Castrol

TRANSMISSION **Gearbox:** Williams six-speed longitudinal semi-automatic **Driveshafts:** Williams **Clutch:** AP (hand-operated)

CHASSIS **Front suspension:** double wishbones, pushrod **Rear suspension:** double wishbones, pushrod **Suspension dampers:** Williams/Penske **Wheel diameter:** front: 13 in.
rear: 13 in. **Wheel rim widths:** front: 12 in. rear: 13.8 in. **Wheels:** OZ **Tyres:** Bridgestone **Brake pads:** Carbone Industrie/Hitco
Brake discs: Carbone Industrie/Hitco **Brake calipers:** AP **Steering:** Williams (power-assisted) **Radiators:** Secan/IMI Marston **Fuel tanks:** ATL **Instruments:** Williams

DIMENSIONS **Wheelbase:** not given **Track:** front: not given rear: not given **Formula weight:** 1322.8 lb/600 kg including driver **Fuel capacity:** not given

according to Head, 'one is looking at a 50–60 horsepower deficit to the front-running engines, you're looking at eight per cent, so it certainly makes quite a big difference depending on what kind of circuit you're on.

'It's not so significantly different at Hungary or Monaco in comparison to Monza or Hockenheim, but it does make a significant difference. But we've known that and accept it and that's the way it is but we start off in a position where we are not going to be as quick as the other cars because of the engine, but then there's the other factor of the handling of the car.

'For those reasons, I don't think we ever hoped to be championship contenders. There was always the possibility

of winning a race and, had it not been for a puncture, that would have happened at Nürburgring [coincidentally, the scene of the introduction of Supertec's spec B engine for qualifying]. But for that bolt [which punctured the tyre] we would have won a race. There was always that possibility, but we never saw ourselves as championship contenders because with the Supertec engine nobody was going to be a championship contender.'

The statistics show that Ralf Schumacher usually outqualified his teammate Zanardi who, sadly, made no contribution to his team's ultimate result. 'It's obviously been a considerable disappointment to us and to him,' says Head of Zanardi's year. 'There have

been a few occasions during the year when he might have been able to get points but for various reasons it hasn't happened, so it's a disappointment to both of us. It's something we both have to work out.'

Head sums up Zanardi's problems thus: 'I think a Formula One car is very edgy on these tyres. It has very little low-speed grip. It relies for its grip very much on its downforce and when you get down to low speed, it's very much on the edge and it's been a difficult adaption for him.'

Looking at the second half of the season, Head had seen light at the end of the tunnel; 'He was reasonably on the pace at Spa and very much on the pace at Monza. [He qualified fourth

Top left: Patrick Head could take some satisfaction from the mid-season improvements which turned the car into a top-six runner.
Paul-Henri Cahier

Top right: Sir Frank Williams and his wife, Virginia. The determined team owner is aiming to get back to the top of the pile with new partner BMW from 2000.
Bryn Williams/Words & Pictures

Above: Ralf Schumacher was a revelation for the team, with a number of scintillating drives.
Paul-Henri Cahier

Left: Patrick Head discusses the intricacies of the car with Ralf Schumacher and Alex Zanardi. The Italian two-time CART Champion endured an embarrassing downturn in fortunes on his Formula 1 return.
Bryn Williams/Words & Pictures

Below: Zanardi's only true front-running performance came at Monza where he was truly competitive before a loose undertray on his Williams dropped him from contention.
Paul-Henri Cahier

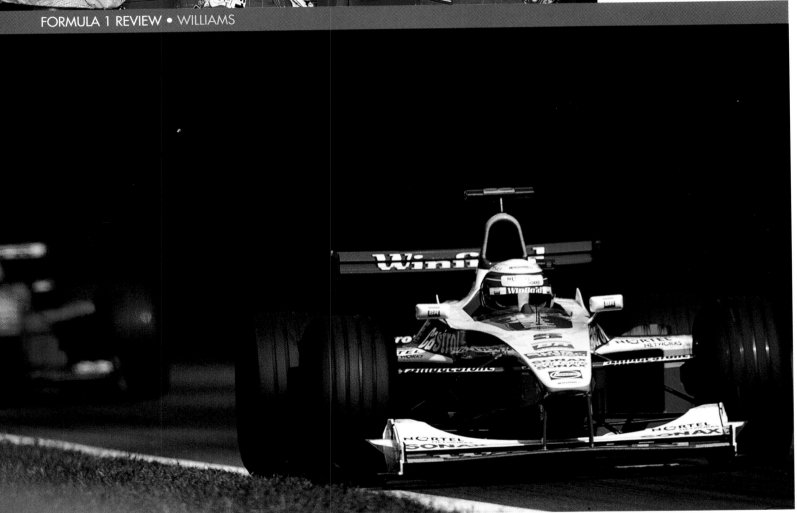

and finished seventh, best of the year.] But at Nürburgring he was looking to be in reasonable shape on the Saturday morning and then he just didn't get it together in the afternoon on the drying track. He was sent out at the right time on the right tyres but he didn't get a clear lap in at the right time.'

There were times early on when he looked to be on a par with his team-mate. He qualified one place behind Ralf at Imola (where Supertec introduced spec A and had some interesting mapping on hand) and was heading for at least one point when he spun out on Herbert's spilt oil. He was five places ahead of Schumacher on the grid at Monaco but finished eighth. He was a place ahead of Ralf in Canada too but while the German finished fourth, Alex retired. Hungary was largely disastrous, a wrong tyre choice says Head, but Alex was again a place ahead of his team-mate. Differential problems, his personal *bête noire*, cost him that race.

Ralf, however, just plugged away at it, doing the best he could with what he had. Grid positions were usually somewhere between 16 and eight in the first two thirds of the season. In Australia and at Silverstone, Ralf got onto the rostrum from eighth on the grid while there were points in Brazil, Spain, Canada, France and Germany.

The aerodynamic changes weren't 'a mega step', admitted Head. Performance improved only spasmodically. 'At Silverstone, we were a bit stronger. We qualified eighth whereas we had been qualifying ninth, tenth, eleventh beforehand. But we were racing with the Jordans who have considerably more power than us and have had all year, generally 40 to 50 horsepower ahead all year.

'Then we had Hockenheim where we qualified badly, mainly because the car wasn't very good at leaping over the kerbs at the chicanes, but we actually raced pretty well, finishing ten seconds or so behind the winner. But we had a really bad race at Hungary where we chose the wrong tyre and basically the car wasn't that good. Then it started coming stronger at Spa and then much stronger at Monza. Against our expectations it was pretty strong at Nürburgring again, and then we had another bad race at Malaysia where we weren't in particularly good shape. It's interesting that quite a few teams – not all, but quite a few – have been strong in some races and not very strong in others.'

With the turn of the new millennium, Williams also heads into a new era. BMW, says Head, will take time to be competitive. 'BMW are new into Formula One. Unlike Mercedes, they have not bought into an existing programme, they have started off, built a factory, built a facility, installed dynos, and it's bound to be that there will be a significant learning period. I think it's going to be a difficult year.'

Gone are the touring cars and BMW's Le Mans programme, not that they were in any way a distraction, emphasises Head. 'Certainly we've decided to focus our attention totally on Formula One for the next few years but I wouldn't say that that in itself is going to mean the resurgence of Williams. It's obviously going to take a very good engine from BMW and Williams improving whatever aspects we've been poor at over the last two or three years.' Typically, the determination is there. It's just a matter of time.

Bob Constanduros

May the force be with you in 2000

For over 50 years, AP Racing have pioneered advancements in clutch and brake technology. Today, the benefits of AP's science are evident in a range of applications for every form of motorsport, from Touring cars to World Rally cars; Formula Ford to Formula 1, where we currently supply 80% of the grid.

Advanced vehicle applications only happen through listening to our customers. And because we listen, they win.

Make sure the force is with you in the new millennium - talk to AP Racing.

the SCIENCE of FRICTION

DAMON HILL

HEINZ-HARALD FRENTZEN

Diana Burnett

Paul-Henri Cahier

THIRD place in the constructors' championship was no less a result than Jordan deserved. In fact, you wonder what might have been had they enjoyed the benefit of regular point-scoring by two drivers instead of one. Heinz-Harald Frentzen was the revelation of 1999, his transformation from a wasted talent made insecure by two years at Williams to a very quick and confident runner was yet another feather in Eddie Jordan's cap.

In opting for Frentzen, they were not only signing him to replace Ralf Schumacher but also denying the team, for the first time, the financial comfort of having at least one pay-driver on board. Employing two former winners such as Frentzen and Damon Hill was another sign of the Irishman's determination to have his team move away from the 'best of the rest' category and join the McLaren–Ferrari elite at the front.

Highlight of the team's history so far had been Damon Hill's victory at Spa in 1998 but, as the new season

kicked into life, there were one or two critics who believed that Spa had been a flash-in-the-pan, an opportunist result at the end of an unusual race. The feeling was that Jordan did not possess the clout and the culture to make such a major step forward. It became the unspoken ambition of Jordan, his managing director, Trevor Foster, and chief designer, Mike Gascoyne, to prove those remaining doubters wrong.

Jordan's notepaper no longer listed a technical director. Gary Anderson, who left the team to eventually join Stewart, had not been replaced when it came to filling this top position. Gascoyne, who had moved from Tyrrell mid-way through 1998, was under probation. His 1999 car, the Jordan Mugen-Honda 199, would therefore be proof of his ability as well as the team's statement of intent. After scoring 61 points, it could be said that both objectives have been achieved.

It was a tough task. Jordan had never before designed and constructed a car without the powerful presence of

Anderson in the drawing office and on the shop floor. Gascoyne encouraged key people – Mark Smith, head of mechanical design, John McQuilliam, in charge of composite design, John Iley, who was made head of aerodynamics, and John Davis, the head of R&D – to assist in a different style of management which allowed for more responsibility in the various departments. The performance of the car would be suitable testimony to the efficiency of this restructuring process.

'We had put a lot of work into the '98 car because we were developing it right up to the last race,' says Gascoyne. 'We were consolidating fourth in the constructors' championship and chasing after third. It was important to the team but, to be honest, it also hurt development of the 1999 car.

'The 199 was a bit of unknown territory for us all. The car was an evolution; it wasn't totally different and we wanted to stress that point. Yes, there were changes, but we understood them. We had a completely new gearbox and I'm very pleased we went

through that exercise; it was reliable from Day 1.

'The aim was to design a car which would start off where we had finished and then do exactly what we had done in the second half of 1998. In other words, we wanted to develop it and push hard so that we would not just be third – which was the minimum we wanted to accept – but also be closer to the top two teams than ever before.'

Unlike the disastrous start to the previous season, the early signs were good as Frentzen qualified fifth in Australia and took second place on a day when the McLarens retired. A strong race to make up for the absence of a clean lap in qualifying in Brazil saw Frentzen make a late stop and finish third place. He was about to repeat that result at Imola when he slid off on oil from Irvine's exploding Ferrari V10 but fourth place at Monaco kept the momentum going.

Then came a blip with mechanical failures for Heinz-Harald in Spain and Canada. The transmission trouble in Barcelona ended a weekend in which

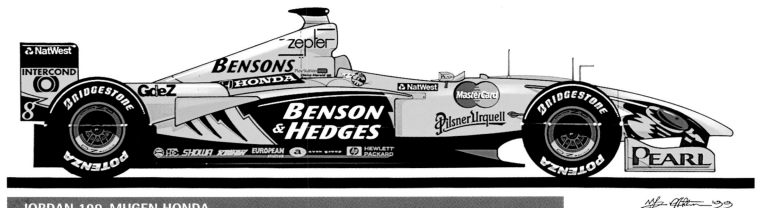

JORDAN 199-MUGEN HONDA

Sponsors: Benson & Hedges, MasterCard, Pearl, Pilsner Urquell, NatWest, Zepter, Intercond, PlayStation, Lucent

Team principal: Eddie Jordan **Technical director:** Mike Gascoyne **Team manager:** Jim Vale **Chief mechanic:** Tim Edwards

ENGINE	Type: Mugen Honda MF301HD	No. of cylinders/vee angle: V10 (72°)	Sparking plugs: NGK	Electronics: Honda PGM F1	Fuel: Elf	Oil: Elf

TRANSMISSION **Gearbox:** Jordan six-speed longitudinal semi-automatic **Driveshafts:** Jordan/Pankl **Clutch:** Jordan/Sachs (hand-operated)

CHASSIS **Front suspension:** double wishbones, pushrod-operated rockers **Rear suspension:** double wishbones, pushrod-operated rockers

Suspension dampers: Penske **Wheel diameter:** front: 13 in. rear: 13 in. **Wheel rim widths:** front: 12 in. rear: 13.7 in. **Wheels:** OZ **Tyres:** Bridgestone

Brake pads: Hitco **Brake discs:** Hitco **Brake calipers:** Brembo **Steering:** Jordan **Radiators:** Secan **Fuel tanks:** ATL **Battery:** Jordan **Instruments:** Jordan

DIMENSIONS **Wheelbase:** 3050 mm **Track:** front: 59.1 in./1500 mm rear: 55.8 in./1418 mm **Gearbox weight:** 110.2 lb/50 kg **Chassis weight (tub):** 88.2 lb/40 kg

Formula weight: 1322.8 lb/600 kg including driver **Fuel capacity:** not given

⌐"Leader of the Pack"♩
by Scania

Scania. Europe's leading truck maker, Jordan's choice for transportation.

Tel.01908 210210 www.scania.co.uk

Right: Eddie Jordan saw his team consolidate their position in the big league with third place in the constructors' championship.

Below: Heinz-Harald Frentzen on his way to winning the Italian Grand Prix at Monza.

All photographs: Paul-Henri Cahier

the team had not been competitive by their standards. But the brake disc failure in Montreal occurred in the closing stages as Frentzen was heading for an excellent second.

'That was a huge disappointment,' admits Gascoyne. 'Barcelona had been our worst performance but, even so, Heinz-Harald would have finished fifth but for a driveshaft bearing failure. We had expected to go well in Canada and that was the case until the brake disc went. I really don't want to say much about that – except that it shouldn't have happened. At that point, we had 16 points and Williams had 12. We were kicking ourselves, thinking we had thrown it away.'

That would turn around dramatically at the next race in France even

though, prior to Magny-Cours, the odds appeared to be against a decent result. Frentzen had injured his leg during the high-speed shunt and he had done no running since Canada. But, in a race of dry–wet–dry conditions, clean driving and clever tactics brought Benson and Hedges Jordan their second Grand Prix victory.

'We had felt from the start of the season that, if we could produce a car that was third best in the field, then we would be able to pick up the odd win that inevitably comes your way,' says Gascoyne. 'But you've got to make sure you're there to collect it! We did that in Magny-Cours. In fact, it was better than that. The strategy was right and we beat the opposition on the road. That was a very pleasing win.'

It would signal the start of a second-half surge as the team became even stronger, particularly during qualifying. With Michael Schumacher having temporarily written himself and Ferrari out of the equation at Silverstone, the Jordan was often vying to be the second-fastest car as Frentzen ran through to the end of the European sector of the season by qualifying inside the top five, usually on the front two rows and, at the Nurburgring, on pole.

Even when a dismal qualifying session occurred at the penultimate round in Malaysia, the team's strength in depth was proved when Frentzen moved from 14th on the grid to finish in the top six, thus securing third place in the constructors' championship. Of

the 60-odd points, Frentzen had scored all but seven of them, which said everything about Hill's disappointing year.

'There's no argument that Damon struggled,' says Gascoyne. 'But these things happen. Very few teams have two drivers who can go at it tooth and nail all season long. You could argue that if Heinz-Harald had, say, 40 points, then if Damon had been up there with him, the team would have scored 80. But it doesn't work that way. One driver would have had 20 and the other 30, or something like that. You've got to take the rough with the smooth.

'Overall, though, the engineers worked well with their drivers, Dino Toso carrying on his association with Damon

and Sam Michael quickly striking up an excellent rapport with the resurgent Heinz-Harald, who has been a revelation. It's been great to see such a nice guy prove it to them all. The quote of the year for me was when "H-H" crossed the line at Magny-Cours, came on the radio and just said "F*** 'em!".'

Jordan's relationship with Mugen-Honda went from strength to strength, the Japanese manufacturer providing an endless stream of modifications and improvements, all of which were shown to be worthwhile and, more to the point, incredibly reliable. What will happen next year as Honda embraces BAR is another story to which no one at Jordan knows the conclusion.

'All we can do is aim to qualify in the top four, finish on the podium and win races,' says Gascoyne. 'It's up to us to perform. If we can do that, then the rest will follow. We want to carry on where we left off this year.

'We achieved a lot in 1999. If you were to ask me which was our best race, I would say the Nürburgring – which might sound strange considering both cars went out with an electrical problem and we won in France and at Monza. But it was a high-downforce circuit and people said we would struggle. And yet the car was quick all weekend, we got it right in qualifying, took pole, made a good start, led the first 35 laps – which

Jordan had never done before – called the pit stop and executed it perfectly to retain the lead.

'Heinz drove an immaculate race. He hasn't put a foot wrong all year and, had the problem not struck just after the pit stop, I don't think he would have made the sort of mistake in the wet conditions which everyone else made.

He didn't finish but Jordan Grand Prix had reached another important milestone. We've just got to make sure there'll be more to follow in 2000. I'm very confident that'll be the case.'

Maurice Hamilton

Top left: Unconfined joy for Heinz-Harald Frentzen and Eddie Jordan after the German's win in the French Grand Prix.

Top right: Down in the dumps. Damon Hill felt the pace during his final season in Formula 1 and his performances with the Jordan *(above)* were, in the main, disappointing.

All photographs: Paul-Henri Cahier

Imagine this is your most important customer.

Now try communicating with him.

As Global Innovation Partner of Jordan Grand Prix, Lucent Technologies is pleased
to partner with the most exciting team in Formula One.
Leading-edge technology from Lucent's Bell Labs gives Jordan access to the most advanced
voice, data and messaging communications in the world.

If we can keep up with them, just think what we can do for you.

Lucent Technologies
Bell Labs Innovations
www.lucent.com

We make the things that make communications work.™

9
BENETTON
10

GIANCARLO FISICHELLA   ALEXANDER WURZ

THE frustration for Benetton is that their car was not as bad as it often looked. But that does little to compensate the former champions for slipping to sixth in the constructors' championship, the British-based team's worst result, probably, since their drivers were in short pants.

We lost count of the times television pictures showed either Giancarlo Fisichella or Alexander Wurz motoring across gravel and, if they were lucky, regaining the track after a lurid moment. If there was to be a prize for perseverance, it would probably go to these two by a short head over the BAR drivers simply because Wurz and Fisichella spent most of the season with a fair idea of where the problem lay but knowing that the team could do little about it.

'No grip' became a familiar mantra each time a Benetton driver pulled off his crash helmet. And, no matter what they tried, there seemed to be no cure. Fisichella's second place in Canada was not a true indicator of form during a season when the Benettons generally appeared to be motoring nowhere.

A new car launch with novel entertainment had started the year on a bright note. Pat Symonds, the technical director, spoke confidently about the team's hopes for the B199, a car which was revolutionary rather than evolutionary thanks to several innovative engineering solutions. The B199 was the second car produced under the leadership of Chief Designer Nick Wirth, who claimed he had been 'aggressive in all areas'.

Not counting wheels, tyres and engines, around 90 per cent of the Mild Seven Benetton Playlife B199 had been made in-house, 'Playlife' being a commercial consideration when it came to badging the Supertec, aka Mecachrome, aka Renault.

Regardless of what you cared to call the engine, Fisichella was the fastest among the customers for the French V10 when he qualified seventh for the opening race in Australia. A tangle with Trulli meant a new nose at the start; fourth place at the finish appearing to be a reasonable reward. But the truth was that the McLarens had retired

and Schumacher's Ferrari was some way behind. It would be a struggle from here on.

'The reason we've been in trouble,' says Symonds, 'is that the aerodynamic performance of the car, as measured on the circuit, had a lower efficiency than we believed it should have based on our wind tunnel testing. In other words, there was a critical area of the aerodynamics that had effectively screwed it up.

'Due to the subtleties of this, it really only came to light around Silverstone time. Certain measurements we had taken led us to believe that everything was okay. But when we started looking for a reason why our performance would never meet what ought to have been possible, we started taking more detailed measurements.

'Since finding that, we did a lot more checking of our aerodynamics on the circuit. Unfortunately, that's a far less controlled experiment than the wind tunnel and, even at a late stage in the season, we hadn't cured the problem. We had found certain ways

of what I would call damage limitation; certain ways of making the problem less harmful. But we hadn't actually cured it.

'On the occasions when we could get things working a bit closer to optimum efficiency – and we didn't achieve what we believed to be close to optimum efficiency by quite a long way – we had a considerable improvement in the performance of the car. Which wasn't surprising, really.

'When we've had that reasonable performance, it really was quite competitive. So my feeling was that the fundamentals of the car were – I don't like to use the word adequate because that's a very wishy-washy expression – but let's just say that the fundamentals of the car were not as bad as its performance made them appear. Just like a chain is only as strong as its weakest link, it was the same with our car. The weak link was its aerodynamic performance.

'Very often the drivers would come in and say "well, we don't really know where we should be working because

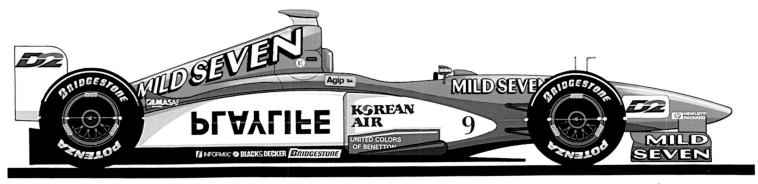

BENETTON B199-PLAYLIFE

Sponsors: Mild Seven, Benetton, Playlife, Agip, FedEx, D2, Korean Air, Cybex, Hewlett Packard, Rauch, Unigraphic Solutions

Team principals: Rocco Benetton   **Technical director:** Pat Symonds   **Team managers:** Joan Villadelprat and Mark Owen   **Chief mechanic:** Michael Ainsley-Cowlishaw

ENGINE   **Type:** Supertec FB01 (Playlife)   **No. of cylinders/vee angle:** V10 (71°)   **Sparking plugs:** Champion   **Electronics:** Magneti Marelli   **Fuel:** Agip   **Oil:** Agip

TRANSMISSION   **Gearbox:** Benetton six-speed longitudinal semi-automatic   **Driveshafts:** Benetton   **Clutch:** AP (hand-operated)

CHASSIS   **Front suspension:** double wishbones, pushrod   **Rear suspension:** double wishbones, pushrod   **Suspension dampers:** Dynamic

     Wheel diameter: front: 13 in.   rear: 13 in.   **Wheel rim widths:** front: not given   rear: not given   **Wheels:** BBS   **Tyres:** Bridgestone   **Brake pads:** Carbone Industrie

     Brake discs: Carbone Industrie   **Brake calipers:** Brembo   **Steering:** Benetton (power-assisted)   **Radiators:** Benetton/IMI Marston   **Fuel tanks:** ATL

     Battery: Benetton   **Instruments:** Benetton

DIMENSIONS   **Wheelbase:** not given   **Track:** front: 58.7 in./1490 mm   rear: 55.3 in./1405 mm   **Formula weight:** 1322.8 lb/600 kg including driver   **Fuel capacity:** not given

the balance is good. But can we have some more grip?" If you piled on wing, you didn't actually get more grip; all you did was get drag.'

Symonds had no complaints about Supertec's role and the continuing packages introduced by the Renault engineers, the development being more like the Renault of old and certainly much better than the progress, or lack of it, in 1998. But, if that had been a pleasant surprise, then the failure of planned performance improvements – such as a Front Torque Transfer system (FTT) – was to be a disappointment.

'After what we experienced in 1998, we felt that if we were going to be at an engine disadvantage in 1999 then it was particularly important to try and gain an advantage in another field,' says Symonds. 'We put a lot of effort into the FTT system and a twin-clutch gearbox. This led to certain design compromises which we felt were worth making in order to have the advantage the systems would give us.

'Both of them proved to be far more troublesome than we first thought. We were really quite happy with the FTT we ran the previous year but, in 1999, we ran into a fundamental mechanical problem which both Xtrac and ourselves were unable to solve.

'Similarly, with the twin-clutch gearbox [introduced with the aim of improving acceleration], we were not in a financial position to make a twin-clutch gearbox and a single-clutch gearbox. We had to make a design that would allow both systems to be used and obviously that compromised the design. Again, we were unable to use the twin-clutch gearbox because its problems were not solved.

'Nonetheless, I think they were brave decisions that, with hindsight, were incorrect. It meant that the car was heavier than we would have liked it to be with regard to having a decent amount of ballast to play with. That has cost us those odd tenths at every single race. But it was nothing compared with the aerodynamic performance loss which cost us many tenths.'

Despite such a desperately difficult season, Symonds is full of praise for the attitude of the team as they cheerfully buckled down to the work each race weekend knowing that the end result, in all probability, would not be close to their pre-season expectations. It was the same for the drivers, particularly Fisichella.

'We're very pleased with Giancarlo's efforts,' says Symonds. 'I felt he was a very good driver in 1998 but he needed to sharpen up in a couple of areas. For instance, I felt that his race performances had tailed off a little bit. We had a feeling that this was due to fitness and we pushed him hard on the fitness front and he has been superb.

'Alex has had a more troubled year. He found the characteristics of the car harder to handle than Giancarlo and he didn't show what we all know he is capable of. We signed him for 2000 because we didn't feel that his poor performances were a reflection of his capabilities; they were more a reflection of our car.'

It is easy to point the finger for such a disappointing season at Rocco Benetton, the scion of the knitwear family who took charge following the departure of David Richards after a 12-month tenure by the Englishman. Rocco Benetton is chief executive while Symonds has total control of the engineering side.

'Rocco looks at the big plan,' says Symonds. 'He looks at strategically where we should be and what we need to be doing in several years' time. For that you need a certain skill, a certain vision and, if you've been in motor racing for years, you could argue that it helps. Equally, you can say that there are advantages with a fresh approach. A good business mind should be able to analyse a specific business and make it work.

'But, in the short term, the day-to-day running of the team, particularly the engineering, is not down to Rocco and therefore it would be totally wrong to blame our aerodynamic problems on him.

'I personally feel it is a big advantage for the team to have the knowledge that the family is directly involved now. The family has been a fantastic supporter of ours over the years and it's nice to know that one of the family members is in the office every day, totally aware of what's going on.

'We have gone through another transition from last year but, fundamentally, Benetton remains a strong team with very good people. We haven't had a season which we can look back on with pride but we've understood our mistakes and obviously taken steps to ensure they don't happen again in 2000. That's as fair an assessment as I can make of a difficult year.'

Maurice Hamilton

Top left: Chief designer Nick Wirth took an 'aggressive in all areas' approach to the design of the 1999 Benetton. Unfortunately the car was afflicted with aerodynamic problems which severely limited its progress.

Top centre: Rocco Benetton took overall control of the team concentrating on the bigger picture, plotting the future direction of the team.

Above: Alex Wurz struggled with the car throughout the year, but retained the confidence of the team and stays on with Fisichella for 2000.

All photographs: Paul-Henri Cahier

11
SAUBER
12

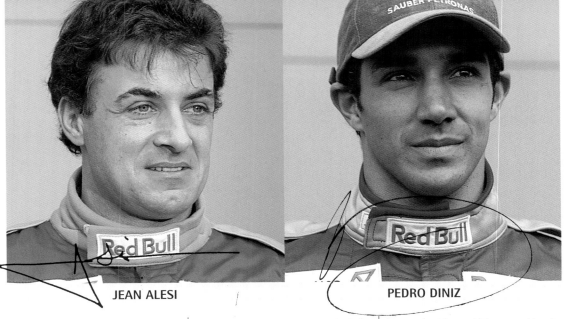

JEAN ALESI   PEDRO DINIZ

Both photographs: Paul-Henri Cahier

IT'S sad when a team feels that it has under-performed but that was certainly the feeling at Sauber in 1999. They scored eight points, the first time that they'd been in single figures since they came into Formula One. The drivers, designer and the team all expected more, so what went wrong?

Perhaps one of the plus points about Sauber is its stability. It doesn't change much; 75 per cent of the mechanics have been with the team since it started in F1 in 1993, some even longer – since the sports car days. Okay, there aren't that many other teams nearby that they can move to. To keep competitive, however, they have to look over their shoulders at other rivals.

In 1999, Peter Sauber changed the structure of the company, and brought in a number two, Jost Capito from Germany. He had joined Sauber from Porsche where he organised the Porsche Pirelli Super Cup and during his early stages with Sauber, and had very successfully developed a road car engine for Petronas.

Taking over an F1 team, then, was an entirely new job for which he had little or no experience. By all accounts, he struggled under considerable pressure, with too much to do. His management style as number two was perhaps a little autocratic and had an adverse effect on the very stability that had been such a bonus in the past.

'There was tension within the team,' said one member. 'The attitude was no longer positive,' said another. 'We lost the spirit, we weren't motivated,' said a third. The sacking of race engineer Tim Preston was laid at his door, and that annoyed Jean Alesi. 'When you are working in a team, you know who you are working with, but I can't understand when someone just outside the team sacks them,' said Alesi. That, and the temptation to work with his old friend Alain Prost meant that the Frenchman was gone at the end of the year.

However, the lack of success of the team cannot be blamed on one man. Sure, the structure of the team changed,

and by the season's end, so had the shareholding, with Peter Sauber's long-time commercial partner Fritz Kaiser selling his share back to Sauber.

At the start of the year, there were several reliability problems, which also frustrated the team. Technical director Leo Ress admitted that three tests weren't enough to make the car reliable. After the first Grand Prix in Melbourne, changes had to be made to the gearbox software. Admittedly there were probably difficulties changing from Goodyear to Bridgestone: 'we probably didn't understand them 100 per cent'.

The second race in Brazil produced the first signs of the potential of the car which would, however, be frustrated throughout the year. Alesi qualified 14th while new team-mate Pedro Diniz was 15th. By lap 21, in spite of a spin, the Frenchman was up to fifth place, but then he had to retire with a gearbox failure. Diniz got up to seventh before a spin, but after the race a puzzled Peter Sauber pleaded 'I don't understand why we are so quick in the race after being so slow

in practice.' It would be something he would get used to.

Alesi reckoned he had the answer. 'The car is on the weight limit,' he explained, 'whereas many others are below the weight limit, carrying ballast for qualifying, which keeps the centre of gravity low. But in the race, they are carrying fuel and not ballast, so we are all the same which gives us an opportunity to race.' And providing his car was handling well, Alesi could always be relied on to do what he does best: race and inspire the team.

The first two races saw three retirements due to the gearbox or transmission, but Alesi scored the team's first point at Imola. Slow corners didn't suit the car, so Monaco was not a success, but then Alesi was fifth on the grid in Barcelona and Diniz 12th, partially thanks to a new diffuser. Neither car finished, due to transmission problems which were becoming a rather too permanent thorn in the team's side.

Alesi again qualified well for Montreal partially thanks to a new-spec Petronas (née Ferrari) engine,

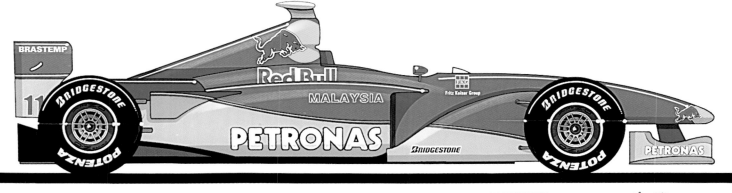

SAUBER C18-PETRONAS

Sponsors: Red Bull, Petronas, Parmalat, Compaq, Bridgestone, Catia Solutions, OZ, Kenwood, Magneti Marelli

Team principal: Peter Sauber **Technical director:** Leo Ress **Team manager:** Beat Zehnder **Chief mechanic:** Urs Kuratle

ENGINE   Type: Petronas (Ferrari) **No. of cylinders/vee angle:** V10 (80°) **Sparking plugs:** Champion **Electronics:** Magneti Marelli **Fuel:** Petronas **Oil:** Petronas

TRANSMISSION   Gearbox: Sauber seven-speed longitudinal semi-automatic **Driveshafts:** Sauber **Clutch:** Sachs (hand-operated)

CHASSIS   Front suspension: double wishbones, pushrod **Rear suspension:** double wishbones, pushrod

Suspension dampers: Sachs **Wheel diameter:** front: 13 in. rear: 13 in. **Wheel rim widths:** front: not given rear: not given **Wheels:** BBS **Tyres:** Bridgestone

Brake pads: Carbone Industrie/Hitco **Brake discs:** Carbone Industrie/Hitco **Brake calipers:** Brembo **Steering:** Sauber **Radiators:** Behr/Secan **Fuel tanks:** ATL

Battery: Champion/SPE **Instruments:** Magneti Marelli

DIMENSIONS   Wheelbase: not given **Track:** front: 58.1 in./1475 mm rear: 55.5 in./1410 mm **Gearbox weight:** not given **Chassis weight (tub):** not given

Formula weight: 1322.8 lb/600 kg including driver **Fuel capacity:** 30.3 gallons/138 litres

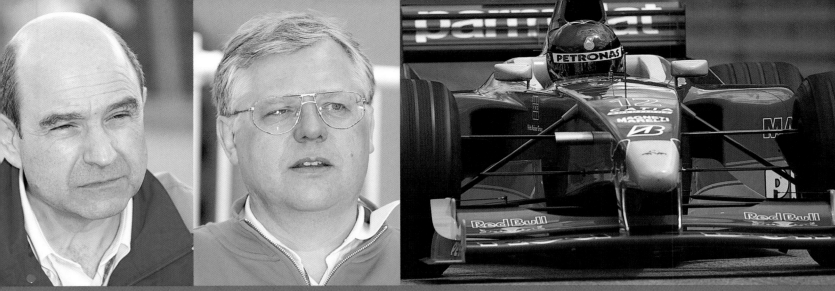

but for the second year running it ended in tears at the first corner. However, team-mate Diniz came through the carnage to score the team's second point. He had started the weekend off with a nasty accident in practice, eventually found to have been caused by a loss of brake fluid due to a cracked brake nipple. Alesi judged the weather just right to start second in Magny-Cours but frustratingly spun out of that place on the wet track just as the safety car came out.

Now came a number of quick circuits to which the car, in theory, was well suited. At Silverstone, the drivers were battling with the Stewarts, but Alesi dropped back, while

Diniz came through to finish sixth. Two weeks later in Austria, the pair stormed through the field on a two-stop strategy, Diniz eventually finishing sixth again, but the low-downforce package initially didn't work for Hockenheim and had to be redesigned for Monza, while a change to the springs and dampers allowed for a more flexible set-up.

Hungary saw the sacking of race engineer Steve Clark after he objected to having to allow his man Diniz to pull over and let team-mate Alesi past. That further heightened tension in the team. The final races of the year didn't really bring anything, apart from a fine sixth place at Suzuka for Alesi in

his farewell race for Sauber. Diniz, too, ended a six-race succession of spins and accidents.

At least there was a determination by this stage to get things right in 2000. By the year's end, a new gearbox was ready to be mated to the latest engine which would be tested in an interim car early in December. Whether the management structure would allow the team to regain its confidence remained to be seen but Ress was determined that technically, they would be better prepared than in 1999.

Bob Constanduros

Top left: Peter Sauber presided over a team which seemed at times to suffer from a degree of disharmony.

Top centre: Leo Ress felt his car underperformed in 1999 and plans are already in hand to rectify the situation for next season.
Lukas Gorys

Top right: Pedro Diniz did his usual solid job of picking up the odd point whenever more fancied runners failed.

Above: Jean Alesi ended the season with a mere two World Championship points. Not surprisingly, the Frenchman has made tracks for Prost.
Paul-Henri Cahier

FLY FIRST CLASS

Ninja **There's no other way to fly.**

And once you've sampled this class of travel you'll want to repeat the experience again and again.

The on board information is supreme and the ride every bit as thrilling as a takeoff from Tokyo.

ZX-12R Ultimate in ultrasports, this bike will make your stopwatch redundant. It's unrivalled blend of class-leading power, high speed stability and swift, responsive handling combines a Concorde speed sensation with Top Gun turning ability.

Fly First Class with Kawasaki. It's the only way.

Kawasaki Motors (UK) Ltd., 1 Dukes Meadow, Millboard Road, Bourne End, Bucks. SL8 5XF. Tel: 01628 856600. Customer Care Line: 01628 856750. Brochure Hotline: 0800 500245.
Ride responsibly within the law and with respect for other road users. Wear an approved helmet and correct protective clothing. Never drink and ride. Remember you are an ambassador for motorcycling and act accordingly.
All new machines designated 250cc and above have two year warranty and one year Kawasaki Riders Club membership & Kawasaki RAC Assist cover.

ZX-9R Right weight. Right power. Right handling… the Right Stuff. The ZX-9R was already a high flier, for Year 2000 its weight has been trimmed, power uprated, steering sharpened and handling made even more precise. Fuel up, get on board and fly.

ZX-6R The unique combination of class leading performance, scalpel sharp handling and legendary long-haul comfort is fine tuned for 2000. A list of upgrades including engine, chassis and styling improvements make this 600cc supersports a first class flyer for an economy fare.

Kawasaki

Let the good times roll.

14

ARROWS

15

PEDRO DE LA ROSA

TORANOSUKE TAKAGI

CASH-strapped and making do, the Arrows team would like to reflect on the 1999 season as a brief stopping point on the road to a brighter future with a bigger budget and a more powerful engine next season. Certainly the past season was an uncomfortable struggle with technical director Mike Coughlan doing his best with very limited resources to develop the A19 chassis which had originally been designed by John Barnard.

Coughlan effectively limited himself to updates required by the technical regulations in developing the A20 which had the same monocoque, oil system and Brian Hart-built V10 engine as its immediate predecessor.

'We designed new front and rear suspension in an effort to alter the weight distribution to cater for the new four-grooved front tyres,' said Coughlan, 'but after that we did almost no development due to lack of money.

'Obviously we had to uprate the impact structures for the '99 rules and the only major change was a new floor for Silverstone which was only subtly different. Then Eghbal Hamedy [Stewart's former aerodynamicist] joined the team and he used his input to make modifications to the floor for the Italian Grand Prix. Beyond that there was not much.'

Lack of finance also precluded any major development on the Hart V10s which were prepared at Hart's Harlow base, and although TWR Engines developed a revised cylinder head this was not raced before the end of the season.

The year ended with a legal dispute between Hart and Walkinshaw over the terms of Arrows' purchase of his business and there remained a question mark over how long the determined privateer engine builder would remain associated with the team into the future.

The season began on a moderately upbeat note with Pedro de la Rosa posting a sixth place finish to take the team's sole championship point of the season in Melbourne.

'De La Rosa was a good find,' insists Coughland. 'He's a good driver and in a top car he could be very good. Tora, on the other hand, can produce a really quick lap but is not so good over a race distance. He was like that at Tyrrell during testing. He starts off quick, but if the car develops a handling imbalance he just drops away down the field rather than adapting his style to cater for the change in the car's behaviour.'

At the start of the season merchant bankers Morgan Grenfell also took a stake in the company and the self-styled Nigerian Prince Malik was also

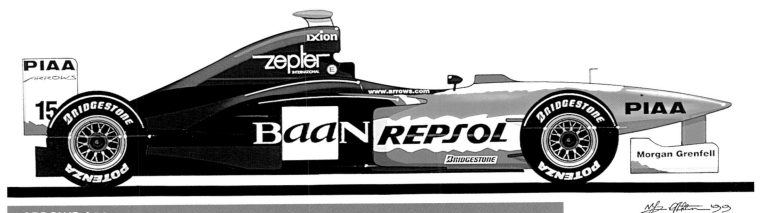

ARROWS A20

Sponsors: Repsol, PIAA, Morgan Grenfell, Zepter, Power Horse, Bridgestone

Team principal: Tom Walkinshaw **Technical director:** Mike Coughlan **Team manager:** Rod Benoist **Chief mechanic:** Stuart Cowie

ENGINE   Type: Arrows **No. of cylinders/vee angle:** V10 (72°) **Sparking plugs:** Champion **Electronics:** Arrows/TAG **Fuel:** Repsol **Oil:** Repsol

TRANSMISSION   Gearbox: Arrows carbon fibre six-speed longitudinal semi-automatic **Driveshafts:** Arrows **Clutch:** AP (hand-operated)

CHASSIS   Front suspension: double wishbones, pushrod **Rear suspension:** double wishbones, pushrod **Suspension dampers:** Dynamic **Wheel diameter:** front: 13 in. rear: 13 in.

Wheel rim widths: front: 12 in. rear: 13.7 in. **Wheels:** BBS **Tyres:** Bridgestone **Brake pads:** Carbone Industrie **Brake discs:** Carbone Industrie **Brake calipers:** AP

Steering: Arrows **Radiators:** Secan/IMI Marston **Fuel tanks:** ATL **Battery:** Arrows **Instruments:** Arrows

DIMENSIONS   Wheelbase: not given **Track:** front: not given rear: not given **Formula weight:** 1322.8 lb/600 kg including driver **Fuel capacity:** not given

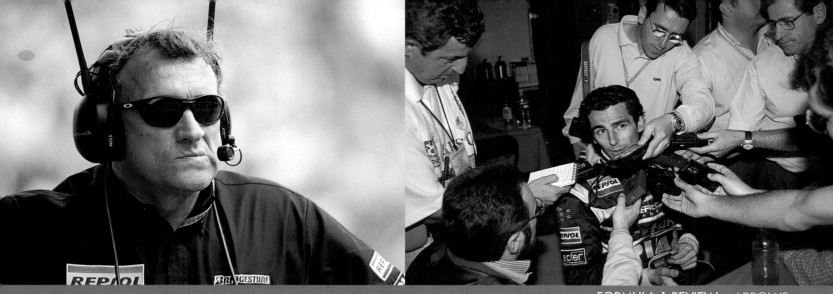

involved trying to promote his T-Minus branding concept as a vehicle for raising major sponsorship for the team. Unfortunately this relationship failed to last the year and Malik was not to be seen in the F1 paddocks by the end of the season.

By the end of the season Coghlan, Hamedy and their colleagues in the design office were flat-out working on a new chassis to take the Supertec V10 engine Arrows will be using next season. For his part, Tom Walkinshaw is pulling out all the stops to attract a major motor manufacturer as a potential partner. He knows that is the only way forward for his team in the long term.

Alan Henry

Opposite centre: Prince Malik disappeared from the team almost as quickly as he had arrived.
Paul-Henri Cahier

Top left: Tom Walkinshaw had plenty to chew on in a tough season.
Paul-Henri Cahier

Top right: Pedro de la Rosa finds himself in demand by journalists after scoring a point on his debut in Australia.
Michael Roberts

Above: The Spanish driver did a good job, given the car's lack of development.
Paul-Henri Cahier

Left: Toranosuke Takagi reflects on his lot as one of the Formula 1 backmarkers.
Paul-Henri Cahier

16 STEWART 17

RUBENS BARRICHELLO **JOHNNY HERBERT**

Both photographs: Diana Burnett

FOR its third season in Formula One, Stewart-Ford's design team was now led by former Jordan technical chief Gary Anderson who took over from Alan Jenkins after the basic architecture of the new SF3 chassis had been decided upon.

The first chassis was being laid up when Anderson arrived at the team's new Milton Keynes headquarters and the first thing he did was to scrap it and start again, citing its lack of torsional rigidity as its biggest problem. There was not time for Anderson to design a totally new car at all, but the subsequent chassis were stiffened up and throughout the season a rolling programme to enhance this aspect of the car continued to good effect.

The new car/engine combination had proved fast but fragile in pre-season testing with V10 failures and a spectacular rear wing breakage at Barcelona dramatically punctuating their progress. Yet the new car was very quick from the start of the season, fast enough to lead the Brazilian Grand Prix at Interlagos before an

engine failure sidelined the car while running in a strong third place.

One rival team director noted: 'The performance of the Stewarts in the early races of the season was an apparent anomaly which I couldn't quite reconcile in my mind. They were out of sequence compared to my perception of their potential.'

This was in fact a compliment stemming from the fact that the cars ran so strongly in the early races of the season. Barrichello's drive to fifth place at Melbourne, starting the spare car from the pit lane after engine bay fires sidelined both his original race car and Johnny Herbert's sister machine, set the tone for the year.

In many ways the Stewart-Ford performance could be regarded as the most impressive of the season. Having struggled badly during its second F1 season in 1998 during which the cars rarely scored points and were beset with continual reliability problems, the SF3 brought with it an upsurge in hope and promise which was not misplaced.

'We sustained a constant progress of refinement through the year with various suspension geometries and combination of geometries,' said Anderson. 'There was nothing we haven't tried out.

'The fuel tank was not really big enough, which hurt our strategy in one or two races, but we tried as much as possible within the structure of the company. We didn't do anything which I could describe as really wrong, but I do feel a bit disappointed that we did not really make the step forward that we should have done. Within the constraints we had, we did a good job.'

That was the point, of course. Stewart was still a young team with an expanding infrastructure in which people were still learning how to work with each other. Nevertheless, at the end of the day Johnny Herbert managed to bag the team its first Grand Prix win at Nürburgring thanks to a clever race strategy which saw the imp-like Englishman selecting the right tyre option at the right moment in the changing track conditions.

It was a golden moment for Jackie and Paul Stewart whose efforts had sometimes privately been scoffed at by other rivals in the pit lane. Yet it had taken their new team less than three seasons to post its maiden Grand Prix victory, an achievement which had taken Jordan eight years and a milestone yet to be achieved by Arrows after 22 seasons.

Cosworth Racing's commitment to the programme was running at a much more intense level now that Ford had decided to purchase the company and this was supplemented by their purchase of Stewart Grand Prix itself in the middle of the summer.

This deal, reputedly worth in the order of 70 million pounds, could be taken as a massive endorsement of faith both in F1 as a whole and the Stewart family in particular, the payoff perhaps for an impeccable 35-year association which Jackie had enjoyed with the Detroit car company.

This new alliance enabled Stewart to send one of its SF3 chassis to Detroit for static rig testing at the motor

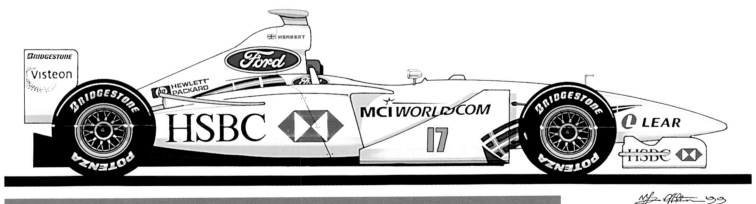

STEWART SF3–FORD

Sponsors: Ford, HSBC, Lear, MCI Worldcom, Visteon, Hewlett Packard, Bride Unigraphic Solutions

Team principals: Jackie and Paul Stewart Technical director: Gary Anderson Team manager: Dave Stubbs Chief mechanic: Dave Redding

ENGINE Type: Ford CR1 No. of cylinders/vee angle: V10 (72°) Sparking plugs: Champion Electronics: Visteon Fuel: Texaco Oil: Texaco

TRANSMISSION Gearbox: Stewart six-speed longitudinal semi-automatic Driveshafts: Stewart Clutch: AP (hand-operated)

CHASSIS Front suspension: double wishbones, pushrod Rear suspension: double wishbones, pushrod Suspension dampers: Stewart/Penske

Wheel diameter: front: 13 in. rear: 13 in. Wheel rim widths: front: not given rear: not given Wheels: BBS Tyres: Bridgestone Brake pads: Carbone Industrie

Brake discs: Carbone Industrie Brake calipers: Brembo Steering: Stewart Radiators: Secan/IMI Marston Fuel tanks: ATL Battery: FIAMM Instruments: Visteon

DIMENSIONS Wheelbase: not given Track: front: not given rear: not given Gearbox weight: not given Chassis weight (tub): not given

Formula weight: 1322.8 lb/600 kg including driver Fuel capacity: not given

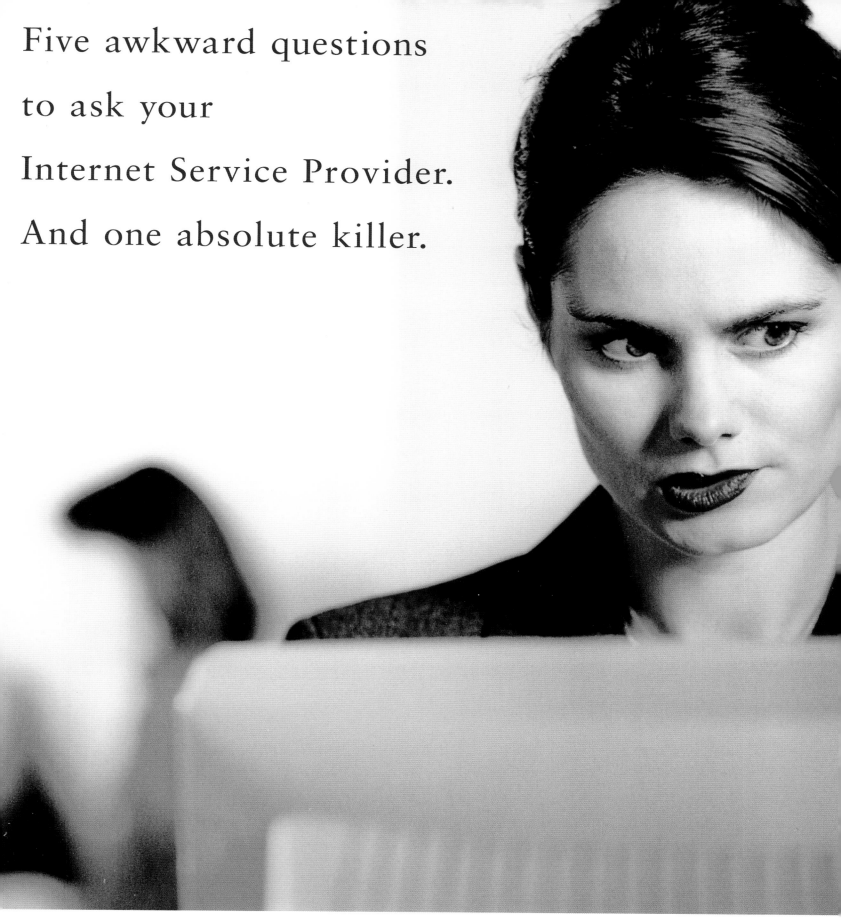

Five awkward questions to ask your Internet Service Provider. And one absolute killer.

A̲sk them • Do they own and manage the largest, most sophisticated and most reliable Internet network in the world? UUNET does • Do they, like UUNET, focus on business customers and business customers alone? Can they, like UUNET, guarantee that you'll always have a network that meets your needs? Whilst delivering the highest levels of service? Can they claim, as UUNET is entitled to, that 77 of the Times Top 100 companies trust them to deliver the quality and resilience they expect, whilst still cutting costs? And now for the absolute killer • Who is their ISP? Chances are, it's UUNET • For more information, including an especially commissioned White Paper on the business potential of the Internet, visit www.uu.net/info •

  www.uu.net/info   **Uniting the world of business**   

Far left: Johnny Herbert celebrates after his win at the European Grand Prix.
Paul-Henri Cahier

Left: Jackie had more reasons than one to smile after the 1999 season.
Paul-Henri Cahier

Below: Rubens Barrichello led the team for the third season and was disappointed not to have clinched a win before his move to Ferrari.
Michael Roberts

company's research and development centre and the suspension design of next year's car would benefit as a result. The CR-1 V10, the smallest F1 engine to be designed by Cosworth, was generally pretty reliable although progressive upgrades during the course of the season caused a few glitches.

'We used the series 3 version from the start,' said Anderson. 'The series 4 was potentially better, although the advantage was pretty small and there were reliability issues which meant that it took some time before we were confident that its performance increment was worth risking in a race.'

On the driver front, Rubens Barrichello generally found himself able to perform better than team-mate Johnny Herbert during the first part of the year, but the introduction of an hydraulic differential improved the general performance of the SF3 from the Austrian Grand Prix onwards and Herbert was able dramatically to close the performance gap to his team-mate from that point on.

'The hydraulic differential certainly helped Johnny onto a competitive level,' Anderson agreed. 'Johnny works the throttle in a more lively fashion than Rubens whose driving style is rather more laid back and economical. It just helped his style and meant that he could get the car into the corners a little easier than before.'

In the middle of the season Barrichello found himself on the receiving end of overtures from Ferrari once it became clear that Eddie Irvine was preparing to strike out on his own, ironically to cut a deal with the Stewart squad now Ford had decided to re-brand the team Jaguar for the 2000 season.

Eventually Barrichello decided that the lure of being the first Brazilian to become a full-time member of the Ferrari F1 team was simply too much to resist. He signed on the dotted line, but not without a genuine pang of regret, for the sensitive and civilised young man from Sao Paulo has really responded well to the Stewart environment and had come to regard Jackie and Paul as members of his employers.

his employers.

For his part, Herbert could reflect on the second half of the season with considerable satisfaction. He'd run well at Hockenheim before his retirement and that second fastest race lap in Austria really confirmed that his old flair had been rekindled. At Nürburgring he was on top of the world and followed that up with a storming drive in Malaysia which almost deprived Mika Häkkinen of third place in the closing stages. Eddie Irvine may have his work cut out dealing with Jaguar's sitting tenant next season.

Alan Henry

It's in the blood

Over four decades of motor

racing heritage has given birth

to some of the world's most

successful racing engines.

Legendary partnerships: high-

performance future.

Visit our website **www.cosworthracing.com** for all the latest updates and info.

Cosworth Racing Limited, The Octagon, St. James Mill Road, Northampton, NN5 5RA

Tel: +44 (0)1604 598300   Fax: +44 (0)1604 598656   e-mail: cmanley@cosworth-racing.co.uk

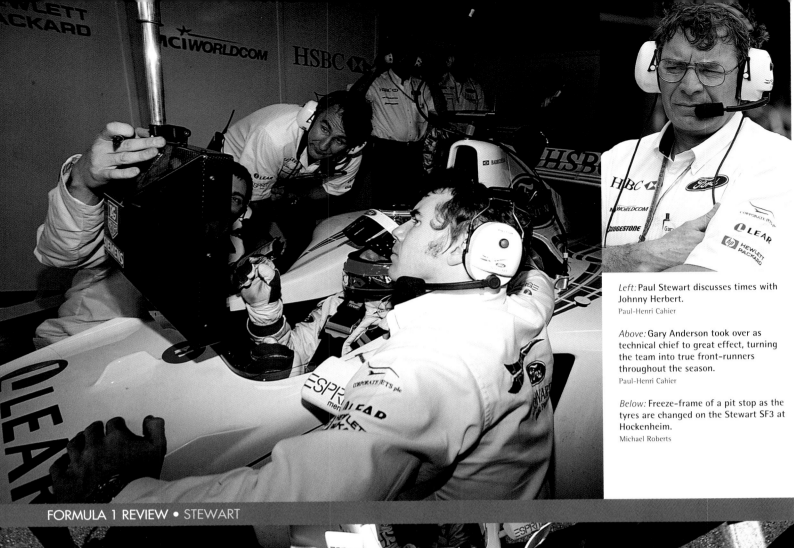

Left: Paul Stewart discusses times with Johnny Herbert.
Paul-Henri Cahier

Above: Gary Anderson took over as technical chief to great effect, turning the team into true front-runners throughout the season.
Paul-Henri Cahier

Below: Freeze-frame of a pit stop as the tyres are changed on the Stewart SF3 at Hockenheim.
Michael Roberts

FORMULA 1 REVIEW • STEWART

since 1967 this is what
we've done in our spare time

18
PROST
19

OLIVIER PANIS

JARNO TRULLI

THE Prost-Peugeot squad continued a process of consolidation during the 1999 season which might not have been immediately obvious viewing from the touchlines considering the French team only managed to squeeze nine constructors' championship points out of its season.

In its second year operating out of its new base at Guyancourt, on the fringes of Paris, Prost expanded its workforce considerably and also recruited a new technical director in the form of Alan Jenkins who had previously worked with the Stewart-Ford squad. He replaced Bernard Dudot in this role just before the French Grand Prix and began a process of further development on the AP02 chassis, originally designed by Loic Bigois, which was supplemented by input from John Barnard's UK-based B3 Technologies design studio.

Barnard had, in fact, been involved as a consultant to the Prost operation ever since the middle of 1998 and had produced most of the front and rear suspension componentry for the AP02.

Jenkins's recruitment – encouraged by Barnard – completed what amounted to a rebirth of the mid-1980s McLaren squad when Prost was Number One driver, Jenkins his race engineer and Barnard the team's technical director. The three men worked well with each other and, more crucially, fully understood each other's *modus operandi*.

Drivers Olivier Panis and Jarno Trulli endured a varied season of achievement. Panis scored the team's first point of the year with a sixth place finish at Interlagos, but then attracted much criticism for the way in which he allegedly held up David Coulthard's McLaren during the San Marino Grand Prix at Imola. This caused a certain cooling of the personal relationship between Olivier and Alain Prost which seemed to bottom out at around the time of the British Grand Prix when it became clear that Panis would probably not be kept on the books beyond the season's end.

'When I joined up, I think it's fair to say that Olivier was something of the black sheep of the family,' said

Jenkins. 'He was on a bit of a downer, but when Didier Coton, who works for Keke Rosberg, came on board as his personal manager it was a really positive development as Didier had a really good influence on him.

'Ironically, when Olivier realised that he was probably not going to be driving for us next year, he seemed to relax and improve considerably. When he was focused he was extremely good, but tended to come off the rails a bit when he was allowed too much latitude with car set-up.

'The other thing which always seemed to get him into a mess was his poor starts. Up until Suzuka, at least, where – contrary to opinion, he was on a two-stop rather than a three-stop strategy – where he got away perfectly and I'm sure he would have kept ahead of Irvine if he'd made it to the finish.'

As for Jarno Trulli, Jenkins feels that his season went in the opposite direction. 'I was really impressed with Jarno at the start of the year, but he certainly seemed to go off the boil

once he decided to leave us.' The Italian posted a sixth place finish in Spain and then bagged the lion's share of the Prost team's points at Nürburgring with second place, splitting the Stewart-Fords of Johnny Herbert and Rubens Barrichello.

Ironically, at the next race in Malaysia, Alain Prost had something of a breach with Trulli whom he accused of not trying after qualifying 18th on the grid. Prost brusquely dismissed Jarno's second place in the European Grand Prix as a lucky moment, while Trulli shot back with 'nothing is ever Alain's fault.' Clearly, Jenkins's assessment that the relationship was all but over well before the end of the year was right on the money.

One of the main problems for Prost during the season was Peugeot's mid-season wobble in terms of future commitment. It looked very probable that the French engine builder would quit its association with the team at the end of 1999, so much so that Prost became deeply involved in detailed discussions with both Supertec and Ferrari over

PROST AP02-PEUGEOT

Sponsors: Gauloises, Peugeot, Alcatel, Canal+, PlayStation, Bic, Agfa, Sodexho, Bridgestone, Total	

Team principal: Alain Prost   **Technical director:** Alan Jenkins   **Team manager:** Jean-Pierre Chatenet   **Chief engineer:** Vincent Gaillardot

ENGINE   Type: Peugeot A18   **No. of cylinders/vee angle:** V10 (72°)   **Sparking plugs:** NGK   **Fuel:** Total   **Oil:** Total

TRANSMISSION   Gearbox: Prost six-speed longitudinal semi-automatic   **Driveshafts:** Prost   **Clutch:** AP (hand-operated)

CHASSIS   Front suspension: double wishbones, pushrod   **Rear suspension:** double wishbones, pushrod   **Suspension dampers:** not given   **Wheels:** BBS   **Tyres:** Bridgestone

Brake pads: not given   **Brake discs:** Carbone Industrie   **Brake calipers:** Brembo   **Steering:** Prost   **Radiators:** not given   **Fuel tanks:** ATL   **Battery:** Fiamm

Instruments: Prost

DIMENSIONS   Wheelbase: not given   **Track:** front: 58.1 in./1475 mm   rear: 55.5 in./1410 mm   **Formula weight:** 1322.8 lb/600 kg including driver

engine supply prospects, to the point that a gearbox design to cater for a Supertec V10 was even started.

There was also some general contact with Mercedes-Benz over the prospect of securing a second supply deal alongside McLaren, but eventually Peugeot decided that it would stick with its programme, at least until the end of 2000.

There was an ingrained streak of conservatism behind Peugeot's whole approach to F1, something which had previously been noticed by McLaren and Jordan, their previous Grand Prix racing partners.

The latest Peugeot A18, 72-degree V10 developed by Jean-Pierre Boudy's team started the season in EV2 specification which was quickly evolved into the EV4 which served as the race engine for most of the year. The EV5 was a qualifying unit which was raced in the final two Grands Prix while the theoretically more powerful again EV7 appeared for qualifying at Nürburgring.

Prost insiders are reluctant to comment in detail about the performance of the Peugeot V10s, but it is reliably believed that the engine specification had to be downrated slightly at the start of the season to improve mechanical reliability and only just edged back to around 770 bhp by the end of the season. This was healthy mid-grid stuff, but hardly approaching the sort of output which was required to run at the front of the field on merit.

Jenkins now feels that the basis for solid improvement is now present. 'John Barnard is full of ideas and getting more so,' he said. 'I think we will get more integrated with B3 on some aspects of the development. I have also known Loic Bigois for a long time. He is a good guy in the wind tunnel and has the sort of overview of the new car's design which is so important to get the best out of our aerodynamic development.

'We also have a great race team. Our pit stops are as good as anybody in the business. The motivation of the mechanics is fantastic and they always seem to be able to complete engine changes up to 20 or 30 minutes ahead of the schedule I have in my mind. Everybody here is working to marshal a collective determination to have a crack at its seriously in 2000.'

Everybody at Prost is impressed with its two new drivers, Jean Alesi and Nick Heidfeld. 'The mechanics and engineers were sorry to see Panis go,' said Jenkins, 'because he was very popular with them. But I am sure Jean will pick up from where he left off.

'As for young Nick, he is very impressive indeed. He's been well prepared by McLaren and will be able to learn a lot more from Alain. He's already been a great hit with the mechanics. I just hope we manage to hang onto him!'

Alan Henry

Top left: Welcome to the real world. Alain Prost finding out that running an F1 team is probably a much tougher challenge than being a racing driver.

Top centre: Alan Jenkins was hired to head up the design team. His pairing with John Barnard *(top right)* should provide a fund of new ideas for the next Prost challenger.

Above: The popular Olivier Panis ended a six-year association with the team which stretched back to its Ligier guise.
All photographs: Paul-Henri Cahier

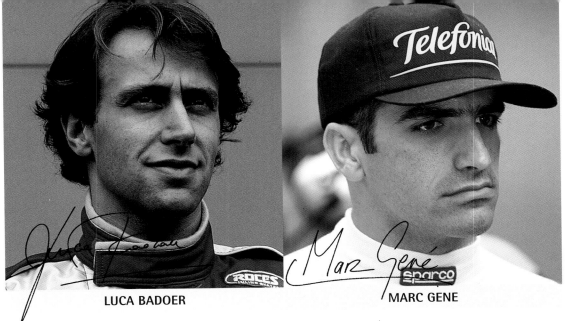

Paul-Henri Cahier

Diana Burnett

LUCA BADOER

MARC GENE

'I MUST say that the level of F1 has increased in the last year more than in the last 30 years. Even if you include Colin Chapman with the wing car, turbocharging, everything, if you take the average of all the cars and how they perform, the level has made its biggest step forward ever. There are only good cars, no bad cars.' So said Minardi's technical director Gustav Brunner as the 1999 Formula One season drew to a close.

Once again, it had driven Formula One's traditional minnow to the brink. Minardi were using Ford engines for the last time. Quite where their power units for 2000 were coming from remained a mystery. The prospect of travel money was in the balance, but Spanish telecommunications company Telefonica were preparing to invest in the team. In their 15th year in Formula One, the popular Faenza team were, as usual, running hard in order to stay in the game – even if at the very back.

It is a measure of the competitiveness of Formula One that Brunner says what he says. This year, unlike years past, Minardi started with a brand new car. They had a 'works' Ford engine deal. And for once, one of their drivers actually had Formula One experience; heavens, Luca Badoer was employed as Ferrari's test driver. The team had continued to grow, now to over 100. They had more things going for them than ever.

And yet at year's end, they were still struggling. Perhaps they wouldn't have it any other way, but this year, for the first time since 1995, they had scored a World Championship point thanks to Marc Gene's sixth place in the European Grand Prix. Indeed, they had actually caught Arrows and were almost resigning their back-of-field position to Tom Walkinshaw's team by the end of the year.

Brunner had actually begun designing the 1999 car within days of rejoining the team early in the spring of 1998. 'It was completely new,' explained Brunner. 'We were quite happy with what we have achieved, looking from inside Minardi, because we have achieved a complete new car, new technology, a good step forward for the team. OK, we didn't get that many results, but we are hopeful that we will make another big step to get back to the others.'

The car was described by some as being 'Ferrari-esque', thanks to the influence of Brunner and his designer George Wrighton, both former Ferrari men. The return of Brunner had also had other effects. Cosworth, who would provide the engine, began talking about its installation as early as August 1998.

They had taken the Stewart engine from the previous year, lowered the sump by 6 mm which meant a new crankcase assembly and then converted it to use Minardi's much-loved Magneti Marelli electronics. This meant a change of pumps. Halfway through the season, the VJM1 became VJM2 with a small loss of weight and top-end modifications that gave it a power increase of about four per cent.

The car, it seems, was quite reasonable. 'We've managed to balance the car reasonably well and it behaves reasonably well,' said Brunner. 'It's pretty stable, it's also good under braking, but there is just not enough grip, which is more likely a lack of downforce, because on the mechanical side we're not worse, or not a lot worse than the others. We don't have enough downforce.

'So our biggest shortcoming was our aerodynamics. We haven't really got the structure in place. The minute we have new owners, new sponsorship for next year, we will invest heavily in aerodynamics as aerodynamics are 70 per cent of car performance.

'We have one and a half aerodynamicists and some part-timers. We need to employ more, produce lots of pieces and test more in the wind tunnel. Our problems were because of lack of finance and lack of personnel. We have done development but it was not that much: new wings, new underwings but they came late, the new underwing for the Austrian Grand Prix. But in a top team you have the first aerodynamic update for Imola – latest – not Austria.'

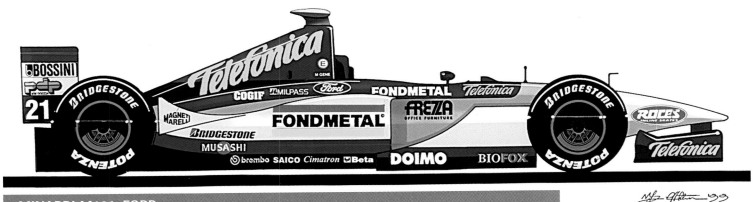

MINARDI M101–FORD

Sponsors: Telefonica, Roces, Doimo, Frezza, Suilhes, PDP, Dreefs, Bossini, RBM, Diemme, Novatex

Team principal: Gabriele Rumi **Technical director:** Gustav Brunner **Team manager:** Cesare Fiorio **Chief mechanic:** Gabriele Pagliarini

ENGINE **Type:** Ford Zetec-R **No. of cylinders/vee angle:** V10 (72°) **Sparking plugs:** Champion **Electronics:** Magneti Marelli **Fuel:** Elf **Oil:** Elf

TRANSMISSION **Gearbox:** Minardi six-speed longitudinal semi-automatic **Driveshafts:** Minardi **Clutch:** AP (hand-operated)

CHASSIS **Front suspension:** double wishbones, pushrod with coaxial spring/damper and torsion bar **Rear suspension:** double wishbones, pushrod

Suspension dampers: Sachs **Wheel diameter:** front: 13 in. rear: 13. **Wheel rim widths:** front: not given

Wheels: not given **Tyres:** Bridgestone **Brake pads:** Carbone Industrie **Brake discs:** Carbone Industrie **Brake calipers:** Brembo **Steering:** Minardi **Radiators:** Secan

Fuel tanks: ATL **Battery:** FIAMM **Instruments:** Magneti Marelli

DIMENSIONS **Wheelbase:** not given **Track:** front: 57.4 in./1459 mm rear: 56.0 in./1421.3 mm **Formula weight:** 1322.8 lb/600 kg including driver **Fuel capacity:** not given

STEPHANE SARRAZIN

Team owner Gabriele Rumi's connection to the Fondmetal wind tunnel concern wasn't a help, it seems. 'He's only the part owner, the main owner is Jean Claude Migeot,' continued Brunner. 'We have to pay for testing time, but the biggest cost is designing and producing the pieces, and that's where we were short of money. Obviously, if you have never created it before, it's creating the know-how and the structure which is costly. This is where the others are well ahead. The design team consists of between four and five people. We have at least doubled it but the newcomers are youngsters and they need to be brought on. It's difficult to get experienced people unless you pinch them from other teams and we are not in a position to do that, so we train youngsters.

'If you look at the bigger teams, they spend nearly the same in aerodynamic development as engine development. It's going that way. Aerodynamic teams are 30-40 people, producing lots of pieces; that's where we are lacking. It's detail in lots of areas of aerodynamics. Cleverness alone is not sufficient any more, you need to have the structure, the culture in place. And the money which goes with it.'

Typically, Minardi chose yet another new pair of drivers, although one of them already had 35 Grands Prix worth of experience, had driven for the team before and was test driver for Ferrari: Luca Badoer. The other was a complete novice. Everyone had encouraged Minardi to take someone with experience, and yet, in the end, it was the newcomer who had the better finishing record even if he usually qualified slower.

'Marc works very hard,' said Brunner. 'Obviously he's not the talent of Luca but he's younger, and he's made fantastic progress. He's our future, and he's growing in confidence.'

After finishing ninth in both Brazil and San Marino, he went into serious decline with a single-handed attempt to demolish the Monaco circuit and then an embarrassing mistake in front of all the Telefonica guests at Barcelona when he attempted to engage gear with 13000 rpm on the clock. He didn't start that race, but then only retired twice from the next ten races, so all was forgiven, particularly when he scored a World Championship point at the Nürburgring.

Of course, it should have been Badoer who scored the points that day.

He was lying fourth when his gearbox failed for the fourth time in the year. He'd had a bad time with injury in a test at Fiorano, and another at Monza. But even so, in spite of better qualifying than Gene, his finishing record was worse. 'I expected more from him,' admitted Brunner.

'He should have had better results. He did a fantastic race and lap time in Nürburgring, and I ask myself why didn't he do this all the time, because most of the time he's not doing it? Maybe it's in the head, he's probably better than his results. If he was managed, or managed himself better, he would be a better sportsman. He could probably improve his fitness too.'

As the millennium ended, the strength of Formula One as a whole meant that Minardi's very presence was a huge financial asset, quite apart from the team's legendary spirit. Therefore there seemed every possibility that they would continue to run and that one day Brunner's dream of catching up would come true.

Bob Constanduros

Top centre: Giancarlo Minardi continued to run a credible Grand Prix team on a miniscule budget.
Diana Burnett

Top right: Gustav Brunner felt the pace of development in Formula 1 has never been so intense.
Diana Burnett

Above: Luca Badoer on the limit in qualifying for the Belgian Grand Prix.
Bryn Williams/Words & Pictures

22

BRITISH AMERICAN RACING

23

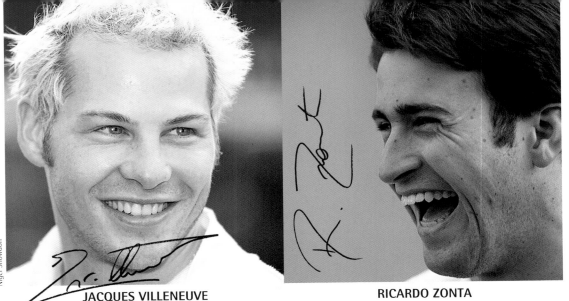

Nigel Snowdon

JACQUES VILLENEUVE

Paul-Henri Cahier

RICARDO ZONTA

DECEMBER 2, 1997. The new British American Racing team is launched and its technical director, Adrian Reynard says 'our aim is to put the car on pole and win the first race.'

October 31, 1999. British American Racing completes its first season without scoring a World Championship point.

Some would say that it only proves you should never believe your own PR. Yet this is a rather cynical way of looking at BAR's first Grand Prix season. Yes, the hype was damaging. The seemingly massive budget suggested the team was chucking away money on the wrong things: the apparently worthless purchase of Tyrrell; the best motorhomes and trucks in the paddock, a fleet that even Eddie Stobart would be proud of. And two cars that were failing to finish.

Back in 1997, BAR also announced that they would be buying Tyrrell and entering Formula One with Reynard in 1999. 'If I had to do it again, I would not say that buying Tyrrell was a worthwhile exercise,' said team principal Craig Pollock at the end of the year. It was, he admitted, a fast track into Formula One's politics.

'The minute we bought into Tyrrell, I participated in the team principal meetings and Malcolm [Oastler, then chief designer] participated as technical delegate. If we hadn't bought the team, we could be excluded from those meetings. It was still a high price to pay.'

Apart from that, there were virtually no material gains, and almost no members of staff moved from Surrey to Oxfordshire to work for the new team.

This left BAR to build up an entirely new workforce and that was always going to be a problem. 'We put together an incredible team of people, but they came out of different cultures: different Formula One teams, Indy Car teams, different F3000 teams. To actually get them into a BAR culture took us a lot longer than we expected,' admitted Pollock. Starting with 180 at the beginning of the year, they were up to nearly 300 by the end.

While they were building a team, they were also putting together a factory and then the cars. They had been designed by Malcolm Oastler, a man whose talent had been proven by his considerable success with Reynard in F3000 and more recently with Indy Cars.

The quality of the parts was certainly tested by the vibrations of the Supertec engine. 'They defy belief,' said chief engineer Steve Farrell. 'It just shook. We have had massive problems. The extra experience of Williams and Benetton may have helped them, but I know that they have had similar problems.

'As Renault have pushed on with development during the year, the vibrations have got worse. Things that lasted 2500 km in March were doing 300 km in August. It was like a bad dream: what's the next thing that's going to break? Rear wings, wishbones, hydraulic fittings, pumps?'

It cost valuable time. 'Our reliability has been pathetic,' summarised Jacques Villeneuve. 'We've never been able to test properly because the car kept breaking down; the same thing during race weekends.' Even so, there was soon a fairly constant flow of new components, albeit with little time to test them.

Villeneuve's engineer Jock Clear, who followed him to BAR from Williams, admitted that 'there always seems to be a good lap in this car somewhere. We always seem to have found it at some stage during the weekend. If we don't find it in qualifying, we find it in the race, the reliability issue aside.' In the third Grand Prix of the year, Villeneuve was fifth on the grid. It was typical that that

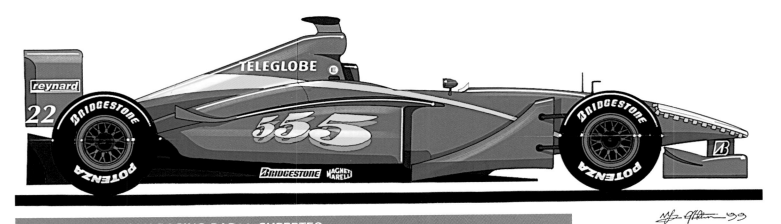

BRITISH AMERICAN RACING BAR01–SUPERTEC

Sponsors: 555, Lucky Strike, Teleglobe

Team principal: Craig Pollock	**Technical director:** Malcolm Oastler	**Team manager:** Robert Synge **Chief engineer:** Steve Farrell

ENGINE   Type: Supertec FB01 **No. of cylinders/vee angle:** V10 (71°) **Sparking plugs:** Champion **Electronics:** BAR/PI/Magneti Marelli **Fuel:** Elf **Oil:** Elf

TRANSMISSION   Gearbox: BAR/Xtrac six-speed longitudinal semi-automatic **Driveshafts:** BAR **Clutch:** Sachs/AP (hand-operated)

CHASSIS   Front suspension: double wishbones, pushrod **Rear suspension:** double wishbones, pushrod **Suspension dampers:** Koni **Wheel diameter:** front: 13 in. rear: 13 in.

Wheel rim widths: front: not given rear: not given **Wheels** OZ **Tyres:** Bridgestone **Brake pads:** not given **Brake discs:** Carbone Industrie/Hitco

Brake calipers: AP **Steering:** BAR **Radiators:** BAR/Marston **Fuel tanks:** ATL **Battery:** Champion **Instruments:** BAR

DIMENSIONS   Wheelbase: not given **Track:** front: not given rear: not given **Formula weight:** 1322.8 lb/600 kg including driver **Fuel capacity:** not given

MIKA SALO

Above left: Team principal Craig Pollock found himself embroiled in a season of turmoil as he strove to get the newly-formed BAR team firing on all cylinders.
Diana Burnett

Above: Designer Malcolm Oastler was thrust into the position of technical director as the season progressed.
Paul-Henri Cahier

Left: Jacques Villeneuve waits for adjustments to be made on his car. Niggling problems blunted progress throughout the season.
Paul-Henri Cahier

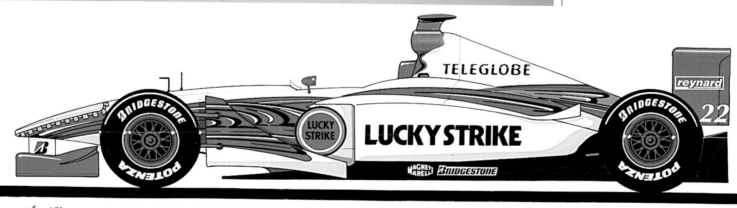

was as far as he got before the gearbox control sheered.

Ironically, Villeneuve's worst qualifying position of the year was 16th in Canada but he was in single figures on the grid for just under half the races. His team-mate, the talented Ricardo Zonta outqualified him with a best of tenth on the grid in the wet in France.

When Zonta was sidelined after a big accident on the bumps at home in Brazil, it was his replacement, Mika Salo, who scored the team's first finish in their fifth race. It wouldn't be until Belgium in August, arguably the team's worst race, that Villeneuve saw the chequered flag.

'Spa was consistent with the rest of the year,' says Farrell of his drivers' massive accidents at Eau Rouge. 'The sort of luck that brings you two huge shunts in 15 minutes has been happening all year. It was just a manifestation of the rest of the programme. I'm fairly convinced it was driver error in each case.' Earlier in the weekend, Villeneuve had suffered a broken front wishbone which was modified and tested overnight and had worked fine ever since.

Two races later, Jacques Villeneuve really did look as though he might finally score points. At Nürburgring he was fifth with five laps to go when a new AP clutch, chosen

because the previous Sachs model had given problems and wasn't producing performance in vital starts, failed. It had done 30-odd starts a week before. In the last race of the year, the team desperate to score points and earn vital travel money, both cars finally finished – but then so did another 12 cars.

The lack of performance had inevitably meant that scapegoats had been sought. Villeneuve castigated Reynard for lack of commitment to the Formula One programme, and Oastler became technical director earlier than planned. The popular team manager Greg Field and two chief mechanics had already been

replaced – in order to improve communication between race and test team. Commercial and other organisational changes had also been made. The politics rumbled on.

As they looked forward to the normally feared second year, the feeling was that it couldn't be worse than the first – even if they would be developing Honda's new engine. 'Next year's car will be bulletproof,' predicted Villeneuve. 'It's been a hard season, but it will pay off next year.'

Alan Henry

PASSION IS THE EMOTION THAT HAS SHAPED MASERATIS OF THE PAST AND WILL DETERMINE THE CARS IN OUR FUTURE – A PASSION FOR PERFORMANCE, FOR SOPHISTICATED STYLE AND FOR UNBRIDLED DRIVING PLEASURE. NOW IS THE TIME TO INDULGE YOUR PASSION...

MASERATI 3200 GT. 370 HORSE POWER AND ROOM FOR FOUR

MARANELLO
SALES LTD

Tower Garage, The By Pass (A30), Egham, Surrey TW20 OAX Telephone: 01784 436431 Facsimile: 01784 436510
Website: www.maserati.it E-Mail: owen@maranellosales.com

Car companies with global ambitions are queuing up to provide power for F1 teams

POWER AND THE GLORY

by Tony Dodgins

TIME was when Formula 1 was all about negotiating an off-the-shelf Cosworth DFV, bolting it into a custom-built chassis and going motor racing. It was the staple diet for many of those at the top of the sport today, men like Ron Dennis and Frank Williams.

Granted, you always had one or two manufacturers, or 'Grandees' as they were called. Overtly sporting, evocative names, such as Ferrari and Alfa Romeo, who traded on their racing heritage. For long periods, Renault, too. But suddenly Grand Prix racing is awash with mainstream manufacturers all prepared to spend the big buck. Why?

'It has come as a result of market research,' says Dennis. 'Cars are becoming more and more legislated.

Bumper heights, A-frame angles, driver safety criteria, headlight position, everything. The end result is becoming more and more similar. If you painted a lot of cars one colour and took the badges off, you'd be surprised how difficult it was to recognise the makes.

'Manufacturers, therefore, are looking for any means to achieve product differentiation. If you win in F1 it is black and white. It signifies advanced technical competence. In my opinion it is a completely logical step for Ford. The volume markets are very much influenced by the public's perception of the brand as a whole.'

Jackie Stewart, however, thinks it was the arrival of Mercedes-Benz, Dennis's current partner but a much lower volume manufacturer, which really rang the bell.

'I think timing is everything,' Stewart says. 'There are commercial benefits from a sport clearly at the sharpest edge of technology. They have always been there. Today though, the consumer is more studious about his or her choice of vehicle. What you are trying to do is influence that choice by making a statement. Formula 1 is glamorous, colourful and exciting and that is what most people want to see from a vehicle they buy. And there has never been a time when the lifestyle of F1 has been so highly profiled or recognised. The sport simply cannot be ignored by the agency people or the marketing and sales directors buried in the bureaucracy of the world's largest companies.

'For me, what really attracted everybody's attention was Mercedes-

Benz coming in when they were extremely vulnerable to being beaten up by, let's say, marques of lesser esteem. And when they came in they were not competitive, either with Sauber or, in the beginning, with McLaren.

Mercedes has admitted that its involvement was clearly designed to generate a more youthful consumer for the brand.

'They knew precisely what they were doing,' Stewart agrees. 'Take the S-Class. The age group buying that car were pretty much in God's waiting room. Mercedes knew it was a very small volume manufacturer in reality, less than a million a year. Ford almost makes more Focuses than that. But they also knew they were not only having a good E-Class car but also an M-Class and an A-Class. Formula 1,

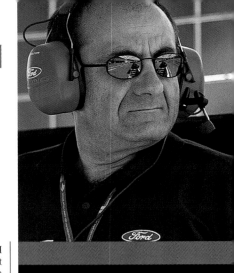

with its technical excellence, appeals to a younger generation market. Suddenly the logic of coming in was not about the Silver Arrows of the fifties or thirties, it was about reaching those people.'

Dennis is in the process of selling a 40 per cent stake in the McLaren group to Mercedes but claims there is no way that McLaren would ever completely sell out to an engine partner, as Stewart sold out to Ford.

'You know that a customer V8 engine is not going to give you a chance of winning the World Championship. But you have to think about what makes you successful in F1,' he says. 'You've got to adapt. Ilmor is probably the finest engine manufacturing facility in the world, but they are totally vertically integrated, which contributes to the speed of reaction and control.

'There is equity participation in Ilmor but it doesn't prevent them from being focused, committed and independent. A large company completely owning a racing organisation to me just doesn't make any sense. You can't look at Ford's involvement with Stewart in isolation. I think you have to see what Honda has done with British American Racing, which is much more than supplying engines. They have found themselves in a position where the chassis engineers and engine technicians have been given the green light for a participation in Grand Prix racing. It is clear that BAR has accepted very clear technical steerage coming from outside their organisation, which would not be possible for this company ever to accept.' Possibly, but some say that the Japanese involvement outside engine work will not be large at BAR.

'Effectively,' Dennis adds, 'you bring all the problems of the large organisation into the small one. If left unshackled by the bureaucratic red tape that you find in large organisations, maybe it will be successful. Time will tell. But good luck to Ford, because companies making a big commitment to F1 is good for the sport.'

So why, in June 1999, did Ford pay a reputed 100 million dollars to buy Stewart when they had already been involved as partners since the outset?

The question was never really satisfactorily answered. Perhaps they did it to justify to their own board the massive spend required by modern day F1. When you are speaking of 100-million dollar sums, directors tend to worry about things like ownership and stock valuation.

Buying Cosworth made sense. By owning it exclusively, Ford can produce not only an F1 engine, but an Indy car engine, an Indy Light/F3000 engine, a touring car engine, a rally engine. At the same time, they can keep all of the secrets to themselves.

Then, by owning the team, maybe they wanted to make decisions beyond the engine programme. They saw the logic of ownership. If push comes to shove and they don't agree with Jackie or Paul, they can snap their fingers and say: excuse me, that's not how we want it done. Not forgetting too, that, via Bernie's commercial dealings and TV ventures, F1 team ownership is now a more lucrative business than ever before. Time was when the only way to make a small fortune out of motor racing was to start with a large one. But times change.

Stewart denies, however, that modern-day F1 is one great cash cow. The lessons of all the early and mid-90s collapses – Brabham, Lotus, Pacific, Simtek – are just as valid. It still needs shrewd management.

'I've never had a business that's lost money. This business had to make money because the only way we could buy new equipment and more expensive people, was to make a profit. That's what private enterprise is about. We made money and we sold the business without an overdraft. There was not one bit of leverage, no other ownership outside of the family trust. It didn't owe the bank anything. We sold a very clean company. We were very cautious. We made money, good money, and we weren't getting television or travel money. We sold it very well and were cautious, canny and conservative.

'I don't know about the other teams but I presume they just spent too much money. Or else the financial investors were small players. They didn't manage it. Right at the beginning the single most important thing that we had was the ability to go out and source money from partner sponsorship. That was more important than the technology, more important than the engineering and more important than the people.

'We couldn't afford any of those without the money. This honeymoon idea that you just go out and get an Adrian Newey is nonsense. Where are you going to get the cash? I could have afforded it, but what good would that have been if I couldn't give him the tools to work with?

Ford has solved that. Stewart thinks the big company ownership issue is a logical one. Then again, so, undoubtedly, does Jackie's bank manager! The surprising thing perhaps is that it didn't happen from the start which, after all, was only three years ago.

'You know, when we started off, I said to Ford: "Are you sure you don't want to own this? We'll do it on a cost-plus basis, and you underwrite the whole thing." But we could never get the board to pass it. Now, it's cost them a great deal more money than when we came in, but at least I had the honour of giving them the opportunity...' He always was a canny Scot.

'Even so,' he adds, 'they were not going to buy in unless they were very comfortable that they were not going to be taken advantage of. Luckily for me, they have been with me for 35 years. I signed in October at Earls Court Motor Show in 1964. They have been very good to me and I've been very good to them. I've never double-billed them, I've never charged them for anything they didn't get. And they know that, so it was a very comfortable negotiation.

So what will Ford–Jaguar do with it? Very much the same as Mercedes, JYS says.

'They have decided that Jaguar also has an ownership average age that is far too high. So now there's an S-type Jaguar as well as an XJ and an XK. And the fourth Jaguar line is going to be a BMW 3-series-type car.

'If you are going to get the message across, how does Jaguar, which has had this older image in recent years, change that around to be dynamic, youthful and competitive? Formula 1 is the perfect platform.

'You look at that and then you address BMW, who don't want to be left behind and are frightened of Mercedes suddenly taking over in their 5-series and 3-series markets. I think it is only a matter of time before Mr Piech [chairman] of Audi/VW realises. And if I were him, I'd do it with Volkswagen.'

Having a range compatible with the F1 image is also important, Stewart thinks. Renault reaped enormous benefit from F1 but didn't take full advantage on the marketing front. Perhaps they didn't bring cars with them that reflected F1, whereas Mercedes have, BMW are and Jaguar will. Honda too. With Toyota coming soon and Peugeot already here, but perhaps not hard or committed enough, it will soon be a question of who's missing, not who's in? General Motors is presently the glaring omission.

One burning question no doubt concerning the BMW board right now: is it enough just to be there? Or, do you have to win? Consider the esteem in which Dennis and Mercedes hold Ilmor, and consider the experience and the strides made by Cosworth on Ford's behalf this year. Munich might be feeling a little naked. On the positive side though, it took Mercedes time.

Above: Jac Nasser, Ford boss who sanctioned the purchase of both Stewart Grand Prix and Cosworth Engineering.
Paul-Henri Cahier

Above centre: The successful Ford-Cosworth CR1 V10.
Bryn Williams/Words & Pictures

Above right: Head of Ford Motorsport Europe, Martin Whitaker, and Jackie Stewart confer. Between them they steered the team to the highest level of F1 in 1999.
Paul-Henri Cahier

Right: Rubens Barrichello in the Stewart SF3.
Paul-Henri Cahier

Below: The ultra-successful partnership of Ron Dennis and Norbert Haug is perhaps the model others must emulate.
Paul-Henri Cahier

Below right: BMW are set to return to Grand Prix racing in 2000 in partnership with Williams. This season has seen a testing programme begin with a 1998 Williams chassis mated to a BMW V10 engine.
BMW

350 Grand Prix Wins
Another Champion performance

The European Grand Prix, Nurburgring, 26th September 1999. History in the making. Stewart-Ford scores its first Grand Prix win. Johnny Herbert, his third. Ford, a remarkable 175th. And Champion - an astonishing 350th. No other spark plug has achieved so much in world motorsport. No other has won 21 F1 World Championships. And no other puts so much world-beating expertise into the spark plugs you fit in your car.

CHAMPION ®

Performance Driven

GRANDS PRIX
1999

Michael Roberts

AUSTRALIAN
grand prix

Left: Eddie Irvine, arms aloft, finally steps from Schumacher's shadow to win his first Grand Prix.
Paul-Henri Cahier

Below far left: Eddie and the Ferrari team celebrate this crucial milestone for the Ulsterman.
Mark Thompson/Allsport

Below left: Winfield–Williams promotions added to the already fevered temperatures on the grid.
Bryn Williams

Below: Ralf Schumacher enhanced his reputation with a fine third on his Williams debut.
Paul-Henri Cahier

IRVINE

FRENTZEN

R. SCHUMACHER

FISICHELLA

BARRICHELLO

DE LA ROSA

IT was a case of topsy-turvy emotions in the immediate aftermath of the Australian Grand Prix. Ferrari had won, yet finished the day acutely aware that its new F399 challenger was not quick enough. Rival McLaren-Mercedes had seen both its cars retire, yet was buoyed by the fact that the new MP4/14s had proved to be the absolute class of the field. In truth, the start of the battle for the 1999 World Championship had been temporarily deferred.

Yet there was one man who was smiling broadly. It is said that everything comes to he who waits, and Eddie Irvine had certainly done more than his fair share of waiting during the previous three years. Now the genial Ulsterman's long established role as Michael Schumacher's patient number two in the Ferrari team had finally paid off, for he had stormed to a convincing victory, a second ahead of runner-up Heinz-Harald Frentzen's Jordan-Mugen Honda.

On the face of it, this success may have seemed fortuitous. Both Ferraris had been struggling to sustain a competitive pace from the start of the season's opening race, and the new McLaren-Mercedes MP4/14s of Mika Häkkinen and David Coulthard proved to be convincingly quicker than the opposition.

As expected, the two McLarens had surged into the distance from the start, but their magic-carpet ride was halted prematurely when Coulthard dropped out with gearchange failure, caused by a hydraulic leak, and Häkkinen succumbed to a throttle bearing failure. Suddenly, Irvine, who had been 18s adrift in third place, found the race presented to him on a plate.

Häkkinen had pipped Coulthard to pole position on the very last lap of qualifying, starting the season as clearly he meant to go on. However, he had to switch to the spare McLaren MP4/14 shortly before the start after his engine developed a misfire.

In fact, the start was preceded by a succession of glitches that could have come from a script for 'the Marx brothers go F1 racing'! As Häkkinen accelerated out of the pit garage to take his place on the grid, an electrical lead became tangled around one of the rear wheels of his McLaren, bringing down the roof gantry on the heads of his mechanics and engineers.

Nevertheless, Mika duly assumed his position on the front row in suitably composed style, but as the cars were being held on the grid just prior to the start, flames were seen issuing from the Stewart-Ford SF3s of Rubens Barrichello – who'd qualified a magnificent fourth – and Johnny Herbert. The start was aborted immediately and both Ford-engined cars hauled out of the line-up.

Subsequent examination revealed that oil seals in both engines had ruptured under pressure, due to the high ambient temperature, which had not been experienced in testing. This had resulted in oil spraying on to the exhaust, in turn causing the rear bodywork to catch alight. It was a bitter disappointment for Herbert who, having only managed to qualify 13th, clearly was not going to beat Barrichello for the use of the spare car at the restart.

More chaos ensued as the pack lined up on the dummy grid for a second try. Michael Schumacher's Ferrari F399 was left on the line due to a problem with the neutral reset button on his steering wheel. For the second straight race, he got away late and had to join in from the back, together with Tora Takagi's late-starting Arrows.

Meanwhile, Häkkinen had edged into the lead from Coulthard at the first corner, with Irvine diving through the gap left by Barrichello's absent Stewart to take an immediate third place. At the second corner, Damon Hill was abruptly turfed into the gravel trap, bringing an early end to his first race of the season, after a brush with Jarno Trulli's Prost.

'All I could see was that as I was turning in for the second corner, someone stuck his nose in,' shrugged Hill. 'There was no way he was going to get through and no way we were going to get round. He got his front wheel in front of my rear wheel, tripped me up and spun me round. Very frustrating.'

Hill wasn't the only one who failed to complete the opening lap, as Jean Alesi's Sauber C18 had been left on the line with a broken transmission

Runners and riders

McLAREN-MERCEDES

Aiming to dominate a second season in a row, McLaren debuted the superbly engineered MP4/14, which was powered by a lightweight Mercedes F0110H 72-degree V10 that produced an estimated 785 bhp at 16,700 rpm. With excess weight trimmed from the entire chassis/engine package, the new car offered even more scope for strategic placement of ballast than its predecessor. Drivers Mika Häkkinen and David Coulthard used MP4/14s from the first race, although consideration had been given to running uprated MP4/13s at the season opener if the new car had not proved quick enough in testing.

FERRARI

The new F399 was touted as an evolutionary version of the 1997 car, but running a seven-speed, longitudinal transmission to make the most of the type 048 V10's 780 bhp at 17,000 rpm extracted from the powerplant by Stefano Domenicali's engine department. Michael Schumacher, entering his fourth season with the team, was partnered by the dutiful Eddie Irvine, whose contract still required him to give the German driver priority in his bid to nail down that elusive World Championship for Maranello.

WILLIAMS-SUPERTEC

Former F1 top dogs obliged to spend another season marking time with customer-specification Supertec V10 (née Mecachrome, née Renault) engines while awaiting the start of a new engine supply partnership with BMW in 2000. Latest FW21 chassis developed by Gavin Fisher and Geoff Willis confidently touted as improvement over 1998 chassis, despite giving away around 20 bhp to top rival teams. All-new driver line-up of seasoned rising star Ralf Schumacher and twice CART Champion Alex Zanardi, returning to F1 for first time since 1994.

JORDAN-MUGEN HONDA

Started season in buoyant mood after positive test results from new Mike Gascoyne-developed Jordan 199 chassis, powered by further uprated Mugen Honda MF301HD engine that pumped out a reputed 765 bhp. Damon Hill continued as team leader, being joined by the man who replaced him at Williams, Heinz-Harald Frentzen. During the off-season, Eddie Jordan had sold a 40 per cent stake in his company to merchant bankers Warburg Pincus.

BENETTON-PLAYLIFE

Now controlled by chief executive Rocco Benetton, and with its Supertec V10s again running under Playlife branding, the Benetton squad aimed to raise the standard of its game, Giancarlo Fisichella and Alexander Wurz remaining as drivers. Kicked off season in Melbourne under the threat that rivals were poised to protest the B199's Nick Wirth-designed torque-transfer system, which employs a clutch mechanism ahead of the front axle line to balance braking loads for optimum effect, despite this system having been given the green light by the FIA technical department.

SAUBER-PETRONAS

Latest Leo Ress-designed Sauber C18 chassis propelled by lighter, lower '98 Monza-spec Ferrari V10 with seven-speed, longitudinal transmission. Well-funded Brazilian Pedro Diniz replaces Johnny Herbert alongside Jean Alesi in driver line-up, despite legal argument over sponsorship payments owed to his previous employer, Arrows.

ARROWS

The future of Tom Walkinshaw's Leafield-based outfit was the subject of endless speculation during the winter, but the team emerged at Melbourne with Mike Coughlan-developed, uprated versions of the John Barnard-designed A19 chassis. Again powered by the team's own Brian Hart-designed V10 engines. Driven this year by Spanish new boy Pedro de la Rosa and Japan's Toranosuke Takagi. Contracted driver Mika Salo was released from his contract 'by mutual agreement' barely a week before the first race.

STEWART-FORD

With former Jordan technical director Gary Anderson taking over from Alan Jenkins at the helm of Stewart design, and an all-new, lightweight Ford CR-1 V10 engine fresh from the drawing board at Cosworth, Rubens Barrichello and new partner Johnny Herbert arrived at Albert Park in a guardedly optimistic mood. New car/engine combination had proved fast, but fragile, in pre-season testing, with V10 failures and a spectacular rear-wing breakage at Barcelona dramatically punctuating their progress.

PROST-PEUGEOT

After a disastrous 1998, Alain Prost's squad emerged from the eye of the storm with a much improved new car developed with input from British designer John Barnard, with whom Prost had worked at McLaren during his championship years of 1985–86. With Peugeot forging ahead on its A18 engine development programme, Prost was aiming to be one of the surprises of the season, enabling rising star Jarno Trulli to unlock some of his obvious potential at long last.

MINARDI-FORD

The use of better-specification Ford Zetec-R V10 engines, which powered the Stewarts in 1998, looked set to boost Giancarlo Minardi in his constant quest for improved performance. Newcomer Marc Gene partnered on the driving front by experienced Italian Luca Badoer – dovetailing this task with job as Ferrari test driver – enjoying his second stint behind the wheel for the small team from Faenza.

BRITISH AMERICAN RACING-SUPERTEC

Ambitious new super-team rising from the ashes of the Tyrrell organisation. Strong on budget, driving talent and engineering resources; weak on experience of working together in a racing environment. Supertec V10 not sufficiently powerful to win from the front, but Jacques Villeneuve and Ricardo Zonta were expected to show respectable form on tracks where power isn't a major issue. First race clouded by summons to appear before FIA World Council regarding rules breach that resulted from dispute over request to run two cars in different liveries.

British American escapes with no penalty

BRITISH American Racing escaped without penalty after appearing before the FIA World Motor Sport Council on 12 April, only five days after the team's race debut in Melbourne. The team had been summoned to answer charges that its management breached the F1 regulations by lodging a complaint about the governing body's behaviour with the European Commission.

British American had originally planned to run its two cars for Jacques Villeneuve and Ricardo Zonta in the liveries of Lucky Strike and 555 State Express respectively. However, the FIA said that this was against its rules, which required both cars run by a team to race in the same livery.

As a signatory of the Concorde agreement, the new team had agreed to abide by the arbitration process at the International Chamber of Commerce to resolve any disputes within the sport. This forum found that the FIA had acted within its rules in prohibiting dual branding, but British American simultaneously lodged its complaint with the EU, which put it in breach of the sport's rules.

Craig Pollock, British American Racing's managing director, admitted to the World Motor Sport Council that, in filing the complaint with the EU, his lawyers had acted without his instruction, and that a number of declarations made in that document did not reflect his personal views.

The FIA accepted Pollock's explanation, with the proviso that it was confirmed in writing to all the parties involved, and that he dissociated himself and British American Racing from the actions, statements and documents published by the lawyers that did not represent his own view.

'We are pleased that the matter is now concluded,' said Pollock. 'I have apologised to the World Motor Sport Council for any misunderstanding concerning our actions and the team can now focus on its preparations for the next Grand Prix in Brazil.'

Regulation changes for '99

CHANGES to the F1 technical regulations were relatively few for the 1999 season when compared to the wholesale upheaval of 12 months earlier, which brought about grooved tyres and dramatically narrower cars.

This season, the addition of a fourth circumferential groove in the front tyre was the main change, but this was set against a background of Bridgestone's newly assumed monopoly on tyre supply. It was also clear that mandating harder tyre compounds was another method that could be deployed if it was necessary to keep a tight rein on lap times in line with the FIA's requirements.

Under the circumstances, it was ironic that the first race under these new rules was won by a driver who had been so openly outspoken about the behaviour of the latest F1 tyres.

'The fourth groove is totally the wrong way to go,' said Irvine before the start of the season. 'By the time you get to the last bit of the corner where you're overtaking, you will have lost the effect of your car's aerodynamic downforce and all the grip from the tyres.

'For sure, if you reduce the amount of rubber in contact with the road, you go slower. But it's not safer, because whenever you spin now, you go a lot further because there is less grip from the harder tyres. For me, it is more dangerous, there's no doubt about that, but the lap times seem to be slower, which pleases the governing body. Everybody thinks it's safer because it's slower, which isn't the case.'

The Ferrari driver found a lot of support for this viewpoint from leading engineers within the F1 business.

'As has been said a number of times before, I, in common with a lot of other people, believe that the FIA is driving up the wrong street,' said Williams technical director Patrick Head. 'My opinion is that they should try to be increasing the mechanical grip – whether it's coming from the tyre compounds or suspension capability – and reducing the overall downforce. But it has been shown in the past that the FIA doesn't attach much value to our opinions, and I really don't see that changing too much in the future.'

By contrast, Prost designer John Barnard felt that the disadvantages of the latest hard-compound Bridgestone tyres may have been exaggerated. 'I think the situation will develop to show that the limitation on tyre performance is going to balance out the aerodynamic and other chassis developments which have been achieved over the winter,' he said.

Other safety improvements for the 1999 season included the mandatory use of seats that could be removed from the cockpit with the driver still in place. Headrests and lateral head supports were improved, and wheels were prevented from flying off the car in a major impact thanks to the adoption of restraining cables made from a special Kevlar rope.

Changes to the engine regulations included revisions that prevented any car from being equipped 'with a system or device which is capable of preventing the driven wheels from spinning or of compensating for excessive throttle demand by the driver.'

In addition, any device that notified the driver of the onset of wheelspin would not be permitted, and changes to the set-up of electronic differentials could only be made while the car was stationary.

Rear wing deflection test for F1 cars

ALL cars competing in the Brazilian GP on 11 April – the second round of the World Championship – were to be subjected to a rigorous rear wing deflection test prior to taking to the circuit, according to an edict from the sport's governing body. This followed strong evidence that certain teams were using rear wings that deflected backwards in an effort to reduce aerodynamic drag at high speed. Intent on nipping this practice in the bud, the FIA's technical department provided all competitors with details of the new test in the week following the Australian Grand Prix.

The test would involve applying a 100-kg rearward pressure on each car's rear wing, which would be permitted 'no more than one degree angular displacement when measured on the top of the rear wing end plate.' The governing body accepted that a certain amount of deflection was inevitable, but was determined to clamp down immediately on what was clearly a breach of the rule forbidding movable aerodynamic devices.

There had been much speculation that teams were experimenting with such devices ever since Johnny Herbert's Stewart-Ford crashed at 180 mph during pre-season testing at Barcelona when its rear wing failed. Despite this, designers disagreed over just how much benefit could be gained from slight flexibility in the rear wing.

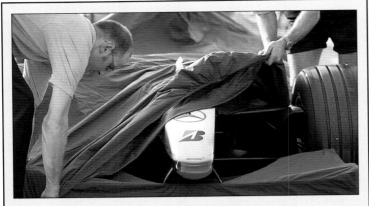

Paul-Henri Cahier

Left: The great McLaren cover-up. The wraps go on the latest MP4/14 to keep prying eyes lenses from seeing Adrian Newey's latest aerodynamic ideas.

Right: A cockpitful of gravel for Michael Schumacher

Below right: Why me? Damon Hill's first race of the season ended on the first lap after tangling with Jarno Trulli's Prost.

MELBOURNE QUALIFYING

Mika Häkkinen's McLaren-Mercedes may have ended up much the worse for wear after an unexpected smash into one of the barriers during Friday's first practice at Albert Park, but the World Champion walked away from the wreck with the unruffled insouciance of a man who knew that his rivals could not depend on such mistakes occurring regularly during the season ahead.

'The new additional head protection in the cockpit worked superbly in the accident, just as it did for Johnny Herbert in his Stewart when he crashed during tests at Barcelona,' said Häkkinen. 'As for me, I was just pushing a little too hard. Naturally, I am very annoyed with myself for going off, but at least I now know the limit of the car.'

David Coulthard capitalised on the Finn's rare error to emerge from the first track session of the new season with fastest time, a fraction ahead of his team-mate. This gave the Scot an early psychological advantage, but both McLaren drivers knew that fresh opposition could come from unexpected quarters this season, as demonstrated by Rubens Barrichello's excellent third-fastest time in the promising new Stewart-Ford SF3.

Yet come Saturday's hour-long qualifying session, Häkkinen duly launched the new season by taking his 11th pole position on the final lap of qualifying, pipping Coulthard, who qualified second, by 0.484s.

'The track felt better and better towards the end, which is usual,' said Häkkinen. 'It is a comfortable gap. I believe I am performing better than last year.'

Coulthard, who was 0.001s quicker than Häkkinen until the Finn popped in his fastest run, admitted that he was extremely disappointed. 'I was surprised that Mika managed another lap just before the flag came out to take pole from me at the last moment, and of course I was disappointed not to have been able to make use of my final lap due to traffic,' said the Scot.

Michael Schumacher was disappointed that his Ferrari F399 could only set Saturday's third-fastest time. 'I think there is more homework we need to do in proper testing,' he said.

Not only did the new Ferrari seem to be suffering from a significant handling imbalance, but Schumacher also lost valuable track time on Friday morning when his car stopped just a few yards beyond the pit lane exit due to gearbox problems. Although mechanics were able to pull the car back into the pit lane, the rules decreed that technically it had stopped out on the circuit and the frustrated German driver was barred from further participation in the session.

Eddie Irvine wound up sixth, saying he would have been quicker had he not made a mistake at the second corner on his final run. However, he was one of only nine drivers who opted for the softer Bridgestone tyres. The following day, he would make them work for him to splendid effect.

Rubens Barrichello qualified the Stewart-Ford SF3 a brilliant fourth, and although his team-mate, Johnny Herbert, trailed in 13th place after a problem with his car's right front shock absorber, the mood in the team's garage was one of absolute elation. 'The car is responsive to changes that the drivers make, and that gives them a lot of confidence,' said Paul Stewart.

Meanwhile, in the Jordan camp, Heinz-Harald Frentzen and Damon Hill adopted differing strategies during qualifying. Frentzen, whose car was fitted with a new engine for this session, ran relatively short stints and wound up fifth, while Hill – who chose longer runs – was four places further back, frustrated by traffic and a spate of yellow flags.

Giancarlo Fisichella's Benetton-Playlife took seventh, the Italian reporting that traffic, yellow flags and a mistake on his last run spoiled his efforts. Alexander Wurz switched to the spare car after quite a heavy accident during the morning, qualifying tenth. The team was unconvinced that its controversial front torque-transfer system would provide benefits on this particular circuit and did not use it in the race.

At Williams, new boy Ralf Schumacher struggled to balance his FW21 on fresh rubber and could only manage eighth on the grid, seven places ahead of Alex Zanardi, who concentrated on making up track time and split his session into two long runs.

Jacques Villeneuve set his 11th-fastest best time on his first run, spinning the British American Racing 01 on his second, then finding too much traffic on his third. Team-mate Ricardo Zonta ended up 19th in the team's other car.

Jarno Trulli complained that his Prost-Peugeot AP02 was suffering from lack of grip and nervous handling en route to 12th place on the grid, eight places ahead of Olivier Panis, who suffered gearbox problems on his race car and made a late switch to the spare before running out of time.

Fuel pressure problems caused Pedro Diniz (14th) to take over the spare Sauber-Petronas, finishing two places ahead of Jean Alesi, who complained that the fresh engine in his car was down on power. The Arrows of Toranosuke Takagi and Pedro de la Rosa were 17th and 18th, while Badoer's Minardi was the last qualifier, as Gene failed to make the 107 per cent cut-off.

after the Frenchman engaged the clutch for the first time. The new Sauber's gearbox had caused concern during pre-season testing, but this setback was especially disappointing for the Swiss team.

By the end of the opening lap, Häkkinen and Coulthard had a remarkable 2.3s in hand over Irvine. Next up was Heinz-Harald Frentzen's Jordan, ahead of Ralf Schumacher's Williams FW21, Giancarlo Fisichella's Benetton B199 and the fast-starting Jacques Villeneuve's British American 01, which had already made up four places from 11th on the grid.

Further back, Barrichello was in last place after starting the spare Stewart-Ford from the pit lane – and even this SF3 was a split second away from another engine-bay fire when the Brazilian accelerated into the fray – while Schumacher's Ferrari was just two places ahead.

Life seemed pretty routine at the front of the field as the McLarens edged into the distance, Coulthard being no less than 8.4s ahead of the third-placed Irvine at the end of lap four. However, Barrichello's comeback drive ensured that there was plenty of action further down the queue.

By lap two, the Brazilian had moved up to 16th and began to concentrate on latching onto the tail of Alexander Wurz's Benetton, a task he had completed by the end of lap seven. On lap eight, he was ahead of the Austrian and storming after the troubled Schumacher's Ferrari. Michael moved ahead of Pedro de la Rosa's Arrows on lap nine, and it took Rubens until lap 12 to find a way past the promising newcomer, by which time Schumacher had moved almost 5s clear.

Not that Michael was having an easy run. Although, from the touchline, he seemed to be picking up the pace nicely, the problem that had prevented him from engaging first gear at the start came back to haunt him during the race. To his extreme frustration, the gearbox began to engage neutral intermittently during cornering, a problem that would not be resolved until the steering wheel was changed much later in the race.

On lap 14, McLaren suffered its first bout of bad luck when Coulthard retired, just as Villeneuve's BAR pirouetted wildly into the wall after its rear wing failed. Thankfully, Jacques was able to stroll away from the impact.

'That's not quite the way I would have liked my first race of the season to end,' he said. 'It's disappointing, because the car was going very well and I was making good progress. It looked

promising for the second half of the race, but just didn't happen this time.'

Villeneuve's shunt brought the safety car out at the head of the pack, at a stroke depriving Häkkinen of an 18.1s lead over Irvine's Ferrari. At the end of lap 17, the cars were unleashed again, although as they accelerated down towards the startline, it was clear that Häkkinen was in trouble: his McLaren wasn't picking up the necessary speed at the head of the queue.

This caused real problems for the other competitors, as the rules state that when the safety car is withdrawn, there must be no overtaking until the pack has passed the start/finish line. For his part, Irvine timed his move to perfection, vaulting ahead of the Finn's crippled McLaren on the approach to the first corner. Further back, however, Barrichello – by then eighth – was wrong-footed and could not avoid tripping the timing beam a fraction ahead of Schumacher's Ferrari, which he had been following up to that point and which had braked abruptly in the chaos. As events transpired, it would turn out to be an expensive mistake.

At the end of lap 18, Häkkinen entered the pits to see if anything could be done to rectify his throttle problem. Engineers plugged in a diagnostic laptop computer in an attempt to solve the glitch, but to no avail. He slogged on for a while before calling it a day with 21 laps completed.

Also in the pits at the end of lap 18 was Fisichella, who had been running fifth, but tangled with Jarno Trulli's Prost at the hesitant restart, damaging his Benetton's nose section, which needed replacing. He rejoined at the tail of the queue and his car ran well for the rest of the afternoon.

'We were encouraged by the performance of the new car and believe that we can achieve the necessary reliability to win races,' said Ron Dennis, McLaren's managing director. 'It was obviously very frustrating, but we know we can get the job done. We just have to be patient for the second race of the season.'

One lap prior to Häkkinen's eventual retirement, Champ Car ace Alex Zanardi's disappointing F1 debut for Williams ended firmly against a retaining wall. Before the start, the Italian had been obliged to take the spare FW21 after encountering a problem with the clutch on his race car. He was clearly disappointed and slightly bewildered.

'I was quite a few seconds off the pace, just turned into a corner and lost the back end,' he explained. 'I certainly

AUSTRALIAN GRAND PRIX

DIARY

November 1998

Speculation suggests that Jaguar branding will replace Ford as the Detroit motor company's F1 flag carrier.

Bernie Ecclestone offers commercial concessions to the European Union in an effort to resolve difficulties over the planned $2 million Eurobond float for his company, F1 Administration.

December 1998

US Grand Prix at Indianapolis confirmed for 2000, on a new track incorporating part of the famous oval circuit.

FIA President Max Mosley hints that all-weather F1 tyres could be introduced by 2001.

Ford extends Stewart engine supply deal by one year to the end of 2001.

Benetton opens new £12-million, full-scale wind tunnel.

January 1999

British American Racing shows new cars in two different liveries.

Brands Hatch Leisure signals interest in bidding for ownership of Silverstone.

International Chamber of Commerce rules that FIA rules on dual branding are valid and British American Racing cannot run two cars in separate liveries.

had more problems this weekend than I thought I would have.'

Out came the safety car for the second time that afternoon, the pack closing up behind the silver Mercedes CLK. When the race proper resumed on lap 24, Irvine was 1.5s ahead of Frentzen, but that was quickly trimmed to below a second by the determined Jordan driver, and it was not until lap 29 that the Ulsterman began to ease clear again. Half a second apart, they both made their single refuelling stops at the end of lap 34, the Ferrari and Jordan briefly being split by Fisichella's hard-charging Benetton as they resumed the chase.

This state of affairs lasted for three laps, after which Fisichella made his stop, but by the time Frentzen retook second place, Irvine had firmly gained the upper hand and never wavered all the way to the finish.

'I must say, Eddie drove a fantastic race,' said an admiring Frentzen. 'He was going really fast and I tried to keep up with him, but it was going to be difficult to beat him today. I thought he was going to make a second stop, as I knew he was on the softer tyre choice, but he just kept going, so my tactic was simply to have my own race.'

Although Irvine joked that he'd never been under serious pressure from the yellow car, things might have been different if an air temperature sensor had not failed in the Jordan's airbox during the second half of the race. This sent an erroneous signal to the electronic control unit, instructing it to enrich the fuel/air mixture in case the engine was in trouble. The unfortunate result was excessive fuel consumption, leaving Heinz-Harald no choice but to change gear earlier than usual towards the finish to avoid running out of fuel.

Behind Frentzen, Ralf Schumacher had a steady run through to third place in the Williams FW21, despite his mount shedding one of its bargeboards in the closing stages of the race. Nevertheless, the young German driver was upbeat and optimistic, reporting that the car 'was well balanced' and that he was 'quite happy with its performance. Even losing the bargeboard did not upset the car's handling.'

Behind Schumacher came Fisichella's Benetton in fourth place, and the latter could well have been a contender for victory had it not been for a succession of minor problems. To start with, the Italian flat-spotted a front tyre on the opening lap, which caused a tiresome front-end vibration. Then he encountered the problems behind the safety car. Under the circumstances, he was quite happy with three points at the end of the day.

Barrichello, however, was the star of the show. While the pace car was out for the second time, he made his first refuelling stop on lap 22, actually making a place by timing his arrival in the pit lane promptly ahead of Marc Gene's Minardi and Jarno Trulli's Prost, which came in next time around – and would collide two laps after resuming the race.

Then, on lap 31, Rubens was finally called in for a 10s stop–go penalty for his over-enthusiastic performance at the first restart, and a lap later he was back for a fuel top-up, a glitch with the rig having short-changed him at the first stop. At this point, he was down in eighth, but tore back to fifth at the chequered flag, setting the second fastest lap of the race – behind Michael Schumacher's Ferrari F399 – as he did so.

'The car handled fantastically,' enthused the Brazilian. 'I think it is going to be a good year.' The only cars behind him at the finish were the promising Arrows A20s of Pedro de la Rosa and Tora Takagi, with Schumacher's Ferrari eighth, one lap down on its victorious stable-mate.

For Michael, the race had been a horror show. Having started last, as he had done in the final race of the 1998 season, he battled manfully through the pack, but was overwhelmed by problems. Despite the gearchange glitch that selected neutral unpredictably and intermittently for much of the race, he had barnstormed his way to third by the end of lap 26 only for his right rear Bridgestone to fly apart, sending him into the pits for fresh rubber.

On lap 37, he made an abortive 'straight through' run down the pit lane – echoing Mika Häkkinen's strategic setback of the previous year – then came in next time around for a replacement steering wheel to be fitted. That overcame the gearchange gremlin and allowed him to post the fastest lap of the day, just two hours from the chequered flag.

Ahead of the teams lay a yawning five-week gap to the second race of the season, the Brazilian Grand Prix at Interlagos. Could Ferrari close the performance gap, or had it missed its window of opportunity in the World Championship? Could McLaren deliver technical reliability at the second race? Or would the Stewart and Jordan teams begin to gatecrash the exclusive McLaren/Maranello party at the very front of the pack?

QANTAS AUSTRALIAN GRAND PRIX

5–7 MARCH 1999

MELBOURNE

Race distance: 57 laps, 187.822 miles/302.271 km

Race weather: Dry, warm and sunny

ROUND
1

MELBOURNE – GRAND PRIX CIRCUIT

CIRCUIT LENGTH: 3.295 miles/5.303 km

Pos.	Driver	Nat.	No.	Entrant	Car/Engine	Laps	Time/Retirement	Speed (mph/km/h)
1	Eddie Irvine	GB	4	Scuderia Ferrari Marlboro	Ferrari F399 048 V10	57	1h 35m 01.659s	118.590/190.852
2	Heinz-Harald Frentzen	D	8	Benson & Hedges Jordan	Jordan 199-Mugen Honda MF301/HD V10	57	1h 35m 02.686s	118.569/190.818
3	Ralf Schumacher	D	6	Winfield Williams	Williams FW21-Supertec FB01 V10	57	1h 35m 08.671s	118.444/190.618
4	Giancarlo Fisichella	I	9	Mild Seven Benetton Playlife	Benetton B199-Playlife V10	57	1h 35m 35.077s	117.899/189.740
5	Rubens Barrichello	BR	16	Stewart Ford	Stewart SF3-Ford CR-1 V10	57	1h 35m 56.357s	117.463/189.038
6	Pedro de la Rosa	ESP	14	Arrows	Arrows A20 V10	57	1h 36m 25.976s	116.862/188.071
7	Toranosuke Takagi	J	15	Arrows	Arrows A20 V10	57	1h 36m 27.947s	116.822/188.007
8	Michael Schumacher	D	3	Scuderia Ferrari Marlboro	Ferrari F399 048 V10	56		
	Ricardo Zonta	BR	23	British American Racing	BAR 01-Supertec FB01 V10	48	Engine	
	Luca Badoer	I	20	Fondmetal Minardi Ford	Minardi M01-Ford Zetec-R V10	42	Gearbox	
	Alexander Wurz	A	10	Mild Seven Benetton Playlife	Benetton B199-Playlife V10	28	Suspension	
	Pedro Diniz	BR	12	Red Bull Sauber Petronas	Sauber C18-Petronas SPE03A V10	27	Transmission	
	Marc Gene	ESP	21	Fondmetal Minardi Ford	Minardi M01-Ford Zetec-R V10	25	Collision with Trulli	
	Jarno Trulli	I	19	Gauloises Prost Peugeot	Prost AP02-Peugeot A18 V10	25	Collision with Gene	
	Olivier Panis	F	18	Gauloises Prost Peugeot	Prost AP02-Peugeot A18 V10	23	Stuck wheel nut	
	Mika Häkkinen	SF	1	West McLaren Mercedes	McLaren MP4/14-Mercedes F0110H V10	21	Throttle	
	Alex Zanardi	I	5	Winfield Williams	Williams FW21-Supertec FB01 V10	20	Accident	
	David Coulthard	GB	2	West McLaren Mercedes	McLaren MP4/14-Mercedes F0110H V10	13	Hydraulics	
	Jacques Villeneuve	CDN	22	British American Racing	BAR 01-Supertec FB01 V10	13	Accident	
	Damon Hill	GB	7	Benson & Hedges Jordan	Jordan 199-Mugen Honda MF301/HD V10	0	Spun off	
	Jean Alesi	F	11	Red Bull Sauber Petronas	Sauber C18-Petronas SPE03A V10	0	Gearbox	
DNS	Johnny Herbert	GB	17	Stewart Ford	Stewart SF3-Ford CR-1 V10		Oil leak	

Fastest lap: M. Schumacher, on lap 55, 1m 32.112s, 128.783 mph/207.256 km/h.

Lap record: Heinz-Harald Frentzen (F1 Williams FW19-Renault V10), 1m 30.585s, 130.929 mph/210.710 km/h (1997).

		1	2	3	4	5	6	7	8	9	10	11	12	13	14	15	16	17	18	19	20	21	22	23	24	25	26	27	28	29	30	31	32	33	34	35	36	37	38	39	40	41	42	43	44
1	HÄKKINEN	1	1	1	1	1	1	1	1	1	1	1	1	1	1	1	1	1	4	4	4	4	4	4	4	4	4	4	4	4	4	4	4	4	4	4	4	4	4	4	4	4	4	4	4
2	COULTHARD	2	2	2	2	2	2	2	2	2	2	2	2	2	4	4	4	4	8	8	8	8	8	8	8	8	8	8	8	8	8	8	8	8	9	9	8	8	8	8	8	8	8	8	8
3	M. SCHUMACHER	4	4	4	4	4	4	4	4	4	4	4	4	4	8	8	8	8	19	19	19	19	6	6	6	6	6	6	6	6	6	6	9	9	8	8	6	6	6	6	6	6	6	6	6
16	BARRICHELLO	8	8	8	8	8	8	8	8	8	8	8	8	8	6	6	6	6	6	6	6	6	3	3	3	3	3	12	16	16	16	15	9	6	6	6	14	14	14	9	9	9	9	9	9
8	FRENTZEN	6	6	6	6	6	6	6	6	6	6	6	6	6	9	9	9	9	3	3	3	3	12	12	12	12	12	16	23	23	23	9	20	14	14	14	9	9	9	14	14	14	16	16
4	IRVINE	9	9	9	9	9	9	9	9	9	9	9	9	9	19	19	19	19	12	12	16	16	10	10	10	10	10	23	15	15	15	20	14	15	15	15	15	15	15	15	15	16	16	14	14
9	FISICHELLA	22	19	19	19	19	19	19	19	19	19	19	19	19	3	3	16	16	16	12	12	23	23	23	23	23	15	9	9	9	14	15	23	23	23	23	23	16	15	15	15	23
6	R. SCHUMACHER	19	22	22	22	22	22	22	22	22	22	22	22	22	23	16	16	3	14	14	14	10	10	15	15	15	15	16	20	20	20	20	16	23	20	16	16	16	16	16	23	23	23	15
7	HILL	12	12	12	12	12	12	12	12	12	12	12	12	12	3	14	14	14	10	10	10	23	18	18	20	20	15	9	14	14	14	23	16	16	20	20	20	20	20	20	20	3	3
10	WURZ	23	23	23	23	23	23	23	23	23	23	23	23	23	16	12	12	12	23	23	23	14	19	20	16	16	20	14	10	3	3	3	3	3	3	3	3	3	3	3	3
22	VILLENEUVE	20	20	14	14	14	14	14	14	3	3	3	3	3	14	15	15	15	15	15	15	15	21	16	14	14	14	10	3
19	TRULLI	14	14	20	20	15	3	3	3	14	14	14	16	16	15	10	10	10	18	18	18	18	16	14	21	21	9	3
17	HERBERT	15	15	15	15	3	15	15	16	16	16	16	14	14	10	18	18	5	5	5	21	20	21	19	19
12	DINIZ	5	10	10	3	20	10	16	15	15	15	15	15	18	23	23	23	21	21	21	20	14	19	9	9
5	ZANARDI	10	3	3	10	10	16	10	10	10	10	10	10	10	20	21	21	21	20	20	20	9	9	9
11	ALESI	18	16	16	16	16	20	20	18	18	18	18	18	18	21	5	5	5	9	9	9	1
15	TAKAGI	3	18	18	18	18	18	18	20	5	5	5	5	20	5	20	20	20	1	1	1
14	DE LA ROSA	21	5	5	5	5	5	5	5	20	20	20	20	21
23	ZONTA	16	21	21	21	21	21	21	21	21	21	21	21	5
18	PANIS													
20	BADOER													
21	GENE													

Pit stop
One lap behind leader

STARTING GRID

1 HÄKKINEN McLaren	**2** COULTHARD McLaren
3* M. SCHUMACHER Ferrari	**16**** BARRICHELLO Stewart
8 FRENTZEN Jordan	**4** IRVINE Ferrari
9 FISICHELLA Benetton	**6** R. SCHUMACHER Williams
7 HILL Jordan	**10** WURZ Benetton
22 VILLENEUVE BAR	**19** TRULLI Prost
17* HERBERT Stewart	**12** DINIZ Sauber
5 ZANARDI Williams	**11** ALESI Sauber
15 TAKAGI Arrows	**14** DE LA ROSA Arrows
23 ZONTA BAR	**18** PANIS Prost
20 BADOER Minardi	**21** GENE Minardi

* started from back of grid
** started from pit lane
*** did not start

47	48	49	50	51	52	53	54	55	56	57	●	
4	4	4	4	4	4	4	4	4	4	4		1
8	8	8	8	8	8	8	8	8	8	8		2
6	6	6	6	6	6	6	6	6	6	6		3
9	9	9	9	9	9	9	9	9	9	9		4
16	16	16	16	16	16	16	16	16	16	16		5
14	14	14	14	14	14	14	14	14	14	14		6
15	15	15	15	15	15	15	15	15	15	15		
23	23	3	3	3	3	3	3	3	3			
3	3											

FOR THE RECORD

First Grand Prix win
Eddie Irvine

First Grand Prix start
Pedro de la Rosa
Marc Gene

50th Grand Prix start
Jacques Villeneuve

TIME SHEETS

QUALIFYING

Weather: Dry, warm and sunny

Pos.	Driver	Car	Laps	Time
1	Mika Häkkinen	McLaren-Mercedes	12	1m 30.462s
2	David Coulthard	McLaren-Mercedes	11	1m 30.946s
3	Michael Schumacher	Ferrari	11	1m 31.781s
4	Rubens Barrichello	Stewart-Ford	12	1m 32.148s
5	Heinz-Harald Frentzen	Jordan-Mugen Honda	11	1m 32.276s
6	Eddie Irvine	Ferrari	12	1m 32.289s
7	Giancarlo Fisichella	Benetton-Playlife	12	1m 32.540s
8	Ralf Schumacher	Williams-Supertec	10	1m 32.691s
9	Damon Hill	Jordan-Mugen Honda	12	1m 32.695s
10	Alexander Wurz	Benetton-Playlife	12	1m 32.789s
11	Jacques Villeneuve	BAR-Supertec	10	1m 32.888s
12	Jarno Trulli	Prost-Peugeot	11	1m 32.971s
13	Johnny Herbert	Stewart-Ford	12	1m 32.991s
14	Pedro Diniz	Sauber-Petronas	9	1m 33.374s
15	Alex Zanardi	Williams-Supertec	12	1m 33.549s
16	Jean Alesi	Sauber-Petronas	10	1m 33.910s
17	Toranosuke Takagi	Arrows	12	1m 34.182s
18	Pedro de la Rosa	Arrows	12	1m 34.244s
19	Ricardo Zonta	BAR-Supertec	11	1m 34.412s
20	Olivier Panis	Prost-Peugeot	10	1m 35.068s
21	Luca Badoer	Minardi-Ford	11	1m 35.316s
22*	Marc Gene	Minardi-Ford	11	1m 37.013s

107 per cent time: 1m 36.794s   * allowed to race

FRIDAY FREE PRACTICE

Weather: Dry, warm and sunny

Pos.	Driver	Laps	Time
1	David Coulthard	30	1m 31.971s
2	Mika Häkkinen	21	1m 31.985s
3	Rubens Barrichello	30	1m 32.947s
4	Heinz-Harald Frentzen	38	1m 33.029s
5	Johnny Herbert	28	1m 33.166s
6	Damon Hill	38	1m 33.420s
7	Michael Schumacher	17	1m 33.576s
8	Jarno Trulli	31	1m 33.870s
9	Alex Zanardi	30	1m 33.951s
10	Ralf Schumacher	26	1m 33.957s
11	Alexander Wurz	31	1m 34.046s
12	Giancarlo Fisichella	25	1m 34.135s
13	Jean Alesi	17	1m 34.541s
14	Eddie Irvine	23	1m 34.595s
15	Olivier Panis	23	1m 34.693s
16	Jacques Villeneuve	25	1m 34.695s
17	Pedro Diniz	24	1m 35.253s
18	Toranosuke Takagi	30	1m 35.699s
19	Pedro de la Rosa	35	1m 35.756s
20	Marc Gene	38	1m 36.481s
21	Luca Badoer	22	1m 37.958s
22	Ricardo Zonta	12	1m 38.075s

SATURDAY FREE PRACTICE

Weather: Dry, warm and sunny

Pos.	Driver	Laps	Time
1	Mika Häkkinen	26	1m 30.324s
2	David Coulthard	30	1m 30.969s
3	Johnny Herbert	26	1m 32.569s
4	Damon Hill	29	1m 32.661s
5	Jacques Villeneuve	20	1m 32.717s
6	Michael Schumacher	25	1m 32.722s
7	Rubens Barrichello	22	1m 32.828s
8	Heinz-Harald Frentzen	23	1m 32.876s
9	Giancarlo Fisichella	28	1m 32.975s
10	Eddie Irvine	24	1m 32.994s
11	Pedro Diniz	22	1m 32.999s
12	Alexander Wurz	16	1m 33.110s
13	Jarno Trulli	21	1m 33.252s
14	Jean Alesi	14	1m 33.305s
15	Ralf Schumacher	24	1m 33.323s
16	Olivier Panis	28	1m 34.129s
17	Pedro de la Rosa	17	1m 34.194s
18	Toranosuke Takagi	28	1m 34.386s
19	Alex Zanardi	7	1m 35.444s
20	Luca Badoer	29	1m 35.839s
21	Marc Gene	19	1m 36.848s
22	Ricardo Zonta	3	1m 48.227s

WARM-UP

Weather: Cool, light overcast

Pos.	Driver	Laps	Time
1	David Coulthard	13	1m 32.560s
2	Mika Häkkinen	14	1m 32.670s
3	Michael Schumacher	14	1m 33.638s
4	Pedro Diniz	14	1m 34.460s
5	Olivier Panis	11	1m 34.518s
6	Alex Zanardi	12	1m 34.556s
7	Johnny Herbert	11	1m 34.707s
8	Ralf Schumacher	9	1m 34.747s
9	Jarno Trulli	15	1m 34.784s
10	Jean Alesi	12	1m 34.805s
11	Alexander Wurz	12	1m 34.973s
12	Giancarlo Fisichella	15	1m 35.013s
13	Rubens Barrichello	13	1m 35.046s
14	Heinz-Harald Frentzen	16	1m 35.085s
15	Pedro de la Rosa	12	1m 35.135s
16	Eddie Irvine	12	1m 35.241s
17	Ricardo Zonta	10	1m 35.294s
18	Toranosuke Takagi	10	1m 35.568s
19	Jacques Villeneuve	8	1m 35.676s
20	Luca Badoer	14	1m 37.289s
21	Marc Gene	12	1m 38.471s
22	Damon Hill	2	16m 57.718s

RACE FASTEST LAPS

Weather: Dry, warm and sunny

Driver	Time	Lap
Michael Schumacher	1m 32.112s	55
Rubens Barrichello	1m 32.894s	29
Mika Häkkinen	1m 33.309s	9
Heinz-Harald Frentzen	1m 33.378s	33
Ralf Schumacher	1m 33.407s	32
Eddie Irvine	1m 33.560s	29
David Coulthard	1m 33.603s	9
Giancarlo Fisichella	1m 33.657s	34
Pedro Diniz	1m 34.748s	13
Ricardo Zonta	1m 34.756s	13
Jacques Villeneuve	1m 34.771s	12
Jarno Trulli	1m 34.980s	21
Pedro de la Rosa	1m 35.220s	39
Toranosuke Takagi	1m 35.877s	50
Olivier Panis	1m 35.910s	13
Alexander Wurz	1m 36.068s	20
Luca Badoer	1m 37.073s	29
Alex Zanardi	1m 37.146s	20
Marc Gene	1m 37.454s	20

CHASSIS LOG BOOK

1	Häkkinen	McLaren MP4/14/1
2	Coulthard	McLaren MP4/14/2
	spare	McLaren MP4/14/4
3	M. Schumacher	Ferrari F399/190
4	Irvine	Ferrari F399/191
	spare	Ferrari F399/192
5	Zanardi	Williams FW21/1
6	R. Schumacher	Williams FW21/3
	spare	Williams FW21/2
7	Hill	Jordan 199/4
8	Frentzen	Jordan 199/3
	spare	Jordan 199/1
9	Fisichella	Benetton B199/4
10	Wurz	Benetton B199/2
	spare	Benetton B199/1
11	Alesi	Sauber C18/3
12	Diniz	Sauber C18/1
	spare	Sauber C18/4
14	de la Rosa	Arrows A20/4
15	Takagi	Arrows A20/2
	spare	Arrows A20/5
16	Barrichello	Stewart SF3/4
17	Herbert	Stewart SF3/3
	spare	Stewart SF3/1
18	Panis	Prost AP02/3
19	Trulli	Prost AP02/2
	spare	Prost AP02/1
20	Badoer	Minardi M01/2
21	Gene	Minardi M01/3
	spare	Minardi M01/1
22	Villeneuve	BAR 01/3
23	Zonta	BAR 01/2
	spare	BAR 01/4

POINTS TABLES

DRIVERS

1	Eddie Irvine	10
2	Heinz-Harald Frentzen	6
3	Ralf Schumacher	4
4	Giancarlo Fisichella	3
5	Rubens Barrichello	2
6	Pedro de la Rosa	1

CONSTRUCTORS

1	Ferrari	10
2	Jordan	6
3	Williams	4
4	Benetton	3
5	Stewart	2
6	Arrows	1

BRAZILIAN
grand prix

FIA WORLD CHAMPIONSHIP • ROUND 2

HÄKKINEN

M. SCHUMACHER

FRENTZEN

R. SCHUMACHER

IRVINE

PANIS

Left: Häkkinen was in total control with the latest McLaren MP4/14-Mercedes.

Below left: Cocooned in his Ferrari cockpit, Eddie Irvine seems to be connected to the outside world by umbilical cords.

IT was business as usual in the Brazilian Grand Prix at Interlagos. Well, almost. A momentary gear-change glitch probably cost Mika Häkkinen one of the most dominant performances of his entire career, although thanks to a superb tactical effort by the entire McLaren-Mercedes team, the Finn still saw off Michael Schumacher's Ferrari F399 to score his tenth Grand Prix victory.

It was a bedrock Häkkinen performance – mature, controlled and decisive – which did much to compensate for the team's disappointment in failing to post a finish for either of its cars in the Australian Grand Prix five weeks earlier.

Yet the great star of the show, as far as the Brazilian crowd was concerned, turned out to be Rubens Barrichello in the Stewart-Ford SF3. Having beaten Michael Schumacher's Ferrari to qualify third on the grid, Rubens took an immediate second place at the start, then surged into the lead when Häkkinen's McLaren slowed fleetingly with that gearchange problem at the start of lap four.

Rubens was never going to win. He wasn't running quickly enough to make a two-stop strategy beat either Häkkinen or Schumacher, but he might have wound up third. As it was, his Ford V10 expired in a cloud of smoke after 42 laps, cruelly dashing his hopes of a well-earned place on the podium.

Unfortunately, the second race of the season also ended with David Coulthard having achieved nothing with the other McLaren MP4/14. This time, the Scot succumbed to gearbox problems after stalling at the start and losing three laps to the leaders.

Häkkinen beat Michael Schumacher's Ferrari into second place by 4.9s, while Heinz-Harald Frentzen's Jordan was third, ahead of Ralf Schumacher's Williams and Melbourne winner Eddie Irvine, who leads the World Championship with 12 points after two races. Behind him are Häkkinen and Frentzen on ten apiece.

Frentzen's car actually ground to a halt on its final lap, having lost fuel pressure, but the German driver retained third place in the race because, at that point, he was running more than a lap ahead of his immediate pursuers.

Having buttoned up a place on the front row of the grid after a great qualifying battle with Häkkinen, Coulthard's legendary ill fortune intervened yet again. As the starting signal was given, his McLaren stalled and was almost hit from behind when

Schumacher's Ferrari weaved around the stationary car as the pack followed Häkkinen's McLaren into the first corner.

'I engaged first gear, had the car held on the handbrake and instead of the revs rising when I expected, it stalled,' he said reflectively. In fact, he had been using a 'parking' brake to keep the car steady off-camber on the inclined Interlagos startline. Despite trying the technique in pre-race testing, it seems he held the brake for a millisecond too long and stalled the Merc V10, pure and simple.

'I was watching in my mirrors, ready for the impact, but everybody avoided me,' he continued. 'I got pushed to the pits and rejoined in amongst the leaders, but three laps down. I was shown a blue flag, even though I was miles ahead of Michael, but eventually I dropped back and let him and Rubens get on with their battle for second.'

Later, Coulthard came into the pits after losing fifth gear. He went straight back out again, but there was no possibility of jumping the offending ratio in the sequential box. When he next selected fifth, the whole gearbox blew apart – almost literally.

At the end of the opening lap, Häkkinen led from Barrichello's Stewart-Ford, Schumacher's Ferrari, Eddie Irvine's Ferrari and the rest of the pack. Coulthard's car was pushed into the pit lane and finally restarted three laps into the race, rejoining in third place on the track, just as Häkkinen slowed momentarily at the head of the field.

For a split second, it seemed as though the McLaren-Mercedes challenge was over for the second race of the season. 'I was accelerating up through the gears, everything going well, when suddenly I couldn't get a high gear,' said Häkkinen. 'I thought the game was over, but suddenly the gears came back and I was able to keep going.'

Almost immediately, the World Champion picked up the pace again, but not before Barrichello had surged into the lead of a Grand Prix for the first time in his career, to the unbridled and vocal delight of the 120,000-strong crowd.

Rubens had rekindled the flame originally lit by fellow *Paulista* Emerson Fittipaldi when he won the 1973 Brazilian Grand Prix for Lotus. Since then, the local fans had developed into F1 sophisticates, their enthusiasm fuelled by the title-winning exploits of Emerson, Nelson Piquet and the great Ayrton Senna. Now they were being

INTERLAGOS QUALIFYING

Mika Häkkinen drove the McLaren-Mercedes MP4/14 to the 12th pole position of his career at Interlagos, ending up 0.147s ahead of team-mate David Coulthard. 'We were trying various set-ups and made some radical changes to the car before qualifying,' said Häkkinen. 'Then I felt more and more confident, but we still haven't reached the maximum potential of the car. It was a very exciting session.'

In reality, it was a close-run thing between the two McLaren drivers during a session that began with the entire field queuing at the pit exit, all anxious to be on their way as the skies threatened to spoil things with a rain shower. In fact, all was well and the rain held off.

Häkkinen set the pace on 1m 17.070s, which eventually he trimmed to 1m 16.568s, but Coulthard almost matched him throughout, and the outcome of the battle for fastest time seemed in doubt right up to their final runs.

David was very pleased with his efforts. 'I am very happy with the way the weekend has gone so far,' he admitted. 'The first time I have really been able to drive the car in the wet was yesterday [Friday's free practice] and it seemed quite well balanced, as it was in the dry.

'The only thing that stood in the way of me trying to take pole position from Mika was a bit of over-driving at the beginning of my final run. I heard a funny noise over the radio and missed my braking [for Turn One]. When you have flat-spotted a tyre, like I did there, if you over-brake again, the tyre will always return to the same flat spot to lock up again, so you have to be careful.'

Rubens Barrichello was delighted to have qualified third in front of his home crowd with the Stewart-Ford. 'I hope this doesn't sound arrogant, but I have been waiting for a good car all my career,' he said.

What was really impressive about Barrichello's performance was the way in which he jousted with Michael Schumacher's Ferrari for third place, losing out to the Italian car, then bouncing back to reassert his position as best of the rest behind the McLarens.

There was precious little wrong with the Ford V10's sheer grunt up the hill before the pits, either, for this was where the Brazilian driver clawed back time from the Ferrari on his crucial final run. His team-mate, Johnny Herbert, wound up tenth. 'I need to improve my pace in qualifying because I was faster in race set-up,' he noted thoughtfully.

Michael Schumacher and Eddie Irvine qualified their Ferrari F399s fourth and sixth. 'We could do better, but there is still something lacking in the Ferrari for qualifying,' said Michael, who was clearly unamused. 'I did not expect to be one second away from pole.'

Irvine added, 'I'm happy to be up on the third row because at one moment I thought I would be much further back.'

Giancarlo Fisichella was delighted to have split the Ferraris with fifth-fastest time in his Benetton B199. 'The car was perfect,' he said. 'Now I must build on this situation in the race.' Alexander Wurz stopped out on the circuit with gearbox problems, ending up ninth after struggling with the handling balance of his car for most of the day.

The Jordan-Mugen Hondas of Damon Hill and Heinz-Harald Frentzen qualified seventh and eighth. 'I did not quite achieve what I expected, which was a place in the top six,' said Hill, 'but I blame that largely on the track time I lost earlier on.' On Friday, both he and Frentzen had problems with the cars' lubrication systems, a malfunction related to a pin in the oil tank impeller, which caused the system to pressurise and blow out most of the oil. 'I will have to go flat out from the start of qualifying,' said Hill after encountering this problem.

Ralf Schumacher wound up 11th in his Williams FW21, commenting, 'We paid the penalty for not testing. I also lost a little time under a yellow flag, but we have a lot of work left to do on the car and engine.' At least this placed him six slots ahead of team-mate Alex Zanardi, after the Italian was obliged to take the spare Williams FW21 and then suffered a suspected engine failure.

The Prost-Peugeot AP02s of Olivier Panis and Jarno Trulli lined up 12th and 13th, both drivers losing valuable set-up action during Saturday morning's truncated free practice session. They complained repeatedly of a lack of traction.

From the Sauber camp, Jean Alesi and Pedro Diniz were 14th and 15th, the Frenchman commenting quite openly, 'No problems, no traffic... that's all we could do.'

F1 debutant Stéphane Sarrazin, Prost's test and F3000 driver, did a good job on loan to Minardi, where he stood in for the injured Luca Badoer, the Italian having broken his hand in a testing shunt at Fiorano. Sarrazin neatly qualified ahead of both Arrows, while Marc Gene brought up the rear of the qualifiers proper, the British American racers having had more than their fair share of alarms and excursions (see sidebar on page 109).

Rubens Barrichello's Stewart leads the Ferraris of Schumacher and Irvine and the Jordans of Frentzen and Hill.
Paul-Henri Cahier

BRAZILIAN GRAND PRIX

Disastrous weekend for F1's newcomers

Paul-Henri Cahier

Clockwise from top left: Olivier Panis scored Prost's first point of the year; Häkkinen and Frentzen take the plaudits; Stéphane Sarrazin's excellent F1 debut in the Minardi ended with a spectacular off-track excursion; the familiar profile of Flavio Briatore (and cigarette) in Supertec guise; Ralf Schumacher finished fourth for Williams; Brazilian beauties abounded on the grid.

given a taste of that heady nationalistic cocktail for the first time since Ayrton brought them to their feet with his second – and last – Brazilian GP win in 1993.

Many onlookers expected Schumacher's Ferrari to pounce immediately, but the Brazilian driver was on top form and retained a steady 3s advantage as he continued his unruffled progress at the head of the field.

In fact, Michael had his hands full during the opening stages of the race. 'We took off some downforce before the start, which made things better once some rubber went down on the racing line,' he explained. 'But until then, it was sliding around quite a lot and very tricky to keep on the road. I didn't want Rubens to get too far ahead, but I also wanted to keep in front of Mika, so that meant using the traffic as much as possible to our advantage.'

On lap 11, everything went wrong for Damon Hill for the second race in a row. The Jordan driver dived decisively inside Alexander Wurz's Benetton B199 as they battled for seventh place entering the first left-hander after the pits. Damon was abreast of his rival, but that didn't stop the Austrian from turning into him. The Jordan driver limped back to the pits to retire his car with deranged suspension. He was not best pleased.

'I was extremely disappointed and rather angry,' he admitted. 'I did not think it was very good driving from Alexander, as I had outbraked him and won the corner and he kept coming over until we hit. Luck has not been on my side for the first two races, but things will get better.'

Wurz was equally frustrated, but perhaps significantly did not attempt to blame his rival. 'It was a difficult race,' he noted after finishing seventh. 'I experienced quite a lot of understeer, and then Damon tried to overtake me and we had a collision. This affected my set-up to drive, and the car became more difficult to drive, and this was followed by a problem with the engine not pulling properly.'

On lap 12, Olivier Panis came in for a 'stop-go' penalty, incurred for jumping the start. It dropped the Frenchman's Prost-Peugeot from seventh to 18th. Four laps later, Johnny Herbert's Stewart SF3 retired from seventh place with hydraulic failure.

'There was a bit of confusion at the start because Coulthard stalled and I picked the wrong line,' shrugged the Englishman. 'I was running well and gained a few places when Hill and Wurz touched, but then I lost all hy-

THE Brazilian Grand Prix was a weekend to forget for the British American Racing team, following a catalogue of disasters, the worst of which left local hero Ricardo Zonta in hospital with foot injuries that eventually would sideline him until the Canadian Grand Prix.

The race itself finally ended for the British American squad when its sole surviving car, driven by Jacques Villeneuve, dropped out from seventh place with a hydraulic failure, having completed 50 of the 72 laps. It was the final chapter in a bitterly disappointing weekend that left F1's newest entrants looking beleaguered and under pressure.

Villeneuve celebrated his 28th birthday on Friday by missing most of free practice after his car developed a fuel tank leak. A new tank was installed for Saturday, but the car failed a fuel check, almost certainly because of contaminants in the new tank. As a result, Villeneuve was moved from 16th place to the back of the starting grid, his qualifying times being disallowed.

Zonta's crash came during Saturday morning's free practice at the uphill Ferradura right-hander, which is approached at around 170mph. 'I think the cockpit head and neck protection saved his life,' said FIA medical delegate Professor Sid Watkins, 'and certainly, at the very least, major head injury. We have no numbers for the forces involved in the impact, but we will have them available later in the year, once we have analysed the data.'

Zonta was taken to hospital with a serious gash in his left foot that contained particles of the carbon fibre chassis, which had entered after it had been punctured by a front suspension member.

draulic pressure and that was the end of it for me.'

Meanwhile, Jean Alesi was giving probably the most remarkable performance of the race. During the race-morning warm-up, he'd been so frustrated with his Sauber C18's performance that he commented, 'It is so bad, I just don't want to talk about it.'

In a bid to retrieve something worthwhile from the weekend, Alesi removed downforce before the start – and simply flew. Despite a second-lap spin that dropped him from 13th to 19th, he simply rocketed through the field to the point where, amazingly, he was running fifth before coming in to refuel at the end of lap 26.

'Today we were able to prove the C18's potential on a track where the driver can also make a difference,' he enthused after the race. 'I twice set fastest lap, but when I made my pit stop, the lollipop man seemed to signal to me twice and I stalled the engine. Not long afterwards, the gearbox broke.' The Frenchman certainly deserved better on a day when his team-mate, Pedro Diniz, also failed to make it to the finish. The Brazilian retired after a tangle with Toranosuke Takagi's Arrows A20.

Meanwhile, Barrichello continued to lead through to lap 27, when he made

his first scheduled refuelling stop, having opted to run the softer of the two available Bridgestone tyre compounds. He resumed in fourth place, but ten laps later surged ahead of Irvine to recover third, then set off at top speed in pursuit of the Ferrari and McLaren.

On lap 32, Stéphane Sarrazin, the Prost test driver who was standing in for the injured Luca Badoer in the Minardi, suddenly swerved violently on the start/finish straight, bouncing off the wall and shedding a wheel after an apparent suspension failure. Thankfully, the young Frenchman walked away from the damaged car, and the debris was hurriedly swept from the track.

At this point, the race settled into a tactical battle between Schumacher and Häkkinen. Both had opted for a single-stop strategy and the harder, more durable tyre compounds. On lap 38, Schumacher decided to stop, but Häkkinen stayed out for another four laps, hammering out a series of really quick circuits that enabled him to get into the pits and out again, on lap 42, before the Ferrari hove into view on the pit straight.

While sitting behind the Ferrari, Mika had gone into what the McLaren squad called 'fuel-consumption mode', with the result that he was able to stay out slightly longer than his rival. Then

he proceeded to beat Schumacher in the same manner as he had done during the previous year's European GP at Nürburgring.

Meanwhile, Fisichella had retired his Benetton with clutch trouble after changing the steering wheel in the mistaken belief that the gearchange controls were at fault.

The Brazilian crowd gasped with dismay on lap 43 as Barrichello's third-placed Stewart retired with engine failure, this time a piston-related breakage. Nevertheless, Rubens was elated with his personal performance.

'I made a good start and was running at a good pace up until the first stop,' he said. 'I lost a bit of consistency with the second set of tyres and I was probably not running well enough to win, but good enough to be on the podium.' It was a huge morale booster for the entire Stewart-Ford team.

On lap 55, Irvine had to make an unscheduled stop from third place to top up the air reservoir feeding the pneumatic valvegear. In the process, he dropped to fifth behind Frentzen and Ralf Schumacher's Williams FW21.

In the closing stages, Irvine came back hard at the young German driver, but Schumacher junior was having none of it and held his place to the chequered flag. 'It was pretty hard to stay in front of Eddie, who was a lot quicker than me,' Ralf admitted. 'He was on new tyres and low fuel, but he was never really a threat.'

As for Ralf's team-mate, Alex Zanardi, his second outing for Williams also ended on a disappointing note. 'I was running a one-stop strategy, but then the differential failed, which made the car extremely difficult to drive,' said the Italian. 'The team asked me to stay out and I drove as fast as I could before the gearbox developed a problem.' He retired on lap 43.

At the end of the day, it seemed as though the McLaren-Mercedes alliance had sustained the performance advantage displayed in Melbourne. Michael Schumacher looked extremely downcast, although he displayed a cautiously upbeat mood at the post-race media conference.

'The team managed to improve the car for the race,' he conceded. 'There are new developments to come in time for Imola, which should help us to close the gap even more. I am not worried about the points situation, as we are still at a very early stage in the season.'

Häkkinen, smiling indulgently, clearly had other ideas.

GRANDE PREMIO MARLBORO DO BRAZIL

9–11 APRIL 1999
INTERLAGOS

Race distance: 72 laps, 192.000 miles/308.994 km

Race weather: Dry, hot and sunny

ROUND **2**

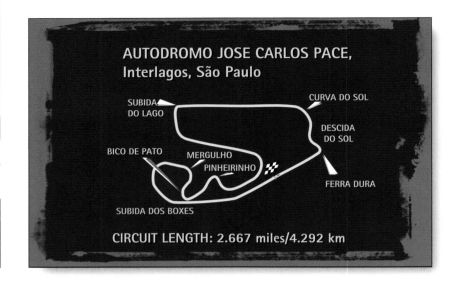

AUTODROMO JOSE CARLOS PACE, Interlagos, São Paulo

SUBIDA DO LAGO — CURVA DO SOL — DESCIDA DO SOL — BICO DE PATO — MERGULHO — PINHEIRINHO — FERRA DURA — SUBIDA DOS BOXES

CIRCUIT LENGTH: 2.667 miles/4.292 km

Pos.	Driver	Nat.	No.	Entrant	Car/Engine	Laps	Time/Retirement	Speed (mph/km/h)
1	Mika Häkkinen	SF	1	West McLaren Mercedes	McLaren MP4/14-Mercedes F0110H V10	72	1h 36m 03.785s	119.921/192.994
2	Michael Schumacher	D	3	Scuderia Ferrari Marlboro	Ferrari F399 048 V10	72	1h 36m 08.710s	119.818/192.829
3	Heinz-Harald Frentzen	D	8	Benson & Hedges Jordan	Jordan 198-Mugen Honda MF301/HD V10	71	Out of fuel	
4	Ralf Schumacher	D	6	Winfield Williams	Williams FW21-Supertec FB01 V10	71		
5	Eddie Irvine	GB	4	Scuderia Ferrari Marlboro	Ferrari F399 048 V10	71		
6	Olivier Panis	F	18	Gauloises Prost Peugeot	Prost AP02-Peugeot A18 V10	71		
7	Alexander Wurz	A	10	Mild Seven Benetton Playlife	Benetton B199-Playlife V10	70		
8	Toranosuke Takagi	J	15	Arrows	Arrows A20 V10	69		
9	Marc Gene	ESP	21	Fondmetal Minardi Ford	Minardi M01-Ford Zetec-R V10	69		
	Pedro de la Rosa	ESP	14	Arrows	Arrows A20 V10	52	Hydraulics	
	Jacques Villeneuve	CDN	22	British American Racing	BAR 01-Supertec FB01 V10	49	Hydraulics	
	Alex Zanardi	I	5	Winfield Williams	Williams FW21-Supertec FB01 V10	43	Transmission	
	Rubens Barrichello	BR	16	Stewart Ford	Stewart SF3-Ford CR-1 V10	42	Engine	
	Pedro Diniz	BR	12	Red Bull Sauber Petronas	Sauber C18-Petronas SPE03A V10	42	Spun off	
	Giancarlo Fisichella	I	9	Mild Seven Benetton Playlife	Benetton B199-Playlife V10	38	Clutch	
	Stéphane Sarrazin	F	20	Fondmetal Minardi Ford	Minardi M01-Ford Zetec-R V10	31	Accident/stuck throttle	
	Jean Alesi	F	11	Red Bull Sauber Petronas	Sauber C18-Petronas SPE03A V10	27	Gearbox	
	David Coulthard	GB	2	West McLaren Mercedes	McLaren MP4/14-Mercedes F0110H V10	22	Gearbox	
	Jarno Trulli	I	19	Gauloises Prost Peugeot	Prost AP02-Peugeot A18 V10	21	Gearbox	
	Johnny Herbert	GB	17	Stewart Ford	Stewart SF3-Ford CR-1 V10	15	Hydraulics	
	Damon Hill	GB	7	Benson & Hedges Jordan	Jordan 199- Mugen Honda MF301/HD V10	10	Accident damage	
DNS	Ricardo Zonta	BR	23	British American Racing	BAR 01-Supertec FB01 V10		Practice accident	

Fastest lap: Häkkinen, on lap 70, 1m 18.448s, 122.386 mph/196.961 km/h.

Lap record: Jacques Villeneuve (F1 Williams FW19-Renault V10), 1m 18.397s, 122.465 mph/197.089 km/h (1997).

Grid order	1	2	3	4	5	6	7	8	9	10	11	12	13	14	15	16	17	18	19	20	21	22	23	24	25	26	27	28	29	30	31	32	33	34	35	36	37	38	39	40	41	42	43	44	45	46	47	48	49	50	51	52	53	54	5
1 HÄKKINEN	1	1	1	16	16	16	16	16	16	16	16	16	16	16	16	16	16	16	16	16	16	16	16	16	16	16	3	3	3	3	3	3	3	3	3	3	1	1	1	1	1	1	1	1	1	1	1	1	1	1	1	1	1	1	1
2 COULTHARD	16	16	16	3	3	3	3	3	3	3	3	3	3	3	3	3	3	3	3	3	3	3	3	3	3	3	1	1	1	1	1	1	1	1	1	1	3	3	3	3	3	3	3	3	3	3	3	3	3	3	3	3	3	3	
16 BARRICHELLO	3	3	3	1	1	1	1	1	1	1	1	1	1	1	1	1	1	1	1	1	1	1	1	1	16	4	4	4	16	16	16	16	16	16	8	8	4	4	4	4	4	4	4	4	4	4	4	4							
3 M. SCHUMACHER	4	4	4	4	4	4	4	4	4	4	4	4	4	4	4	4	4	4	4	4	4	4	4	4	4	4	16	16	16	16	16	16	16	4	4	4	4	8	8	4	4	4	8	8	8	8	8	8	8	8	8	8	8		
9 FISICHELLA	9	9	9	9	9	9	9	9	9	9	9	9	9	9	9	9	9	9	9	9	9	11	11	11	11	11	11	9	9	9	9	9	9	9	8	8	8	4	6	6	6	6	6	6	6	6	6	6	6	6					
4 IRVINE	8	8	8	8	8	8	8	8	8	8	8	8	8	8	8	8	8	8	11	11	9	9	9	9	9	9	8	8	8	8	8	8	8	8	9	6	6	6	22	18	18	18	18	18	18	18	18	18	18	18	1				
7 HILL	10	10	10	10	10	10	10	10	10	18	18	17	17	17	11	11	11	11	8	8	8	8	8	8	8	6	6	6	6	6	6	6	6	6	12	12	12	12	18	22	22	22	22	22	10	10	10	10	10	10	1				
8 FRENTZEN	7	7	7	7	7	7	7	7	17	17	11	11	11	6	6	6	6	6	6	6	6	6	6	6	12	12	12	12	12	12	12	12	12	12	22	22	22	10	10	10	10	10	14	14	14	14	15	15	1						
10 WURZ	18	18	18	18	18	18	18	18	18	6	6	6	19	19	19	10	10	10	12	12	14	14	14	14	14	14	22	22	22	22	14	14	14	14	14	14	22	15	15	15	21	21	2												
17 HERBERT	17	17	17	17	17	17	17	17	6	6	18	19	19	10	10	10	12	12	14	14	18	18	18	18	22	22	22	22	22	14	14	14	14	10	18	10	10	15	21	21	21	21	15	21	21										
6 R. SCHUMACHER	6	6	6	6	6	6	6	6	19	19	10	10	12	12	14	14	22	22	18	14	14	14	14	20	20	20	10	10	10	10	10	10	18	14	14	14	21	15	15	15	15	15													
18 PANIS	19	19	19	19	19	19	19	19	11	10	10	10	12	12	14	14	22	22	18	18	22	22	22	22	22	10	10	10	18	18	18	18	18	18	18	15	15	15	5	5															
19 TRULLI	11	12	12	12	11	11	11	11	19	5	12	12	14	14	22	22	22	20	18	19	20	20	20	20	20	20	21	21	21	21	21	21	15	15	15	15	5	5	5	15															
11 ALESI	12	5	5	5	12	12	12	5	12	14	22	22	20	20	18	18	18	10	10	10	18	18	18	18	15	15	15	5	5	5	5	21	21	21	21																				
12 DINIZ	20	14	14	14	11	5	5	5	12	14	22	22	20	18	18	18	10	10	10	21	21	21	21	21	21	15	15	15	5	5	5	21	21	21	21																				
5 ZANARDI	5	21	21	11	14	14	14	14	22	5	21	21	21	21	21	21	21	21	15	15	15	15	15	15	15	5	5	5	5																										
20 SARRAZIN	14	15	15	21	21	21	21	21	21	21	20	15	15	15	15	15	15	5	5	5	5	5	5																																
14 DE LA ROSA	21	22	11	15	15	15	22	22	22	20	20	15	18	18	5	5	5	5	5	5	19	2																																	
15 TAKAGI	15	11	22	22	22	22	20	20	20	15	5	5	5	17	2	2	2	2	2	2																																			
21 GENE	22	20	20	20	20	20	15	15	15	7	2	2	2	2	2																																								
22 VILLENEUVE	2	2	2	2	2	2	2	2	2	2																																													

Pit stop

One lap behind leader

STARTING GRID

2 **COULTHARD** McLaren	1 **HÄKKINEN** McLaren
3 **M. SCHUMACHER** Ferrari	16 **BARRICHELLO** Stewart
4 **IRVINE** Ferrari	9 **FISICHELLA** Benetton
8 **FRENTZEN** Jordan	7 **HILL** Jordan
17 **HERBERT** Stewart	10 **WURZ** Benetton
18 **PANIS** Prost	6 **R. SCHUMACHER** Williams
11 **ALESI** Sauber	19 **TRULLI** Prost
5 **ZANARDI** Williams	12 **DINIZ** Sauber
14 **DE LA ROSA** Arrows	20 **SARRAZIN** Minardi
21 **GENE** Minardi	15 **TAKAGI** Arrows
	22 **VILLENEUVE** BAR

Did not start:

ZONTA (BAR)

58 59 60 61 62 63 64 65 66 67 68 69 70 71 72	
1 1 1 1 1 1 1 1 1 1 1 1 1 1 1	1
3 3 3 3 3 3 3 3 3 3 3 3 3 3 3	2
8 8 8 8 8 8 8 8 8 8 8 8 8 8	3
6 6 6 6 6 6 6 6 6 6 6 6 6 6	4
4 4 4 4 4 4 4 4 4 4 4 4 4 4	5
18 18 18 18 18 18 18 18 18 18 18 18 18 18 18	6
10 10 10 10 10 10 10 10 10 10 10 10 10 10	
15 15 15 15 15 15 15 15 15 15 15 15	
21 21 21 21 21 21 21 21 21 21 21 21	

TIME SHEETS

QUALIFYING

Weather: Dry and overcast.

Pos.	Driver	Car	Laps	Time
1	Mika Häkkinen	McLaren-Mercedes	12	1m 16.568s
2	David Coulthard	McLaren-Mercedes	12	1m 16.715s
3	Rubens Barrichello	Stewart-Ford	11	1m 17.305s
4	Michael Schumacher	Ferrari	11	1m 17.578s
5	Giancarlo Fisichella	Benetton-Playlife	12	1m 17.810s
6	Eddie Irvine	Ferrari	11	1m 17.843s
7	Damon Hill	Jordan-Mugen Honda	11	1m 17.884s
8	Heinz-Harald Frentzen	Jordan-Mugen Honda	11	1m 17.902s
9	Alexander Wurz	Benetton-Playlife	12	1m 18.334s
10	Johnny Herbert	Stewart-Ford	12	1m 18.374s
11	Ralf Schumacher	Williams-Supertec	12	1m 18.506s
12	Olivier Panis	Prost-Peugeot	12	1m 18.636s
13	Jarno Trulli	Prost-Peugeot	12	1m 18.684s
14	Jean Alesi	Sauber-Petronas	12	1m 18.716s
15	Pedro Diniz	Sauber-Petronas	11	1m 19.194s
16	Alex Zanardi	Williams-Supertec	10	1m 19.452s
17	Stéphane Sarrazin	Minardi-Ford	12	1m 20.016s
18	Pedro de la Rosa	Arrows	11	1m 20.075s
19	Toranosuke Takagi	Arrows	12	1m 20.096s
20	Marc Gene	Minardi-Ford	11	1m 20.710s
21*	Jacques Villeneuve	BAR-Supertec		times disallowed

* allowed to race

FRIDAY FREE PRACTICE

Weather: Wet, then slowly drying

Pos.	Driver	Laps	Time
1	Mika Häkkinen	26	1m 18.881s
2	David Coulthard	24	1m 19.352s
3	Michael Schumacher	28	1m 19.621s
4	Eddie Irvine	24	1m 19.772s
5	Giancarlo Fisichella	32	1m 20.309s
6	Rubens Barrichello	28	1m 20.338s
7	Jarno Trulli	36	1m 20.359s
8	Heinz-Harald Frentzen	32	1m 20.431s
9	Olivier Panis	34	1m 20.562s
10	Ralf Schumacher	38	1m 20.671s
11	Alexander Wurz	37	1m 20.779s
12	Jean Alesi	25	1m 20.824s
13	Johnny Herbert	24	1m 20.934s
14	Ricardo Zonta	28	1m 21.009s
15	Pedro Diniz	39	1m 21.116s
16	Alex Zanardi	19	1m 21.773s
17	Marc Gene	29	1m 21.897s
18	Toranosuke Takagi	36	1m 22.355s
19	Pedro de la Rosa	26	1m 22.494s
20	Stéphane Sarrazin	38	1m 22.578s
21	Damon Hill	17	1m 32.229s
22	Jacques Villeneuve	11	1m 36.568s

SATURDAY FREE PRACTICE

Weather: Dry and overcast

Pos.	Driver	Laps	Time
1	David Coulthard	15	1m 17.035s
2	Mika Häkkinen	14	1m 17.246s
3	Heinz-Harald Frentzen	25	1m 17.962s
4	Rubens Barrichello	18	1m 17.979s
5	Michael Schumacher	22	1m 18.110s
6	Jean Alesi	22	1m 18.383s
7	Damon Hill	26	1m 18.415s
8	Ralf Schumacher	20	1m 18.480s
9	Johnny Herbert	15	1m 18.605s
10	Giancarlo Fisichella	18	1m 18.635s
11	Eddie Irvine	23	1m 18.682s
12	Pedro Diniz	23	1m 18.738s
13	Alexander Wurz	25	1m 18.896s
14	Alex Zanardi	23	1m 18.930s
15	Jarno Trulli	24	1m 19.037s
16	Jacques Villeneuve	18	1m 19.459s
17	Olivier Panis	21	1m 19.578s
18	Ricardo Zonta	13	1m 19.662s
19	Stéphane Sarrazin	21	1m 19.984s
20	Toranosuke Takagi	22	1m 20.008s
21	Pedro de la Rosa	22	1m 20.295s
22	Marc Gene	12	1m 21.033s

WARM-UP

Weather: Dry and sunny

Pos.	Driver	Laps	Time
1	Mika Häkkinen	13	1m 17.709s
2	David Coulthard	13	1m 17.749s
3	Michael Schumacher	16	1m 18.295s
4	Olivier Panis	15	1m 18.497s
5	Rubens Barrichello	16	1m 19.011s
6	Heinz-Harald Frentzen	19	1m 19.108s
7	Damon Hill	17	1m 19.112s
8	Eddie Irvine	12	1m 19.171s
9	Jacques Villeneuve	12	1m 19.216s
10	Ralf Schumacher	19	1m 19.389s
11	Alex Zanardi	14	1m 19.541s
12	Pedro Diniz	15	1m 19.565s
13	Johnny Herbert	13	1m 19.605s
14	Giancarlo Fisichella	18	1m 19.612s
15	Jean Alesi	18	1m 19.710s
16	Jarno Trulli	13	1m 19.715s
17	Pedro de la Rosa	15	1m 19.994s
18	Alexander Wurz	17	1m 20.418s
19	Toranosuke Takagi	10	1m 20.593s
20	Stéphane Sarrazin	18	1m 20.764s
21	Marc Gene	16	1m 21.274s

RACE FASTEST LAPS

Weather: Dry, hot and sunny

Driver	Time	Lap
Mika Häkkinen	1m 18.448s	70
Michael Schumacher	1m 18.616s	65
Eddie Irvine	1m 18.816s	63
Jean Alesi	1m 18.897s	25
Heinz-Harald Frentzen	1m 19.009s	61
David Coulthard	1m 19.310s	3
Olivier Panis	1m 19.386s	29
Ralf Schumacher	1m 19.395s	67
Rubens Barrichello	1m 19.477s	25
Alexander Wurz	1m 20.145s	65
Johnny Herbert	1m 20.324s	14
Giancarlo Fisichella	1m 20.484s	35
Jacques Villeneuve	1m 20.727s	39
Pedro Diniz	1m 20.833s	30
Jarno Trulli	1m 20.969s	15
Damon Hill	1m 21.140s	9
Stéphane Sarrazin	1m 21.225s	20
Alex Zanardi	1m 21.473s	8
Toranosuke Takagi	1m 21.598s	37
Pedro de la Rosa	1m 21.698s	36
Marc Gene	1m 21.731s	60

CHASSIS LOG BOOK

1	Häkkinen	McLaren MP4/14/1
2	Coulthard	McLaren MP4/14/2
	spare	McLaren MP4/14/3
3	M. Schumacher	Ferrari F399/193
4	Irvine	Ferrari F399/191
	spare	Ferrari F399/192
5	Zanardi	Williams FW21/2
6	R. Schumacher	Williams FW21/4
	spare	Williams FW21/3
7	Hill	Jordan 199/4
8	Frentzen	Jordan 199/3
	spare	Jordan 199/1
9	Fisichella	Benetton B199/4
10	Wurz	Benetton B199/5
	spare	Benetton B199/2
11	Alesi	Sauber C18/1
12	Diniz	Sauber C18/3
	spare	Sauber C18/2
14	de la Rosa	Arrows A20/4
15	Takagi	Arrows A20/4
	spare	Arrows A20/5
16	Barrichello	Stewart SF3/4
17	Herbert	Stewart SF3/3
	spare	Stewart SF3/2
18	Panis	Prost AP02/3
19	Trulli	Prost AP02/2
	spare	Prost AP02/1
20	Sarrazin	Minardi M01/1
21	Gene	Minardi M01/3
	spare	Minardi M01/2
22	Villeneuve	BAR 01/3
23	Zonta	BAR 01/2
	spare	BAR 01/4

POINTS TABLES

DRIVERS

1	Eddie Irvine	12
2 =	Mika Häkkinen	10
2 =	Heinz-Harald Frentzen	10
4	Ralf Schumacher	7
5	Michael Schumacher	6
6	Giancarlo Fisichella	3
7	Rubens Barrichello	2
8 =	Pedro de la Rosa	1
8 =	Olivier Panis	1

CONSTRUCTORS

1	Ferrari	18
2 =	McLaren	10
2 =	Jordan	10
4	Williams	7
5	Benetton	3
6	Stewart	2
7 =	Arrows	1
7 =	Prost	1

M. SCHUMACHER

COULTHARD

BARRICHELLO

HILL

FISICHELLA

ALESI

FIA WORLD CHAMPIONSHIP • ROUND 3

SAN MARINO
grand prix

IMOLA

Top left: It was Ferrari's day and the *tifosi* duly responded in style.

Below far left: Schumacher's win was Ferrari's first for 16 years at Imola's Autodromo Enzo e Dino Ferrari.

Below left: Schumacher once again conquered the might of McLaren.

IT was on lap 37 of the San Marino Grand Prix that Ron Dennis's patience finally snapped. The McLaren boss deserted his position on the pit wall and strode purposefully down towards his old friend and former employee, Alain Prost.

He didn't have to complete the journey to complain that French driver Olivier Panis was costing David Coulthard a lot of time in his chase of Michael Schumacher's leading Ferrari. Prost waved his hand in acknowledgement and got on the radio to tell Panis – who was about to be lapped by Coulthard's McLaren – to get out of the way. His man duly complied next time around.

Unfortunately, having got ahead of the Prost, Coulthard immediately slid wide over the kerb at the tricky downhill Rivazza corner, allowing the French car past again. It was the story of Coulthard's race.

Perhaps it would be an over-simplification to single out the backmarkers, Coulthard's rather tentative driving or the Ferrari team's race strategy as a cause of McLaren's defeat. In truth, it was a combination of these factors, coming hard on the heels of Mika Häkkinen's departure from the race when he made a rare error and crashed while leading.

In practice, the McLaren team had concluded that there was little to choose between a one- and two-stop strategy, so the team wisely hedged its bets. Häkkinen ran to a two-stop plan, taking an immediate lead from Coulthard – on a one-stopper – as the pack jostled into the Tamburello chicane.

Michael Schumacher's Ferrari F399 led the pursuit as Jacques Villeneuve's British American 01 – which had qualified a splendid fifth – was left stranded on the grid for good with a gearbox electronics malfunction.

'I'm not really sure what happened,' said Jacques, with an understandable air of impatience as his car was pushed into the pit lane. 'The engine was running, but there was a problem with the gearbox electronics and it just wouldn't move. We're going to have to make sure that things like this don't happen again.'

Meanwhile, in the first-lap scrum, Pedro de la Rosa's Arrows made firm contact with Jarno Trulli's Prost, damaging the former's front suspension, but eliminating Trulli on the spot with broken rear suspension.

By the end of the opening lap, Häkkinen was already 1.75s ahead of Coulthard. Then came the Ferraris of Schumacher and Eddie Irvine, Rubens Barrichello's Stewart-Ford, Heinz-Har-

IMOLA QUALIFYING

With Ferrari making a big push to undermine McLaren's superior performance, qualifying at Imola would become something of a high-speed chess game, the two teams eyeing each other like hawks as each attempted to second-guess the other's strategy.

McLaren seemed to retain the edge, but on the face of it, Ferrari was getting closer. Both Schumacher and Irvine were armed with newly-redesigned front wings that sharpened the F399's turn-in. On closer examination, however, the McLaren-Mercs appeared to retain the upper hand. With two minutes of the session still to run, Michael's Ferrari led the two McLarens out for one last effort at dislodging Häkkinen from pole position.

Neatly spaced, the three cars began their final lap between 21 and 8s before the chequered flag was shown at the start/finish line. The order remained the same – Häkkinen, Coulthard, Schumacher – as they finished that final lap.

Thus Häkkinen successfully buttoned up the 13th pole position of his career. 'It was very interesting,' he said, 'I knew David could go quicker; it is not an easy track on which to go quickly. You have to be very aggressive and, at the same time, very smooth, which is very difficult.'

Coulthard was second fastest. 'I knew our car was capable of going for the pole,' he said, 'but I lost time behind a BAR car, and on my last run I pushed too hard on the first part of the lap and overheated my tyres.'

David had been guardedly confident from the outset that he would gain the upper hand over his team-mate at the Autodromo Enzo e Dino Ferrari, where he had scored his last F1 win during the 1998 season.

'It is not easy to work out a good handling balance on this circuit,' said the Scot, 'but when you do manage that, the lap times flow quite easily. I have always been quite good at balancing the car's needs between high- and slow-speed corners, and that's what helps me here.' But things didn't quite go to plan.

For his part, Michael Schumacher also believed that he could have snatched pole had he not made a slight error on his last run. 'I am disappointed with myself because I never did a good lap,' he said. 'The car is nearly perfect.'

Eddie Irvine wound up fourth, believing that he could have been a little quicker had it not been for a couple of yellow flags, but not quick enough to gain another place.

Jacques Villeneuve set an encouraging fifth-fastest time in his British American 01. 'I am delighted for the entire team that our performance and reliability is improving,' said Craig Pollock. 'It is just a shame that Mika [Salo] had problems.' The Finn suffered a hydraulic failure after six laps and was only able to complete another single lap in Villeneuve's spare car, ending up 19th.

There was also much optimism in the Stewart-Ford camp, even though the Cosworth-built CR-1 engine was being run again at a reduced 16,700 rpm limit, rather than the 17,250 rpm that had been used at Interlagos.

Rubens Barrichello began the weekend with a very bullish attitude towards his prospects of running in the top six and just managed to achieve that ambition. 'I was quite aggressive on my last lap, which was full of incidents,' he said. 'I hit the kerb quite hard at Rivazza, and then the lap was further spoiled by a slower car. I could have gone a little quicker, but only enough to move up a single place.'

By contrast, Johnny Herbert simply could not reproduce the times he had recorded in the morning. 'It is a little difficult to understand,' he confessed. 'I guess I just didn't use the information about the car's characteristics very well this afternoon.'

Heinz-Harald Frentzen pipped his Jordan team-mate Damon Hill for eighth-fastest time, despite the German driver having flat-spotted a set of tyres in a dramatic moment under braking for Rivazza after a left rear pushrod broke. Hill, who slid into the gravel on his final run, admitted that he was very disappointed and that his problems were simply caused by over-driving.

The Williams-Supertecs of Ralf Schumacher and Alex Zanardi wound up ninth and tenth fastest, placing second and third behind Villeneuve in the customer Supertec engine race.

In 11th place was Olivier Panis's Prost-Peugeot, which stopped out on the circuit with an oil-system problem. The Frenchman's team-mate, Jarno Trulli, could not better 14th-fastest time, trouble with the electronic throttle bugging his progress.

Jean Alesi and Pedro Diniz qualified 13th and 15th in their Saubers, both men reporting that the cars felt nicely balanced, but were just too slow. The Benetton B199s were bugged by inconsistent handling, with the result that Giancarlo Fisichella and Alexander Wurz started 16th and 17th – not what they had been hoping for in front of the team's home crowd.

was two short, as de la Rosa's Arrows and Alexander Wurz's Benetton had tangled while battling for 17th place at the uphill Tosa left-hander, both cars retiring on the spot.

'Pedro was in front of me, he slid wide, I tried to go past on the inside and we collided,' shrugged Wurz. 'For me, it was the end of a very difficult weekend, full of problems.' De la Rosa saw it differently. 'My car had been difficult to drive since I'd touched wheels with Trulli,' he said, 'but I continued until I was rear-ended by Wurz, which I really think was unnecessary.'

By lap ten, Häkkinen was 8.3s ahead of Coulthard, with Schumacher another 3s behind in third place. The Ferrari team leader was not close enough to take advantage of a momentary lapse by Coulthard, which saw him shave the grass at Rivazza four laps later.

On lap 15, Jean Alesi brought his Sauber C18 in for the first refuelling stop of the race, the Frenchman having decided that a three-stop strategy would offer the best prospect of making up worthwhile ground from 13th on the grid. He dropped from ninth to 15th, but soon began to make up ground as others pitted or hit trouble.

Then the unthinkable happened. Coming up to complete lap 17, Häkkinen slid wide over the high kerb as he entered the start/finish straight. The McLaren displayed what initially seemed nothing more than a routine wobble, but suddenly it snapped left into the wall, losing its left front wheel.

'I made a mistake,' he admitted. 'I was pushing too hard.' What more could be said in the face of such an honest admission? 'He's won nine out of the last 19 races for us,' said one McLaren team member sympathetically, 'and he probably won't make another mistake for another couple of years.'

Later, Ron Dennis echoed those sentiments. 'It is very unusual for either of our drivers to make mistakes,' he said, 'but Mika made one today – better now than at the end of last year. David's chance to win the race was taken away by the behaviour of several backmarkers, and I am disappointed in the lack of sporting behaviour from their team managers.'

Häkkinen's retirement left Coulthard to pick up McLaren's fallen standard. Initially, he looked in good shape, well able to consolidate his advantage over Schumacher at between 3 and 4s. Like Häkkinen, the two remaining contenders for victory were in the small minority running Bridgestone's harder tyres – Fisichella was the other member of the quartet – and both were on

ald Frentzen's Jordan, Ralf Schumacher's Williams and Damon Hill's Jordan.

With a clear track ahead and a light fuel load, Häkkinen could easily dictate the pace and was well on his team's pre-planned schedule, having opened a 4.24s advantage by the end of lap five. Next time around, the pack

tate the pace and was well on his team's pre-planned schedule, having opened a 4.24s advantage by the end of lap five. Next time around, the pack

Right: David Coulthard at speed.
Paul-Henri Cahier

Inset: Ron Dennis and DC. The McLaren boss believed that backmarkers prevented his man from taking a run at Schumacher's Ferrari.
Michael Cooper/Allsport

HARVEY POSTLETHWAITE

HARVEY Postlethwaite died suddenly on 13 April from a heart attack, robbing Grand Prix racing of one of its most prolific and versatile designers who had been a familiar face in the F1 pit lane for more than a quarter of a century.

At the time of his death Harvey had been working on Honda's prototype F1 car which was being developed in preparation for a Grand Prix return by the Japanese car maker next season. Shortly afterwards, Honda announced that this programme was being abandoned in favour of a partnership with British American Racing.

Postlethwaite first made his mark as an F1 designer in 1975 as the architect of Lord Hesketh's 308 at the wheel of which the late James Hunt won the Dutch Grand Prix at Zandvoort, beating world championship favourite Niki Lauda's Ferrari in a straight fight. Yet in motor racing circles he will probably best be remembered for updating the Ferrari team's chassis technology to levels which matched those of the top British teams in the early 1980s.

After qualifying from Birmingham University with a BSc in mechanical engineering, Postlethwaite then spent another three years on a course which led to a PhD for investigation and original studies in the very specialised field of automotive crash research.

Paul-Henri Cahier

He worked for March on non-F1 projects from 1970 onwards, but his sights were always set on the sport's most senior category. Thus when Alexander Hesketh acquired an F1 March 731 car for James Hunt to drive, Harvey accepted Hesketh's offer to join the ambitious young team as chief engineer.

On the surface, Hesketh Racing projected a wild champagne and caviar image, but in reality it was extremely serious about its racing. Based on the knowledge gained from developing the March, Postlethwaite developed the Hesketh 308 which competed for the next two seasons and delivered Hunt his memorable, maiden Grand Prix victory in Holland.

By the end of 1975 Hesketh had run out of funds and the team closed its doors. Postlethwaite then moved to Austro–Canadian oil magnate Walter Wolf's emergent team and designed the Wolf WR1 which South African driver Jody Scheckter took to second place in the 1977 world championship. He was briefly reunited with Hunt at the start of 1979 when the Englishman switched to Wolf from McLaren, but James's best days were over and he retired from racing after only a handful of races.

In 1981 Postlethwaite brought state-of-the-art British technology to Ferrari which had been lagging behind badly. He designed the Italian team's chassis which won the 1982 and 1983 constructors' world championships.

'After you have worked with all these facilities and resources, it's a bit difficult to envisage going back to work with any other F1 team in this game,' said Postlethwaite of the Ferrari organisation. He stayed on at Maranello until 1988, then left to join Tyrrell, only to return to the Italian team from 1982 to 1985. He then went briefly to the Swiss Sauber squad and back to Tyrrell where he stayed until the team was closed at the end of 1998 following its purchase by the new British American Racing organisation.

Not only was Postlethwaite knowledgeable and passionately enthusiastic about his chosen business, he was also unstinting in the assistance and guidance he offered to his younger colleagues. Many amongst the emerging generation of F1 engineers benefited from his generous and gregarious spirit.

a one-stop strategy. Everything looked good for Coulthard to repeat his 1998 win at Imola.

Strung out behind at the lap-20 mark were Irvine, Barrichello, Frentzen, Ralf Schumacher, Damon Hill, Johnny Herbert and Pedro Diniz.

The next ten laps saw a spate of refuelling stops. On lap 24, Barrichello made his first stop, dropping from fourth to seventh, while three laps later Frentzen came in, falling from fourth to eighth. On the next lap, Ralf Schumacher stopped from fourth place, but hardly had the German driver accelerated back into the fray than his Williams rolled to a halt, a fire in the airbox having burned the wiring loom of the injectors.

On lap 29, Hill made his first refuelling stop, dropping from fourth to seventh, while Irvine also came in, retaining third place. Almost unnoticed, Toranosuke Takagi retired the other Arrows A20 from 16th place with loss of fuel pressure, while next time around, Alesi brought the Sauber in for its second stop, dropping from eighth to 11th.

Then came the sequence of events that swung the race in Ferrari's favour. Realising that he was about to become entangled in traffic, Michael Schumacher agreed with Ross Brawn to pit the second-place Ferrari for its first (6.9s) stop on lap 31. He rejoined in second place and, a couple of corners later, had a near miss with Pedro Diniz when the Brazilian got into a huge slide right in front of the Ferrari after his gearchange electronics began to play up.

At this point, opinions from the touchline began to diverge. Would it have been wise to bring Coulthard in immediately, the lap after Schumacher stopped, for his own refuelling stop? McLaren judged otherwise, sticking to its original strategy, and David stayed out in the lead until the end of lap 35, when he made a 9.2s stop that put him back in the race 5.2s behind Schumacher's Ferrari. By now, Irvine was third, ahead of Barrichello, Frentzen and Hill.

However, Coulthard rejoined in heavy traffic and everything went wrong. Thanks to that unyielding clutch of slower cars, the deficit between him and Schumacher grew alarmingly from 6.8s on lap 37 to 9.2s on lap 38, and a frustrating 13.05s on lap 39.

Having gone from a position where he could easily breeze back into the lead when Schumacher made his second stop, Coulthard was approaching the point where it was touch and go. Sensing his vulnerability, Schumacher put the hammer down. He piled on the pressure, opening a 21.8s lead before stopping again at the end of lap 45. With 17 laps to go, he accelerated back into the race 4.7s ahead of Coulthard, and from then on the capacity crowd cheered him home to the Italian team's first win in 16 years at the emotionally titled Autodromo Enzo e Dino Ferrari.

'Especially during that middle run, I was probably doing qualifying speeds,' said Schumacher. 'For the first 30 laps, it was important to take everything smoothly, make sure that you didn't destroy the tyres and keep the gap as close as you could afford to allow it. After that, it was more or less qualifying speeds. Then the last stint was a matter of carrying the car to the finish and driving it home.

'Basically we went for a strategy which would give us two options, and we took the option according to the way the race was going. Obviously Ross Brawn is in charge of the final decision on that, and we communicated a bit, but I left the choice to him. I knew he had a better appreciation of what would be the ideal strategy, and it was he who decided.'

For Coulthard, it was a bitterly disappointing outcome to a race that he'd pinned his hopes on winning, particularly after Häkkinen dropped out. Yet he also knew that, prior to Imola, he had no championship points on the board and needed to get his score off the ground.

'It definitely felt better as the race went on, and the second set of tyres worked much better for me,' he said. 'I struggled with a bit of oversteer on the first set. It is always difficult to judge how much change [in handling] there is going to be between warm-up and the race, especially when the temperature goes up as much as it did today. With hindsight, maybe I could have taken a little more mechanical grip off the nose, but otherwise I had no problems.

'I think that our one-stop strategy was the right one, and would have been good enough to win me the race apart from the obvious difficulties of getting through the traffic. It seemed

SAN MARINO GRAND PRIX

Far left: Alesi picked up his first point of the season.

Centre left: Jacques Villeneuve's BAR was left stranded on the grid after a promising qualifying performance.

Left: Barrichello once again showed the progress of the Stewart-Ford with a podium place.

Below left: Small car – big stage. Damon Hill got his stuttering start to the season under way with fourth for Jordan.

All photographs: Paul-Henri Cahier

particularly bad here – worse than I can ever remember – and a couple of the drivers didn't seem to respond to the blue flags.

'Yes, I am disappointed. Today I lost a race that I should have won, but because of other factors apart from the car and my driving, we didn't win it. That doesn't take anything away from the achievements of Michael or Ferrari, but we had the correct strategy and a quick enough package to have won.'

Unfortunately, Eddie Irvine was not around at the finish to consolidate his third place and gain a spot on the podium, the Ulsterman's Ferrari having dropped out with 15 laps to go due to engine failure.

'I felt the engine tighten about 100 metres before it failed,' he said. 'It was a pity because this is the second consecutive race where I have missed out on an almost certain podium finish. In the early stages, I was having trouble with the car's handling, as it was moving around a lot on the soft-compound tyres, but after that it stabilised and my lap times came down again.'

Right behind Irvine at the moment of his departure from the race was Frentzen, at that stage running 22s ahead of Barrichello. The oil slick dropped by the Ferrari was not flagged in time, and Heinz-Harald pirouetted into retirement.

'I was about to come in for my second stop and I think, if it had been as quick as my first, I think I could have got out ahead of Rubens,' he said. 'That was really disappointing because I think I could have finished on the podium again.'

That left Barrichello to bag a terrific third place for Stewart and touchingly dedicate the result to 'my friend Ayrton Senna, wherever he may be.' He crossed the finishing line just 0.9s ahead of Damon Hill, although both cars were a lap down on the winner.

'I was closing on Barrichello towards the end,' said Damon, 'but with all the backmarkers and then having to let Michael through, I was not able to catch him. But this is the first race I have completed since Suzuka last year and it felt great, although exhausting in that heat.'

With five laps to go, Johnny Herbert was running in fifth place ahead of Fisichella's Benetton and Zanardi's Williams only for the Stewart to suffer engine failure. 'It was a shame, because everything had been going well and there was no indication that the engine was about to fail,' he said.

It was certainly a pity for Zanardi, for although Fisichella nipped through to take fifth, the former CART ace spun into retirement and left the way open for the hard-charging Jean Alesi to grab the final point on offer.

In seventh place came BAR stand-in Mika Salo after a steady performance, while the Minardis of Luca Badoer and Marc Gene were the only others running at the chequered flag.

No fewer than 16 years had passed since Patrick Tambay had clinched Ferrari's previous victory in front of a home crowd at Imola. In that year, the team went on to win the constructors' championship, an entry in the pages of F1 history that has almost become overlooked.

Schumacher's victory, however, was seen at Ferrari as a crucial step on the road to another constructors' title. If the team achieved that, the win would be altogether more memorable, and the San Marino Grand Prix might come to be seen as the crucial turning point.

Williams-BMW tests at Miramas

THE first Williams-BMW F1 test car underwent its first three days of preliminary trials during the week before the San Marino Grand Prix at the Miramas test track, near Marseilles. Jörg Müller drove the FW20 chassis fitted with the Munich-built V10 engine in conditions of considerable secrecy. However, Williams technical director Patrick Head explained that the engines ran for around 350 km over the three days before one started to tighten up and the test team returned to Munich to strip them down and check them over.

'We are very satisfied with the work we have completed,' said BMW motorsport chief Gerhard Berger, 'although there is still a long way to go.'

Sources close to the German manufacturer confirmed that BMW fully understood just how far it still needed to progress with the development of the new power plant. To that end, some energetic head-hunting had been carried out on BMW's behalf among the other F1 engine makers.

It was understood that the engine developed quite reasonable power at this early stage in the programme, and at 15,000 rpm it was producing what the Supertec V10 was managing at 17,000 rpm. However, major torsional stiffness problems with the cylinder block remained to be addressed, this being a major technical challenge in the race to make F1 engines as light as possible.

GRAN PREMIO WARSTEINER DI SAN MARINO

30 APRIL – 2 MAY 1999

IMOLA

Race distance: 62 laps, 189.784 miles/305.428 km

Race weather: Dry, hot and sunny

FIA FORMULA 1 WORLD CHAMPIONSHIP

ROUND 3

IMOLA – AUTODROMO DINO E ENZO FERRARI

Piratella · Tosa · Variante Alfa · Acque Minerale · Villeneuve · Rivazza · Traguardo · Tamburello · Variante Bassa

CIRCUIT LENGTH: 3.061 miles/4.926 km

Pos.	Driver	Nat.	No.	Entrant	Car/Engine	Laps	Time/Retirement	Speed (mph/km/h)
1	Michael Schumacher	D	3	Scuderia Ferrari Marlboro	Ferrari F399 048 V10	62	1h 33m 44.792s	121.466/195.481
2	David Coulthard	GB	2	West McLaren Mercedes	McLaren MP4/14-Mercedes F0110H V10	62	1h 33m 49.057s	121.374/195.333
3	Rubens Barrichello	BR	16	Stewart Ford	Stewart SF3-Ford CR-1 V10	61		
4	Damon Hill	GB	7	Benson & Hedges Jordan	Jordan 199-Mugen Honda MF301/HD V10	61		
5	Giancarlo Fisichella	I	9	Mild Seven Benetton Playlife	Benetton B199-Playlife V10	61		
6	Jean Alesi	F	11	Red Bull Sauber Petronas	Sauber C18-Petronas SPE03A V10	61		
7	Mika Salo	SF	23	British American Racing	BAR 01-Supertec FB01 V10	59	Electrics	
8	Luca Badoer	I	20	Fondmetal Minardi Ford	Minardi M01-Ford Zetec-R V10	59		
9	Marc Gene	ESP	21	Fondmetal Minardi Ford	Minardi M01-Ford Zetec-R V10	59		
10	Johnny Herbert	GB	17	Stewart Ford	Stewart SF3-Ford CR-1 V10	58	Engine	
11	Alex Zanardi	I	5	Winfield Williams	Williams FW21-Supertec FB01 V10	58	Spun off	
	Pedro Diniz	BR	12	Red Bull Sauber Petronas	Sauber C18-Petronas SPE03A V10	49	Spun off	
	Olivier Panis	F	18	Gauloises Prost Peugeot	Prost AP02-Peugeot A18 V10	48	Throttle	
	Eddie Irvine	GB	4	Scuderia Ferrari Marlboro	Ferrari F399 048 V10	46	Engine	
	Heinz-Harald Frentzen	D	8	Benson & Hedges Jordan	Jordan 199-Mugen Honda MF301/HD V10	46	Accident	
	Toranosuke Takagi	J	15	Arrows	Arrows A20 V10	29	Fuel pressure	
	Ralf Schumacher	D	6	Winfield Williams	Williams FW21-Supertec FB01 V10	28	Throttle	
	Mika Häkkinen	SF	1	West McLaren Mercedes	McLaren MP4/14-Mercedes F0110H V10	17	Accident	
	Pedro de la Rosa	ESP	14	Arrows	Arrows A20 V10	5	Collision with Wurz	
	Alexander Wurz	A	10	Mild Seven Benetton Playlife	Benetton B199-Playlife V10	5	Collision with de la Rosa	
	Jacques Villeneuve	CDN	22	British American Racing	BAR 01-Supertec FB01 V10	0	Transmission	
	Jarno Trulli	I	19	Gauloises Prost Peugeot	Prost AP02-Peugeot A18 V10	0	Collision	

Fastest lap: M. Schumacher, on lap 45, 1m 28.547s, 124.544 mph/200.435 km/h.

Lap record: Heinz-Harald Frentzen (F1 Williams FW19-Renault V10), 1m 25.531s, 128.936 mph/207.503 km/h (1997).

Grid order	1	2	3	4	5	6	7	8	9	10	11	12	13	14	15	16	17	18	19	20	21	22	23	24	25	26	27	28	29	30	31	32	33	34	35	36	37	38	39	40	41	42	43	44	45	46	4
1 HÄKKINEN	1	1	1	1	1	1	1	1	1	1	1	1	1	1	1	1	1	2	2	2	2	2	2	2	2	2	2	2	2	2	2	2	2	2	2	3	3	3	3	3	3	3	3	3	3	3	
2 COULTHARD	2	2	2	2	2	2	2	2	2	2	2	2	2	2	2	2	3	3	3	3	3	3	3	3	3	3	3	3	3	3	3	3	3	3	3	2	2	2	2	2	2	2	2	2	2	2	
3 M. SCHUMACHER	3	3	3	3	3	3	3	3	3	3	3	3	3	3	3	3	4	4	4	4	4	4	4	4	4	4	4	4	4	4	4	4	4	4	4	4	4	4	4	4	4	4	4	4	4	4	
4 IRVINE	4	4	4	4	4	4	4	4	4	4	4	4	4	4	4	4	16	16	16	16	16	16	8	8	8	6	7	16	16	16	16	16	16	16	16	16	16	16	16	16	16	16	16	16	8	8	8	1
22 VILLENEUVE	16	16	16	16	16	16	16	16	16	16	16	16	16	16	16	16	8	8	8	8	8	8	6	6	6	7	16	17	17	8	8	8	8	8	8	8	8	8	8	8	8	7	7	7	1		
16 BARRICHELLO	8	8	8	8	8	8	8	8	8	8	8	8	8	8	8	8	6	6	6	6	6	6	7	7	7	16	17	8	8	7	7	7	7	7	7	7	7	7	7	7	7	16	16	16			
8 FRENTZEN	6	6	6	6	6	6	6	6	6	6	6	6	6	6	6	6	7	7	7	7	7	7	16	16	16	17	8	7	7	9	9	9	9	17	17	17	17	17	17	17	17	17					
7 HILL	7	7	7	7	7	7	7	7	7	7	7	7	7	7	7	7	17	17	17	17	17	17	17	17	17	8	5	11	9	17	17	17	17	5	5	5	5	5	5	5	5	5	1				
6 R. SCHUMACHER	11	11	11	11	11	11	11	11	11	11	11	11	11	11	17	17	5	5	12	12	12	12	12	5	5	5	9	5	5	5	5	11	11	11	11	11	11	11	11	11	9	2					
5 ZANARDI	17	17	17	17	17	17	17	17	17	17	17	17	17	17	5	5	12	12	5	5	5	5	5	9	11	11	9	5	12	11	11	11	11	9	9	9	9	9	9	9	9						
18 PANIS	5	5	5	5	5	5	5	5	5	5	5	5	5	5	12	12	9	9	9	9	9	9	9	11	9	9	12	12	11	12	12	18	18	18	18	18	23	23	23	23	23	2					
17 HERBERT	9	9	9	12	12	12	12	12	12	12	12	12	12	12	9	9	11	11	11	11	11	11	11	18	12	12	18	18	18	18	23	23	23	23	18	20	18	18	18	2							
11 ALESI	12	12	12	9	9	9	9	9	9	9	9	9	9	9	15	15	23	23	23	23	23	23	18	12	18	18	23	23	23	23	12	20	20	20	20	18	20	20	20	1							
19 TRULLI	23	23	23	23	18	18	18	18	18	18	15	15	15	15	23	23	18	18	18	18	18	18	23	23	23	20	20	20	20	20	21	21	21	21	21	21	21	21	21								
12 DINIZ	18	18	18	18	23	23	23	23	23	23	18	18	18	18	11	11	20	20	21	15	20	20	20	15	21	21	12	12	12	12	12	12	12	12	12	12											
9 FISICHELLA	15	15	15	15	15	23	23	23	23	23	18	18	18	18	18	18	21	21	21	15	20	21	21	15	15	15																					
10 WURZ	14	14	14	14	14	20	20	20	20	20	20	20	20	20	20	20	15	15	15	20	21	15	15	21																							
14 DE LA ROSA	10	10	10	10	10	21	21	21	21	21	21	21	21	21	21	21	21																														
23 SALO	20	20	20	20	20																																										
15 TAKAGI	21	21	21	21	21																																										
21 GENE																																															
20 BADOER																																															

Pit stop
One lap behind leader

STARTING GRID

1 HÄKKINEN McLaren	**2** COULTHARD McLaren
3 M. SCHUMACHER Ferrari	**4** IRVINE Ferrari
22 VILLENEUVE BAR	**16** BARRICHELLO Stewart
8 FRENTZEN Jordan	**7** HILL Jordan
6 R. SCHUMACHER Williams	**5** ZANARDI Williams
18 PANIS Prost	**17** HERBERT Stewart
11 ALESI Sauber	**19** TRULLI Prost
12 DINIZ Sauber	**9** FISICHELLA Benetton
10 WURZ Benetton	**14** DE LA ROSA Arrows
23 SALO BAR	**15** TAKAGI Arrows
21 GENE Minardi	**20** BADOER Minardi

50	51	52	53	54	55	56	57	58	59	60	61	62	
3	3	3	3	3	3	3	3	3	3	3	3	3	1
2	2	2	2	2	2	2	2	2	2	2	2	2	2
16	16	16	16	16	16	16	16	16	16	16	16		3
7	7	7	7	7	7	7	7	7	7	7	7		4
17	17	17	17	17	17	17	17	17	9	9	9		5
9	9	9	9	9	9	9	9	9	11	11	11		6
5	5	5	5	5	5	5	5	23					
11	11	11	11	11	11	11	11	11	11				20
23	23	23	23	23	23	23	23	21					
20	20	20	20	20	20	20	20	20					
21	21	21	21	21	21	21	21	21					

FOR THE RECORD

100th Grand Prix start Rubens Barrichello

TIME SHEETS

QUALIFYING

Weather: Dry, hot and sunny.

Pos.	Driver	Car	Laps	Time
1	Mika Häkkinen	McLaren-Mercedes	11	1m 26.362s
2	David Coulthard	McLaren-Mercedes	10	1m 26.384s
3	Michael Schumacher	Ferrari	12	1m 26.538s
4	Eddie Irvine	Ferrari	11	1m 26.993s
5	Jacques Villeneuve	BAR-Supertec	12	1m 27.313s
6	Rubens Barrichello	Stewart-Ford	11	1m 27.409s
7	Heinz-Harald Frentzen	Jordan-Mugen Honda	10	1m 27.613s
8	Damon Hill	Jordan-Mugen Honda	11	1m 27.708s
9	Ralf Schumacher	Williams-Supertec	12	1m 27.770s
10	Alex Zanardi	Williams-Supertec	11	1m 28.142s
11	Olivier Panis	Prost-Peugeot	12	1m 28.205s
12	Johnny Herbert	Stewart-Ford	11	1m 28.246s
13	Jean Alesi	Sauber-Petronas	12	1m 28.253s
14	Jarno Trulli	Prost-Peugeot	6	1m 28.403s
15	Pedro Diniz	Sauber-Petronas	12	1m 28.599s
16	Giancarlo Fisichella	Benetton-Playlife	12	1m 28.750s
17	Alexander Wurz	Benetton-Playlife	11	1m 28.765s
18	Pedro de la Rosa	Arrows	11	1m 29.293s
19	Mika Salo	BAR-Supertec	7	1m 29.451s
20	Toranosuke Takagi	Arrows	12	1m 29.656s
21	Marc Gene	Minardi-Ford	12	1m 30.035s
22	Luca Badoer	Minardi-Ford	12	1m 30.945s

FRIDAY FREE PRACTICE

Weather: Dry, hot and sunny

Pos.	Driver	Laps	Time
1	Mika Häkkinen	34	1m 28.467s
2	David Coulthard	27	1m 28.605s
3	Eddie Irvine	33	1m 29.046s
4	Damon Hill	48	1m 29.452s
5	Michael Schumacher	27	1m 29.534s
6	Alex Zanardi	42	1m 29.614s
7	Ralf Schumacher	34	1m 29.630s
8	Jacques Villeneuve	24	1m 29.765s
9	Rubens Barrichello	28	1m 29.792s
10	Jarno Trulli	42	1m 29.808s
11	Jean Alesi	36	1m 30.182s
12	Olivier Panis	29	1m 30.408s
13	Pedro Diniz	32	1m 30.482s
14	Mika Salo	23	1m 30.569s
15	Alexander Wurz	38	1m 30.830s
16	Giancarlo Fisichella	20	1m 30.854s
17	Heinz-Harald Frentzen	26	1m 30.991s
18	Johnny Herbert	21	1m 31.046s
19	Pedro de la Rosa	35	1m 31.257s
20	Luca Badoer	30	1m 31.547s
21	Toranosuke Takagi	15	1m 31.557s
22	Marc Gene	14	1m 33.529s

SATURDAY FREE PRACTICE

Weather: Dry, hot and sunny

Pos.	Driver	Laps	Time
1	David Coulthard	32	1m 26.509s
2	Mika Häkkinen	26	1m 26.750s
3	Michael Schumacher	33	1m 26.834s
4	Eddie Irvine	26	1m 27.193s
5	Rubens Barrichello	27	1m 27.429s
6	Johnny Herbert	28	1m 27.734s
7	Ralf Schumacher	28	1m 27.986s
8	Heinz-Harald Frentzen	36	1m 28.196s
9	Damon Hill	39	1m 28.209s
10	Alex Zanardi	28	1m 28.364s
11	Jarno Trulli	31	1m 28.405s
12	Pedro Diniz	34	1m 28.447s
13	Jean Alesi	29	1m 28.468s
14	Alexander Wurz	36	1m 28.565s
15	Giancarlo Fisichella	25	1m 28.569s
16	Mika Salo	27	1m 28.596s
17	Jacques Villeneuve	19	1m 28.702s
18	Olivier Panis	27	1m 28.956s
19	Toranosuke Takagi	26	1m 29.300s
20	Pedro de la Rosa	31	1m 29.762s
21	Marc Gene	23	1m 30.497s
22	Luca Badoer	18	1m 31.347s

WARM-UP

Weather: Dry, hot and sunny

Pos.	Driver	Laps	Time
1	David Coulthard	13	1m 28.642s
2	Eddie Irvine	15	1m 28.749s
3	Mika Häkkinen	12	1m 28.838s
4	Michael Schumacher	14	1m 29.084s
5	Johnny Herbert	14	1m 29.573s
6	Damon Hill	16	1m 29.596s
7	Jarno Trulli	10	1m 29.615s
8	Heinz-Harald Frentzen	18	1m 29.683s
9	Pedro Diniz	14	1m 29.703s
10	Jacques Villeneuve	9	1m 29.779s
11	Mika Salo	10	1m 30.014s
12	Alexander Wurz	15	1m 30.023s
13	Olivier Panis	13	1m 30.036s
14	Jean Alesi	15	1m 30.145s
15	Rubens Barrichello	12	1m 30.191s
16	Giancarlo Fisichella	15	1m 30.303s
17	Ralf Schumacher	11	1m 30.410s
18	Pedro de la Rosa	11	1m 30.806s
19	Toranosuke Takagi	12	1m 30.904s
20	Alex Zanardi	15	1m 30.967s
21	Marc Gene	16	1m 32.096s
22	Luca Badoer	14	1m 32.545s

RACE FASTEST LAPS

Weather: Dry, hot and sunny

Driver	Time	Lap
Michael Schumacher	1m 28.547s	45
Mika Häkkinen	1m 29.145s	15
David Coulthard	1m 29.199s	52
Eddie Irvine	1m 29.726s	45
Olivier Panis	1m 30.081s	28
Damon Hill	1m 30.140s	37
Heinz-Harald Frentzen	1m 30.229s	46
Alex Zanardi	1m 30.254s	55
Jean Alesi	1m 30.442s	39
Rubens Barrichello	1m 30.564s	21
Ralf Schumacher	1m 30.737s	22
Pedro Diniz	1m 30.908s	24
Giancarlo Fisichella	1m 30.977s	33
Mika Salo	1m 31.007s	44
Johnny Herbert	1m 31.238s	24
Toranosuke Takagi	1m 31.587s	29
Luca Badoer	1m 32.851s	35
Marc Gene	1m 33.175s	38
Pedro de la Rosa	1m 33.328s	3
Alexander Wurz	1m 33.337s	3

CHASSIS LOG BOOK

1	Häkkinen	McLaren MP4/14/5
2	Coulthard	McLaren MP4/14/4
	spare	McLaren MP4/14/2
3	M. Schumacher	Ferrari F399/193
4	Irvine	Ferrari F399/191
	spare	Ferrari F399/192
5	Zanardi	Williams FW21/5
6	R. Schumacher	Williams FW21/4
	spare	Williams FW21/2
7	Hill	Jordan 199/4
8	Frentzen	Jordan 199/5
	spare	Jordan 199/3
9	Fisichella	Benetton B199/6
10	Wurz	Benetton B199/5
	spare	Benetton B199/4
11	Alesi	Sauber C18/5
12	Diniz	Sauber C18/4
	spare	Sauber C18/1
14	de la Rosa	Arrows A20/4
15	Takagi	Arrows A20/5
	spare	Arrows A20/7
16	Barrichello	Stewart SF3/4
17	Herbert	Stewart SF3/5
	spare	Stewart SF3/3
18	Panis	Prost AP02/3
19	Trulli	Prost AP02/2
	spare	Prost AP02/5
20	Badoer	Minardi M01/1
21	Gene	Minardi M01/4
	spare	Minardi M01/3
22	Villeneuve	BAR 01/3
23	Salo	BAR 01/5
	spare	BAR 01/4

POINTS TABLES

DRIVERS

1	Michael Schumacher	16
2	Eddie Irvine	12
3 =	Mika Häkkinen	10
3 =	Heinz-Harald Frentzen	10
5	Ralf Schumacher	7
6 =	David Coulthard	6
6 =	Rubens Barrichello	6
8	Giancarlo Fisichella	5
9	Damon Hill	3
10 =	Pedro de la Rosa	1
10 =	Olivier Panis	1
10 =	Jean Alesi	1

CONSTRUCTORS

1	Ferrari	28
2	McLaren	16
3	Jordan	13
4	Williams	7
5	Stewart	6
6	Benetton	5
7 =	Arrows	1
7 =	Prost	1
7 =	Sauber	1

Right: Look, no hands. Michael Schumacher pumps his fists in celebration as he completes his slowing down lap.
Diana Burnett

Far right: Mika Häkkinen muses on his third place while Schumacher and Todt celebrate.
Lukas Gorys

Below: The Monte Carlo kerbs were well covered in rubber by the time the racing was over.
Paul-Henri Cahier

MONACO
grand prix

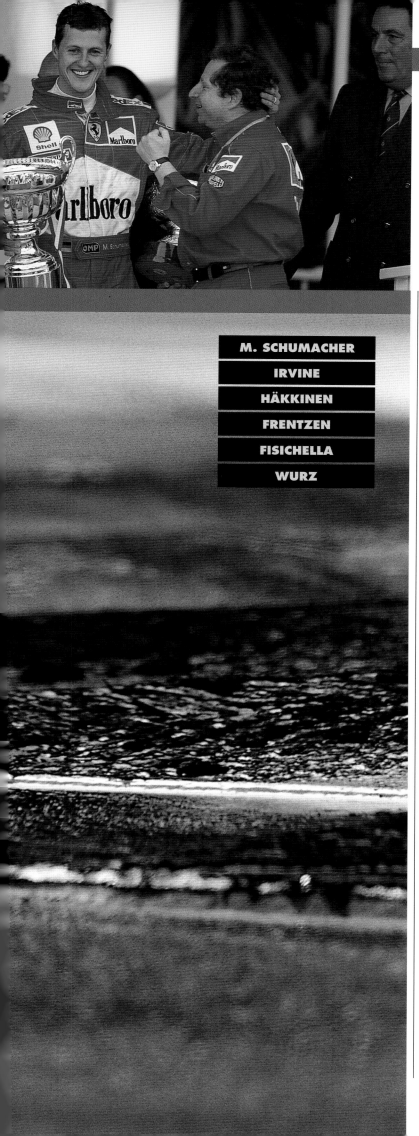

DIARY

Gianni Agnelli, Ferrari's honorary President, backed Eddie Irvine as the most likely and sensible choice as number-two driver in the Italian team for the 2000 season.

Honda poised to confirm long-term engine supply contract with British American Racing.

Juan Pablo Montoya wins CART race in Rio, ahead of Dario Franchitti and Christian Fittipaldi.

French GP tipped for return to Paul Ricard after Bernie Ecclestone buys the circuit.

Eddie Jordan joins Ireland's overseas tourism promotions team as sporting ambassador.

M. SCHUMACHER

IRVINE

HÄKKINEN

FRENTZEN

FISICHELLA

WURZ

MICHAEL Schumacher claimed one of Niki Lauda's most celebrated records in a typically eventful race through the streets of Monte Carlo, when he won his 16th World Championship Grand Prix at the wheel of a Ferrari, eclipsing the famous Austrian driver's previous record of 15 wins between 1974 and 1977.

To add more icing to the cake, Michael headed Eddie Irvine across the line for Ferrari's first ever 1–2 finish in this most famous of races, in which the first Ferrari had actually competed 52 years earlier. It was also Schumacher's 35th career victory, achieved in decisive fashion, as the McLaren-Mercedes challenge was demolished completely. At least for the time-being.

Having qualified in pole position, World Champion Mika Häkkinen trailed home a defeated third, puzzled because his McLaren MP4/14 felt strange and unpredictable for much of the race. Initially, it seemed as though he had suffered a minor problem with the car's steering, which knocked his confidence on a circuit where that quality is of paramount importance.

'Up to my refuelling stop, I was pushing hard to build up my advantage,' said Schumacher, 'and after the stop I just drove it home. There was not so much flexibility within my own race strategy, but I made sure that the gap never dropped below 20 seconds. I squeezed ahead of Mika going into the first corner which, to be honest, made it all much easier from the start.'

As for Häkkinen, he effectively lost the race in the initial sprint to Ste Dévote. Schumacher edged around the outside of him to take the lead, while Mika was scrupulously fair, not squeezing the German driver in the slightest.

'I made a really bad start, with too much wheelspin,' he shrugged, 'and during the race I suffered with inconsistent handling, coupled with a very heavy steering load, which probably means I had some sort of front-end failure.'

However, after a detailed technical post-mortem had been carried out on the Finn's MP4/14, no specific reason could be found for the problem, and the McLaren team was left scratching its corporate head. With a gearbox oil leak having caused David Coulthard's third retirement in the four races run so far in the season, it was a grim day indeed for the World Champions from Woking.

Häkkinen had started the race with significantly more fuel in his McLaren than Schumacher's Ferrari, the plan being that the Finn would take the lead at the first corner, consolidate his advantage as the fuel load reduced and then pull away. Unfortunately, Schumacher demolished that strategy and left Häkkinen with his hands full fending off Irvine.

By the end of the opening lap, Michael's Ferrari was 1.3s ahead of Häkkinen, who was followed by the second Ferrari of Eddie Irvine, David Coulthard's McLaren, Rubens Barrichello's Stewart, Jarno Trulli's Prost and Giancarlo Fisichella's Benetton. On the second time around, he had stretched his lead to 1.9s, while a remarkable 6.6s separated the Ferrari from Rubens Barrichello's Stewart-Ford in sixth place.

By lap four, Damon Hill's acutely frustrating weekend had finally run its course. He had attempted to squeeze his Jordan inside Ralf Schumacher's Williams, under braking for the chicane, while battling for a lowly 15th place. The cars made contact, and Hill was out on the spot, leaving his former Jordan team-mate to resume 21st and last.

'The incident was my fault,' said Hill. 'I was simply being too ambitious. Starting in 17th place, I had to be very aggressive with my strategy, and I decided after two laps that I just had to try and overtake. Ralf was defending his line, so I do not blame him at all.'

By lap ten, Michael Schumacher had broken Häkkinen's challenge and was running 6.1s ahead of the Finn's McLaren. Such was his speed in the early stages that he was 13.7s ahead of Coulthard in fourth place, and an amazing 20.9s in front of Rubens Barrichello.

There were more problems for the frustrated Williams team on lap 14, when Zanardi slid down one of the escape roads, dropping from tenth to 16th. Later, it emerged that the Italian driver's progress had been hampered by a broken seat, which made it difficult for him to handle hard braking.

'I had another black day, even if it was almost funny,' said Zanardi. 'I felt like I was floating in the cockpit. I made several mistakes due to this big problem, as I often overshot the corners because I didn't have any feel on the brake pedal. Sometimes I couldn't even reach the pedals!'

By lap 17, Coulthard's fourth-place McLaren had begun to trail smoke, an ominous portent of his ultimate fate, while he steadily dropped back from the leading bunch. Another five laps saw Schumacher 15s ahead of his

Paul-Henri Cahier

Qualifying through the streets of Monaco is traditionally a nail-biting affair, but the hour-long session in preparation for this year's race was one of the most gripping in recent memory.

Having recovered from its defeat by the Ferraris at Imola, McLaren was expected to sustain the MP4/14's proven performance edge, but the team took the wrong route on Thursday by opting for soft tyres. Ron Dennis freely admitted that this had been the wrong choice. Häkkinen and Coulthard were left battling poor handling balance, and it wasn't until they made the change to tyres of a harder compound that they began to make up for lost time.

On Saturday morning, Coulthard experienced even more problems. He'd started the weekend with a bad limp after hurting a foot during a charity football match, then sustained another self-inflicted wound when he slid his car's right rear wheel into the pit wall on the exit from the last corner during Saturday morning's free practice.

David pulled off into the pit lane exit, and the car was eventually pushed back to have its broken right rear suspension toe-link repaired. However, on close examination, it was apparent that the impact had also cracked the lightweight cylinder block of the Mercedes V10, which meant that a fresh engine had to be installed for qualifying.

At least Coulthard could console himself that he was in good company. After setting fastest time of the session, Schumacher had clipped the inside kerb at Ste Dévote and slid headlong into the opposite barrier, damaging his car's monocoque beyond repair. Damon Hill also crashed heavily at Rascasse and, although the Jordan crew worked heroically to rebuild the shattered machine in 50 minutes, the fizz had definitely gone out of the Brit's weekend and he never picked up his earlier pace.

Then came the battle for grid positions. Despite feeling that his spare F399 wasn't quite as crisp as his original chassis, Schumacher scorched around in 1m 20.611s to clinch what looked like a commanding pole. Meanwhile, Häkkinen gained second on 1m 21.126 s, but was still suffering from a slight handling imbalance, which was costing him time in the final sector.

McLaren made a last-moment change to the chassis set-up and Mika launched into his final lap, only 14s before the chequered flag was waved. At the first split, he was a scant 0.008s up, and it didn't look enough. Surely it would all ebb away through the final sector of the lap. But no, he successfully carried his speed through to a brilliant 14th career pole on 1m 20.547s.

Häkkinen completed his quickest lap while a stationary yellow flag was displayed at Tabac for Damon Hill's abandoned Jordan. 'I obviously had to be cautious,' he said, 'and if I'd really been flat out, I could have been another one-tenth quicker. I put my hand up to acknowledge the flag at that point.'

In fact, the stationary yellow flag was not an issue. Since the start of the season, only waved yellow warning flags had any validity under the rules; the stationary yellow, previously used as a caution flag, had effectively been struck from the rule book. With that in mind, it was disappointing that Schumacher should hint that Häkkinen's behaviour had been less than impeccable. Mika was above board, no question.

Meanwhile, David Coulthard vaulted up to third place in the closing stages of the session. 'I was obviously very happy to jump so far forward at the end,' he said. 'It was a bit of a relief.'

So Schumacher ended up second on the grid, although he claimed his third run would have been his fastest, 'but I was held up by Panis right at the last corner.' Eddie Irvine said he made a mistake on his third run, but felt confident for the race after qualifying fourth.

Best of the rest in qualifying was Rubens Barrichello, who celebrated the 35th anniversary of Jackie Stewart's victory in the Monaco F3 race by qualifying fifth, ahead of Heinz-Harald Frentzen's Jordan. 'H-H' continued his role as revelation of the season, looking as forceful and confident during his qualifying runs as team-mate Hill looked tentative and uncomfortable.

Ford's CR-1 V10 had been restored to its 17,250 rpm operating limit for this race, for only the second time in the season, after a promising full-race distance had been tested at Nogaro. For the Sunday only at Monaco, further revised versions of the V10, with new pistons, were installed in the cars.

'To have done that behind McLaren and Ferrari is very satisfying,' said Barrichello, 'but if we are to do better than that, we must get more grip from the car.' Johnny Herbert wound up 13th, explaining that he could have been eighth if he had not come up behind Damon Hill on his best lap.

Frentzen was quite satisfied with his sixth-fastest time, although he admitted to an unusual mistake. 'On my fastest lap, I got my hand jammed between the steering wheel and the side of the monocoque at the chicane and could hardly turn,' he said. 'I have never experienced that before.' Damon Hill was a dejected 17th, having never been able to obtain a decent balance from his repaired chassis. Eventually, he stopped on the circuit with a gearbox problem.

Further back, Jarno Trulli was second fastest at one point, but he spun at Ste Dévote and had to take the spare Prost, ending up seventh. Jacques Villeneuve and Mika Salo were eighth and 12th for the BAR team. 'I am very satisfied because both cars are intact, and to have performed like this on our first visit to Monaco is very satisfying,' said Craig Pollock.

rivals, just as Alexander Wurz's Benetton, by then running in tenth place, began to shed part of its rear wing tail flap.

On lap 23, Marc Gene's Minardi crashed out of 19th place at Ste Dévote, rounding off a difficult weekend for the young Spanish driver, who had already suffered two previous accidents during the meeting.

Ten laps later, the Stewart-Ford team was on the receiving end of its first dose of trouble when Johnny Herbert lost control coming out of Casino Square and zig-zagged to a spectacular halt at Mirabeau. The Englishman successfully fought to keep his car away from the barrier all the way down the hill.

'There was no warning at all,' said Herbert. 'I was coming out of Casino Square and something gave up on the right rear suspension.' Subsequent examination revealed that a rear suspension toe-link had broken. It would not be the first time that day. Meanwhile, Jacques Villeneuve's BAR – running on soft tyres – retired from a promising eighth place with a hydraulic fluid leak.

At the end of lap 37, Irvine made his first refuelling stop in 6.7s, retaining third place, just as Coulthard pulled in for good. 'I started to have a gear selection problem,' he shrugged, 'and the team advised me that the gearbox had lost oil pressure. They told me to come in which, of course, was the right thing to do because otherwise a terminal failure would have been inevitable.'

It was certainly a busy lap because, back around the circuit, Mika Salo's BAR slid into the guard rail at the Loews hairpin, retiring on the spot from 11th place. 'I first started to have brake trouble as early as lap three,' he said. 'I had to back off a little and couldn't push really hard. I was still fighting as hard as I could with Jean Alesi as I was coming up to the Loews when I felt the pedal go completely soft. Unfortunately, there was nothing I could do except drive straight into the wall.'

On lap 39, Häkkinen encountered a sequence of events that would cost him any chance of finishing even in second place. Almost half a minute down, he suddenly found himself obliged to take to the escape road at the tricky downhill Mirabeau corner, just beyond Casino Square, after skidding on oil dropped by Toranosuke Takagi's Arrows, which had suffered a major engine failure.

'The incident must have just happened when I arrived there,' said

Right: Mika Häkkinen locks his brakes behind Michael Schumacher as the pair lead the field into Ste Dévote. Behind them, Irvine and Coulthard jockey for position.

Mika. 'When I tried to turn into Mirabeau, the rear wheels began to lock, so I decided to steer down the escape road rather than risk spinning into the barrier.'

That little drama left him 45.5s behind Schumacher, allowing the latter to make his sole 9.9s refuelling stop at the end of lap 42 without remotely jeopardising his advantage. He resumed 24.2s ahead of the McLaren, but when Mika made his own 7.4s stop at the end of lap 50, Eddie Irvine was able to slip through into second place.

On lap 56, Eddie brought the Ferrari in for its second stop (6.8s) and managed to nip back out again ahead of Häkkinen, whose fate was sealed. To round off his miserable day, Häkkinen had another nasty moment on lap 65, when his engine suddenly began to sound like a bag of nails – so much so, that he held his radio link open as he passed the pits so that his pit crew could hear it. Happily, what may have been a fleeting electrical problem seemed to fix itself, and two laps later he was able to set the fastest lap of the race.

Understandably, Irvine was well satisfied with second place on the podium, which consolidated his second place in the championship points.

'I made a great start,' he said, 'and the car felt better and better as the fuel load lightened. What you need here at Monaco is a very well balanced car, and that's what we had. We need a little more work on the aerodynamics and we should be able to maintain this form in Spain in two weeks' time.

'Before the race, we had to look at various [strategic] situations to see what would be the best thing to do. This is where we can play our ace card, which is Ross [Brawn]. He does a fantastic job sorting that problem and, as at Imola, the strategy seemed to work out well for us today.

'Early on, Mika seemed to hit some traffic, but I managed to nip through it quite nicely. That helped me to close the gap, and once I got to him, I could see that I was a lot faster than he was. But because overtaking is so difficult round here, we had to do the overtaking on strategy, which we achieved.'

Fourth place fell to Heinz-Harald Frentzen after a consistently impressive drive in his Jordan. 'My race was against Rubens, and we won that comfortably,' he said. 'I did not expect to be able to take him at the start, so we decided that I should stay close to him and make up the time when he made his pit stop.

Left: Another strong race for Giancarlo Fisichella who finished fifth.

Below left: Damon Hill near the back of the field heads into Loews hairpin inside the Prost of Olivier Panis. Behind them are Takagi, Badoer, Gene and de la Rosa.

Right: Eddie Irvine produced another tremendous drive to take second place behind team leader Schumacher.

Controversy as Brands Hatch signs for British Grand Prix

ON the Friday before the Monaco Grand Prix, Brands Hatch announced that it had secured the British Grand Prix for 2002,' marking a return of F1 racing to the Kent circuit for the first time since 1986.

At press conferences held at Brands Hatch and in Monaco, Nicola Foulston, chief executive of Brands Hatch Leisure plc, confirmed that she had signed the normal undertakings required by the Grand Prix organisers, guaranteeing that Bernie Ecclestone's Formula One Administration organisation will receive payment for the race in three years' time.

'I am delighted to have secured the future of Grand Prix racing in Britain beyond 2001,' she said. The planned new track will have its pit complex on the straight before the current Hawthorns right-hander on the old Grand Prix circuit, and this whole area will be levelled out to accommodate a new paddock area at that point.

The plans prompted a dismissive response from the British Racing Drivers' Club, owners of Silverstone, which believed that Foulston could over-stretch herself with the £20 million investment needed to upgrade Brands Hatch.

The club's opposition to the move was echoed by McLaren's Ron Dennis, who slammed the plans as a deliberate attempt on Foulston's part to destabilise the BRDC. 'There is a very emotional and hotly debated issue over this in Britain, but some people have to stand up and be counted,' he said. 'What is happening is wrong. The media needs to understand that the BRDC has got some relatively mature people at the top, who are perhaps a little too mature and need to stop fighting by Queensbury rules and take a more aggressive stance in defending their club.'

Dennis's main objection centred on the fact that Silverstone's operators are 'almost unique' in reinvesting their money in the sport, and he believes that this would change dramatically if the race moved to Brands Hatch. He also claimed that the changes required to update the Kent circuit to the appropriate FIA standards would probably trigger a public inquiry, with the result that Brands Hatch Leisure would be unable to meet the deadline for the first race in 2002.

Foulston, however, was robust in defending her company's position. 'This is not the same situation as McLaren has with their new factory,' she said. 'I am not applying to build anything in green-belt land. Brands Hatch is already designated as a race circuit and there is no change of use.

'I have the support of Brands Hatch shareholders, my bankers and the local government. I have not wasted all this work over the last three months just as an exercise to wind people up.'

'As soon as he pitted, I was able to pull away. I was gaining on Häkkinen, but getting close to him and overtaking are two different things, of course.'

Rubens stopped on lap 51, dropping to fifth behind Frentzen, while Heinz-Harald did not come in for another six laps, by which time he'd built up a sufficient cushion to be able to get back into the race ahead of the Brazilian in the Stewart.

Sadly, the Stewart-Ford team's hopes of a top-six finish were dashed when Barrichello succumbed to the same right rear suspension failure that earlier had sidelined his team-mate, Johnny Herbert. 'The car ran reasonably well,' said Rubens, 'although I wasn't able to find consistency after my pit stop.'

In fifth and sixth places were the Benetton B199s of Giancarlo Fisichella and Alexander Wurz, although the Italian driver admitted that he'd been hoping to finish higher on this tight track. Wurz explained that he'd lost a lot of time behind Zanardi in the opening stages of the race, and was only able to pass him on lap 14 when the Italian made one of his unscheduled detours.

Jarno Trulli finished seventh for the Prost team, while Alex Zanardi was eighth in the only remaining Williams, and the last competitor running at the end of a gruelling race, which had seen both Sauber C18s succumb to accidents and Olivier Panis suffer an engine failure in his Prost-Peugeot.

While Schumacher, Irvine and the Ferrari team celebrated, it fell to McLaren International's managing director, Martin Whitmarsh, to sum up his team's dilemma after the race. 'Everybody here at McLaren reflects a mood of grim determination,' he said. 'I think we have to concede that at Monaco we were not on target in terms of both traction and drivability. It is something we intend to address with all the resources at our disposal and are aiming for a very different outcome at Barcelona.'

Nobody doubted him for a second.

Paul-Henri Cahier

Main picture: The best seat in the house, for those lucky enough to have access to a yacht in the harbour. Mika Häkkinen guides his McLaren along the waterfront.
Pamela Lauesen/FOSA

Left: The remains of Damon Hill's Jordan after his tangle with Ralf Schumacher.
Pamela Lauesen/FOSA

Below: Alexander Wurz survived the afternoon to finish sixth.
Pamela Lauesen/FOSA

Bottom right: Jarno Trulli was able to qualify the Prost-Peugeot seventh, a position he had held onto at the end of the race.
Paul-Henri Cahier

Bottom centre: A grim-faced Ralf Schumacher strides back to the pits.
Michael Cooper/Allsport

Bottom far left: Ferrari steering wheel.
Paul-Henri Cahier

MONACO GRAND PRIX

GRAND PRIX DE MONACO

13–16 MAY 1999

MONTE CARLO

Race distance: 78 laps, 163.187 miles/262.624 km

Race weather: Dry, hot and sunny

ROUND
4

MONACO – MONTE CARLO Grand Prix Circuit

Ste Devote · Montée De Beau Rivage · Mirabeau · Tabac · Nouvelle Chicane · Loews · Virage Du Portier · Virage Anthony Noghes · Tunnel · La Rascasse

CIRCUIT LENGTH: 2.092 miles/3.367 km

Pos.	Driver	Nat.	No.	Entrant	Car/Engine	Laps	Time/Retirement	Speed (mph/km/h)
1	Michael Schumacher	D	3	Scuderia Ferrari Marlboro	Ferrari F399 048 V10	78	1h 49m 31.812s	89.393/143.864
2	Eddie Irvine	GB	4	Scuderia Ferrari Marlboro	Ferrari F399 048 V10	78	1h 50m 02.288s	88.980/143.200
3	Mika Häkkinen	SF	1	West McLaren Mercedes	McLaren MP4/14-Mercedes F0110H V10	78	1h 50m 09.295s	88.887/143.050
4	Heinz-Harald Frentzen	D	8	Benson & Hedges Jordan	Jordan 199-Mugen Honda MF301/HD V10	78	1h 50m 25.821s	88.665/142.693
5	Giancarlo Fisichella	I	9	Mild Seven Benetton Playlife	Benetton B199-Playlife V10	77		
6	Alexander Wurz	A	10	Mild Seven Benetton Playlife	Benetton B199-Playlife V10	77		
7	Jarno Trulli	I	19	Gauloises Prost Peugeot	Prost AP02-Peugeot A18 V10	77		
8	Alex Zanardi	I	5	Winfield Williams	Williams FW21-Supertec FB01 V10	76		
9	Rubens Barrichello	BR	16	Stewart Ford	Stewart SF3-Ford CR-1 V10	71	Suspension/accident	
	Ralf Schumacher	D	6	Winfield Williams	Williams FW21-Supertec FB01 V10	54	Accident	
	Jean Alesi	F	11	Red Bull Sauber Petronas	Sauber C18-Petronas SPE03A V10	50	Hit wall	
	Pedro Diniz	BR	12	Red Bull Sauber Petronas	Sauber C18-Petronas SPE03A V10	49	Accident	
	Olivier Panis	F	18	Gauloises Prost Peugeot	Prost AP02-Peugeot A18 V10	40	Engine	
	David Coulthard	GB	2	West McLaren Mercedes	McLaren MP4/14-Mercedes F0110H V10	36	Oil leak	
	Mika Salo	SF	23	British American Racing	BAR 01-Supertec FB01 V10	36	Brakes	
	Toranosuke Takagi	J	15	Arrows	Arrows A20 V10	36	Engine	
	Jacques Villeneuve	CDN	22	British American Racing	BAR 01-Supertec FB01 V10	32	Oil leak	
	Johnny Herbert	GB	17	Stewart Ford	Stewart SF3-Ford CR-1 V10	32	Suspension	
	Pedro de la Rosa	ESP	14	Arrows	Arrows A20 V10	30	Gearbox	
	Marc Gene	ESP	21	Fondmetal Minardi Ford	Minardi M01-Ford Zetec-R V10	24	Accident	
	Luca Badoer	I	20	Fondmetal Minardi Ford	Minardi M01-Ford Zetec-R V10	10	Gearbox	
	Damon Hill	GB	7	Benson & Hedges Jordan	Jordan 199-Mugen Honda MF301/HD V10	3	Collision with R. Schumacher	

Fastest lap: Häkkinen, on lap 67, 1m 22.259s, 91.562 mph/147.355 km/h (record).

Previous lap record: Mika Häkkinen (F1 McLaren MP4/13-Mercedes V10), 1m 22.948s, 90.801 mph/146.130 km/h (1998).

Grid order	1	2	3	4	5	6	7	8	9	10	11	12	13	14	15	16	17	18	19	20	21	22	23	24	25	26	27	28	29	30	31	32	33	34	35	36	37	38	39	40	41	42	43	44	45	46	47	48	49	50	51	52	53	54	55	56	57	58	59	60
1 HÄKKINEN	3	3	3	3	3	3	3	3	3	3	3	3	3	3	3	3	3	3	3	3	3	3	3	3	3	3	3	3	3	3	3	3	3	3	3	3	3	3	3	3	3	3	3	3	3	3	3	3	3	3	3	3	3	3	3	3	3	3	3	3
3 M. SCHUMACHER	1	1	1	1	1	1	1	1	1	1	1	1	1	1	1	1	1	1	1	1	1	1	1	1	1	1	1	1	1	1	1	1	1	1	1	1	1	1	1	1	1	1	1	1	1	1	1	4	4	4	4	4	4	4	4	4	4	4	4	4
2 COULTHARD	4	4	4	4	4	4	4	4	4	4	4	4	4	4	4	4	4	4	4	4	4	4	4	4	4	4	4	4	4	4	4	4	4	4	4	4	4	4	4	4	4	4	4	1	1	1	1	1	1	1	1	1	1	1	1	1	1	1	1	1
4 IRVINE	2	2	2	2	2	2	2	2	2	2	2	2	2	2	2	2	2	2	2	2	2	2	2	2	2	2	2	2	2	2	2	2	16	16	16	16	16	16	16	16	16	16	16	16	16	16	16	8	8	8	8	8	8	8	8	8	8	8	8	8
16 BARRICHELLO	16	16	16	16	16	16	16	16	16	16	16	16	16	16	16	16	16	16	16	16	16	16	16	16	16	16	16	16	16	16	16	16	8	8	8	8	8	8	8	8	8	8	8	8	16	16	16	16	16	16	16	16	16	16	16	16	16	16	16	16
8 FRENTZEN	8	8	8	8	8	8	8	8	8	8	8	8	8	8	8	8	8	8	8	8	8	8	8	8	8	8	8	8	8	8	8	8	9	9	9	9	9	9	19	19	19	19	19	19	19	19	19	9	9	9	9	9	9	9	9	9	9	9	9	9
19 TRULLI	19	19	19	19	19	19	19	19	19	19	19	19	19	19	19	19	19	19	19	9	9	9	9	9	9	9	9	9	9	9	9	9	19	19	19	19	19	19	9	9	9	9	9	9	9	9	9	19	19	19	19	19	19	19	19	19	19	19	19	19
22 VILLENEUVE	9	9	9	9	9	9	9	9	9	9	9	9	9	9	9	9	9	9	9	22	22	22	22	22	22	22	22	22	22	22	19	19	10	10	10	10	10	10	10	10	10	10	10	10	11	11	11	11	12	10	10	10	10	10	10	10	10	10	10	10
9 FISICHELLA	22	22	22	22	22	22	22	22	22	22	22	22	22	22	22	22	22	22	22	19	19	19	19	19	19	19	19	19	19	19	10	10	10	10	10	10	10	10	11	11	11	11	11	11	10	12	12	12	10	5	5	5	5	5	5	5	5	5	5	5
10 WURZ	5	5	5	5	5	5	5	5	5	5	5	5	10	10	10	10	10	10	10	10	10	10	10	10	10	10	10	10	10	10	23	11	11	11	12	12	12	12	12	12	12	12	12	10	10	10	10	11	6	6	6	6								
5 ZANARDI	10	10	10	10	10	10	10	10	10	10	10	10	17	17	17	17	17	17	17	17	17	17	17	17	17	17	17	17	11	23	23	23	5	5	5	5	5	5	5	5	5	5	5	5	5	11														
23 SALO	17	17	17	17	17	17	17	17	17	17	17	17	23	23	23	23	23	23	23	23	23	23	23	23	23	23	23	23	12	12	12	12	12	18	18	18	18	6	6	6	6	6	6	6	6															
17 HERBERT	23	23	23	23	23	23	23	23	23	23	23	23	11	11	11	11	11	11	11	11	11	11	11	11	11	11	11	11	5	5	5	5	6	6	6	6																								
11 ALESI	12	12	12	11	11	11	11	11	11	11	11	11	12	12	12	12	12	12	12	12	12	12	12	12	12	12	12	12	18	18	18	18																												
12 DINIZ	11	11	11	12	12	12	12	12	12	12	12	12	18	18	18	18	18	18	18	18	18	18	18	18	18	18	5	5	5	5	15	15	15	15																											
6 R. SCHUMACHER	6	6	6	18	18	18	18	18	18	18	18	18	5	5	5	5	5	5	5	5	5	5	5	5	18	18	18	18	18	6	6	6	6																												
7 HILL	7	7	7	15	15	15	15	15	15	15	15	15	15	15	15	15	15	15	15	15	15	15	15	15	15	15	15	15	15	15																															
18 PANIS	18	18	18	20	20	20	20	20	20	21	21	21	21	21	6	6	6	6	6	6	6	6	6	6	6	6																																			
15 TAKAGI	15	15	15	21	21	21	21	21	21	14	14	6	6	6	21	21	21	21	21	21	21	14	14	14	14	14																																			
20 BADOER	20	20	20	14	14	14	14	6	6	14	14	14	14	14	14	14	14	14	14	14																																								
14 DE LA ROSA	21	21	21	6	6	6	6	6	6																																																				
21 GENE	14	14	14																																																											

Pit stop

One lap behind leader

STARTING GRID

	1 HÄKKINEN McLaren
3 M. SCHUMACHER Ferrari	
	2 COULTHARD McLaren
4 IRVINE Ferrari	
	16 BARRICHELLO Stewart
8 FRENTZEN Jordan	
	19 TRULLI Prost
22 VILLENEUVE BAR	
	9 FISICHELLA Benetton
10 WURZ Benetton	
	5 ZANARDI Williams
23 SALO BAR	
	17 HERBERT Stewart
11 ALESI Sauber	
	12 DINIZ Sauber
6 R. SCHUMACHER Williams	
	7 HILL Jordan
18 PANIS Prost	
	15 TAKAGI Arrows
20 BADOER Minardi	
	14 DE LA ROSA Arrows
21 GENE Minardi	

Lap chart (bottom left)

64	65	66	67	68	69	70	71	72	73	74	75	76	77	78	
3	3	3	3	3	3	3	3	3	3	3	3	3	3	3	1
4	4	4	4	4	4	4	4	4	4	4	4	4	4	4	2
1	1	1	1	1	1	1	1	1	1	1	1	1	1	1	3
8	8	8	8	8	8	8	8	8	8	8	8	8	8	8	4
16	16	16	16	16	16	16	16	16	9	9	9	9	9	9	5
9	9	9	9	9	9	9	9	10	10	10	10	10	10	10	6
10	10	10	10	10	10	10	10	10	19	19	19	19	19	19	
19	19	19	19	19	19	19	19	19	5	5	5	5	5		
5	5	5	5	5	5	5	5								

TIME SHEETS

QUALIFYING

Weather: Dry, hot and sunny.

Pos.	Driver	Car	Laps	Time
1	Mika Häkkinen	McLaren-Mercedes	12	1m 20.547s
2	Michael Schumacher	Ferrari	11	1m 20.611s
3	David Coulthard	McLaren-Mercedes	12	1m 20.956s
4	Eddie Irvine	Ferrari	12	1m 21.011s
5	Rubens Barrichello	Stewart-Ford	12	1m 21.530s
6	Heinz-Harald Frentzen	Jordan-Mugen Honda	12	1m 21.556s
7	Jarno Trulli	Prost-Peugeot	11	1m 21.769s
8	Jacques Villeneuve	BAR-Supertec	12	1m 21.827s
9	Giancarlo Fisichella	Benetton-Playlife	11	1m 21.938s
10	Alexander Wurz	Benetton-Playlife	12	1m 21.968s
11	Alex Zanardi	Williams-Supertec	12	1m 22.152s
12	Mika Salo	BAR-Supertec	12	1m 22.241s
13	Johnny Herbert	Stewart-Ford	12	1m 22.248s
14	Jean Alesi	Sauber-Petronas	12	1m 22.354s
15	Pedro Diniz	Sauber-Petronas	12	1m 22.659s
16	Ralf Schumacher	Williams-Supertec	11	1m 22.719s
17	Damon Hill	Jordan-Mugen Honda	12	1m 22.832s
18	Olivier Panis	Prost-Peugeot	12	1m 22.916s
19	Toranosuke Takagi	Arrows	11	1m 23.290s
20	Luca Badoer	Minardi-Ford	12	1m 23.765s
21	Pedro de la Rosa	Arrows	12	1m 24.260s
22	Marc Gene	Minardi-Ford	11	1m 24.914s

THURSDAY FREE PRACTICE

Weather: Dry and bright

Pos.	Driver	Laps	Time
1	Michael Schumacher	32	1m 22.718s
2	Mika Häkkinen	37	1m 22.854s
3	Olivier Panis	40	1m 23.318s
4	Eddie Irvine	41	1m 23.396s
5	Giancarlo Fisichella	30	1m 23.458s
6	David Coulthard	37	1m 23.503s
7	Rubens Barrichello	32	1m 23.545s
8	Mika Salo	32	1m 23.793s
9	Jacques Villeneuve	35	1m 23.862s
10	Johnny Herbert	31	1m 23.865s
11	Damon Hill	48	1m 23.874s
12	Jarno Trulli	25	1m 23.958s
13	Alex Zanardi	53	1m 24.065s
14	Alexander Wurz	35	1m 24.263s
15	Jean Alesi	49	1m 24.492s
16	Ralf Schumacher	10	1m 24.906s
17	Pedro Diniz	41	1m 25.094s
18	Pedro de la Rosa	44	1m 26.148s
19	Heinz-Harald Frentzen	12	1m 26.336s
20	Toranosuke Takagi	23	1m 27.618s
21	Marc Gene	48	1m 27.667s
22	Luca Badoer	26	1m 28.316s

SATURDAY FREE PRACTICE

Weather: Dry, overcast and warm

Pos.	Driver	Laps	Time
1	Michael Schumacher	28	1m 21.249s
2	Eddie Irvine	30	1m 21.521s
3	Mika Häkkinen	26	1m 21.919s
4	Rubens Barrichello	29	1m 21.974s
5	Heinz-Harald Frentzen	38	1m 22.166s
6	Jacques Villeneuve	29	1m 22.252s
7	Ralf Schumacher	32	1m 22.372s
8	Giancarlo Fisichella	34	1m 22.599s
9	Alex Zanardi	33	1m 22.654s
10	Johnny Herbert	34	1m 22.971s
11	Alex Wurz	32	1m 23.123s
12	Jean Alesi	31	1m 23.145s
13	David Coulthard	9	1m 23.160s
14	Jarno Trulli	31	1m 23.384s
15	Pedro Diniz	37	1m 23.641s
16	Olivier Panis	31	1m 23.751s
17	Damon Hill	24	1m 23.929s
18	Toranosuke Takagi	34	1m 24.143s
19	Pedro de la Rosa	31	1m 24.380s
20	Luca Badoer	29	1m 24.588s
21	Marc Gene	32	1m 24.818s
22	Mika Salo	16	1m 24.917s

WARM-UP

Weather: Dry, hot and sunny

Pos.	Driver	Laps	Time
1	Michael Schumacher	14	1m 23.792s
2	Eddie Irvine	14	1m 24.259s
3	Mika Häkkinen	12	1m 24.268s
4	David Coulthard	15	1m 24.270s
5	Damon Hill	15	1m 24.764s
6	Ralf Schumacher	18	1m 24.780s
7	Heinz-Harald Frentzen	16	1m 25.389s
8	Rubens Barrichello	15	1m 25.408s
9	Johnny Herbert	14	1m 25.485s
10	Alexander Wurz	15	1m 25.579s
11	Jarno Trulli	15	1m 25.793s
12	Jean Alesi	14	1m 26.002s
13	Pedro Diniz	16	1m 26.070s
14	Giancarlo Fisichella	14	1m 26.260s
15	Olivier Panis	14	1m 26.510s
16	Jacques Villeneuve	10	1m 26.669s
17	Alex Zanardi	12	1m 27.722s
18	Mika Salo	12	1m 27.880s
19	Pedro de la Rosa	11	1m 27.962s
20	Luca Badoer	11	1m 29.358s
21	Marc Gene	8	1m 30.881s
22	Toranosuke Takagi	3	1m 38.064s

RACE FASTEST LAPS

Weather: Dry, hot and sunny

Driver	Time	Lap
Mika Häkkinen	1m 22.259s	67
Michael Schumacher	1m 22.288s	32
Heinz-Harald Frentzen	1m 22.471s	64
Eddie Irvine	1m 22.572s	62
Pedro Diniz	1m 22.637s	48
Ralf Schumacher	1m 22.837s	47
David Coulthard	1m 22.883s	31
Alexander Wurz	1m 23.236s	68
Alex Zanardi	1m 23.294s	49
Jean Alesi	1m 23.417s	47
Giancarlo Fisichella	1m 23.473s	67
Jacques Villeneuve	1m 23.537s	31
Rubens Barrichello	1m 23.583s	55
Jarno Trulli	1m 23.646s	49
Olivier Panis	1m 24.480s	24
Mika Salo	1m 24.787s	31
Johnny Herbert	1m 24.919s	25
Toranosuke Takagi	1m 26.482s	26
Marc Gene	1m 26.864s	18
Pedro de la Rosa	1m 26.914s	23
Luca Badoer	1m 28.691s	8
Damon Hill	1m 28.848s	3

CHASSIS LOG BOOK

1	Häkkinen	McLaren MP4/14/2
2	Coulthard	McLaren MP4/14/4
	spare	McLaren MP4/14/1
3	M. Schumacher	Ferrari F399/193
4	Irvine	Ferrari F399/191
	spare	Ferrari F399/192
5	Zanardi	Williams FW21/5
6	R. Schumacher	Williams FW21/4
	spare	Williams FW21/1 & 2
7	Hill	Jordan 199/4
8	Frentzen	Jordan 199/6
	spare	Jordan 199/3
9	Fisichella	Benetton B199/6
10	Wurz	Benetton B199/5
	spare	Benetton B199/4 & 1
11	Alesi	Sauber C18/5
12	Diniz	Sauber C18/4
	spare	Sauber C18/1 & 6
14	de la Rosa	Arrows A20/4
15	Takagi	Arrows A20/2
	spare	Arrows A20/5
16	Barrichello	Stewart SF3/4
17	Herbert	Stewart SF3/5
	spare	Stewart SF3/3
18	Panis	Prost AP02/3
19	Trulli	Prost AP02/2
	spare	Prost AP02/5
20	Badoer	Minardi M01/1
21	Gene	Minardi M01/4
	spare	Minardi M01/3
22	Villeneuve	BAR 01/3
23	Salo	BAR 01/5
	spare	BAR 01/4

POINTS TABLES

DRIVERS

1	Michael Schumacher	26
2	Eddie Irvine	18
3 =	Mika Häkkinen	14
3 =	Heinz-Harald Frentzen	13
5 =	Ralf Schumacher	7
5 =	Giancarlo Fisichella	7
7 =	David Coulthard	6
7 =	Rubens Barrichello	6
9	Damon Hill	3
10 =	Pedro de la Rosa	1
10 =	Olivier Panis	1
10 =	Jean Alesi	1
10 =	Alexander Wurz	1

CONSTRUCTORS

1	Ferrari	44
2	McLaren	20
3	Jordan	16
4	Benetton	8
5	Williams	7
6	Stewart	6
7 =	Arrows	1
7 =	Prost	1
7 =	Sauber	1

SPANISH
grand prix

| HÄKKINEN |
| COULTHARD |
| M. SCHUMACHER |
| IRVINE |
| R. SCHUMACHER |
| TRULLI |

DIARY

Bernie Ecclestone's F1 Eurobond issue launched successfully in the run-up to the Spanish Grand Prix, benefiting family trusts established by the multi-millionaire to the tune of an estimated $875 million.

Damon Hill dismisses talk of retiring at the end of the season as 'premature and predictable'.

FIA technical chief Charlie Whiting turns down offer to run Benetton team.

Kenny Bräck wins Indy 500 as rival Robby Gordon runs out of fuel on the final lap.

MIKA Häkkinen and David Coulthard swung the tide decisively in the McLaren-Mercedes team's favour with a commanding 1-2 victory in the Spanish Grand Prix. It was the first time that the two drivers had dominated the podium since the 1998 German Grand Prix at Hockenheim.

On this occasion, Michael Schumacher and Eddie Irvine had to be satisfied with third and fourth places. However, the high degree of mechanical reliability from their Ferrari F399s ensured that Schumacher and the team emerged from the weekend still comfortably leading the World Championship points tables.

Häkkinen qualified brilliantly in pole position in the final moments of Saturday's hour-long qualifying session and stamped his mastery on the race from the start. The Finn led all but four of the race's 65 laps, only relinquishing the advantage fleetingly to Coulthard when he made his two routine refuelling stops.

During the middle sector of the race, Coulthard was frustrated by inconsistent handling, which caused him to lose a lot of time, allowing Schumacher's Ferrari to close within a second at one point. Coulthard also confessed that he did little to help his cause by overshooting his pit at the first refuelling stop, a slip that cost him an extra 5s, which he could ill afford.

'Remember, that was only the second pit stop I have done all year,' he said, referring to his retirements in three of the previous five races. 'I called in over the radio to say that I was experiencing too much oversteer on my first set of tyres, so a pressure adjustment was made for the second set, but I still had oversteer in the low-speed and understeer in the high-speed corners.

'That enabled Michael to start catching me and I also had quite a lot of traffic in the closing stages after my second stop, and the handling balance felt better on my last set of tyres. I didn't have problems with traffic like I did at Imola, but I did spend about a lap behind Damon [Hill] and was just starting to get a bit frustrated, thinking he should know better, when he moved over out of my way.'

Schumacher may have been hoping for some tactical assistance from Irvine at the start, but as Häkkinen got cleanly away from pole position, it was Coulthard who came bursting through the front row to ease out the Ulsterman in the sprint down to the first corner.

As Schumacher found himself boxed in behind David and Eddie, Jacques

CATALUNYA QUALIFYING

Mika Häkkinen won the 15th pole position of his career – and his fifth in the first five races of the 1999 season – when he qualified his McLaren-Mercedes fastest at the Circuit de Catalunya.

'The track conditions improved for me during the session,' he said, 'and the engineers made great changes to the set-up during the session. David [Coulthard] was faster than me during the morning, and this was a good experience of the team – and David and I – working together to get to the point where my car could take pole.'

Coulthard was a slightly disappointed third fastest: 'The car was oversteering too much at the start of the session; I changed the set-up and it changed to understeer. I should have left it as it was.'

The Scot had done a good job after suffering a frightening moment during Saturday's free practice, from which he emerged fastest, despite a spectacular spin on the penultimate corner of the lap after a rear suspension pushrod broke. David was able to control the car and coax it back into the pit lane. Nevertheless, he was extremely happy with his lap time.

'It was a crack like a rifle shot and I instantly knew what had happened,' he said. Slight modifications were made to all the McLarens and the team remained confident that the problem would not be repeated.

Eddie Irvine split the McLarens to set second-fastest time in his Ferrari F399. 'If anyone had told me before the weekend that I would be starting this race from second place on the grid, I don't think I would have believed it,' he said.

'I am very pleased, because for some strange reason the car has been much better this weekend than it was during testing here, when it was a complete disaster. Everywhere we have been this year, the car had been really well balanced, but when we came here for the final test last week, I was a long way off the pace.

'I just couldn't drive the car fast then. But when we came here yesterday, the car felt good straight away. Today, pole position was a definite possibility, but I couldn't get the car good enough at both the start and the finish of the lap. It could only be one or the other.'

As for Michael Schumacher, fourth place on the grid was hardly what he had become accustomed to. 'My car was very well balanced in the morning, but for reasons which we must now investigate, it was not as good in qualifying,' he shrugged. 'No matter what we tried, the lap times stayed pretty much the same.'

Jean Alesi was briefly fastest early in the session and eventually wound up fifth in his Sauber-Petronas. 'This is an absolute dream,' said the Frenchman, 'the first time this year we have used 100 per cent of the car's potential.' Pedro Diniz ended up 12th, reporting that he had been unable to find a good balance. 'I had understeer at the start and ended up with oversteer,' he said.

In the British American camp, Jacques Villeneuve emerged as the fastest of the Supertec-engined runners, in sixth place. The Canadian had suffered problems with the car during the morning, which were traced to a defective plug in the wiring loom. During qualifying, he was happy with the outcome, although an excursion on the grass during his best lap certainly cost him time. Mika Salo ended up 16th, his best lap being disallowed after a yellow flag infringement during the morning.

Rubens Barrichello was seventh in the Stewart-Ford. He briefly tried the spare car, which was set up for team-mate Johnny Herbert (14th), after his race car developed an engine vibration.

Heinz-Harald Frentzen and Damon Hill were eighth- and 11th-fastest for Jordan. 'No real problems,' said Frentzen, 'and I am not too worried because there are a few guys ahead of me who have chosen the softer tyre choice.' Ralf Schumacher managed tenth in the Williams FW21, commenting, 'It could have been worse. This is about our limit at present, and it will take another three or four races to improve things.' Team-mate Alex Zanardi was a disappointed 17th, reporting that his car was handling poorly and 'trying to make it better had the opposite effect.'

Villeneuve compounded the problem for the German ace by storming down the outside to get ahead of both Ferraris under braking for the first right-hander. Back on the startline, meanwhile, Marc Gene's hopes of a decent showing in front of his home crowd ended prematurely when his Minardi suffered clutch failure, while Olivier Panis's Prost-Peugeot was pushed into the pits after the engine stalled. He joined in a lap behind the leaders.

At the end of the opening lap, Häkkinen was 1.2s ahead of Coulthard, with Villeneuve, Schumacher, Irvine, Jarno Trulli (Prost) and Jean Alesi (Sauber) next up. Villeneuve was driving superbly, and his strong performance with the British American 01 was effectively handing the race to the McLaren duo.

By lap three, Häkkinen was 2.7s ahead of Coulthard, but the battle for third was already 5.6s behind the Scot; by lap six, 10.2s separated Mika from the Canadian driver, who was doing such a good job of keeping the Ferraris under control.

'I had taken off quite well from the second row of the grid,' said Schumacher, 'but I was blocked in by Eddie and David ahead of me and had to brake to avoid going into them. That gave Villeneuve the chance to pass me, and that was it really.

'I could perhaps have passed him at turn five on the first lap, but it would have meant a lot of risk. Being behind him cost me around 50 seconds, but I caught up until the second pit stop, but then I lost more time when I had to follow a slower Arrows into the pit lane.'

Undeniably, it was a processional and rather predictable race from the outset. Häkkinen led through to lap 23, when he made a 6.8s first refuelling stop, dropping back to 12.0s behind his team-mate. Then Coulthard made his own first stop at the end of lap 26, taking 12.8s after he overshot his pit.

Schumacher finally got his break on lap 24, when he and Villeneuve came in for their first refuelling stop, the Ferrari driver vaulting ahead to take third while Villeneuve resumed in fifth, behind Irvine. Villeneuve was slightly disappointed at this. 'I made a great start, which surprised me, as all my practice starts this weekend hadn't been so good, but that was a lucky one,' he grinned. 'The car was really good and I was running strongly, easily able to hold off Michael until the first pit stop. But in spite of a great effort by my crew, he managed to pass me in the pit lane.'

That same lap saw the retirement of Olivier Panis with failure of his Prost's gearbox hydraulics, while Alex Zanardi also pulled in from 13th place after his Williams suffered transmission failure. The latter, who had raced the spare Williams FW21, was poised to resume the race after his first refuelling stop. 'I selected first gear, but I heard a strange noise. Then when I released the clutch, nothing happened,' he shrugged. 'I think the main drive of my gearbox failed.'

It was Alesi's turn to depart the race on lap 28. Running ninth behind Trulli, the Frenchman got too close to the Prost and flicked down through the gears so violently that he broke the Sauber's transmission.

On lap 30, Häkkinen was leading by 13.7s from Coulthard, with Schumacher another 14s adrift in third, and

SPANISH GRAND PRIX

Right: Alex Zanardi had another frustrating weekend in the Williams FW21.

Left: Jacques Villeneuve burns rubber as he leaves the pits. The BAR driver drove a strong race, leading Michael Schumacher in the early stages.

Below left: Trying his hardest, Michael Schumacher's Ferrari had no answer to the speed of the McLarens.

Irvine 4s further back in a dutiful fourth. Villeneuve was fifth, ahead of Trulli, with Ralf Schumacher's Williams and Heinz-Harald Frentzen's Jordan next up.

Both Jordan drivers were experiencing difficulties, having opted to run the harder of the two available Bridgestone compounds. 'It was disappointing,' said Frentzen, who retired after 35 laps with a driveshaft failure. 'I was not able to pass Ralf, and the soft tyres, which many of our competitors were on, did not seem to drop off as much as we had hoped.'

On lap 40, Johnny Herbert's Stewart-Ford retired with transmission failure. 'As I was coming in for my first pit stop, I had felt the gear shifting was a little strange,' he reflected. 'Just before my second stop, I felt something break and attempted to crawl back to the pits, but I just couldn't make it.'

That same lap saw Pedro Diniz retire his Sauber with transmission problems, while Jacques Villeneuve made it three in a row when he came in for an unscheduled stop from fifth place to remove a loose tail flap from his rear wing. The mechanics wrestled to remove the flap, becoming increasingly frustrated, after which Villeneuve stalled the car when first gear broke as he tried to rejoin the race.

It was a great shame, for Villeneuve had driven with an unruffled assurance throughout, delivering a fine performance that did much to restore the 1997 World Champion's F1 image after a difficult few races with the new British American team.

By lap 42, Schumacher's Ferrari was only 0.8s behind Coulthard, and it seemed possible that he had a chance of leaping ahead of the McLaren driver as they prepared for their second refuelling stops. Michael came in on lap 43, but had to follow Toranosuke Takagi's slower Arrows into the pit lane, which cost him a few crucial seconds.

Häkkinen made his second (7.9s) stop on lap 44, while Coulthard came in for a 7.4s stop next time around, just squeezing back into the race 1.2s ahead of Schumacher's Ferrari. From that point on, it was all done and dusted, Häkkinen stroking it home to his 11th Grand Prix victory.

Schumacher was philosophical about the outcome. 'We knew this was going to be a difficult circuit for us,' he said, 'but all weekend we performed better than I had expected, and a big part of that is down to the team. Thanks to them, I managed to pick up another four valuable points, and it is good to know that we are not far off the pace

F1 rules slammed by top names

BOTH Damon Hill and Williams technical director Patrick Head spoke out at Barcelona to criticise the current F1 technical regulations, which make overtaking almost impossible and cause the cars to be unpredictable and uncomfortable to drive.

On the eve of one of the most processional and unremarkable Grands Prix in recent memory, they called on the FIA to rethink its current policy of restricting speed by simply reducing tyre grip.

'I'm not happy with these cars,' said Hill, referring to the incorporation of a fourth groove in the hard-compound front tyres used from the start of the year. 'I have driven Grand Prix cars under three [sets of] regulations and have driven much nicer cars than these. I find them completely frustrating at the moment. They are all dependent on their aerodynamic performance, and anything which upsets that is throwing a real spanner in the works. They are too heavily dependent on aerodynamic downforce.'

His view was energetically supported by Head, who complained that the new rules, which have been vigorously endorsed by FIA President Max Mosley, have produced 'a dominance of aerodynamics over tyres [performance].' He added, 'Imagine being a tyre supplier and effectively being told, "Go away and make some lousy tyres for these cars."'

Head explained that CART Champion Alex Zanardi was struggling this year in F1 at least in part because of the new four-groove front tyres. 'Alex is a pushy driver who likes to chisel away at his lap times throughout a race,' he said. 'But he has found our current F1 car to be so on edge the whole time – entering a corner and driving through it – that he has had to change his driving style quite a lot.

'He is very frustrated he cannot be more aggressive with the car. This is explained by the dominance of aerodynamics over the grip from the tyre, and by the cars having been made narrower. I believe one solution would be to trim back the aerodynamics.'

as we now head for circuits which should suit our car better.'

In fourth place, Eddie Irvine admitted that the race had been rather dull, blaming too much testing at Barcelona. 'I don't think we should have done so much testing at the same track the week before a Grand Prix, as it always seems to make for a dull race,' he said. 'I wish I had my stereo in the car to keep me amused.'

Behind Irvine, Ralf Schumacher produced an encouraging fifth place for Williams, the German driver climbing up from tenth on the grid. 'Ralf drove a fantastic race,' said Patrick Head, 'and fifth place is certainly as good as we can expect at the moment if two McLarens and two Ferraris finish the race.

'It is now up to us to try and improve the car and give him a better chance to be closer to the front of the grid in qualifying. In the closing laps, we thought we had a problem in the cooling system of Ralf's car, so we asked him to slow down just to be certain of his fifth place.'

Completing the top six was Jarno Trulli's Prost-Peugeot, while Damon Hill slipped his Jordan ahead of Rubens Barrichello's Stewart-Ford with just two laps to run to take seventh at the chequered flag.

'The best part of the race was going round the outside of Rubens!' said Hill. 'I had been trying to catch up with him in the middle part of the race, but I just missed out making up enough time to get him in the pit stops, so it was satisfying to overtake him.

'I could see all the blue flags at the end of the race, and my race engineer was very good at telling me what was going on. I just had to find the place where I would lose the least amount of time. The race itself was not as difficult as I had expected, but there was not enough advantage in running on hard tyres.'

For his part, Barrichello was acutely disappointed – not only because he had lost seventh place, but also because he believed he should have finished sixth, ahead of Trulli.

'I had one real chance to make sixth towards the end, but overall the performance of the car during the whole weekend did not measure up to what we had achieved in the previous races,' he said. 'With the second set of tyres, I was able to push and regain the time I lost with the backmarkers and blue flags. But with the third set, the car became very unstable.'

Barrichello's annoyance was compounded when, subsequently, his

Stewart SF3 was disqualified after it was found that the metal ballast fixed beneath the centre of the car was too low and was in danger of coming loose.

Into ninth place went Mika Salo's BAR after a solid run with the Benettons of Giancarlo Fisichella and Alexander Wurz. The latter pair struggled home in the next two places.

'I am frustrated with this result and with the car's performance altogether,' said Fisichella. 'The testing we did here last week didn't help us as much as it should have for this race, and we have had many difficulties since Friday.'

Both Benetton drivers had run on soft tyres and adopted a three-stop strategy in an effort to vault up from their lowly grid positions. However, lack of grip during the race thwarted their ambitions.

For its part, the McLaren team left Barcelona in a mood of guarded optimism. On the one hand, Häkkinen and Coulthard were delighted to be back as front-runners again; on the other, there was no way that the Ferrari threat could be discounted as the team faced the next few races in the calendar. Ferrari may have been down at Barcelona, but it could hardly have been counted out.

SPANISH GRAND PRIX

Clockwise from top left:
Blue mood: Olivier Panis under increasing pressure to perform at Prost.
Paul-Henri Cahier

Irvine's Ferrari at speed past the pits.
Michael Roberts

Reflections on a transporter: Ferrari versus McLaren-Mercedes.
Michael Roberts

Giancarlo Fisichella checks the qualifying times.
Paul-Henri Cahier

www.pedrodelarosa.com: de la Rosa keeps pace with technology.
Paul-Henri Cahier

Right: Jean Alesi kitted up and ready to go out in his Sauber.
Paul-Henri Cahier

REPSOL t minus

www.pedrodelarosa.com

GRAN PREMIO MARLBORO DE ESPAÑA

28–30 MAY 1999
CATALUNYA

Race distance: 65 laps, 190.882 miles/307.196 km

Race weather: Dry, hot and sunny

ROUND 5

CATALUNYA Circuit – Barcelona

Campsa
Repsol
Würth
Elf
La Caixa

CIRCUIT LENGTH: 2.938 miles/4.728 km

Pos.	Driver	Nat.	No.	Entrant	Car/Engine	Laps	Time/Retirement	Speed (mph/km/h)
1	Mika Häkkinen	SF	1	West McLaren Mercedes	McLaren MP4/14-Mercedes F0110H V10	65	1h 34m 13.665s	121.544/195.608
2	David Coulthard	GB	2	West McLaren Mercedes	McLaren MP4/14-Mercedes F0110H V10	65	1h 34m 19.903s	121.411/195.393
3	Michael Schumacher	D	3	Scuderia Ferrari Marlboro	Ferrari F399 048 V10	65	1h 34m 24.510s	121.313/195.234
4	Eddie Irvine	GB	4	Scuderia Ferrari Marlboro	Ferrari F399 048 V10	65	1h 34m 43.847s	120.899/194.569
5	Ralf Schumacher	D	6	Winfield Williams	Williams FW21-Supertec FB01	65	1h 35m 40.873s	119.699/192.637
6	Jarno Trulli	I	19	Gauloises Prost Peugeot	Prost AP02-Peugeot A18 V10	64		
7	Damon Hill	GB	7	Benson & Hedges Jordan	Jordan 199-Mugen Honda MF301/HD V10	64		
DQ	Rubens Barrichello	BR	16	Stewart Ford	Stewart SF3-Ford CR-1 V10	64	Illegal undertray	
8	Mika Salo	SF	23	British American Racing	BAR 01-Supertec FB01 V10	64		
9	Giancarlo Fisichella	I	9	Mild Seven Benetton Playlife	Benetton B199-Playlife V10	64		
10	Alexander Wurz	A	10	Mild Seven Benetton Playlife	Benetton B199-Playlife V10	64		
11	Pedro de la Rosa	ESP	14	Arrows	Arrows A20 V10	63		
12	Toranosuke Takagi	J	15	Arrows	Arrows A20 V10	62		
	Luca Badoer	I	20	Fondmetal Minardi Ford	Minardi M01-Ford Zetec-R V10	50	Spun off	
	Jacques Villeneuve	CDN	22	British American Racing	BAR 01-Supertec FB01 V10	40	Transmission	
	Pedro Diniz	BR	12	Red Bull Sauber Petronas	Sauber C17-Petronas SPE03A V10	40	Gearbox	
	Johnny Herbert	GB	17	Stewart Ford	Stewart SF3-Ford CR-1 V10	40	Transmission	
	Heinz-Harald Frentzen	D	8	Benson & Hedges Jordan	Jordan 199-Mugen Honda MF301/HD V10	35	Differential	
	Jean Alesi	F	11	Red Bull Sauber Petronas	Sauber C17-Petronas SPE03A V10	27	Transmission	
	Alex Zanardi	I	5	Winfield Williams	Williams FW21-Supertec FB01 V10	24	Transmission	
	Olivier Panis	F	18	Gauloises Prost Peugeot	Prost AP02-Peugeot A18 V10	24	Gearbox hydraulics	
	Marc Gene	ESP	21	Fondmetal Minardi Ford	Minardi M01-Ford Zetec-R V10	0	Gearbox	

Fastest lap: M. Schumacher, on lap 29, 1m 24.982s, 124.452 mph/200.287 km/h.

Previous lap record: Giancarlo Fisichella (F1 Jordan 197-Peugeot V10), 1m 22.242s, 128.919 mph/207.475 km/h (1997).

Grid order	1	2	3	4	5	6	7	8	9	10	11	12	13	14	15	16	17	18	19	20	21	22	23	24	25	26	27	28	29	30	31	32	33	34	35	36	37	38	39	40	41	42	43	44	45	46	47	48	49
1 HÄKKINEN	1	1	1	1	1	1	1	1	1	1	1	1	1	1	1	1	1	1	1	1	1	1	1	2	2	2	1	1	1	1	1	1	1	1	1	1	1	1	1	1	1	1	1	1	2	1	1	1	1
4 IRVINE	2	2	2	2	2	2	2	2	2	2	2	2	2	2	2	2	2	2	2	2	2	2	2	1	1	1	2	2	2	2	2	2	2	2	2	2	2	2	2	2	2	2	1	2	2	2	2	2	
2 COULTHARD	22	22	22	22	22	22	22	22	22	22	22	22	22	22	22	22	22	22	22	22	22	22	22	11	11		3	3	3	3	3	3	3	3	3	3	3	3	3	3	3	3	3	3	3	3	3	3	3
3 M. SCHUMACHER	3	3	3	3	3	3	3	3	3	3	3	3	3	3	3	3	3	3	3	3	3	3	3	6	6	6	4	4	4	4	4	4	4	4	4	4	4	4	4	4	4	4	4	4	4	4	4	4	4
11 ALESI	4	4	4	4	4	4	4	4	4	4	4	4	4	4	4	4	4	4	4	4	4	11	11	8	3	4	22	22	22	22	22	22	22	22	22	22	22	22	19	6	6	6	7	7	7	7	7		
22 VILLENEUVE	19	19	19	19	19	19	19	19	19	19	19	19	19	19	19	19	19	19	19	19	19	19	6	3	4	22	19	19	19	19	19	19	19	19	19	19	19	19	6	19	16	7	6	6	6	6	6		
16 BARRICHELLO	11	11	11	11	11	11	11	11	11	11	11	11	11	11	11	11	11	11	11	11	11	6	8	4	8	12	6	6	6	6	6	6	6	6	6	6	6	16	16	7	19	19	19	19	19	1			
8 FRENTZEN	6	6	6	6	6	6	6	6	6	6	6	6	6	6	6	6	6	6	6	6	6	4	22	22	19	8	8	8	8	8	8	16	16	16	16	7	7	19	16	16	16	16	1						
19 TRULLI	8	8	8	8	8	8	8	8	8	8	8	8	8	8	8	8	8	8	8	8	8	8	16	16	12	11	16	16	16	16	16	12	12	12	12	23	23	23	23	23	23	23	2						
6 R. SCHUMACHER	16	16	16	16	16	16	16	16	16	16	16	16	16	16	16	16	16	16	16	16	4	12	12	16	8	12	12	12	12	12	12	7	7	7	7	9	9	9	9	9	9	10							
7 HILL	17	17	17	17	17	17	17	17	17	17	17	17	17	17	17	12	12	12	12	12	7	7	19	16	7	7	7	7	7	7	17	17	17	17	10	10	10	10	10	10	9	1							
12 DINIZ	12	12	12	12	12	12	12	12	12	12	12	12	12	12	12	7	7	7	7	7	19	7	7	17	17	17	17	17	17	23	23	23	23	14	14	14	14	14	14	14	1								
9 FISICHELLA	7	7	7	7	7	7	7	7	7	7	7	7	7	7	7	17	5	5	5	5	5	17	17	9	9	9	9	9	9	9	9	9	9	9	15	15	15	15	15	15	15	1							
17 HERBERT	9	9	9	9	9	9	9	9	9	9	9	9	9	9	9	9	17	17	9	9	9	23	23	23	23	23	23	9	10	10	10	10	10	20	20	20	20	20	20	20	2								
18 PANIS	5	5	5	5	5	5	5	5	5	5	5	5	5	5	9	9	9	23	23	23	9	9	9	23	23	10	10	10	10	10	10	10	14	14	14	14													
23 SALO	10	10	10	23	23	23	23	23	23	23	23	23	23	23	23	23	10	17	17	23	23	10	10	10	14	14	14	14	14	14	15	15	15	15															
5 ZANARDI	23	23	23	10	10	10	10	10	10	10	10	10	10	10	10	17	15	10	10	10	10	14	14	15	15	15	15	15	15	20	20	20	20																
10 WURZ	14	14	14	14	14	14	14	14	14	14	14	14	14	15	15	10	15	15	14	14	15	15	15	15	15	20	20	20																					
14 DE LA ROSA	15	15	15	15	15	15	15	15	15	15	15	15	15	14	14	14	14	14	15	20	20	20																											
15 TAKAGI	20	20	20	20	20	20	20	20	20	20	20	20	20	20	20	20	14	20	20	20	20																												
21 GENE	18	18	18	18	18	18	18	18	18	18	18	18	18	18	18	18	18	18																															
20 BADOER																																																	

Pit stop

One lap behind leader

STARTING GRID

1 HÄKKINEN McLaren		4 IRVINE Ferrari
2 COULTHARD McLaren		3 M. SCHUMACHER Ferrari
11 ALESI Sauber		22 VILLENEUVE BAR
16 BARRICHELLO Stewart		8 FRENTZEN Jordan
19 TRULLI Prost		6 R. SCHUMACHER Williams
7 HILL Jordan		12 DINIZ Sauber
9 FISICHELLA Benetton		17 HERBERT Stewart
18 PANIS Prost		23 SALO BAR
5 ZANARDI Williams		10 WURZ Benetton
14 DE LA ROSA Arrows		15 TAKAGI Arrows
21 GENE Minardi		20 BADOER Minardi

Lap chart numbers:
53 54 55 56 57 58 59 60 61 62 63 64 65

```
1  1  1  1  1  1  1  1  1  1  1  1  1   1
2  2  2  2  2  2  2  2  2  2  2  2  2   2
3  3  3  3  3  3  3  3  3  3  3  3  3   3
4  4  4  4  4  4  4  4  4  4  4  4  4   4
6  6  6  6  6  6  6  6  6  6  6  6  6   5
19 19 19 19 19 19 19 19 19 19 19 19 19  6
16 16 16 16 16 16 16 16 16 16 17 7  7
7  7  7  7  7  7  7  7  7  7  16 16
23 23 23 23 23 23 23 23 23 23 23 23
9  9  9  9  9  9  9  9  9  9  9  9
10 10 10 10 10 10 10 10 10 10 10 10
14 14 14 14 14 14 14 14 14 14 14 14
15 15 15 15 15 15 15 15 15
```

TIME SHEETS

QUALIFYING

Weather: Dry, hot and sunny

Pos.	Driver	Car	Laps	Time
1	Mika Häkkinen	McLaren-Mercedes	11	1m 22.088s
2	Eddie Irvine	Ferrari	12	1m 22.219s
3	David Coulthard	McLaren-Mercedes	11	1m 22.244s
4	Michael Schumacher	Ferrari	11	1m 22.277s
5	Jean Alesi	Sauber-Petronas	9	1m 22.388s
6	Jacques Villeneuve	BAR-Supertec	11	1m 22.703s
7	Rubens Barrichello	Stewart-Ford	11	1m 22.920s
8	Heinz-Harald Frentzen	Jordan-Mugen Honda	11	1m 22.938s
9	Jarno Trulli	Prost-Peugeot	12	1m 23.194s
10	Ralf Schumacher	Williams-Supertec	12	1m 23.303s
11	Damon Hill	Jordan-Mugen Honda	12	1m 23.317s
12	Pedro Diniz	Sauber-Petronas	12	1m 23.331s
13	Giancarlo Fisichella	Benetton-Playlife	12	1m 23.333s
14	Johnny Herbert	Stewart-Ford	11	1m 23.505s
15	Olivier Panis	Prost-Peugeot	12	1m 23.559s
16	Mika Salo*	BAR-Supertec	12	1m 23.683s
17	Alex Zanardi	Williams-Supertec	12	1m 23.703s
18	Alexander Wurz	Benetton-Playlife	11	1m 23.824s
19	Pedro de la Rosa	Arrows	12	1m 24.619s
20	Toranosuke Takagi	Arrows	11	1m 25.280s
21	Marc Gene	Minardi-Ford	11	1m 25.672s
22	Luca Badoer	Minardi-Ford	12	1m 25.833s

* fastest lap disallowed

FRIDAY FREE PRACTICE

Weather: Dry, hot and sunny

Pos.	Driver	Laps	Time
1	Eddie Irvine	25	1m 23.577s
2	Heinz-Harald Frentzen	27	1m 23.790s
3	Michael Schumacher	36	1m 23.895s
4	Mika Häkkinen	22	1m 23.982s
5	Alex Zanardi	41	1m 24.312s
6	Damon Hill	30	1m 24.318s
7	David Coulthard	32	1m 24.339s
8	Rubens Barrichello	26	1m 24.347s
9	Jacques Villeneuve	34	1m 24.458s
10	Ralf Schumacher	29	1m 24.559s
11	Jean Alesi	15	1m 24.571s
12	Pedro Diniz	22	1m 24.823s
13	Jarno Trulli	38	1m 24.957s
14	Olivier Panis	40	1m 25.140s
15	Giancarlo Fisichella	32	1m 25.448s
16	Johnny Herbert	27	1m 25.667s
17	Alexander Wurz	32	1m 25.901s
18	Mika Salo	12	1m 25.990s
19	Pedro de la Rosa	36	1m 26.595s
20	Toranosuke Takagi	42	1m 27.296s
21	Luca Badoer	25	1m 27.314s
22	Marc Gene	27	1m 27.506s

SATURDAY FREE PRACTICE

Weather: Dry, hot and sunny

Pos.	Driver	Laps	Time
1	David Coulthard	19	1m 22.138s
2	Michael Schumacher	26	1m 22.212s
3	Mika Häkkinen	24	1m 22.257s
4	Heinz-Harald Frentzen	30	1m 22.836s
5	Jean Alesi	26	1m 22.917s
6	Jacques Villeneuve	15	1m 23.074s
7	Rubens Barrichello	27	1m 23.106s
8	Damon Hill	24	1m 23.125s
9	Johnny Herbert	29	1m 23.136s
10	Mika Salo	22	1m 23.196s
11	Ralf Schumacher	27	1m 23.208s
12	Pedro Diniz	33	1m 23.272s
13	Giancarlo Fisichella	26	1m 23.346s
14	Jarno Trulli	30	1m 23.493s
15	Alex Zanardi	30	1m 23.574s
16	Alexander Wurz	26	1m 23.633s
17	Eddie Irvine	17	1m 23.839s
18	Olivier Panis	28	1m 23.911s
19	Pedro de la Rosa	31	1m 25.042s
20	Marc Gene	29	1m 25.663s
21	Toranosuke Takagi	22	1m 25.948s
22	Luca Badoer	18	1m 26.535s

WARM-UP

Weather: Dry, hot and sunny

Pos.	Driver	Laps	Time
1	Mika Häkkinen	13	1m 24.031s
2	David Coulthard	14	1m 24.328s
3	Michael Schumacher	13	1m 24.431s
4	Jean Alesi	9	1m 24.452s
5	Eddie Irvine	13	1m 24.745s
6	Damon Hill	15	1m 24.784s
7	Jarno Trulli	16	1m 24.816s
8	Heinz-Harald Frentzen	17	1m 24.897s
9	Ralf Schumacher	16	1m 24.958s
10	Pedro Diniz	16	1m 25.057s
11	Jacques Villeneuve	9	1m 25.297s
12	Johnny Herbert	19	1m 25.479s
13	Olivier Panis	14	1m 25.594s
14	Giancarlo Fisichella	13	1m 25.734s
15	Rubens Barrichello	14	1m 25.797s
16	Alex Zanardi	17	1m 25.870s
17	Pedro de la Rosa	11	1m 25.955s
18	Alexander Wurz	13	1m 26.099s
19	Mika Salo	7	1m 26.228s
20	Marc Gene	11	1m 26.963s
21	Luca Badoer	15	1m 27.597s
22	Toranosuke Takagi	10	1m 27.836s

RACE FASTEST LAPS

Weather: Dry, hot and sunny

Driver	Time	Lap
Michael Schumacher	1m 24.982s	29
Mika Häkkinen	1m 25.209s	7
Eddie Irvine	1m 25.343s	40
David Coulthard	1m 25.487s	8
Rubens Barrichello	1m 26.006s	40
Pedro Diniz	1m 26.315s	20
Damon Hill	1m 26.348s	47
Jarno Trulli	1m 26.505s	25
Ralf Schumacher	1m 26.520s	35
Jean Alesi	1m 26.542s	24
Jacques Villeneuve	1m 26.675s	9
Heinz-Harald Frentzen	1m 26.894s	35
Mika Salo	1m 27.004s	58
Alexander Wurz	1m 27.029s	35
Giancarlo Fisichella	1m 27.098s	59
Olivier Panis	1m 27.175s	20
Alex Zanardi	1m 27.248s	19
Pedro de la Rosa	1m 27.409s	33
Johnny Herbert	1m 27.442s	17
Toranosuke Takagi	1m 29.184s	7
Luca Badoer	1m 29.632s	39

CHASSIS LOG BOOK

1	Häkkinen	McLaren MP4/14/5
2	Coulthard	McLaren MP4/14/4
	spare	McLaren MP4/14/2
3	M. Schumacher	Ferrari F399/194
4	Irvine	Ferrari F399/191
	spare	Ferrari F399/192
5	Zanardi	Williams FW21/5
6	R. Schumacher	Williams FW21/4
	spare	Williams FW21/2
7	Hill	Jordan 199/4
8	Frentzen	Jordan 199/6
	spare	Jordan 199/3
9	Fisichella	Benetton B199/6
10	Wurz	Benetton B199/5
	spare	Benetton B199/1
11	Alesi	Sauber C18/5
12	Diniz	Sauber C18/6
	spare	Sauber C18/4
14	de la Rosa	Arrows A20/4
15	Takagi	Arrows A20/2
	spare	Arrows A20/5
16	Barrichello	Stewart SF3/4
17	Herbert	Stewart SF3/5
	spare	Stewart SF3/6
18	Panis	Prost AP02/5
19	Trulli	Prost AP02/6
	spare	Prost AP02/3
20	Badoer	Minardi M01/1
21	Gene	Minardi M01/4
	spare	Minardi M01/3
22	Villeneuve	BAR 01/5
23	Salo	BAR 01/6
	spare	BAR 01/3

POINTS TABLES

DRIVERS

1	Michael Schumacher	30
2	Mika Häkkinen	24
3	Eddie Irvine	21
4	Heinz-Harald Frentzen	13
5	David Coulthard	12
6	Ralf Schumacher	9
7	Giancarlo Fisichella	7
8	Rubens Barrichello	6
9	Damon Hill	3
10 =	Pedro de la Rosa	1
10 =	Olivier Panis	1
10 =	Jean Alesi	1
10 =	Alexander Wurz	1
10 =	Jarno Trulli	1

CONSTRUCTORS

1	Ferrari	51
2	McLaren	36
3	Jordan	16
4	Williams	9
5	Benetton	8
6	Stewart	6
7	Prost	2
8 =	Arrows	1
8 =	Sauber	1

CANADIAN

grand prix

HÄKKINEN

FISICHELLA

IRVINE

R. SCHUMACHER

HERBERT

DINIZ

Left: On top of the world, Mika. Häkkinen celebrates as he takes the lead in the championship for the first time during the season.

MIKA Häkkinen took the lead in the drivers' championship for the first time in the 1999 season by winning the Canadian Grand Prix, on a day when Michael Schumacher seemed, marginally, to have the upper hand only to crash spectacularly while running ahead of the Finn. That left Mika to pick a cautious and well-judged path through the misfortunes that befell most of his rivals at the front of the pack to post his third win of the season in fine style.

In the battle for second place, Heinz-Harald Frentzen appeared to be on course to gain the honour, but his Jordan-Mugen Honda crashed heavily on lap 66 after a brake disc exploded. That provided the capacity crowd with the remarkable spectacle of a World Championship Grand Prix finishing with the safety car leading the field around the final lap at much reduced speed.

Frentzen was taken to hospital with concussion, held overnight as a precaution and then released to fly back to Europe to recuperate. Another couple of weeks would pass before it was discovered that he had damaged a knee in the accident – but, by then, the German driver would have emerged victorious from the French Grand Prix at Magny-Cours.

Heinz-Harald's late retirement in Montreal left Giancarlo Fisichella's Benetton B199 to finish second – as it had done the previous year – ahead of Eddie Irvine's Ferrari F399, Ralf Schumacher's Williams FW21 and the Stewart-Ford of Johnny Herbert. The number of incidents reignited the simmering controversy over the poor grip developed by the current grooved tyres and the manner in which they aggravate the aerodynamic instability of the narrow-track cars when running in close company.

After qualifying second on the grid, World Champion Häkkinen was content to run second from the start until he was presented with an unexpected bonus when Michael Schumacher, who had led from pole position, made a rare error and smashed into a concrete retaining wall. Häkkinen's win meant that, with six of the season's 16 races having been run, he led the title chase with 34 points to Schumacher's 30. However, the race brought no luck for his McLaren-Mercedes team-mate, David Coulthard, who finished seventh after being docked a 10s stop-go penalty for mistakenly overtaking the safety car on the circuit.

At the start, Schumacher had chopped his Ferrari hard across the nose of Häkkinen's McLaren in a bid to dis-

MONTREAL QUALIFYING

'They're some of the most uncomfortable looking racing cars I've ever seen,' said Le Mans veteran Derek Bell after watching F1 qualifying from the trackside. 'They seem to lack fluidity, and nobody seems to get into any flowing rhythm.'

Bell, attending a Grand Prix for the first time in more than two years, had put his finger on the problem. The sudden drop-off in adhesion from Bridgestone's soft-compound rubber continued to keep everyone on their toes, yet it was Michael Schumacher who coped with every slip and heart-stopping slide to nail his first pole of the season.

In so doing, the German ace broke Häkkinen's run of five straight poles since the start of the year. McLaren struggled from the outset, and the sight of the World Champion twice ploughing through a gravel trap and wiping off his rear wing after a pirouette during Saturday's practice left the silver cars looking distinctly ruffled.

By the same token, Coulthard revelled in the characteristic of this track, which played to the strongest card in his driving deck, namely his uncanny precision and judgement when it comes to braking from very high speed. Häkkinen is better at slowing for medium-speed turns, so on this occasion it seemed as though the Scot would be carrying the McLaren-Merc challenge to the Maranello camp.

In the event, it was Mika who joined Schumacher on the front row, after David's edge slipped away unaccountably during qualifying. The Ferraris had a definite advantage, having harnessed the latest version of the type 048B engine for Saturday's practice and qualifying. This offered a 6 kg weight saving, a slightly lower installation and an estimated 16 bhp extra on tap. But in reality, it was still too close to call at the sharp end of the action.

'After my first run, I was not happy with the handling and came in to have a bodywork securing stay repaired,' said Schumacher. 'Then I went back to the original set-up and then encountered a series of yellow flags.' Eddie Irvine qualified third, but reckoned he could have been quicker had it not been for the customary flurry of yellow flags.

Häkkinen and Coulthard qualified second and fourth. 'I'm very pleased indeed,' said Mika. 'I was not able to go fast this morning, but the car was much better this afternoon. It was a pity I had too much traffic on my last run. The car is generally extremely difficult to drive in low-downforce trim.'

Coulthard added, 'I am confident in our race set-up, but I was slower than I had been this morning when I was running a heavier fuel load. I am a little confused as to what caused that drop-off in performance.'

In the Stewart-Ford camp, Rubens Barrichello was very satisfied at having qualified his Stewart-Ford fifth fastest, but Johnny Herbert was puzzled as to precisely why he could not do better than an eventual tenth. 'I was initially close behind Rubens, but then dropped away,' he mused. 'It was very disappointing.'

Heinz-Harald Frentzen qualified sixth, a good effort considering the Jordan team had to change an engine in his car after the morning session. He also had a close call when he almost tailgated Diniz's Sauber on the long straight back towards the pits. By contrast, a dejected Damon Hill wound up 14th.

'I started in my race car, then had an engine problem,' he said. 'I switched to the spare, but the brakes felt different and I didn't feel fully confident in it.'

Giancarlo Fisichella's Benetton B199 was seventh fastest, despite the fact that he lost control and glanced a barrier, slightly injuring a knee. Alexander Wurz set 11th-fastest time, again being frustrated by yellow flags.

Jean Alesi's Sauber C18 ended up eighth fastest, only to clip a kerb, damaging the undertray and causing him to stop on the circuit. Jarno Trulli was ninth, ahead of Herbert, while Alex Zanardi at least managed to boost his self confidence by narrowly out-qualifying his Williams team-mate, Ralf Schumacher.

'Overall, I can't say that I am totally depressed with the performance,' said Zanardi. 'I am still not where I wanted to be, but today the car at least ran reliably, which is what it is supposed to do.'

In the British American camp, there was a mood of deep frustration, Jacques Villeneuve having struggled to line up 16th in front of his home crowd, one place ahead of his returning team-mate Ricardo Zonta.

'Today didn't go well for us,' said Jacques grimly. 'We didn't have any mechanical problems, we just didn't get it right. We will have to take some risks in the warm-up to see if we can improve things for the race.'

abuse the Finn of any notion of grabbing an immediate lead. The move was not illegal, just uncompromising and rather aggressive.

Häkkinen held second place from Irvine, while Fisichella nosed ahead of Coulthard. Further back, by an amaz-

ing coincidence, the first corner at Montreal would prove the undoing of the same two competitors for the second straight Canadian GP – Jarno Trulli's Prost collided with Jean Alesi's Sauber, eliminating both competitors from the race.

This time, the Italian spun across the inside of the corner, tagging Rubens Barrichello's Stewart SF3 before slamming into the hapless Alesi. The two principal victims went out on the spot, while Barrichello pitted to have damaged bodywork patched up, resuming one lap down.

'I was braking hard to avoid Coulthard,' said Rubens, 'when I was hit by Trulli. It was a pretty big impact; it even took a piece out of my helmet. I think it was a dangerous move at that specific part of the circuit.'

Further around the opening lap, Alexander Wurz marked the second anniversary of his F1 debut by pulling off with a broken driveshaft. 'I didn't collide with anyone, it just failed,' he said. 'It was really frustrating, as I had pulled up to eighth from 11th after the start.'

Rather than red-flag the race, the organisers deployed the safety car at the end of the opening lap. It was withdrawn the next time around, yet hardly had Schumacher leaped away into the lead than it was out again on lap four, after Ricardo Zonta had become the first of several celebrated names to slam into the wall opposite the pits as he accelerated out of the fast, final ess-bend.

On lap seven, the safety car was withdrawn again and Schumacher accelerated into an immediate 14s lead ahead of Häkkinen, Irvine, Coulthard, Fisichella – the Scot had nipped ahead of the Benetton mid-way around the first lap – Frentzen, Johnny Herbert and Ralf Schumacher.

With a clear track ahead, Schumacher really piled on the pressure, but Häkkinen was virtually a match for the Ferrari team leader. Having completed 12 laps, Schumacher had eased open a 2.1s advantage over his main rival, but Irvine was already 5.5s down in third place and working hard to keep Coulthard under control.

On lap 15, Damon Hill became the second casualty of the tricky final corner, pasting his Jordan 199 into the scenery with a brisk impact. 'I made a mistake,' he shrugged candidly. 'I lost control and the car hit the wall. The track was slippery, but it was my mistake to have crashed.'

Barrichello pulled in to retire from 18th and last place on the same lap. 'Because of the accident, the car was completely out of shape,' he reported. 'There was a big problem with the steering column because the car was pulling to the left. I tried to carry on, but the car was undrivable.'

On lap 24, the upbeat Herbert, in the other Stewart, made the first of two re-

Hill to retire from racing

ONLY three days after crashing into the wall at Montreal, Damon Hill announced that he would be retiring from Grand Prix racing at the end of the year. 'After much reflection, I have decided not to continue racing in Formula 1 after the end of the 1999 season,' he said. 'Despite being a late starter to Formula 1, at the age of 32, I am very proud of my record. F1 has afforded me many incredible opportunities, and I will cherish some fantastic memories. I have fulfilled my ambitions and consider myself very fortunate to have done so.'

The decision reflected Hill's acute dislike of the current breed of F1 car, with its distinct lack of grip and sensitivity to side winds. It had also been aggravated by the speed of his new Jordan team-mate, Heinz-Harald Frentzen, ironically the man who replaced him in the Williams team when he was dropped at the end of his 1996 World Championship season.

Eddie Jordan immediately commented, 'This is a sad, but typically brave and honest decision by one of Britain's great sporting heroes. Damon was a great World Champion and a wonderful ambassador for motor sport worldwide. His results will always show he was one of the sport's great winners.'

Eddie Irvine, who memorably described Hill as a 'sad old man' after accusing the Jordan driver of balking him during last year's British Grand Prix, also complimented his old rival. 'Well, he's had a good run and been World Champion,' he said. 'All I can say is I hope he enjoys his retirement and wish him good luck.'

However, unbeknown to everyone during the week after the Canadian GP, the Damon Hill retirement saga still had a few unexpected twists to deliver.

Ford buys Stewart Grand Prix

FORD pointed the way for car manufacturers to become involved with top Grand Prix teams by its not altogether surprising announcement at Montreal that it was buying the Stewart team for an estimated £60 million. The deal was announced on the eve of Jackie Stewart's 60th birthday and was widely hailed as the crowning achievement of the Scot's 35-year association with the global car giant.

'Our goal at Ford is to race to win,' said Neil Ressler, Ford's chief technical officer and Vice President for Research and Vehicle Technology, who is also a director of Stewart Grand Prix. 'By buying our own team, and applying the company's comprehensive technical resources to it, I believe the Stewart-Ford team will become increasingly more successful. In addition, F1 provides hands-on engineering experience for many of our youngest and most talented engineers.'

As if to emphasise the increased technical support applied to Ford's F1 project, a Stewart SF3 had recently been taken to the Research and Vehicle Technology Centre in Detroit, where a detailed assessment of its chassis strength, rigidity, bump control and aerodynamic efficiency had been carried out. Such highly sophisticated tests will benefit the design of the team's car for the 2000 season.

Ford's commercial influence was also expected to have a positive effect on the team's ability to attract additional sponsorship from companies that do business with the car maker. This is particularly important because Ford is believed to have taken a policy decision against seeking sponsorship from a tobacco company, although there has been no official confirmation of this stance.

'Ford's increased commitment to Formula 1 is great news for the team,' said Jackie Stewart. 'To be competitive in F1 these days, and to win the great benefits available, teams need strong financial and technical support. Ford can offer that.'

fuelling stops, dropping from seventh to tenth, as Schumacher continued to edge away from Häkkinen at the head of the field. The Ferrari team leader's advantage was 3.9s on lap 26, then 4.2s next time around, and 4.6s on lap 28.

Then came disaster for Maranello. Michael came through the left-hand exit of the final ess-bend, approaching the end of lap 30, and his Ferrari F399 seemed to drift into an understeering slide. There wasn't sufficient space for

him to correct it and he slammed into the wall – hard.

Schumacher released his belts, climbed out and stalked away with a face like thunder. He had had a lucky escape from physical injury. However, a crane had hardly winched the wrecked Ferrari to safety than local hero Jacques Villeneuve became the third former World Champion to come unstuck at the same spot, lurching almost head-on into the unyielding concrete at the wheel of his BAR 01.

At least Michael was refreshingly open in taking complete responsibility for the unfortunate episode. 'I lost control of the car because I went off the racing line, got on to the dirt and ended up in the wall,' he said. 'This was clearly my mistake. I apologise to the team, who again did a great job this weekend. It was a shame because the car was working perfectly. I usually make one mistake a year; I hope that this incident was the last for the season!'

Villeneuve's similar shunt eliminated the second British American contender from a promising eighth place. The safety car was deployed while the debris was cleared up, and many runners took the opportunity to make their refuelling stops.

Fisichella, Frentzen, Diniz, Ralf Schumacher and Herbert all came in – in fourth to ninth places respectively – on lap 36 and resumed in the same order. Häkkinen and Irvine, now first and third, came in next time, allowing

Coulthard through into first place, but he stopped at the end of lap 38.

On resuming the race, Coulthard misread the flashing blue/green lights at the end of the pit lane, which indicated that the safety car and its accompanying 'train' had come into view on the start/finish straight. This obliged him to wait in the pits, but the Scot mistakenly rejoined the queue in company with Irvine's Ferrari.

Later, David would collect the mandatory 10s stop–go penalty for this misdemeanour. Before that could be imposed, however, he and Irvine touched at the first corner going into lap 41, while battling for third place. They spun back to tenth and eighth respectively.

'I had managed to get half a car length ahead of Eddie going into that corner,' said Coulthard later, 'so I was a bit surprised when he went round the outside and turned into me. We touched as I didn't have anywhere to go. I guess in reality it was really a 50–50 situation. After that, I came in for a quick wheel check [lap 41], as I must have bent the suspension a bit, as I was crabbing down the straight.'

While Coulthard faded – being obliged to come in for his stop–go penalty at the end of lap 49 – Irvine picked up the pace, revelling in the feel of his Ferrari F399 on this occasion. On lap 43, he moved ahead of Alex Zanardi's Williams for seventh – the Italian would soon incur a penalty for the same rule infringement as Coulthard –

then was up to sixth, ahead of Diniz in the remaining Sauber-Petronas, on lap 46.

On lap 53, Irvine elbowed his way through to fifth, ahead of Herbert, who was a little bit wary about his tactics when the Ferrari driver forced his way in front going into the final ess-bend, both cars effectively straight-lining the corner across the grass as they had braked so late.

'I kept him at bay for a few laps, but when we came to the chicane, I

CANADIAN GRAND PRIX

Main picture: Irvine tails Häkkinen with Coulthard and Fisichella behind. Meanwhile Trulli takes to the grass to eventually collide with Alesi and Barrichello.
Pamela Lauesen/FOSA

Below far left: Luca Badoer made it to the finish for once with the Minardi, but not quite in the points.
Peter Nygaard/GP Photo

Below centre left: Happy 60th birthday Jackie! Wife Helen, Johnny Herbert, Rubens Barrichello and Paul join in.
Brandon Malone/Action Images

Below: Coulthard tags the back of Irvine.
Steve Etherington/EPI

thought he was too far back to make a passing move,' Herbert said. 'When he [finally] went down the inside, he was going in too quickly to make the chicane. I had to steer away to avoid him and we both went through the grass. It was a good battle while it lasted. I was able to keep a gap between us in the slower corners on braking, but it's a shame I couldn't hold him off.'

Meanwhile, Häkkinen continued on his way, over 10s ahead of the opposition, while Frentzen hunted down Fisichella for second place. He managed to push ahead as they came up to finish lap 43, when Olivier Panis's Prost and Luca Badoer's Minardi wrong-footed the Benetton driver as he came up to lap the slower cars out of the final chicane.

Frentzen began to edge away confidently until his brake disc exploded and he slid into the barrier. With three laps remaining, the safety car was deployed yet again and that was the end of the story.

Eventually, Irvine came home a strong third behind Fisichella, while Ralf Schumacher was fourth, ahead of Herbert, Diniz and the slightly disappointed Coulthard. Marc Gene, Panis and Badoer were the only others still running at the chequered flag.

At the beginning of the afternoon, it seemed as though nothing would stand in the way of the expected battle between the Ferrari and McLaren teams. Then came Michael Schumacher's abrupt departure from the contest, after which the race began to unravel for almost everyone else in the pack. Apart from the unflustered and serene Mika Häkkinen, that is.

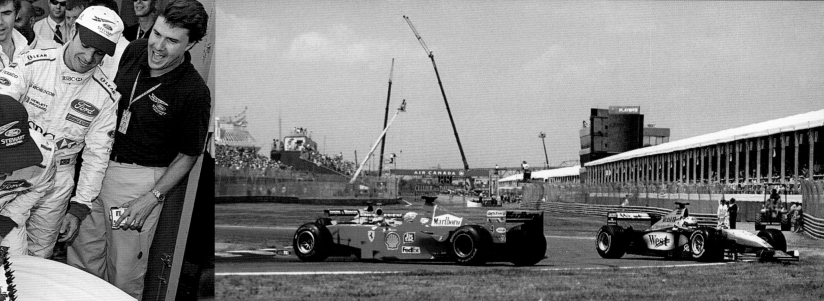

AIR CANADA
GRAND PRIX
DU CANADA
11–13 JUNE 1999
MONTREAL

Race distance: 69 laps, 189.548 miles/305.049 km

Race weather: Dry, very hot and sunny

ROUND 6

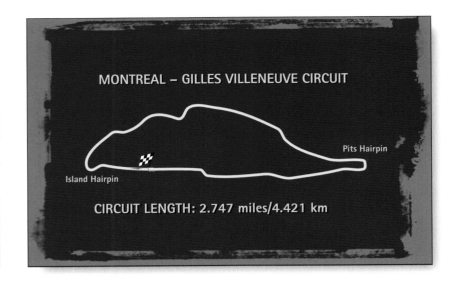

MONTREAL – GILLES VILLENEUVE CIRCUIT

Pits Hairpin

Island Hairpin

CIRCUIT LENGTH: 2.747 miles/4.421 km

Pos.	Driver	Nat.	No.	Entrant	Car/Engine	Laps	Time/Retirement	Speed (mph/km/h)
1	Mika Häkkinen	SF	1	West McLaren Mercedes	McLaren MP4/14-Mercedes F0110H V10	69	1h 41m 35.727s	111.943/180.155
2	Giancarlo Fisichella	I	9	Mild Seven Benetton Playlife	Benetton B199-Playlife V10	69	1h 41m 36.509s	111.929/180.132
3	Eddie Irvine	GB	4	Scuderia Ferrari Marlboro	Ferrari F399 V10	69	1h 41m 37.524s	111.910/180.102
4	Ralf Schumacher	D	6	Winfield Williams	Williams FW21-Supertec FB01 V10	69	1h 41m 38.119s	111.899/180.084
5	Johnny Herbert	GB	17	Stewart Ford	Stewart SF3-Ford CR-1 V10	69	1h 41m 38.532s	111.891/180.072
6	Pedro Diniz	BR	12	Red Bull Sauber Petronas	Sauber C17-Petronas SPE03A V10	69	1h 41m 39.438s	111.875/180.045
7	David Coulthard	GB	2	West McLaren Mercedes	McLaren MP4/14-Mercedes F0110H V10	69	1h 41m 40.731s	111.851/180.007
8	Marc Gene	ESP	21	Fondmetal Minardi Ford	Minardi M01-Ford Zetec-R V10	68		
9	Olivier Panis	F	18	Gauloises Prost Peugeot	Prost AP02-Peugeot A18 V10	68		
10	Luca Badoer	I	20	Fondmetal Minardi Ford	Minardi M01-Ford Zetec-R V10	67		
11	Heinz-Harald Frentzen	D	8	Benson & Hedges Jordan	Jordan 199-Mugen Honda MF301/HD V10	65	Accident/brakes	
	Alex Zanardi	I	5	Winfield Williams	Williams FW21-Supertec FB01 V10	50	Transmission	
	Toranosuke Takagi	J	15	Arrows	Arrows A20 V10	41	Transmission	
	Jacques Villeneuve	CDN	22	British American Racing	BAR 01-Supertec FB01 V10	34	Accident	
	Michael Schumacher	D	3	Scuderia Ferrari Malboro	Ferrari F399 V10	29	Accident	
	Pedro de la Rosa	ESP	14	Arrows	Arrows A20 V10	22	Transmission	
	Damon Hill	GB	7	Benson & Hedges Jordan	Jordan 199-Mugen Honda MF301/HD V10	14	Accident	
	Rubens Barrichello	BR	16	Stewart Ford	Stewart SF3-Ford CR-1 V10	14	Collision damage	
	Ricardo Zonta	BR	23	British American Racing	BAR 01-Supertec FB01 V10	2	Accident	
	Jean Alesi	F	11	Red Bull Sauber Petronas	Sauber C17-Petronas SPE03A V10	0	Collision with Trulli	
	Jarno Trulli	I	19	Gauloises Prost Peugeot	Prost AP02-Peugeot A18 V10	0	Collision with Alesi	
	Alexander Wurz	A	10	Mild Seven Benetton Playlife	Benetton B199-Playlife V10	0	Driveshaft	

Fastest lap: Irvine, on lap 62, 1m 20.382s, 123.031 mph/197.999 km/h.

Lap record: Michael Schumacher (F1 Ferrari F300 V10), 1m 19.379s, 124.586 mph/200.501 km/h (1998).

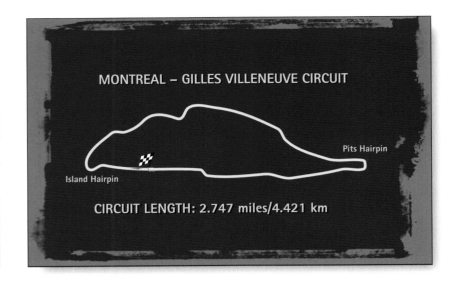

All results and data © FIA 1999

Grid order	1	2	3	4	5	6	7	8	9	10	11	12	13	14	15	16	17	18	19	20	21	22	23	24	25	26	27	28	29	30	31	32	33	34	35	36	37	38	39	40	41	42	43	44	45	46	47	48	49	50	51	52	53
3 M. SCHUMACHER	3	3	3	3	3	3	3	3	3	3	3	3	3	3	3	3	3	3	3	3	3	3	3	3	3	3	3	3	3	1	1	1	1	1	1	1	1	1	1	1	1	1	1	1	1	1	1	1	1	1	1	1	1
1 HÄKKINEN	1	1	1	1	1	1	1	1	1	1	1	1	1	1	1	1	1	1	1	1	1	1	1	1	1	1	1	1	1	4	4	4	4	4	2	4	4	9	8	8	8	8	8	8	8	8	8	8	8	8	8	8	8
4 IRVINE	4	4	4	4	4	4	4	4	4	4	4	4	4	4	4	4	4	4	4	4	4	4	4	4	4	4	4	4	4	2	2	2	2	4	4	2	8	8	9	9	9	9	9	9	9	9	9	9	9	9	9	9	
2 COULTHARD	9	9	2	2	2	2	2	2	2	2	2	2	2	2	2	2	2	2	2	2	2	2	2	2	2	2	2	2	2	9	9	9	9	9	9	9	9	9	6	6	6	6	6	6	6	6	6	6	6	6	6	6	
16 BARRICHELLO	2	2	9	9	9	9	9	9	9	9	9	9	9	9	9	9	9	9	9	9	9	9	9	9	9	9	9	9	9	8	8	8	8	8	8	8	8	8	17	17	17	17	17	17	17	17	17	17	17				
8 FRENTZEN	8	8	8	8	8	8	8	8	8	8	8	8	8	8	8	8	8	8	8	8	8	8	8	8	8	8	8	8	6	6	6	12	12	12	12	12	12	12	12	12	12	12	12	12	4	4	4	4	4	12			
9 FISICHELLA	17	17	17	17	17	17	17	17	17	17	17	17	17	17	17	17	17	17	17	17	17	6	6	6	6	6	6	12	12	6	6	6	6	6	6	6	5	5	4	4	4	12	12	12	12	12	12	12	12				
11 ALESI	5	5	6	6	6	6	6	6	6	6	6	6	6	6	6	6	6	6	6	6	6	12	12	12	12	12	22	22	22	22	22	17	17	17	17	17	4	4	5	5	5	2	5	5	2	21	21	21					
19 TRULLI	6	6	12	12	12	12	12	12	12	12	12	12	12	12	12	12	12	12	12	12	12	22	22	22	22	22	17	17	17	17	17	20	5	15	15	15	15	15	2	2	2	2	2	2	5	2	2	21	21				
17 HERBERT	12	12	12	22	22	22	22	22	22	22	22	22	22	22	22	22	22	22	22	22	22	17	17	17	17	17	20	20	20	20	20	5	15	5	5	5	5	2	20	20	20	20	18	18	18	21	21	18	18				
10 WURZ	22	22	22	7	7	7	7	7	7	7	7	7	7	14	14	14	14	14	14	14	15	15	15	15	15	20	5	5	5	5	5	15	20	20	20	20	20	18	18	18	21	21	21	18	20	20	20						
5 ZANARDI	7	7	7	14	14	14	14	14	14	14	14	14	14	15	15	15	15	15	15	15	20	20	20	20	5	5	15	15	15	15	15	18	18	18	18	18	18	21	21	21	21	20	20	20	20								
6 R. SCHUMACHER	23	23	14	20	20	20	20	20	20	20	20	20	15	20	20	20	20	20	20	18	18	18	18	5	15	15	18	18	18	18	18	21	21	21	21	21																	
7 HILL	14	14	20	15	15	15	15	15	15	15	15	15	20	18	18	18	18	18	5	5	5	5	18	18	18	18	21	21	21	21																							
18 PANIS	20	20	15	21	21	21	21	21	21	21	21	18	18	5	5	5	5	5	5	5	21	21	21	21	21																												
22 VILLENEUVE	15	15	21	18	18	18	18	18	18	18	18	21	5	5	21	21	21	21	21	21																																	
23 ZONTA	21	21	18	5	5	5	5	5	5	5	5	5	21	21																																							
12 DINIZ	18	18	16	16	16	16	16	16	16	16	16	16	16																																									
15 TAKAGI	16	16																																																			
14 DE LA ROSA																																																					
20 BADOER																																																					
21 GENE																																																					

Pit stop

One lap behind leader

3	1
M. SCHUMACHER	**HÄKKINEN**
Ferrari	McLaren
4	2
IRVINE	**COULTHARD**
Ferrari	McLaren
16	8
BARRICHELLO	**FRENTZEN**
Stewart	Jordan
9	11
FISICHELLA	**ALESI**
Benetton	Sauber
19	17
TRULLI	**HERBERT**
Prost	Stewart
10	5
WURZ	**ZANARDI**
Benetton	Williams
6	7
R. SCHUMACHER	**HILL**
Williams	Jordan
18	22
PANIS	**VILLENEUVE**
Prost	BAR
23	12
ZONTA	**DINIZ**
BAR	Sauber
15	14
TAKAGI	**DE LA ROSA**
Arrows	Arrows
20	21
BADOER	**GENE**
Minardi	Minardi

Lap chart (bottom left):

56	57	58	59	60	61	62	63	64	65	66	67	68	69	
1	1	1	1	1	1	1	1	1	1	1	1	1	1	1
8	8	8	8	8	8	8	8	8	8	9	9	9	9	2
9	9	9	9	9	9	9	9	9	9	4	4	4	4	3
6	6	4	4	4	4	4	4	4	4	6	6	6	6	4
4	4	6	6	6	6	6	6	6	6	17	17	17	17	5
17	17	17	17	17	17	17	17	17	17	12	12	12	12	6
12	12	12	12	12	12	12	12	12	12	2	2	2	2	
2	2	2	2	2	2	2	2	2	21	21	21			
21	21	21	21	21	21	21	21	21	21	18	18	18		
18	18	18	18	18	18	18	18	18	18	20	20			
20	20	20	20	20	20	20	20	20	20					

QUALIFYING

Weather: Dry, very hot and sunny

Pos.	Driver	Car	Laps	Time
1	Michael Schumacher	Ferrari	7	1m 19.298s
2	Mika Häkkinen	McLaren-Mercedes	12	1m 19.327s
3	Eddie Irvine	Ferrari	11	1m 19.440s
4	David Coulthard	McLaren-Mercedes	11	1m 19.729s
5	Rubens Barrichello	Stewart-Ford	11	1m 19.930s
6	Heinz-Harald Frentzen	Jordan-Mugen Honda	12	1m 20.158s
7	Giancarlo Fisichella	Benetton-Playlife	7	1m 20.378s
8	Jean Alesi	Sauber-Petronas	10	1m 20.459s
9	Jarno Trulli	Prost-Peugeot	11	1m 20.557s
10	Johnny Herbert	Stewart-Ford	12	1m 20.829s
11	Alexander Wurz	Benetton-Playlife	11	1m 21.000s
12	Alex Zanardi	Williams-Supertec	12	1m 21.076s
13	Ralf Schumacher	Williams-Supertec	10	1m 21.081s
14	Damon Hill	Jordan-Mugen Honda	12	1m 21.094s
15	Olivier Panis	Prost-Peugeot	11	1m 21.252s
16	Jacques Villeneuve	BAR-Supertec	11	1m 21.302s
17	Ricardo Zonta	BAR-Supertec	12	1m 21.467s
18	Pedro Diniz	Sauber-Petronas	12	1m 21.571s
19	Toranosuke Takagi	Arrows	11	1m 21.693s
20	Pedro de la Rosa	Arrows	12	1m 22.613s
21	Luca Badoer	Minardi-Ford	12	1m 22.808s
22	Marc Gene	Minardi-Ford	12	1m 23.387s

FRIDAY FREE PRACTICE

Weather: Dry, very hot and sunny

Pos.	Driver	Laps	Time
1	Eddie Irvine	35	1m 20.576s
2	David Coulthard	36	1m 20.664s
3	Michael Schumacher	35	1m 21.276s
4	Jean Alesi	37	1m 21.510s
5	Giancarlo Fisichella	27	1m 21.724s
6	Ricardo Zonta	31	1m 21.810s
7	Mika Häkkinen	19	1m 21.950s
8	Heinz-Harald Frentzen	35	1m 22.002s
9	Jacques Villeneuve	40	1m 22.021s
10	Rubens Barrichello	28	1m 22.167s
11	Jarno Trulli	41	1m 22.454s
12	Ralf Schumacher	22	1m 22.506s
13	Alexander Wurz	31	1m 22.649s
14	Damon Hill	36	1m 22.734s
15	Olivier Panis	18	1m 22.892s
16	Johnny Herbert	40	1m 23.177s
17	Luca Badoer	30	1m 23.778s
18	Alex Zanardi	20	1m 23.824s
19	Marc Gene	47	1m 23.826s
20	Pedro de la Rosa	46	1m 23.996s
21	Toranosuke Takagi	35	1m 24.131s
22	Pedro Diniz	5	1m 24.462s

SATURDAY FREE PRACTICE

Weather: Dry, very hot and sunny

Pos.	Driver	Laps	Time
1	Michael Schumacher	33	1m 19.281s
2	David Coulthard	32	1m 19.543s
3	Mika Häkkinen	27	1m 19.568s
4	Eddie Irvine	29	1m 19.631s
5	Heinz-Harald Frentzen	36	1m 19.940s
6	Giancarlo Fisichella	33	1m 20.162s
7	Rubens Barrichello	28	1m 20.261s
8	Ralf Schumacher	35	1m 20.275s
9	Jarno Trulli	37	1m 20.396s
10	Jean Alesi	25	1m 20.485s
11	Alex Zanardi	35	1m 20.754s
12	Damon Hill	40	1m 20.785s
13	Johnny Herbert	30	1m 20.861s
14	Alexander Wurz	32	1m 20.919s
15	Jacques Villeneuve	33	1m 20.924s
16	Olivier Panis	28	1m 20.935s
17	Pedro Diniz	34	1m 21.022s
18	Ricardo Zonta	22	1m 21.235s
19	Toranosuke Takagi	29	1m 21.810s
20	Pedro de la Rosa	31	1m 22.039s
21	Marc Gene	24	1m 22.205s
22	Luca Badoer	30	1m 22.730s

WARM-UP

Weather: Dry, very hot and sunny

Pos.	Driver	Laps	Time
1	David Coulthard	15	1m 20.614s
2	Rubens Barrichello	15	1m 21.012s
3	Johnny Herbert	13	1m 21.059s
4	Mika Häkkinen	15	1m 21.244s
5	Giancarlo Fisichella	19	1m 21.530s
6	Eddie Irvine	14	1m 21.534s
7	Michael Schumacher	14	1m 21.560s
8	Damon Hill	13	1m 21.709s
9	Ralf Schumacher	19	1m 21.845s
10	Alexander Wurz	15	1m 21.950s
11	Pedro Diniz	16	1m 21.984s
12	Olivier Panis	14	1m 22.027s
13	Heinz-Harald Frentzen	17	1m 22.156s
14	Jarno Trulli	18	1m 22.228s
15	Toranosuke Takagi	13	1m 22.323s
16	Pedro de la Rosa	12	1m 22.469s
17	Jean Alesi	15	1m 22.472s
18	Alex Zanardi	16	1m 22.535s
19	Luca Badoer	16	1m 22.691s
20	Jacques Villeneuve	12	1m 22.898s
21	Ricardo Zonta	9	1m 23.256s
22	Marc Gene	5	1m 26.279s

RACE FASTEST LAPS

Weather: Dry, very hot and sunny

Driver	Time	Lap
Eddie Irvine	1m 20.382s	62
Michael Schumacher	1m 20.709s	28
David Coulthard	1m 20.961s	35
Mika Häkkinen	1m 21.047s	28
Heinz-Harald Frentzen	1m 21.284s	65
Giancarlo Fisichella	1m 21.345s	65
Pedro Diniz	1m 21.864s	63
Ralf Schumacher	1m 22.002s	28
Johnny Herbert	1m 22.078s	64
Olivier Panis	1m 22.100s	57
Jacques Villeneuve	1m 22.283s	29
Toranosuke Takagi	1m 22.792s	26
Marc Gene	1m 22.888s	60
Pedro de la Rosa	1m 23.280s	19
Luca Badoer	1m 23.394s	32
Alex Zanardi	1m 23.442s	27
Rubens Barrichello	1m 23.785s	11
Damon Hill	1m 23.953s	12
Ricardo Zonta	2m 03.038s	2

1	Häkkinen	McLaren MP4/14/5
2	Coulthard	McLaren MP4/14/6
	spare	McLaren MP4/14/2
3	M. Schumacher	Ferrari F399/194
4	Irvine	Ferrari F399/191
	spare	Ferrari F399/192
5	Zanardi	Williams FW21/5
6	R. Schumacher	Williams FW21/4
	spare	Williams FW21/2
7	Hill	Jordan 199/4
8	Frentzen	Jordan 199/6
	spare	Jordan 199/3
9	Fisichella	Benetton B199/6
10	Wurz	Benetton B199/5
	spare	Benetton B199/3
11	Alesi	Sauber C18/3
12	Diniz	Sauber C18/5
	spare	Sauber C18/4
14	de la Rosa	Arrows A20/4
15	Takagi	Arrows A20/2
	spare	Arrows A20/5
16	Barrichello	Stewart SF3/4
17	Herbert	Stewart SF3/5
	spare	Stewart SF3/3
18	Panis	Prost AP02/5
19	Trulli	Prost AP02/6
	spare	Prost AP02/3
20	Badoer	Minardi M01/1
21	Gene	Minardi M01/4
	spare	Minardi M01/3
22	Villeneuve	BAR 01/3
23	Zonta	BAR 01/6
	spare	BAR 01/5

POINTS TABLES

DRIVERS

1	Mika Häkkinen	34
2	Michael Schumacher	30
3	Eddie Irvine	25
4 =	Heinz-Harald Frentzen	13
4 =	Giancarlo Fisichella	13
6 =	David Coulthard	12
6 =	Ralf Schumacher	12
8	Rubens Barrichello	6
9	Damon Hill	3
10	Johnny Herbert	2
11 =	Pedro de la Rosa	1
11 =	Olivier Panis	1
11 =	Jean Alesi	1
11 =	Alexander Wurz	1
11 =	Jarno Trulli	1
11 =	Pedro Diniz	1

CONSTRUCTORS

1	Ferrari	55
2	McLaren	46
3	Jordan	16
4	Benetton	14
5	Williams	12
6	Stewart	8
7 =	Prost	2
7 =	Sauber	2
9	Arrows	1

FRENTZEN
HÄKKINEN
BARRICHELLO
R. SCHUMACHER
M. SCHUMACHER
IRVINE

FRENCH
grand prix

Left: Heinz-Harald Frentzen typically shows quiet satisfaction with his unexpected win while Eddie Jordan is naturally in boisterous mood.

Below left: Frentzen's tactical approach to the race in treacherous conditions paid dividends as others floundered.

HEINZ-HARALD Frentzen delivered the Jordan team its second F1 victory in the French Grand Prix at Magny-Cours after an outstanding tactical performance in treacherous conditions, only a fortnight after surviving a high-speed accident in the Canadian race at Montreal.

The 32-year-old German driver was still nursing a stiff right knee, the result of slamming into one of the tyre barriers in Montreal at around 110 mph after a brake disc failed just when it looked as though second place was in the bag. Yet despite having been obliged to spend a night in a Canadian hospital, suffering from mild concussion, Frentzen was in peak form in the French race, qualifying an excellent fifth before going on to a well-earned win.

It was one of the most fascinating Grands Prix of recent years, thanks to torrential rain, which injected a tantalising element of unpredictability into qualifying and the race itself. Frentzen seized the lead, with only seven of the race's 72 laps left to run, when Mika Häkkinen's McLaren-Mercedes dodged into the pits for a last minute 'splash and dash'.

Thus Heinz-Harald was able to beat the World Champion by 11.092s, Häkkinen easing off in the closing stages to make sure of his six points. It might have been even closer – or perhaps the outcome would have been completely different – if Häkkinen hadn't indulged in a quick spin during his otherwise meteoric climb through the field.

That said, the result might also have been different if David Coulthard's McLaren-Mercedes had not pulled off with electrical failure mid-way around lap ten. The Scot, who qualified a brilliant fourth at the peak of Saturday's rain shower, was in the lead and pulling away from the pack by the end of lap six, when his now legendary ill fortune intervened once again.

The second F1 victory of Frentzen's career came only nine months after Damon Hill had scored the Jordan team's maiden victory in a similarly rain-soaked Belgian Grand Prix at Spa. On this occasion, however, Hill retired after 31 laps, following a qualifying effort that briefly had seen him – and indeed several others – outside the 107 per cent qualifying cut-off point. After the race, there was much speculation over whether Hill might advance his retirement decision and not even compete in his home Grand Prix at Silverstone.

MAGNY-COURS QUALIFYING

After days of scorching sunshine, which had lasted throughout the previous week's test programme at the Circuit de Nevers, the teams' careful pre-planning went out of the window for two reasons. Firstly, the wind direction changed dramatically during Friday's free practice. Secondly, the heavens opened on Saturday afternoon and qualifying took place in monsoon conditions.

'We really should reduce testing,' said Eddie Irvine. 'On Friday, my car felt totally different than it had done in the test. I just didn't recognise it. The traction disappeared and there was just no point in chasing the wind direction and just wasting sets of tyres.'

As the rain sluiced down on Saturday afternoon, McLaren and Ferrari unaccountably took a siesta. Despite precise local weather forecasts to the effect that the rain would not stop until 2.15 pm – 15 minutes after the end of the session – neither of F1's top teams took advantage of the brief spell of less intense rain. As a result, Rubens Barrichello surfed to the second pole position of his career – and the first ever for the Stewart-Ford team – on the second flying lap of the session.

'I thought it was best to get a time in the bank because my information was that the weather would deteriorate,' said Rubens. 'When I saw Jean Alesi go out so early, I said to the crew, "Let's go." It worked in my favour because the rain persisted.'

Alesi's Sauber joined the Brazilian on the front row, on the tenth anniversary of the French driver's F1 debut in a Tyrrell-Ford at Paul Ricard. 'It was the best present I could have had,' said Alesi, choking back tears.

If Stewart and Sauber could work out that it was sensible to get a lap under their belts early in the session, one wondered what on earth McLaren and Ferrari were up to.

In fact, Coulthard did brilliantly, storming around to set a fourth-fastest 1m 40.403s best which, considering the prevailing conditions, was an outstanding performance by anybody's standards. Between his and sixth-place Michael Schumacher's Ferrari was Frentzen's Jordan. Häkkinen, however, never managed a clear lap and had to settle for 14th in the final line-up, three places ahead of Irvine.

'David did a brilliant job,' said Ron Dennis. 'Mika must have fallen foul of every yellow flag and spinning car on the circuit. We are not too worried about the fastest qualifiers. We are out to win the World Championship, and that means beating our main competitors.'

Elsewhere in the line-up, Olivier Panis qualified his Prost-Peugeot third fastest, thanks in part to an accurate meteorological forecast from the team's experts. Jarno Trulli ran slightly later in the session and wound up eighth fastest.

Frentzen qualified his Jordan 199 in fifth place. 'The conditions were terrible,' he said. 'We experienced a lot of aquaplaning and it was certainly a mistake to wait for 20 minutes before going out.' Damon Hill qualified outside the 107 per cent cut-off point after suffering broken exhausts on both his race car and the spare.

For his part, Michael Schumacher wrestled his Ferrari F399 to sixth. 'The conditions were horrible,' he said. 'I lost control on the straight. I waited too long in the pits because I thought that two or three cars might clear the racing line.'

Eddie Irvine lined up 17th. 'The aquaplaning was unbelievable,' he said. 'I also had three spins and lost time when I was called in for two weight checks during the session.'

The crucial moment that won Frentzen the race came at the end of lap 22, three laps before the safety car was deployed to slow the field after the rain intensified. The period of reduced speed enforced on the field behind the safety car allowed the Jordan driver to run non-stop through to the chequered flag.

Heavy rain had also disrupted qualifying, giving the starting line-up a distinctly unfamiliar look. At the start, Rubens Barrichello's Stewart-Ford SF3 grabbed an immediate lead from pole position, ahead of Jean Alesi's Sauber C18 and David Coulthard's McLaren, which had accelerated into third place from fourth on the grid, passing Olivier Panis's Prost. At the same time, Frentzen's Jordan squeezed out Michael Schumacher's Ferrari for fifth.

Way back down the grid order, things could hardly have been worse for Eddie Irvine. He'd qualified 17th at the height of the downpour and came around 18th on the opening lap.

'Everything that could go wrong did go wrong today,' he said. 'I was in neutral at the start and lost time as I had to select first again. I knew it was going to rain, so I decided to take it carefully at first.'

Second time around, Coulthard dived neatly inside Alesi to relieve the Sauber driver of second place under braking for the Adelaide hairpin. By the end of the lap, Barrichello still held a slender 0.6s lead from the Scot, with Mika Häkkinen in the other McLaren-Mercedes having reached eighth from his original starting position of 14th.

Things may have been going swimmingly for Barrichello, but again Johnny Herbert was poised to experience a bitterly disappointing day at the wheel of the other Stewart SF3, which lasted only until lap five before its gearbox broke.

'I was half-way through the first lap when I lost second gear,' he explained. 'After a few more laps, I lost the other gears, and the only option left was to cruise back to the pits and watch the rest of the race from there.'

On lap six, Coulthard duly deprived Barrichello of his lead under braking for the Adelaide hairpin and really began to streak away from the pack. He was 3.5s ahead on lap seven, and 5.5s in front on lap eight. Then, on lap nine, he came through 7.6s before the Stewart. Unfortunately, that was the last his pit crew saw of him, as the McLaren had coasted to a halt out on the circuit on lap ten, following an electrical failure.

As always, Coulthard concealed his acute disappointment beneath a veneer of dignity and restrained good manners. Yet McLaren managing director Ron Dennis didn't forget his efforts when commenting on the race. 'The pleasure that all the team gained from seeing Mika recover from his spin and the discipline with which he accepted second place doesn't match the disappointment that we feel for David,' he said. 'His opening laps were some of his best ever seen, and these moments are sometimes forgotten, but not by us.'

Barrichello retook the lead, 3.9s ahead of Alesi, with Frentzen third, followed by Häkkinen, Michael Schumacher and Panis.

On lap 21, we were treated to a repeat of the previous afternoon's weather, the rain beginning to fall heavily, so Panis's Prost, Irvine's Ferrari, the Benettons of Giancarlo Fisichella and Alexander Wurz, Jacques Villeneuve's British American 01, Damon Hill's Jordan, Pedro de la Rosa's and Toranosuke Takagi's Arrows and Marc Gene's Minardi all scrambled in for the first routine refuelling stops and a switch to wet-weather rubber.

Hill was clipped by de la Rosa as he resumed the race, damaging a rear wheel, which caused Damon to spin with a punctured tyre. He returned to the pits for repairs next time around.

Irvine, who by that stage had climbed to ninth place, found himself on the receiving end of the afternoon's second helping of misfortune. 'I knew it was going to rain,' he said, 'so I decided to take it carefully at first. Then I started picking off cars one by one.

Insets (left to right): Sooner or later? Todt, Schumacher and Brawn in discussion about when to time the Ferrari's runs in qualifying; Eddie Irvine's weekend yielded a single point which could have proved costly as the championship battle unfolded; Olivier Panis explains his problems to Prost.

Main picture: Rubens Barrichello held pole but could not hold off Frentzen or Häkkinen in the race.

All photographs: Paul-Henri Cahier

Left: David Coulthard seemed to have control of the race, only for his McLaren to fail him.

Below left: Ralf Schumacher produced yet another convincing performance to edge out big brother Michael and pick up fourth place.

'When the rain came, I radioed the team, saying, "Pits, pits." I thought they might not be 100 per cent ready, but we had agreed that I should come in anyway. It was a bad stop, and without it I might have finished higher.'

Irvine was being diplomatic in the extreme. In fact, the Ferrari mechanics had begun to fit another set of dry-weather tyres before realising their error and putting on a set of wet tyres. As a result, a stop that should have taken around 9s took a shambolic 42.9s, effectively writing the Ulster-man out of the equation.

On lap 22, Barrichello, Häkkinen, Alesi, Frentzen, Michael Schumacher, Ralf Schumacher (Williams), Trulli, Zonta (BAR), Zanardi (Williams) and Badoer (Minardi) all made their first refuelling stops. Barrichello resumed in the lead, ahead of Häkkinen.

'When I came in, I noticed the guys taking a long time refuelling,' recalled Frentzen. 'I got very nervous about this long stop, but then I realised the strategy had been changed to give a long second stint.

'Shortly after I rejoined, it began to rain, then I saw Alesi off the road and started screaming into the radio for them to bring out the safety car.

'After it went in, the car felt very heavy and was aquaplaning everywhere because of the big fuel load. I had to ease off and save fuel at one point, and I had a moment when I thought the gearbox had broken when I had to go tight into the hairpin to avoid one of the Arrows.'

The pack resumed in the order of Barrichello, Häkkinen and Alesi, but as the rain intensified, it became clear that it would be only a matter of time before the safety car was deployed. That happened on lap 25, but it wasn't soon enough to save Alesi, who spun off at the Estoril right-hander moments beforehand.

'Today I had no luck,' shrugged the dejected Frenchman. 'I was able to stay strongly in touch with Barrichello, but just before it started to rain, I had to let David Coulthard by. The car and engine were going really well and, after my pit stop, in which we switched to wet tyres, I was able to rejoin still in third place.

'Unfortunately, the track was really wet and there was a lot of standing water. When I braked for a corner, the car spun into the gravel. It was my mistake.'

The safety car remained out for ten laps, but this did not prevent Wurz and Villeneuve from spinning off on lap 26. 'The rain was coming down

hard and I saw Villeneuve spin off in front of me on the straight, so I dropped to half speed,' said Wurz. 'But the car was really low and there was so much aquaplaning – not from the wheels, but from the underside of the car – that I had no control and slid off on the straight.'

When the safety car was finally withdrawn on lap 35, Barrichello leaped into a half-second lead. On lap 38, Häkkinen made a bid for the lead, diving inside Barrichello at Adelaide only for the McLaren to snap into a spin. Mika resumed seventh, leaving Barrichello to handle Michael Schumacher's Ferrari, which duly went through into the lead on lap 44.

Michael pulled steadily away, opening an 8.7s lead by lap 50 only to come around next time less than a second ahead of Barrichello. 'This was a pretty chaotic race for me,' he said later. 'My radio stopped working early on, so I tried to communicate with the pits with hand signals.

'My first problem was that I was having trouble changing gear, and the reason I slowed a lot at one point was that I only had first and second gear. So I came in and changed the steering wheel, but from this point on things did not really improve.'

Michael's stop for a replacement steering wheel came on lap 54, allowing Barrichello back into a 2.1s lead over Frentzen and Häkkinen. On lap

57, Häkkinen made it back into second place, ahead of Frentzen, but Barrichello would be a much harder nut to crack.

Häkkinen dived inside the Stewart at Adelaide on lap 59, but Rubens kept his nerve and accelerated back ahead through the exit of the turn. Next time around, Häkkinen made it stick, coming through at the end of lap 60 with a 2.7s lead over the Stewart.

Barrichello was consistently quick, precise and very disciplined. He raced hard without playing dirty. Only a late refuelling stop deprived him of a possible second place. Schumacher's Ferrari had a long third stop while the front wing settings were adjusted and the steering wheel was replaced after the German had suffered a repeat of the gearchange glitch that effectively wrote him out of the points in the Australian Grand Prix.

As the race wore on, Rubens was troubled increasingly by oversteer and locking rear brakes. 'It was quite difficult to drive,' he said, 'and I was having to concentrate hard, but even so I was losing time to the McLarens, Ferraris and Jordans.'

On lap 65, Häkkinen and Barrichello made their second refuelling stops, allowing Frentzen his free run to victory. Mika and Rubens picked up again in second and third places, while Ralf Schumacher came storming

through to finish fourth, after getting the upper hand in a skirmish with big brother Michael. The Ferrari driver found that his car simply didn't work properly in the drying conditions.

Having caught up with Michael in the closing stages, Irvine was not amused to be told to keep behind the troubled German as young Ralf scampered away to take a fourth place that Irvine clearly thought could easily have been his. Nevertheless, he remained diplomatic as far as the record was concerned.

'The car was okay and I found I could catch up with Michael quite easily,' he said. 'I could have done a one-stop race, as we had started with a lot of fuel [he made his second stop on lap 50]. Basically, we made too many mistakes due to the difficult conditions, which is not normally the case. Our car was quicker than our main competitors and we missed an opportunity.'

Outside the top six, the Prosts of Jarno Trulli and Olivier Panis finished seventh and eighth. Trulli admitted that his set-up was not ideal in the wet, producing rather too much understeer for his taste. Panis reckoned his car handled well in the rain and he had precious little to complain about. It was the first time in 1999 that the Prost-Peugeot squad had had both cars running at the chequered flag.

Ricardo Zonta's ninth place for the British American team came as something of a consolation after Villeneuve's pirouette into retirement just after a perfectly timed refuelling stop, which otherwise might have seen him on course for a podium finish. 'When the track started to dry, I changed back to dry tyres and was really able to push then,' said the Brazilian. 'I'm only sorry that it started to rain again, because I was catching Panis very quickly and I think I could have finished much higher. When the rain came again, I had to back off and just get to the end.'

Luca Badoer's Minardi and the Arrows of Toranosuke Takagi and Pedro de la Rosa completed the list of finishers on this bonus day for the Jordan team, when slick strategy and some first-rate driving from Heinz-Harald Frentzen had produced a marvellous success.

Yet Häkkinen's pace underlined the fact that the Finn was still favourite for the World Championship. Surely his run of success had only been stalled momentarily by the rain at the Circuit de Nevers. He would pick up the winning thread at Silverstone. Wouldn't he?

Jordan vetoes Irvine for 2000

EDDIE Jordan effectively torpedoed any prospect of his old colleague, Eddie Irvine, rejoining his team next year as successor to Damon Hill. 'To be truthful, I think Eddie Irvine would be better off not coming back here,' he said, 'and I think it would be better for us if he didn't come back either. We are still very good friends. I think Eddie would be better staying where he is. The fans at Ferrari adore him. He drove a great race in Canada and he is a darling of the crowd.'

Such a move would have given the 33-year-old Ulsterman the opportunity of establishing himself as a number-one driver in his own right, rekindling his links with the team for which he drove from 1993 to 1995.

However, Irvine remained characteristically relaxed and philosophical about the situation, and would give nothing away. 'I'm paid [at Ferrari] to help another guy win races and world championships,' he said. 'But at the same time, I'm getting a very competitive car to drive.

'Damon's retirement changes nothing for me. It doesn't make any difference to what I'm going to do. I think he's been thinking of retirement for a lot longer than perhaps seems obvious.

'I'm fairly relaxed. I'm under no pressure, nobody has given me any deadlines. It's not an easy decision to make. Every alternative [team] has an upside and a downside.

'I didn't come into F1 to help Michael win championships, but that's my job at the moment. It's a job I have to do because, if I want to drive a Ferrari, it's the only option I have. But it's not the perfect job. Michael's got the perfect job.'

Yet Eddie Jordan said he believed Irvine's popularity with Ferrari exceeded that of the German driver. 'I think they [the fans] are getting a bit fed up with Michael, and Eddie is more their kind of person,' said Jordan. 'Eddie has had a great season. If I was the boss of Ferrari, I cannot believe that I would want him to go. Eddie wants to win races. Where does he have a better chance of doing so than Ferrari?'

Those were to prove prescient words indeed.

147

GRAND PRIX MOBIL 1
DE FRANCE
25–27 JUNE 1999
NEVERS MAGNY-COURS

Race distance: 72 laps, 190.024 miles/305.814 km

Race weather: Dry and overcast, then heavy rain

ROUND 7

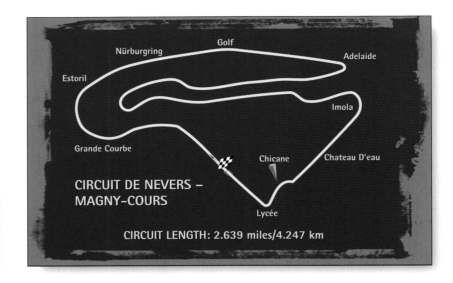

CIRCUIT DE NEVERS – MAGNY-COURS

CIRCUIT LENGTH: 2.639 miles/4.247 km

Pos.	Driver	Nat.	No.	Entrant	Car/Engine	Laps	Time/Retirement	Speed (mph/km/h)
1	Heinz-Harald Frentzen	D	8	Benson & Hedges Jordan	Jordan 199-Mugen Honda MF301/HD V10	72	1h 58m 24.343s	96.291/154.965
2	Mika Häkkinen	SF	1	West McLaren Mercedes	McLaren MP4/14-Mercedes F0110H V10	72	1h 58m 35.435s	96.141/154.724
3	Rubens Barrichello	BR	16	Stewart Ford	Stewart SF3-Ford CR-1 V10	72	1h 59m 07.775s	95.706/154.024
4	Ralf Schumacher	D	6	Winfield Williams	Williams FW21-Supertec FB01 V10	72	1h 59m 09.818s	95.679/153.980
5	Michael Schumacher	D	3	Scuderia Ferrari Marlboro	Ferrari F399 048 V10	72	1h 59m 12.224s	95.646/153.928
6	Eddie Irvine	GB	4	Scuderia Ferrari Marlboro	Ferrari F399 048 V10	72	1h 59m 13.244s	95.633/153.906
7	Jarno Trulli	I	19	Gauloises Prost Peugeot	Prost AP02-Peugeot A18 V10	72	1h 59m 22.114s	95.514/153.715
8	Olivier Panis	F	18	Gauloises Prost Peugeot	Prost AP02-Peugeot A18 V10	72	1h 59m 22.874s	95.504/153.699
9	Ricardo Zonta	BR	23	British American Racing	BAR 01-Supertec FB01 V10	72	1h 59m 53.107s	95.103/153.053
10	Luca Badoer	I	20	Fondmetal Minardi Ford	Minardi M01-Ford Zetec-R V10	71		
11	Toranosuke Takagi	J	15	Arrows	Arrows A20 V10	71	Illegal tyres	
12	Pedro de la Rosa	ESP	14	Arrows	Arrows A20 V10	71		
	Giancarlo Fisichella	I	9	Mild Seven Benetton Playlife	Benetton B199-Playlife V10	42	Spun off	
	Damon Hill	GB	7	Benson & Hedges Jordan	Jordan 199-Mugen Honda MF301/HD V10	31	Engine	
	Alex Zanardi	I	5	Winfield Williams	Williams FW21-Supertec FB01 V10	26	Engine	
	Jacques Villeneuve	CDN	22	British American Racing	BAR 01-Supertec FB01 V10	25	Spun off	
	Alexander Wurz	A	10	Mild Seven Benetton Playlife	Benetton B199-Playlife V10	25	Spun off	
	Marc Gene	ESP	21	Fondmetal Minardi Ford	Minardi M01-Ford Zetec-R V10	25	Spun off	
	Jean Alesi	F	11	Red Bull Sauber Petronas	Sauber C18-Petronas SPE03A V10	24	Spun off	
	David Coulthard	GB	2	West McLaren Mercedes	McLaren MP4/14-Mercedes F0110H V10	9	Alternator	
	Pedro Diniz	BR	12	Red Bull Sauber Petronas	Sauber C18-Petronas SPE03A V10	6	Transmission	
	Johnny Herbert	GB	17	Stewart Ford	Stewart SF3-Ford CR-1 V10	4	Gearbox	

Fastest lap: Coulthard, on lap 8, 1m 19.227s, 119.996 mph/193.115 km/h.

Lap record: Nigel Mansell (F1 Williams FW14B-Renault V10), 1m 17.070s, 123.355 mph/198.521 km/h (1992).

Grid order																																																							
16 BARRICHELLO	16 16 16 16 16	2 2 2 2	16 16 16 16 16 16 16 16 16 16 16 16 16 16 16	16 16 16 16 16 16 16 16 16 16 16 16 16 16 16 16 16 16 16 16 16 16 16 16	3 3 3 3 3 3 3 3 3 3 3 1
11 ALESI	11 2 2 2	16 16 16 16 11 11 11 11 11 11 11 11	1 1 1 1 1 1 1 1 1 1 1 1 1 1 1	8 3 3 3 3 16 16 16 16 16 16 16 16 16 16 16
18 PANIS	2 11 11 11 11 11 11 11 11 11	8 8 8 8 8 8 1 1 1 11 11 11 11 11 11 11	8 8 8 8 8 8 8 8 8 8 8 8	3 8 8 8 8 8 8 8 8 8 8 8 8 8
2 COULTHARD	8 8 8 8 8 8 8 8 8	1 1 1 1 8 8 8 8 8 8 8 8 8 8 3 3 3 3 3 3 3 3 3 3 3 18 18 18 18 18 18 18 18 18 18 18 18	6 6 1 1 1 18
8 FRENTZEN	3 3 3 3 3 3 3 3 3 3 3 3 3 3 3 3 3 3 3 3 3 3 18 18 18 18 18 18 18 18 18 18 18 18 18 19 19 19	6 6 6 6 6 6 18 1 18 18 18 1
3 M. SCHUMACHER	18 18 18 18	1 1 1 1 1 18 18 18 18 18 18 18 18 18 18 18 18 19 6 18 18 19 19 19 19 19 19 19 19 19 19 19 19 19 19	6 6 6 19 4 4 4 4 4 4 1 18 6 19 19
9 FISICHELLA	19 19 1 1 18 18 18 18 18 19 19 19 19 19 19 19 19 19 6 19 19 19 6 6 6 6 6 6 6 6 6 6 1 1 1 4 19 19 1 1 1 1 4 19 19 6 6
19 TRULLI	9 1 19 19 19 19 19 19 9 9 9 9 9 9 6 6 6 6 18 18 6 6 9 9 9 9 9 9 9 9 9 9 4 4 1 1 1 19 19 19 19 19 19 4 4 23 2
17 HERBERT	1 9 9 9 9 9 9 9 9 6 6 6 6 6 6 6 9 9 9 4 4 23 9 9 22 4 4 4 4 4 4 4 4 23 23 23 4 4 9 9 9 23 23 23 23 23 23 4 23 23 4
23 ZONTA	10 10 10 10 10 10 10 10 6 10 10 10 10 10 10 4 4 4 4 9 9 9 22 22 4 23 23 23 23 23 23 23 23 23 14 4 4 23 23 23 23 23 20 20 20 20 20 20 20 20 20 20 20
12 DINIZ	17 12 12 12 12 12 6 6 10 22 22 22 4 4 4 10 10 10 10 10 10 5 4 4 23 5 14 14 14 14 14 14 14 14 14 20 20 20 20 20 20 20 14 14 14 14 14 14 14 14 14 14 14 14 1
22 VILLENEUVE	12 6 6 6 6 6 22 22 22 5 4 4 22 22 22 22 22 22 22 22 22 23 22 23 10 14 20 20 20 20 20 20 20 15 14 14 14 14 14 14 15 15 15 15 15 15 15 15 15 15 15 1
10 WURZ	22 22 22 22 22 22 5 5 5 5 5 23 23 23 23 23 23 23 23 23 22 4 10 10 5 20 15 15 15 15 15 15 15 4 15 15 15 15 15 15
1 HÄKKINEN	6 5 5 5 5 5 23 23 23 23 23 23 23 23 5 5 5 5 5 5 14 5 14 7 7 7 7 7
5 ZANARDI	23 23 23 23 23 23 7 7 4 7 7 7 7 7 7 7 7 7 7 20 14 14 21 7
6 R. SCHUMACHER	5 17 7 7 7 7 4 4 7 14 14 14 14 14 14 14 14 14 14 14 21 21 20
4 IRVINE	7 7 4 4 4 4 14 14 14 15 15 15 15 15 15 15 15 15 20 21 20 20 15
7 HILL	4 4 17 14 14 14 15 15 20 20 20 20 20 20 20 20 20 15 15 15 15 7
14 DE LA ROSA	14 14 14 15 15 15 20 20 21 21 21 21 21 21 21 21 21 21 21 7 7 7
15 TAKAGI	15 15 15 20 20 20 21 21 21
20 BADOER	20 21 21 21 21 21
21 GENE	21 20 20 17

Pit stop
One lap behind leader

STARTING GRID

11 **ALESI** Sauber	**16** **BARRICHELLO** Stewart
2 **COULTHARD** McLaren	**18** **PANIS** Prost
3 **M. SCHUMACHER** Ferrari	**8** **FRENTZEN** Jordan
19 **TRULLI** Prost	**9** **FISICHELLA** Benetton
23 **ZONTA** BAR	**17** **HERBERT** Stewart
22 **VILLENEUVE** BAR	**12** **DINIZ** Sauber
1 **HÄKKINEN** McLaren	**10** **WURZ** Benetton
6 **R. SCHUMACHER** Williams	**5** **ZANARDI** Williams
7* **HILL** Jordan	**4** **IRVINE** Ferrari
15* **TAKAGI** Arrows	**14*** **DE LA ROSA** Arrows
21* **GENE** Minardi	**20*** **BADOER** Minardi

* these drivers were allowed to race, but were allocated grid positions by the race stewards, according to their practice times.

58	59	60	61	62	63	64	65	66	67	68	69	70	71	72	
16	16	1	1	1	1	1	8	8	8	8	8	8	8	8	1
1	1	16	16	16	16	16	8	1	1	1	1	1	1	1	2
8	8	8	8	8	8	8	16	16	16	16	16	16	16	16	3
19	19	3	3	3	3	3	3	3	3	3	6	6	6	6	4
3	3	6	6	6	6	6	6	6	6	6	4	3	3	3	5
6	6	18	18	4	4	4	4	4	4	4	6	4	4	4	6
18	18	4	4	18	19	19	19	19	19	19	19	19	19	19	
4	4	19	19	19	18	18	18	18	18	18	18	18	18	18	
23	23	23	23	23	23	23	23	23	23	23	23	23	23	23	
20	20	20	20	20	20	20	20	20	20	20	20	20	20		
14	14	14	15	15	15	15	15	15	15	15	15	15	15		
15	15	15	14	14	14	14	14	14	14	14	14	14	14		

TIME SHEETS

QUALIFYING

Weather: Very heavy rain

Pos.	Driver	Car	Laps	Time
1	Rubens Barrichello	Stewart-Ford	5	1m 38.441s
2	Jean Alesi	Sauber-Petronas	6	1m 38.881s
3	Olivier Panis	Prost-Peugeot	5	1m 40.400s
4	David Coulthard	McLaren-Mercedes	11	1m 40.403s
5	Heinz-Harald Frentzen	Jordan-Mugen Honda	10	1m 40.690s
6	Michael Schumacher	Ferrari	10	1m 41.127s
7	Giancarlo Fisichella	Benetton-Playlife	9	1m 41.825s
8	Jarno Trulli	Prost-Peugeot	8	1m 42.096s
9	Johnny Herbert	Stewart-Ford	7	1m 42.199s
10	Ricardo Zonta	BAR-Supertec	9	1m 42.228s
11	Pedro Diniz	Sauber-Petronas	8	1m 42.942s
12	Jacques Villeneuve	BAR-Supertec	10	1m 43.748s
13	Alexander Wurz	Benetton-Playlife	10	1m 44.319s
14	Mika Häkkinen	McLaren-Mercedes	8	1m 44.368s
15	Alex Zanardi	Williams-Supertec	11	1m 44.912s
16	Ralf Schumacher	Williams-Supertec	9	1m 45.189s
17	Eddie Irvine	Ferrari	7	1m 45.218s
	Damon Hill*	Jordan-Mugen Honda	10	1m 45.334s
	Marc Gene*	Minardi-Ford	10	1m 46.324s
	Luca Badoer*	Minardi-Ford	8	1m 46.784s
	Pedro de la Rosa*	Arrows	9	1m 48.215s
	Toranosuke Takagi*	Arrows	10	1m 48.322s

107 per cent time: 1m 45.331s   * allowed to race

FRIDAY FREE PRACTICE

Weather: Dry, hot and gusty

Pos.	Driver	Laps	Time
1	Michael Schumacher	9	1m 17.912s
2	Eddie Irvine	10	1m 18.199s
3	Mika Häkkinen	18	1m 18.251s
4	David Coulthard	21	1m 18.468s
5	Alex Zanardi	35	1m 18.746s
6	Heinz-Harald Frentzen	31	1m 18.779s
7	Jean Alesi	13	1m 18.908s
8	Rubens Barrichello	20	1m 18.950s
9	Ralf Schumacher	15	1m 19.069s
10	Johnny Herbert	24	1m 19.266s
11	Alexander Wurz	22	1m 19.491s
12	Damon Hill	26	1m 19.591s
13	Giancarlo Fisichella	34	1m 19.651s
14	Jacques Villeneuve	40	1m 20.002s
15	Jarno Trulli	39	1m 20.121s
16	Olivier Panis	34	1m 20.285s
17	Pedro Diniz	24	1m 20.528s
18	Pedro de la Rosa	38	1m 20.655s
19	Ricardo Zonta	22	1m 20.681s
20	Toranosuke Takagi	26	1m 21.418s
21	Luca Badoer	33	1m 21.506s
22	Marc Gene	44	1m 21.928s

SATURDAY FREE PRACTICE

Weather: Dry and overcast, then rain

Pos.	Driver	Laps	Time
1	Rubens Barrichello	18	1m 17.232s
2	David Coulthard	21	1m 17.283s
3	Mika Häkkinen	21	1m 17.386s
4	Ralf Schumacher	14	1m 17.496s
5	Eddie Irvine	19	1m 17.520s
6	Michael Schumacher	20	1m 17.698s
7	Heinz-Harald Frentzen	23	1m 18.030s
8	Damon Hill	20	1m 18.170s
9	Alex Zanardi	27	1m 18.255s
10	Ricardo Zonta	22	1m 18.484s
11	Johnny Herbert	13	1m 18.516s
12	Jean Alesi	15	1m 18.595s
13	Giancarlo Fisichella	20	1m 18.671s
14	Jacques Villeneuve	20	1m 18.777s
15	Toranosuke Takagi	19	1m 18.887s
16	Jarno Trulli	24	1m 19.075s
17	Pedro Diniz	27	1m 19.171s
18	Pedro de la Rosa	19	1m 19.214s
19	Alexander Wurz	16	1m 19.375s
20	Olivier Panis	22	1m 19.403s
21	Luca Badoer	20	1m 20.388s
22	Marc Gene	29	1m 20.681s

WARM-UP

Weather: Dry and overcast

Pos.	Driver	Laps	Time
1	David Coulthard	13	1m 32.091s
2	Eddie Irvine	15	1m 32.111s
3	Michael Schumacher	12	1m 32.449s
4	Heinz-Harald Frentzen	16	1m 32.621s
5	Ralf Schumacher	12	1m 33.465s
6	Mika Häkkinen	11	1m 33.613s
7	Olivier Panis	13	1m 34.003s
8	Jean Alesi	12	1m 34.022s
9	Rubens Barrichello	13	1m 34.355s
10	Jarno Trulli	14	1m 34.478s
11	Giancarlo Fisichella	12	1m 34.892s
12	Johnny Herbert	11	1m 34.924s
13	Jacques Villeneuve	12	1m 34.951s
14	Alexander Wurz	13	1m 35.099s
15	Damon Hill	12	1m 35.484s
16	Pedro Diniz	13	1m 35.611s
17	Toranosuke Takagi	11	1m 36.830s
18	Alex Zanardi	14	1m 37.288s
19	Ricardo Zonta	12	1m 37.415s
20	Luca Badoer	13	1m 38.415s
21	Pedro de la Rosa	10	1m 38.636s
22	Marc Gene	12	1m 38.824s

RACE FASTEST LAPS

Weather: Dry and overcast, then heavy rain

Driver	Time	Lap
David Coulthard	1m 19.227s	8
Mika Häkkinen	1m 19.758s	20
Ralf Schumacher	1m 20.313s	19
Eddie Irvine	1m 20.328s	17
Jean Alesi	1m 20.848s	17
Rubens Barrichello	1m 20.878s	4
Ricardo Zonta	1m 20.881s	19
Heinz-Harald Frentzen	1m 20.994s	17
Michael Schumacher	1m 21.014s	12
Jarno Trulli	1m 21.330s	15
Olivier Panis	1m 21.403s	20
Alexander Wurz	1m 21.409s	19
Giancarlo Fisichella	1m 21.423s	19
Jacques Villeneuve	1m 21.461s	18
Alex Zanardi	1m 21.983s	19
Damon Hill	1m 22.021s	19
Pedro de la Rosa	1m 22.535s	19
Pedro Diniz	1m 22.629s	3
Toranosuke Takagi	1m 22.664s	19
Marc Gene	1m 22.844s	13
Luca Badoer	1m 22.900s	16
Johnny Herbert	1m 25.608s	3

CHASSIS LOG BOOK

1	Häkkinen	McLaren MP4/14/5
2	Coulthard	McLaren MP4/14/6
	spare	McLaren MP4/14/2
3	M. Schumacher	Ferrari F399/193
4	Irvine	Ferrari F399/191
	spare	Ferrari F399/192
5	Zanardi	Williams FW21/5
6	R. Schumacher	Williams FW21/3
	spare	Williams FW21/2
7	Hill	Jordan 199/4
8	Frentzen	Jordan 199/5
	spare	Jordan 199/6
9	Fisichella	Benetton B199/3
10	Wurz	Benetton B199/5
	spare	Benetton B199/2
11	Alesi	Sauber C18/6
12	Diniz	Sauber C18/5
	spare	Sauber C18/4
14	de la Rosa	Arrows A20/4
15	Takagi	Arrows A20/2
	spare	Arrows A20/5
16	Barrichello	Stewart SF3/4
17	Herbert	Stewart SF3/5
	spare	Stewart SF3/3
18	Panis	Prost AP02/5
19	Trulli	Prost AP02/7
	spare	Prost AP02/3
20	Badoer	Minardi M01/1
21	Gene	Minardi M01/4
	spare	Minardi M01/3
22	Villeneuve	BAR 01/7
23	Zonta	BAR 01/6
	spare	BAR 01/5

POINTS TABLES

DRIVERS

1	Mika Häkkinen	40
2	Michael Schumacher	32
3	Eddie Irvine	26
4	Heinz-Harald Frentzen	23
5	Ralf Schumacher	15
6	Giancarlo Fisichella	13
7	David Coulthard	12
8	Rubens Barrichello	10
9	Damon Hill	3
10	Johnny Herbert	2
11 =	Pedro de la Rosa	1
11 =	Olivier Panis	1
11 =	Jean Alesi	1
11 =	Alexander Wurz	1
11 =	Jarno Trulli	1
11 =	Pedro Diniz	1

CONSTRUCTORS

1	Ferrari	58
2	McLaren	52
3	Jordan	26
4	Williams	15
5	Benetton	14
6	Stewart	12
7 =	Prost	2
7 =	Sauber	2
9	Arrows	1

BRITISH
grand prix

| COULTHARD |
| IRVINE |
| R. SCHUMACHER |
| FRENTZEN |
| HILL |
| DINIZ |

FIA WORLD CHAMPIONSHIP • ROUND 8

Far left top: Michael Schumacher's title ambitions for 1999 were ended at Silverstone when the German speared into the tyre wall.
Bruce Grant-Braham

Far left centre: His wrecked Ferrari, hoisted onto a flat-bed truck, clearly shows the extent of frontal damage.
Clive Mason/Allsport

Far left bottom: Takagi smokes his Bridgestones.
Michael Cooper/Allsport

Left: The drivers await the second start with Schumacher's grid position vacant.
Paul-Henri Cahier

Below left: Johnny Herbert lost a possible championship point after a stop–go penalty.
Paul-Henri Cahier

Below centre: Ralf Schumacher's performances in the Williams grew ever-more impressive as the season unfolded. His third place was thoroughly merited.
Paul-Henri Cahier

Schumacher accident raises run-off concerns

EVEN before the Ferrari team had established that a loss of hydraulic pressure to the rear brakes had been the cause of Michael Schumacher's accident, questions were again being asked about the effectiveness of gravel traps in arresting Grand Prix cars that are out of control.

'I've been saying for years they've got to slope upwards,' said Eddie Irvine. 'If they don't, they don't do anything. You've got to be forced into the gravel. It's something the Grand Prix Drivers' Association keeps pushing for and it doesn't happen.'

However, the FIA issued a statement saying, 'The gravel trap performed satisfactorily in a worst-case situation. There are no simple answers to slowing an out-of-control car.'

The Ferrari team did not take long to establish the cause of the problem with Schumacher's rear braking circuit, tracing the loss of pressure to a fluid leak from the left rear caliper. However, there was no information as to precisely why the brake bleed nipple on that caliper had become loose. Ferrari has accepted the assurance of Brembo, its brake supplier, that there was no inherent fault with the component concerned.

Schumacher's accident happened at probably the worst place on the Silverstone circuit to suffer any sort of brake failure. Once he left the tarmac, trying desperately to brake at around 160 mph, there was absolutely nothing he could do, but hang on grimly. Had the failure occurred at any one of a number of other points on the circuit – say the Bridge, Priory, Brooklands or Luffield corners – in all probability, he would have spun to a halt in a cloud of tyre smoke, undone his belt and walked away.

Main photograph: Paul-Henri Cahier

DIARY

Arrows agrees deal to use Supertec V10 engines for 2000 season.

Mercedes-Benz announces plans to take a 40 per cent stake in the TAG McLaren Group. This will lead to the German car maker building its new SLR sports car at McLaren's Paragon technical centre, currently under construction near Woking.

Bernie Ecclestone refutes claims published in the Sunday Times *that F1 cars may have been used to smuggle drugs around the world.*

US race car constructor Don Panoz buys the British G-Force organisation, builder of chassis for the Indy Racing League.

Christian Fittipaldi scores first ever CART win at Elkhart Lake in Newman/Haas Swift-Ford.

Right: Many thousands of Damon Hill's fans turned up in support of the 1996 World Champion on his farewell Silverstone appearance. They had a brief sight of their hero leading a lap late in the race.
Paul-Henri Cahier

Far right and below right: Battling Damon had the satisfaction of a much-improved performance which brought him fifth place at the finish.
Michael Cooper/Allsport (far right) and
Paul-Henri Cahier

SILVERSTONE QUALIFYING

It was a familiar story in qualifying. Even Michael Schumacher's efforts in the Ferrari to outgun Mika Häkkinen's McLaren for pole position were thwarted by lack of grip through the tight Priory/Brooklands/Luffield section.

Häkkinen's sixth pole of the season came in characteristically unruffled fashion, the Finn getting the best out of his soft-compound Bridgestones as the track temperature steadied at a sweltering 36 degrees. But for David Coulthard – out to reverse his recent run of misfortune – third on the grid was mildly disappointing.

'The car was not really changed that much since last week's test,' said Häkkinen. 'I was quite happy with the balance. We did some small changes to the set-up, but I think we timed the run just right. The first 20 minutes or so were the quickest.'

Coulthard added, 'I was quite happy with my high-speed balance, but mechanically, I haven't been able to replicate the form which we had at last week's test.

'I've lacked a bit of confidence in the braking areas, so under the circumstances I'm rather happy I finished third. But the car was actually much better today than yesterday, but when I try to carry more speed into the corners, I've been running wide. I would be surprised if I was so far away with full tanks as I was in qualifying.'

For his part, Michael Schumacher set second-fastest time with the Ferrari F399 on his first qualifying run. 'I don't know how much the wind or the temperature changed, but I had more difficulty keeping it under control on the infield,' he said. 'Irvine said he didn't do sufficient testing last week on the latest tyres, so he had to change the set-up of his car.

'I can't complain about being on the second row,' he shrugged. 'I had too much understeer until we found the solution for my final run. I pushed as hard as I could, but by the end of the session, the track was getting slower.'

Over at Jordan, the self-generated, will-he-won't-he speculation over Hill's retirement was beginning to tax the patience of even the most philosophical team members. Yet Damon ran well from the start of practice. With an uprated D-spec Mugen Honda V10 available for qualifying, and a new lightweight gearbox that enhanced the rear-end aerodynamics and gave better weight distribution, he stormed to an encouraging sixth place on the grid. The team did not use the new gearboxes in the race, as there was concern over the durability of the new rear wing mount, which was part of the revised package.

Hill qualified behind French GP winner Heinz-Harald Frentzen, but by less than 0.1s on this occasion. Truth be told, the gap might have been bigger. Frentzen was on course to knock Eddie Irvine's Ferrari from fourth place on the grid – almost matching David Coulthard's third-place McLaren to the second timing split – only for the speed to slip away from him through the last three corners.

Rubens Barrichello finished the day in a rather disappointed mood after qualifying seventh. 'I had expected to be at least in the top six after last week's test,' he said, 'but the car was very difficult to drive.' Johnny Herbert wound up 11th, unhappy with his set-up.

Williams had incorporated some major aerodynamic changes in the FW21s for this race, including repositioned exhaust exits and changes to the exit ducting from the side pods. Ralf Schumacher used this revised configuration to set eighth-fastest time, five places ahead of team-mate Alex Zanardi.

The German driver was moderately satisfied. 'I think we were reasonably confident after the test that we would be next best after Jordan, so the fact that we have qualified eighth says we still need to so some more work on the car,' he said. 'But it is certainly much better in the new set-up.'

D AVID Coulthard won perhaps the most significant race of his career at Silverstone with a measured drive to victory in the British Grand Prix, bringing to an end a bleak interval in his career that had lasted for more than a year. The McLaren-Mercedes team gave him a helping hand with a couple of briskly conducted refuelling stops that allowed him to take full advantage of an error made by his key rival, Ferrari driver Eddie Irvine, who lost crucial seconds when he overshot his pit during his first refuelling stop.

Irvine finished second on a day that was marred by a first-lap accident, which left Michael Schumacher with a broken right leg after he crashed heavily at Stowe corner, while Mika Häkkinen's McLaren was withdrawn from the battle after shedding its left rear wheel.

Coulthard's McLaren had the performance advantage over Irvine's Ferrari, and the Scot drove with great restraint and self-discipline to conserve his machinery, edging away from the Ulsterman in the closing stages when he realised that the race was all but won.

Although the day was clouded by the sombre sight of Ferrari's brilliant team leader clattering away to Northampton hospital in a 'medevac' helicopter, Coulthard's win represented a crucial moment of restoration for the easy-going 28-year-old, who had last tasted victory champagne at the 1998 San Marino Grand Prix.

Schumacher's nightmare began in the first few yards of the race, where any potential benefit of his second-row starting position evaporated as Häkkinen and Coulthard accelerated cleanly into first and second places. As if to add insult to injury, Eddie Irvine's Ferrari surged decisively around the outside going into Copse, pushing him back to fourth place.

Down through the quick and tricky Becketts section, Schumacher came back hard at Irvine and slipstreamed on to his tail as the two Ferraris accelerated to almost 190 mph. Irvine glanced in his mirror and dutifully allowed just enough room for Schumacher to have a look down the inside into Stowe. But Eddie was not handing him the position on a plate; he was also braking as late as he could, trying to keep pace with the flying McLaren-Mercedes.

Suddenly everything went wrong. Instead of cutting a gentle arc to the right, Michael locked his front brakes. From then on, everything was lost. The Ferrari left the tarmac still travelling at around 90 mph. With its rear wheels still apparently driving it onwards, the car skated across the gravel trap, reducing speed slightly to around 66 mph at the point of impact with the tyre barrier.

The tyres, which were not tethered together, were scattered in all directions, allowing the Ferrari to hit the unyielding barrier behind them. The impact ripped off the front end of the Ferrari monocoque. As Schumacher caught his breath and went to lift himself from the shattered car, it became clear that all was not well. After a moment's effort, he slumped back into the cockpit as marshals swarmed around the car.

Michael had sustained a double fracture below his right knee and had to wait for the ambulance to arrive before he was released from the wreckage and taken to the circuit medical centre, jauntily waving to his fans from the stretcher. He underwent a 90-minute operation, which was a complete success, surgeon Bill Ribbans revealing that only one pin had been needed to hold the bones in place, both of them having sustained clean breaks.

'I know I'm going to be out of action for two to three months and I realise that I've absolutely no chance of the championship this year,' said Schumacher. 'But I'm confident that I'll be back driving a Ferrari in Formula 1 before the end of the season.'

It was cruelly ironic that, at the stage when Schumacher's Ferrari speared off the road, the race had already been red flagged to a halt, as Jacques Villeneuve's British American 01 and Alex Zanardi's Williams had stalled on the starting grid. The McLaren pit informed both Häkkinen and Coulthard of the situation by radio, but Irvine explained that he had heard nothing from his pit.

'I had to touch the brakes to avoid David (Coulthard) going into Becketts on the first lap, and it's possible that Michael may have touched me and damaged his front wing,' said Irvine. 'All I know is that he came flying past me all locked up. I think he just out-braked himself.'

At first, this view was shared by many others. Schumacher had been frustrated by the handling of his car during the morning's warm-up session and had made a quick change to the set-up in an effort to improve things. Then he was jumped by Irvine going into Copse and simply might have taken one risk too many as he slammed into Stowe in a bad mood.

However, having examined all the technical data at its disposal, the Ferrari team concluded that a rear brake malfunction had caused the accident. Eventually, a leaking nipple was identified as the culprit.

'The results from the telemetry are very clear,' said Ferrari spokesman Claudio Berro. 'The braking on the rear wheels [of Schumacher's car] was zero. All this talk about steering and throttle problems is just not right. The result is clear, but now we have to find the precise cause.'

At the restart, Häkkinen again surged into an immediate lead from Irvine, Coulthard, Frentzen, Ralf Schumacher and Hill. Meanwhile, there were more problems on the grid as Pedro de la Rosa's Arrows A20 refused to budge with gearbox failure, bringing out the safety car at the end of the opening lap to cover the Spaniard's removal from the track.

The restart had given a second chance to Zanardi, Villeneuve (who took the spare British American 01) and Olivier Panis, who switched to the spare Prost AP02 after suffering hydraulic problems with his race car.

On lap six, Luca Badoer brought his Minardi into the pits to clear debris

from his radiator ducting after Toranosuke Takagi's Arrows had pushed him on to the grass. The Italian resumed the chase momentarily, but stopped with engine failure just beyond the pit exit.

By lap ten, Häkkinen had built up a lead of 3.8s over Irvine in what seemed to be turning into a procession. The leading trio was so far ahead of its pursuers that Coulthard was disappearing around Copse before Heinz-Harald Frentzen's Jordan tripped the timing line.

On lap 23, Hill was the first front-runner to make a refuelling stop, taking 8.5s and dropping from seventh to eighth. Next time around, Coulthard made his first stop (7.6s), resuming third behind Irvine and Häkkinen, the Finn making a 9.2s stop on the following lap. Frentzen and Ralf Schumacher also stopped from fourth and fifth places, the latter's Williams FW21 just getting the jump on his rival to vault ahead as they accelerated back into the race.

Häkkinen's stop had certainly taken a fraction too long, the mechanics working on the left rear wheel appearing to have had some trouble in securing the replacement. As he accelerated back down the pit lane, Mika gently swerved the McLaren from side to side, as if to reassure himself that all was well. But clearly it wasn't.

Next time around, Mika was back in the pits for a 17.6s additional stop to deal with that left rear wheel, which had worked loose. He resumed 11th. On the same lap, Irvine came in for the first time, slightly overshooting his refuelling rig and taking 12s for his stop as a result. He resumed a crucial 0.8s behind Coulthard.

'It was the first time I had come into the pits when the McLaren guys were already waiting for their driver,' he said. 'Once I had got past them, I suddenly realised how close my guys were to them, and it was pretty obvious I wasn't going to be able to get stopped in time to get into my pit in the right position. I just overshot, which is why they weren't immediately able to get the fuel hose on the nozzle. Ultimately, that mistake cost us the race.'

Häkkinen, however, was still in trouble. Coming out of the final right-hander of the lap, his McLaren shed its left rear wheel, but he still managed to dodge across to the pit entrance and three-wheel back in for more attention from his crew. Meanwhile, the safety car was deployed as the wayward wheel bounced against the trackside barrier, then back on to the circuit, where it narrowly missed several cars.

When Häkkinen finally resumed the race, he was running 19th and last. He was through to 16th by lap 35, at which point the McLaren pit signalled him to come back in, whereupon his car was retired. 'We decided to retire the car as a precaution against a similar problem with the left-hand rear wheel,' said Ron Dennis. 'But we will fully investigate this.'

On lap 41, Irvine made his second stop, dropping from second to fifth. Next time around, Coulthard also made his second stop (in 6.3s) and just managed to squeeze back into the race ahead of the Ferrari. Thereafter, although Irvine gave it his best shot, Coulthard retained the upper hand.

'As soon as my team got me back into the race ahead of Eddie at my second stop, I realised that by keeping out of trouble I could win this one,' said the Scot. 'It was more nerve-racking than any race at any other point in my career. Otherwise, Eddie and I were pretty evenly matched; he was a little quicker at the beginning, I was a little quicker at the end. Whoever had track position today was going to win this race.'

For the moment, however, they were running third and fourth, as Frentzen was briefly leading, ahead of Hill, in an impressive, if misleading, Jordan 1-2. On lap 45, Heinz-Harald made his second stop in 6.8s, allowing Damon to surge into the lead for one glorious lap before making his own refuelling stop on the next circuit.

At this stage, the order was Coulthard, Irvine, Ralf Schumacher, Frentzen, Hill and Johnny Herbert in the Stewart-Ford. However, Johnny's hopes for a point from his home Grand Prix were dashed on lap 49, when he came in to take a 10s 'stop-go' penalty, apparently for prematurely overtaking Jean Alesi's Sauber at the end of the second safety-car period on lap 32.

'It's such a shame to come away from Silverstone empty handed,' he shrugged after the race. 'We put in a lot of hard work over the last two days and I was feeling quite comfortable with the car. It was pretty disheartening when I saw the pit board telling me I had a penalty.'

Herbert finished 12th, four places behind his equally luckless team-mate, Rubens Barrichello who, at one point, looked as though he might challenge Frentzen for fourth. Then the Brazilian suffered a deflated left front tyre – apparently caused by a stone piercing the wheel rim – and was obliged to make an unscheduled third stop with only 13 of the race's 60 laps to run.

All that was left was for Coulthard to reel off the remaining laps to the chequered flag and make a return to the top step of the rostrum, which he felt was far too long overdue. 'It was absolutely fantastic,' he said. 'When I came out of my last [refuelling] stop ahead of Eddie, it was the most nerve-racking moment of my career. This is the British Grand Prix and I would trade all other wins for this.'

Behind Irvine, Ralf Schumacher put in a simply storming performance to finish third. 'When the first race was red flagged, at first I didn't realise what had happened,' said Ralf. 'Then, as soon as I realised it was Michael involved, the team told me he was out of the car and it didn't look bad. Obviously, it's not very nice to have to get back in the car when your brother has had an accident, but on the other hand, the team is relying on me and I have to do my job.

'I have to say the team did a great job with the revised aero-package, because with the old set-up we'd been nowhere in the pre-race test here. Then suddenly we were a lot closer, and in the race my pit crew did an incredible job to get me back out in front of Heinz-Harald.'

In the Jordan camp, Damon Hill drove superbly to wind up fifth behind team-mate Heinz-Harald Frentzen, but had to ease back in the closing stages when a warning light signalled a loss of pneumatic pressure from the valve-gear. He had to short-shift to keep the V10 in one piece.

'There was a lot of pressure before the race, so I am very happy to have come through the trials and tribulations to finish fifth,' he admitted. 'The plan is now to have a few beers and think about the future. I am not going to make any decisions today.'

Completing the top six was Pedro Diniz's Sauber after a strong battle with Giancarlo Fisichella's Benetton, which the former beat across the line by less than a second. Jean Alesi, in the other Sauber, had grappled with a major throttle potentiometer problem, which had obliged him to make an extra stop at the end of lap 34 for the team to adjust the computer software programme. He resumed the chase, but could only finish in 14th place, two laps down.

Behind Fisichella came the luckless Barrichello's Stewart-Ford, then Jarno Trulli's Prost and Alex Zanardi's Williams FW21. 'I am glad I finished the race, but of course I'm not excited about my performance,' said the former CART Champion. 'I will have to work on this and try to improve.'

THE RAC BRITISH GRAND PRIX

9–11 JULY 1999
SILVERSTONE

Race distance: 60 laps, 191.566 miles/308.296 km

Race weather: Dry, hot and sunny

FIA FORMULA 1 WORLD CHAMPIONSHIP

Mobil 1

ROUND 8

SILVERSTONE – GRAND PRIX CIRCUIT

Copse · Maggotts · Chapel · Hangar Straight · Brooklands · Priory · Bridge · The Vale · Stowe Corner · Woodcote · Luffield · Abbey Curve · Club Corner

CIRCUIT LENGTH: 3.194 miles/5.140 km

Pos.	Driver	Nat.	No.	Entrant	Car/Engine	Laps	Time/Retirement	Speed (mph/km/h)
1	David Coulthard	GB	2	West McLaren Mercedes	McLaren MP4/14-Mercedes F0110G V10	60	1h 32m 30.144s	124.256/199.971
2	Eddie Irvine	GB	4	Scuderia Ferrari Marlboro	Ferrari F399 048B V10	60	1h 32m 31.973s	124.215/199.905
3	Ralf Schumacher	D	6	Winfield Williams	Williams FW21-Supertec FB01 V10	60	1h 32m 57.555s	123.645/198.988
4	Heinz-Harald Frentzen	D	8	Benson & Hedges Jordan	Jordan 199-Mugen Honda MF301/HD V10	60	1h 32m 57.933s	123.637/198.975
5	Damon Hill	GB	7	Benson & Hedges Jordan	Jordan 199-Mugen Honda MF301/HD V10	60	1h 33m 08.750s	123.397/198.589
6	Pedro Diniz	BR	12	Red Bull Sauber Petronas	Sauber C18-Petronas SPE03A V10	60	1h 33m 23.787s	123.066/198.056
7	Giancarlo Fisichella	I	9	Mild Seven Benetton Playlife	Benetton B199-Playlife V10	60	1h 33m 24.758s	123.045/198.022
8	Rubens Barrichello	BR	16	Stewart Ford	Stewart SF3-Ford CR-1 V10	60	1h 33m 38.734s	122.739/197.530
9	Jarno Trulli	I	19	Gauloises Prost Peugeot	Prost AP02-Peugeot A18 V10	60	1h 33m 42.189s	122.664/197.409
10	Alexander Wurz	A	10	Mild Seven Benetton Playlife	Benetton B199-Playlife V10	60	1h 33m 42.267s	122.662/197.406
11	Alex Zanardi	I	5	Winfield Williams	Williams FW21-Supertec FB01 V10	60	1h 33m 47.268s	122.552/197.229
12	Johnny Herbert	GB	17	Stewart Ford	Stewart SF3-Ford CR-1 V10	60	1h 33m 47.853s	122.540/197.209
13	Olivier Panis	F	18	Gauloises Prost Peugeot	Prost AP02-Peugeot A18 V10	60	1h 33m 50.636s	122.479/197.111
14	Jean Alesi	F	11	Red Bull Sauber Petronas	Sauber C18-Petronas SPE03A V10	59		
15	Marc Gene	ESP	21	Fondmetal Minardi Ford	Minardi M01-Ford Zetec-R V10	58		
16	Toranosuke Takagi	J	15	Arrows	Arrows A20 V10	58		
	Ricardo Zonta	BR	23	British American Racing	BAR 01-Supertec FB01 V10	41	Suspension	
	Mika Häkkinen	SF	1	West McLaren Mercedes	McLaren MP4/14-Mercedes F0110G V10	35	Wheel hub	
	Jacques Villeneuve	CDN	22	British American Racing	BAR 01-Supertec FB01 V10	29	Gearbox	
	Luca Badoer	I	20	Fondmetal Minardi Ford	Minardi M01-Ford Zetec-R V10	6	Gearbox	
	Pedro de la Rosa	ESP	14	Arrows	Arrows A20 V10	0	Gearbox	
DNS	Michael Schumacher	D	3	Scuderia Ferrari Marlboro	Ferrari F399 048B V10		Accident at first start	

Fastest lap: Häkkinen, on lap 28, 1m 28.309s, 130.200 mph/209.537 km/h.

Lap record: M. Schumacher (F1 Ferrari F3108 V10), 1m 24.475s, 136.109 mph/219.047 km/h (1997).

Grid order	1	2	3	4	5	6	7	8	9	10	11	12	13	14	15	16	17	18	19	20	21	22	23	24	25	26	27	28	29	30	31	32	33	34	35	36	37	38	39	40	41	42	43	44	45	46
1 HÄKKINEN	1	1	1	1	1	1	1	1	1	1	1	1	1	1	1	1	1	1	1	1	1	1	1	1	4	4	2	2	2	2	2	2	2	2	2	2	2	2	2	2	2	2	8	8	7	2
3 M. SCHUMACHER	4	4	4	4	4	4	4	4	4	4	4	4	4	4	4	4	4	4	4	4	4	4	4	4	1	2	4	4	4	4	4	4	4	4	4	4	4	4	8	7	7	8	4			
2 COULTHARD	2	2	2	2	2	2	2	2	2	2	2	2	2	2	2	2	2	2	2	2	2	2	2	2	2	1	6	6	6	6	6	6	6	6	6	6	6	6	6	8	7	2	2	2	2	7
4 IRVINE	8	8	8	8	8	8	8	8	8	8	8	8	8	8	8	8	8	8	8	8	8	8	8	8	16	6	8	8	8	8	8	8	8	8	8	8	8	8	16	16	4	4	4	6		
8 FRENTZEN	6	6	6	6	6	6	6	6	6	6	6	6	6	6	6	6	6	6	6	6	6	6	6	16	6	8	7	7	7	7	7	7	16	16	16	16	16	16	7	4	6	6	6	8		
7 HILL	7	7	7	7	7	7	7	7	7	7	7	7	7	7	7	7	7	7	7	7	7	7	16	6	8	7	16	16	16	16	16	7	7	7	7	7	7	7	9	9	16	16	16	16		
16 BARRICHELLO	16	16	16	16	16	16	16	16	16	16	16	16	16	16	16	16	16	16	16	16	16	16	7	12	7	22	22	22	11	11	11	17	17	17	17	17	12	6	17	17	17	12				
6 R. SCHUMACHER	11	11	11	11	11	11	11	11	11	11	11	11	11	11	11	11	11	11	11	11	17	12	7	22	16	11	11	17	17	17	12	12	12	12	12	12	17	10	17	12	12	12				
22 VILLENEUVE	12	12	17	17	17	17	17	17	17	17	17	17	17	17	17	17	17	17	17	11	12	17	22	11	11	17	17	12	12	12	9	9	9	9	9	9	9	6	12	9	9	9				
11 ALESI	17	17	12	12	12	12	12	12	12	12	12	12	12	12	12	12	12	12	12	22	22	23	18	17	12	12	22	9	9	9	5	5	5	5	5	10	10	17	19	19	19	19				
17 HERBERT	22	22	22	22	22	22	22	22	22	22	22	22	22	22	22	22	22	22	19	19	11	17	12	1	1	9	5	5	5	10	10	10	10	10	5	19	19	10	10	10	10	10				
12 DINIZ	5	5	5	5	5	5	5	5	5	5	5	5	5	5	5	5	5	5	23	23	19	23	18	9	9	5	19	10	18	18	18	18	18	19	5	5	5	5	5	5						
5 ZANARDI	19	19	19	19	19	19	19	19	19	19	19	19	19	19	19	19	19	19	18	11	18	12	9	5	5	19	10	18	11	19	19	19	18	18	18	18	18	18	18	18						
19 TRULLI	9	9	9	9	9	9	9	9	9	9	9	9	9	9	9	9	9	9	9	23	23	5	18	17	2	5	19	19	10	23	18	19	23	23	23	23	23	23	11	11	11	11	11			
18 PANIS	10	10	23	23	23	23	23	23	23	23	23	23	23	23	23	23	23	10	18	11	9	9	5	19	10	23	18	23	23	11	11	11	11	11	11	11	11	21	21	21	21					
23 ZONTA	23	23	10	10	10	10	10	10	10	10	10	10	10	10	10	10	10	18	10	9	5	19	10	23	18	15	15	1	1	1	15	15	15	15	15	15	15	15	15	15						
9 FISICHELLA	18	18	18	18	18	18	18	18	18	18	18	18	18	18	18	18	18	9	9	10	10	10	23	18	1	21	21	15	15	15	21	21	21	21	21											
10 WURZ	15	15	15	15	15	15	15	15	15	15	15	15	15	15	15	15	15	15	15	15	15	15	15	15	1	1	21	21	21																	
15 TAKAGI	21	21	21	21	21	21	21	21	21	21	21	21	21	21	21	21	21	21	21	21	21	21	21	21																						
14 DE LA ROSA	20	20	20	20	20	20																																								
20 BADOER																																														
21 GENE																																														

Pit stop

One lap behind leader

STARTING GRID

1 HÄKKINEN McLaren	**3*** M. SCHUMACHER Ferrari
2 COULTHARD McLaren	**4** IRVINE Ferrari
8 FRENTZEN Jordan	**7** HILL Jordan
16 BARRICHELLO Stewart	**6** R. SCHUMACHER Williams
22 VILLENEUVE BAR	**11** ALESI Sauber
17 HERBERT Stewart	**12** DINIZ Sauber
5 ZANARDI Williams	**19** TRULLI Prost
18 PANIS Prost	**23** ZONTA BAR
9 FISICHELLA Benetton	**10** WURZ Benetton
15 TAKAGI Arrows	**14** DE LA ROSA Arrows
20 BADOER Minardi	**21** GENE Minardi

* did not take restart

TIME SHEETS

QUALIFYING

Weather: Overcast and very warm

Pos.	Driver	Car	Laps	Time
1	Mika Häkkinen	McLaren-Mercedes	9	1m 24.804s
2	Michael Schumacher	Ferrari	11	1m 25.223s
3	David Coulthard	McLaren-Mercedes	12	1m 25.594s
4	Eddie Irvine	Ferrari	12	1m 25.677s
5	Heinz-Harald Frentzen	Jordan-Mugen Honda	11	1m 25.991s
6	Damon Hill	Jordan-Mugen Honda	12	1m 26.099s
7	Rubens Barrichello	Stewart-Ford	12	1m 26.194s
8	Ralf Schumacher	Williams-Supertec	12	1m 26.438s
9	Jacques Villeneuve	BAR-Supertec	11	1m 26.719s
10	Jean Alesi	Sauber-Petronas	11	1m 26.761s
11	Johnny Herbert	Stewart-Ford	12	1m 26.873s
12	Pedro Diniz	Sauber-Petronas	12	1m 27.196s
13	Alex Zanardi	Williams-Supertec	12	1m 27.223s
14	Jarno Trulli	Prost-Peugeot	10	1m 27.227s
15	Olivier Panis	Prost-Peugeot	11	1m 27.543s
16	Ricardo Zonta	BAR-Supertec	11	1m 27.699s
17	Giancarlo Fisichella	Benetton-Playlife	12	1m 27.857s
18	Alexander Wurz	Benetton-Playlife	12	1m 28.010s
19	Toranosuke Takagi	Arrows	11	1m 28.037s
20	Pedro de la Rosa	Arrows	12	1m 28.148s
21	Luca Badoer	Minardi-Ford	11	1m 28.695s
22	Marc Gene	Minardi-Ford	12	1m 28.772s

FRIDAY FREE PRACTICE

Weather: Dry and overcast

Pos.	Driver	Laps	Time
1	Mika Häkkinen	26	1m 26.981s
2	Ralf Schumacher	32	1m 27.004s
3	Eddie Irvine	27	1m 27.061s
4	David Coulthard	28	1m 27.155s
5	Rubens Barrichello	35	1m 27.158s
6	Michael Schumacher	24	1m 27.327s
7	Damon Hill	31	1m 27.381s
8	Pedro Diniz	40	1m 27.931s
9	Jacques Villeneuve	38	1m 27.981s
10	Alex Zanardi	32	1m 28.162s
11	Ricardo Zonta	34	1m 28.238s
12	Jean Alesi	20	1m 28.472s
13	Giancarlo Fisichella	26	1m 28.546s
14	Heinz-Harald Frentzen	29	1m 28.595s
15	Alexander Wurz	17	1m 28.740s
16	Jarno Trulli	7	1m 28.883s
17	Luca Badoer	36	1m 29.130s
18	Johnny Herbert	28	1m 29.201s
19	Marc Gene	36	1m 29.416s
20	Pedro de la Rosa	29	1m 29.439s
21	Toranosuke Takagi	27	1m 29.630s
22	Olivier Panis	6	1m 30.372s

SATURDAY FREE PRACTICE

Weather: Dry, warm and sunny

Pos.	Driver	Laps	Time
1	Mika Häkkinen	22	1m 24.489s
2	David Coulthard	28	1m 25.151s
3	Michael Schumacher	29	1m 25.301s
4	Heinz-Harald Frentzen	24	1m 25.406s
5	Damon Hill	30	1m 25.600s
6	Eddie Irvine	19	1m 25.742s
7	Rubens Barrichello	25	1m 25.946s
8	Ralf Schumacher	30	1m 26.250s
9	Johnny Herbert	35	1m 26.311s
10	Jacques Villeneuve	18	1m 26.531s
11	Pedro Diniz	36	1m 26.564s
12	Jean Alesi	28	1m 26.676s
13	Ricardo Zonta	29	1m 27.157s
14	Alexander Wurz	35	1m 27.193s
15	Alex Zanardi	26	1m 27.250s
16	Giancarlo Fisichella	28	1m 27.254s
17	Jarno Trulli	26	1m 27.309s
18	Toranosuke Takagi	26	1m 27.782s
19	Olivier Panis	29	1m 27.864s
20	Pedro de la Rosa	27	1m 27.977s
21	Luca Badoer	29	1m 28.376s
22	Marc Gene	29	1m 28.421s

WARM-UP

Weather: Dry, hot and sunny

Pos.	Driver	Laps	Time
1	Mika Häkkinen	14	1m 26.788s
2	David Coulthard	12	1m 27.286s
3	Michael Schumacher	13	1m 27.497s
4	Damon Hill	15	1m 28.105s
5	Rubens Barrichello	14	1m 28.265s
6	Eddie Irvine	12	1m 28.295s
7	Heinz-Harald Frentzen	12	1m 28.381s
8	Ralf Schumacher	15	1m 28.382s
9	Jean Alesi	13	1m 28.431s
10	Jarno Trulli	12	1m 28.733s
11	Johnny Herbert	17	1m 28.785s
12	Alex Zanardi	11	1m 29.038s
13	Alexander Wurz	17	1m 29.260s
14	Giancarlo Fisichella	16	1m 29.480s
15	Jacques Villeneuve	12	1m 29.537s
16	Ricardo Zonta	9	1m 29.645s
17	Toranosuke Takagi	11	1m 29.828s
18	Pedro Diniz	16	1m 29.845s
19	Pedro de la Rosa	10	1m 30.018s
20	Luca Badoer	15	1m 30.128s
21	Olivier Panis	11	1m 30.217s
22	Marc Gene	14	1m 30.381s

RACE FASTEST LAPS

Weather: Dry, hot and sunny

Driver	Time	Lap
Mika Häkkinen	1m 28.309s	28
Eddie Irvine	1m 28.782s	54
David Coulthard	1m 28.846s	47
Damon Hill	1m 29.252s	48
Heinz-Harald Frentzen	1m 29.330s	47
Ralf Schumacher	1m 29.414s	26
Rubens Barrichello	1m 29.493s	49
Pedro Diniz	1m 29.819s	27
Johnny Herbert	1m 30.103s	53
Giancarlo Fisichella	1m 30.296s	54
Jean Alesi	1m 30.334s	37
Alex Zanardi	1m 30.522s	41
Ricardo Zonta	1m 30.611s	27
Alexander Wurz	1m 30.625s	40
Olivier Panis	1m 30.793s	41
Jarno Trulli	1m 30.964s	52
Jacques Villeneuve	1m 31.342s	18
Marc Gene	1m 31.612s	44
Luca Badoer	1m 32.409s	3
Toranosuke Takagi	1m 32.442s	22

CHASSIS LOG BOOK

1	Häkkinen	McLaren MP4/14/5
2	Coulthard	McLaren MP4/14/6
	spare	McLaren MP4/14/2
3	M. Schumacher	Ferrari F399/192
4	Irvine	Ferrari F399/191
	spare	Ferrari F399/193
5	Zanardi	Williams FW21/5
6	R. Schumacher	Williams FW21/3
	spare	Williams FW21/2
7	Hill	Jordan 199/4
8	Frentzen	Jordan 199/5
	spare	Jordan 199/6
9	Fisichella	Benetton B199/7
10	Wurz	Benetton B199/5
	spare	Benetton B199/4
11	Alesi	Sauber C18/6
12	Diniz	Sauber C18/5
	spare	Sauber C18/3
14	de la Rosa	Arrows A20/3
15	Takagi	Arrows A20/2
	spare	Arrows A20/5
16	Barrichello	Stewart SF3/4
17	Herbert	Stewart SF3/5
	spare	Stewart SF3/3
18	Panis	Prost AP02/5
19	Trulli	Prost AP02/7
	spare	Prost AP02/3
20	Badoer	Minardi M01/1
21	Gene	Minardi M01/4
	spare	Minardi M01/3
22	Villeneuve	BAR 01/7
23	Zonta	BAR 01/6
	spare	BAR 01/5

POINTS TABLES

DRIVERS

1	Mika Häkkinen	40
2 =	Michael Schumacher	32
2 =	Eddie Irvine	32
4	Heinz-Harald Frentzen	26
5	David Coulthard	22
6	Ralf Schumacher	19
7	Giancarlo Fisichella	13
8	Rubens Barrichello	10
9	Damon Hill	5
10 =	Johnny Herbert	2
10 =	Pedro Diniz	2
12 =	Pedro de la Rosa	1
12 =	Olivier Panis	1
12 =	Jean Alesi	1
12 =	Alexander Wurz	1
12 =	Jarno Trulli	1

CONSTRUCTORS

1	Ferrari	64
2	McLaren	62
3	Jordan	31
4	Williams	19
5	Benetton	14
6	Stewart	12
7	Sauber	3
8	Prost	2
9	Arrows	1

49	50	51	52	53	54	55	56	57	58	59	60	
2	2	2	2	2	2	2	2	2	2	2	2	1
4	4	4	4	4	4	4	4	4	4	4	4	2
6	6	6	6	6	6	6	6	6	6	6	6	3
8	8	8	8	8	8	8	8	8	8	8	8	4
7	7	7	7	7	7	7	7	7	7	7	7	5
12	12	12	12	12	12	12	12	12	12	12	12	6
17	9	9	9	9	9	9	9	9	9	9	9	
9	19	19	19	19	19	19	19	19	19	16	16	
19	10	10	10	10	10	10	10	10	16	19	19	
10	5	5	5	5	5	16	16	10	10	10	10	
5	18	18	18	18	16	5	5	5	5	5	5	
18	16	16	16	16	18	18	18	18	17	17	17	
16	17	17	17	17	17	17	17	17	18	18	18	
11	11	11	11	11	11	11	11	11	11	11	11	
21	21	21	21	21	21	21	21	21	21			
15	15	15	15	15	15	15	15	15	15			

SPIELBERG 1999

IRVINE
COULTHARD
HÄKKINEN
FRENTZEN
WURZ
DINIZ

FIA WORLD CHAMPIONSHIP • ROUND 9

AUSTRIAN
grand prix

DIARY

Prost rumoured to be negotiating to use customer Ferrari engines in 2000 in the event of Peugeot withdrawing from F1 at the end of the season.

Britain's ITV television channel still fails to finalise deal with Bernie Ecclestone over the terms of its live Grand Prix qualifying coverage.

Jean Alesi in talks with both Prost and Sauber over possible deals for the 2000 season.

Jarno Trulli moves closer to deal with Jordan team to succeed Damon Hill next season as team-mate to Heinz-Harald Frentzen.

Left: Luck of the Irish? Eddie Irvine won the Austrian Grand Prix and Mika Häkkinen was unimpressed with his hard won third place.

Below left: David Coulthard tips team-mate Häkkinen's McLaren into the second corner spin which shaped the race.

IT was one of the most disappointing moments of David Coulthard's F1 career. Two corners after the start of the Austrian Grand Prix at the A1-Ring, the Scot tarnished the golden memories of that Silverstone victory a fortnight before by shunting his McLaren-Mercedes team-mate Mika Häkkinen into a spin right in front of the entire pack.

It was every driver's nightmare, but it could have been worse. Both McLaren MP4/14s amazingly survived with such superficial damage that neither driver judged it necessary to make a precautionary pit stop to check for further damage. Thus, while Coulthard got on with the business of leading the race, Häkkinen got his head down in preparation for a memorable charge through from the back of the field.

At the end of the day, Coulthard found himself beaten into second place by Eddie Irvine's Ferrari F399, the Ulsterman perhaps making up for his pit lane slip at Silverstone which had prevented him from winning there. On the face of it, one could have been forgiven for thinking that Coulthard had simply been out-raced by the Ferrari driver, but McLaren boss Ron Dennis admitted that the team took some of the responsibility for not keeping David fully informed of how the race was developing.

Häkkinen had qualified superbly on pole position and duly took the lead into the first corner. Coulthard was close behind on the uphill run to the tricky right-hand Remus Kurve, where he decided to have a stab down the inside under braking.

'When I went off the line I thought there might be a chance to pass Mika into the first corner,' said Coulthard. 'When I realised that wouldn't be possible, I came back across on to my line, and thought it might be possible to [try it again there] under braking, because all weekend I had been a little bit better [than Mika] under brakes into turn two.

'But clearly I misjudged that completely. It has always been a nightmare scenario to run into Mika when we got to the apex, but unfortunately he was turning in as I tried to stop. And disaster happened.'

Coulthard managed to squeeze through into the lead going onto the top straight as Häkkinen spun to a halt, mercifully not having slid beyond the narrow strip of grass separating the tarmac from the gravel run-off area. Rubens Barrichello's Stewart SF3 pulled level with Coulthard along the top straight, but David just retained the advantage, while, further back,

A1-RING QUALIFYING

From the outset, there had been precious little doubt that the main issue in Austria was set to be contested by the two McLaren-Mercedes drivers and Ferrari's lone standard bearer. Mika Salo couldn't be expected to deliver much on his first outing as Michael Schumacher's understudy.

A fuel pump problem caused Häkkinen's car to stop on its first out lap during the hour-long qualifying session, but the well-oiled McLaren machine ensured that his spare MP4/14 was ready the moment he returned to the paddock on a motorcycle pillion. David Coulthard, meanwhile, had also had an electronic glitch on his own out lap and came straight back in to have the system re-programmed. From then on the McLaren duo never missed a beat.

Häkkinen's fastest lap was truly remarkable. Yet again the Finn's performance radiated such shimmering, audacious confidence that you just knew his seventh pole position of the season was a foregone conclusion.

Coulthard was a strong second with Irvine a slightly disappointed third, believing that his Ferrari F399 had the potential to carry him onto the outside of the front row.

'We underperformed, to be honest,' said Eddie. 'We should have been a little quicker, but I just couldn't use the brakes. On one lap I would lock the fronts at one corner and go straight on, then on the next lap the rears would lock. That won't be an issue in the race because the temperatures will be more stabilised. I'm expecting to give the McLarens a good run for their money.'

Tyres did not prove to be a major issue during qualifying. The low-grip track surface was pretty raw after torrential thunderstorms doused most of Austria on Thursday and most quick teams had to keep an eye open for graining front covers as the track gradually picked up grip on Friday morning.

Virtually the entire field went for the softer Bridgestone option, the cars performing better on scrubbed rubber which delivered less in the way of understeer than a brand new set of tyres.

In fourth place on the grid, Heinz-Harald Frentzen was well pleased with his 1m 12.266s best. 'After a difficult morning trying to find the right set-up, I had not expected to finish so high up,' he admitted.

'This is the best result we have had all season and I am very pleased with the job we did. This morning we were struggling to find a balance but we made the right modifications in time for a successful qualifying session.'

By contrast, Damon Hill lost his way on chassis set-up with the initially promising feel he had experienced on Friday slipping away from him. He wound up 11th. 'Whatever we had yesterday did not work today,' he said.

Rubens Barrichello and Johnny Herbert qualified the Stewart-Fords strongly in fifth and sixth places. Rubens encountered traffic on his last run, but shared Herbert's satisfaction. 'The car was very well balanced,' said the Brazilian.

Mika Salo set seventh fastest time in the other Ferrari, satisfied enough with his performance although he admitted he had not yet really amassed enough confidence or experience to get the best out of the car.

In the Williams camp, both Ralf Schumacher and Alex Zanardi were using carbon-fibre brakes for qualifying after Alex had experimented with steel discs, but eighth and 14th on the grid respectively reflected the fact that neither driver could get things to gel properly throughout the hour-long session.

Behind Ralf, Jacques Villeneuve wound up ninth on 1m 12.833s, his efforts with the BAR thwarted when he caught a flurry of yellow warning flags on his best lap, while his team-mate Ricardo Zonta wound up 15th after sliding into a gravel trap.

Meanwhile, Alexander Wurz's Benetton lined up tenth, the Austrian feeling quite satisfied with the feel of his car but believing he could have gone slightly quicker had he enjoyed a clear, traffic-free run. Giancarlo Fisichella was 12th after finding his B199 particularly difficult to drive on the limit in low-downforce configuration.

Uncharacteristically off the pace were both Sauber C18s, Pedro Diniz (1m 13.223s) and Jean Alesi (1m 13.226s) winding up 16th and 17th. Diniz was continually frustrated by an inability to work out a decent handling balance on new tyres while Alesi had engine problems and was forced to switch from his race chassis to the spare car.

Ferrari new boy Mika Salo had dislodged the front wing of his F399 in an impact which had snapped off the rear wing of Johnny Herbert's Stewart.

Despite a broken front wing endplate, Coulthard led the opening lap by 1.2s from Barrichello, with Eddie Irvine's Ferrari third. Then came Heinz-Harald Frentzen's Jordan 199, Salo, Jacques Villeneuve's British American Racing 01 and Ralf Schumacher's Williams FW21. At the tail of the field

Herbert pitted for repairs just as Häkkinen came through in 22nd, and last, place.

On lap three Salo finally came in to have his Ferrari's nose section changed, by which time Coulthard had opened his advantage to 4.017s over Barrichello. Salo dropped from seventh to 20th, by which time Häkkinen was up to 18th.

On lap nine Ralf Schumacher made the first driving error of his 1999 season when he spun off after outbraking Pedro Diniz's Sauber C18 for fifth place. Unfortunately, the German youngster failed to make the move stick and ended up with his Williams FW21's rear wheels firmly stuck in the gravel.

'I came into a corner and Diniz was very close behind and trying to overtake,' shrugged Ralf. 'I was trying to hold him off, but I braked too late and began to slide on the track, which was quite dirty at that point. I could not then avoid spinning and going into the gravel.'

By lap ten Coulthard had opened his advantage by 9.8s from Barrichello with Irvine seemingly unable to do anything about the Stewart SF3 in third place. In fact, he was taking an overtly tactical approach, running as gently as he dared.

'I had actually been saving fuel at the start of the race and I was hoping the car wasn't going to break down then, because at that stage I was behind Barrichello and driving very slowly,' he later explained.

'If I had broken down then, the Italian press would have murdered me! But I just had to save the fuel and try to save the brakes. Later I started pushing and pushing and it was when Barrichello went in [for his stop] that I really put the hammer down. That is what got us ahead of DC.'

Further back, two drivers were making a major impression on the lap charts. Not only had Häkkinen stormed back from 22nd to 12th in the first ten laps, but Jean Alesi's Sauber C18 had also climbed from 17th to tenth during that period, the Frenchman running on a two-stop strategy in contrast to the McLaren-Mercedes drivers' one-stop plan.

For his part, Häkkinen was absolutely flying, overtaking car after car in decisively surgical fashion, with perfect judgement and no obvious drama. If he was inwardly seething over the events of the opening lap, he certainly didn't seem to be showing it.

On lap 24 Diniz brought his Sauber in from fifth place to make the first refuelling stop of the race, allowing

161

Red on Green. Eddie Irvine's Ferrari provides the focal point in the majestic scenery surrounding the A1-Ring.
Paul-Henri Cahier

Häkkinen to take his track position some 35s behind Coulthard's leading sister McLaren. Within another four laps Häkkinen was piling the pressure on Frentzen's Jordan, and the Finn eventually dived inside his rival to take fourth place with a decisive move under braking for the first right-hander going into lap 34.

Next time round, Villeneuve's encouraging run with the British American 01 ended when he retired from sixth place with a broken driveshaft. 'I was pleased with my start and in the early part of the race there was a lot of action,' he said. 'We were on a one-stop strategy and decided to make it as late as possible.

'The car was easy to drive and things were looking good, until lap 34 when something in the differential broke and I could only drive slowly back to the pits.'

For Coulthard, a crucial turning point came on lap 36 when he briefly found himself balked by Alex Zanardi's Williams as it rolled to a halt out on the circuit. The Italian's car had run out of fuel due to a problem with the radio link between the car and the pit wall.

'I was concentrating on overtaking Diniz and only saw the pit board on the third time it was shown to me,' shrugged Alex. 'But it was too late.'

Coulthard lost 2.5s at this point and later lambasted Zanardi in front of the media. 'The race is lost now, but I had already had a word with him this morning, because I think he is not being entirely professional on the track in terms of getting out of the way of quicker cars,' said David.

'I don't know why he was in the middle of turn six, on line and going slowly [when I came to lap him], but both I and the driver ahead of me had to run very wide, onto the marbles, to overtake him. Then he parked it on the exit of the corner. But that's racing. Sometimes you have to expect to find idiots in the way.'

On lap 39 Coulthard made his 10.9s refuelling stop, dropping to second behind Irvine who now really began to pile the pressure, pulling out a 22.6s lead before himself diving into the pits for an 8.6s stop at the end of lap 44. The net result was that Irvine accelerated back into the fray 1.9s ahead of Coulthard. It seemed as though McLaren had lost.

There were still 25 laps to go and Coulthard tried everything to close the gap. He gradually edged his silver McLaren closer to the red Ferrari, but it was clear that any change in the order at the head of the field would depend on Irvine making a slip. But the Ulsterman was keeping his head magnificently under this intense pressure and wasn't about to oblige, despite the occasional puffs of smoke coming from his car.

'It was probably coming from my brain, I was so overloaded,' he joked afterwards. 'I had problems with the brakes and the car was understeering like a pig on the second set of tyres, so I was really struggling to get [competitive] lap times. Then it started to get a bit better, but we still had the brake problem and I had to ease off. Because of that, DC began to catch me a bit too quick, so then I had to forget about the brakes and start pushing.'

Coulthard gave it everything he had in the closing stages, but Irvine hung doggedly onto his advantage to win the second grand prix of his career by three-tenths of a second. On their slowing down lap, while Irvine thumped the air with both fists, Coulthard just drove on with scarcely an acknowledgement to the modestly-sized crowd.

Häkkinen slammed home a magnificent third. 'You don't really expect me to tell you about it from start to finish, do you?' he said, concealing his disappointment behind a wry grin. 'But, after all, the result was acceptable. Whatever happened in the second corner is not important at the moment, in this situation, but generally it was very enjoyable to be overtaking lots of other cars again.'

Frentzen finished a strong fourth with Alexander Wurz having a good run to fifth with the Benetton B199 in front of his home crowd. 'I really found my rhythm with the circuit,' he said. 'My first set of tyres wasn't so good, and I was sliding quite a lot, but my second set was much better and I could really push.'

Rubens Barrichello had retired on lap 56 with engine failure while running in fourth place. 'The car felt good and my pace was consistent,' he said. 'We have lost points too often this year when we have been well placed.'

Pedro Diniz completed the top six after a good run, but Alesi ran out of fuel in almost exactly the same circumstances as Zanardi. 'What can I say?' the Frenchman shrugged in sheer frustration.

Giancarlo Fisichella's Benetton looked set for seventh, but engine failure three laps from the finish dropped him to 12th in the final order, leaving Jarno Trulli's Prost to finish just out of the points, lapped by the leader. Damon Hill's Jordan was seventh ahead of the recovering Ferrari of Salo, who was frustrated by a lack of straight-line speed after his early unscheduled delay.

Olivier Panis's Prost finished tenth ahead of Marc Gene's Minardi, the luckless Fisichella, Luca Badoer's Minardi and the great unsung star of the show, Johnny Herbert. After resuming four laps down once his replacement rear wing had been fitted, he drove brilliantly to post the second fastest lap of the race.

Meanwhile, on the rostrum, Coulthard looked haunted and disbelieving. Not only had he cost Häkkinen what would otherwise have been an easy victory, but he had given a boost to the McLaren team's number one rival just at a point where they were at potentially their most vulnerable.

After the rostrum ceremony, Coulthard and Häkkinen, who had driven brilliantly to finish third after resuming dead last, disappeared into the Mercedes motorhome with team chief Ron Dennis, Mercedes motorsport director Norbert Haug and Jurgen Schrempp, the chairman of the huge Daimler-Chrysler combine which a fortnight previously took a 40 per cent stake in the McLaren team.

What was said behind closed doors was certainly not shared with the news-hungry media jostling around the paddock outside. However it is known that Coulthard apologised to Häkkinen for his error, the World Champion accepted graciously and the two men agreed to put the incident behind them.

'David hit some bad traffic for two or three laps before his pit stop,' said Ron Dennis, 'but we felt we had more than enough margin [to keep ahead].

'Then we had a throttle cut on David's car. It didn't cost him much in terms of track time, but it turned the engine off for about a second, and then he was a little cautious, just making sure that he didn't have a problem.

'The bottom line is that we could have cruised the race if it hadn't been for the incident. If you've got two competitive drivers in your team you've got a choice, and personally I think that the choice we make – which is to let the drivers race – is the right one.'

Perhaps he was correct. Yet it must have taken a very philosophical stance on Häkkinen's part to subscribe to that generous view at the end of this extremely frustrating afternoon.

McLaren boss cautious over Irvine's prospects

EDDIE Irvine may have dished out a defeat to David Coulthard at the A1-Ring, but McLaren-Mercedes team chief Ron Dennis finished the weekend feeling that the fundamental balance of F1 power had remained unchanged following Michael Schumacher's accident at Silverstone.

'I find it in one way amusing, and in another quite perplexing, that Eddie Irvine has been so vocal about so many things,' he said, 'and specifically, the difference it [the accident] is going to make to his position and to Ferrari's World Championship efforts.

'The simple fact is that he has been outqualified by Michael at every Grand Prix this year up to Silverstone. The only time his contractual obligation to finish behind Schumacher has played any part in the outcome of a Grand Prix was in France, where he finished fifth behind him.

'I must therefore presume that Eddie, for whose abilities I have a very healthy respect, has been giving every effort to his Grand Prix results up until the Silverstone race. So I cannot really see why he is going to find something [extra] within himself that he wasn't able to find before.'

That said, Dennis seemed to understand that Irvine faced a difficult task and that the manner in which Ferrari's Sporting Director Jean Todt deserted the pit wall at Silverstone after Schumacher's accident, rushing instead to hospital in Northampton to be with his number one driver, did not send the most sympathetic message to the man left carrying the team's hopes.

'I have a great deal of sympathy for Irvine's position,' he said. 'Elements of his team left Silverstone prior to the Grand Prix recommencing. That doesn't send a very professional or supportive message to him.

'I also understand that he [Irvine] needs to rally the team around him in the best way that he sees fits. But as has often been the case with other drivers who've found themselves in this position, I don't think they find the right people around them to give them the right guidance as to how they should behave and approach the unique situation they find themselves in.

'The realities haven't changed, so if we at McLaren continue to do a competent job, there is no reason to think that Eddie's position relative to our cars on the grid will change unless, of course, Ferrari will improve their cars. In any event, the outcome of the World Championship will probably be as much about reliability as pure performance, and we are all mindful of that fact.'

PlayStation
PlayStation

MILD SEVEN
KicKers
Agip
KOREAN AIR
10
BRIDGESTONE
UNITED COLORS OF BENETTON.

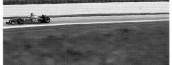

GROSSER PREIS VON ÖSTERREICH

23–25 JULY 1999

A1-RING

Race distance: 71 laps, 190.543 miles/306.649 km

Race weather: Overcast and warm

ROUND 9

A1-RING – ZELTWEG
CIRCUIT LENGTH: 2.684 miles/4.319 km

Remus Kurve · Niki Lauda Kurve · Gösser Kurve · Power Horse Kurve · Jochen Rindt Kurve · Castrol Kurve · Mobilkom Kurve

Pos.	Driver	Nat.	No.	Entrant	Car/Engine	Laps	Time/Retirement	Speed (mph/km/h)
1	Eddie Irvine	GB	4	Scuderia Ferrari Marlboro	Ferrari F399 048B V10	71	1h 28m 12.438s	129.610/208.587
2	David Coulthard	GB	2	West McLaren Mercedes	McLaren MP4/14-Mercedes F0110G V10	71	1h 28m 12.751s	129.602/208.575
3	Mika Häkkinen	SF	1	West McLaren Mercedes	McLaren MP4/14-Mercedes F0110G V10	71	1h 28m 34.720s	129.066/207.712
4	Heinz-Harald Frentzen	D	8	Benson & Hedges Jordan	Jordan 199-Mugen Honda MF301/HD V10	71	1h 29m 05.241s	128.329/206.526
5	Alexander Wurz	A	10	Mild Seven Benetton Playlife	Benetton B199-Playlife V10	71	1h 29m 18.796s	128.005/206.004
6	Pedro Diniz	BR	12	Red Bull Sauber Petronas	Sauber C18-Petronas SPE03A V10	71	1h 29m 23.371s	127.895/205.828
7	Jarno Trulli	I	19	Gauloises Prost Peugeot	Prost AP02-Peugeot A18 V10	70		
8	Damon Hill	GB	7	Benson & Hedges Jordan	Jordan 199-Mugen Honda MF301/HD V10	70		
9	Mika Salo	SF	3	Scuderia Ferrari Marlboro	Ferrari F399 048B V10	70		
10	Olivier Panis	F	18	Gauloises Prost Peugeot	Prost AP02-Peugeot A18 V10	70		
11	Marc Gene	ESP	21	Fondmetal Minardi Ford	Minardi M01-Ford Zetec-R V10	70		
12	Giancarlo Fisichella	I	9	Mild Seven Benetton Playlife	Benetton B199-Playlife V10	68	Engine	
13	Luca Badoer	I	20	Fondmetal Minardi Ford	Minardi M01-Ford Zetec-R V10	68		
14	Johnny Herbert	GB	17	Stewart Ford	Stewart SF3-Ford CR-1 V10	67		
15	Ricardo Zonta	BR	23	British American Racing	BAR 01-Supertec FB01 V10	63	Clutch	
	Rubens Barrichello	BR	16	Stewart Ford	Stewart SF3-Ford CR-1 V10	55	Engine	
	Jean Alesi	F	11	Red Bull Sauber Petronas	Sauber C18-Petronas SPE03A V10	49	Out of fuel	
	Pedro de la Rosa	ESP	14	Arrows	Arrows A20 V10	38	Spun off	
	Alex Zanardi	I	5	Winfield Williams	Williams FW21-Supertec FB01 V10	35	Out of fuel	
	Jacques Villeneuve	CDN	22	British American Racing	BAR 01-Supertec FB01 V10	34	Broken driveshaft	
	Toranosuke Takagi	J	15	Arrows	Arrows A20 V10	25	Engine	
	Ralf Schumacher	D	6	Winfield Williams	Williams FW21-Supertec FB01 V10	8	Spun off	

Fastest lap: Häkkinen, on lap 39, 1m 12.107s, 133.986 mph/215.629 km/h.

Lap record: Jacques Villeneuve (F1 Williams FW19-Renault V10), 1m 11.814s, 134.657 mph/216.709 km/h (1997).

Grid order	1 2 3 4 5 6 7 8 9 10 11 12 13 14 15 16 17 18 19 20 21 22 23 24 25 26 27 28 29 30 31 32 33 34 35 36 37 38 39 40 41 42 43 44 45 46 47 48 49 50 51 52 53
1 HÄKKINEN	2 2 2 2 2 2 2 2 2 2 2 2 2 2 2 2 2 2 2 2 2 2 2 2 2 2 2 2 2 2 2 2 2 2 2 2 2 2 2 4 4 4 4 4 4 4 4 4 4 4 4 4 4
2 COULTHARD	16 16 16 16 16 16 16 16 16 16 16 16 16 16 16 16 16 16 16 16 16 16 16 16 16 16 16 16 16 16 16 16 16 16 16 16 16 16 16 16 16 16 16 16 16 16 16 16 16 16 16 16 16 16
4 IRVINE	4 4 4 4 4 4 4 4 4 4 4 4 4 4 4 4 4 4 4 4 4 4 4 4 4 4 4 4 4 4 4 4 4 4 4 4 4 4 4 1 2 2 2 8 8 8 8 8 16 16 16 16 1 1 1 1
8 FRENTZEN	8 8 8 8 8 8 8 8 8 8 8 8 8 8 8 8 8 8 8 8 8 8 8 8 8 8 8 8 8 8 8 8 8 8 8 8 8 8 8 1 1 1 1 8 8 16 16 16 16 1 1 1 1 16 16 16 16
16 BARRICHELLO	3 3 22 22 22 22 22 22 22 22 12 12 12 12 12 12 12 12 12 12 12 12 12 1 1 1 1 1 1 1 8 8 8 8 8 16 16 1 1 1 1 8 8 8 8 8 8 8 8
17 HERBERT	22 22 6 6 6 6 6 6 12 12 22 22 22 22 22 22 11 11 11 11 11 11 11 22 22 22 22 22 22 22 9 9 9 9 9 9 9 9 9 10 11 11 11 11 11 11 11 12 12 12 10
3 SALO	6 6 3 12 12 12 12 12 9 9 9 9 9 9 9 9 9 11 22 1 1 1 1 22 9 9 9 9 9 10 10 10 10 10 10 10 10 10 19 19 12 12 12 12 10 10 10 9
6 R. SCHUMACHER	9 12 12 9 9 9 9 23 23 23 23 23 11 11 11 9 1 22 22 22 22 22 9 10 10 10 19 19 19 19 19 19 19 19 7 10 10 10 10 9 9 9 12 1
22 VILLENEUVE	12 9 9 23 23 23 23 10 10 10 10 11 11 23 1 1 9 9 9 9 10 19 19 19 19 19 19 19 19 7 7 7 7 7 7 11 12 9 9 19 19 19 1 1
10 WURZ	10 23 23 10 10 10 10 10 11 11 11 11 1 1 1 23 23 23 23 10 10 10 10 10 10 19 7 7 7 7 7 7 7 23 23 23 23 11 11 11 11 11 11 12 10 18 19 19 19 7 7 7 7
7 HILL	19 10 10 19 19 11 11 11 19 19 1 1 10 10 10 10 10 10 19 19 19 19 7 23 23 23 23 23 23 23 11 11 11 11 23 12 12 12 12 9 9 19 7 7 7 23 23 23 23 2
9 FISICHELLA	23 19 19 11 11 19 19 1 1 19 19 19 19 19 19 19 19 23 7 7 7 7 23 11 11 11 11 11 11 11 22 12 12 12 12 3 3 18 18 18 18 18 7 23 23 23 3 3 3 3
19 TRULLI	7 7 7 7 1 7 7 1 7 7 7 7 7 7 7 7 7 7 23 23 23 12 12 12 12 12 12 12 5 3 3 18 18 3 23 23 23 23 23 3 3 18 18 18 18 18
5 ZANARDI	14 11 11 14 14 1 1 7 14 14 14 14 14 14 14 14 14 14 14 14 5 5 5 5 3 18 18 18 23 23 23 3 3 3 3 3 18 18 18 21 21 21 21 2
23 ZONTA	20 14 14 15 15 14 14 15 15 15 15 15 15 15 15 15 15 15 15 15 15 5 5 5 14 21 21 21 21 21 21 21 21 21 21 21 21 21 21 20 20 20 2
12 DINIZ	11 15 15 1 1 15 15 5 5 5 5 5 5 5 5 5 5 5 21 21 21 21 3 3 3 18 14 14 14 20 20 20 20 20 20 20 17 17 17 17
11 ALESI	15 5 5 5 5 5 5 21 21 21 21 21 21 21 21 21 21 21 18 18 18 18 18 18 18 18 14 20 20 17 17 17 17 17 17 17 17 17
18 PANIS	21 21 1 21 21 21 21 18 18 18 18 18 18 18 18 18 18 18 3 3 3 3 3 14 14 14 14 20 17 17 17
20 BADOER	5 18 21 18 18 18 18 3 3 3 20 20 20 20 20 20 20 17 17 17 17 17 17 17 17 17 17
15 TAKAGI	18 1 18 3 3 3 3 20 20 20 20 20 20 20 20 20 20 17 17 17 17 17 17 17 17 17
14 DE LA ROSA	17 20 20 20 20 20 20 20 17 17 17 17 17 17 17 17 17 17 17 17 17
21 GENE	1 17 17 17 17 17 17 17

Pit stop

One lap behind leader

STARTING GRID

1 **HÄKKINEN** McLaren	**2** **COULTHARD** McLaren
4 **IRVINE** Ferrari	**8** **FRENTZEN** Jordan
16 **BARRICHELLO** Stewart	**17** **HERBERT** Stewart
3 **SALO** Ferrari	**6** **R. SCHUMACHER** Williams
22 **VILLENEUVE** BAR	**10** **WURZ** Benetton
7 **HILL** Jordan	**9** **FISICHELLA** Benetton
19 **TRULLI** Prost	**5** **ZANARDI** Williams
23 **ZONTA** BAR	**12** **DINIZ** Sauber
11 **ALESI** Sauber	**18** **PANIS** Prost
20 **BADOER** Minardi	**15** **TAKAGI** Arrows
14 **DE LA ROSA** Arrows	**21** **GENE** Minardi

TIME SHEETS

QUALIFYING

Weather: cloudy and bright

Pos.	Driver	Car	Laps	Time
1	Mika Häkkinen	McLaren-Mercedes	10	1m 10.954s
2	David Coulthard	McLaren-Mercedes	12	1m 11.153s
3	Eddie Irvine	Ferrari	12	1m 11.973s
4	Heinz-Harald Frentzen	Jordan-Mugen Honda	12	1m 12.266s
5	Rubens Barrichello	Stewart-Ford	12	1m 12.342s
6	Johnny Herbert	Stewart-Ford	12	1m 12.488s
7	Mika Salo	Ferrari	12	1m 12.514s
8	Ralf Schumacher	Williams-Supertec	10	1m 12.515s
9	Jacques Villeneuve	BAR-Supertec	11	1m 12.833s
10	Alexander Wurz	Benetton-Playlife	12	1m 12.850s
11	Damon Hill	Jordan-Mugen Honda	11	1m 12.901s
12	Giancarlo Fisichella	Benetton-Playlife	11	1m 12.924s
13	Jarno Trulli	Prost-Peugeot	11	1m 12.999s
14	Alex Zanardi	Williams-Supertec	12	1m 13.101s
15	Ricardo Zonta	BAR-Supertec	12	1m 13.172s
16	Pedro Diniz	Sauber-Petronas	12	1m 13.223s
17	Jean Alesi	Sauber-Petronas	11	1m 13.226s
18	Olivier Panis	Prost-Peugeot	12	1m 13.457s
19	Luca Badoer	Minardi-Ford	12	1m 13.606s
20	Toranosuke Takagi	Arrows	12	1m 13.641s
21	Pedro de la Rosa	Arrows	11	1m 14.139s
22	Marc Gene	Minardi-Ford	10	1m 14.363s

FRIDAY FREE PRACTICE

Weather: Cloudy and bright

Pos.	Driver	Laps	Time
1	Damon Hill	49	1m 13.303s
2	Mika Häkkinen	34	1m 13.325s
3	David Coulthard	37	1m 13.376s
4	Ricardo Zonta	43	1m 13.685s
5	Jean Alesi	36	1m 13.696s
6	Ralf Schumacher	39	1m 13.711s
7	Pedro Diniz	46	1m 13.740s
8	Jacques Villeneuve	43	1m 13.840s
9	Eddie Irvine	41	1m 13.883s
10	Rubens Barrichello	35	1m 13.923s
11	Johnny Herbert	47	1m 14.008s
12	Alex Zanardi	53	1m 14.049s
13	Luca Badoer	44	1m 14.203s
14	Marc Gene	45	1m 14.333s
15	Heinz-Harald Frentzen	27	1m 14.558s
16	Mika Salo	32	1m 14.608s
17	Jarno Trulli	50	1m 14.724s
18	Giancarlo Fisichella	35	1m 14.785s
19	Olivier Panis	36	1m 15.028s
20	Alexander Wurz	32	1m 15.107s
21	Pedro de la Rosa	26	1m 15.651s
22	Toranosuke Takagi	19	1m 16.067s

SATURDAY FREE PRACTICE

Weather: Cloudy and bright

Pos.	Driver	Laps	Time
1	David Coulthard	39	1m 11.801s
2	Mika Häkkinen	32	1m 11.854s
3	Eddie Irvine	43	1m 11.926s
4	Johnny Herbert	36	1m 12.139s
5	Giancarlo Fisichella	44	1m 12.679s
6	Heinz-Harald Frentzen	44	1m 12.693s
7	Rubens Barrichello	30	1m 12.745s
8	Ralf Schumacher	36	1m 12.801s
9	Mika Salo	41	1m 12.832s
10	Jarno Trulli	40	1m 12.928s
11	Jacques Villeneuve	33	1m 12.946s
12	Jean Alesi	34	1m 12.966s
13	Alexander Wurz	44	1m 13.065s
14	Pedro Diniz	40	1m 13.262s
15	Olivier Panis	38	1m 13.270s
16	Ricardo Zonta	31	1m 13.316s
17	Alex Zanardi	40	1m 13.326s
18	Damon Hill	43	1m 13.350s
19	Luca Badoer	23	1m 13.553s
20	Marc Gene	40	1m 13.851s
21	Toranosuke Takagi	27	1m 13.941s
22	Pedro de la Rosa	29	1m 14.091s

WARM-UP

Weather: Overcast and warm

Pos.	Driver	Laps	Time
1	Mika Häkkinen	14	1m 13.264s
2	David Coulthard	16	1m 13.603s
3	Jacques Villeneuve	16	1m 13.645s
4	Pedro Diniz	18	1m 13.796s
5	Jean Alesi	18	1m 14.079s
6	Damon Hill	16	1m 14.119s
7	Eddie Irvine	11	1m 14.236s
8	Johnny Herbert	20	1m 14.266s
9	Alexander Wurz	19	1m 14.395s
10	Rubens Barrichello	18	1m 14.432s
11	Jarno Trulli	19	1m 14.558s
12	Giancarlo Fisichella	16	1m 14.585s
13	Heinz-Harald Frentzen	19	1m 14.613s
14	Pedro de la Rosa	13	1m 14.624s
15	Mika Salo	16	1m 14.701s
16	Olivier Panis	15	1m 14.835s
17	Toranosuke Takagi	17	1m 14.850s
18	Luca Badoer	18	1m 14.916s
19	Ralf Schumacher	15	1m 15.137s
20	Ricardo Zonta	14	1m 15.390s
21	Marc Gene	15	1m 15.605s
22	Alex Zanardi	17	1m 15.739s

RACE FASTEST LAPS

Weather: Sunny and warm

Driver	Time	Lap
Mika Häkkinen	1m 12.107s	39
Johnny Herbert	1m 12.641s	67
Eddie Irvine	1m 12.787s	43
David Coulthard	1m 12.855s	69
Pedro Diniz	1m 13.093s	49
Heinz-Harald Frentzen	1m 13.176s	42
Jean Alesi	1m 13.228s	47
Rubens Barrichello	1m 13.278s	36
Olivier Panis	1m 13.465s	67
Mika Salo	1m 13.481s	67
Giancarlo Fisichella	1m 13.579s	41
Alexander Wurz	1m 13.654s	42
Damon Hill	1m 13.960s	63
Jacques Villeneuve	1m 13.977s	33
Ricardo Zonta	1m 14.063s	36
Jarno Trulli	1m 14.112s	37
Alex Zanardi	1m 14.381s	31
Marc Gene	1m 14.517s	34
Luca Badoer	1m 14.622s	63
Pedro de la Rosa	1m 14.914s	29
Toranosuke Takagi	1m 15.361s	25
Ralf Schumacher	1m 16.173s	8

CHASSIS LOG BOOK

	Driver	Chassis
1	Häkkinen	McLaren MP4/14/5
2	Coulthard	McLaren MP4/14/7
	spare	McLaren MP4/14/2
3	Salo	Ferrari F399/195
4	Irvine	Ferrari F399/191
	spare	Ferrari F399/194
5	Zanardi	Williams FW21/5
6	R. Schumacher	Williams FW21/6
	spare	Williams FW21/2
7	Hill	Jordan 199/4
8	Frentzen	Jordan 199/5
	spare	Jordan 199/6
9	Fisichella	Benetton B199/7
10	Wurz	Benetton B199/5
	spare	Benetton B199/4
11	Alesi	Sauber C18/6
12	Diniz	Sauber C18/5
	spare	Sauber C18/4
14	de la Rosa	Arrows A20/4
15	Takagi	Arrows A20/2
	spare	Arrows A20/5
16	Barrichello	Stewart SF3/4
17	Herbert	Stewart SF3/5
	spare	Stewart SF3/3
18	Panis	Prost AP02/5
19	Trulli	Prost AP02/7
	spare	Prost AP02/3
20	Badoer	Minardi M01/1
21	Gene	Minardi M01/4
	spare	Minardi M01/3
22	Villeneuve	BAR 01/7
23	Zonta	BAR 01/5
	spare	BAR 01/3

POINTS TABLES

DRIVERS

1	Mika Häkkinen	44
2	Eddie Irvine	42
3	Michael Schumacher	32
4	Heinz-Harald Frentzen	29
5	David Coulthard	28
6	Ralf Schumacher	19
7	Giancarlo Fisichella	13
8	Rubens Barrichello	10
9	Damon Hill	5
10 =	Alexander Wurz	3
10 =	Pedro Diniz	3
12	Johnny Herbert	2
13 =	Pedro de la Rosa	1
13 =	Olivier Panis	1
13 =	Jean Alesi	1
13 =	Jarno Trulli	1

CONSTRUCTORS

1	Ferrari	74
2	McLaren	72
3	Jordan	34
4	Williams	19
5	Benetton	16
6	Stewart	12
7	Sauber	4
8	Prost	2
9	Arrows	1

57	58	59	60	61	62	63	64	65	66	67	68	69	70	71		
4	4	4	4	4	4	4	4	4	4	4	4	4	4	4		1
2	2	2	2	2	2	2	2	2	2	2	2	2	2	2		2
1	1	1	1	1	1	1	1	1	1	1	1	1	1	1		3
8	8	8	8	8	8	8	8	8	8	8	8	8	8	8		4
10	10	10	10	10	10	10	10	10	10	10	10	10	10	10		5
12	12	12	12	12	12	12	12	12	12	12	12	12	12	12		6
9	9	9	9	9	9	9	9	9	9	9	9	19	19			
19	19	19	19	19	19	19	19	19	19	19	7	7				
7	7	7	7	7	7	7	7	7	7	3	3					
23	23	23	23	23	23	3	3	3	3	18	18					
3	3	3	18	18	18	18	18	21	21							
18	18	18	18	18	18	21	21	21	21							
21	21	21	21	21	21	20	20	20	20							
20	20	20	20	20	20	17	17	17	17							
17	17	17	17	17	17											

GERMAN

IRVINE

SALO

FRENTZEN

R. SCHUMACHER

Running free. Ferrari's Eddie Irvine took his second consecutive victory to throw the World Championship wide open.
Paul-Henri Cahier

Paul-Henri Cahier

Left: Mika Häkkinen stands on the pit wall and takes the applause for his pole position. Sadly for the Finn, a massive tyre failure pitched him off the circuit during the race.

Right: Undoubted star of the weekend was Mika Salo who moved over to let team leader Irvine take victory.

Below right: At the end of the race, Eddie Irvine was first to acknowledge the debt he owed to his Finnish team mate.

IT almost seemed as though nothing could get in the way of his great good fortune. Only seven days after winning in Austria, Eddie Irvine surged majestically into the lead of the World Championship by heading a Ferrari 1–2 grand slam in the German Grand Prix. As the sidelined Michael Schumacher watched proceedings on television from his Swiss villa, Irvine was followed across the line by the German driver's substitute, Mika Salo.

It was a success which propelled Irvine comfortably ahead of his rivals in the title chase with 52 points, ahead of Mika Häkkinen's 44 and Heinz-Harald Frentzen, whose Jordan finished third at Hockenheim, on 33 with only six of the season's 16 races remaining.

For the third successive race, the expected McLaren-Mercedes domination seemed to self-destruct. Häkkinen qualified brilliantly on pole position only to crash out of the race at 190 mph after a rear tyre failure coming into the stadium section of the circuit.

Irvine, who learned from his tenure in Schumacher's shadow how it feels to adhere to team orders, now found himself the beneficiary of such instructions in his new role of *de facto* Ferrari team leader. Salo had been quicker from the start, running in second place, but briefly found himself in the lead after Häkkinen's accident.

'He did a fantastic job,' said Irvine in acknowledging that Salo had let him through to win.

'I know what it feels like, but I never made the call [for Salo to move over], thank goodness. What a star Mika was today. This was his race and he will be getting the trophy. I would feel bad if it was sitting on my mantelpiece instead of his. He's a boy wonder and he did an absolutely fantastic job today. Incredible!'

Häkkinen got cleanly away from pole position, his McLaren MP4/14 leading into the first right-hander out of the packed stadium with Salo rocketing his Ferrari F399 through from the second row to take an immediate second place from David Coulthard, Frentzen's Jordan and Irvine.

Further back, Marc Gene, who had done an excellent job qualifying his Minardi in 19th place, made an unfortunate error as he accelerated away from the grid, clipping Jacques Villeneuve's British American 01 and pitching the Canadian into a collision with Pedro Diniz's Sauber. Villeneuve and Diniz were out on the spot, but Gene survived to race on.

Further round the opening lap, Jean Alesi's Sauber C18 ran into the back of Olivier Panis's Prost, dislodging the

HOCKENHEIM QUALIFYING

Hockenheim is a track which imposes very significant loadings on the tyres, leading to significant degradation of the rear covers in particular, as some people would find out to their cost in due course.

Yet there was still the question of refuelling strategy and many believed that the call was finely balanced between one or two stops, unlike in Austria the previous weekend, when one stop was the only competitive option. The teams were playing their cards close to their chest.

The softer of the two relatively hard available Bridgestone tyre compounds proved to be the favoured option, but they would be getting a little ragged after 20 laps, so a one-stop option would probably mean a short opening stint and a longer second run through to the chequered flag after 45 racing laps.

Jarno Trulli did some grandstanding for the Prost team on Friday, emerging with an unrepresentative fastest time thanks to the simple expedient of slapping on a new set of tyres in the closing moments of free practice. It was not representative of what was to follow in the serious business of Saturday qualifying.

The track temperature hovered at 31 degrees at the start of qualifying, soaring to 37 degrees by the time Häkkinen posted provisional pole with 1m 43.093s just 14 minutes into the session, ahead of Trulli's admittedly promising Prost by a margin of 1.2s.

By 1.30 pm the track temperature was up to 42 degrees, but ten minutes later a few clouds momentarily masked the sun and it was down to 40 degrees as Frentzen produced a perfectly timed run to set a new benchmark on 1m 43.000s.

Jordan's low-downforce aerodynamic set-up has a proven record of performing well, as Heinz-Harald demonstrated at Montreal – before his unfortunate shunt – and again at the recent Monza test. Aided by another upgraded Mugen Honda qualifying-specification V10 the German driver was right on the pace.

Yet Häkkinen managed to ease back ahead for the eighth pole position of his season – and the team's 100th since 1966 – when he wound up 0.05s faster than Frentzen at the end of qualifying.

'It was an extremely enjoyable session,' he said, 'but in fact my advantage should have been bigger. My second-last run was going well until the second-last corner where someone had put sand down and there was no grip at all.'

David Coulthard was third on 1m 43.288s. He said he was quite happy with his first run, after which he lost a front tyre tread and came slowly back to the pits. He took the spare and then went back into the race chassis towards the end 'but struggled a bit to get up to speed.'

Mika Salo was well satisfied with fourth fastest in the Ferrari F399 on 1m 43.557s, but Eddie Irvine had a frustrating time to qualify fifth on 1m 43.769s. He slid off coming into the stadium section on his first run and then changed the set-up, but he had gone in the wrong direction and there was not time to change it back again.

'My last run was still looking very good,' he reflected, 'but I lost a second behind Villeneuve and Diniz in T2. Adding up all my sector times would have put me 0.3s off pole which is less than we normally are. I didn't want fourth; fifth is the place to be because it's very dirty on the inside line.'

Right behind him, Rubens Barrichello's Stewart-Ford completed the top six qualifiers on 1m 43.938s. 'To start in the top six is not that bad, but I had a car today which was capable of being in the top four,' he said. He was at least much more satisfied than his team-mate Johnny Herbert who wound up 17th on 1m 45.454s, having insufficient time to set up the car after a raft of problems during the morning, most notably a rear wing failure which pitched him into a high-speed spin before the Ostkurve chicane.

Olivier Panis wound up seventh (1m 43.979s) in his Prost-Peugeot while team-mate Jarno Trulli was ninth (1m 44.209s) after suffering an engine failure with his race car and then stopping out on the circuit with his spare.

Separating the two Prosts was Damon Hill on 1m 44.001s.

'On my second run I made a mistake in the stadium,' he said. 'On my first I ran over debris and on my fourth I had traffic.'

Fisichella's Benetton lined up tenth ahead of Ralf Schumacher's Williams, Jacques Villeneuve's BAR, Alexander Wurz's Benetton and Alex Zanardi in the other Williams. For once, the Italian F1 returnee had a relatively trouble-free time.

Swiss car's nose cone and sending Alesi into the pit lane for a replacement first time round. Meanwhile, Häkkinen led by 1.0s ahead of Salo, Coulthard, Rubens Barrichello's Stewart and Irvine.

On the third lap Barrichello successfully dived inside Frentzen's Jordan-Mugen Honda to take fourth place coming into the stadium while, a few seconds later, Giancarlo Fisichella in the Benetton B199 slid off the road from ninth place at the same point while battling furiously with team-mate Alexander Wurz and resumed 20th.

It was to be a short-lived upsurge in fortune for Barrichello who would roll to a halt with hydraulic failure on lap seven while the autocrossing Fisichella would survive for just another lap before the legacy of that earlier excursion manifested itself in a front suspension failure.

Irvine, meanwhile, was taking things relatively easy in the opening stages. 'I tried to keep out of people's slipstream because the oil temperature warning light was on, so I backed off and ran in clean air as much as I could. It was a matter of letting the race come back to me.'

Coulthard had spent the opening laps getting very close to Salo, but continually being thwarted in his efforts to overtake. Then on lap 10 the McLaren driver got a touch too close to the Ferrari under braking for the Ostkurve chicane and lost part of the MP4/14's nose section in the inevitable impact.

David trailed in for repairs, resuming 10th, but later denied he was ever trying seriously to pass Salo at that point. 'He braked quite early and I had to cut to the inside to avoid hitting him,' he explained.

'I don't know whether I carried too much speed into the corner, but he just seemed to stop. I wasn't making a move. In circumstances like this you really do rely on cars in front running at the same pace. The [piece of] wing hit my helmet as it went by.'

On lap 14, Damon Hill came in to retire after a troubled afternoon. He had run in the top eight in the opening sprint, but dropped back to 11th after a couple of lurid-looking off-course excursions. Then he came to announce that he was not happy with the feel of his Jordan's brakes. He climbed out of the cockpit.

As the frustrated Damon stormed back to the Jordan motorhome, jostling BBC radio reporter Peter Slater in the process, team manager Trevor Foster confirmed that there was nothing mechanically wrong with Hill's car.

'Damon made us look a bit silly,' he said. 'We asked him on the radio if he wanted to pit and he said nothing, then he came in suddenly and compounded that by stopping ten feet short of our pit.

'We changed the tyres, inspected and refuelled the car and put on a new nose as a precaution, and then he cut the engine and said he didn't want to continue.'

Damon later explained; 'We had to change the brake material between the warm-up and the race, and I had problems with it. I was finding it difficult

DIARY

Eddie Irvine reportedly signs to drive for the new Jaguar-branded Stewart F1 team for the 2000 season.

Mika Häkkinen and David Coulthard sign new contracts to remain with the McLaren-Mercedes team into the 2000 season.

Speculation suggests that Toyota may defer its F1 debut until 2002 at the earliest.

Former Stewart F1 driver Jan Magnussen poised for CART racing return with Patrick Racing.

Right: Eddie Irvine and Mika Salo provided Ferrari with an unexpected 1-2 finish. Two races after Schumacher's Silverstone accident saw the Ulsterman a serious championship contender.
Paul-Henri Cahier

Below left: Despite his enforced absence, Michael Schumacher's presence was still felt at Hockenheim.

Ecclestone: F1 bigger than one person

WITH speculation over the prospects for Michael Schumacher's recovery at the top of the agenda on the eve of the German Grand Prix, F1 Commercial Rights Holder Bernie Ecclestone claimed that the sport is bigger than any of its participants and will continue to thrive despite any accidents which may befall its leading competitors.

'Regretfully what I am going to say will upset a few people, but Formula One is certainly bigger than any single person belonging to it,' he insisted. 'People said after the death of Ayrton Senna that F1 would be finished, but it's not true.

'Obviously we will miss Michael and there will be no real threat to the McLarens for a few races. But the Austrian Grand Prix last weekend turned out to be a great race even without Michael.

'Michael is a racer. He will always be at ten-tenths. He is always on his personal limit and, if he could not be, I think he would rather stop racing.'

For all the inevitable discussion over whether Schumacher might now call it a day and retire, the overwhelming opinion in the F1 paddock was that the 33-year old German ace would soon be back in business.

Schumacher's fellow drivers certainly believed he would soon return. Johnny Herbert, who partnered him in the Benetton-Renault team back in 1995, felt that his rival would return even more motivated and committed than before his accident.

'I really would doubt whether he will have any problems whatsoever coming back to race,' said the 34-year old who himself battled back to health after badly smashing both ankles when he crashed a Formula 3000 Reynard at Brands Hatch in 1988.

'After all, it is only a clean break. If he had mashed up his feet like I did, or perhaps suffered the sort of head injuries that Mika [Häkkinen] did in his crash at Adelaide [in 1995] then there might be some question mark over it. But there won't be.

'I also believe that Michael is not motivated by money. He's still hungry for success and is motivated by the desire to be remembered as the man who brought Ferrari right back to the top again. There is no question in my mind that he will be back at the wheel and as good as ever.'

Ecclestone also reiterated his stance against the current F1 tyre regulations which had been championed by FIA President Max Mosley.

'I don't think that grooved tyres make a race better or worse,' said Bernie. 'Personally I think they are unnecessary because they don't achieve anything and they look silly. I believe we should have wet tyres or slicks. F1 cars have to look aggressive and convey the fascination of the sport.

'I would suggest it would be better to have wide slicks. The idea behind the grooved tyres was to make the cars slower in the corners because they offer less grip. But less grip also means less safety. So in fact the grooved tyres are adding to the dangers of F1 rather than making it safer.'

Bernie also stated, in reference to Michael Schumacher's Silverstone accident, it was his belief that gravel traps are 'quite useless'.

He added: 'They do not brake the cars down effectively. Michael's Ferrari could not dig into the gravel because it was up in the air for most of the time.

'What we need is a run-off area with an extremely rough asphalt surface and the track surface itself should be rougher too, so that the cars don't slide as much. That way they could be slowed down more efficiently.'

to stop the car and thought it pointless to continue. The team wanted me to, but I took the decision that it was not safe for me to carry on.'

A mechanical problem during the race morning warm-up meant that Hill could not use his preferred type of brakes during the race itself. Prior to the start he had made the point to his team that he did not like the feel of the brakes during the session.

Inevitably, Hill's retirement from the race reignited much fevered speculation over the possibility of his quitting the cockpit for good before the end of the season, but a couple of days after the race the Jordan team made it clear that the issue was at an end and that Damon had their complete confidence.

On lap 21, Frentzen made a 10.5s refuelling stop, dropping from third to fifth place. 'My start wasn't the best,' he later recalled. 'Rubens was very fast early on and I let him through as well. After the fourth or fifth lap I also flat-spotted a tyre and had to cope with a vibration.'

On lap 22 it was Irvine's turn to make a 9.4s stop, dropping from third to fourth – crucially getting out of the pit lane ahead of Frentzen who'd stopped on the previous lap – and the other Ferrari followed him in next time round, Salo making a 10.0s stop which dropped him from second to third.

Häkkinen, meanwhile, had only been edging gently away from the pack. After ten laps he was 4.4s ahead of Salo and just 6.4s ahead of his fellow Finn when the spate of refuelling stops began around the lap 20 mark.

The leading McLaren came in for its stop at the end of lap 24, but there was a problem with the refuelling rig failing to engage with the car-mounted nozzle, so the mechanics had to shuffle Coulthard's rig into place and use that instead. As a result, the stop lasted a protracted 24.3s and Häkkinen resumed the race a disappointed fourth.

On lap 26 Häkkinen overtook Frentzen for third place, then suffered a massive failure of his left rear tyre coming into the braking area for the right-hander into the stadium. This spectacular incident pitched him into a tyre barrier with the same dreadful suddenness as Michael Schumacher had experienced at Silverstone.

Thankfully the Finn was unhurt and walked back to the pits with a philosophical expression on his face which belied the fact that outside forces had now deprived him of three straight Grand Prix wins this season.

The Finn had been extremely fortunate not to have smashed into the concrete wall on the right of the circuit

and there was little in the way of discernible retardation as the McLaren pirouetted wildly on the tarmac and then skated across the top of the gravel bed en route to its appointment with the tyre barrier.

The tyre failure was identical to one suffered by Coulthard during Saturday qualifying and was immediately investigated in detail by both McLaren and Bridgestone technicians.

By the end of Sunday evening there was speculation that some deflection of the McLaren's rear wing might have cut the tyre, causing the disastrous delamination, but the team and tyre maker were both keeping their views to themselves until a more detailed analysis could be completed.

It was eventually decided that the fragments of the failed tyre should be

Bryn Williams/Words & Pictures

returned to Bridgestone's research and development centre in Japan for detailed analysis.

On the Tuesday following the race McLaren Managing Director Martin Whitmarsh commented; 'We have reached no conclusion, and it would be unwise to speculate, but the Bridgestone engineers have told us that they could find no cuts on David Coulthard's tyre.

'It has also been confirmed by a Bridgestone engineer that they do not believe that a rear wing failure caused the subsequent tyre problem on Häkkinen's car during the race.'

Rival teams speculated that McLaren might have been trying to run their cars with particularly low tyre pressures in an effort to enhance grip out of the corners. Ferrari reputedly considered doing this but decided that it would be prudent to run higher pressures which apparently cause less tyre 'growth' at high speeds.

However, McLaren made it very clear that they would not compromise the operational safety of their cars by racing them in a configuration which they did not believe was the best and most secure under the circumstances.

Whatever the cause, Häkkinen's retirement was effectively the end of the race, as such. Salo went through into the lead, but immediately dropped back behind Irvine, and the two Ferraris stroked home to claim another generous helping of 16 points towards the constructors' championship.

Frentzen came home a good third, while Coulthard's frustrations were not over yet. During his recovery, he cut across the Ostkurve chicane kerb in the process of overtaking Olivier Panis's Prost. This resulted in his incurring a 10s stop–go penalty and, after a third stop to top up with fuel in the closing stages, the Scot eventually finished fifth behind Ralf Schumacher's Williams.

At his final refuelling stop David tore back into the race somewhat over-zealously and had a close wheel-to-wheel moment with Alexander Wurz's Benetton as a result. There was talk of a further penalty for the Scot, this time for crossing the yellow line which delineates the pit lane exit at the start of the first straight. But no action was taken.

Schumacher had driven a sensational race, his underpowered Williams qualifying 11th and then storming through to finish within 13s of Irvine's victorious Ferrari at the chequered flag. Panis was sixth ahead of Wurz, the frustrated Alesi, the Minardis of Gene and Badoer, while Johnny Herbert looked on course for a place in the top six when his gearbox broke on lap 41 and he wound up classified 11th.

At the end of the day, Irvine confessed that he didn't really feel like celebrating his third Grand Prix victory of the year. 'It is ten points,' he agreed, 'but we didn't take the race to the McLarens – they rather shot themselves in the foot.

'Obviously it isn't great to be qualifying on the second and third rows, but at the moment McLaren seems to have the legs on us. The next race, in Hungary, is on a very different type of circuit, so I'm hoping we will be quicker there.'

Top left: Ralf Schumacher continued to perform miracles with the Williams.
Paul-Henri Cahier

Above left: Jacques Villeneuve giving his all despite the lack of results.
Paul-Henri Cahier

Above: Mika Salo put his name on the wanted list for a number of other F1 teams with his scintillating performance.
Paul-Henri Cahier

Left: Jackie Stewart: just one of the team owners on the phone to Mika Salo's manager Mike Greasley?
Paul-Henri Cahier

Right: Eddie Irvine, typically underwhelmed by the questions at a Hockenheim press conference, appears to doze off.
Steve Etherington/EPI

GERMAN GRAND PRIX

GROSSER MOBIL 1 PREIS VON DEUTSCHLAND

30 JULY–1 AUGUST 1999
HOCKENHEIM

Race distance: 45 laps, 190.782 miles/307.035 km

Race weather: Dry, hot and sunny

FORMULA 1 WORLD CHAMPIONSHIP

ROUND 10

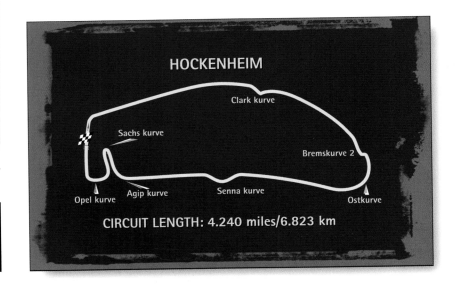

HOCKENHEIM

Clark kurve
Sachs kurve
Bremskurve 2
Senna kurve
Opel kurve
Agip kurve
Ostkurve

CIRCUIT LENGTH: 4.240 miles/6.823 km

Pos.	Driver	Nat.	No.	Entrant	Car/Engine	Laps	Time/Retirement	Speed (mph/km/h)
1	Eddie Irvine	GB	4	Scuderia Ferrari Marlboro	Ferrari F399 048B V10	45	1h 21m 58.594s	139.636/224.723
2	Mika Salo	SF	3	Scuderia Ferrari Marlboro	Ferrari F399 048B V10	45	1h 21m 59.601s	139.608/224.677
3	Heinz-Harald Frentzen	D	8	Benson & Hedges Jordan	Jordan 199-Mugen Honda MF301/HD V10	45	1h 22m 03.789s	139.489/224.486
4	Ralf Schumacher	D	6	Winfield Williams	Williams FW21-Supertec FB01 V10	45	1h 22m 11.403s	139.274/224.140
5	David Coulthard	GB	2	West McLaren Mercedes	McLaren MP4/14-Mercedes F0110G V10	45	1h 22m 15.417s	139.160/223.957
6	Olivier Panis	F	18	Gauloises Prost Peugeot	Prost AP02-Peugeot A18 V10	45	1h 22m 28.473s	138.794/223.367
7	Alexander Wurz	A	10	Mild Seven Benetton Playlife	Benetton B199-Playlife V10	45	1h 22m 31.927s	138.697/223.211
8	Jean Alesi	F	11	Red Bull Sauber Petronas	Sauber C18-Petronas SPE03A V10	45	1h 23m 09.885s	137.642/221.513
9	Marc Gene	ESP	21	Fondmetal Minardi Ford	Minardi M01-Ford Zetec-R V10	45	1h 23m 46.912s	136.628/219.881
10	Luca Badoer	I	20	Fondmetal Minardi Ford	Minardi M01-Ford Zetec-R V10	44		
11	Johnny Herbert	GB	17	Stewart Ford	Stewart SF3-Ford CR-1 V10	40	Gearbox	
	Pedro de la Rosa	ESP	14	Arrows	Arrows A20 V10	37	Accident	
	Mika Häkkinen	SF	1	West McLaren Mercedes	McLaren MP4/14-Mercedes F0110G V10	25	Accident	
	Alex Zanardi	I	5	Winfield Williams	Williams FW21-Supertec FB01 V10	21	Differential	
	Ricardo Zonta	BR	23	British American Racing	BAR 01-Supertec FB01 V10	20	Engine	
	Toranosuke Takagi	J	15	Arrows	Arrows A20 V10	15	Engine	
	Damon Hill	GB	7	Benson & Hedges Jordan	Jordan 199-Mugen Honda MF301/HD V10	13	Brakes	
	Jarno Trulli	I	19	Gauloises Prost Peugeot	Prost AP02-Peugeot A18 V10	10	Engine	
	Giancarlo Fisichella	I	9	Mild Seven Benetton Playlife	Benetton B199-Playlife V10	7	Suspension	
	Rubens Barrichello	BR	16	Stewart Ford	Stewart SF3-Ford CR-1 V10	6	Hydraulics	
	Jacques Villeneuve	CDN	22	British American Racing	BAR 01-Supertec FB01 V10	0	Collision with Diniz	
	Pedro Diniz	BR	12	Red Bull Sauber Petronas	Sauber C18-Petronas SPE03A V10	0	Collision with Villeneuve	

Fastest lap: Coulthard, on lap 43, 1m 45.270s, 144.985 mph/233.331 km/h (record).

Previous lap record: Gerhard Berger (F1 Benetton B197-Renault V10), 1m 45.747s, 144.331 mph/232.278 km/h (1997).

Grid order	1	2	3	4	5	6	7	8	9	10	11	12	13	14	15	16	17	18	19	20	21	22	23	24	25	26	27	28	29	30	31	32	33	34	35	36	37	38	39	40	41	42	43	44	45	
1 HÄKKINEN	1	1	1	1	1	1	1	1	1	1	1	1	1	1	1	1	1	1	1	1	1	1	1	1	3	4	4	4	4	4	4	4	4	4	4	4	4	4	4	4	4	4	4	4	1	
8 FRENTZEN	3	3	3	3	3	3	3	3	3	3	3	3	3	3	3	3	3	3	3	3	3	3	3	6	6	3	3	3	3	3	3	3	3	3	3	3	3	3	3	3	3	3	3	3	2	
2 COULTHARD	2	2	2	2	2	2	2	2	8	8	8	8	8	8	8	8	8	8	8	8	8	4	4	6	3	8	8	8	8	8	8	8	8	8	8	8	8	8	8	8	8	8	8	8	3	
3 SALO	8	8	16	16	16	8	8	8	8	2	4	4	4	4	4	4	4	4	4	4	8	6	4	4	1	2	6	6	6	6	6	6	6	6	6	6	6	6	6	6	6	6	6	6	4	
4 IRVINE	16	16	8	8	8	4	4	4	4	6	6	6	6	6	6	6	6	6	6	6	6	8	8	2	6	18	18	18	18	2	2	2	2	2	2	2	2	2	17	2	2	2	2	2	5	
16 BARRICHELLO	4	4	4	4	4	6	6	6	6	10	10	10	10	10	10	10	10	17	17	17	17	2	2	6	18	2	2	2	2	17	17	17	17	17	17	17	17	18	18	18	18	18	18	18	6	
18 PANIS	6	6	6	6	6	10	10	10	10	7	7	17	17	17	17	18	18	18	18	2	2	2	10	17	10	17	17	17	17	10	10	10	10	18	18	18	10	10	10	10	11	11	11	11		
7 HILL	10	10	10	10	10	7	7	7	7	17	17	7	7	7	18	18	2	2	2	10	10	10	17	10	17	10	10	10	10	18	18	18	18	10	10	10	11	11	11	11						
19 TRULLI	9	9	7	7	7	17	17	17	17	18	18	2	2	2	18	18	18	18	18	18	10	10	11	11	11	11	11	11	11	11	11	11	11	11	11	11	21	21	21	21						
9 FISICHELLA	7	7	19	19	17	19	19	18	18	18	2	2	23	23	23	5	5	5	5	14	20	11	11	11	21	21	21	21	21	21	21	21	21	21	21	21	20	20	20	20						
6 R. SCHUMACHER	19	19	17	17	19	18	18	19	19	19	23	23	7	5	5	11	14	14	14	20	14	20	21	21	14	14	14	14	14	14	14	14	14	14	14	20	20	20								
22 VILLENEUVE	17	17	18	18	18	5	5	5	23	23	5	5	5	11	11	14	20	20	20	5	11	21	14	14	20	20	20	20	20	20	20	20	20	20												
10 WURZ	18	18	5	5	5	23	23	23	5	5	14	14	11	14	14	20	21	21	11	11	5	14	20	20	20																					
5 ZANARDI	5	5	23	23	23	14	14	14	14	14	11	11	14	20	20	21	11	11	11	21	21																									
21 GENE	21	21	14	14	14	20	20	20	20	20	20	20	20	21	21	23	23	23	23	23																										
12 DINIZ	23	23	20	20	20	21	21	21	21	21	21	21	15	15																																
17 HERBERT	14	14	21	21	21	15	11	11	11	11	15	15	15																																	
23 ZONTA	20	20	9	15	15	11	15	15	15	15																																				
20 BADOER	11	15	15	11	11	16	9																																							
14 DE LA ROSA	15	11	11	9	9	9																																								
11 ALESI																																														
15 TAKAGI																																														

Pit stop
One lap behind leader

STARTING GRID

1 **HÄKKINEN** McLaren	**8** **FRENTZEN** Jordan
2 **COULTHARD** McLaren	**3** **SALO** Ferrari
4 **IRVINE** Ferrari	**16** **BARRICHELLO** Stewart
18 **PANIS** Prost	**7** **HILL** Jordan
19 **TRULLI** Prost	**9** **FISICHELLA** Benetton
6 **R. SCHUMACHER** Williams	**22** **VILLENEUVE** BAR
10 **WURZ** Benetton	**5** **ZANARDI** Williams
21 **GENE** Minardi	**12** **DINIZ** Sauber
17 **HERBERT** Stewart	**23** **ZONTA** BAR
20 **BADOER** Minardi	**14** **DE LA ROSA** Arrows
11 **ALESI** Sauber	**15** **TAKAGI** Arrows

TIME SHEETS

QUALIFYING

Weather: Dry, hot and sunny

Pos.	Driver	Car	Laps	Time
1	Mika Häkkinen	McLaren-Mercedes	11	1m 42.950s
2	Heinz-Harald Frentzen	Jordan-Mugen Honda	11	1m 43.000s
3	David Coulthard	McLaren-Mercedes	12	1m 43.288s
4	Mika Salo	Ferrari	11	1m 43.577s
5	Eddie Irvine	Ferrari	11	1m 43.769s
6	Rubens Barrichello	Stewart-Ford	12	1m 43.938s
7	Olivier Panis	Prost-Peugeot	12	1m 43.979s
8	Damon Hill	Jordan-Mugen Honda	12	1m 44.001s
9	Jarno Trulli	Prost-Peugeot	10	1m 44.209s
10	Giancarlo Fisichella	Benetton-Playlife	11	1m 44.338s
11	Ralf Schumacher	Williams-Supertec	12	1m 44.468s
12	Jacques Villeneuve	BAR-Supertec	10	1m 44.508s
13	Alexander Wurz	Benetton-Playlife	11	1m 44.522s
14	Alex Zanardi	Williams-Supertec	12	1m 45.034s
15	Marc Gene	Minardi-Ford	12	1m 45.331s
16	Pedro Diniz	Sauber-Petronas	12	1m 45.335s
17	Johnny Herbert	Stewart-Ford	11	1m 45.454s
18	Ricardo Zonta	BAR-Supertec	12	1m 45.460s
19	Luca Badoer	Minardi-Ford	12	1m 45.917s
20	Pedro de la Rosa	Arrows	12	1m 45.935s
21	Jean Alesi	Sauber-Petronas	12	1m 45.962s
22	Toranosuke Takagi	Arrows	12	1m 46.209s

FRIDAY FREE PRACTICE

Weather: Very hot and sunny

Pos.	Driver	Laps	Time
1	Jarno Trulli	33	1m 45.677s
2	Eddie Irvine	22	1m 46.225s
3	Giancarlo Fisichella	32	1m 46.243s
4	David Coulthard	28	1m 46.411s
5	Rubens Barrichello	31	1m 46.418s
6	Olivier Panis	31	1m 46.516s
7	Mika Salo	32	1m 46.542s
8	Damon Hill	33	1m 46.851s
9	Alexander Wurz	35	1m 46.859s
10	Mika Häkkinen	28	1m 46.866s
11	Marc Gene	34	1m 46.913s
12	Alex Zanardi	32	1m 47.043s
13	Ralf Schumacher	23	1m 47.334s
14	Pedro Diniz	16	1m 47.513s
15	Jacques Villeneuve	21	1m 47.513s
16	Jean Alesi	9	1m 47.551s
17	Heinz-Harald Frentzen	24	1m 47.802s
18	Johnny Herbert	20	1m 47.985s
19	Luca Badoer	23	1m 48.953s
20	Ricardo Zonta	20	1m 48.978s
21	Toranosuke Takagi	26	1m 49.059s
22	Pedro de la Rosa	27	1m 49.207s

SATURDAY FREE PRACTICE

Weather: Very hot and sunny

Pos.	Driver	Laps	Time
1	Damon Hill	28	1m 43.918s
2	Mika Häkkinen	24	1m 44.001s
3	Rubens Barrichello	23	1m 44.119s
4	Heinz-Harald Frentzen	24	1m 44.142s
5	Olivier Panis	30	1m 44.442s
6	David Coulthard	24	1m 44.526s
7	Eddie Irvine	26	1m 44.695s
8	Jarno Trulli	27	1m 44.726s
9	Mika Salo	25	1m 44.839s
10	Jacques Villeneuve	27	1m 44.860s
11	Ralf Schumacher	21	1m 44.960s
12	Giancarlo Fisichella	29	1m 45.428s
13	Alexander Wurz	29	1m 45.651s
14	Marc Gene	19	1m 45.651s
15	Alex Zanardi	29	1m 45.709s
16	Pedro Diniz	33	1m 45.838s
17	Ricardo Zonta	17	1m 45.894s
18	Jean Alesi	22	1m 46.156s
19	Pedro de la Rosa	21	1m 46.224s
20	Luca Badoer	14	1m 46.543s
21	Toranosuke Takagi	18	1m 46.732s
22	Johnny Herbert	5	11m 15.684s

WARM-UP

Weather: Very hot and sunny

Pos.	Driver	Laps	Time
1	David Coulthard	12	1m 45.557s
2	Olivier Panis	12	1m 45.788s
3	Mika Häkkinen	9	1m 45.941s
4	Jarno Trulli	13	1m 46.384s
5	Rubens Barrichello	11	1m 46.727s
6	Johnny Herbert	14	1m 46.804s
7	Damon Hill	13	1m 46.896s
8	Jacques Villeneuve	11	1m 46.959s
9	Eddie Irvine	12	1m 47.004s
10	Ralf Schumacher	13	1m 47.189s
11	Jean Alesi	10	1m 47.259s
12	Mika Salo	12	1m 47.347s
13	Giancarlo Fisichella	14	1m 47.374s
14	Heinz-Harald Frentzen	13	1m 47.387s
15	Luca Badoer	10	1m 47.397s
16	Alexander Wurz	13	1m 47.580s
17	Ricardo Zonta	12	1m 47.793s
18	Pedro Diniz	13	1m 47.979s
19	Alex Zanardi	11	1m 48.327s
20	Pedro de la Rosa	9	1m 48.534s
21	Marc Gene	11	1m 48.749s
22	Toranosuke Takagi	13	1m 48.800s

RACE FASTEST LAPS

Weather: Dry, hot and sunny

Driver	Time	Lap
David Coulthard	1m 45.270s	43
Olivier Panis	1m 46.823s	20
Mika Häkkinen	1m 47.433s	6
Heinz-Harald Frentzen	1m 47.619s	17
Eddie Irvine	1m 47.687s	17
Giancarlo Fisichella	1m 47.785s	5
Rubens Barrichello	1m 47.788s	5
Mika Salo	1m 47.945s	4
Ralf Schumacher	1m 48.083s	29
Jean Alesi	1m 48.334s	4
Johnny Herbert	1m 48.408s	29
Alexander Wurz	1m 48.455s	44
Damon Hill	1m 48.925s	9
Ricardo Zonta	1m 49.179s	14
Jarno Trulli	1m 49.285s	6
Alex Zanardi	1m 49.835s	5
Marc Gene	1m 49.894s	28
Luca Badoer	1m 49.942s	28
Toranosuke Takagi	1m 50.286s	6
Pedro de la Rosa	1m 50.534s	14

CHASSIS LOG BOOK

1	Häkkinen	McLaren MP4/14/5
2	Coulthard	McLaren MP4/14/7
	spare	McLaren MP4/14/2
3	Salo	Ferrari F399/195
4	Irvine	Ferrari F399/191
	spare	Ferrari F399/193
5	Zanardi	Williams FW21/5
6	R. Schumacher	Williams FW21/6
	spare	Williams FW21/2
7	Hill	Jordan 199/4
8	Frentzen	Jordan 199/5
	spare	Jordan 199/6
9	Fisichella	Benetton B199/7
10	Wurz	Benetton B199/5
	spare	Benetton B199/4
11	Alesi	Sauber C18/6
12	Diniz	Sauber C18/5
	spare	Sauber C18/4
14	de la Rosa	Arrows A20/4
15	Takagi	Arrows A20/2
	spare	Arrows A20/5
16	Barrichello	Stewart SF3/4
17	Herbert	Stewart SF3/5
	spare	Stewart SF3/3
18	Panis	Prost AP02/5
19	Trulli	Prost AP02/7
	spare	Prost AP02/3
20	Badoer	Minardi M01/1
21	Gene	Minardi M01/4
	spare	Minardi M01/3
22	Villeneuve	BAR 01/7
23	Zonta	BAR 01/5
	spare	BAR 01/3

POINTS TABLES

DRIVERS

1	Eddie Irvine	52
2	Mika Häkkinen	44
3	Heinz-Harald Frentzen	33
4	Michael Schumacher	32
5	David Coulthard	30
6	Ralf Schumacher	22
7	Giancarlo Fisichella	13
8	Rubens Barrichello	10
9	Mika Salo	6
10	Damon Hill	5
11 =	Alexander Wurz	3
11 =	Pedro Diniz	3
13 =	Johnny Herbert	2
13 =	Olivier Panis	2
15 =	Pedro de la Rosa	1
15 =	Jean Alesi	1
15 =	Jarno Trulli	1

CONSTRUCTORS

1	Ferrari	90
2	McLaren	74
3	Jordan	38
4	Williams	22
5	Benetton	16
6	Stewart	12
7	Sauber	4
8	Prost	3
9	Arrows	1

HUNGARIAN

grand prix

HÄKKINEN

COULTHARD

IRVINE

FRENTZEN

BARRICHELLO

HILL

HUNGARORING QUALIFYING

The Hungaroring is a tight little track with short straights and few overtaking opportunities, requiring a finely balanced mix of a high-downforce aerodynamic configuration for maximum grip in the corners and firm discipline from the drivers, who must avoid straying far from the racing line lest they skid on the build-up of dust and end up twiddling their thumbs in a gravel trap.

In 1998, Michael Schumacher conjured up a brilliant win for Ferrari thanks to a three-stop strategy and helped by a rash of self-inflicted technical and strategic problems experienced by key rivals McLaren. This year, however, McLaren arrived in Hungary absolutely determined to get Häkkinen's World Championship challenge back on the rails again after a disastrous run of misfortune culminating with the Finn's lucky escape at Hockenheim after a high-speed tyre failure.

Despite a spin in Friday's rain-slicked free practice, Häkkinen looked confident from the start and neatly tucked away pole position with a best lap in 1m 18.156s.

'I was happy with the balance,' said Mika, 'but my third run was spoiled when I came up behind Herbert who had bits and pieces flying all over the place from his car. It was a pity, because it was a really good lap.'

It was not an easy run by any means, for Irvine was bang on form with the Ferrari and shaved his way down to 1m 18.263s, easily good enough to push Coulthard onto the second row.

'There are no long straights so I thought that if there was anywhere we could qualify on pole, it would be here,' said Irvine. 'In fact the sector [of the lap] where we are losing out is the first section with two straights.

'All the same, it is good to be on the front row, even if it means I am on the dirty side of the track. But in the past I have made great starts from both sides of the track – and the start will be everything in this race.'

Both McLaren and Ferrari opted to run the harder of the two relatively soft Bridgestone tyre compounds available for this race, although Mika Salo, inexplicably, just couldn't string things together and wound up a desolate 18th on the grid, 2.1s away from Irvine's best.

'Eddie will be fighting on his own tomorrow,' said a slightly disapproving Jean Todt. He was unable to explain why Salo had been unable to match his Saturday free practice times – set on well used rubber – when it came to the crucial hour of qualifying.

Using the softer tyre choice, Giancarlo Fisichella's Benetton B199 (1m 18.515s) just pipped the similarly equipped Jordan 199s of Heinz-Harald Frentzen (1m 18.664s) and Damon Hill (1m 18.667s). It was a promising performance from Benetton who had previously been lacking speed in high-downforce trim. Technical chief Pat Symonds speculated that they had been helped by running a full-sized car in their £12 million wind tunnel at Enstone for the first time the previous week.

'Fourth place is a good result, but more than anything else I am really happy with the performance of the car,' enthused Fisichella, who had to make a brief visit to hospital on Saturday morning after getting some dirt in one of his eyes.

'The modifications we made after the Danielsson test [straight line running on the Lurcy-Levis aerodrome near Magny-Cours]

have helped to cure many of the set-up problems that have troubled us for the first half of the season. Now the car is well balanced and has good grip.'

Alexander Wurz wound up seventh on 1m 18.733s, also quite happy with his car, but the two Benettons were split by the Jordans of Heinz-Harald Frentzen (1m 18.664s) and Damon Hill (1m 18.667s).

'I'm slightly disappointed,' said Frentzen. 'We had a problem with the balance on my first run, but my second was trouble-free and the car felt fine. We then made some modifications but had a problem because a gurney flap came off, causing a bit of understeer, so I had to wait until my final run only then to encounter traffic. I think Herbert and I touched at one point, so it was quite eventful.'

For his part, Hill felt he had got the optimum out of the car 'but I picked up too much understeer at the last corner'. In eighth place Rubens Barrichello was a little disappointed that he could only squeeze a 1m 19.095s out of his Stewart-Ford SF3.

'I was hoping for a top-four position today, which was realistic, given the way the car had been performing,' said the Brazilian. 'However the car was very nervous and I experienced a lot more understeer this afternoon. I can't really explain it because I was not happy with the set-up before qualifying.'

Team-mate Johnny Herbert ended up tenth fastest on 1m 19.095s after Frentzen ran over his nose wing as the Englishman was trying to make room for him to come through. 'A bit annoying,' shrugged Herbert with masterly understatement.

Jacques Villeneuve's British American 01 qualified ninth on 1m 19.127s after experimenting with several different chassis set-ups. 'The car is still competitive, and it allows me to battle my way, but we're lacking some speed,' he admitted.

The Sauber C18s of Jean Alesi (1m 19.390s) and Pedro Diniz (1m 19.782s) lined up 11th and 12th, although, in truth, the Frenchman was fortunate to have taken any part in qualifying at all. During the Saturday morning free practice session he crashed heavily avoiding Pedro de la Rosa's Arrows which had slowed to walking pace on the exit of the first corner.

'He did three things wrong,' said Alesi after returning from a brief stint of hospital treatment. 'First he was going slowly, second he was on the line and third he lifted off. That's a very long corner and I had no chance to brake.

'I just had to swerve to avoid him and escape a collision. But he came to apologise later. He didn't do it on purpose, he just made an incorrect evaluation.'

Despite this, both Saubers lined up ahead of the Prost-Peugeots of Jarno Trulli and Olivier Panis, while the Williams team also had a frustrating time. Alex Zanardi wound up 15th (1m 19.924s) after having one run spoiled by an Arrows, another by Johnny Herbert, and then a mistake on his third run. Ralf Schumacher qualified in 16th place (1m 19.945s), and was worried by a lack of grip.

'I can't understand what really happened, but the car felt completely different to before,' said Schumacher. 'I didn't have any grip and maybe even a damper failed. Whatever it was we have now to find it out.'

Left: Have a drink on me boys! Mika Häkkinen drops his magnum of Moët down to his McLaren crew.

Below right: Jacques Villeneuve qualified the BAR inside the top ten, a welcome improvement in fortune for the Brackley team.

MIKA Häkkinen and David Coulthard firmly applied the brake to Eddie Irvine's World Championship aspirations with a convincing McLaren-Mercedes grand slam in the Hungarian Grand Prix. The Ulsterman, forced into a slight driving error through a combination of pressure from Coulthard and a handling problem on his Ferrari F399, dropped from second to third in the closing stages to see his title lead slashed dramatically from eight points to two by the end of the afternoon.

It was certainly a reassuring moment for Häkkinen who had not been first past the chequered flag since the Canadian Grand Prix at Montreal. After the abject disappointments of Silverstone, the A1-Ring and Hockenheim, this dominant performance at the Hungaroring seemed to signal that normal service had been resumed at the head of the field.

Irvine, who qualified second behind Häkkinen, was unlucky not to finish second. Running ahead of Coulthard's McLaren in the closing stages, Irvine momentarily slid off the road with 14 of the race's 77 laps still to run. It only cost him about 4s, but it was enough for his old rival to nip through to take a second place he held to the chequered flag.

'I managed to keep ahead of DC at our second refuelling stop when we came in together,' said Irvine, 'after which I pushed like mad because I didn't want him on my tail for the last 20 or so laps.

'The tyres felt good for two or three laps, then they went off in a big way. I was struggling with the front and rear of the car. It was jumping around too much and we were only hanging on by the skin of our teeth.' Ferrari insiders ended the weekend speculating that a problem with the car's differential may have been the key to Irvine's handling problems.

The start of the race had been uneventful, the first plunging downhill right-hander for once not claiming a single victim as the pack sprinted away from the grid. Häkkinen made a clean getaway from pole to lead from Irvine, Giancarlo Fisichella's Benetton B199, Heinz-Harald Frentzen's Jordan 199 and David Coulthard in the other McLaren MP4/14.

Mika was not messing about. He produced a 1.3s lead by the end of the opening lap and, with seven laps under his belt, was already 5.1s ahead of the seemingly breathless Ferrari. On lap 11, Alex Zanardi's Williams FW21 suddenly skidded luridly onto the grass, recovered and then came slowly

Bryn Williams/Words & Pictures

into the pits to retire. The sensors in the electronic differential had gone haywire and nothing could be quickly done to rectify the situation.

Coulthard had qualified third, but a slow start saw him rather bogged down in traffic on this tight circuit where overtaking is extremely difficult and his task was made even more difficult by a slight gearbox downchange problem.

'It locked the rear wheels several times under braking,' he said, 'but they told me they were monitoring the situation and I heard no more about it.'

Nevertheless, David paid the price for his poor getaway. Boxed in behind Frentzen's fourth-place Jordan, with ten laps completed he was already 19.1s behind Häkkinen and even Fisichella's Benetton was 4s ahead in third place, the Italian pulling steadily away from the rest of the pack.

For his part, Häkkinen was simply rattling away fastest laps, seemingly as the mood took him. Meanwhile, at the back of the pack, the other Mika was having an absolutely wretched time in the second Ferrari, unable to offer any worthwhile support to Irvine.

Having qualified an almost incomprehensible 18th, the team decided that Salo should carry a heavy fuel load from the outset and make a relatively late single stop. It simply did not work, because he was unable to find a way past the slower cars during the early stages of the race. Salo was just left floundering, and he knew it.

By lap 17 Häkkinen was being shown the 'PUSH' signal from the pit, indicating that he should sustain as quick a pace as possible up to his first scheduled refuelling stop, to prevent himself temporarily dropping back into the clutches of slower cars on a one-stop strategy who might hold him up artificially during their run-up to their own arrival in the pit lane.

Häkkinen duly responded, easing open the gap to 8.8s over Irvine by the end of lap 20. Meanwhile, further back in the pack, Pedro Diniz spun off in sheer frustration after being asked to let team-mate Jean Alesi through into ninth place.

'I made a good start and ran ahead of Jean for the first 19 laps,' shrugged the Brazilian. 'But then Mr Sauber told me to let him by. I did this, at the chicane at the top of the hill, but I was upset and lost my concentration and spun under braking. The car was oversteering in any case, and I let myself get caught out.'

On lap 28 Fisichella made his first refuelling stop in 8.8s, dropping from third to ninth. Next time round Irvine came in for an 8.3s stop, dropping

from second to third, while Damon Hill's Jordan also came in, dropping from fifth to eighth.

Frentzen came in on lap 30 for a 6.4s first stop, resuming sixth, while next time round Häkkinen made a flawless 7.4s refuelling stop which saw him squeeze back into the race 2.7s ahead of Coulthard who had yet to make his stop.

Coulthard made his first refuelling stop on lap 33 in 7.3s, dropping from second to fourth. As the pack now settled down again, on lap 34 Häkkinen led by 20.6s from Irvine with Rubens Barrichello's Stewart SF3 third – but on a one-stop strategy and yet to come in – ahead of Coulthard, Fisichella, Frentzen and Hill.

On lap 40, Barrichello came in for an 11.1s single refuelling stop and resumed in eighth position. Now Coulthard had a clear track to Irvine and

DIARY

Ralf Schumacher turns down invitation to drive alongside Eddie Irvine in forthcoming Jaguar F1 team.

F1 Commercial Rights Holder Bernie Ecclestone denies speculation that he is keen to purchase an interest in Everton Football Club.

Juan Pablo Montoya scores decisive win in Mid Ohio CART race, finishing ahead of Team Green running mates Paul Tracey and Dario Franchitti.

Former Stewart aerodynamicist Eghbal Hamedy joins the Arrows F1 team.

Left: Mika Häkkinen took control of the championship race once more with a decisive win at the Hungaroring.
Michael Roberts

tyres, until he made a mistake. That was exactly what I needed.'

From that point on, the race ran to an uneventful finish. Häkkinen won by 9.7s from his team-mate with the frustrated Irvine trailing in third another 17.5s down. 'I am a little surprised that the McLarens proved to be so much quicker,' he admitted, 'although there are a couple of [technical] things on the car that we need to look at.

'Maybe we got something wrong. We need to look at everything very carefully in the de-brief, because it is very unusual for us not to be quick in the race. And here we were struggling.'

Behind Irvine it was left to Heinz-Harald Frentzen to finish fourth ahead of Rubens Barrichello and Damon Hill in the other Jordan. In contrast to the German Grand Prix at Hockenheim a fortnight ago, Hill was quite satisfied with his performance on the circuit where he scored his maiden F1 victory for Williams six years ago.

'The start went well and, on the strategy we had, a short middle stint of the race looked very promising,' said Damon. 'I ought to have come out ahead of Rubens, but we hadn't counted on him making just one stop.

'I was able to catch up and get to within a second of him, but I couldn't get closer than that. I could have had a chance if he had been blocked by a backmarker, or made a mistake, but about five laps from the end I had to back off because we had an air pressure problem with the engine. It was a

tough race, but it's good to finish and score a championship point.'

Alexander Wurz's Benetton finished seventh, the Austrian frustrated over his car's nervous handling, possibly the long-term legacy of a bump with a rival on the first corner. The Prost-Peugeots of Jarno Trulli and Olivier Panis sandwiched Ralf Schumacher's ninth-place Williams FW21, the young German making the best of a difficult job to climb up from 16th on the grid.

Johnny Herbert's Stewart SF3 took 11th place ahead of perhaps the most disappointed man of the day, Mika Salo, the Finnish driver who finished a storming second at Hockenheim as stand-in for the injured Michael Schumacher.

This time, Salo qualified 18th and struggled round to finish a lapped 12th, unable to make any impression on his rivals. 'To be honest, I am embarrassed by my performance and feel I have let the team down,' he said.

On a day when 23 plane-loads of Finnish fans arrived in Budapest to cheer his compatriot Häkkinen to victory, Salo's was a stunningly honest admission.

At the opposite end of the field, Häkkinen was enjoining his countrymen to party. 'This is fabulous and the atmosphere is great,' said the World Champion.

'I am sure the Finnish people here will have a great evening tonight. They have good reason to celebrate and to be proud of Finland and proud of McLaren.'

really began to pile on the pressure. On lap 41 he was just 3.5s behind the Ferrari and had sliced that back to a single second in another four laps. From then on, David was scarcely more than half a second behind the Ferrari as the rivals raced towards what could be their crucial second refuelling stops.

On lap 52, Fisichella's superb run in third place came to an end when his Benetton's engine died through an apparent loss of fuel pressure as he came in for his second stop. Despite every effort, the Supertec V10 flatly refused to fire up again, so that was that.

'The choice to use the super soft tyre choice proved the right one,' said Giancarlo. 'As the race progressed, their performance stabilised and the car became very well balanced. I was in third position and felt there was a good possibility we could get on the

podium, but then the engine suddenly lost power a few hundred metres before my second stop.'

On lap 55, Häkkinen made his second refuelling stop in 7.4s and resumed in first, steadily reeling off the laps towards his fourth win of the season. Three laps later Irvine (6.8s) and Coulthard (6.2s) made their second refuelling stops from second and third places, resuming in the same order.

On lap 63, Irvine ran wide onto the grass on a medium-speed right-hander at the back of the circuit. 'It would have been very difficult to have attacked and passed him without the mistake,' said Coulthard.

'Before the [second] pit stop I was trying to stay as close to him as possible, to put him under pressure and to be able to hope for a mistake from him. But after the stop he was obviously much quicker on his fresh set of

McLaren chief slams Bridgestone press release

McLAREN team chief Ron Dennis described as 'wholly unacceptable' the decision by tyre supplier Bridgestone to issue an official communiqué on the subject of Mika Häkkinen's tyre failure at Hockenheim which could be interpreted as implying that the World Champion team was guilty of operational errors.

It had been speculated by rivals in the paddock that, in order to enhance grip out of medium-speed corners, the McLaren had been running tyre pressures lower than those specified by the supplier. After a detailed examination of the tiny remnants of rubber retrieved after the 195 mph failure which pitched the World Champion out of the German Grand Prix just over a lap after his scheduled refuelling stop, Bridgestone concluded:

'There was no failure of the tyre consistent with incorrect or faulty construction [and] there was no structural failure on the McLaren car.' The release continued to speculate that tyre pressures, a cut in the tyre, or a blister could have caused the problem.

'Our cars are heavily instrumented,' replied Dennis, 'so we can absolutely determine whether or not there was a failure on the car. There was no structural failure at all with either Mika or David's car.

'As far as tyre pressures were concerned the only data we had was the starting pressures and those fell within the operational parameters laid down.

'We have been with Bridgestone for a little while, we've won a World Championship with them. We know their strengths and weaknesses and they know ours.

'It is wholly inappropriate [for them] to put forward to the media a solution that is black and white if the solution is not black and white. And there is nothing black and white about what happened at Hockenheim.'

Left: Ricardo Zonta ploughs a lonely furrow in his BAR. The Brazilian's debut season had been character-building to say the least.
Bryn Williams/Words & Pictures

Right: Also waiting for a change in fortune was Johnny Herbert, so far largely overshadowed by Barrichello.
Bryn Williams/Words & Pictures

Below left: Irvine and Ferrari had no answers to McLaren.
Michael Cooper/Allsport

Below right: Irvine leaves the post-mortem to Häkkinen.
Lukas Gorys

Bottom: Alex Zanardi kicks up the dust in his Williams. The double CART champion was forced into retirement by electronic failure.
Mark Thompson/Allsport

MARLBORO MAGYAR NAGYDÍJ
13–15 AUGUST 1999
HUNGARORING

Race distance: 77 laps, 190.090 miles/305.921 km

Race weather: Dry, hot and sunny

ROUND **11**

HUNGARORING CIRCUIT

CIRCUIT LENGTH: 2.468 miles/3.972 km

Pos.	Driver	Nat.	No.	Entrant	Car/Engine	Laps	Time/Retirement	Speed (mph/km/h)
1	Mika Häkkinen	SF	1	West McLaren Mercedes	McLaren MP4/14-Mercedes F0110G V10	77	1h 46m 23.536s	107.201/172.524
2	David Coulthard	GB	2	West McLaren Mercedes	McLaren MP4/14-Mercedes F0110G V10	77	1h 46m 33.242s	107.038/172.262
3	Eddie Irvine	GB	4	Scuderia Ferrari Marlboro	Ferrari F399 048B V10	77	1h 46m 50.764s	106.746/171.791
4	Heinz-Harald Frentzen	D	8	Benson & Hedges Jordan	Jordan 199-Mugen Honda MF301/HD V10	77	1h 46m 55.351s	106.669/171.668
5	Rubens Barrichello	BR	16	Stewart Ford	Stewart SF3-Ford CR-1 V10	77	1h 47m 07.344s	106.471/171.348
6	Damon Hill	GB	7	Benson & Hedges Jordan	Jordan 199-Mugen Honda MF301/HD V10	77	1h 47m 19.262s	106.274/171.031
7	Alexander Wurz	A	10	Mild Seven Benetton Playlife	Benetton B199-Playlife V10	77	1h 47m 24.548s	106.187/170.891
8	Jarno Trulli	I	19	Gauloises Prost Peugeot	Prost AP02-Peugeot A18 V10	76		
9	Ralf Schumacher	D	6	Winfield Williams	Williams FW21-Supertec FB01 V10	76		
10	Olivier Panis	F	18	Gauloises Prost Peugeot	Prost AP02-Peugeot A18 V10	76		
11	Johnny Herbert	GB	17	Stewart Ford	Stewart SF3-Ford CR-1 V10	76		
12	Mika Salo	SF	3	Scuderia Ferrari Marlboro	Ferrari F399 048B V10	75		
13	Ricardo Zonta	BR	23	British American Racing	BAR 01-Supertec FB01 V10	75		
14	Luca Badoer	I	20	Fondmetal Minardi Ford	Minardi M01-Ford Zetec-R V10	75		
15	Pedro de la Rosa	ESP	14	Arrows	Arrows A20 V10	75		
16	Jean Alesi	F	11	Red Bull Sauber Petronas	Sauber C18-Petronas SPE03A V10	74	Fuel pressure	
17	Marc Gene	ESP	21	Fondmetal Minardi Ford	Minardi M01-Ford Zetec-R V10	74		
	Jacques Villeneuve	CDN	22	British American Racing	BAR 01-Supertec FB01 V10	60	Clutch	
	Giancarlo Fisichella	I	9	Mild Seven Benetton Playlife	Benetton B199-Playlife V10	52	Fuel pressure	
	Toranosuke Takagi	J	15	Arrows	Arrows A20 V10	26	Gearbox	
	Pedro Diniz	BR	12	Red Bull Sauber Petronas	Sauber C18-Petronas SPE03A V10	19	Spun off	
	Alex Zanardi	I	5	Winfield Williams	Williams FW21-Supertec FB01 V10	10	Differential	

Fastest lap: Coulthard, on lap 69, 1m 20.699s, 110.129 mph/177.236 km/h.

Previous lap record: Nigel Mansell (F1 Williams FW14B-Renault V10), 1m 18.308s, 113.349 mph/182.418 km/h (1992).

Grid order																																																											
1 HÄKKINEN	1 1 1 1 1 1 1 1 1 1 1 1 1 1 1 1 1 1 1 1 1 1 1 1 1 1 1 1 1 1 1 1 1 1 1 1 1 1 1 1 1 1 1 1 1 1 1 1 1 1 1 1 1 1 1 1 1 1 1
4 IRVINE	4 4 4 4 4 4 4 4 4 4 4 4 4 4 4 4 4 4 4 4 4 4 4 4 4 4 4 4 4 2 2 2 2 4 4 4 4 4 4 4 4 4 4 4 4 4 4 4 4 4 4 4 4 4 4 4 4 4 4
2 COULTHARD	9 9 9 9 9 9 9 9 9 9 9 9 9 9 9 9 9 9 9 9 9 9 9 9 9 9 9 8 8 4 4 4 16 16 16 16 16 16 2 2 2 2 2 2 2 2 2 2 2 2 2 2 2 2 2 2 2 2
9 FISICHELLA	8 8 8 8 8 8 8 8 8 8 8 8 8 8 8 8 8 8 8 8 8 8 8 8 8 2 4 16 16 16 2 2 2 2 2 16 9 9 9 9 9 9 9 9 9 9 9 9 11 11 11 8 8 8 8
8 FRENTZEN	2 2 2 2 2 2 2 2 2 2 2 2 2 2 2 2 2 2 2 2 2 2 2 2 2 7 16 11 9 9 9 9 9 9 9 9 8 8 8 8 8 8 8 8 8 11 9 8 8 16 16 16 16
7 HILL	7 7 7 7 7 7 7 7 7 7 7 7 7 7 7 7 7 7 7 7 7 7 7 7 7 16 11 9 8 8 8 8 8 8 8 8 7 7 7 7 7 7 7 11 11 8 8 16 16 7 7 7 7
10 WURZ	16 16 16 16 16 16 16 16 16 16 16 16 16 16 16 16 16 16 16 16 16 16 16 16 16 11 9 8 11 7 7 7 7 7 7 7 11 11 11 11 11 11 11 11 11 16 16 16 16 7 7 11 11 11 11 11 11
16 BARRICHELLO	10 10 10 10 10 10 10 10 10 10 10 10 10 10 10 10 10 10 10 10 10 10 10 10 10 7 7 7 11 11 11 11 11 11 11 11 16 16 16 16 16 16 16 16 16 10 10 7 7 10 10 10 10 10
22 VILLENEUVE	12 12 12 12 12 12 12 12 12 12 12 12 12 12 12 12 12 11 11 10 10 10 10 11 11 11 11 11 9 10 10 10 10 10 10 10 10 10 10 10 10 10 10 10 10 7 7 10 10 19 19 19 19 19
17 HERBERT	11 11 11 11 11 11 11 11 11 11 11 11 11 11 11 11 11 19 19 19 19 19 19 19 19 19 17 17 17 17 17 17 19 19 19 19 19 19 19 19 19 19 19 6 6 6 6 6
11 ALESI	19 19 19 19 19 19 19 19 19 19 19 19 19 19 19 19 17 17 17 17 17 17 17 18 18 18 18 18 18 18 17 3 3 3 3 3 6 6 6 6 6 6 18 18 18 18 18 18
12 DINIZ	17 17 17 17 17 17 17 17 17 17 17 17 17 17 17 17 22 22 22 23 23 23 23 23 18 19 19 19 19 19 19 18 22 6 6 6 22 22 22 22 22 22 18 22 22 22 22 22
19 TRULLI	22 22 22 22 22 22 22 22 22 22 22 22 22 22 22 22 23 23 6 6 18 18 18 6 3 3 3 3 3 22 22 22 3 18 18 18 18 22 22 17 17 17 17 17 17 17
18 PANIS	23 23 23 23 23 23 23 23 23 23 23 23 23 23 23 6 6 22 18 18 18 6 3 22 22 22 22 22 22 18 18 18 18 17 17 17 17 17 17 17 17 23 23 23 23
5 ZANARDI	5 5 5 5 5 5 5 5 6 6 6 6 6 6 18 18 18 18 20 20 20 20 20 22 6 6 6 6 6 6 17 17 17 17 17 3 3 3 3 3 3 23 23 23 23 23
6 R. SCHUMACHER	6 6 6 6 6 6 6 18 18 18 18 18 18 18 18 18 20 20 20 20 14 14 14 3 20 23 23 23 20 20 20 20 20 20 20 20 20 20 20 20 23 20 20 20 20 20
23 ZONTA	18 18 18 18 18 18 18 18 5 20 20 20 20 20 20 20 14 14 14 3 3 3 22 6 20 20 20 23 23 23 23 23 23 23 23 23 23 23 14 14 14 14 14 14
3 SALO	20 20 20 20 20 20 20 20 14 14 14 14 14 14 14 14 3 3 3 22 22 22 14 14 14 14 14 14 14 14 14 14 14 14 14 14 20 21 21 21 21 21
20 BADOER	14 14 14 14 14 14 14 3 3 3 21 21 21 21 21 21 21 21 21 21 21 21 21 21 21 21 21 21 21 21 21 21 21
14 DE LA ROSA	3 3 3 3 3 3 3 21 21 21 21 21 21 21 21 21 15 15 15 15 15 15
15 TAKAGI	15 15 15 21 21 21 21 21 15 15 15 15 15 15 15 15 15 15
21 GENE	21 21 21 15 15 15 15 15 15 5

STARTING GRID

1 **HÄKKINEN** McLaren	4 **IRVINE** Ferrari
2 **COULTHARD** McLaren	9 **FISICHELLA** Benetton
8 **FRENTZEN** Jordan	7 **HILL** Jordan
10 **WURZ** Benetton	16 **BARRICHELLO** Stewart
22 **VILLENEUVE** BAR	17 **HERBERT** Stewart
11 **ALESI** Sauber	12 **DINIZ** Sauber
19 **TRULLI** Prost	18 **PANIS** Prost
5 **ZANARDI** Williams	6 **R. SCHUMACHER** Williams
23 **ZONTA** BAR	3 **SALO** Ferrari
20 **BADOER** Minardi	14 **DE LA ROSA** Arrows
15 **TAKAGI** Arrows	21 **GENE** Minardi

62 63 64 65 66 67 68 69 70 71 72 73 74 75 76 77	
1 1 1 1 1 1 1 1 1 1 1 1 1 1 1 1	1
4 2 2 2 2 2 2 2 2 2 2 2 2 2 2 2	2
2 4 4 4 4 4 4 4 4 4 4 4 4 4 4 4	3
8 8 8 8 8 8 8 8 8 8 8 8 8 8 8 8	4
6 16 16 16 16 16 16 16 16 16 16 16 16 16 16 16	5
7 7 7 7 7 7 7 7 7 7 7 7 7 7 7 7	6
1 11 11 11 11 11 11 11 10 10 10 10 10 10 10 10	
0 10 10 10 10 10 10 11 11 9 11 11 11 11 19 19	
9 19 19 19 19 19 19 19 1 11 11 19 19 6 6	
6 6 6 6 6 6 6 6 6 6 6 6 18 18	
8 18 18 18 18 18 18 18 18 18 18 18 18 18 17 17	
7 17 17 17 17 17 17 17 17 17 17 17 17 17 3 3	
3 3 3 3 3 3 3 3 3 3 3 3 3 23	
3 23 23 23 23 23 23 23 23 23 23 23 23 20	
0 20 20 20 20 20 20 20 20 20 20 20 20 14	
4 14 14 14 14 14 14 14 14 14 14 14 14	
1 21 21 21 21 21 21 21 21 21 21 21 21	

Pit stop
One lap behind leader

TIME SHEETS

QUALIFYING
Weather: Dry, hot and sunny

Pos.	Driver	Car	Laps	Time
1	Mika Häkkinen	McLaren-Mercedes	11	1m 18.156s
2	Eddie Irvine	Ferrari	11	1m 18.263s
3	David Coulthard	McLaren-Mercedes	12	1m 18.384s
4	Giancarlo Fisichella	Benetton-Playlife	11	1m 18.515s
5	Heinz-Harald Frentzen	Jordan-Mugen Honda	12	1m 18.664s
6	Damon Hill	Jordan-Mugen Honda	11	1m 18.667s
7	Alexander Wurz	Benetton-Playlife	11	1m 18.733s
8	Rubens Barrichello	Stewart-Ford	11	1m 19.095s
9	Jacques Villeneuve	BAR-Supertec	11	1m 19.127s
10	Johnny Herbert	Stewart-Ford	11	1m 19.389s
11	Jean Alesi	Sauber-Petronas	12	1m 19.390s
12	Pedro Diniz	Sauber-Petronas	11	1m 19.782s
13	Jarno Trulli	Prost-Peugeot	12	1m 19.788s
14	Olivier Panis	Prost-Peugeot	12	1m 19.841s
15	Alex Zanardi	Williams-Supertec	11	1m 19.924s
16	Ralf Schumacher	Williams-Supertec	12	1m 19.945s
17	Ricardo Zonta	BAR-Supertec	12	1m 20.060s
18	Mika Salo	Ferrari	12	1m 20.369s
19	Luca Badoer	Minardi-Ford	12	1m 20.961s
20	Pedro de la Rosa	Arrows	12	1m 21.328s
21	Toranosuke Takagi	Arrows	11	1m 21.675s
22	Marc Gene	Minardi-Ford	12	1m 21.867s

FRIDAY FREE PRACTICE
Weather: Overcast, cool, intermittent light rain

Pos.	Driver	Laps	Time
1	Eddie Irvine	25	1m 19.476s
2	Mika Häkkinen	19	1m 19.722s
3	David Coulthard	28	1m 20.117s
4	Rubens Barrichello	32	1m 20.547s
5	Mika Salo	31	1m 20.989s
6	Heinz-Harald Frentzen	30	1m 21.185s
7	Alex Zanardi	33	1m 21.251s
8	Alexander Wurz	34	1m 21.456s
9	Ralf Schumacher	29	1m 21.481s
10	Johnny Herbert	21	1m 21.486s
11	Jacques Villeneuve	29	1m 21.504s
12	Olivier Panis	34	1m 21.525s
13	Luca Badoer	39	1m 21.635s
14	Giancarlo Fisichella	30	1m 21.673s
15	Jean Alesi	40	1m 22.009s
16	Damon Hill	21	1m 22.182s
17	Ricardo Zonta	39	1m 22.290s
18	Jarno Trulli	25	1m 22.360s
19	Marc Gene	33	1m 22.380s
20	Pedro Diniz	17	1m 23.096s
21	Toranosuke Takagi	25	1m 23.216s
22	Pedro de la Rosa	37	1m 24.064s

SATURDAY FREE PRACTICE
Weather: sunny and bright

Pos.	Driver	Laps	Time
1	Mika Häkkinen	23	1m 18.219s
2	David Coulthard	28	1m 18.890s
3	Heinz-Harald Frentzen	21	1m 19.012s
4	Johnny Herbert	29	1m 19.164s
5	Rubens Barrichello	26	1m 19.186s
6	Jacques Villeneuve	33	1m 19.332s
7	Damon Hill	34	1m 19.356s
8	Jarno Trulli	31	1m 19.518s
9	Giancarlo Fisichella	16	1m 19.641s
10	Alexander Wurz	37	1m 19.715s
11	Eddie Irvine	17	1m 19.817s
12	Ralf Schumacher	30	1m 19.825s
13	Olivier Panis	31	1m 19.920s
14	Alex Zanardi	36	1m 19.926s
15	Mika Salo	21	1m 20.139s
16	Ricardo Zonta	31	1m 20.152s
17	Jean Alesi	8	1m 20.323s
18	Pedro Diniz	40	1m 20.342s
19	Pedro de la Rosa	29	1m 21.398s
20	Luca Badoer	22	1m 21.523s
21	Marc Gene	32	1m 21.568s
22	Toranosuke Takagi	24	1m 22.213s

WARM-UP
Weather: Sunny and bright

Pos.	Driver	Laps	Time
1	David Coulthard	14	1m 20.420s
2	Mika Häkkinen	13	1m 20.435s
3	Heinz-Harald Frentzen	18	1m 20.454s
4	Giancarlo Fisichella	15	1m 20.704s
5	Eddie Irvine	14	1m 21.083s
6	Jean Alesi	14	1m 21.083s
7	Alexander Wurz	17	1m 21.154s
8	Jacques Villeneuve	15	1m 21.211s
9	Jarno Trulli	18	1m 21.364s
10	Johnny Herbert	18	1m 21.549s
11	Olivier Panis	15	1m 21.561s
12	Rubens Barrichello	15	1m 21.671s
13	Pedro Diniz	15	1m 21.853s
14	Mika Salo	13	1m 22.226s
15	Damon Hill	12	1m 22.321s
16	Alex Zanardi	16	1m 22.530s
17	Luca Badoer	14	1m 22.849s
18	Ricardo Zonta	11	1m 22.889s
19	Toranosuke Takagi	11	1m 23.364s
20	Pedro de la Rosa	14	1m 23.812s
21	Marc Gene	14	1m 24.065s
22	Ralf Schumacher	3	5m 07.280s

RACE FASTEST LAPS
Weather: Dry, hot and sunny

Driver	Time	Lap
David Coulthard	1m 20.699s	69
Mika Häkkinen	1m 20.744s	44
Jean Alesi	1m 20.830s	45
Heinz-Harald Frentzen	1m 20.991s	71
Eddie Irvine	1m 21.010s	62
Damon Hill	1m 21.180s	31
Ricardo Zonta	1m 21.343s	32
Giancarlo Fisichella	1m 21.469s	51
Alexander Wurz	1m 21.539s	71
Rubens Barrichello	1m 21.707s	38
Ralf Schumacher	1m 21.745s	48
Jarno Trulli	1m 21.936s	45
Jacques Villeneuve	1m 21.975s	49
Pedro Diniz	1m 22.452s	19
Johnny Herbert	1m 22.455s	70
Olivier Panis	1m 22.587s	59
Mika Salo	1m 22.681s	49
Luca Badoer	1m 23.456s	45
Pedro de la Rosa	1m 23.520s	47
Alex Zanardi	1m 24.297s	7
Marc Gene	1m 24.807s	28
Toranosuke Takagi	1m 25.483s	11

CHASSIS LOG BOOK

1	Häkkinen	McLaren MP4/14/4
2	Coulthard	McLaren MP4/14/6
	spare	McLaren MP4/14/2
3	Salo	Ferrari F399/195
4	Irvine	Ferrari F399/191
	spare	Ferrari F399/193
5	Zanardi	Williams FW21/5
6	R. Schumacher	Williams FW21/6
	spare	Williams FW21/2
7	Hill	Jordan 199/4
8	Frentzen	Jordan 199/5
	spare	Jordan 199/6
9	Fisichella	Benetton B199/7
10	Wurz	Benetton B199/5
	spare	Benetton B199/4
11	Alesi	Sauber C18/4
12	Diniz	Sauber C18/7
	spare	Sauber C18/3
14	de la Rosa	Arrows A20/7
15	Takagi	Arrows A20/4
	spare	Arrows A20/5
16	Barrichello	Stewart SF3/4
17	Herbert	Stewart SF3/5
	spare	Stewart SF3/3
18	Panis	Prost AP02/5
19	Trulli	Prost AP02/7
	spare	Prost AP02/3
20	Badoer	Minardi M01/1
21	Gene	Minardi M01/4
	spare	Minardi M01/3
22	Villeneuve	BAR 01/8
23	Zonta	BAR 01/5
	spare	BAR 01/3

POINTS TABLES

DRIVERS

1	Eddie Irvine	56
2	Mika Häkkinen	54
3 =	David Coulthard	36
3 =	Heinz-Harald Frentzen	36
5	Michael Schumacher	32
6	Ralf Schumacher	22
7	Giancarlo Fisichella	13
8	Rubens Barrichello	12
9 =	Mika Salo	6
9 =	Damon Hill	6
11 =	Alexander Wurz	3
11 =	Pedro Diniz	3
13 =	Johnny Herbert	2
13 =	Olivier Panis	2
15 =	Pedro de la Rosa	1
15 =	Jean Alesi	1
15 =	Jarno Trulli	1

CONSTRUCTORS

1	Ferrari	94
2	McLaren	90
3	Jordan	42
4	Williams	22
5	Benetton	16
6	Stewart	14
7	Sauber	4
8	Prost	3
9	Arrows	1

BELGIAN
grand prix

FIA WORLD CHAMPIONSHIP • ROUND 12

Above left: David Coulthard took control of the Belgian Grand Prix after beating team-mate Mika Häkkinen into the first corner.
Peter Nygaard/GP Photo

Above: Häkkinen fails to see the funny side of things despite Adrian Newey's demeanour.
Paul-Henri Cahier

Left: Coulthard enjoys his Moët moment.
Bryn Williams/Words & Pictures

Main picture: Coulthard against the verdant Spa backdrop.
Paul-Henri Cahier

SPA QUALIFYING

As early as Friday morning, Coulthard had flagged his intentions by setting fastest time in the first free practice session on this most dramatic of circuits through the pine forests of the Hautes Fagnes region close to the German border.

Qualifying saw the pole position battle resolved in Häkkinen's favour by a mere 0.1s – nothing on a circuit which, at 4.3 miles to the lap, is almost twice as long as most tracks on the championship schedule.

The entire field opted for the softer of Bridgestone's two available tyre compounds and, for much of the session, it really seemed as though Coulthard might end up ahead. He was quicker than Häkkinen through the first and third sectors of the lap, but then Mika dug deep and went quicker on the crucial first sector.

He sustained his speed through the second sector, where he was always quick, and was 0.2s up at the second timing split. He lost another tenth on the run back to the start/finish line, but it was still enough to get the job done with a whisker in hand.

'Sometimes you can be one or two tenths of a second faster and it is very satisfying,' he said, 'But when it is one second faster it is a little difficult to understand. Good car, brilliant driver, I guess!'

Coulthard was also well satisfied with second place on the grid. 'I was also slightly surprised when I saw the gap to the others,' he said. 'I changed the car [set-up] for the last run. It was slightly better, but I made a couple of mistakes.'

In the Jordan camp, Heinz-Harald Frentzen qualified third on 1m 51.332s fractionally ahead of his team-mate Damon Hill who managed 1m 51.372s.

'On my first run the rear end of the car felt slightly nervous,' said Frentzen, 'so I made some changes, but lost the second run to Jacques Villeneuve's accident and the third one I lost when Zonta crashed in the same place. I took new tyres for the last run and found a good compromise set-up which was not too soft, preventing the car from bottoming out up the hill from Eau Rouge.' For his part, Hill merely smiled and commented; 'I am very happy and satisfied that the gap to Heinz-Harald is so small.'

Ralf Schumacher was very happy with fifth fastest on 1m 51.414s with his Williams FW21. 'The car was well balanced and I think I could have gone a fraction quicker,' he said, 'but I was held up by an Arrows on my last run.' Alex Zanardi qualified eighth on 1m 52.014s, still complaining that he was not totally happy with the brake balance on his car.

Eddie Irvine was extremely disappointed with a sixth-fastest time of 1m 51.895s in the Ferrari F399. Neither he nor team-mate Mika Salo, who qualified ninth on 1m 52.124s, were sufficiently quick in any of the sectors of the lap. 'I thought it would be difficult to beat McLaren,' said Irvine, 'but I had expected to be closer.'

The Stewart SF3 drivers Rubens Barrichello and Johnny Herbert were struggling with grip and could only manage seventh and tenth fastest times, but the British American duo Jacques Villeneuve and Ricardo Zonta wound up 11th and 14th feeling moderately satisfied considering the catalogue of misfortune which had beset the team on Friday and Saturday.

The team found its resilience tested to the limit with two massive accidents and one unnerving structural failure besetting its cars.

The first setback came in Friday free practice. Jacques Villeneuve, who in 1998 had crashed his Williams trying to realise a personal ambition by trying to get through the challenging Eau Rouge turn without lifting from the throttle, this time had to watch from the cockpit of his BAR 01 as its right front suspension collapsed when he went on the brakes at 200 mph for the Les Combes right-hander at the top of the circuit.

The car spun at high speed, clipped the guard rail and then shuddered to a halt. Villeneuve, cool and philosophical as ever, undid his belts and hopped out to reflect on this latest turn of ill fortune in a difficult debut season for the all-new British American Racing team.

'I was on the straight and there was a lot of space, so it wasn't very dangerous,' he said. 'Nothing compared with last year, but it gave me a surprise as it happened without warning.'

It was also nothing compared with what lay in store for him and team-mate Ricardo Zonta the following day. Eau Rouge was the scene of their spectacular departures from the circuit, another demonstration of how cars spin too far on grooved tyres and the fact that gravel traps are of questionable value in such dramatic circumstances.

Villeneuve said; 'I was flat out, but I thought I would come through, but the rear end let go.' Zonta said he was not certain why he lost control. Craig Pollock explained that immediately he saw the first accident he telephoned the team's factory in Brackley and told them to redirect the team's two test cars which were heading for the following week's Monza test. Talk about thinking on your feet.

It was the qualifying session from hell for BAR as both Jacques Villeneuve *(opposite)* and Ricardo Zonta *(above)* had massive accidents at Eau Rouge. Both drivers were unhurt.
Both photographs: Michael Cooper/Allsport

Below left: Craig Pollock talks to JV before he returned to the track in the spare car.
Paul-Henri Cahier

Below: Jacques, shaken but not stirred, reflects on his lucky escape.
Paul-Henri Cahier

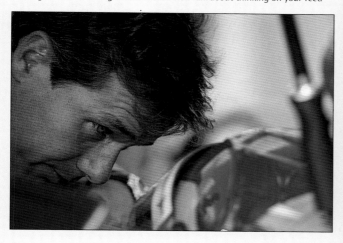

ONLY a fortnight after Mika Häkkinen's runaway victory at Budapest, David Coulthard muscled in on the winning action to make his own late bid for the World Championship with an unchallenged victory in the Belgian Grand Prix at Spa-Francorchamps.

Heinz-Harald Frentzen finished third in the Jordan Mugen-Honda, while Eddie Irvine's Ferrari F399 wound up fourth after some controversial collaboration on the part of team-mate Mika Salo to keep Ralf Schumacher's Williams back in fifth place.

These tactics produced vociferous criticism from an outraged Williams technical director Patrick Head who did not stint from telling the world exactly what he thought of the Italian team.

'Unfortunately Ralf fell foul of Ferrari's cynical approach running a one-car team with a blocking tactic to protect Irvine's position and I am very surprised that Mika Salo was prepared to accept such orders from the pits,' he said.

'Ferrari has been doing this for the last number of years and I have to say that I very much appreciate the more sporting approach of McLaren in running a two-car team. They will thoroughly deserve the drivers' and the manufacturers' championship which I hope they will achieve this year.'

At the end of the day, it was another dominant 1–2 for the McLaren-Mercedes squad, but this time with Coulthard taking the chequered flag ahead of the reigning World Champion in a success which left team principal Ron Dennis defending his organisation's approach to team tactics. This was in part prompted by a controversial first corner incident when the two McLarens briefly collided at the first corner of the race.

Häkkinen had qualified on pole position for the tenth time out of 11 races so far this season, but was slow off the mark after making a slight false start in his McLaren MP4/14. Coulthard accelerated away down the outside from second place on the grid, then turned into the tight right-hand La Source hairpin where he inadvertently bumped Häkkinen's car.

'There has been criticism from some sections of the media when we re-signed David,' said Dennis robustly, 'and now he drives a superb race and there is criticism of our team tactics.

'The first corner incident was a close call, but David was clearly ahead before the braking point. Any change in the end position would have cost us our long-established reputation for dealing totally even-handedly with our drivers.'

Many F1 insiders took the view that this was all very well, but felt that Dennis's even-handed strategy comes hand-in-hand with the risk that his two drivers might race each other out of the World Championship stakes with only four races left to run. It was suggested that McLaren might live to regret not imposing team orders if Häkkinen, who admitted that he settled for second place at Spa and abandoned his chase of Coulthard after a few laps, should fail to retain his title by less than four points.

The Spa success result transformed Coulthard into a strong title contender with 46 points, only 14 behind Häkkinen with 40 points left to compete for.

After Häkkinen was slow away, Coulthard pulled cleanly ahead going into the first turn and then came across only for the Finn to keep coming on the inside line.

'I was in front going into the first corner,' explained David, 'and it is very difficult to judge in your mirrors where your competitor is in those circumstances. I felt contact, moved away slightly to give Mika room and continued on my way.

'I am delighted to have finally won here at Spa which has always been my favourite track and a great challenge for every driver.'

This slight tangle meant that both McLarens ran wide out of the corner and, for a fleeting moment, it seemed as though Heinz-Harald Frentzen's Jordan 199 might be able to out-accelerate them both from his tighter inside line. But then Coulthard and Häkkinen got themselves sorted out, Mercedes V10 power told its own story and the two silver cars duly led the plunge past the old pit complex down to Eau Rouge.

Back on the grid, Toranosuke Takagi's Arrows retired virtually before the start with clutch trouble while Ricardo Zonta stalled his British American 01 and started so late that he would be lapped by Coulthard's leading McLaren just before the end of the Scot's third lap.

By the end of the second lap David was already a comfortable 2.1s ahead of Häkkinen with Frentzen, Eddie Irvine's Ferrari F399 and the Williams FW21s of Ralf Schumacher and Alex Zanardi running well next up.

By lap five Coulthard had extended his lead to 3.0s and, two laps later, he was 4.7s ahead of Häkkinen and a massive 15.8s in front of Irvine's fourth-place Ferrari. Further back, after a slow start, Damon Hill's Jordan 199 was all over the rear wing of Zanardi's Williams challenging for sixth place and, by lap 11, this duo had become a cosy threesome with Salo's Ferrari hauling up behind the 1996 World Champion.

Damon found himself facing an increasing struggle on his first set of tyres. 'I had a (slow) puncture on my first set of tyres, so I had no traction out of the slow corners,' he explained,

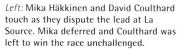

Left: Mika Häkkinen and David Coulthard touch as they dispute the lead at La Source. Mika deferred and Coulthard was left to win the race unchallenged.
Paul-Henri Cahier

Below: Ferrari mechanics are watched over by a surreal Mika Salo graphic.
Bryn Williams/Words and Pictures

Bottom: Salo's defensive tactics kept Ralf Schumacher at bay, much to the chagrin of Patrick Head.
Bryn Williams/Words and Pictures

DIARY

Nick Heidfeld signs to partner Jean Alesi in the Prost-Peugeot squad for the 2000 season.

Jarno Trulli signs a two-year deal to drive for the Jordan Mugen-Honda squad.

Mika Salo and Pedro Diniz are confirmed as the Sauber-Petronas drivers for next season.

Jason Watt won the Spa Formula 3000 round after a race-long tussle with runner-up Gonzalo Rodriguez.

Left: Eddie Irvine's Ferrari in unusual guise after the tobacco ban was put into effect at the Belgian Grand Prix for the first time.

'and then at the end of the main straight I was running up onto the rev limiter which meant I could not pass.' Things were better after his first stop on lap 16 and thereafter he picked up the pace with more confidence on the track where he'd scored Jordan's maiden Grand Prix victory only 12 months earlier.

On lap 17 the two leading McLarens were 10.2s apart as Frentzen came in from third place for his first refuelling stop, dropping to sixth. On lap 18 Häkkinen made his 7.7s first refuelling stop, dropping to third behind Ralf Schumacher's Williams which was on a one-stop strategy. Irvine also made his first (6.9s) stop, dropping from fourth to sixth.

Next time round it was Coulthard's turn to come in, the race leader making a flawless stop which put him back into the fray 10.0s ahead of Häkkinen who forced his way ahead of Schumacher's Williams which had briefly moved into second place.

On the next lap, Pedro Diniz spun his Sauber spectacularly into retirement out of a distant 18th place at Eau Rouge, the Brazilian having made his first refuelling stop on lap 15.

On lap 21, Zanardi came in for what was supposed to be his sole 9.2s refuelling stop, the Williams mechanics also adjusting the FW21's nose wings. The Italian dropped from fourth to eighth, but seemed well on course for his first finish in the points until it became clear that a glitch with the refuelling rig had prevented all the allotted fuel from going into the car. As a result, on lap 31, Alex was back again for a top-up.

On lap 22, Schumacher brought the other Williams in for its sole refuelling stop, dropping from fourth to seventh. This left Coulthard leading by 8.1s with Frentzen third, Irvine fourth ahead of Hill, Salo and Schumacher's Williams which was now just 2s behind the number two Ferrari.

What happened next prompted Patrick Head's explosive indignation. On lap 28 Salo suddenly slowed his lap times from 1m 55.940s to 1m 58.313s. Salo had been running just 13s behind team-mate Eddie Irvine on lap 27, but over the next few laps he dropped back to 22s behind, deliberately boxing in Schumacher's Williams in an effort to give Irvine a sufficient time cushion to get in and out of his second scheduled refuelling stop without relinquishing fourth place to his German rival.

These somewhat questionable tactics worked a treat. Irvine duly made his second (8.0s) stop from fourth

Tobacco row threatens Belgian GP future

THE Belgian Grand Prix weekend took place against speculation that the race might be dropped from the F1 World Championship calendar next season after a major row over tobacco advertising resulted in the cars running in unbranded livery throughout the 1999 event.

The problem had its roots in a dispute between the national, predominantly Flemish government in Brussels and the regional government of the Walloonia area in which the Spa-Francorchamps circuit is situated. The local government was prepared to allow tobacco advertising, effectively in line with the EU directive which is working towards a total ban in 2006, but the national government intervened to overrule this.

The Walloonia economic minister Serge Kubla met with lawyer Didier Pietzeys, acting on behalf of the F1 teams, in an effort to break the deadlock without success.

'The penalties for a breach of these national tobacco laws are pretty draconian and, understandably, no team was prepared to do it,' said McLaren boss Ron Dennis. 'But I think this is seriously likely to jeopardise the Belgian Grand Prix in the future.

'Much work has been done at Estoril and there is a strong desire for a Grand Prix in China. So there are options. But there is a choice [for the Belgian government], an opportunity for them to adopt a position consistent with the EU directive. Being pulled into a battle between the two factions is not what the teams wanted.'

place on lap 32 and squeezed back into the queue a couple of seconds ahead of the Williams. In fact, the whole episode was extremely close because, as Irvine accelerated back out of the pits, Salo had to take to the dust on the edge of the track to squeeze ahead momentarily into fourth place, so fleetingly it was Salo (fourth), Irvine (fifth) and the frustrated Schumacher (in sixth).

Just beyond Les Combes on lap 33 Salo let Irvine ahead again and, his disruptive tactics now completed, he peeled off to make his own second refuelling stop at the end of lap 34.

While all this drama had been taking place, the two McLarens sailed through their second refuelling stops, Häkkinen and Coulthard coming in on laps 31 and 32 respectively before resuming in their familiar positions at the head of the field.

A couple of laps before his second stop Coulthard had experienced his only mildly unsettling moment of the race when he was chopped rather abruptly by Marc Gene's Minardi as he came up to lap the slower car at Blanchimont. The episode cost David a sudden 3s, but made no material difference to the outcome of the race.

Further back, Johnny Herbert's disappointing afternoon was finally rounded off when his Stewart-Ford spun off the road due to a brake problem caused by a wheel bearing seizure.

'I went off on the grass at Pouhon, because of a brake problem,' he later explained. 'I pumped the pedal, and it all seemed fine, but at the next corner, Fagnes, it felt like I lost the brakes and I went straight into the gravel trap and hit the barrier backwards. Before that I was bothered by understeer and a general lack of grip.'

Thereafter Coulthard raced home to score the sixth F1 victory of his career by the margin of 10.4s over Häkkinen whose second place at least enabled him to scrape back into the lead of the World Championship by just a single point ahead of fourth place finisher Eddie Irvine.

Yet it was clear for the world to see that the Finn was very much less than impressed. Having already lost six points in Austria when Coulthard pushed him into a spin on the second corner of the race, he was not in a conciliatory mood when the two cars pulled into the paddock area.

The two men stoically ignored each other after climbing from their silver McLarens and Häkkinen kept well out of the picture when it came to the ritual champagne spraying on the victory rostrum. Ron Dennis moved quickly to defuse the situation and was seen having a few words with his two hirelings after the rostrum ceremony and before they went into the media conferences after the race.

As a result, Häkkinen kept his emotions under tight rein. 'It was an experience again,' said the Finn, referring obliquely to their Austrian collision, 'and not a very pleasant one. No further comment to be honest.'

Later he added: 'The way the race went generally, overtaking is not something I would consider when you have two very competitive drivers running at equal speeds. It didn't make any sense for me to try to stay close to David either, because the engine doesn't cool very well when you're following closely and you can be taking unnecessary risks because you don't have the best possible downforce in the car.' It sounded like the company line.

In third place, Frentzen was well satisfied with the outcome of his afternoon's endeavours. 'I am happy with the result, although unfortunately I lost a place in the drivers' championship to David,' he grinned.

'In the race I tried to keep up with Mika, or at least not lose too much ground to him, and I was able to push much harder on new tyres after the pit stop, but the McLarens were unbeatable today.'

In fourth place, Irvine was happy to have merely kept in play for the World Championship. 'Considering our situation today, I am happy I am only one point behind, as I thought it could be a bigger gap,' he admitted.

'We have not been fast enough all weekend and it was very hard to do good lap times in the race. But this was actually a good result for me; thanks to a good start and a good strategy, we managed to keep the position and pick up a few points.'

Behind the frustrated Schumacher, Damon Hill's Jordan-Mugen Honda came through to finish sixth ahead of Salo in the other Ferrari F399 and the luckless, delayed Zanardi. Jean Alesi's Sauber C18 was ninth ahead of a frustrated Rubens who continued to bemoan his Stewart's continuing acute lack of mechanical grip through to the end of the weekend.

Giancarlo Fisichella and Alexander Wurz wound up 11th and 14th, sandwiching the Prost-Peugeots of Jarno Trulli and Olivier Panis, neither Benetton driver working out a worthwhile set-up all weekend. The Italian complained of poor grip while Wurz, who switched to the spare car before the start, struggled all the way with locking rear brakes which made his car feel particularly nervous.

In 15th place Jacques Villeneuve finally posted his first finish for British American Racing at the end of a bruising weekend for the team. 'It's difficult to get satisfaction from finishing in 15th, but at least it's a finish,' he shrugged.

'My first set of tyres did not work at all and I was running with a very heavy fuel load, which was perhaps not the best solution, as the car was not going well. Eight laps before the end I was told to take it easy and make the finish, and that's what I did.'

Elsewhere in the paddock, as the McLaren-Mercedes squad celebrated, the most prescient words of the afternoon came from Frentzen 'I think we will be very strong at Monza,' he said thoughtfully, 'so I am looking forward to that race and to trying to beat the McLarens there.'

FOSTER'S
BELGIAN
GRAND PRIX
27–29 AUGUST 1999
SPA–FRANCORCHAMPS

Race distance: 44 laps, 190.498 miles/306.577 km

Race weather: Dry, hot and sunny

ROUND
12

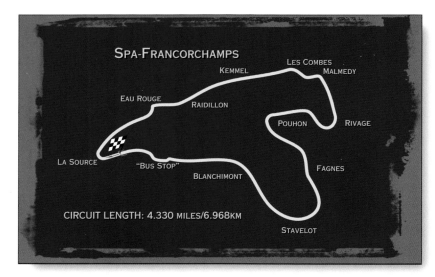

SPA-FRANCORCHAMPS

CIRCUIT LENGTH: 4.330 miles/6.968km

Pos.	Driver	Nat.	No.	Entrant	Car/Engine	Laps	Time/Retirement	Speed (mph/km/h)
1	David Coulthard	B	2	West McLaren Mercedes	McLaren MP4/14-Mercedes F0110G V10	44	1h 25m 43.057s	133.343/214.595
2	Mika Hakkinen	SF	1	West McLaren Mercedes	McLaren MP4/14-Mercedes F0110G V10	44	1h 25m 53.526s	133.072/214.159
3	Heinz-Harald Frentzen	D	8	Benson & Hedges Jordan	Jordan 199-Mugen Honda MF301/HD V10	44	1h 26m 16.490s	132.482/213.209
4	Eddie Irvine	GB	4	Scuderia Ferrari Marlboro	Ferrari F399 048B V10	44	1h 26m 28.005s	132.188/212.736
5	Ralf Schumacher	D	6	Winfield Williams	Williams FW21-Supertec FB01 V10	44	1h 26m 31.124s	132.108/212.608
6	Damon Hill	GB	7	Benson & Hedges Jordan	Jordan 199-Mugen Honda MF301/HD V10	44	1h 26m 37.973s	131.934/212.328
7	Mika Salo	SF	3	Scuderia Ferrari Marlboro	Ferrari F399 048B V10	44	1h 26m 39.306s	131.900/212.273
8	Alex Zanardi	I	5	Winfield Williams	Williams FW21-Supertec FB01 V10	44	1h 26m 50.079s	131.628/211.835
9	Jean Alesi	F	11	Red Bull Sauber Petronas	Sauber C18-Petronas SPE03A V10	44	1h 26m 56.905s	131.455/211.557
10	Rubens Barrichello	BR	16	Stewart Ford	Stewart SF3-Ford CR-1 V10	44	1h 27m 03.799s	131.282/211.278
11	Giancarlo Fisichella	I	9	Mild Seven Benetton Playlife	Benetton B199-Playlife V10	44	1h 27m 15.252s	130.995/210.816
12	Jarno Trulli	I	19	Gauloises Prost Peugeot	Prost AP02-Peugeot A18 V10	44	1h 27m 19.211s	130.896/210.657
13	Olivier Panis	F	18	Gauloises Prost Peugeot	Prost AP02-Peugeot A18 V10	44	1h 27m 24.600s	130.761/210.44014
14	Alexander Wurz	A	10	Mild Seven Benetton Playlife	Benetton B199-Playlife V10	44	1h 27m 40.802s	130.359/209.792
15	Jacques Villeneuve	CDN	22	British American Racing	BAR 01-Supertec FB01 V10	43		
16	Marc Gene	ESP	21	Fondmetal Minardi Ford	Minardi M01-Ford Zetec-R V10	43		
	Pedro de la Rosa	ESP	14	Arrows	Arrows A20 V10	35	Transmission	
	Luca Badoer	I	20	Fondmetal Minardi Ford	Minardi M01-Ford Zetec-R V10	33	Suspension	
	Ricardo Zonta	BR	23	British American Racing	BAR 01-Supertec FB01 V10	33	Gearbox	
	Johnny Herbert	GB	17	Stewart Ford	Stewart SF3-Ford CR-1 V10	27	Wheel bearing/brakes	
	Pedro Diniz	BR	12	Red Bull Sauber Petronas	Sauber C18-Petronas SPE03A V10	19	Spun off	
	Toranosuke Takagi	J	15	Arrows	Arrows A20 V10	0	Clutch	

Fastest lap: Hakkinen, on lap 23, 1m 53.955s, 136.781 mph/220.128 km/h.

Previous lap record: Alain Prost (F1 Williams FW15C-Renault V10), 1m 51.095s, 140.424 mph/225.990 km/h (1993).

Grid order	1	2	3	4	5	6	7	8	9	10	11	12	13	14	15	16	17	18	19	20	21	22	23	24	25	26	27	28	29	30	31	32	33	34	35	36	37	38	39	40	41	42	43	44	●
1 HÄKKINEN	2	2	2	2	2	2	2	2	2	2	2	2	2	2	2	2	2	2	2	2	2	2	2	2	2	2	2	2	2	2	2	2	2	2	2	2	2	2	2	2	2	2	2	1	
2 COULTHARD	1	1	1	1	1	1	1	1	1	1	1	1	1	1	1	1	1	6	1	1	1	1	1	1	1	1	1	1	1	1	1	1	1	1	1	1	1	1	1	1	1	1	1	2	
8 FRENTZEN	8	8	8	8	8	8	8	8	8	8	8	8	8	8	8	4	6	1	6	6	8	8	8	8	8	8	8	8	8	8	8	8	8	8	8	8	8	8	8	8	8	8	8	3	
7 HILL	4	4	4	4	4	4	4	4	4	4	4	4	4	4	4	8	4	5	5	8	4	4	4	4	4	4	4	4	4	4	4	4	4	4	4	4	4	4	4	4	4	4	4	4	
6 R. SCHUMACHER	6	6	6	6	6	6	6	6	6	6	6	6	6	6	6	6	5	8	8	5	4	7	7	7	7	7	3	3	3	3	6	6	6	6	6	6	6	6	6	6	6	6	6	5	
4 IRVINE	5	5	5	5	5	5	5	5	5	5	5	5	5	5	5	5	8	4	4	4	7	3	3	3	3	3	6	6	6	6	7	7	7	7	7	7	7	7	7	7	7	7	7	6	
16 BARRICHELLO	7	7	7	7	7	7	7	7	7	7	7	7	7	7	3	3	9	7	7	7	3	6	6	6	6	6	5	5	7	7	3	3	3	3	3	3	3	3	3	3	3	3	3		
5 ZANARDI	3	3	3	3	3	3	3	3	3	3	3	3	3	3	3	16	16	7	9	9	3	5	5	5	5	5	5	7	7	5	16	5	5	5	5	5	5	5	5	5	5	5	5		
3 SALO	16	16	16	16	16	16	16	16	16	16	16	16	16	16	16	7	9	3	3	3	9	11	11	11	11	11	11	16	16	16	5	11	11	11	11	11	11	11	11	11	11	11	11		
17 HERBERT	17	17	17	17	17	17	11	11	11	11	11	11	11	11	9	9	7	10	10	10	16	16	16	16	16	11	11	11	11	16	16	16	16	16	16	16	16	16	16	16	16	16			
22 VILLENEUVE	9	9	9	9	11	11	17	17	17	17	17	17	17	9	10	10	10	11	11	11	10	22	22	22	22	18	19	19	19	19	9	9	9	9	9	9	9	9	9	9	9	9			
19 TRULLI	10	11	11	11	9	9	9	9	9	9	9	9	9	17	22	22	22	22	16	16	16	18	18	18	18	19	18	9	9	9	19	19	19	19	19	19	19	19	19	19	19	19			
9 FISICHELLA	11	10	10	10	10	10	10	10	10	19	19	19	19	10	11	11	11	16	22	22	22	10		9	18	18	18	18	18	18	18	18	18	18	18	18	18	18	18	18	18	18			
23 ZONTA	22	19	19	19	19	19	19	19	19	10	10	10	10	22	17	18	18	19	18	19	19	19	19	9	9	9	17	10	10	10	10	10	10	10	10	10	10	10	10	10	10	10			
10 WURZ	10	22	22	22	18	18	18	18	18	18	10	10	22	22	12	16	16	19	19	19	19	9	17	17	10	22	22	22	22	22	22	22	22	22	22	22	22	22							
11 ALESI	12	18	18	18	22	22	22	22	22	12	12	12	20	19	18	17	17	17	17	17	17	10	10	10	10	22	21	21	20	20	20	20	21	21	21	21	21	21	21	21	21				
18 PANIS	18	20	20	20	20	20	20	20	18	20	18	18	19	20	20	20	20	20	20	21	21	20	20	21	21	21	21	14	14																
12 DINIZ	20	12	12	12	12	12	12	12	12	12	20	12	21	20	12	21	21	21	21	20	20	14	14	14	14	14	14																		
15 TAKAGI	21	21	21	21	21	21	21	21	21	18	20	21	21	21	21	14	14	14	14	14	14	23	23	23	23	23																			
20 BADOER	14	14	14	14	14	14	14	14	14	14	14	14	14	14	14	23	23	23	23	23	23																								
21 GENE	23	23	23	23	23	23	23	23	23	23	23	23	23	23	23	23	23	23																											
14 DE LA ROSA																																													

Pit stop

One lap behind leader

1 **HÄKKINEN** McLaren		**4** **IRVINE** Ferrari	
2 **COULTHARD** McLaren		**9** **FISICHELLA** Benetton	
8 **FRENTZEN** Jordan		**7** **HILL** Jordan	
10 **WURZ** Benetton		**16** **BARRICHELLO** Stewart	
22 **VILLENEUVE** BAR		**17** **HERBERT** Stewart	
11 **ALESI** Sauber		**12** **DINIZ** Sauber	
19 **TRULLI** Prost		**18** **PANIS** Prost	
5 **ZANARDI** Williams		**6** **R. SCHUMACHER** Williams	
23 **ZONTA** BAR		**3** **SALO** Ferrari	
20 **BADOER** Minardi		**14** **DE LA ROSA** Arrows	
15 **TAKAGI** Arrows		**21** **GENE** Minardi	

TIME SHEETS

QUALIFYING
Weather: Dry, hot and sunny

Pos.	Driver	Car	Laps	Time
1	Mika Häkkinen	McLaren-Mercedes	11	1m 18.156s
2	Eddie Irvine	Ferrari	11	1m 18.263s
3	David Coulthard	McLaren-Mercedes	12	1m 18.384s
4	Giancarlo Fisichella	Benetton-Playlife	11	1m 18.515s
5	Heinz-Harald Frentzen	Jordan-Mugen Honda	12	1m 18.664s
6	Damon Hill	Jordan-Mugen Honda	11	1m 18.667s
7	Alexander Wurz	Benetton-Playlife	11	1m 18.733s
8	Rubens Barrichello	Stewart-Ford	11	1m 19.095s
9	Jacques Villeneuve	BAR-Supertec	11	1m 19.127s
10	Johnny Herbert	Stewart-Ford	11	1m 19.389s
11	Jean Alesi	Sauber-Petronas	12	1m 19.390s
12	Pedro Diniz	Sauber-Petronas	11	1m 19.782s
13	Jarno Trulli	Prost-Peugeot	12	1m 19.788s
14	Olivier Panis	Prost-Peugeot	12	1m 19.841s
15	Alex Zanardi	Williams-Supertec	11	1m 19.924s
16	Ralf Schumacher	Williams-Supertec	12	1m 19.945s
17	Ricardo Zonta	BAR-Supertec	12	1m 20.060s
18	Mika Salo	Ferrari	12	1m 20.369s
19	Luca Badoer	Minardi-Ford	12	1m 20.961s
20	Pedro de la Rosa	Arrows	12	1m 21.328s
21	Toranosuke Takagi	Arrows	11	1m 21.675s
22	Marc Gene	Minardi-Ford	12	1m 21.867s

FRIDAY FREE PRACTICE
Weather: Overcast, cool, intermittent light rain

Pos.	Driver	Laps	Time
1	Eddie Irvine	25	1m 19.476s
2	Mika Häkkinen	19	1m 19.722s
3	David Coulthard	28	1m 20.117s
4	Rubens Barrichello	32	1m 20.547s
5	Mika Salo	31	1m 20.989s
6	Heinz-Harald Frentzen	30	1m 21.185s
7	Alex Zanardi	33	1m 21.251s
8	Alexander Wurz	34	1m 21.456s
9	Ralf Schumacher	29	1m 21.481s
10	Johnny Herbert	21	1m 21.486s
11	Jacques Villeneuve	29	1m 21.504s
12	Olivier Panis	34	1m 21.525s
13	Luca Badoer	39	1m 21.635s
14	Giancarlo Fisichella	30	1m 21.673s
15	Jean Alesi	40	1m 22.009s
16	Damon Hill	21	1m 22.182s
17	Ricardo Zonta	39	1m 22.290s
18	Jarno Trulli	25	1m 22.360s
19	Marc Gene	33	1m 22.380s
20	Pedro Diniz	17	1m 23.096s
21	Toranosuke Takagi	25	1m 23.216s
22	Pedro de la Rosa	37	1m 24.064s

SATURDAY FREE PRACTICE
Weather: Sunny and bright

Pos.	Driver	Laps	Time
1	Mika Häkkinen	23	1m 18.219s
2	David Coulthard	28	1m 18.890s
3	Heinz-Harald Frentzen	21	1m 19.012s
4	Johnny Herbert	29	1m 19.164s
5	Rubens Barrichello	26	1m 19.186s
6	Jacques Villeneuve	33	1m 19.332s
7	Damon Hill	34	1m 19.356s
8	Jarno Trulli	31	1m 19.518s
9	Giancarlo Fisichella	16	1m 19.641s
10	Alexander Wurz	37	1m 19.715s
11	Eddie Irvine	17	1m 19.817s
12	Ralf Schumacher	30	1m 19.825s
13	Olivier Panis	31	1m 19.920s
14	Alex Zanardi	36	1m 19.926s
15	Mika Salo	21	1m 20.139s
16	Ricardo Zonta	31	1m 20.152s
17	Jean Alesi	8	1m 20.323s
18	Pedro Diniz	40	1m 20.342s
19	Pedro de la Rosa	29	1m 21.398s
20	Luca Badoer	22	1m 21.523s
21	Marc Gene	32	1m 21.568s
22	Toranosuke Takagi	24	1m 22.213s

WARM-UP
Weather: Sunny and bright

Pos.	Driver	Laps	Time
1	David Coulthard	14	1m 20.420s
2	Mika Häkkinen	13	1m 20.435s
3	Heinz-Harald Frentzen	18	1m 20.454s
4	Giancarlo Fisichella	15	1m 20.704s
5	Eddie Irvine	14	1m 21.083s
6	Jean Alesi	14	1m 21.083s
7	Alexander Wurz	17	1m 21.154s
8	Jacques Villeneuve	15	1m 21.211s
9	Jarno Trulli	18	1m 21.364s
10	Johnny Herbert	18	1m 21.549s
11	Olivier Panis	15	1m 21.561s
12	Rubens Barrichello	15	1m 21.671s
13	Pedro Diniz	15	1m 21.853s
14	Mika Salo	13	1m 22.226s
15	Damon Hill	12	1m 22.321s
16	Alex Zanardi	16	1m 22.530s
17	Luca Badoer	14	1m 22.849s
18	Ricardo Zonta	11	1m 22.889s
19	Toranosuke Takagi	11	1m 23.364s
20	Pedro de la Rosa	14	1m 23.812s
21	Marc Gene	14	1m 24.065s
22	Ralf Schumacher	3	5m 07.280s

RACE FASTEST LAPS
Weather: Dry, hot and sunny

Driver	Time	Lap
David Coulthard	1m 20.699s	69
Mika Häkkinen	1m 20.710s	44
Jean Alesi	1m 20.830s	45
Heinz-Harald Frentzen	1m 20.991s	71
Eddie Irvine	1m 21.010s	62
Damon Hill	1m 21.180s	31
Ricardo Zonta	1m 21.343s	32
Giancarlo Fisichella	1m 21.469s	51
Alexander Wurz	1m 21.539s	71
Rubens Barrichello	1m 21.707s	38
Ralf Schumacher	1m 21.745s	48
Jarno Trulli	1m 21.936s	45
Jacques Villeneuve	1m 21.975s	49
Pedro Diniz	1m 22.452s	19
Johnny Herbert	1m 22.455s	70
Olivier Panis	1m 22.587s	59
Mika Salo	1m 22.681s	49
Luca Baoder	1m 23.456s	45
Pedro de la Rosa	1m 23.520s	47
Alex Zanardi	1m 24.297s	7
Marc Gene	1m 24.807s	28
Toranosuke Takagi	1m 25.483s	11

CHASSIS LOG BOOK

1	Häkkinen	McLaren MP4/14/4
2	Coulthard	McLaren MP4/14/6
	spare	McLaren MP4/14/2
3	Salo	Ferrari F399/195
4	Irvine	Ferrari F399/191
	spare	Ferrari F399/193
5	Zanardi	Williams FW21/5
6	R. Schumacher	Williams FW21/6
	spare	Williams FW21/2
7	Hill	Jordan 199/4
8	Frentzen	Jordan 199/5
	spare	Jordan 199/6
9	Fisichella	Benetton B199/7
10	Wurz	Benetton B199/5
	spare	Benetton B199/4
11	Alesi	Sauber C18/4
12	Diniz	Sauber C18/7
	spare	Sauber C18/3
14	de la Rosa	Arrows A20/7
15	Takagi	Arrows A20/4
	spare	Arrows A20/5
16	Barrichello	Stewart SF3/4
17	Herbert	Stewart SF3/5
	spare	Stewart SF3/3
18	Panis	Prost AP02/5
19	Trulli	Prost AP02/7
	spare	Prost AP02/3
20	Badoer	Minardi M01/1
21	Gene	Minardi M01/4
	spare	Minardi M01/3
22	Villeneuve	BAR 01/8
23	Zonta	BAR 01/5
	spare	BAR 01/3

POINTS TABLES

DRIVERS

1	Eddie Irvine	56
2	Mika Häkkinen	54
3 =	David Coulthard	36
3 =	Heinz-Harald Frentzen	36
5	Michael Schumacher	32
6	Ralf Schumacher	22
7	Giancarlo Fisichella	13
8	Rubens Barrichello	12
9 =	Mika Salo	6
9 =	Damon Hill	6
11 =	Alexander Wurz	3
11 =	Pedro Diniz	3
13 =	Johnny Herbert	2
13 =	Olivier Panis	2
15 =	Pedro de la Rosa	1
15 =	Jean Alesi	1
15 =	Jarno Trulli	1

CONSTRUCTORS

1	Ferrari	94
2	McLaren	90
3	Jordan	42
4	Williams	22
5	Benetton	16
6	Stewart	14
7	Sauber	4
8	Prost	3
9	Arrows	1

FRENTZEN

R. SCHUMACHER

SALO

BARRICHELLO

COULTHARD

IRVINE

ITALIAN
grand prix

A win in the sun for Heinz-Harald Frentzen and for Jordan Mugen-Honda.
Paul-Henri Cahier

Right: Five red lights are about to go out and the 22-car field is about to be unleashed on the Monza track.
Michael Roberts

MONZA QUALIFYING

From the start of the weekend there was an underlying feeling that things were slipping away from Ferrari and that Irvine's distant fourth place in the Belgian Grand Prix a fortnight earlier was probably as much as the Italian team could realistically hope for.

This reality produced a distinctly subdued mood, both amongst the fans and around the lavish Ferrari encampment of multi-million dollar motorhomes in the paddock. This was supposed to be the weekend when the *tifosi* welcomed back their hero Michael Schumacher after an heroic recovery from a broken leg sustained on the opening lap of the British Grand Prix at Silverstone two months ago.

Yet the ground was cut from beneath the feet of Ferrari's loyal race fans during last week's test here when Michael suddenly realised he could not endure the pain and needed more time to recover fully.

You could see his point. Monza is all about ferocious braking from high speed. Into the first chicane beyond the pits, the top runners were still hard on the throttle at the 100-metre board. By any standards, that is serious stuff indeed.

The circuit also requires the second-lowest downforce settings of the season after Hockenheim and puts a premium on monitoring brake disc wear, particularly in view of the thinner discs which the rules require this season. Something to seriously keep in mind on a circuit where Häkkinen's McLaren MP4/14 went through the speed trap 252 metres before the first chicane during qualifying at 220.7 mph.

It was also Häkkinen who emerged on top at the end of qualifying, clinching his 11th pole position of the season with a lap in 1m 22.432s, just 0.491s faster than Heinz-Harald Frentzen's Jordan which joined him on the front row.

'My second run was good and my third was fantastic,' said Häkkinen. 'It was one of the most enjoyable qualifying sessions I can remember and I couldn't believe that I could do that time. We changed the car throughout the session and all the changes worked, but the team adapted the car to suit my style through the first sector where I was initially losing time.'

David Coulthard wound up third on 1m 23.177s, commenting; 'I didn't come away from last week's test with a set-up I was totally happy with. This afternoon I had to abort my third run and then had a yellow flag on my last run. If we go through the first two corners [of the race] in grid order it will be difficult to catch Heinz before the pit stops.' This turned out to be a highly optimistic assessment of the Scot's chances.

Of course, Frentzen had fallen victim to such a brake disc failure in the closing moments of the Canadian Grand Prix, but the Jordan team had no such worries at Monza. 'H-H' was predicting great things from his Jordan 199 after a very successful pre-race test demonstrated the benefits of revised, lower-drag front brake-cooling ducts and he came close to pushing Häkkinen's McLaren off pole position in a fraught qualifying session punctuated by plenty of spins and yellow flags.

Frentzen reckoned that three four-lap runs was the most effective qualifying strategy, having discovered that he could squeeze out a quicker time on a second flying lap than on the first. A combination of traffic, a driving error and yellow flags respectively conspired to thwart his efforts.

By contrast, Damon Hill could only manage ninth fastest time, admitting that he was disappointed and did not get the best out of the car. 'I lost one run because of yellow flags, but that was the case for most drivers,' he said. 'Then I tried too hard on my last attempt and went over the chicane.'

Yet the real story of qualifying was the manner in which Williams had fine-tuned their FW21s to get even better form out of their proven, efficient low-downforce configuration.

With their Supertec V10s giving away around 50 bhp to the 775 bhp Mugen-Hondas powering the Jordans and around 75 bhp to the pace-setting Mercs, Williams produced a fine effort to line up fourth and fifth with Alex Zanardi at last getting the hang of things to pip teammate Ralf Schumacher.

'Alex has had to re-think his approach and has dug deep to solve his previous problems,' said Patrick Head. 'He did a fine job today.'

Alex said: 'It would have been very difficult if we had started behind a Ferrari tomorrow going into the first chicane. I am happy with the car which we have improved sensibly and it is good to be on the second row after all the problems this season.'

Ralf added: 'I am moderately satisfied. Twice I had to stop for yellow flags and then had to stop on my last flying lap.' A dashboard warning light came on and Ralf was told to switch off the engine.

If Williams was elated, home team Ferrari finished qualifying in a dejected frame of mind. Mika Salo lined up sixth on 1m 23.657s, fractionally quicker than Eddie Irvine who was two places further back on 1m 23.765s.

Salo reckoned his car felt quite good, but Irvine was slightly befuddled. 'The car is a little better than yesterday,' he admitted. 'It is more consistent, but not much quicker. On my last run I was slowed by a yellow flag but it would not have affected my time very much.'

'Basically, we have not made enough progress with the car over the last three or four races. We have some improvements coming for the next race but we cannot fix the problem overnight.'

HEINZ-HARALD Frentzen turned the battle for the World Championship into a four-way affair at Monza with a dramatic and extremely impressive second win of his season for the Jordan Mugen-Honda squad, the German ace smoothly taking over the lead after Mika Häkkinen inexplicably spun off while in a dominant position for the second time this year.

Reviving painful memories of his Imola error, Häkkinen blew his hopes of all-but clinching the title when he skidded off the road while running seven seconds ahead of Frentzen with 30 of the race's 53 laps completed. It was a mistake which threw a lifeline to the off-the-pace Eddie Irvine who finished sixth for Ferrari, thereby moving him back into the joint World Championship lead alongside the hapless Finn.

Almost unbelievably, Häkkinen selected first rather than second gear as he changed down under braking for the tight chicane beyond the pits. The McLaren's rear wheels momentarily locked and he pirouetted gently to a halt on the gravel run-off area.

The emotion of the moment was all too much for the Finn who has endured such a lurid season of dramatically changing fortunes. He leaped from the car, threw away its steering wheel in acute frustration and hurled his gloves to the ground. A few moments later he could be seen crouched at the edge of the circuit, head bowed over his knees in a combination of frustration and annoyance at his momentary lapse.

'I just couldn't believe it,' said Frentzen. 'Mika had a consistent seven-second lead in front of me. At the beginning I tried to keep up with him, but couldn't quite hold him. I was slightly worried about the very long opening stint [he refuelled on lap 35 of the 53-lap race] from the viewpoint of tyre wear, but once I was in the lead I was able to save the brakes, tyres and engine and just bring it home.'

Meanwhile, Frentzen's success left team owner Eddie Jordan laughing all

the way to the bank. He had placed a £2000 each-way bet on Heinz-Harald winning at Monza, something he had also cleverly anticipated to his financial benefit when Damon Hill scored the team's first win in Belgium last year.

'We were powerful all weekend,' said Jordan. 'Heinz-Harald told me that if Honda could produce the sort of engine they said they could, then we had a chance of pole position and winning the race. I was so optimistic that I placed the bet.'

The win also carried the German driver to within ten points of Mika Häkkinen and Eddie Irvine. This was in sad contrast to the fortunes of his Jordan team-mate Damon Hill who on this occasion trailed home tenth after losing crucial time at his refuelling stop when he accidentally switched off his engine.

Häkkinen had pulled comfortably into the lead at the start with the impressive Alex Zanardi's Williams FW21 squeezing briefly into second place as the pack scrambled into the

first chicane. It was a glorious moment of self-justification for the Italian driver, but it didn't last long as Frentzen sliced through on the inside of the Curva Grande to take second place under braking for the next chicane.

Ralf Schumacher was fourth from David Coulthard's McLaren with Mika Salo's Ferrari scrambling all over them as they came down the straight towards the Variante Ascari in a ragged, closely-fought group. Coulthard then made a slight mistake on the fast chicane, losing momentum which allowed Salo to nip neatly through into fifth on the following sprint down to Parabolica.

At the end of lap one Häkkinen led by 1.3s from Frentzen, Zanardi, Ralf Schumacher, Salo, Coulthard and Rubens Barrichello's Stewart-Ford SF3. Marc Gene's Minardi had already crashed out of the race and, going into the second lap, Giancarlo Fisichella's Benetton B199 spun out of 15th place at the first turn after a nudge from behind while Pedro Diniz's Sauber spun

away 12th having just overtaken Alexander Wurz's Benetton.

To say it wasn't the Benetton team's day at its home race would be something of a major understatement. By the end of the afternoon they were left considering whether or not to sue the Monza track authorities for compensation after Fisichella's abandoned car was virtually wrecked by souvenir-hunting fans who poured onto the track immediately after the race was over.

In an orgy of pillaging, the car was subjected to extremely serious damage. The engine cover, rear wing, brake cooling ducts, rear electrical loom, fuel hatch cover and side crash structures were all ripped off. In addition, the driver's seat was snapped in two and one half taken away as a trophy.

By lap four Häkkinen's lead had opened to 2.2s with Frentzen another 2.1s ahead of Zanardi, the Italian having smacked his Williams over a chicane kerb early in the race and dislodged his car's undertray. Next time round he had dropped another 0.3s to

Frentzen, prompting Ralf Schumacher, who was running fourth, to ask over the radio link to the Williams pit if they could tell Zanardi to move over as the German driver was convinced he had the potential of lapping faster than his team-mate.

In fact, while the team was considering its tactical position, Schumacher made a slight mistake and dropped back a few lengths further behind Zanardi. By lap five Häkkinen had set his fourth successive fastest lap of the race to lead by 3.0s with Frentzen still 2.5s in front of Zanardi. Schumacher, Salo, Coulthard and Barrichello remained in tight formation with a small gap opening to Eddie Irvine's Ferrari F399.

Barrichello had been delighted from the outset with the precise feel of his car and was really hounding Coulthard, the McLaren driver, by contrast, still struggling with poor balance. In particular, Rubens was able to whistle confidently through the Parabolica right-hander and, going into lap 11, had sufficient momentum to draw

199

DIARY

Leading Formula 3000 contender Gonzalo Rodriguez killed practising his Penske team Lola-Mercedes for the CART race at Laguna Seca.

FIA plans $48 million deposit requirement for new teams planning to compete in F1 World Championship.

Bernie Ecclestone makes no comment on speculation that he wishes to sell a stake in his F1 Administration empire to the Japanese bank Nomura.

Brands Hatch Leisure formally applies for detailed planning permission to upgrade the Kent circuit to full FIA F1 specification.

level with the McLaren on the outside going into the first chicane. Barrichello made the move stick and emerged with sixth place.

On lap 15 Häkkinen had increased his lead to 6.9s with Frentzen now 3.5s ahead of a slowing Zanardi. Three laps later, Alex moved over to allow Ralf Schumacher past and the young German immediately celebrated by setting the fastest lap up to that point. 'Without his help I don't think I would have finished second today,' said Ralf after the race.

'Alex and I have an agreement; if somebody is quicker, we help each other, because at the end of the day we are driving for the team to get the best result. He made it incredibly easy for me to get by him to drive my [own] race. He deserves a big share of my second place today.'

Next time round and Barrichello overtook Salo for fifth place under braking for the second chicane. By lap 20 Häkkinen had stabilised his lead at 7.8s and although he seemed to be well in command of the race, there was no doubt that Frentzen was keeping him honest and not allowing him to relax for a second.

On lap 24 Toranosuke Takagi's Arrows collided with Luca Badoer's Minardi at the first corner, the Minardi being eliminated on the spot while the Japanese driver made it back to the pits for repairs. It was the second Minardi to be eliminated in a collision with an Arrows and team boss Gabriele Rumi certainly didn't stint when it came to making a very precise observation about these episodes.

'The Arrows, our direct rival, no more in the condition to compete with us in terms of performances, adopted the only way they could afford – they eliminated us,' he said firmly. 'This morning I had already expressed my fears about this. Unfortunately, I wasn't wrong.'

On lap 26 Barrichello overtook Zanardi to take fourth place, then three laps later made his first refuelling stop and dropped to tenth. One lap prior to this Coulthard went inside Zanardi under braking for the first chicane, but Alex was not having it and held the position.

Then, going into lap 30, the unbelievable moment of the race finally arrived. Swinging into the first chicane, it seemed as though Häkkinen had missed his braking point, still tried to make the turn and locked his rear wheels. But the explanation was more simple. The World Champion had changed down one gear too many, engaged first instead of second gear and

Jaguar confirms for F1 in 2000

JAGUAR, one of the most famous names in British motoring history was confirmed as an entrant into the Grand Prix arena for the 2000 season, it was announced at the Frankfurt Motor Show on the Tuesday after the Italian Grand Prix.

'Jaguar has a long and distinguished record in motor sport,' said Dr Wolfgang Reitzle, Chairman of Jaguar. 'We have won Le Mans seven times and we have twice been sports car world champions. We have also won the Monte Carlo Rally as well as countless other events. The next logical move is F1.

'The move into F1 will undoubtedly benefit Jaguar technologically. It will also clearly promote a wider recognition of the Jaguar brand as we significantly expand our product range over the next few years.'

In one of the most audacious pieces of re-branding yet seen in motor racing's most senior category, Ford – which purchased Jaguar ten years ago – would rename the Stewart Grand Prix team Jaguar Racing and confirmed that Eddie Irvine, who, after the Italian Grand Prix, was tying for the lead at the top of this year's championship points table, will be the Number One driver from the start of 2000.

'I'm overjoyed,' said Irvine. 'I've been waiting for this opportunity for the past two years. I'm lucky to be involved in such a fantastic project. Through my experience in the rebuilding of Ferrari, I believe I can make a significant contribution to Jaguar Racing.'

The emergence of Jaguar as an F1 contender is highly significant on two counts. Firstly, it revives the sporting pedigree of a company whose links with frontline motor sport stretch back to the immediate post-war years. Secondly, it serves as another major endorsement of Grand Prix racing's commercial pulling power amongst the world's major car makers.

At a time when tobacco sponsorship in Grand Prix racing is being scaled down prior to a complete ban from 2006 onwards, Jaguar would now go head-to-head with Mercedes, who have an option to purchase a 40 per cent holding in McLaren, and BMW, the Williams team's engine supplier from the start of next season, in a battle which could end with more major car makers owning many of the top Grand Prix teams.

Commented Neil Ressler, Ford Motor Company's Vice President and Chief Technical Officer; 'Jaguar's input to the F1 programme will begin immediately.

'The Coventry-based engineering teams can certainly contribute to the racing programme and I also believe that Jaguar's production car engineers can learn a great deal from the racing team.

'The need to solve problems quickly breeds a nimble and innovative culture which we will be able to transfer to the road car development programmes. I regard the technology transfer as one of the biggest single benefits of Jaguar's decision to enter F1.'

It was confirmed that the team's F1 engines would continue to be designed, developed and built by Cosworth Racing which is wholly owned by Ford. Trevor Crisp, Jaguar's Group Chief Engineer for power train engineering, will head up the F1 engine development programme.

slid to a shuddering halt onto the gravel and grass on the left-hand side of the circuit.

Despite the anti-stall mechanism on the McLaren MP4/14, Mika still managed to end up with the engine stopped. There was nothing to do but to walk back to the pits, mourning the loss of another certain 10 points without which the retention of his World Championship was seriously beginning to look a very much more shaky prospect.

On lap 31 Zanardi made his sole refuelling stop, dropping from sixth to tenth and two laps later Schumacher brought the other Williams FW21 in for an 8.7s stop which dropped him from second to fifth.

On lap 35 Heinz-Harald brought the leading Jordan in for a 7.5s refuelling stop, resuming in third place behind Salo and Coulthard. Next time round Salo (6.9s) and Coulthard (7.0s) came in nose-to-tail for their own refuelling stops and although Mika's Ferrari just

squeezed out ahead of Barrichello's Stewart, a touch of over-anxiety on the Scot's part lost him vital fractions which meant that he accelerated back into the race behind the Stewart-Ford.

This allowed Frentzen back through into the lead and although Schumacher picked up the pace in the closing stages, the Jordan driver was now well in command and conserving his machinery as the chequered flag beckoned. On the face of it, this had seemed an absolutely trouble-free run for the German driver. Only when the Jordan was subsequently stripped down back at base did the team discover that one of its clutch plates had broken. So it was a closer call than it looked from the touchlines.

On lap 41 Johnny Herbert rounded off another disappointing race when his Stewart-Ford retired with clutch problems from 11th place, the Englishman having fought back from 20th on the opening lap after lightly touching Olivier Panis's Prost AP02 which had

momentarily slowed to walking pace immediately ahead of him.

Frentzen duly ran out the race to win by 3.2s from Ralf Schumacher, the Williams squad left quietly pondering just what the outcome might have been had they asked Zanardi to move over on the second or third lap.

For his part, Salo was well pleased with his third place. 'This is an unbelievable result after two difficult days in practice. It was fantastic to be on the podium again and it was particularly emotional here in front of all the Italian fans.'

Barrichello was similarly satisfied with fourth while Coulthard at least got his McLaren to the finish, but fifth place from third on the starting grid was far from what the Scot had been hoping for after his victory at Spa a fortnight earlier.

Irvine also had a difficult run to sixth place, changes to the car set-up meaning that his Ferrari was quicker on the straight but bad on the kerbs. 'We knew we would struggle here,' he explained. 'In the end, though, I got one point and my nearest rival got none. We got out of jail today.' It had certainly been a damage limitation exercise for Ferrari, but McLaren had let them off the hook and gave them much-needed breathing space to fight another day.

Zanardi dropped to seventh at the end but Jacques Villeneuve was buoyed after a good run to eighth in the BAR 01. 'The car was competitive from the first to the last lap so that I was able to keep pushing,' he reported.

'At the start I was probably a bit cautious and could have made up a couple of places if I had been more aggressive, but then I felt that everything was going well and I was sure that I could finish so I was not worrying about the reliability.'

Ninth place fell to Jean Alesi's Sauber C18 with the delayed Damon Hill, who found that his Jordan's power steering failed after his refuelling stop, and Olivier Panis's Prost completing the list of classified finishers.

It had definitely been a great day for Heinz-Harald Frentzen and the most impressive of the three Grand Prix wins recorded thus far by the Jordan team.

'We put a little pressure on Mika – not a lot, but enough – and he made a mistake because he had to push harder,' said an ecstatic Eddie Jordan. 'Those quick laps prior to the pit stop that Heinz drove were really crucial and he did exactly what was expected of him. We always knew we had a good strategy and we knew that if we were leading at the pit stop we would be OK.'

ITALIAN GRAND PRIX

Right: Ralf exhibits pure joy at his second place on the podium.
Paul-Henri Cahier

Below and bottom: Takagi rides over the rear wheel of Luca Badoer's Minardi
Both photographs: Sporting Pictures (UK) Ltd

Far right and bottom right: Mika muffs it and spins out whilst the unbelieving *tifosi* go wild. The Finn hurls his glove to ground in disgust at his error.
Both photographs: Bryn Williams/Words & Pictures

Bottom centre: No win for Ferrari but the flag was proudly displayed nonetheless.
Paul-Henri Cahier

ITALIAN GRAND PRIX

GRAN PREMIO CAMPARI D'ITALIA
10–12 SEPTEMBER 1999
MONZA

Race distance: 53 laps, 189.858 miles/305.548 km

Race weather: Dry, hot and sunny

ROUND 13

MONZA – GRAND PRIX CIRCUIT

Curva di Lesmo
Curva del Serraglio
Seconda Variante
Variante Ascari
Parabolica
Curva Grande
Variante Goodyear

CIRCUIT LENGTH: 3.585 miles/5.770 km

Pos.	Driver	Nat.	No.	Entrant	Car/Engine	Laps	Time/Retirement	Speed (mph/km/h)
1	Heinz-Harald Frentzen	D	8	Benson & Hedges Jordan	Jordan 199-Mugen Honda MF301/HD V10	53	1h 17m 02.923s	147.848/237.938
2	Ralf Schumacher	D	6	Winfield Williams	Williams FW21-Supertec FB01 V10	53	1h 17m 06.195s	147.743/237.770
3	Mika Salo	SF	3	Scuderia Ferrari Marlboro	Ferrari F399 048B V10	53	1h 17m 14.855s	147.467/237.326
4	Rubens Barrichello	BR	16	Stewart Ford	Stewart SF3-Ford CR-1 V10	53	1h 17m 20.553s	147.286/237.034
5	David Coulthard	GB	2	West McLaren Mercedes	McLaren MP4/14-Mercedes F0110G V10	53	1h 17m 21.065s	147.270/237.008
6	Eddie Irvine	GB	4	Scuderia Ferrari Marlboro	Ferrari F399 048B V10	53	1h 17m 30.325s	146.976/236.536
7	Alex Zanardi	I	5	Winfield Williams	Williams FW21-Supertec FB01 V10	53	1h 17m 30.970s	146.956/236.503
8	Jacques Villeneuve	CDN	22	British American Racing	BAR 01-Supertec FB01 V10	53	1h 17m 44.720s	146.523/235.806
9	Jean Alesi	F	11	Red Bull Sauber Petronas	Sauber C18-Petronas SPE03A V10	53	1h 17m 45.121s	146.510/235.786
10	Damon Hill	GB	7	Benson & Hedges Jordan	Jordan 199-Mugen Honda MF301/HD V10	53	1h 17m 59.182s	146.070/235.078
11	Olivier Panis	F	18	Gauloises Prost Peugeot	Prost AP02-Peugeot A18 V10	52	DNF	
	Johnny Herbert	GB	17	Stewart Ford	Stewart SF3-Ford CR-1 V10	40	Clutch	
	Toranosuke Takagi	J	15	Arrows	Arrows A20 V10	35	Spun off	
	Pedro de la Rosa	ESP	14	Arrows	Arrows A20 V10	35	Accident damage	
	Mika Häkkinen	SF	1	West McLaren Mercedes	McLaren MP4/14-Mercedes F0110G V10	29	Spun off	
	Jarno Trulli	I	19	Gauloises Prost Peugeot	Prost AP02-Peugeot A18 V10	29	Gearbox	
	Ricardo Zonta	BR	23	British American Racing	BAR 01-Supertec FB01 V10	25	Wheel bearing	
	Luca Badoer	I	20	Fondmetal Minardi Ford	Minardi M01-Ford Zetec-R V10	23	Collision with Takagi	
	Alexander Wurz	A	10	Mild Seven Benetton Playlife	Benetton B199-Playlife V10	11	Electrics	
	Pedro Diniz	BR	12	Red Bull Sauber Petronas	Sauber C18-Petronas SPE03A V10	1	Spun off	
	Giancarlo Fisichella	I	9	Mild Seven Benetton Playlife	Benetton B199-Playlife V10	1	Accident	
	Marc Gene	ESP	21	Fondmetal Minardi Ford	Minardi M01-Ford Zetec-R V10	0	Collision	

Fastest lap: R. Schumacher, on lap 48, 1m 25.579s, 150.821 mph/242.723 km/h.

Lap record: Mika Häkkinen (F1 McLaren MP4/12-Mercedes V10), 1m 24.808s, 152.192 mph/244.929 km/h (1997).

Grid order	1	2	3	4	5	6	7	8	9	10	11	12	13	14	15	16	17	18	19	20	21	22	23	24	25	26	27	28	29	30	31	32	33	34	35	36	37	38	39	40
1 HÄKKINEN	1	1	1	1	1	1	1	1	1	1	1	1	1	1	1	1	1	1	1	1	1	1	1	1	1	1	1	1	1	8	8	8	8	8	8	3	8	8	8	8
8 FRENTZEN	8	8	8	8	8	8	8	8	8	8	8	8	8	8	8	8	8	8	8	8	8	8	8	8	8	8	8	8	8	6	6	6	3	2	6	6	6	6		
2 COULTHARD	5	5	5	5	5	5	5	5	5	5	5	5	5	5	5	5	5	6	6	6	6	6	6	6	6	6	6	6	3	3	3	3	2	2	8	3	3	3		
5 ZANARDI	6	6	6	6	6	6	6	6	6	6	6	6	6	6	6	6	5	5	5	5	5	5	5	5	16	16	16	16	5	2	2	2	4	4	6	16	16	16		
6 R. SCHUMACHER	3	3	3	3	3	3	3	3	3	3	3	3	3	3	3	3	3	16	16	16	16	16	16	16	5	5	3	3	2	4	4	4	7	6	16	2	2	2		
3 SALO	2	2	2	2	2	2	2	2	2	2	16	16	16	16	16	16	16	3	3	3	3	3	3	3	3	3	5	5	4	5	7	7	6	22	4	4	4	4		
16 BARRICHELLO	16	16	16	16	16	16	16	16	16	16	2	2	2	2	2	2	2	2	2	2	2	2	2	2	2	2	2	2	7	7	22	22	22	16	5	5	5	5		
4 IRVINE	4	4	4	4	4	4	4	4	4	4	4	4	4	4	4	4	4	4	4	4	4	4	4	4	4	4	4	4	22	22	11	11	16	5	22	22	22	22		
7 HILL	7	7	7	7	7	7	7	7	7	7	7	7	7	7	7	7	7	7	7	7	7	7	7	7	7	7	7	7	11	11	16	16	5	7	7	7	7	7		
18 PANIS	22	22	22	22	22	22	22	22	22	22	22	22	22	22	22	22	22	22	22	22	22	22	22	22	22	22	22	22	16	16	5	5	11	11	11	11	11	11		
22 VILLENEUVE	10	10	10	10	10	10	10	11	11	11	11	11	11	11	11	11	11	11	11	11	11	11	11	11	11	11	11	11	18	18	18	17	17	17	17	17	17	17		
19 TRULLI	12	11	11	11	11	11	11	10	19	19	19	19	19	19	19	19	17	17	17	17	17	17	17	17	17	17	18	18	17	17	17	18	18	18	18	18	18	18		
11 ALESI	11	18	18	19	19	19	19	19	18	10	18	18	18	18	18	17	19	23	23	23	23	23	23	19	19	19	19	17	15	15	15	15	15	15	15					
10 WURZ	18	19	19	18	18	18	18	18	10	18	17	17	17	17	17	18	23	19	19	19	19	19	19	18	18	18	17	19	14	14	14	14	14	14						
17 HERBERT	9	23	23	23	23	23	23	23	23	23	23	23	23	23	23	18	18	18	18	18	18	18	18	23	15	15	15	15												
12 DINIZ	19	17	17	17	17	17	17	17	17	17	20	20	20	20	20	20	20	20	20	20	20	20	20	15	15	14	14	14	14											
9 FISICHELLA	23	20	20	20	20	20	20	20	20	20	15	15	15	15	15	15	15	15	15	15	15	15	14	14																
23 ZONTA	20	15	15	15	15	15	15	15	15	10	14	14	14	14	14	14	14	14	14	14																				
20 BADOER	17	14	14	14	14	14	14	14	14	14																														
21 GENE	15																																							
14 DE LA ROSA	14																																							
15 TAKAGI																																								

Pit stop
One lap behind leader

STARTING GRID

1 **HÄKKINEN** McLaren	**8** **FRENTZEN** Jordan
2 **COULTHARD** McLaren	**5** **ZANARDI** Williams
6 **R. SCHUMACHER** Williams	**3** **SALO** Ferrari
16 **BARRICHELLO** Stewart	**4** **IRVINE** Ferrari
7 **HILL** Jordan	**18** **PANIS** Prost
22 **VILLENEUVE** BAR	**19** **TRULLI** Prost
11 **ALESI** Sauber	**10** **WURZ** Benetton
17 **HERBERT** Stewart	**12** **DINIZ** Sauber
9 **FISICHELLA** Benetton	**23** **ZONTA** BAR
20 **BADOER** Minardi	**21** **GENE** Minardi
14 **DE LA ROSA** Arrows	**15** **TAKAGI** Arrows

43	44	45	46	47	48	49	50	51	52	53	
8	8	8	8	8	8	8	8	8	8	8	1
6	6	6	6	6	6	6	6	6	6	6	2
3	3	3	3	3	3	3	3	3	3	3	3
16	16	16	16	16	16	16	16	16	16	16	4
2	2	2	2	2	2	2	2	2	2	2	5
4	4	4	4	4	4	4	4	4	4	4	6
5	5	5	5	5	5	5	5	5	5	5	
22	22	22	22	22	22	22	22	22	22	22	
7	7	7	7	7	7	11	11	11	11	11	
11	11	11	11	11	11	7	7	7	7	7	
18	18	18	18	18	18	18	18	18	18		

TIME SHEETS

QUALIFYING

Weather: Dry, hot and sunny

Pos.	Driver	Car	Laps	Time
1	Mika Häkkinen	McLaren-Mercedes	10	1m 22.432s
2	Heinz-Harald Frentzen	Jordan-Mugen Honda	11	1m 22.926s
3	David Coulthard	McLaren-Mercedes	12	1m 23.177s
4	Alex Zanardi	Williams-Supertec	12	1m 23.432s
5	Ralf Schumacher	Williams-Supertec	12	1m 23.636s
6	Mika Salo	Ferrari	12	1m 23.657s
7	Rubens Barrichello	Stewart-Ford	11	1m 23.739s
8	Eddie Irvine	Ferrari	12	1m 23.765s
9	Damon Hill	Jordan-Mugen Honda	11	1m 23.979s
10	Olivier Panis	Prost-Peugeot	12	1m 24.016s
11	Jacques Villeneuve	BAR-Supertec	11	1m 24.188s
12	Jarno Trulli	Prost-Peugeot	11	1m 24.293s
13	Jean Alesi	Sauber-Petronas	12	1m 24.591s
14	Alexander Wurz	Benetton-Playlife	12	1m 24.593s
15	Johnny Herbert	Stewart-Ford	12	1m 24.594s
16	Pedro Diniz	Sauber-Petronas	11	1m 24.596s
17	Giancarlo Fisichella	Benetton-Playlife	12	1m 24.862s
18	Ricardo Zonta	BAR-Supertec	12	1m 25.114s
19	Luca Badoer	Minardi-Ford	11	1m 25.348s
20	Marc Gene	Minardi-Ford	12	1m 25.695s
21	Pedro de la Rosa	Arrows	11	1m 26.383s
22	Toranosuke Takagi	Arrows	12	1m 23.509s

FRIDAY FREE PRACTICE

Weather: Sunny and very hot

Pos.	Driver	Laps	Time
1	Ralf Schumacher	36	1m 24.507s
2	Jarno Trulli	41	1m 24.692s
3	Alex Zanardi	46	1m 24.823s
4	Jean Alesi	21	1m 25.030s
5	Mika Häkkinen	33	1m 25.103s
*6	Olivier Panis	33	1m 25.138s
7	Jacques Villeneuve	22	1m 25.307s
8	David Coulthard	36	1m 25.347s
9	Pedro Diniz	42	1m 25.388s
10	Damon Hill	31	1m 25.397s
11	Rubens Barrichello	37	1m 25.499s
12	Johnny Herbert	37	1m 25.551s
13	Heinz-Harald Frentzen	16	1m 25.577s
14	Giancarlo Fisichella	24	1m 25.701s
15	Alexander Wurz	40	1m 25.742s
16	Eddie Irvine	36	1m 25.897s
17	Mika Salo	39	1m 25.931s
18	Marc Gene	27	1m 26.069s
19	Ricardo Zonta	29	1m 26.181s
20	Luca Badoer	28	1m 26.633s
21	Pedro de la Rosa	23	1m 27.542s
22	Toranosuke Takagi	33	1m 27.931s

* fastest time disallowed

SATURDAY FREE PRACTICE

Weather: Sunny and very hot

Pos.	Driver	Laps	Time
1	Heinz-Harald Frentzen	34	1m 23.142s
2	David Coulthard	27	1m 23.412s
3	Mika Häkkinen	27	1m 23.482s
4	Alex Zanardi	31	1m 23.721s
5	Jarno Trulli	35	1m 23.833s
6	Rubens Barrichello	18	1m 23.837s
7	Ralf Schumacher	27	1m 23.863s
8	Damon Hill	32	1m 23.921s
9	Johnny Herbert	32	1m 23.971s
10	Mika Salo	30	1m 24.091s
11	Olivier Panis	33	1m 24.240s
12	Eddie Irvine	29	1m 24.330s
13	Jacques Villeneuve	23	1m 24.412s
14	Alexander Wurz	24	1m 24.576s
15	Pedro Diniz	38	1m 24.739s
16	Jean Alesi	23	1m 24.770s
17	Giancarlo Fisichella	22	1m 24.995s
18	Marc Gene	24	1m 25.595s
19	Luca Badoer	30	1m 25.605s
20	Ricardo Zonta	8	1m 25.761s
21	Pedro de la Rosa	32	1m 26.617s
22	Toranosuke Takagi	19	1m 26.631s

WARM-UP

Weather: Sunny and very hot

Pos.	Driver	Laps	Time
1	Rubens Barrichello	17	1m 25.397s
2	David Coulthard	13	1m 25.667s
3	Mika Häkkinen	12	1m 25.854s
4	Pedro Diniz	15	1m 26.119s
5	Johnny Herbert	18	1m 26.126s
6	Jacques Villeneuve	12	1m 26.137s
7	Ralf Schumacher	10	1m 26.166s
8	Olivier Panis	14	1m 26.310s
9	Giancarlo Fisichella	16	1m 26.404s
10	Heinz-Harald Frentzen	16	1m 26.446s
11	Jarno Trulli	14	1m 26.603s
12	Ricardo Zonta	12	1m 26.704s
13	Alex Zanardi	15	1m 26.712s
14	Eddie Irvine	16	1m 27.096s
15	Damon Hill	14	1m 27.131s
16	Jean Alesi	9	1m 27.226s
17	Alexander Wurz	13	1m 27.425s
18	Mika Salo	5	1m 27.665s
19	Marc Gene	13	1m 27.825s
20	Toranosuke Takagi	12	1m 27.973s
21	Luca Badoer	9	1m 28.185s
22	Pedro de la Rosa	13	1m 28.488s

RACE FASTEST LAPS

Weather: Dry, hot and sunny

Driver	Time	Lap
Ralf Schumacher	1m 25.579s	48
Mika Salo	1m 25.630s	44
Rubens Barrichello	1m 25.825s	51
David Coulthard	1m 25.832s	32
Jean Alesi	1m 25.911s	52
Heinz-Harald Frentzen	1m 25.917s	32
Olivier Panis	1m 25.953s	31
Alex Zanardi	1m 26.047s	51
Mika Häkkinen	1m 26.060s	24
Johnny Herbert	1m 26.253s	18
Jacques Villeneuve	1m 26.338s	48
Damon Hill	1m 26.342s	41
Eddie Irvine	1m 26.387s	48
Jarno Trulli	1m 26.493s	23
Ricardo Zonta	1m 26.945s	24
Alexander Wurz	1m 28.338s	6
Pedro de la Rosa	1m 28.516s	15
Luca Badoer	1m 28.914s	10
Toranosuke Takagi	1m 29.216s	12

CHASSIS LOG BOOK

1	Häkkinen	McLaren MP4/14/5
2	Coulthard	McLaren MP4/14/7
	spare	McLaren MP4/14/2
3	Salo	Ferrari F399/196
4	Irvine	Ferrari F399/191
	spare	Ferrari F399/193
5	Zanardi	Williams FW21/5
6	R. Schumacher	Williams FW21/6
	spare	Williams FW21/2
7	Hill	Jordan 199/4
8	Frentzen	Jordan 199/5
	spare	Jordan 199/6
9	Fisichella	Benetton B199/7
10	Wurz	Benetton B199/4
	spare	Benetton B199/5
11	Alesi	Sauber C18/4
12	Diniz	Sauber C18/7
	spare	Sauber C18/3
14	de la Rosa	Arrows A20/7
15	Takagi	Arrows A20/5
	spare	Arrows A20/2
16	Barrichello	Stewart SF3/4
17	Herbert	Stewart SF3/5
	spare	Stewart SF3/3
18	Panis	Prost AP02/5
19	Trulli	Prost AP02/2
	spare	Prost AP02/3
20	Badoer	Minardi M01/1
21	Gene	Minardi M01/4
	spare	Minardi M01/3
22	Villeneuve	BAR 01/6
23	Zonta	BAR 01/7
	spare	BAR 01/3

POINTS TABLES

DRIVERS

1 =	Mika Häkkinen	60
1 =	Eddie Irvine	60
3	Heinz-Harald Frentzen	50
4	David Coulthard	48
5	Michael Schumacher	32
6	Ralf Schumacher	30
7	Rubens Barrichello	15
8	Giancarlo Fisichella	13
9	Mika Salo	10
10	Damon Hill	7
11 =	Alexander Wurz	3
11 =	Pedro Diniz	3
13 =	Johnny Herbert	2
13 =	Olivier Panis	2
15 =	Pedro de la Rosa	1
15 =	Jean Alesi	1
15 =	Jarno Trulli	1

CONSTRUCTORS

1	McLaren	108
2	Ferrari	102
3	Jordan	57
4	Williams	30
5	Stewart	17
6	Benetton	16
7	Sauber	4
8	Prost	3
9	Arrows	1

EUROPEAN
grand prix

HERBERT

TRULLI

BARRICHELLO

R. SCHUMACHER

HÄKKINEN

GENE

FIA WORLD CHAMPIONSHIP • ROUND 14

Paul-Henri Cahier

Left: Johnny Herbert took a surprise maiden victory for the Stewart-Ford team after his perfect reading of the changing weather conditions put him in a position to challenge for a win.

Below left: Jarno Trulli cuts across the grass as he staightlines the chicane. The Italian claimed second place for Prost.

BRITISH veteran Johnny Herbert produced a perfect strategy and avoided every pitfall to score the Stewart-Ford team's maiden F1 victory in a chaotic, action-packed European Grand Prix which saw all the regular leading runners dogged by misfortune and freak incidents in the unpredictable weather conditions.

It was the 35-year old's third Grand Prix win in his 142nd outing and his first since 1995 when he won both the British and Italian races at the wheel of a Benetton-Renault. Herbert finished a commanding 22.6s ahead of Jarno Trulli's Prost-Peugeot with the other Stewart-Ford, driven by Brazil's Rubens Barrichello, a few feet behind in third place.

One of the great stars of the weekend was Ralf Schumacher who seemed on course to give the British Williams team its first win for two seasons only for a punctured tyre to drop him to fourth. In the early stages of the race Schumacher had pulled the overtaking move of the race when he passed David Coulthard's McLaren by going offline onto the wet while running on dry weather tyres under hard braking for the first corner after the pits.

'It was pretty marginal when I switched to wet tyres at my first stop,' admitted Herbert after the race. 'It took a bit of guesswork, because it just rained on the lap when I was coming in.'

This crucial middle stint on wet tyres from laps 35 to 47 was the key to Herbert's remarkable climb from 14th place on the starting grid to the top step of the podium.

By contrast, fellow Briton David Coulthard's World Championship bid ended on an ignominious note when he slid out of the race and into a tyre barrier while leading comfortably after 38 of the race's 66 laps.

It was a day on which F1's outsiders enjoyed their moment of glory as the established top contenders, both drivers and teams, flapped and floundered. Mika Häkkinen was fortunate to recover to grab fifth place and a two-point championship lead over Eddie Irvine after his McLaren-Mercedes dropped from second to 14th after the team mistakenly switched his car from dry to wet weather tyres during a brief rain shower, only for the track to dry out again almost immediately.

The initial start had been aborted after Marc Gene's Minardi and Alex Zanardi's Williams got themselves out of grid order, but when the race finally got underway it was Frentzen who accelerated away perfectly to fend off both McLarens on the run down to the first corner.

Ralf Schumacher's Williams followed through in fourth place, while suddenly all hell let loose in the middle of the pack as Damon Hill's Jordan suddenly slowed with a terminal electrical fault.

Alexander Wurz suddenly found himself faced with the Jordan's dramatically slowing yellow rear wing and had no option but to swerve right, pitching Pedro Diniz's Sauber into a frightening roll over the Benetton's right front wheel.

The Sauber crashed down on its rollover bar and then skidded sideways across the high kerb and over the grassy run-off area. The safety car was immediately deployed as marshals cleared up the debris and Diniz was removed from the wrecked car.

For a few minutes the whole episode looked worryingly serious so the sighs of relief were almost audible as the Brazilian waved to the crowd from the stretcher carrying him to the ambulance. Amazingly, he had survived with a few cuts and bruises.

'I had a good start, but when I came out of the first corner I had no power and could not get out of the way,' explained Hill. 'The ensuing accident was very nasty; I saw it happening and there was nothing I could do. I saw Pedro fly past me and was very worried, as I was on the scene when they were tending to him. I am very relieved to hear that he is OK.'

Not until the end of lap six was the safety car withdrawn and Frentzen vaulted straight into a half-second lead ahead of the two McLarens. With Ralf Schumacher hanging on to the back of the train, the leading quartet picked up the pace to such immediate effect that the gap from Ralf back to Giancarlo Fisichella's fifth-place Benetton B199 was already 1.8s at the end of lap seven.

That same lap also saw Eddie Irvine's Ferrari F399 pass Olivier Panis's Prost for sixth place after which he quickly closed the gap to Fisichella, pressuring the Benetton hard from lap 11 onwards.

On the same lap Alex Zanardi's Williams and Pedro de la Rosa's Arrows collided and spun on the final corner of the lap. De la Rosa recovered, but Zanardi pressed his Williams's neutral-reset button, accidentally buzzing the Supertec V10 round to 17,000 rpm before pulling for a gear which, perhaps understandably, broke the car's transmission.

Irvine was getting extremely frustrated in his pursuit of Fisichella. The Italian driver was certainly driving very defensively although most of his

Heinz-Harald Frentzen and the Jordan team had come to Nürburgring following an extremely positive test at Magny-Cours, but from the outset it seemed as though nothing could go right for the German driver in front of his home fans.

Firstly, the Italian GP winner lost valuable set-up time during Friday free practice with a gearbox oil pump failure which required a fresh gearbox to be fitted. Then on Saturday morning his Mugen-Honda V10 suffered a pneumatic valvegear failure after only 12 laps.

The Jordan mechanics duly embarked on an engine change which they judged would be completed in time to allow Frentzen about 20 minutes' running before the end of the session. Unfortunately a problem with the oil tank installation then cropped up and he eventually only got back on the circuit a couple of minutes before the chequered flag.

Yet the promising signs were already there. Although there was insufficient time for a single flying lap, Heinz ran the first two sectors virtually as fast as Häkkinen's McLaren before backing off and peeling into the pit lane. The car felt good.

A heavy rain shower during the Saturday lunch break left the track glistening with puddles prior to the start of practice. It was a time for cool judgement and considerable nerve.

Conditions were drying all the time as demonstrated by the fact that at 1.05 pm Damon Hill managed a fastest time of 1m 35.119s but Rubens Barrichello was down to 1m 31.703s barely 15 minutes later.

With half an hour to go the racing line was seriously drying and at 1.42 pm Häkkinen raised the stakes with a 1m 25.084s and then followed that with a 1m 22.973s. Then Coulthard went quickest on 1m 22.204s and Ralf Schumacher slammed the Williams FW21 into contention with 1m 22.688s, second-fastest with ten minutes left.

The front runners had set such a blistering pace that Frentzen, who'd only done three laps up to this point, was actually outside the 107 per cent qualifying cut-off point with only nine minutes of qualifying left.

His engineer Sam Michael had wanted him to go out early and get some provisional quick laps under his belt, but Heinz-Harald argued strenuously in favour of holding back until the last moment. With Bridgestone's soft option rubber producing its best time on its first flying lap – and dropping off thereafter – the team prepared for a race-pace tyre change after Frentzen's first run and the strategy worked a treat.

With four minutes to go, the times continued to tumble. Ralf Schumacher went quickest on 1m 20.444s, then Häkkinen 1m 20.376s then Coulthard 1m 20.176s. Finally, almost as the chequered flag was unfurled, Frentzen posted a 1m 19.910s. It was all over and the German driver celebrated only the second pole position of his career.

'I have to apologise to my team,' grinned Frentzen. 'We had some friction between us about choosing the right moment to go out and at one stage we were all shouting at one another.

'It's very difficult to make the decision that is going to be right at the end. We had already changed the set-up so many times during the session, and at the end I was fuelled for seven timed laps, so I was [really] carrying too much fuel because I had decided to come into the pits again for that change of tyres.'

The McLaren MP4/14s of Coulthard (1m 20.176s) and Mika Häkkinen (1m 20.376s) wound up second and third on the grid. 'Thankfully my engineer didn't listen to me at all because I was convinced the track wouldn't dry out,' said Coulthard.

'This time I was absolutely delighted he took no notice of me and under the circumstances I am reasonably happy with the outcome. Heinz-Harald was very fair; he pulled way off line to let me past, so thanks for that.'

Häkkinen was obviously disappointed. 'Even if I had managed to get a clear lap I don't think I would have managed pole,' he admitted.

In the Williams camp, Ralf Schumacher set fourth fastest time on 1m 20.444s in the Williams FW21 using the latest B-spec engine which all the Supertec runners were using this weekend just for qualifying. Ralf used his spare FW21 set up for the wet for his first run, then switched to the race car for his runs in drier conditions. Alex Zanardi (18th/1m 22.284s) did not time his runs to best advantage and also got caught up in traffic.

Eddie Irvine hardly helped his cause with an ill-timed spin which dropped him back to ninth on the grid, unable to better 1m 20.842s.

'I am very disappointed because we were capable of getting on the front row,' he admitted. 'On my penultimate lap I was held up by traffic, then on the last lap I locked my rear brakes on a damp patch and that was the end of it. The race will be a different story.' Not as things transpired.

Separating the Ferraris from the front runners was Olivier Panis who managed fifth on 1m 20.638s in the Prost-Peugeot while Damon Hill lined up an encouraging seventh behind Giancarlo Fisichella's on-form Benetton B199. Jacques Villeneuve really raised hopes in the British American camp by posting eighth fastest on 1m 20.825s to slip ahead of Irvine while Jarno Trulli completed the top ten on 1m 20.965s, the Italian admitting that he had made a mistake in the final sector of what should have been his best lap.

Over in the Stewart-Ford camp, Johnny Herbert (1m 21.379s) and Rubens Barrichello (1m 21.490s) qualified a disappointed 14th and 15th. Rubens got himself stuck behind a Minardi on his best lap and Herbert took the spare SF3, set up for Barrichello, but found it difficult to get on with the rather sensitive throttle response on this particular car.

Sauber satisfied with C18 impact resistance

IMMEDIATELY after returning to its Swiss base, the Sauber team carried out a detailed analysis of the structural damage sustained by Pedro Diniz's Sauber C18 during its first corner accident in the European Grand Prix.

The roll hoop was subjected to 'severe dynamic forces', the first impact taking place at approximately 95 kph and the energy was absorbed as predicted. After that, the roll hoop structure hit the kerb laterally and further energy was dissipated by the hoop and its supporting structure.

According to Sauber's engineers; 'This high lateral loads, far behind the requested safety limits [sic], consequently caused the rupture of the roll hoop. As the car rolled over again, the driver was protected by a secondary structure to the top of the survival cell, which is a special feature of the C18 chassis. Final protection was also provided by the high head support as recommended by the FIA.'

Far left: Pedro Diniz rolls his Sauber to destruction.

Below left: Miraculously, the Brazilian escaped almost unscathed from the accident which left his car minus its roll-over bar.

Bottom left: Ralf Schumacher contributed another sensational drive for Williams.
All photographs: Paul-Henri Cahier

moves were quite legitimate given that he was defending his track position. Nevertheless, Irvine wanted to be through and away. They were 6.7s behind Schumacher's Williams on lap 13 and 7.2s adrift on lap 16, but 'Fisi' made a slight error as a light rain shower began to brush the circuit next time round which allowed the Ferrari driver to slip ahead into fifth without any further drama.

As the rain began to make the track really treacherous, so Schumacher lunged ahead of Coulthard on lap 20 just as McLaren signalled Häkkinen into the pits for wet rubber. It was absolutely the wrong call and Mika resumed in tenth place, dropping back to 12th before coming back into the pits at the end of lap 24 to refit dry weather tyres.

This left Frentzen leading superbly from Schumacher and Coulthard, for if McLaren had experienced problems with Häkkinen's car this was as nothing compared with the drama surrounding Ferrari which also began on lap 20 when Mika Salo brought his F399 in to have a damaged nose section replaced.

Seconds after the Finn had been dispatched back into the race a distant 17th, knowing immediately that his switch to wets had been a mistake, so Irvine radioed in that he would be stopping next time round. The pit crew had wet tyres ready, but at the last moment Eddie said that he wanted another set of dries which meant there was a mad, Keystone Cops-style scramble to get the tyres into position as Ferrari number four pulled to a halt.

Amazingly, the replacement right rear tyre seemed to have gone 'walkabout'. With Jean Todt and Ross Brawn watching from the pit wall with expressions of incomprehension etched on their faces, the mechanics belatedly located the missing wheel and Irvine accelerated back into the race now 13th after an unforgivably protracted 28.2s stop.

On lap 27 Schumacher made a 7.0s refuelling stop from second place, resuming fourth behind Fisichella, then on lap 31, Frentzen, Coulthard and Fisichella came in from first, second and third places for what was scheduled to be their sole refuelling stop.

Frentzen beat Coulthard back into the fray, only for the leading Jordan to roll to a halt with terminal electrical problems at almost precisely the same point on the circuit where Hill had retired on the opening lap. As the disbelieving Heinz-Harald climbed from the cockpit, Coulthard and Ralf Schumacher went through into first and second places.

'It feels awful to drop out of the race when you are leading,' shrugged Frentzen. 'Everything had gone so well for the first half of the race and the team did a fantastic job in the pits to get me out ahead of David, but as I came out I seemed to have an electrical problem.' Technical director Mike Gascoyne would later confirm that both cars had retired from the battle with 'electronic problems caused by a certain degree of finger trouble – but not on the part of the drivers!'

Shortly after Frentzen's departure from the race the rain began to fall heavily again. Slightly further back in the pack, Johnny Herbert was now up to fifth place and decided that he would switch to wets when he came in for his first stop at the end of lap 35.

'The way I looked at it, there was a cloud dead in front of me' said Herbert. 'Everything had been coming that way, so I just guessed and hoped that it would come straight over the track. And it did.'

While all this was happening, Coulthard was pulling steadily away from the opposition. He really didn't need to push quite so hard and was being cautioned about this regularly over the radio link. Unfortunately the tricky track surface caught him out and he slid gently off into a tyre barrier.

'I'm very disappointed to have gone off in these conditions,' said David, 'as I had a good lead and it is more acceptable to go off whilst you are chasing than when you are leading. I am sorry for the team for that. It is the first time I have put the car off in a race this year, but that is little consolation.'

Schumacher now went through into the lead ahead of Fisichella and Herbert. On lap 44 Ralf brought the Williams FW21 in for its second stop, resuming third behind Fisichella's Benetton and Herbert's Stewart. On lap 47 Herbert made his second stop in 6.2s, switching to slicks and dropping briefly behind Jarno Trulli's Prost which came in next time round.

On lap 49 Fisichella's hopes of victory were dashed when he spun off the road, the Italian almost unable to contain his tears, while, almost immediately afterwards, Schumacher radioed in to say he thought he had picked up a right rear puncture.

The Williams pit crew immediately told him to come into the pits, but by the time he'd heard the message, Ralf was abreast the pit entry lane. In any event, he wasn't *quite* sure he'd got a problem. Only when he accelerated through the final right hander onto the start/finish straight at the end of lap 49 could he properly discern the dreaded imbalance which confirmed that a tyre was losing pressure.

Ralf continued through the next two corners only for the right rear tyre to fly apart, launching him across a gravel trap from which he emerged almost intact, the Williams hobbling back to the pits for repairs on three wheels. He resumed in fifth place, all prospects of a worthy victory now evaporated.

Now Herbert surged into a lead he would never lose ahead of Trulli and Barrichello. The hapless Schumacher's

Williams resumed in fourth place with the Minardis of Luca Badoer and Marc Gene next up. On lap 55, Badoer's hopes of scoring his first ever helping of championship points evaporated in a cloud of smoke as his Minardi's gearbox broke. A bitter blow indeed, and the Italian driver was another unable to contain his emotion at the heart-rending shame of it all.

That left Gene in a storming fifth place, but the Spaniard was a little taken aback to see signals telling him to push as hard as he could. When asked precisely why this was necessary, his pit responded by advising him that Häkkinen's McLaren followed by Irvine's Ferrari were next in line behind him.

Häkkinen had been behind Irvine until lap 63 when he finally forced his way ahead of the Ferrari and stormed off in pursuit of Gene whom he finally relegated to sixth just two laps from the chequered flag. With Irvine unable to catch the Minardi before the chequered flag, Häkkinen at least managed to edge into a valuable two-point championship lead with only two races left to run.

Herbert duly took the chequered flag 22.61s ahead of Trulli who fought every inch of the way to keep Barrichello at bay over the last few laps. The young Italian had adopted a three-stop strategy and it worked well for him.

'The nicest point of the race came when it started to rain and most of the drivers decided to come in for wet tyres,' he explained. 'Even my team called me up to bring me in, but I decided to stay out on the dry tyres. This was very important. Yes, we did make three stops in all, but I almost forgot [that] because I was fighting so much that I am still a bit confused.'

Ralf Schumacher had to be content with fourth ahead of a frustrated Häkkinen, the delighted Gene and a philosophical Irvine. 'Our strategy was a bit wrong,' he said after making two more stops, one for wets on lap 40, and then a switch back to dry rubber nine laps later.

'It was another great opportunity missed. As for my first pit stop, it is difficult when you have one group of mechanics serving two cars. We should have been attacking ahead, instead of covering Häkkinen, but there were too many mistakes. Even so, we have got off lightly.'

Jean Todt summed it up diplomatically; 'This is not a time for recriminations. If we want to fight to the end of the championship we must not stumble like this in the remaining races.'

Left and below: Marc Gene scored possibly the season's most valuable point for Minardi, which will bring the Faenza team millions of dollars as part of the FOCA package. The Spaniard scored his own first World Championship point.
Both photographs: Paul-Henri Cahier

Bottom: Luckless Minardi team-mate Luca Badoer was eliminated with gearbox trouble after holding fourth place.
Michael Roberts

Next page: Herbert, Stewart and Barrichello celebrate their 1–3 finish. For JYS it was a dream come true, winning a Grand Prix in a car bearing his name before the team becomes Jaguar in the year 2000.
Paul-Henri Cahier

DIARY

Ricardo Zonta renews his contract with British American Racing for the 2000 season.

Arrows boss Tom Walkinshaw confirms that his team will continue development of its own V10 engine even though the team will use Supertec engines in 2000.

Brands Hatch Leisure chief executive Nicola Foulston vigorously denies rumours in the financial press that she might consider moving the British Grand Prix outside the UK.

Speculation that the Portuguese Grand Prix might return to the F1 World Championship calendar in 2000 intensifies.

EUROPEAN
GRAND PRIX
24–26 SEPTEMBER 1999
NÜRBURGRING

Race distance: 66 laps, 186.833 miles/300.679 km

Race weather: Dry, then showers

FIA FORMULA 1 WORLD CHAMPIONSHIP

ROUND 14

NÜRBURGRING – GRAND PRIX CIRCUIT

Bit Kurve
Veedol Schikane
Shell Kurve
Castrol S
Dunlop Kehre
Röhmer Kurve

CIRCUIT LENGTH: 2.831 miles/4.556 km

Pos.	Driver	Nat.	No.	Entrant	Car/Engine	Laps	Time/Retirement	Speed (mph/km/h)
1	Johnny Herbert	GB	17	Stewart Ford	Stewart SF3-Ford CR-1 V10	66	1h 41m 54.314s	110.004/177.034
2	Jarno Trulli	I	19	Gauloises Prost Peugeot	Prost AP02-Peugeot A18 V10	66	1h 42m 16.933s	109.599/176.381
3	Rubens Barrichello	BR	16	Stewart Ford	Stewart SF3-Ford CR-1 V10	66	1h 42m 17.180s	109.594/176.374
4	Ralf Schumacher	D	6	Winfield Williams	Williams FW21-Supertec FB01 V10	66	1h 42m 33.822s	109.297/175.897
5	Mika Häkkinen	SF	1	West McLaren Mercedes	McLaren MP4/14-Mercedes F0110H V10	66	1h 42m 57.264s	108.883/175.230
6	Marc Gene	ESP	21	Fondmetal Minardi Ford	Minardi M01-Ford Zetec-R V10	66	1h 42m 59.468s	108.844/175.167
7	Eddie Irvine	GB	4	Scuderia Ferrari Marlboro	Ferrari F399 048B V10	66	1h 43m 00.997s	108.817/175.124
8	Ricardo Zonta	BR	23	British American Racing	BAR 01-Supertec FB01 V10	65		
9	Olivier Panis	F	18	Gauloises Prost Peugeot	Prost AP02-Peugeot A18 V10	65		
10	Jacques Villeneuve	CDN	22	British American Racing	BAR 01-Supertec FB01 V10	61	Clutch	
	Luca Badoer	I	20	Fondmetal Minardi Ford	Minardi M01-Ford Zetec-R V10	53	Gearbox	
	Pedro de la Rosa	ESP	14	Arrows	Arrows A20 V10	52	Gearbox	
	Giancarlo Fisichella	I	9	Mild Seven Benetton Playlife	Benetton B199-Playlife V10	48	Spun off	
	Mika Salo	SF	3	Scuderia Ferrari Marlboro	Ferrari F399 048B V10	44	Brakes	
	Toranosuke Takagi	J	15	Arrows	Arrows A20 V10	42	Spun off	
	David Coulthard	GB	2	West McLaren Mercedes	McLaren MP4/14-Mercedes F0110H V10	37	Spun off	
	Jean Alesi	F	11	Red Bull Sauber Petronas	Sauber C18-Petronas SPE03A V10	35	Driveshaft	
	Heinz-Harald Frentzen	D	8	Benson & Hedges Jordan	Jordan 199-Mugen Honda V10	32	Electrics	
	Alex Zanardi	I	5	Winfield Williams	Williams FW21-Supertec FB01 V10	10	Transmission	
	Damon Hill	GB	7	Benson & Hedges Jordan	Jordan 199-Mugen Honda V10	0	Electrics	
	Alexander Wurz	A	10	Mild Seven Benetton Playlife	Benetton B199-Playlife V10	0	Collision with Diniz	
	Pedro Diniz	BR	12	Red Bull Sauber Petronas	Sauber C18-Petronas SPE03A V10	0	Collision with Wurz	

Fastest lap: Häkkinen, on lap 64, 1m 21.282s, 125.384 mph/201.786 km/h.

Lap record: Heinz-Harald Frentzen (F1 Williams FW19-Renault V10), 1m 18.805s, 129.325 mph/208.128 km/h (1997).

Grid order	1	2	3	4	5	6	7	8	9	10	11	12	13	14	15	16	17	18	19	20	21	22	23	24	25	26	27	28	29	30	31	32	33	34	35	36	37	38	39	40	41	42	43	44	45	46	47	48	49	50
8 FRENTZEN	8	8	8	8	8	8	8	8	8	8	8	8	8	8	8	8	8	8	8	8	8	8	8	8	8	8	8	8	8	8	8	2	2	2	2	6	6	6	6	6	6	9	9	9	9	6	17			
2 COULTHARD	1	1	1	1	1	1	1	1	1	1	1	1	1	1	1	1	1	1	1	6	6	6	6	6	6	2	2	2	2	2	6	6	6	6	9	9	9	9	9	9	17	17	19							
1 HÄKKINEN	2	2	2	2	2	2	2	2	2	2	2	2	2	2	2	2	2	2	2	2	2	2	2	6	9	9	9	9	9	16	16	16	16	9	17	17	17	17	17	17	6	6	17	19	19	19				
6 R. SCHUMACHER	6	6	6	6	6	6	6	6	6	6	6	6	6	6	6	6	6	6	1	9	9	9	9	9	6	6	6	6	9	9	9	9	16	16	19	19	19	19	19	19	19	19	19	17	16					
18 PANIS	9	9	9	9	9	9	9	9	9	9	9	9	9	9	9	9	4	4	4	4	16	16	16	16	16	16	16	16	16	16	17	17	17	17	19	16	16	16	16	16	16	16	16	20	20					
9 FISICHELLA	18	18	18	18	18	18	4	4	4	4	4	4	4	4	4	9	9	9	9	16	19	19	19	19	19	19	19	17	17	17	17	22	19	19	22	19	22	22	22	22	22	20	20	20	20	22	22			
7 HILL	4	4	4	4	4	4	18	18	18	18	18	18	18	18	18	18	18	18	18	19	17	11	11	11	17	17	11	11	22	22	22	19	20	20	4	4	4	20	20	4	4	4	4	4	21	21				
22 VILLENEUVE	22	22	22	22	22	22	22	22	22	22	22	22	22	22	22	22	22	18	19	11	11	17	17	17	11	11	17	17	11	19	19	19	22	19	4	21	21	21	21	21	4	22	22	22	22	4				
4 IRVINE	3	3	3	3	3	3	3	3	3	3	3	3	3	3	3	3	3	3	17	11	22	22	22	22	22	22	20	20	20	20	11	11	4	21	21	20	20	20	4	4	21	21	21	21	21	1				
19 TRULLI	11	11	11	11	11	11	11	11	11	11	16	16	16	16	16	16	16	16	3	22	1	20	20	20	20	20	11	11	11	11	4	4	11	20	20	1	1	1	23	23	23	1	1	1	23	23				
10 WURZ	16	16	16	16	16	16	16	16	16	16	19	19	19	19	19	19	19	19	11	1	20	21	21	21	21	21	21	21	4	4	21	21	1	1	18	18	18	1	1	1	23	23	23	23	18	18				
3 SALO	19	19	19	19	19	19	19	19	19	19	17	17	17	17	17	17	17	17	22	20	21	1	4	4	4	4	4	4	21	21	1	1	18	14	23	23	18	18	18	18	18	18	18	18	14	14				
12 DINIZ	17	17	17	17	17	17	17	17	17	17	23	23	23	23	23	11	11	11	23	11	11	4	1	14	14	14	14	14	14	14	23	18	14	23	14	14	14	14	14	14	14	14	14	14						
17 HERBERT	14	14	14	14	14	14	14	14	14	14	15	11	11	11	11	11	14	23	20	18	18	23	23	1	1	1	1	1	1	14	14	23	23	14	23	23	3	3	3	3	3									
16 BARRICHELLO	15	15	15	15	15	15	23	23	23	23	11	15	15	15	15	15	15	20	21	23	23	18	14	23	23	23	23	23	23	18	18	18	3	3	15	15	15	15												
11 ALESI	23	23	23	23	23	23	15	15	15	15	20	20	20	20	20	20	15	23	18	3	14	18	18	18	18	18	18	18	18	3	15	3	15	15																
23 ZONTA	20	20	20	20	20	20	20	5	5	5	21	21	21	21	21	21	21	21	15	3	14	3	3	3	3	3	3	3	3	15	3	15																		
5 ZANARDI	21	21	21	21	21	21	5	5	20	20	14	14	14	14	14	14	14	14	14	15	15	15	15	15	15	15	15	15	15																					
20 BADOER	5	5	5	5	5	5	21	21	21	21																																								
21 GENE																																																		
15 TAKAGI																																																		
14 DE LA ROSA																																																		

Pit stop
One lap behind leader

8 **FRENTZEN** Jordan	2 **COULTHARD** McLaren
1 **HÄKKINEN** McLaren	6 **R. SCHUMACHER** Williams
18 **PANIS** Prost	9 **FISICHELLA** Benetton
7 **HILL** Jordan	22 **VILLENEUVE** BAR
4 **IRVINE** Ferrari	19 **TRULLI** Prost
10 **WURZ** Benetton	3 **SALO** Ferrari
12 **DINIZ** Sauber	17 **HERBERT** Stewart
16 **BARRICHELLO** Stewart	11 **ALESI** Sauber
23 **ZONTA** BAR	5 **ZANARDI** Williams
20 **BADOER** Minardi	21 **GENE** Minardi
15 **TAKAGI** Arrows	14 **DE LA ROSA** Arrows

53	54	55	56	57	58	59	60	61	62	63	64	65	66	●	
17	17	17	17	17	17	17	17	17	17	17	17	17	17	17	1
19	19	19	19	19	19	19	19	19	19	19	19	19	19	19	2
16	16	16	16	16	16	16	16	16	16	16	16	16	16		3
20	6	6	6	6	6	6	6	6	6	6	6	6	6	6	4
6	22	22	22	22	22	22	22	22	21	21	21	1	1		5
22	21	21	21	21	21	21	21	21	1	1	1	21	21	6	
21	4	4	4	4	4	4	4	4	4	4	4	4	4		
4	1	1	1	1	1	1	1	1	23	23	23	23			
1	23	23	23	23	23	23	23	23	18	18	18	18			
23	18	18	18	18	18	18	18	18	18						
18															

FOR THE RECORD

First Grand Prix win
Stewart

First championship point
Marc Gene

QUALIFYING

Weather: Damp track, drying steadily

Pos.	Driver	Cars	Laps	Time
1	Heinz-Harald Frentzen	Jordan-Mugen Honda	9	1m 19.910s
2	David Coulthard	McLaren-Mercedes	12	1m 20.176s
3	Mika Häkkinen	McLaren-Mercedes	12	1m 20.376s
4	Ralf Schumacher	Williams-Supertec	12	1m 20.444s
5	Olivier Panis	Prost-Peugeot	12	1m 20.638s
6	Giancarlo Fisichella	Benetton-Playlife	11	1m 20.781s
7	Damon Hill	Jordan-Mugen Honda	11	1m 20.818s
8	Jacques Villeneuve	BAR-Supertec	10	1m 20.825s
9	Eddie Irvine	Ferrari	11	1m 20.842s
10	Jarno Trulli	Prost-Peugeot	12	1m 20.965s
11	Alexander Wurz	Benetton-Playlife	12	1m 21.144s
12	Mika Salo	Ferrari	12	1m 21.314s
13	Pedro Diniz	Sauber-Petronas	11	1m 21.345s
14	Johnny Herbert	Stewart-Ford	11	1m 21.379s
15	Rubens Barrichello	Stewart-Ford	12	1m 21.490s
16	Jean Alesi	Sauber-Petronas	11	1m 21.634s
17	Ricardo Zonta	BAR-Supertec	10	1m 22.267s
18	Alex Zanardi	Williams-Supertec	12	1m 22.284s
19	Luca Badoer	Minardi-Ford	11	1m 22.631s
20	Marc Gene	Minardi-Ford	12	1m 22.760s
21	Toranosuke Takagi	Arrows	11	1m 23.401s
22	Pedro de la Rosa	Arrows	10	1m 23.698s

FRIDAY FREE PRACTICE

Weather: Sunny and breezy

Pos.	Driver	Laps	Time
1	Mika Häkkinen	27	1m 20.758s
2	Mika Salo	38	1m 20.920s
3	Olivier Panis	28	1m 21.134s
4	Eddie Irvine	30	1m 21.338s
5	Ralf Schumacher	29	1m 21.385s
6	David Coulthard	33	1m 21.461s
7	Rubens Barrichello	34	1m 21.505s
8	Giancarlo Fisichella	41	1m 21.636s
9	Jarno Trulli	43	1m 21.750s
10	Jacques Villeneuve	41	1m 21.850s
11	Jean Alesi	27	1m 21.884s
12	Heinz-Harald Frentzen	22	1m 21.933s
13	Johnny Herbert	39	1m 21.982s
14	Damon Hill	28	1m 22.207s
15	Luca Badoer	36	1m 22.311s
16	Alex Zanardi	45	1m 22.321s
17	Alexander Wurz	46	1m 22.427s
18	Pedro Diniz	32	1m 22.462s
19	Pedro de la Rosa	21	1m 22.853s
20	Marc Gene	38	1m 22.872s
21	Ricardo Zonta	34	1m 23.604s
22	Toranosuke Takagi	32	1m 24.282s

SATURDAY FREE PRACTICE

Weather: Overcast and cool

Pos.	Driver	Laps	Time
1	Mika Häkkinen	24	1m 18.945s
2	Ralf Schumacher	26	1m 19.401s
3	Eddie Irvine	33	1m 19.666s
4	David Coulthard	31	1m 19.667s
5	Rubens Barrichello	31	1m 19.812s
6	Damon Hill	35	1m 19.919s
7	Jacques Villeneuve	31	1m 19.979s
8	Giancarlo Fisichella	35	1m 20.012s
9	Alex Zanardi	34	1m 20.109s
10	Jean Alesi	26	1m 20.123s
11	Alexander Wurz	38	1m 20.151s
12	Pedro Diniz	38	1m 20.211s
13	Olivier Panis	34	1m 20.313s
14	Mika Salo	28	1m 20.385s
15	Jarno Trulli	33	1m 20.389s
16	Johnny Herbert	35	1m 20.410s
17	Heinz-Harald Frentzen	14	1m 20.643s
18	Luca Badoer	28	1m 21.163s
19	Ricardo Zonta	29	1m 21.224s
20	Marc Gene	36	1m 21.811s
21	Toranosuke Takagi	19	1m 22.026s
22	Pedro de la Rosa	27	1m 22.191s

WARM-UP

Weather: Damp track, drying steadily

Pos.	Driver	Laps	Time
1	Giancarlo Fisichella	13	1m 26.935s
2	David Coulthard	12	1m 27.305s
3	Heinz-Harald Frentzen	18	1m 27.604s
4	Ralf Schumacher	13	1m 27.986s
5	Olivier Panis	14	1m 28.168s
6	Mika Häkkinen	14	1m 28.297s
7	Alexander Wurz	14	1m 28.317s
8	Mika Salo	16	1m 28.558s
9	Jarno Trulli	12	1m 28.640s
10	Eddie Irvine	14	1m 28.728s
11	Pedro Diniz	15	1m 28.760s
12	Rubens Barrichello	15	1m 28.941s
13	Jacques Villeneuve	11	1m 28.969s
14	Jean Alesi	16	1m 29.021s
15	Ricardo Zonta	10	1m 29.376s
16	Alex Zanardi	13	1m 29.425s
17	Marc Gene	13	1m 29.643s
18	Johnny Herbert	16	1m 29.703s
19	Pedro de la Rosa	12	1m 30.291s
20	Luca Badoer	12	1m 30.611s
21	Damon Hill	15	1m 30.626s
22	Toranosuke Takagi	12	1m 30.852s

RACE FASTEST LAPS

Weather: Dry, then showers

Driver	Time	Lap
Mika Häkkinen	1m 21.282s	64
David Coulthard	1m 21.835s	29
Heinz-Harald Frentzen	1m 22.082s	29
Ralf Schumacher	1m 22.237s	64
Giancarlo Fisichella	1m 22.244s	31
Eddie Irvine	1m 22.332s	65
Jacques Villeneuve	1m 22.564s	32
Rubens Barrichello	1m 22.960s	32
Johnny Herbert	1m 23.010s	32
Ricardo Zonta	1m 23.067s	64
Jean Alesi	1m 23.097s	15
Mika Salo	1m 23.404s	31
Marc Gene	1m 23.657s	30
Jarno Trulli	1m 23.742s	30
Luca Badoer	1m 23.745s	33
Olivier Panis	1m 23.905s	16
Alex Zanardi	1m 24.300s	9
Toranosuke Takagi	1m 24.848s	30
Pedro de la Rosa	1m 24.857s	8

1	Häkkinen	McLaren MP4/14/4
2	Coulthard	McLaren MP4/14/6
	spare	McLaren MP4/14/5
3	Salo	Ferrari F399/195
4	Irvine	Ferrari F399/196
	spare	Ferrari F399/193
5	Zanardi	Williams FW21/5
6	R. Schumacher	Williams FW21/6
	spare	Williams FW21/2
7	Hill	Jordan 199/4
8	Frentzen	Jordan 199/5
	spare	Jordan 199/6
9	Fisichella	Benetton B199/7
10	Wurz	Benetton B199/4
	spare	Benetton B199/3
11	Alesi	Sauber C18/4
12	Diniz	Sauber C18/7
	spare	Sauber C18/3
14	de la Rosa	Arrows A20/7
15	Takagi	Arrows A20/5
	spare	Arrows A20/2
16	Barrichello	Stewart SF3/4
17	Herbert	Stewart SF3/5
	spare	Stewart SF3/3
18	Panis	Prost AP02/5
19	Trulli	Prost AP02/7
	spare	Prost AP02/3
20	Badoer	Minardi M01/1
21	Gene	Minardi M01/4
	spare	Minardi M01/3
22	Villeneuve	BAR 01/6
23	Zonta	BAR 01/7
	spare	BAR 01/4

POINTS TABLES

DRIVERS

1	Mika Häkkinen	62
2	Eddie Irvine	60
3	Heinz-Harald Frentzen	50
4	David Coulthard	48
5	Ralf Schumacher	33
6	Michael Schumacher	32
7	Rubens Barrichello	19
8	Giancarlo Fisichella	13
9	Johnny Herbert	12
10	Mika Salo	10
11 =	Jarno Trulli	7
11 =	Damon Hill	7
13 =	Alexander Wurz	3
13 =	Pedro Diniz	3
15	Olivier Panis	2
16 =	Pedro de la Rosa	1
16 =	Jean Alesi	1
16 =	Marc Gene	1

CONSTRUCTORS

1	McLaren	110
2	Ferrari	102
3	Jordan	57
4	Williams	33
5	Stewart	31
6	Benetton	16
7	Prost	9
8	Sauber	4
9 =	Arrows	1
9 =	Minardi	1

MALAYSIAN

grand prix

FIA WORLD CHAMPIONSHIP • ROUND 15

Left: David Coulthard pushes his McLaren inside the Ferrari of Michael Schumacher during the early stages of the race. The German driver was in no position to mix it with the Scot, as he had to help Irvine in his championship quest.

Below left: Michael Schumacher and Eddie Irvine celebrate while Mika Häkkinen has to be content with third. Michael's control of the race was masterly.

Below right: A Ferrari takes the Turn 15 hairpin by the Tower, the shape of which represents the hibiscus, the national flower of Malaysia.

DIARY

Frank Williams continues to maintain that Alex Zanardi's place in his F1 line-up for the 2000 season is guaranteed despite the Italian's poor performances. Marc Gene agrees to stay with the Minardi team for the 2000 season.

Dario Franchitti dominates Surfers Paradise CART race to take title points lead with only one race of the season to go.

Olivier Panis flies back from Malaysia to try McLaren-Mercedes at Magny-Cours in preparation for possible test driving role with the team in 2000.

MIKA Häkkinen was poised on the verge of his second world championship title after a sensational Malaysian Grand Prix which ended with the Ferraris of Eddie Irvine and Michael Schumacher being disqualified for a technical infringement after finishing in first and second places.

This apparently devastating news for Irvine came less than two hours after he had celebrated the fact that he would be going into the final race of the season at Suzuka four points ahead of Häkkinen and with a strong chance of becoming Ferrari's first world champion driver for 20 years. The Ferrari team promptly gave notice of their intention to appeal against this penalty and the FIA confirmed that it would act quickly to convene a court of appeal hearing in Paris in time to resolve the issue prior to the final race of the season in Japan.

At post-race scrutineering the Ferraris were found to have infringed the bodywork rules by having aerodynamic deflectors on the side of the chassis – the 'bargeboards' – which infringed the permitted dimensions. FIA F1 technical delegate Jo Bauer submitted a report to the stewards of the meeting saying that, in his view, the two Ferrari F399s therefore did not conform with the technical rules.

When checking the bodywork facing the ground, it was noticed that parts of the deflector panels 'did not lie on either the reference or step planes' as they are required to do.

The rules require that the flat bottom of the car – between the front and rear wheels – should effectively 'mirror' all the appendages on the chassis. Therefore the undertray profile should have covered the entire aerodynamic deflectors – or barge boards – which, in the Ferrari's case, they did not.

Bauer submitted this information to the three independent stewards, in this case by Bryan Brophy, Derek Ledger and Dr K Kanagalingam. They took less than an hour to decide that the Ferraris had indeed infringed the rules and therefore had to be disqualified from the race subject to appeal.

Prior to this drama, Schumacher had loyally assisted Irvine in what was variously described as a brilliantly orchestrated demonstration of team tactics by some – and criticised by others as blatantly unsportsmanlike for his blocking of Mika Häkkinen's McLaren-Mercedes MP4/14 which came home third.

Twice during the course of the 56-lap inaugural race on the magnificent new Sepang circuit, Schumacher gifted the lead to Irvine and spent much of the afternoon keeping Häkkinen boxed up in third place all the way to the chequered flag.

On the face of it, the Ferrari squad dramatically out-manoeuvred McLaren in terms of race tactics and while Häkkinen was clearly bitterly disappointed that he had to settle for third place, he made no overt criticism of Ferrari's tactics.

'It was the hardest race of my life.' said the Finn. 'I was flat out all the way. Ferrari had brilliant tactics and I don't really blame them. I spent most of the race behind Michael but could not get past him.

'The reason for that was that I had to drive very cautiously as I did not want to get caught out by his inconsistent driving patterns. He was lifting in high speed corners and fluctuating his speed, so I had to be careful not to run into him.'

However, the Finn was less than amused when Ferrari subsequently used these comments in a manner which seemed to indicate that he did not wish to win the World Championship by means of a disqualification and believed the race had been won fairly by the Italian team.

'I am very upset to see that my post race press conference comments in which I said that we had been soundly and fairly beaten have been used to give the impression that they were made after I learnt that Ferrari had been in an infringement of the regulations and therefore excluded from the race,' he later added.

'This is totally wrong. The comments I made were in respect of Ferrari's performance in the race. This was before I was informed that Ferrari had been excluded, following which I left the circuit.'

Häkkinen was the only driver on the grid to opt for the harder of the two Bridgestone tyre compounds in the interests of durability in the sweltering conditions. With that in mind, and the fact that he spent so much time being slowed by Schumacher, McLaren's failure to switch him to the same one stop refuelling strategy identical to that adopted by Ferrari for Schumacher certainly raised a few eyebrows.

On the final parade lap, Jarno Trulli's Prost rolled to a halt with engine failure but the French car was pushed away behind the barrier in time for the start to take place without any delay.

When the lights went out Schumacher's pole-position Ferrari eased confidently into the lead as the pack jostled into the first tight right hander with Irvine slotting in neatly behind. Further back, Damon Hill was tapped

SEPANG QUALIFYING

There was much speculation over just how Michael Schumacher would perform on his return to the cockpit of the Ferrari F399 at Sepang. The run-up to the race had produced an unpredictable cocktail of 'will-he-won't-he' speculation revolving round whether or not he was sufficiently fit, whether or not he was pressured into returning, whether or not he would help Irvine.

In the end, he answered all those nagging doubts with a brilliant 22nd career pole position, his fastest lap of 1m 39.688s being 0.94s quicker than Eddie Irvine could manage to claim second place on the front row of the grid.

It was a truly awesome performance which inevitably had the cynics casting sideways glances and wondering whether there was some sort of illicit control system on the F399. Yet even his rival drivers were impressed.

'I expected we would be strong here,' said Schumacher, 'but to be one second ahead is certainly surprising. It is a combination of better mechanical set-up and some aerodynamic development. Physically I am in good condition, my neck is fine and I have no worries for the race. I did only eight laps as I could see my time would not be beaten and I wanted to keep as many tyres as possible to have greater flexibility in the race.'

For his part Irvine had a spin, but admitted he had precious little chance of beating his team-mate. Meanwhile, on the second row, David Coulthard managed a 1m 40.806s to pip his McLaren MP4/14 team-mate Mika Häkkinen to third place, the Scot making a last minute switch to the softer of the two Bridgestone compounds while Mika remained the only competitor on the grid to take the harder option.

Both drivers had problems fine tuning their chassis balance. 'We haven't got the combination of fast, slow and medium balance we need,' said Coulthard, 'and I had too much understeer in the second to last corner. In the race I will obviously let Mika past to improve his chances for the championship.'

The Stewart SF3s of Johnny Herbert (1m 40.937s) and Rubens Barrichello (1m 41.351s) wound up fifth and sixth fastest, the Brazilian finishing the session in aggrieved frame of mind after being accused by Jean Alesi of ruining his final run by holding him up even though the Stewart driver was allegedly on an 'out' lap.

Needless to say, Barrichello saw it otherwise and the two men were involved in a frank exchange of views after the session was over. Rubens ended up just pipping Alexander Wurz who did a good job of qualifying his Benetton seventh on 1m 41.444s.

In the Williams camp, although Ralf Schumacher strung together a strong final lap to qualify eighth on 1m 41.558s, both he and Alex Zanardi – 16th on 1m 42.885s – struggled with their cars. 'The handling characteristics of our cars over the last two years shows up at their worst on these types of circuit,' explained Patrick Head.

Wurz was separated from his 11th-placed team-mate Giancarlo Fisichella by Damon Hill's Jordan 199 (1m 42.050s) and Jacques Villeneuve's British American 01 (1m 42.087s) which had set the pace with fastest time during Friday's free practice session.

For once Hill had managed to qualify ahead of the beleaguered Heinz-Harald Frentzen who was back in an unaccustomed 14th on 1m 42.050s. Both cars had been struggling for balance throughout free practice, but Frentzen's particular problems began when his headrest came loose under braking for the first corner of qualifying which pitched him into a sudden spin.

He then took the spare Jordan 199 and had to abort his second run due to a problem with the left front brake caliper. This had to be replaced and, with only two sets of tyres left, he drove a three-lap and five-lap stint to produce his best time of 1m 42.380s on his final lap. At least things would get better for Heinz-Harald come the race.

Heinz-Harald Frentzen charges his
Jordan against the backdrop of the
giant stands.
Paul-Henri Cahier

Court of Appeal reinstates Ferrari 1-2

THE television vans, tangled electrical cables, satellite dishes and aerials crammed the Place de la Concorde in Paris outside the offices of the Automobile Club de France as the massed ranks of the world motor sporting media crammed into a second-floor conference room in a mood of fevered anticipation on the Saturday morning following the Malaysian Grand Prix.

They convened to hear FIA President Max Mosley, sandy-haired and sober-suited, announce that the previous day's FIA Court of Appeal had overturned the stewards' decision from the Malaysian Grand Prix and reinstated the Ferrari F399s of Eddie Irvine and Michael Schumacher to first and second places. 'Ferrari came here with an accurate jig to show that all the relevant dimensions of the bargeboards on the car were within the permitted 5-mm tolerance' he explained.

Mosley said that the International Court of Appeal confirmed that the dimensions of the turning vane (bargeboard) was within the 5-mm tolerance 'provided the vane was properly attached to the car.'

The court also stated that 'the 10 mm dimension referred to in the technical delegate's report resulted from a method of measurement which was not necessarily in strict conformity with the regulations' [and] 'the measuring equipment available to the FIA scrutineers at the Malaysian Grand Prix was not sufficiently accurate to call into question Ferrari's statement that the turning vane was indeed properly attached to the car.'

Mosley explained: 'on an F1 car there are a large number of dimensions which fall into two categories. There are those which are a maximum or a minimum, and those with specific dimensions.

'When you have a maximum dimension you cannot flout that by even the smallest amount, but if you have a simple dimension such as the flat bottom, you have a tolerance and we are satisfied that the tolerance of the Ferrari bargeboards fell into those tolerances, possibly by less than 1 mm, but nevertheless conformed.'

Irvine, who had flown back from Asia to attend the hearing, had just arrived back in Tokyo when he received the news.

'Never once did I ever believe Ferrari would have done something illegal to gain an advantage,' he said. 'That doesn't mean I wasn't worried, mind you, because you never know what can happen. This is great news, although after Ferrari put its case to the Appeal Court yesterday I already felt confident we had proved our point.

'This is the best possible result for Ferrari, for me and for the sport

of Formula 1. We are now going to have a cracking final weekend in Suzuka, which is my all-time favourite race track.

'After flying back from Paris to Japan, I got to the Hotel President around 2 in the afternoon local time. I knew I would have to wait until six o'clock for the news and believe me, they were the longest four hours of my life!'

His obvious elation was shared by Ferrari chairman Luca di Montezemolo who claimed that 'this verdict reaffirms the values of the sport which have inspired Ferrari over 50 years and restores to us and our fans the great victory achieved on the track, which confirms the quality of our work.'

Unsurprisingly, McLaren – and many other rival teams – were concerned about the manner in which the 5-mm plus/minus tolerance, which most engineers had taken to apply only to vertical movement in the flat underfloor, had now apparently been extended to cover other elements of the car's design.

McLaren issued a statement saying that in accepting the invitation to attend the Court of Appeal hearing 'it was our understanding that there was an oral and written acceptance that there had been a breach of the Technical Regulations. In a case of a breach of the Technical Regulations during a race the penalty that has been consistently applied is the one that was given in Malaysia, namely that of exclusion.

'We were very surprised to learn the day before the hearing that Ferrari had decided to argue that they had, contrary to their previous admissions, not infringed the Technical Regulations at all. This argument was based on a submission that the FIA technical equipment and procedures were inadequate and an interpretation of the Technical Regulations in conflict with the previous accepted understanding within Formula One, including that of the FIA Race Director and FIA F1 Technical Delegate.'

Ron Dennis added: 'I believe, along with probably every technical director in Formula One, that the manufacturing tolerance referred to under article 3:12:6 of the Technical Regulations has no bearing on any other aspect of the car other than the vertical flatness of the horizontal surfaces that form the underside of the vehicle.'

Both McLaren and Stewart, whose cars stood to be elevated to second and third place if the disqualification stood, sent eminent barristers to argue their corner.

None of the legal representatives wanted to be quoted on the record after the hearing, but some of them left the premises facing the Place de la Concorde unimpressed with the manner in which the whole proceedings had been conducted.

Right: Jacques Villeneuve gave all in the BAR. The French Canadian *(inset)* endured a nightmare season, but the mood remained upbeat with the promise of Honda power for 2000.

Left: Max Mosley delivers the verdict for which the motor racing world had waited nearly a week.
Dave Rogers/Allsport

to 11.6s by lap 21, but then Michael put the hammer down and cut a couple of fastest race laps to close the margin to 8.0s on lap 24.

Next time round, Irvine made his first refuelling stop, the Ulsterman's Ferrari remaining stationary for 7.2s. That allowed Michael to go through in the lead, his Ferrari running a one-stop strategy, and on lap 21 of the 56-lap race, Häkkinen made a 7.5s refuelling stop from second place. He just failed to get back into the fray ahead of Irvine, while on lap 28 Schumacher brought the Ferrari in for a long 10.4s stop with Johnny Herbert's Stewart following him in from what was a fleeting second place.

All this shuffling around left Irvine 5.1s ahead of Schumacher with Häkkinen still boxed in third. Barrichello and Herbert were next up in the Stewarts, but for McLaren the race was now lost. From the touchlines there was still a nagging suspicion that Häkkinen's team had done it just right and that he might be able to squeeze through to the finish without stopping again, but nine laps to go, Mika had to come in for a 6.9s 'splash and dash' which dropped him behind Herbert.

As the two Ferraris of Irvine and Schumacher reeled off their final few laps towards the chequered flag, Häkkinen pushed as hard as he knew how to get through. His determination was rewarded just three laps from the chequered flag when Johnny's Stewart ran wide at one corner and the McLaren nipped by to claim third place on the rostrum.

Herbert and Barrichello were delighted with fourth and fifth while Frentzen's charge through to take the final point on offer with sixth place had certainly been one of the great performances of the afternoon.

Immediately after the race Ron Dennis and Adrian Newey went down to the scrutineering area poised to protest the Ferraris for finishing the race with what amounted to slick tyres on their cars, as the grooves were no longer visible in the rubber, having worn off completely, in contravention of Article 81 of the sporting code.

'I'm not under any illusions,' said Dennis. 'I don't expect anything to be done about that, but it's clear that they were able to go out at their fastest when the grooves were worn out, and that's now what the regulation is about.' However, Dennis's concern was overtaken by events as the scrutineers began to measure the Ferrari bargeboards, and the more pressing issue of their questionable dimensions became the burning topic of the day.

into retirement thanks to a shove from Giancarlo Fisichella's Benetton which had to pit at the end of the opening lap for repairs. Further round the opening lap Ricardo Zonta's BAR and Pedro Diniz's Sauber also spun but managed to continue.

At the end of the opening lap Schumacher led by 1.7s from Irvine with David Coulthard's McLaren third ahead of Häkkinen. Then came the Stewart SF3s of Rubens Barrichello and Johnny Herbert with Alexander Wurz's Benetton next up.

Having proved his point at the head of the pack, Schumacher eased back from a 3.1s lead second time round to allow Irvine ahead on lap four. On the following lap Eddie set a new fastest lap as Coulthard aggressively and effectively forced his way ahead of Michael's Ferrari to set off in pursuit of the Ulsterman, making light contact with the Italian car which would leave Michael grappling with a touch of understeer on his second stint.

By lap seven Coulthard had narrowed Irvine's advantage to just a second

and Eddie was having to drive with great precision to avoid permitting the Scot any ambitious ideas

On lap six, Jean Alesi's Sauber C18 overtook Jacques Villeneuve's BAR and Ralf Schumacher's Williams to move into eighth place while, next time round Coulthard reduced the gap to Irvine's leading Ferrari. Further back on the same lap, Ricardo Zonta's BAR seized its engine due to a water leak and he pirouetted gently off the track into retirement.

Ralf Schumacher was pressing hard in ninth place, confident that he was in good shape on a one-stop strategy which would see him make up ground in the middle of the race. However, the young German driver's exuberance got the better of him mid-way round lap eight as he pushed too hard and joined the increasing list of those who spun off

Coulthard was clearly set to be as much a 'spoiler' for McLaren as Schumacher was for Ferrari. Running a low- drag aerodynamic set-up, once DC elbowed his way through into second place he quickly hauled up onto

Irvine's tail. Eddie said he was amazed how good the McLaren seemed to be under late braking, but it didn't last for long as Coulthard retired with fuel pump failure on lap 15.

Meanwhile, Heinz-Harald Frentzen was really charging through the pack from his disappointing 14th place on the grid. By the end of the opening lap he had moved up to 11th, then tenth on lap eight and ninth on lap 15. With more rubber down on the racing line, 'H-H' reported that his Jordan 199 felt better and better as the race progressed.

'The more I pushed, the better it felt,' he said. 'I had hoped for rain, but it all seemed to be working out well without it.'

Coulthard's departure from the fray had left the Ferraris running in 1–2 formation at the head of the pack and now Michael Schumacher really began to play the Maranello team card. With Häkkinen boxed in behind him, he began to fall back from Irvine and drop the Finn out of contention.

The gap between Irvine and Schumacher expanded from 4.5s on lap 16

The faces tell all just after the finish of the Malaysian Grand Prix. Eddie Irvine *(below)* couldn't be more pleased with the outcome, whereas Mika Häkkinen *(right)* feels the pressure of defending his championship.
Both photographs: Paul-Henri Cahier

PETRONAS MALAYSIAN GRAND PRIX
15–17 OCTOBER 1999
SEPANG

Race distance: 56 laps, 192.844 miles/310.352 km

Race weather: Hot, humid and sunny

FORMULA 1 WORLD CHAMPIONSHIP

ROUND 15

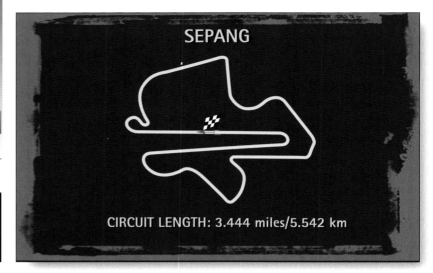

SEPANG

CIRCUIT LENGTH: 3.444 miles/5.542 km

Pos.	Driver	Nat.	No.	Entrant	Car/Engine	Laps	Time/Retirement	Speed (mph/km/h)
1	Eddie Irvine	GB	4	Scuderia Ferrari Marlboro	Ferrari F399 048B V10	56	1h 36m 38.494s	119.727/192.682
2	Michael Schumacher	D	3	Scuderia Ferrari Marlboro	Ferrari F399 048B V10	56	1h 36m 39.534s	119.705/192.647
3	Mika Häkkinen	SF	1	West McLaren Mercedes	McLaren MP4/14-Mercedes F0110H V10	56	1h 36m 48.237s	119.526/192.359
4	Johnny Herbert	GB	17	Stewart Ford	Stewart SF3-Ford CR-1 V10	56	1h 36m 56.032s	119.366/192.101
5	Rubens Barrichello	BR	16	Stewart Ford	Stewart SF3-Ford CR-1 V10	56	1h 37m 10.790s	119.064/191.615
6	Heinz-Harald Frentzen	D	8	Benson & Hedges Jordan	Jordan 199-Mugen Honda MF301/HD V10	56	1h 37m 13.378s	119.011/191.530
7	Jean Alesi	F	11	Red Bull Sauber Petronas	Sauber C18-Petronas SPE03A V10	56	1h 37m 32.902s	118.614/190.891
8	Alexander Wurz	A	10	Mild Seven Benetton Playlife	Benetton B199-Playlife V10	56	1h 37m 39.428s	118.482/190.678
9	Marc Gene	ESP	21	Fondmetal Minardi Ford	Minardi M01-Ford Zetec-R V10	55		
10	Alex Zanardi	I	5	Winfield Williams	Williams FW21-Supertec FB01 V10	55		
11	Giancarlo Fisichella	I	9	Mild Seven Benetton Playlife	Benetton B199-Playlife V10	52		
	Jacques Villeneuve	CDN	22	British American Racing	BAR 01-Supertec FB01 V10	48	Hydraulics	
	Pedro Diniz	BR	12	Red Bull Sauber Petronas	Sauber C18-Petronas SPE03A V10	44	Spun off	
	Pedro de la Rosa	ESP	14	Arrows	Arrows A20 V10	30	Engine	
	Luca Badoer	I	20	Fondmetal Minardi Ford	Minardi M01-Ford Zetec-R V10	15	Overheating	
	David Coulthard	GB	2	West McLaren Mercedes	McLaren MP4/14-Mercedes F0110H V10	14	Fuel pressure	
	Ralf Schumacher	D	6	Winfield Williams	Williams FW21-Supertec FB01 V10	7	Spun off	
	Toranosuke Takagi	J	15	Arrows	Arrows A20 V10	7	Driveshaft	
	Ricardo Zonta	BR	23	British American Racing	BAR 01-Supertec FB01 V10	6	Engine	
	Olivier Panis	F	18	Gauloises Prost Peugeot	Prost AP02-Peugeot A18 V10	5	Engine	
	Damon Hill	GB	7	Benson & Hedges Jordan	Jordan 199-Mugen Honda MF301/HDV10	0	Collision with Fisichella	
DNS	Jarno Trulli	I	19	Gauloises Prost Peugeot	Prost AP02-Peugeot A18 V10		Engine	

Fastest lap: M. Schumacher, on lap 25, 1m 40.267s, 123.640 mph/198.980 km/h (record).

Grid order	1	2	3	4	5	6	7	8	9	10	11	12	13	14	15	16	17	18	19	20	21	22	23	24	25	26	27	28	29	30	31	32	33	34	35	36	37	38	39	40	41	42
3 M. SCHUMACHER	3	3	3	4	4	4	4	4	4	4	4	4	4	4	4	4	4	4	4	4	4	4	4	4	4	3	3	3	4	4	4	4	4	4	4	4	4	4	4	4	4	3
4 IRVINE	4	4	4	3	2	2	2	2	2	2	2	2	2	2	3	3	3	3	3	3	3	3	3	3	3	1	1	17	3	3	3	3	3	3	3	3	3	3	3	3	3	1
2 COULTHARD	2	2	2	2	3	3	3	3	3	3	3	3	3	3	1	1	1	1	1	1	1	17	17		4	1	1	1	1	1	1	1	1	1	1	1	1	1	1	1	1	4
1 HÄKKINEN	1	1	1	1	1	1	1	1	1	1	1	1	1	1	16	16	16	16	17	17	17	17	17	17	4	4	1	16	16	16	16	16	16	16	16	16	16	17	17	17	1	
17 HERBERT	16	16	16	16	16	16	16	16	16	16	16	16	16	16	17	17	17	17	17	11	11	22	16	16	16	16	16	16	17	17	17	17	17	17	17	17	17	11	11	16	1	
16 BARRICHELLO	17	17	17	17	17	17	17	17	17	17	17	17	17	17	10	10	10	11	11	10	22	16	8	8	8	8	8	8	11	11	11	11	11	11	11	11	11	16	16	8		
10 WURZ	10	10	10	10	10	10	10	10	10	10	10	10	10	10	11	11	11	10	10	22	16	8	11	11	11	11	11	11	10	10	10	10	10	10	10	8	8	11	1			
6 R. SCHUMACHER	6	6	6	6	6	11	11	11	11	11	11	11	11	11	22	22	22	22	22	16	8	12	10	10	10	10	10	10	22	22	22	22	22	22	8	10	10	10	1			
7 HILL	22	22	22	22	22	6	6	22	22	22	22	22	22	22	8	8	8	8	8	8	12	11	22	22	22	22	22	22	12	12	12	12	12	12	12	12	12	12	1			
22 VILLENEUVE	11	11	11	11	11	22	22	8	8	8	8	8	8	8	12	12	12	12	12	12	10	10	12	12	12	12	12	12	8	8	8	8	8	8	22	22	22	22	2			
9 FISICHELLA	8	8	8	8	8	8	8	21	21	12	12	12	12	12	21	21	21	21	21	21	21	21	21	21	5	21	21	21	21	21	21	21	21	21	21	21	21	21	2			
18 PANIS	21	21	21	21	21	21	21	12	12	21	21	21	21	21	14	14	14	14	14	14	14	14	14	5	5	5	21	14	14	5	5	5	5	5	5	5	5	5	5			
23 ZONTA	5	5	15	15	15	15	12	14	14	14	14	14	14	14	5	5	5	5	5	5	5	5	14	14	14	5	5	9	9	9	9	9	9	9	9	9	9	9				
8 FRENTZEN	20	20	20	20	12	12	14	5	5	5	5	5	5	5	20	9	9	9	9	9	9	9	9	9	9	9	9															
11 ALESI	15	15	18	18	18	23	5	20	20	20	20	20	20	9																												
5 ZANARDI	18	18	5	12	23	14	20	9	9	9	9	9	9																													
12 DINIZ	14	14	12	14	14	5	15																																			
19 TRULLI	12	12	14	23	20	20	9																																			
21 GENE	23	23	23	5	5	9																																				
14 DE LA ROSA	9	9	9	9	9																																					
20 BADOER																																										
15 TAKAGI																																										

Pit stop
One lap behind leader

3
M. SCHUMACHER   4
Ferrari   **IRVINE**
                       Ferrari

2
COULTHARD   1
McLaren   **HÄKKINEN**
                       McLaren

17
HERBERT   16
Stewart   **BARRICHELLO**
                       Stewart

10
WURZ   6
Benetton   **R. SCHUMACHER**
                       Williams

7
HILL   22
Jordan   **VILLENEUVE**
                       BAR

9
FISICHELLA   18
Benetton   **PANIS**
                       Prost

23
ZONTA   8
BAR   **FRENTZEN**
                       Jordan

11
ALESI   5
Sauber   **ZANARDI**
                       Williams

12
DINIZ   19*
Sauber   **TRULLI**
                       Prost

21
GENE   14
Minardi   **DE LA ROSA**
                       Arrows

20
BADOER   15
Minardi   **TAKAGI**
                       Arrows

* did not start

46	47	48	49	50	51	52	53	54	55	56	
3	3	3	3	3	3	3	4	4	4	4	1
1	1	4	4	4	4	3	3	3	3	3	2
4	4	17	17	17	17	17	17	1	1	1	3
17	17	1	1	1	1	1	1	17	17	17	4
16	16	16	16	16	16	16	16	16	16	16	5
8	8	8	8	8	8	8	8	8	8	8	6
11	11	11	11	11	11	11	11	11	11	11	
10	10	10	10	10	10	10	10	10	10	10	
22	22	22	21	21	21	21	21	21	21		
21	21	21	5	5	5	5	5	5	5		
5	5	5	9	9	9	9	9				
9	9	9									

QUALIFYING

Weather: Dry, humid and sunny

Pos.	Driver	Cars	Laps	Time
1	Michael Schumacher	Ferrari	8	1m 39.688s
2	Eddie Irvine	Ferrari	8	1m 40.635s
3	David Coulthard	McLaren-Mercedes	12	1m 40.806s
4	Mika Häkkinen	McLaren-Mercedes	11	1m 40.866s
5	Johnny Herbert	Stewart-Ford	12	1m 40.937s
6	Rubens Barrichello	Stewart-Ford	12	1m 41.351s
7	Alexander Wurz	Benetton-Playlife	12	1m 41.444s
8	Ralf Schumacher	Williams-Supertec	11	1m 41.558s
9	Damon Hill	Jordan-Mugen Honda	11	1m 42.050s
10	Jacques Villeneuve	BAR-Supertec	11	1m 42.087s
11	Giancarlo Fisichella	Benetton-Playlife	11	1m 42.110s
12	Olivier Panis	Prost-Peugeot	12	1m 42.208s
13	Ricardo Zonta	BAR-Supertec	11	1m 42.310s
14	Heinz-Harald Frentzen	Jordan-Mugen Honda	12	1m 42.380s
15	Jean Alesi	Sauber-Petronas	12	1m 42.522s
16	Alex Zanardi	Williams-Supertec	12	1m 42.885s
17	Pedro Diniz	Sauber-Petronas	12	1m 42.933s
18	Jarno Trulli	Prost-Peugeot	12	1m 42.948s
19	Marc Gene	Minardi-Ford	12	1m 43.563s
20	Pedro de la Rosa	Arrows	12	1m 43.579s
21	Luca Badoer	Minardi-Ford	12	1m 44.321s
22	Toranosuke Takagi	Arrows	12	1m 44.637s

FRIDAY FREE PRACTICE

Weather: Wet track, drying slowly

Pos.	Driver	Laps	Time
1	Jacques Villeneuve	28	1m 42.407s
2	David Coulthard	38	1m 42.519s
3	Jean Alesi	35	1m 42.701s
4	Eddie Irvine	40	1m 42.725s
5	Michael Schumacher	37	1m 42.875s
6	Pedro Diniz	35	1m 43.006s
7	Rubens Barrichello	40	1m 43.042s
8	Mika Häkkinen	34	1m 43.153s
9	Alexander Wurz	42	1m 43.311s
10	Johnny Herbert	37	1m 43.349s
11	Giancarlo Fisichella	27	1m 43.403s
12	Damon Hill	38	1m 43.417s
13	Olivier Panis	22	1m 43.500s
14	Heinz-Harald Frentzen	44	1m 43.677s
15	Jarno Trulli	34	1m 43.793s
16	Luca Badoer	17	1m 44.818s
17	Ricardo Zonta	15	1m 44.968s
18	Ralf Schumacher	26	1m 45.164s
19	Pedro de la Rosa	28	1m 45.397s
20	Alex Zanardi	40	1m 45.833s
21	Toranosuke Takagi	37	1m 46.690s
22	Marc Gene	22	1m 49.451s

SATURDAY FREE PRACTICE

Weather: Very hot and sunny

Pos.	Driver	Laps	Time
1	Michael Schumacher	28	1m 40.424s
2	Eddie Irvine	24	1m 40.506s
3	Mika Häkkinen	24	1m 41.107s
4	Johnny Herbert	32	1m 41.111s
5	David Coulthard	31	1m 41.269s
6	Jacques Villeneuve	29	1m 41.560s
7	Rubens Barrichello	29	1m 41.608s
8	Jean Alesi	25	1m 42.042s
9	Ralf Schumacher	26	1m 42.153s
10	Heinz-Harald Frentzen	26	1m 42.282s
11	Giancarlo Fisichella	25	1m 42.292s
12	Pedro Diniz	15	1m 42.473s
13	Ricardo Zonta	24	1m 42.578s
14	Alexander Wurz	27	1m 42.755s
15	Damon Hill	30	1m 42.861s
16	Jarno Trulli	24	1m 42.946s
17	Alex Zanardi	26	1m 43.108s
18	Pedro de la Rosa	30	1m 43.729s
19	Luca Badoer	24	1m 43.981s
20	Olivier Panis	12	1m 44.032s
21	Marc Gene	15	1m 44.937s
22	Toranosuke Takagi	22	1m 44.978s

WARM-UP

Weather: Overcast and humid

Pos.	Driver	Laps	Time
1	Rubens Barrichello	13	1m 41.679s
2	David Coulthard	13	1m 41.765s
3	Mika Häkkinen	11	1m 41.818s
4	Eddie Irvine	14	1m 42.243s
5	Michael Schumacher	13	1m 42.563s
6	Johnny Herbert	13	1m 42.681s
7	Alexander Wurz	11	1m 42.745s
8	Pedro Diniz	14	1m 42.846s
9	Olivier Panis	14	1m 43.540s
10	Jean Alesi	10	1m 43.686s
11	Giancarlo Fisichella	13	1m 43.725s
12	Ralf Schumacher	9	1m 43.835s
13	Ricardo Zonta	11	1m 43.894s
14	Heinz-Harald Frentzen	11	1m 43.950s
15	Jarno Trulli	10	1m 44.032s
16	Jacques Villeneuve	11	1m 44.079s
17	Alex Zanardi	15	1m 44.347s
18	Damon Hill	12	1m 44.663s
19	Luca Badoer	11	1m 44.677s
20	Pedro de la Rosa	12	1m 44.941s
21	Toranosuke Takagi	12	1m 45.288s
22	Marc Gene	13	1m 45.341s

RACE FASTEST LAPS

Weather: Hot, humid and sunny

Driver	Time	Lap
Michael Schumacher	1m 40.267s	25
Heinz-Harald Frentzen	1m 40.631s	53
Rubens Barrichello	1m 40.810s	55
Giancarlo Fisichella	1m 40.960s	36
Mika Häkkinen	1m 41.103s	49
Eddie Irvine	1m 41.254s	38
Jean Alesi	1m 41.328s	56
Johnny Herbert	1m 41.383s	50
Pedro Diniz	1m 41.639s	20
Jacques Villeneuve	1m 41.769s	35
Alexander Wurz	1m 41.950s	36
Alex Zanardi	1m 42.056s	27
Marc Gene	1m 42.490s	54
David Coulthard	1m 42.940s	11
Pedro de la Rosa	1m 43.885s	22
Luca Badoer	1m 46.367s	9
Ralf Schumacher	1m 46.418s	5
Toranosuke Takagi	1m 46.441s	4
Ricardo Zonta	1m 46.444s	2
Olivier Panis	1m 46.874s	4

CHASSIS LOG BOOK

1	Häkkinen	McLaren MP4/14/4
2	Coulthard	McLaren MP4/14/6
	spare	McLaren MP4/14/2 & 5
3	M. Schumacher	Ferrari F399/195
4	Irvine	Ferrari F399/196
	spare	Ferrari F399/193
5	Zanardi	Williams FW21/5
6	R. Schumacher	Williams FW21/6
	spare	Williams FW21/2
7	Hill	Jordan 199/4
8	Frentzen	Jordan 199/5
	spare	Jordan 199/6
9	Fisichella	Benetton B199/7
10	Wurz	Benetton B199/4
	spare	Benetton B199/3
11	Alesi	Sauber C18/4
12	Diniz	Sauber C18/5
	spare	Sauber C18/6
14	de la Rosa	Arrows A20/7
15	Takagi	Arrows A20/5
	spare	Arrows A20/2
16	Barrichello	Stewart SF3/4
17	Herbert	Stewart SF3/5
	spare	Stewart SF3/6
18	Panis	Prost AP02/5
19	Trulli	Prost AP02/7
	spare	Prost AP02/3
20	Badoer	Minardi M01/1
21	Gene	Minardi M01/4
	spare	Minardi M01/3
22	Villeneuve	BAR 01/6
23	Zonta	BAR 01/7
	spare	BAR 01/4

POINTS TABLES

DRIVERS

1	Eddie Irvine	70
2	Mika Häkkinen	66
3	Heinz-Harald Frentzen	51
4	David Coulthard	48
5	Michael Schumacher	38
6	Ralf Schumacher	33
7	Rubens Barrichello	21
8	Johnny Herbert	15
9	Giancarlo Fisichella	13
10	Mika Salo	10
11 =	Jarno Trulli	7
11 =	Damon Hill	7
13 =	Alexander Wurz	3
13 =	Pedro Diniz	3
15	Olivier Panis	2
16 =	Pedro de la Rosa	1
16 =	Jean Alesi	1
16 =	Marc Gene	1

CONSTRUCTORS

1	Ferrari	118
2	McLaren	114
3	Jordan	58
4	Stewart	36
5	Williams	33
6	Benetton	16
7	Prost	9
8	Sauber	4
9 =	Arrows	1
9 =	Minardi	1

JAPANESE
grand prix

HÄKKINEN

M. SCHUMACHER

IRVINE

FRENTZEN

R. SCHUMACHER

ALESI

DIARY

Greg Moore killed in final CART Championship round at Fontana, California.

British American Racing faces potential internal power struggle with Adrian Reynard bidding to replace Craig Pollock as chairman of the new F1 team.

McLaren boss Ron Dennis furious that a FOCA TV cameraman took photographs of a piece of paper giving away details of his team's refuelling tactics in the Japanese Grand Prix.

Jordan technical director Mika Gascoyne refutes rumours that he has received an approach to join the Ferrari F1 design team.

MIKA Häkkinen drove a flawless race to dominate the Japanese Grand Prix and clinch his second World Championship title, a result which brought a collective sigh of relief from the McLaren-Mercedes team after a nerve-wracking week following the reinstatement of the Ferraris to their 1–2 result in Malaysia a fortnight before.

His achievement made him only the seventh driver in the 50-year history of the World Championship to win back-to-back titles, a feat previously managed by Alberto Ascari, Juan Manuel Fangio, Jack Braham, Alain Prost, Ayrton Senna and Michael Schumacher.

Meanwhile, second and third places for Michael Schumacher and Eddie Irvine was enough to win Ferrari its first constructors' World Championship since 1983, even though the drivers' title eluded Irvine despite the additional boost given by the FIA appeal court's decision the previous week to reinstate him and Michael Schumacher to first and second places in the Malaysian Grand Prix.

The Finn went into the race trailing Irvine by four points knowing that if he won, he would take the title whatever the Ulsterman managed to achieve. Yet if neither finished, of course, Irvine would be World Champion.

There were also three mathematical situations in which Häkkinen and Irvine could end up in a dead heat on points, the Finn winning in each case on a tie-decider.

If Häkkinen won and Irvine was second, they would be equal on 76 points with Mika taking the crown with five wins to Irvine's fourth. If Häkkinen managed second, with Irvine fifth, they would dead-heat on 72 points with Mika coming out on top with three second places to Irvine's two. Finally, if Häkkinen was third and Irvine retired, they would be equal on 70 points with Häkkinen winning again on the same basis.

However, Mika was leaving nothing to chance and blitzed his opposition. 'This has been a very difficult year,' said the elated Finn. 'All the way through from the start of the season we've missed finishing races and lost a lot of points. To have won the Championship in the last Grand Prix is nerve-wracking. It's an experience which I can't recommend to anyone. I experienced it with Michael last year and again with Eddie this year. I hope that's enough for a day...'

Outclassed and outdriven, Irvine remained gracious in the extreme after being beaten into third place by the McLaren-Mercedes team leader and Michael Schumacher in the other Ferrari F399.

'We knew there were going to be games played today,' he said with a sardonic grin, referring to the way in which David Coulthard had steadily held him up from third place, trying to push him back into the clutches of Heinz-Harald Frentzen's Jordan and the Williams FW21 of Ralf Schumacher.

'We made small mistakes at some races this season, like Silverstone and the Nürburgring, which certainly cost us some points. It was a fantastic drive by Mika [today] to win the race but he has certainly done his best to help me [have a chance] of winning the World Championship, no doubt about that, but we didn't quite make it.'

Häkkinen made a copybook getaway from second place on the grid, accelerating into the first corner six lengths ahead of Michael Schumacher's pole-position Ferrari F399.

'The start is always difficult here at Suzuka because it is downhill,' he later reflected. 'I knew I could do well and was very confident. When the lights changed, I immediately knew I had an advantage over Michael, and at the moment I shifted into second gear, I was already one car's length ahead in the lead. At that point I knew that all I had to do was keep that position.'

For his part, Schumacher acknowledged that he had made a very bad start. 'I had a problem when I went off the grid on the parade lap and a similar problem during the race start,' he said. 'I went into wheelspin and made a mess of it while Mika just got a very good start, without making a mistake.'

At the end of the opening lap Häkkinen was already 0.8s ahead of Schumacher with Olivier Panis holding a seemingly remarkable third place in his Prost-Peugeot which had dodged through from sixth place on the grid as Coulthard had attempted to block Irvine on the run to the first corner.

Unfortunately, all David managed to do was to block Heinz-Harald Frentzen's Jordan by moving across to the right, leaving plenty of room on the left for Irvine to sweep round the outside of the McLaren into an immediate fourth place.

Panis, who was leaving Prost immediately after the race and was close to inking a deal as McLaren-Mercedes test driver next season, was not expected to run hard with the leaders for many laps but he kept his head above water in respectable style during the opening phase of the race.

With four laps completed Häkkinen was already 2.6s ahead of Schumacher with Panis third and Irvine fourth, the

SUZUKA QUALIFYING

David Coulthard set the ball rolling just 14 minutes into qualifying by posting a competitive benchmark time of 1m 38.871s and ten minutes later the dazzling scarlet Ferraris of Schumacher and Eddie Irvine trickled down the pit lane in formation to start their bid for grid positions.

Michael was right on the pace from the start. On his first flying lap he was a startling 0.7s inside Coulthard's best at the first timing split and maintained that advantage right through to the end of the lap. It would have been even quicker had he not got into a slight twitch coming through the fast left-hander onto the return straight.

The Ferrari ace stopped the clocks at 1m 38.032s after which Häkkinen emerged from the pit and equalled his time to three places of decimals. This put everybody in mind of that amazing day at Jerez two years ago where Jacques Villeneuve's Williams, Schumacher's Ferrari and Heinz-Harald Frentzen's Williams set identical times to take the first three places on the grid.

This seemed to be the F1 show gone mad, even though a shrewd bookie would probably tell you there was as much chance of a dead heat as the cars producing any other combination of time. Surely Bernie Ecclestone's showmanship qualities didn't extend to fiddling the timing mechanism? It was certainly a compelling thought, but hardly one which stood up to bold scrutiny.

Häkkinen, meanwhile. had thrust aside the somewhat preoccupied demeanour which had clouded his efforts over the past three races. He seemed back on form, relaxed and more confident than ever. Just as he'd seemed 12 months earlier when he arrived to clinch his first world title.

The Finn was set to counter-attack in a bid to oust Schumacher from pole when he was floored by an accidental punch from an unexpected source. Trickling slowly through the pits chicane, trying to ensure plenty of track space ahead for a really quick lap, the Finn suddenly found Jean Alesi's Sauber bearing down on him at speed, the Frenchman hard at work on a quick lap.

Alesi lost downforce, straight-lined the chicane, reappeared on the circuit ahead of Häkkinen, immediately spinning which forced Mika to do likewise. Each was extremely fed-up with the other, but most observers agreed it was just one of those unfortunate things.

'As a result of this I didn't get a chance to try and improve my time,' said Häkkinen. 'I had to ease up slightly because I didn't want to catch Frentzen, who was ahead of me, too quickly. I think Jean may have got too close and possibly lost front aerodynamics. He went straight on and spun. It was a strange situation for somebody as experienced as he is.'

Eddie Irvine wound up fifth on 1m 38.975s with the other Ferrari after crashing his race car heavily under braking for the Spoon curve. He took over the spare F399 when he was holding fourth place and then dropped one further place to Heinz-Harald Frentzen's Jordan. 'Having been passed by Frentzen cost me 10 per cent of my potential to become World Champion,' he said.

Frentzen was quite content with the outcome. 'I am happy with the result,' he said, 'but I did not expect Ferrari to be that strong. My goal in the race is a place on the podium as there is still a race between David [Coulthard] and myself for third place in the championship.' Damon Hill struggled with problems under braking for the chicane, ending up 12th on 1m 40.140s.

Olivier Panis (1m 39.623s) and Jarno Trulli (1m 39.644s) wound up sixth and seventh in their Prost-Peugeots ahead of Johnny Herbert's Stewart SF3 on 1m 39.706s, the Englishman admitting he thought he should have been quicker although the car felt better on slow-speed corners. Rubens Barrichello, 13th on 1m 40.140s, suffered a water leak on his race car, took the spare and then reverted to his race chassis.

Champion style. When the chips were down, Mika Häkkinen produced a top-drawer performance to take his second championship in as many years.
Bryn Williams/Words & Pictures

Irvine loses out on bonus

EDDIE Irvine stood to collect a 2-million dollar (1.25 million pound) bonus if he had clinched the drivers' World Championship at the Japanese Grand Prix, it was revealed during the week after the race by Ferrari chairman Luca di Montezemolo.

Speaking at the team's Fiorano test track, Montezemolo praised Irvine, saying 'I don't think money is Eddie's sole motivation because he is so honest. He told me it was so hard to work with Michael Schumacher because it felt like being hit with a pneumatic hammer.'

He continued to explain that he was very happy for Irvine when he won the Austrian and German Grands Prix and added that he expected his replacement, Rubens Barrichello 'to stimulate Michael Schumacher. I don't expect him to be his butler or servant.'

Right: Olivier Panis was a surprise front-runner, sitting comfortably in third place during the race's early stages.

Below right: Out with a whimper. Damon Hill's prolonged retirement plans were brought forward when the Jordan driver gave up his unequal struggle on lap 22.

All photographs: Paul-Henri Cahier

Montezemolo, in reviewing Ferrari's 1999 season, said he was extremely disappointed at implications that the team had boycotted Irvine's bid for the championship. 'How can you think that Ferrari would do less than its best for the drivers. Ferrari always wants to win. I was the happiest man in the world when Eddie those two races in the summer.'

However, he did admit that one of the reasons that Irvine didn't win the race was that Häkkinen drove extremely well and that Irvine was not quite as fast as the Finn.

'If you want to win in F1, you have to fend for yourself rather like Senna did. But we won the constructors' championship ahead of a team which was described as superman and beat the Mercedes-Benz brand.'

He also said that the period surrounding the appeal against the team's exclusion from first and second places in the Malaysian Grand Prix was a 'difficult time' for the team and criticised both McLaren and its engine supplier Mercedes-Benz for their stance after the appeal.

'I didn't like the way McLaren responded to it all,' said Montezemolo. 'I didn't like what was said about our cars by people who don't know how to lose.'

Ulsterman now 9s behind the leading McLaren. Coulthard, meanwhile, was trying to make up for his poor getaway by harrying Irvine as hard as he could, anxious to overtake the Ulsterman and start trying to control his rival's pace in the interests of protecting Häkkinen's title challenge.

By lap nine Häkkinen had extended his lead to 5.5s and some observers believed that McLaren might be intending him to make three refuelling stops, such was the apparent speed with which he was pulling away from Schumacher. Others thought that Michael was perhaps so comparatively slow because he was running a heavy fuel load and perhaps intending to get through to the finish with just one stop.

That this was not the case and that both front runners were stopping twice was demonstrated on lap 18. Häkkinen, by now 8.3s ahead of the Ferrari, came in for an 8.8s first refuelling stop at the end of lap 18, dropping to second place behind Schumacher and then regained the lead when Michael stopped at the end of lap 22.

Thereafter Mika extended his lead to 27.5s over Schumacher when he came in for a second stop in 7.4s at the end of lap 38, Michael having made his own second stop on the previous lap. He resumed 9.6s ahead and raced on to the finish, lapping everybody but the four cars behind him.

Vaulting Coulthard ahead of Irvine was clearly going to call for a degree of creative strategy on the part of the McLaren team. On lap 22 McLaren signalled Coulthard to come in for his first refuelling stop. The Scot's car was stationary for 7.1s and when Irvine came in for his first stop next time round the Ferrari was at rest for precisely the same time.

However, a slightly faster lap in and out of the pits enabled Coulthard just to squeeze ahead of Irvine going into the first corner at the start of lap 24.

Coulthard now played the tactical card on McLaren's behalf for some of the race, although he moved the wrong way at the start and allowed Irvine to get ahead of him on the run to the first corner. Eventually squeezing ahead of the Ulsterman's Ferrari as Eddie emerged from his first refuelling stop, Coulthard then tried to push him back into the clutches of Heinz-Harald Frentzen's Jordan and Ralf Schumacher's Williams.

It didn't quite work, but Irvine lost 18s in six laps before diving into the pits to get rid of the problem with an early second stop on lap 32. Then Coulthard, who had been grappling with gearchange problems in his McLaren, caused by an oil leak, spun off and glanced a barrier. He got the car back to the pits for repairs, resumed, briefly held up Michael Schumacher's Ferrari and then quit for good as the gearchange problems worsened.

Schumacher, however, emerged from the cockpit of his Ferrari in an extremely sour mood and took a considerably less indulgent view of what he judged to be indefensible driving on Coulthard's part as he came up to lap the McLaren driver.

'It was a different thing between me and Mika in Malaysia where I was actually racing for position and had not been lapped,' he said. 'In that position you can play tactics. But if you have been lapped, you should give space.

'David had passed many blue flags, and he had some kind of a problem, but he was really zig-zagging. Actually I am not sure now whether I should believe that what happened at Spa last year wasn't done purposely, the way he behaved today. The situation cost me, I think, about 10 seconds.'

In fact, this was a gross exaggeration. Coulthard had held him up for about three corners and lost the Ferrari team leader just over 3s. Schumacher's complaint was not only unreasonable, it was also inaccurate. Yet for him to have referred to their Spa collision in 1998 was definitely below the belt and prompted a trenchant response from Coulthard.

'If he doesn't apologise, I'm going to sue him,' said Coulthard immediately after the race. I didn't want to do it [hold him up] today and it's not a nice thing to do.

'But I am very disappointed with Michael Schumacher's comments especially the way he has questioned my integrity over the incident at Spa. I have never tried to endanger any driver on the track and in fact fight within the Grand Prix Drivers' Association for driver safety.

McLaren chief Ron Dennis added: 'After what he put Mika Häkkinen through in Malaysia I don't want to hear one word from Michael Schumacher about being held up. He should look at his own races and some of the things he's done himself. David is truthful and has a high level of integrity. Those remarks do not do any credit to Michael.'

Coulthard also responded by suggesting that Schumacher hadn't really

wanted Irvine to win the drivers' championship anyway, preferring to reserve that Ferrari privilege for himself in 2000. In the event Coulthard withdrew his threat of legal action after Michael had toned down his own remarks. Even so, it had been a tense episode which many people took to reflect the fact that Schumacher reckoned there was one law for him and another for everybody else on the circuit.

In the end, Schumacher was 5.0s behind at the finish with Irvine a soundly beaten third, losing out on the championship by two points and admitting that he had just not been able to keep up.

Heinz-Harald Frentzen's Jordan and Ralf Schumacher's Williams had a good tussle to finish less than a second apart in fourth and fifth places, while Jean Alesi's Sauber completed the top six.

Frentzen's splendid run consolidated both his and the Jordan team's third place in their respective championships. It was a dramatic contrast to the manner in which Damon Hill slipped off the F1 stage almost unnoticed, parking his car in the garage after 21 laps.

'I spun off just before I was due in for my pit stop and had to change the nose cone which lost me lots of time,' he admitted. 'After that I decided there was too little to gain and too much to lose by carrying on. I have to acknowledge that F1 for me is a thing of the past and that I have made the right decision to retire.'

Outside the top six, Johnny Herbert and Rubens Barrichello wound up seventh and eighth in the final outing for the Stewart-Ford team prior to its rebranding as Jaguar Racing, while British American Racing rounded off a disastrous season with Jacques Villeneuve trailing home ninth.

The newest team on the F1 block ended its freshman year with a further notional loss of 6.3 million pounds – in addition to a significant over-spend on the racing budget – which represented the money they failed to secure for next year in travel and other benefits by failing to post a single championship point over the 16-race series.

Thus the season ended with Ferrari and McLaren effectively splitting the spoils. The constructors' title was probably a better consolation prize than Ferrari might reasonably have expected after Michael Schumacher's mid-season accident, but Häkkinen's success in retaining the drivers' crown was unreservedly applauded along the length of the pit lane. It was hard to argue against the notion that the right man had won.

Mixed emotions on the Suzuka podium: Michael can be well satisfied with his performance, Mika is rightly proud of his superb drive, and Eddie is left to think just how close he came to the World Championship.
Paul-Henri Cahier

FUJI TELEVISION
JAPANESE
GRAND PRIX
29–31 OCTOBER 1999
SUZUKA

Race distance: 53 laps, 192.986 miles/310.581 km

Race weather: Dry, warm and sunny

ROUND
16

SUZUKA RACING CIRCUIT

First Curve · S curve · Degner Curve · Underpass · Chicane · Hairpin · Spoon Curve

CIRCUIT LENGTH: 3.641 miles/5.860 km

Pos.	Driver	Nat.	No.	Entrant	Car/Engine	Laps	Time/Retirement	Speed (mph/km/h)
1	Mika Häkkinen	SF	1	West McLaren Mercedes	McLaren MP4/14-Mercedes FO110H V10	53	1h 31m 18.785s	126.813/204.086
2	Michael Schumacher	D	3	Scuderia Ferrari Marlboro	Ferrari F399 048B V10	53	1h 31m 23.800s	126.697/203.899
3	Eddie Irvine	GB	4	Scuderia Ferrari Marlboro	Ferrari F399 048B V10	53	1h 32m 54.473s	124.636/200.583
4	Heinz-Harald Frentzen	D	8	Benson & Hedges Jordan	Jordan 199-Mugen Honda MF301/HD V10	53	1h 32m 57.420s	124.570/200.477
5	Ralf Schumacher	D	6	Winfield Williams	Williams FW21-Supertec FB01 V10	53	1h 32m 58.279s	124.551/200.446
6	Jean Alesi	F	11	Red Bull Sauber Petronas	Sauber C18-Petronas SPE03A V10	52		
7	Johnny Herbert	GB	17	Stewart Ford	Stewart SF3-Ford CR-1 V10	52		
8	Rubens Barrichello	BR	16	Stewart Ford	Stewart SF3-Ford CR-1 V10	52		
9	Jacques Villeneuve	CDN	22	British American Racing	BAR 01-Supertec FB01 V10	52		
10	Alexander Wurz	A	10	Mild Seven Benetton Playlife	Benetton B199-Playlife V10	52		
11	Pedro Diniz	BR	12	Red Bull Sauber Petronas	Sauber C18-Petronas SPE03A V10	52		
12	Ricardo Zonta	BR	23	British American Racing	BAR 01-Supertec FB01 V10	52		
13	Pedro de la Rosa	ESP	14	Arrows	Arrows A20 V10	51		
14	Giancarlo Fisichella	I	9	Mild Seven Benetton Playlife	Benetton B199-Playlife V10	47	Engine	
	Toranosuke Takagi	J	15	Arrows	Arrows A20 V10	43	Gearbox	
	Luca Badoer	I	20	Fondmetal Minardi Ford	Minardi M01-Ford Zetec-R V10	43	Engine	
	David Coulthard	GB	2	West McLaren Mercedes	McLaren MP4/14-Mercedes FO110H V10	39	Gearbox	
	Marc Gene	ESP	21	Fondmetal Minardi Ford	Minardi M01-Ford Zetec-R V10	31	Gearbox	
	Damon Hill	GB	7	Benson & Hedges Jordan	Jordan 199-Mugen Honda MF301/HD V10	21	Driver	
	Olivier Panis	F	18	Gauloises Prost Peugeot	Prost AP02-Peugeot A18 V10	19	Gearbox	
	Jarno Trulli	I	19	Gauloises Prost Peugeot	Prost AP02-Peugeot A18 V10	3	Engine	
	Alex Zanardi	I	5	Winfield Williams	Williams FW21-Supertec FB01 V10	0	Electrics	

Fastest lap: M. Schumacher, on lap 31, 1m 41.319s, 129.466 mph/208.355 km/h.

Lap record: Heinz-Harald Frentzen (F1 Williams FW19-Renault V10), 1m 38.942s, 132.576 mph/213.361 km/h (1997).

Grid order	1	2	3	4	5	6	7	8	9	10	11	12	13	14	15	16	17	18	19	20	21	22	23	24	25	26	27	28	29	30	31	32	33	34	35	36	37	38	39	40
3 M. SCHUMACHER	1	1	1	1	1	1	1	1	1	1	1	1	1	1	1	1	1	1	1	3	3	3	1	1	1	1	1	1	1	1	1	1	1	1	1	1	1	1	1	1
1 HÄKKINEN	3	3	3	3	3	3	3	3	3	3	3	3	3	3	3	3	3	3	3	1	1	1	3	3	3	3	3	3	3	3	3	3	3	3	3	3	3	3	3	3
2 COULTHARD	18	18	18	18	18	18	18	18	18	18	18	18	18	18	18	18	18	18	18	4	4	4	4	4	2	2	2	2	2	2	2	17	4	4	4	4	4	4	4	4
8 FRENTZEN	4	4	4	4	4	4	4	4	4	4	4	4	4	4	4	4	4	4	2	2	2	2	2	4	4	4	4	4	4	4	17	17	4	17	8	8	8	8	8	8
4 IRVINE	2	2	2	2	2	2	2	2	2	2	2	2	2	2	2	2	8	8	8	6	8	8	8	8	8	8	8	8	8	6	6	4	4	11	11	6	6	6	6	6
18 PANIS	8	8	8	8	8	8	8	8	8	8	8	8	8	8	8	8	6	6	6	8	6	6	6	6	6	6	6	6	6	8	17	11	11	8	8	11	11	11	11	11
19 TRULLI	6	6	6	6	6	6	6	6	6	6	6	6	6	6	6	6	11	11	11	16	17	17	17	17	17	17	17	17	17	17	11	8	8	6	6	17	17	17	17	17
17 HERBERT	11	11	11	11	11	11	11	11	11	11	11	11	11	11	11	11	17	18	16	17	11	11	11	11	11	11	11	11	11	11	8	6	6	16	16	16	16	16	16	16
6 R. SCHUMACHER	19	19	19	17	17	17	17	17	17	17	17	17	17	17	17	17	22	16	12	22	22	22	22	22	22	22	22	22	22	22	2	2	22	22	2	2	2	2	10	10
11 ALESI	17	17	17	22	22	22	22	22	22	22	22	22	22	22	22	18	18	12	17	11	16	16	16	16	16	16	16	16	16	16	16	22	2	2	2	10	10
22 VILLENEUVE	22	22	22	10	10	10	10	10	10	10	10	10	10	10	10	10	16	16	17	22	10	10	10	10	10	10	10	10	10	10	10	10	12	12	12	10	2	12
7 HILL	10	10	10	16	16	16	16	16	16	16	16	16	16	16	16	16	12	12	22	10	12	12	12	12	12	12	12	12	12	12	12	10	10	10	12	12	12	23
16 BARRICHELLO	16	16	16	7	7	7	7	7	7	7	7	7	7	7	12	10	10	10	23	23	23	23	23	23	23	23	23	23	23	23	23	23	23	23	23	23	9
9 FISICHELLA	7	7	7	12	12	12	12	12	12	12	12	12	12	12	23	23	23	23	18	21	21	21	21	21	21	21	21	21	9	9	9	14	9	9	9	9	14
10 WURZ	12	12	12	23	23	23	23	23	23	23	23	23	23	23	21	21	14	14	9	9	9	9	9	9	9	9	9	9	14	14	9	14	14	14	14	14	15
5 ZANARDI	9	9	9	21	21	21	21	21	21	21	21	21	21	14	14	14	15	21	15	14	14	14	14	14	14	14	14	20	15	15	15	20	20	20	15	20
12 DINIZ	23	23	23	14	14	14	14	14	14	14	14	14	14	9	9	21	20	9	7	7	20	20	20	20	20	20	20	15	20	20	20	15	15	15	20
23 ZONTA	21	21	21	15	15	15	15	15	15	15	9	9	9	7	15	20	9	14	20	20	15	15	15	15	15	15	15	15
15 TAKAGI	14	14	14	20	9	9	9	9	9	9	15	15	15	20	9	14	7	15	15
21 GENE	15	15	15	9	9	20	20	20	20	20	20	20	20	20	7	7	7	20
14 DE LA ROSA	20	20	20
20 BADOER																																Pit stop							
																																One lap behind leader							

STARTING GRID

3 **M. SCHUMACHER** Ferrari	1 **HÄKKINEN** McLaren
2 **COULTHARD** McLaren	8 **FRENTZEN** Jordan
4 **IRVINE** Ferrari	18 **PANIS** Prost
19 **TRULLI** Prost	17 **HERBERT** Stewart
6 **R. SCHUMACHER** Williams	11 **ALESI** Sauber
22 **VILLENEUVE** BAR	7 **HILL** Jordan
16 **BARRICHELLO** Stewart	9 **FISICHELLA** Benetton
10 **WURZ** Benetton	5 **ZANARDI** Williams
12 **DINIZ** Sauber	23 **ZONTA** BAR
15 **TAKAGI** Arrows	21 **GENE** Minardi
14 **DE LA ROSA** Arrows	20 **BADOER** Minardi

43	44	45	46	47	48	49	50	51	52	53	●
1	1	1	1	1	1	1	1	1	1	1	1
3	3	3	3	3	3	3	3	3	3	3	2
4	4	4	4	4	4	4	4	4	4	4	3
8	8	8	8	8	8	8	8	8	8	8	4
6	6	6	6	6	6	6	6	6	6	6	5
11	11	11	11	11	11	11	11	11	11	11	6
17	17	17	17	17	17	17	17	17	17	17	
16	16	16	16	16	16	16	16	16	16		
22	22	22	22	22	22	22	22	22	22		
10	10	10	10	10	10	10	10	10	10		
12	12	12	12	12	12	12	12	12			
23	23	23	23	23	23	23	23	23			
9	9	9	9	9	14	14	14	14			
14	14	14	14	14							
15											
20											

TIME SHEETS

QUALIFYING
Weather: Dry, sunny and warm

Pos.	Driver	Car	Laps	Time
1	Michael Schumacher	Ferrari	11	1m 37.470s
2	Mika Häkkinen	McLaren-Mercedes	9	1m 37.820s
3	David Coulthard	McLaren-Mercedes	12	1m 38.239s
4	Heinz-Harald Frentzen	Jordan-Mugen Honda	12	1m 38.696s
5	Eddie Irvine	Ferrari	11	1m 38.975s
6	Olivier Panis	Prost-Peugeot	11	1m 39.623s
7	Jarno Trulli	Prost-Peugeot	12	1m 39.644s
8	Johnny Herbert	Stewart-Ford	12	1m 39.706s
9	Ralf Schumacher	Williams-Supertec	11	1m 39.717s
10	Jean Alesi	Sauber-Petronas	10	1m 39.721s
11	Jacques Villeneuve	BAR-Supertec	12	1m 39.732s
12	Damon Hill	Jordan-Mugen Honda	12	1m 40.140s
13	Rubens Barrichello	Stewart-Ford	11	1m 40.140s
14	Giancarlo Fisichella	Benetton-Playlife	10	1m 40.261s
15	Alexander Wurz	Benetton-Playlife	12	1m 40.303s
16	Alex Zanardi	Williams-Supertec	12	1m 40.403s
17	Pedro Diniz	Sauber-Petronas	11	1m 40.740s
18	Ricardo Zonta	BAR-Supertec	11	1m 40.861s
19	Toranosuke Takagi	Arrows	11	1m 41.067s
20	Marc Gene	Minardi-Ford	12	1m 41.529s
21	Pedro de la Rosa	Arrows	11	1m 41.708s
22	Luca Badoer	Minardi-Ford	8	1m 42.515s

FRIDAY FREE PRACTICE
Weather: Dry, warm and sunny

Pos.	Driver	Laps	Time
1	Mika Häkkinen	31	1m 41.746s
2	David Coulthard	19	1m 41.894s
3	Michael Schumacher	27	1m 42.215s
4	Rubens Barrichello	34	1m 42.529s
5	Alex Zanardi	36	1m 42.718s
6	Olivier Panis	32	1m 42.925s
7	Giancarlo Fisichella	27	1m 42.953s
8	Jacques Villeneuve	24	1m 43.047s
9	Heinz-Harald Frentzen	30	1m 43.235s
10	Eddie Irvine	33	1m 43.375s
11	Ralf Schumacher	27	1m 43.399s
12	Alexander Wurz	33	1m 43.430s
13	Jean Alesi	36	1m 43.485s
14	Pedro de la Rosa	37	1m 43.599s
15	Marc Gene	39	1m 43.652s
16	Damon Hill	22	1m 43.720s
17	Ricardo Zonta	40	1m 43.776s
18	Toranosuke Takagi	39	1m 43.804s
19	Jarno Trulli	33	1m 43.916s
20	Johnny Herbert	29	1m 44.179s
21	Pedro Diniz	32	1m 44.423s
22	Luca Badoer	36	1m 45.543s

SATURDAY FREE PRACTICE
Weather: Dry, warm and sunny

Pos.	Driver	Laps	Time
1	Michael Schumacher	24	1m 39.085s
2	Mika Häkkinen	22	1m 39.579s
3	Johnny Herbert	31	1m 40.134s
4	Heinz-Harald Frentzen	21	1m 40.139s
5	Damon Hill	32	1m 40.175s
6	Rubens Barrichello	26	1m 40.334s
7	David Coulthard	21	1m 40.377s
8	Jarno Trulli	29	1m 40.535s
9	Ralf Schumacher	12	1m 40.570s
10	Jean Alesi	27	1m 40.632s
11	Olivier Panis	29	1m 40.656s
12	Eddie Irvine	20	1m 40.667s
13	Giancarlo Fisichella	22	1m 41.001s
14	Alex Zanardi	25	1m 41.363s
15	Alexander Wurz	18	1m 41.562s
16	Pedro Diniz	33	1m 41.584s
17	Ricardo Zonta	20	1m 41.596s
18	Jacques Villeneuve	17	1m 41.938s
19	Pedro de la Rosa	28	1m 42.156s
20	Toranosuke Takagi	11	1m 42.222s
21	Marc Gene	22	1m 42.895s
22	Luca Badoer	23	1m 43.077s

WARM-UP
Weather: Dry, warm and sunny

Pos.	Driver	Laps	Time
1	Mika Häkkinen	13	1m 40.630s
2	Michael Schumacher	14	1m 40.761s
3	Heinz-Harald Frentzen	15	1m 41.372s
4	Ralf Schumacher	12	1m 41.680s
5	David Coulthard	12	1m 41.714s
6	Eddie Irvine	14	1m 42.060s
7	Rubens Barrichello	13	1m 42.522s
8	Jarno Trulli	7	1m 42.629s
9	Jacques Villeneuve	12	1m 42.844s
10	Olivier Panis	13	1m 42.919s
11	Damon Hill	13	1m 43.023s
12	Johnny Herbert	14	1m 43.051s
13	Alexander Wurz	12	1m 43.333s
14	Pedro Diniz	12	1m 43.339s
15	Giancarlo Fisichella	12	1m 43.551s
16	Marc Gene	11	1m 43.708s
17	Alex Zanardi	12	1m 43.757s
18	Jean Alesi	9	1m 43.896s
19	Pedro de la Rosa	10	1m 44.411s
20	Ricardo Zonta	12	1m 44.816s
21	Toranosuke Takagi	11	1m 45.508s
22	Luca Badoer	12	1m 45.596s

RACE FASTEST LAPS
Weather: Dry, warm and sunny

Driver	Time	Lap
Michael Schumacher	1m 41.319s	31
Mika Häkkinen	1m 41.577s	31
David Coulthard	1m 42.106s	33
Ralf Schumacher	1m 42.567s	22
Heinz-Harald Frentzen	1m 42.972s	22
Olivier Panis	1m 43.188s	4
Eddie Irvine	1m 43.297s	26
Rubens Barrichello	1m 43.496s	22
Jean Alesi	1m 43.669s	3
Johnny Herbert	1m 43.706s	5
Jacques Villeneuve	1m 43.898s	6
Damon Hill	1m 43.939s	14
Alexander Wurz	1m 43.963s	11
Pedro Diniz	1m 44.112s	22
Jarno Trulli	1m 44.304s	3
Giancarlo Fisichella	1m 44.379s	12
Ricardo Zonta	1m 44.869s	30
Marc Gene	1m 45.359s	29
Luca Badoer	1m 45.377s	30
Pedro de la Rosa	1m 45.556s	25
Toranosuke Takagi	1m 46.150s	27

CHASSIS LOG BOOK

1	Häkkinen	McLaren MP4/14/4
2	Coulthard	McLaren MP4/14/6
	spare	McLaren MP4/14/2 and 5
3	M. Schumacher	Ferrari F399/195
4	Irvine	Ferrari F399/196
	spare	Ferrari F399/194 and 193
5	Zanardi	Williams FW21/5
6	R. Schumacher	Williams FW21/6
	spare	Williams FW21/2
7	Hill	Jordan 199/4
8	Frentzen	Jordan 199/6
	spare	Jordan 199/5
9	Fisichella	Benetton B199/7
10	Wurz	Benetton B199/4
	spare	Benetton B199/5
11	Alesi	Sauber C18/4
12	Diniz	Sauber C18/5
	spare	Sauber C18/6
14	de la Rosa	Arrows A20/4
15	Takagi	Arrows A20/2
	spare	Arrows A20/5
16	Barrichello	Stewart SF3/4
17	Herbert	Stewart SF3/6
	spare	Stewart SF3/3
18	Panis	Prost AP02/5
19	Trulli	Prost AP02/7
	spare	Prost AP02/3
20	Badoer	Minardi M01/3
21	Gene	Minardi M01/4
	spare	Minardi M01/1
22	Villeneuve	BAR 01/6
23	Zonta	BAR 01/7
	spare	BAR 01/3

POINTS TABLES

DRIVERS

1	Mika Häkkinen	76
2	Eddie Irvine	74
3	Heinz-Harald Frentzen	54
4	David Coulthard	48
5	Michael Schumacher	44
6	Ralf Schumacher	35
7	Rubens Barrichello	21
8	Johnny Herbert	15
9	Giancarlo Fisichella	13
10	Mika Salo	10
11 =	Jarno Trulli	7
11 =	Damon Hill	7
13 =	Alexander Wurz	3
13 =	Pedro Diniz	3
15 =	Olivier Panis	2
15 =	Jean Alesi	2
17 =	Pedro de la Rosa	1
17 =	Marc Gene	1

CONSTRUCTORS

1	Ferrari	128
2	McLaren	124
3	Jordan	61
4	Stewart	36
5	Williams	35
6	Benetton	16
7	Prost	9
8	Sauber	5
9 =	Arrows	1
9 =	Minardi	1

Paul-Henri Cahier

DRIVERS' POINTS TABLE

Compiled by Nick Henry

Place	Driver	Nationality	Date of birth	Car	Australia	Brazil	San Marino	Monaco	Spain	Canada	France	Britain	Austria	Germany	Hungary	Belgium	Italy	Europe	Malaysia	Japan	Points total
1	Mika Häkkinen	SF	28/9/68	McLaren-Mercedes	Rp	1pf	Rp	3pfs	1ps	1	2s	Rpfs	3pf	Rp	1p	2pfs	Rp	5fs	3s	1	76
2	Eddie Irvine	GB	10/11/65	Ferrari	1	5	R	2b	4	3f	6	2	1	1	3	4	6b	7b	1	3	74
3	Heinz–Harald Frentzen	D	18/5/67	Jordan-Mugen Honda	2	3*b	R	4	R	11*	1	4	4	3	4	3	1	Rp	6	4	54
4	David Coulthard	GB	27/3/71	McLaren-Mercedes	R	Rs	2	R	2	7s	Rf	1	2	5fb	2fsb	1	5s	R	R	R	48
5	Michael Schumacher	D	3/1/69	Ferrari	8fs	2	1fsb	1	3f	Rp	5	DNS	–	–	–	–	–	–	2pf	2pf	44
6	Ralf Schumacher	D	30/6/75	Williams-Supertec	3	4	R	R	5	4	4	3	R	4	9	5	2f	4	R	5	35
7	Rubens Barrichello	BR	23/5/72	Stewart-Ford	5	R	3	9*	DQ	R	3p	8	R	R	5	10	4	3	5	8	21
8	Johnny Herbert	GB	25/6/64	Stewart-Ford	R	R	10*	R	R	5	R	12	14	11*	11	R	R	1	4	7	15
9	Giancarlo Fisichella	I	14/1/73	Benetton-Playlife	4	R	5	5	9	2	R	7	12*	R	R	11	R	R	11	14*	13
10	Mika Salo	SF	30/11/66	BAR-Supertec	–	–	7*	R	8	–	–	–	–	–	–	–	–	–	–	–	
				Ferrari	–	–	–	–	–	–	–	–	9	2	12	7	3	R	–	–	10
11=J	Jarno Trulli	I	13/7/74	Prost-Peugeot	R	R	R	7	6	R	7	9	7	R	8	12	R	2	DNS	R	7
11=	Damon Hill	GB	17/9/60	Jordan-Mugen Honda	R	R	4	R	7	R	R	5b	8	R	6	6	10	R	R	R	7
13=	Alexander Wurz	A	15/2/74	Benetton-Playlife	R	7	R	6	10b	R	10	5s	7	7	14	R	R	R	8	10b	3
13=	Pedro Diniz	BR	22/5/70	Sauber-Petronas	R	R	R	R	R	6	R	6	6b	R	R	R	R	R	R	11	3
15=	Olivier Panis	F	2/9/66	Prost-Peugeot	R	6	R	R	R	9b	8	13	10	6	10	13	11*	9	R	R	2
15=	Jean Alesi	F	11/6/64	Sauber-Petronas	R	R	6	R	R	R	R	14	R	8s	16*	9	9	R	7	6	2
17=	Pedro de la Rosa	ESP	24/2/71	Arrows	6b	R	R	R	11	R	12	R	R	R	15	R	R	R	R	13	1
17=	Marc Gene	ESP	29/3/74	Minardi-Ford	R	9	9	R	R	8	R	15	11	9	17	16	R	6	9	R	1
	Luca Badoer	I	25/1/71	Minardi-Ford	R	–	8	R	R	10	10b	R	13	10	14	R	R	R	R	R	0
	Stéphane Sarrazin	F		Minardi-Ford	–	R															0
	Toranosuke Takagi	J	12/2/72	Arrows	7	8	R	R	12	R	11	16	R	R	R	R	R	R	R	R	0
	Jacques Villeneuve	CDN	9/4/71	BAR-Supertec	R	R	R	R	R	R	R	R	R	R	R	R	15	8	10*	R	0
	Alex Zanardi	I	23/10/66	Williams-Supertec	R	R	11*	8	R	R	R	11	R	R	R	8b	7	R	10b	R	0
	Ricardo Zonta	BR	23/3/76	BAR-Supertec	R	DNS	–	–	–	R	9	R	15*	R	13	R	R	8	R	12	0

KEY

p	pole position	b	fastest pit stop (entrance–exit)
f	fastest lap	*	classified but not running at the finish
s	fastest speed through speed trap	R	retired

DQ	disqualified
DNS	did not start
DNQ	did not qualify

POINTS & PERCENTAGES

Compiled by David Hayhoe

GRID POSITIONS: 1999

Pos.	Driver	Starts	Best	Worst	Average
1	Mika Häkkinen	16	1	14	2.25
2	Michael Schumacher	10	1	6	2.70
3	David Coulthard	16	2	4	2.75
4	Heinz-Harald Frentzen	16	1	14	5.31
5	Eddie Irvine	16	2	17	5.37
6	Rubens Barrichello	16	1	15	6.56
7	Damon Hill	16	4	18	9.75
8	Ralf Schumacher	16	4	16	9.81
9	Giancarlo Fisichella	16	4	17	10.50
10	Jacques Villeneuve	16	5	21	10.56
11	Johnny Herbert	16	5	17	11.06
12	Jarno Trulli	16	7	18	11.25
13	Mika Salo	9	4	19	11.44
14=	Alexander Wurz	16	7	18	12.37
14=	Olivier Panis	16	3	20	12.37
16	Jean Alesi	16	2	21	12.56
17	Alessandro Zanardi	16	4	18	13.37
18	Pedro Diniz	16	11	18	14.81
19	Ricardo Zonta	12	10	19	16.00
20	Stéphane Sarrazin	1	17	17	17.00
21	Toranosuke Takagi	16	17	22	19.87
22	Pedro de la Rosa	16	18	22	20.06
23	Luca Badoer	15	19	22	20.40
24	Marc Gene	16	15	22	20.69

CAREER PERFORMANCES: 1999 DRIVERS

Driver	Nationality	Races	Championships	Wins	2nd places	3rd places	4th places	5th places	6th places	Pole positions	Fastest laps	Points
Jean Alesi	F	167	–	1	16	15	11	14	9	2	4	236
Luca Badoer	I	49	–	–	–	–	–	–	–	–	–	–
Rubens Barrichello	BR	113	–	–	2	4	9	9	4	2	–	77
David Coulthard	GB	90	–	6	18	6	4	6	5	8	11	221
Pedro de la Rosa	E	16	–	–	–	–	–	1	–	–	–	1
Pedro Diniz	BR	82	–	–	–	–	2	6	–	–	–	10
Giancarlo Fisichella	I	57	–	–	4	1	4	3	3	1	1	49
Heinz-Harald Frentzen	D	97	–	3	3	9	11	8	9	2	6	142
Marc Gene	E	16	–	–	–	–	–	1	–	–	–	1
Mika Häkkinen	FIN	128	2	14	7	16	8	9	6	21	13	294
Johnny Herbert	GB	145	–	3	1	3	11	6	5	–	–	98
Damon Hill	GB	116	1	22	15	5	7	2	5	20	19	360
Eddie Irvine	GB	97	–	4	6	14	8	6	5	–	1	173
Olivier Panis	F	91	–	1	3	1	3	4	7	–	–	56
Mika Salo	FIN	77	–	–	1	1	1	5	2	–	–	25
Stéphane Sarrazin	F	1	–	–	–	–	–	–	–	–	–	–
Michael Schumacher	D	128	2	35	22	14	6	5	4	23	39	570
Ralf Schumacher	D	49	–	–	2	4	5	8	3	–	1	62
Tora Takagi	J	32	–	–	–	–	–	–	–	–	–	–
Jarno Trulli	I	46	–	–	1	–	1	–	2	–	–	11
Jacques Villeneuve	CDN	65	1	11	5	5	3	4	3	13	9	180
Alexander Wurz	D	35	–	–	1	5	2	1	–	1	–	24
Alessandro Zanardi	I	41	–	–	–	–	–	1	–	1	–	1
Ricardo Zonta	BR	12	–	–	–	–	–	–	–	–	–	–

Note: Drivers beginning the formation lap are deemed to have made a start

UNLAPPED: 1999

Number of cars on same lap as leader

Grand Prix	Starters	at ¼ distance	at ½ distance	at ¾ distance	at full distance
Australia	22	17	10	8	7
Brazil	21	17	7	4	2
San Marino	22	17	8	4	2
Monaco	22	15	6	6	4
Spain	22	20	13	8	5
Canada	22	16	8	9	7
France	22	19	13	11	9
Britain	22	19	15	14	13
Austria	22	19	13	10	6
Germany	22	17	13	12	9
Hungary	22	19	10	8	7
Belgium	22	20	18	15	14
Italy	22	17	14	12	10
Europe	22	18	11	8	7
Malaysia	22	14	13	10	8
Japan	22	20	12	5	5

LAP LEADERS: 1999

Grand Prix	Mika Häkkinen	Michael Schumacher	David Coulthard	Eddie Irvine	Rubens Barrichello	Heinz-Harald Frentzen	Johnny Herbert	Ralf Schumacher	Giancarlo Fisichella	Mika Salo	Damon Hill	Total
Australia	17	–	–	40	–	–	–	–	–	–	–	57
Brazil	38	11	–	–	23	–	–	–	–	–	–	72
San Marino	17	27	18	–	–	–	–	–	–	–	–	62
Monaco	–	78	–	–	–	–	–	–	–	–	–	78
Spain	61	–	4	–	–	–	–	–	–	–	–	65
Canada	40	29	–	–	–	–	–	–	–	–	–	69
France	6	11	4	–	44	7	–	–	–	–	–	72
Britain	24	–	31	2	–	2	–	–	–	–	1	60
Austria	–	–	39	32	–	–	–	–	–	–	–	71
Germany	24	–	–	20	–	–	–	–	–	1	–	45
Hungary	77	–	–	–	–	–	–	–	–	–	–	77
Belgium	–	–	44	–	–	–	–	–	–	–	–	44
Italy	29	–	–	–	–	23	–	–	–	1	–	53
Europe	–	–	5	–	–	32	17	8	4	–	–	66
Malaysia	–	17	–	39	–	–	–	–	–	–	–	56
Japan	50	3	–	–	–	–	–	–	–	–	–	53
Total	383	176	145	133	67	64	17	8	4	2	1	1000
(Per cent)	38.3	17.6	14.5	13.3	6.7	6.4	1.7	0.8	0.4	0.2	0.1	(100)

RETIREMENTS: 1999

Number of cars to have retired

Grand Prix	Starters	at ¼ distance	at ½ distance	at ¾ distance	at full distance	percentage
Australia	22	5	12	13	14	63.6
Brazil	21	2	6	12	13	61.9
San Marino	22	4	7	9	14	63.6
Monaco	22	2	9	13	14	63.6
Spain	22	1	4	8	9	40.9
Canada	22	6	9	11	12	54.5
France	22	3	9	10	10	45.5
Britain	22	3	4	6	6	27.3
Austria	22	1	4	6	9	40.9
Germany	22	5	9	10	12	54.5
Hungary	22	2	3	4	6	27.3
Belgium	22	1	2	5	6	27.3
Italy	22	4	6	10	12	54.5
Europe	22	4	5	10	13	59.1
Malaysia	22	7	8	9	11	50.0
Japan	22	2	4	6	9	40.9

HEIDFELD'S

YEAR

by Simon Arron

Left: After coming close to the F3000 title in 1998, Nick Heidfeld made no mistake in his second attempt with the West Competition team demolishing the opposition.

Bottom row: Formula 1 will welcome Heidfeld next season. The German *(left)* takes a seat in the Prost team which, ironically, could have gone to Stéphane Sarrazin *(centre)*. Bruno Junqueira *(right)* showed searing pace, but also a few rough edges, and should be a leading F3000 contender in 2000.

All photographs: Paul-Henri Cahier

I T is unlikely there was any worthier racing champion than Nick Heidfeld in 1999. Thrust into an apparent no-win situation, he emerged with his reputation enhanced in a series that put pressure on young drivers like never before.

Heidfeld started the year as clear favourite for the FIA Formula 3000 Championship crown, an inevitable by-product of his having run previous title-holder Juan Pablo Montoya so close in 1998. He had the benefit of continuity with West Competition, junior arm of McLaren-Mercedes, but simply winning the title would not be enough; that much was expected. If he wanted credit for his achievements, nothing less than total domination would do. And he was utterly convincing in what was arguably the year's most competitive form of racing.

The FIA F3000 series scaled new heights of popularity in 1999. A curtain-raiser at all European Grands Prix bar Monza, it attracted more than 20 teams – when the sport's power-brokers ideally wanted a maximum of 15. Within the framework of the TV-sensitive F1 timetable, just two 45-minute qualifying sessions were possible – and drivers were split into groups to practise just once each. There was no scope for fussing about set-ups or technical minutiae. It was a case of jumping in and making the most of what you had. And while Heidfeld readily admitted his West Lola wasn't always quite to his taste, it only once stopped him qualifying in the top six. Of more than 40 drivers who took part, he was one of only eight who made the cut for every race. And he was unique in always being at the front.

'Our car tended to be slightly better in a racing situation than it was in qualifying,' said David Brown, head of the West team and former F1 engineer for the likes of Ayrton Senna, Alain Prost, Nigel Mansell and Damon Hill. 'The great thing about Nick was that he was always able to drag a time from it – and that's a mark of class.'

At the start of the year the 22-year-old German was formidable in the races and four wins from the first six of 10 rounds had more or less put him out of rivals' reach by July. Had he not been penalised for speeding past a caution flag in Monaco, he would have won five of the first six races. Given that the whole field was seldom covered by much more than one second per lap, his ability to find that vital last fraction of speed was awesome.

Having the backing from McLaren, Mercedes and West was all very well – but there were better-heeled teams out

there that struggled to compete at anything like the same level.

'It doesn't matter how good your equipment is,' Heidfeld said, 'you still have to use it properly. We had the right people and a good team that worked very, very hard. That was the key. Just painting the car silver isn't enough to win you races.'

Some believed Heidfeld benefited because the team was focused entirely on him – and pointed to the fact that his highly-rated team-mate, 1998 British F3 champion Mario Haberfeld, failed to qualify for half the races and didn't score a single point.

Brown winced at the suggestion. 'I want both cars up there at the front,' he said. 'The trouble is that the ultra-short qualifying gives new drivers very little chance if they have a problem – and Mario wasn't the only F3 graduate to suffer as a result.'

To prove the point about parity, Heidfeld took over Haberfeld's car after his was sidelined during one qualifying session – and promptly lapped at the same speed he had with his own.

Heidfeld made just one conspicuously silly mistake all season – when he crashed while trying to take the lead at Hockenheim – and clinched the title by applying a common-sense approach when it was called for. He leaves the formula with a share of Montoya's record as the most successful FIA F3000 racer of all time (with seven career victories) and a Prost Grand Prix contract in his pocket. That's the good news – but it needs to be the start of a trend. The fact remains that Heidfeld is the first FIA F3000 champion to graduate directly to F1 since 1993 – which is not a great statistic for a formula with one-make rules conceived to make it easier to identify the stars of the future.

Back-to-back victories in the final two races salvaged a difficult season for Jason Watt (Super Nova) and made him distant runner-up to Heidfeld, but the Dane took little pleasure in the final outcome.

Second place had seemed certain to go to the popular Uruguayan Gonzalo Rodriguez (Astromega), but his death while practising for a Champ Car race in September cast a pall over the season. Rodriguez, 27, had scored the third F3000 victory of his career at Monaco earlier in the year but lost ground to Heidfeld during a mid-season lull that no title contender could afford.

Gonzalo's final start, at Spa, was a fitting epitaph to a charismatic, no-nonsense racer. Scything through from the fifth row of the grid, he passed a clutch of people before spinning and having to pass them again. He then

239

FORMULA 3000 REVIEW

Jason Watt took end-of-season victories at Spa *(left)* and Nürburgring. Sadly, the talented Danish driver *(below)* subsequently suffered serious injuries in a road accident which ended his career.

Bottom far left: Studies in concentration: of Max Wilson *(above)* and Nick Heidfeld *(below)*.

Bottom centre: Nicolas Minassian powers away from the Silverstone grid to score a memorable win for Kid Jensen racing.

All photographs: Paul-Henri Cahier

completed the last few laps with precious little water in his engine and the temperature gauge off the clock – but still finished second. His post-race smile said it all and that's how we will remember him.

Clearly moved, Watt dedicated his subsequent Nürburgring win to Rodriguez's memory – a classy and appropriate gesture.

Barely had the season finished, however, than the series was dealt a fresh blow when the Dane suffered paralysing injuries in a motorcycle crash. For the second time in as many months, the F3000 community was left reeling.

Heidfeld might have landed a Prost deal next year, but the French team was officially supposed to be grooming Stéphane Sarrazin for F1. Its junior arm, Gauloises Formula, made a sluggish start, however, and Sarrazin didn't show race-winning potential until the second half of the season – known in the trade as 'too late'. His sole win in Hungary owed a little to opportunism in traffic, but it was the least he deserved. He generally drove well – and going from 26th to sixth at the A1-Ring was exceptional – but he still demonstrated an occasional impetuous streak. With a little polish, however, he'll make it.

Brazilian Bruno Junqueira (Petrobras) is already favoured to succeed Heidfeld after a slightly rough-and-tumble season that underlined his searing pace and adventurous racecraft. His lone win, at Hockenheim, was just reward after he zipped past team-mate Max Wilson at about 170 mph... with two wheels on the grass. It was one hell of a move, and, to many, he was the revelation of the season. A few too many scrapes scotched his title chances, but it was an impressive year nonetheless.

The only other winner was Frenchman Nicolas Minassian, who gave disc jockey Kid Jensen's fledgling team a memorable lights-to-flag victory at Silverstone. This was probably the most painful moment of the season for team West, which had sacked Minassian the previous autumn on the grounds that he apparently wasn't fast enough...

As for the rest, there were flashes of real promise from several rookies, notably Rodriguez's team-mate Justin Wilson and Frenchman Franck Montagny (DAMS), and the fact that 23 drivers scored points finishes underlined the closeness of the competition. Only one driver, however, stood out on a consistent basis – and he scored almost twice as many points as his closest challenger. Truly, this was Nick Heidfeld's year.

Gonzalo Rodriguez

Paul-Henri Cahier

ON October 5 1999, the church in Silverstone village was packed as the racing world paid tribute to Gonzalo Rodriguez, who was killed at Laguna Seca, California on September 11, while practising for what would have been his second Champ Car race.

The 27-year-old Uruguayan had been a popular member of the British racing community since 1994 – and had established his credentials as a star of the future with some fine performances during three seasons in the FIA F3000 series.

He was dovetailing a limited Champ Car programme with his F3000 commitments as reward for some excellent testing performances with top American team Penske Racing, and had already created a fine impression. Influential people were working behind the scenes to secure him a top drive Stateside in 2000 and Gonzalo was looking to the future with rightful optimism.

Despite his success, Gonzalo Rodriguez never forgot those who helped him in his early days. He had time – and a ready smile – for everyone whose path he crossed. The sport has lost a real character and a great natural talent – and I am but one of many that will miss him sorely.

Simon Arron

TO THE MANOR BORN

by Marcus Simmons

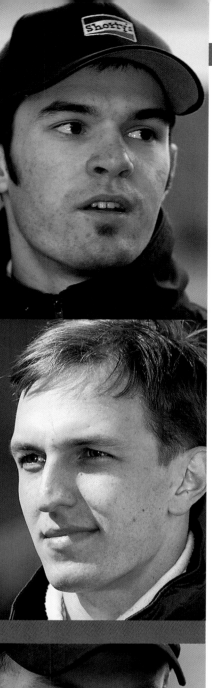

Top left: **A fairy-tale win for one of the less well-financed of teams, Manor Motorsports and Marc Hynes** *(above, top).* **The 21-year old driver from Gloucestershire was a worthy champion.**
Both photographs: Lorenzo Bellanca/LAT Photographic

Above, centre: **The excellent Luciano Burti driving for Paul Stewart Racing was runner-up.**
Gary Hawkins/LAT Photographic

Left and above: **Star of the future? Jenson Button took three wins in his maiden F3 season. The youngster has the talent and backing to reach the top.**
Both photographs: Lorenzo Bellanca/LAT Photographic

THE 1999 season was one of both ignominy and huge promise for Formula 3. While the category's class of 1998 largely failed miserably in Formula 3000, the 1999 crop produced a spellbinding season and at least five drivers who could have the potential to not only star in the more senior class, but make it right to the very top.

Nowhere was the action more compelling than in Britain, where homegrown talent Marc Hynes waged a thrilling battle for the championship with Brazilian Luciano Burti. To these two, add teenage sensation Jenson Button, Dutchman Christijan Albers – who took the German series by storm – and British expat Darren Manning (the runaway Japanese champion) for your most likely quintet of future superstars.

The Hynes versus Burti duel in Britain was one right out of the same mould which brought the classic Senna–Brundle season of 1983, and even Piquet–Warwick in 1978. In the Senna/Piquet corner, 24-year old Burti was entering his second year in F3, remaining with the Stewart Racing squad with which he had made such a good impression during his rookie campaign. In the Brundle/Warwick camp, 21-year old Hynes had switched from the Promatecme team to Manor Motorsport, an outfit virtually unbeatable in Formula Renault but which had never started an F3 race.

New to F3 they may have been, but the Manor boys were old friends to Hynes, who had won his Renault title in 1997 with them before embarking on his disappointing maiden F3 season. For the 21-year-old from Gloucestershire, this would be the last chance to remain on the bandwagon of rated racing talent.

Armed with the ubiquitous Italian Dallara chassis (used by nearly everyone in British F3) and the Neil Brown-tuned Mugen Honda engine (again, as raced by the majority in the series), Hynes got off to a flying start by winning the first two rounds. That gave him the foundations to build on during the season. Three more wins were to come his way, one of them in the prestigious British Grand Prix support race, as well as the showcase Marlboro Masters of F3 'European championship' at Dutch track Zandvoort.

Hynes finally wrapped up the title with a scrappy fourth place in the final round at Thruxton to complete a fairy-tale season for Manor, one in which team boss and chief engineer John Booth proved you don't need huge budgets or banks of data to succeed in F3. In fact, Hynes probably spent barely a third of some others on his season and tested less than most of the rest of the field. He drove beautifully, bringing the car home in the points in every one of the 16 races. When he was off the pace, his cool head brought its reward. A really deserving champion.

Burti also deserved the championship, but ultimately was pipped into the runner-up spot. For much of the season the Stewart team was in trouble. The new-for-1999 Dallara was sufficiently different to all that had gone before to render much of the veteran team's set-up information useless, so that Burti's spectacular driving style, right up until September, was required to drag competitive times out of his Dallara-Mugen. Then his racecraft would nearly always allow him a place in the top three.

Nowhere was this more evident than at Brands Hatch, where an inspired Burti shook off everything a train of five following cars could throw at him to win in what appeared to be one of the slowest cars in the field.

By autumn Stewart, after some intensive testing, had figured out the F399 Dallara and Burti was back on form to battle with Hynes at both Spa and Silverstone. But the *Sao Paulista* was a touch too ruthless in both events, and was excluded from third place at the latter track for swerving into Hynes at the start. It's easy to say that this is what cost the crown, but a championship is decided over 16 races, not just one. In reality, the driver's and team's inability to get its car as consistently close to the pace as Hynes and Manor is what decided the contest.

Best of the rest was Button, who took three wins in his rookie F3 season with the Renault-powered Promatecme team. The 19-year-old from Somerset made plenty of mistakes, but this was only his second season out of karts. Button has blistering pace and, allied to that, probably the best set-up chassis in F3, although there were always question marks over its French powerplant, preparation of which was handed over for 1999 from RPM to the Renault touring car engine tuner Sodemo.

This young man exudes star quality and, at the end of the season, was agonising over the tricky decision of whether to stay in F3 for a second season (for which he would be clear title favourite) or make an early step to Formula 3000.

The other two to win a race in Britain were Dane Kristian Kolby and Indian Narain Karthikeyan. The former lined up for his second season with Fortec Motorsport and took a lucky victory at Pembrey when Button was penalised for an alleged jump start. Too often Kolby and his talented British rookie team mate Matt Davies were left struggling in qualifying and would need to use their tremendous racecraft to battle into prominent race positions.

Karthikeyan hooked up with Carlin Motorsport, with which he'd run a half-season in 1998, and scored two brilliant wins at Brands Hatch, but was inconsistent elsewhere.

Other drivers of whom much had been expected had awful seasons. Scottish Formula Opel ace Andrew Kirkaldy seemed to suffer a crisis of confidence in the second Stewart seat, South African Toby Scheckter – son of 1979 F1 World Champion Jody – only got into the swing of things in the middle of summer with Speedsport, while charming Brazilian Aluizio Coelho stepped up as British Formula Renault champ to Promatecme and showed speed but little in the way of racecraft.

The National Class for year-old cars was, as expected, dominated by the brilliant Martin O'Connell in his Rowan Racing Dallara-Toyota, although he was beaten twice in late-season races by impressive Japanese newcomer Takuma Sato, who looks an excellent prospect.

In the German championship, Albers shook off some persistently bad luck to win the title with a race to spare in his Bertram Schafer Racing Dallara-Opel. Chief among his rivals were Swiss Marcel Fassler, lining up with the new-to-F3 Bemani team, Thomas Jager and Austrian Robert Lechner. All were regular front-runners, but had no answer to Albers's blinding speed.

A Magny-Cours-built Martini-Opel chassis won the French title for the first time since Yannick Dalmas in 1986, the bespectacled La Filière driver Sebastien Bourdais doing the deed. His main opposition came from the Signature Dallara-Renault squad of Jonathan Cochet and Benoit Treluyer, who won the Pau street race against both domestic and Italian opposition.

The Italian championship went to Swede Peter Sundberg in the Prema Power Dallara-Opel from the similar RC Motorsport-run car of Gianluca Calcagni. This series turned nasty in mid-summer at Enna-Pergusa, when Calcagni forced Sundberg off the road and briefly had his racing licence under threat, and culminated when they tangled at Imola's Tamburello chicane in the final round.

Manning cruised to the Japanese title with six wins in a row in his TOM'S Dallara-Toyota. There were four other 'gai-jin' westerners in the series, but they were all beaten by local talents Toshihiro Kaneishi and Tsugio Matsuda.

Lastly, the South American championship had a vintage year which ended with ex-British Formula Renault Championship racer Hoover Orsi vanquishing far better-funded rivals in his Cesario Formula Dallara-Mugen.

HIGH-FLYERS

by Gary Watkins

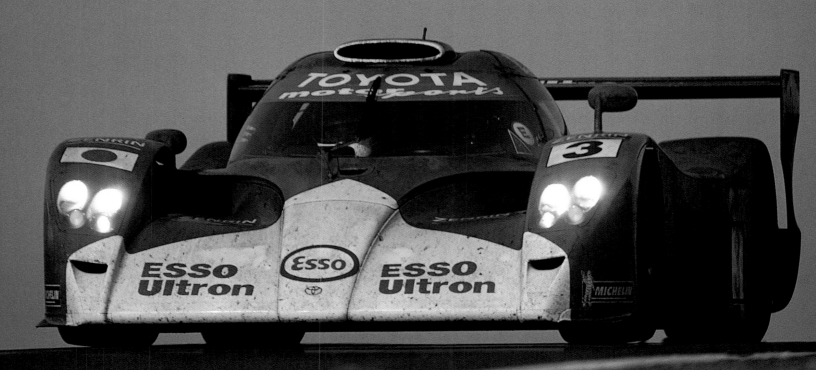

Left (from top): Spectators watch TV pictures of Peter Dumbreck's Mercedes CLR launching itself into orbit; Ukyo Katayama waits patiently during a pit stop as the Toyota is repaired following a contretemps with a privateer BMW; a scheduled stop for the Number 2 Toyota of Boutsen, McNish and Kelleners; Audi returned with the R8R, a formidable contender.

Top far left: Glorious victory at Le Mans for BMW and Pierluigi Martini (pictured) with team-mates Yannick Dalmas and Jo Winkelhock.

Bottom far left: Toyota ran the Munich marque close with the Number 3 car of Ukyo Katayama, Toshio Suzuki and Keiichi Tsuchia.

All photographs: Paul-Henri Cahier

THE 67th running of the Le Mans 24 Hours had all the makings of a classic. The best in the history of the event, some predicted. More manufacturers than ever before lined up for a shot at sports car racing's big prize, more money was thrown at the event by the mega-buck factory teams, and more top-line drivers were brought in from around the world. When it all came down to it, the race didn't live up to expectation, though it assured its place in the history books for all the wrong reasons.

The final Le Mans of the 20th century will be remembered not for the race itself, but for the series of aerial accidents that hit the AMG Mercedes team. Three times did one of the German squad's CLR GT racers take off while nudging 200 mph, three times the airborne car flipped and, miraculously, three times the driver was able to walk from his silver wreck.

Mercedes sports boss Norbert Haug claimed that the manufacturer 'had done everything possible to prepare for the race', but the Three-Pointed Star's campaign started to come off the rails almost before it had begun. In Le Mans pre-qualifying in May, Australian Mark Webber crashed at high-speed on the Mulsanne Straight after a wishbone pulled out of the monocoque. What's more, the other two CLRs languished down the times, and the paddock pundits were already claiming that, come the race, the Silver Arrows would be no match for pre-event favourites Toyota and BMW.

For a while, it looked as though the Mercs wouldn't even take the start in June. Webber suffered his second major accident in a CLR in Thursday's second qualifying session when his car took off while following another car through the series of flat-out kinks between the Mulsanne and Indianapolis corners. He repeated his somersault on his first lap out of the pits after the car had been repaired in time for Saturday morning's race day warm-up. As the Australian clambered from his upside-down wreck, the prospects of either of the two remaining Mercs starting the race looked slim.

However, the go-ahead was given to start the event, though with minor aerodynamic modifications made to both cars and instructions given to the drivers not to follow other cars too closely. Just over four hours into the race, it looked like a fateful decision. Scot Peter Dumbreck somersaulted out of the slipstream of Thierry Boutsen's Toyota. The car narrowly missed an overhead advertising 'bridge' and landed on the wrong side of the barriers.

The remaining CLR was immediately withdrawn. Haug claimed the three crashes were isolated incidents. 'With the data we had on Saturday morning, we were convinced of having made the right decision to start,' he said.

The Mercedes' problem is believed to have been a multifaceted one. Modern GT cars, with their long bodywork overhangs, are extremely pitch sensitive. In fact, a Porsche sustained a similar accident in the 1998 Petit Le Mans race at Road Atlanta in the US. Merc's car appears to have been more sensitive than the rest, a problem exacerbated by running the rear end soft to try to increase straight-line speed. What's more, the majority of AMG's testing had been undertaken at the Fontana oval in the US, a track far removed from Le Mans.

The full reason for the accidents might never be known, but what is clear is that the incident brought Merc's short return to sports car racing to an abrupt end. By now, the prospects of a revival of the DTM touring car series in Germany was gaining momentum, giving the marque the perfect pretext to slide silently from the stage.

Amid the controversy, it was easy to forget there was a race at Le Mans this year, and one that kept the crowd on the edge of its seats for much of the way. The only problem was that the event turned into a two-horse race almost from the start. Toyota and BMW were the only manufacturers in with a chance, although it's worth noting that Dumbreck was challenging for second when he crashed.

Formula 1 racer-turned-commentator Martin Brundle notched up his first Le Mans pole in an illustrious sports car career, but his designs on victory were again dogged by ill-fortune. The Toyota GT-One driver led the early laps before hydraulic problems forced the car out of contention.

After Brundle's Toyota dropped back, the race then developed into a straight fight between the lead BMW V12 LMR of J.J. Lehto, Jörg Müller and Tom Kristensen and the GT-One Thierry Boutsen shared with Allan McNish and Ralf Kelleners. The two crews swapped the lead back and forth into the hours of darkness until Boutsen suffered a monumental accident at the Dunlop Chicane from which he was lucky to emerge with his life. Within 36 hours the three-time Grand Prix winner had announced his retirement from the sport.

The Toyota's retirement left Lehto and co. with a massive advantage over the second Schnitzer BMW of Yannick Dalmas, Piérluigi Martini and Jo Winkelhock. The lead V12 LMR was three laps up when the most bizarre of problems robbed Lehto and Kristensen of second Le Mans victories, Müller of his first. An anti-roll bar broke and swung down into the pedal assembly, jamming open Lehto's loud pedal and forcing him into the barriers with not inconsiderable force.

The departure of one Williams-built BMW left another in the lead, though the sole-surviving Toyota was not far behind. The Japanese crew of Ukyo Katayama, Toshio Suzuki and Keiichi Tsuchiya kept the Schnitzer squad under pressure to the end. Remarkably, both teams kept their best to last, and Martini ended up with a new lap record courtesy of his efforts to keep ahead.

In fact, the Toyota Team Europe squad believed that Katayama could have overhauled Martini had he not had to make an unscheduled tyre stop after he was unceremoniously put on the kerbs by a privateer BMW. 'In all my years in motor racing I have never seen anything like that,' said TTE boss Ove Andersson after his Toyota took the chequered flag the line a lap behind the winner.

Le Mans 1999 was the year of the tortoise. The slowest of the BMW and Toyota entries finished first and second, while third and fourth positions were taken by a manufacturer that also set a conservative pace. Le Mans debutant Audi's R8R prototypes could not match the speed of the BMWs and Toyotas, but a steady run from Frank Biela, Didier Theys and Emanuele Pirro netted a podium for the marque on its debut. The second Joest-managed car's run was no more competitive, and not as reliable. No fewer than three changes of gearbox left it four laps behind its sister.

Audi's R8R had began its competition career in the Sebring 12 Hours, the first round of the new American Le Mans Series. The German marque was expected to contest some races after the French enduro, but decided instead to concentrate on Le Mans 2000.

BMW did take the plunge, however, and entered the second half of the championship, which ran to the same rule book as the 24 Hours in France. Schnitzer had already contested – and won – Sebring, but its full-time participation in series began on a sour note when it withdrew both its cars from round three at Mosport in Canada, citing circuit safety. This withdrawal, coupled with the fact that Lehto was robbed of his Sebring points by an administration error, meant the Finn faced an almost impossible uphill battle

The atmosphere of Le Mans 1999.

Above: The Audi R8R blasts down the main straight past the pits.

Left: The Mercedes CLR of Bouchut, Heidfeld and Dumbreck lay second at one stage before its spectacular accident.

Top right: The new Nissan R391 overtakes the Courage-Porsche of Pescarolo, Ferte and Gay. Pescarolo was taking part in his 33rd Sarthe start.

Classy rear ends! The CLR *(above right)* dwarfed by the Viper through one of the chicanes, while the traditional bevy of Hawaiian Tropic beauties *(right)* surround the Audi.

All photographs: Paul-Henri Cahier

Left: Don Panoz's faith in his front-engined monsters was richly rewarded throughout the season.
Paul-Henri Cahier

Below left: Karl Wendlinger *(left)*, enjoying his racing again, dominated the GT2 class with Olivier Beretta and their Chrysler Viper *(right)*.
Both photographs: Shutterspeed Fotografik

Bottom left: Emmanuel Collard and Vincente Sospiri campaigned their Ferrari 333SP *(left)* in the newly-tagged SportsRacing World Cup. Lola *(right)* provided a successful challenger in the hands of DAMS regular Eric Bernard.
Both photographs: Dave Cundy

GT RACING REVIEW

if he was going to claim the title. His cause wasn't helped when team-mate Jörg Müller, one of the Sebring winners, spun out of the lead of Petit Le Mans with only three laps to go. The German driver's mistake handed a third victory in the series to Panoz.

The ALMS, founded by Don Panoz, was undoubtedly sports car racing's success story in 1999. The series attracted monster entries and the racing at the front was always close. With the promise of more manufacturers and four races outside North America, the ALMS looked set to go from strength to strength in 2000. The only cloud on the horizon was a rival series set up by NASCAR's ruling family. Grand-Am, which encompassed the Daytona 24 Hours, threatened to steal away many of the smaller teams.

Factory-supported sports car racing was fairly thin on the ground in Europe in 1999. The withdrawal of Mercedes and Porsche at the end of last year forced the FIA GT Championship to downgrade to a series for slower GT2-type cars, such as Chrysler Vipers and Porsche 911s. The former was the dominant car over the 10-race series in the hands of the ORECA factory team. Such was its supremacy that it took until round eight, at Homestead in the US, for the French squad to suffer its first defeat. The team still had something to celebrate in Florida, though, because former Grand Prix drivers Olivier Beretta and Karl Wendlinger wrapped up the title.

The International SportsRacing Series, now in its second full year, continued to grow, if unspectacularly. A couple of races into the year the championship got a new name in the SportsRacing World Cup. Even without its new tag, it still edged the FIA GT Championship for the title of the most prestigious sports car series in Europe. Grids fluctuated dramatically, but at least defending champions Emmanuel Collard and Vincenzo Sospiri didn't have all things their own way in the JB team Ferrari 333SP, in which they won all bar one race in 1998. Two more crews relying on the ageing Italian chassis notched up race wins, while the French DAMS squad claimed a mid-season hat-trick with its new Lola B98/10.

A classic year for sports car racing? Few would claim that for 1999. A typical one? Most definitely. The seeds of recovery were there but, as ever in this arena, fraction and schism served to keep a good sport down. That's probably why the last 12 months of sports car racing's first century will be remembered for airborne Mercedes.

VOLVO
6 YEARS AT THE TOP

by Marcus Simmons

IN future years, when motorsport nostalgia freaks look back at the British Touring Car Championship's vintage Super Touring era, two driver and car combinations will stand out as the most consistently successful.

While the fortunes of Alfa Romeo, Audi, Vauxhall and BMW waxed and waned, Volvo and Renault – represented by tin-top superstars Rickard Rydell and Alain Menu respectively – have won races year after year, and each has netted a BTCC title.

The 1998 season was a real *tour de force* for Rydell and his Volvo S40. As well as taking the BTCC crown, he took victory in the classic Bathurst 1000 endurance race at Australia's mighty Mount Panorama circuit, sharing with veteran local hero Jim Richards.

It all started back in 1994, when the respected TWR organisation joined forces with Volvo for their first season in the BTCC with the 850 Estate. It may have been an unlikely

weapon, but it allowed a learning year in the hotly competitive arena, with no outside expectations of race wins and a lot of publicity wherever the team went.

Experienced Dutchman Jan Lammers, a Le Mans 24-Hours winner with the TWR Jaguar squad, was signed as lead driver, with Swedish single-seater ace Rydell as his back-up.

'I was a bit of an unknown in touring cars, but touring cars were unknown for me as well,' remembers Rydell. 'I had never raced a front-wheel drive car. Jan knew a lot of the people in the team and had the chief designer engineering his car, but I got someone who was new to touring cars at the time.'

That 'someone' was ex-Formula 1 engineer John Gentry, who would go on to design the 850 saloon and do the initial work on the title-winning S40. 'I was lucky because we struck up a good relationship,' says Rydell. 'Some people have more problems adapting

to touring cars than others I guess, but I thought it was really easy. The Estate was perhaps not the best car, but it was the right thing to do at the time.'

In fact, Rydell's results were good enough to seriously worry other teams. That year, 1994, Alfa Romeo also entered the BTCC with the spectacular bewinged 155. It forced a rules clarification in which manufacturers were told they could run with front and rear aerodynamics. It wasn't lost on TWR that the 850 Estate would be impossible to convert to such a specification...

'If we'd made an estate car for 1995 it would have been very good,' opines Rydell. 'That's one reason why they introduced the wings I believe, because it didn't look very good for the others with the Volvo beating them!'

That promise was backed up in 1995 with the saloon, which Rydell took to a record number of pole positions and third place in the championship. 'We were on Dunlop tyres,' recounts Rydell, 'and they were very

Top (from left): The 850 Estate which caught the imagination of the public in Volvo's first BTCC campaign way back in 1994; the highly competitive 850 saloon which took a record number of pole positions the following year; and its successor, the S40, which crosses the line to the delight of the team on the pit wall as Rydell claims the car's first win in 1996.

Above: The S40 in its final season with Volvo's star driver Rickard Rydell at the wheel.

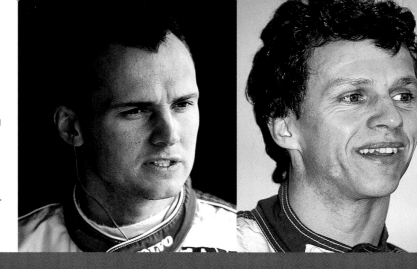

Right (from left): Volvo's roster of driving talent over the past six years of the BTCC: Rickard Rydell, Jan Lammers, Tim Harvey, Kelvin Burt, Gianni Morbidelli and Vincent Radermecker.

Below (from left): The 850 saloon in action at Silverstone, 1995; Rydell gives the S40 its first win at Brands Hatch in 1996; a successful trip to Australia – Volvo win the highly-prized Bathurst race.

Bottom: Rydell and Volvo S40 show the rest a clean pair of heels as the Swede heads for the 1998 BTCC title.

good in qualifying, but they didn't last very well over a race distance. We were close to winning the championship anyway.'

Tim Harvey, the 1992 Champion, backed up Rydell that year and took a fine fifth in the title chase. 'I learnt quite a lot from him,' the Swede declares. 'He's a very fun guy, really good with the sponsors and team and good at motivating the mechanics. He was always up there.'

Sadly for Harvey, his career took a downswing with a move to Peugeot for 1996, his replacement coming from the world of single-seaters. But for new boy Kelvin Burt it was a tough time in touring cars. He took Volvo's first win of 1996 at Silverstone, but then had a massive accident at Oulton Park which he was lucky to survive. Even now the Briton admits he returned to the cockpit too soon, and he was put well into the shade by his team leader through the remainder of that season and 1997.

The 1996 campaign was still a good one for Rydell. Now on Michelins, he again took third in the rankings, but the boxy shape of the 850 was beginning to tell. 'There was a lot of development going on and the Volvo was quite big compared to most of the other cars,' explains Rydell. 'They all improved more than we thought they would, especially the championship-winning Audi.'

Into the ring came the swoopy S40, a svelte machine which was heralded as a potential 1997 champion, but Rydell refused to get carried away: 'A lot of cars went faster that year and Alain Menu was very quick and won the championship. It's always the case when you build a car for the first time – you're not going to get 100% out of

it because you notice things that you could have done better, which we did with the S40.' Nevertheless, fourth in the championship brought reward after a difficult season marked by the departure of Gentry, who was replaced as designer by his former TWR understudy Brendan Gribben.

His work produced a masterpiece for 1998, the second S40 taking Rydell to the title. 'After our first test with that car we thought we had something in hand,' remembers the Swede. 'At the first race we were closer to 100% than the others. We did really well, with 17 podium places out of 26 races and no mechanical failures.'

Italian team mate Gianni Morbidelli didn't show so well. The ex-Grand Prix driver struggled to get to grips with contemporary Super Tourers and the battling style of his BTCC opposition, and returned home to lick his wounds at the end of the year.

Relatively unknown Belgian Vincent Radermecker was drafted in as his replacement for 1999 after impressing in a test. He did a good job backing up Rydell throughout the season, playing his part in a strong title defence which ended with the Volvo number one occupying third place in the manufacturer's last season of its six-year stint in the BTCC.

With Nissan getting its act together with the Primera, which boasted a supremely powerful engine, the other makes had to update their now ageing powerplants to squeeze yet more speed out of them.

'The Nissan Primera was a faster car,' says Rydell, 'so the team needed to improve the engine a lot for 1999. You win some and lose some, but we had a very good season.'

In fact, six very good seasons.

RICKARD RYDELL: SPEEDY SWEDE

NOW 32, Rickard Rydell has packed a great deal into his car racing career. From a family of Stockholm florists, as a teenager he attracted the attention of Swedish racing veteran Picko Troberg, who pushed his young protégé from local Formula 3 racing into the hotbed of the British series.

Troberg is still Rydell's manager today, his familiar white walrus moustache doing its best to hide an always beaming face which looks down on his superstar in much the same way as would a kindly uncle.

Rydell was an instant success in Britain, winning his first F3 race in the country in early 1989 for the Eddie Jordan Racing team. He stayed in the UK for three seasons, also racing in Formula 3000, before moving to Japan in 1992.

That season he battled for the title with future BTCC rival Anthony Reid, who would fight him for the tin-top crown in 1998, and a young Canadian by the name of Jacques Villeneuve... The future touring car stars triumphed, Reid winning the championship and Rydell the blue riband Macau Grand Prix. A second year brought him more success, before the call came from TWR to drive its new Volvo Estate.

'I might have been in F1 if I'd stayed in Japan to do F3000!' grins Rydell. 'There are a lot of drivers in F1 that I've raced against that I know I could beat, but having said that I'm really pleased to have done the BTCC.

'It's a good fun championship and I've been working with Volvo all the time. I hope to continue that relationship. I couldn't really ask for any more – it's been perfect.'

Volvo may be out of the BTCC for now, but Rydell has been loaned to parent company Ford for next season. 'If Volvo do have another programme then I will be their driver. They're still keen on motor racing and wanted to keep me, which is one of the reasons why I'm driving for Ford. If it hadn't been for that I would have gone to another series.'

FORM AN ORDERLY QUEUE

by Charles Bradley

TOURING CAR RACING REVIEW

Far left: The Nissans of Laurent Aïello and David Leslie head the pack at Oulton Park. The Primera was the dominant car of the 1999 season.
Shutterspeed Fotografik

Above left: Matt Neal a privateer winner at Donington on the podium with Rickard Rydell.

Left: John Cleland finally called time on his touring car career.
Both photographs: Bothwell Photographic

Above: Laurent Aïello was the class act of the BTCC series and thoroughly deserved his title.
Bothwell Photographic

Left: Rickard Rydell fought tooth and nail to retain the driver's crown but enjoyed little luck in the Volvo.
Dave Cundy

TOURING car racing has been one of the biggest success stories of the 1990s. Manufacturers have flocked to the FIA-mandated, two-litre Super Touring regulations like moths around a 100-watt light-bulb as they have provided fans (i.e.: the car buying public) with a breath-taking and, more importantly, tele-genic spectacle. A kind of all-singing, all-dancing garage forecourt, if you like.

But when you're playing for high stakes, only the big money competitors are going to win. Suddenly, manufacturers began to pull the plug on their increasingly expensive touring car programmes.

The first cracks appeared last year when both Audi and Peugeot – stalwarts of both the British and German championships – elected to withdraw its multi-million-pound works support from both. The German Supertourenwagen Cup (STW) also lost its factory BMW, Ford and Nissan backing to boot over a period of just two seasons, leaving it with only Opel and Honda to see it through 1999. It is currently in turmoil, with series organiser, the ADAC, joining forces with the Italian CSAI to promote a Euro-STW series in 2000. Italy, too, was forced to struggle on this year with interest from just Alfa Romeo and the Italian BMW and Audi importers. It is simply a case of the championships joining forces to avoid plunging into the abyss.

More bad news for the German series is the resurrection of the big-banger DTM series for five-litre, V8-powered cars. Mercedes and Opel are once again behind the movement and expect Alfa Romeo to follow suit. If the movement can keep a lid on costs this time, the German Super Touring series should start packing its bags and move to Italy full time.

Even the flagship British championship, long regarded as the benchmark by which all others are measured, has hit hard times. The withdrawal of Nissan, Volvo and Renault – ironically the marques behind the last three champion drivers (a coincidence or too much overspending?) – is a severe body blow for the new millennium. But it is hardly a surprising one, and the reasons for it are numerous.

First and foremost, the Super Touring regulations have outgrown their usefulness. Eight years of constant development has seen teams of the calibre of TWR and Williams push the boundaries to their limit, so the only way to go that all-important little bit further is to throw substantial amounts of money around.

Secondly, the trend of manufacturer buy-outs has diluted the competition. Ford has bought into Volvo, Renault has bought into Nissan, and so on. It doesn't take a rocket scientist to work out that bosses at the top of the management tree are soon going to be asking why they're paying twice as much as they need to, just to see two of their own companies try to outdo each other.

Another telling explanation is that Formula One has drawn in so many of the corporate giants that there's precious little money left to spend on mere national championships. The boardroom decision on whether a manufacturer races in touring cars isn't taken in by sportsmen but hard-nosed, account-driven marketing staff. If there's no apparent return from the cost of doing it, then they simply won't.

Many scoffed at Ford's decision to hire Nigel Mansell for a ludicrous six-figure sum to contest just half a dozen races in 1998. But its big chiefs were turning somersaults on Monday morning after he led the Donington Park race, which was beamed live into millions of homes around the country.

The value equation has steadily become less rewarding for manufacturers, and has meant that touring car racing has plunged into a nose-dive. This year we've seen the sad demise of a once virile and exciting formula, but there is light at the end of the tunnel: direct action that could reverse the trend and put the category back in the spotlight for the right reasons.

Last year, British Touring Car Championship organiser TOCA had the foresight to announce new regulations aimed at slashing the costs of touring car racing by half. Daring claims need bold solutions, and it planned to do this by forcing all teams to use a list of 29 common components – from wheels to gearboxes – to ensure that teams could offer their services to manufacturers for less. A reduction in available downforce from aerodynamic devices, plus an all-round wishbone policy and a more open engine formula, should mean that eligible base models that weren't particularly suited to touring cars will no longer be inferior.

This more open playing field should result in increased scope to run more cars for less money. The revolution will occur in Britain in 2001, and TOCA hopes that the combined German and Italian series will adopt its brave new world.

In the meantime, the BTCC will adopt the highly artificial success bal-

last method to slow any runaway winners. This year's fugitive from the chasing pack was Laurent Aïello, who added the British crown to his French and German titles. This was Aïello's first season in Britain and despite a nightmarish start at Donington – where he didn't score a point – a brace of victories on (for him) the virgin soil of the highly testing Thruxton circuit had his opposition quite rightly shaking in their boots.

The reason for his instant success was the supremacy of the Nissan Primera. Even after a ruling which banned its rear wishbone suspension (forcing them to use a less favourable beam axle) and the poaching by Ford of its star from 1998, Anthony Reid, the combined might of Nissan Motorsports Europe and race team Ray Mallock Ltd kept the Primera at the top of the evolutionary scale.

Only last year's champion, TWR Volvo's Rickard Rydell, could hold a torch to them but that was too often extinguished by niggling mechanical failures which he simply didn't suffer the year before when he just beat Reid to the crown. The Swede said he didn't know what bad luck was in '98. He does now, and finished the season in third, just ahead of Honda's James Thompson.

Aïello's biggest opposition in the championship, however, also came from within the Nissan stable. David Leslie, a long-time Mallock cohort and often credited with excellent chassis development skills, finished as runner-up. But the Scot only ever looked like winning the series if Aïello threw it away. The Frenchman had a cutting edge that Leslie simply lacked, and David always looked more prone to getting dragged into any rough-and-tumble antics that were going on around him.

Only a badly-handled team orders fiasco threatened to overshadow Aïello's and Nissan's season. Hours after Laurent was tagged into the Donington pit wall by Renault's Jason Plato, which destroyed his regular race car, Aïello was told to stay behind Leslie in the day's second race – even though he was obviously quicker. Cue many a Gallic shrug for the TV cameras and the odd temper tantrum behind closed doors.

He needn't have worried, though. Despite an unnecessary clash with Plato at Knockhill that got him excluded from the race, Aïello's path was only ruffled by a couple of mechanical dramas in the middle of the season, which merely served to delay his confirmation as Champion until

TEN OUT OF TEN FOR AIELLO PLUS TOP MARKS FOR NEAL

The 1999 Auto Trader BTCC champion Laurent Aiello notched up ten victories and ten pole positions in his Michelin-shod Nissan Primera GT. At the same time, Matt Neal in his Team Dynamics Nissan Primera, also on Michelin, took the Independents' title, winning no fewer than 20 of the 26 races and achieving pole position on 25 occasions. The facts speak for themselves. Fit the tyres fit for champions - Michelin.

The more we progress, the further you go.

www.michelin.co.uk

Right: James Thompson was as brave as ever in the Honda Accord.
Dave Cundy

Below right (from top): Alain Menu struggled with the Ford Mondeo; Snetterton's night race was a big success; Renault are the latest manufacturer to take their leave of the BTCC.

All photographs: Bothwell Photographic

the final round. He even took time out to finish fourth at Le Mans in an Audi – a class act.

Honda looks set to take the leading role in next year's BTCC (barring any independent Nissans with Aïello at the wheel) as its Yorkshire terrier Thompson proved his bravery behind the wheel of a sometimes evil-looking car. Its curvaceous rear windscreen robbed the boot-mounted wing of aerodynamic efficiency and thus starved the back-end of grip, causing Thompson and Peter Kox the odd heart flutter or two in fast corners.

Kox hit the headlines when he won the BTCC's first-ever night race at Snetterton which was a resoundingly successful affair. Fine weather, brilliant racing and a festival atmosphere all added up to a superb event which will be replicated for the Silverstone finale as well next season. TOCA invested about £80,000 in the evening and hired floodlights which cost almost half-a-million pounds each which turned the second half of the circuit into virtual daylight, while the rest was in darkness. Another innovation next year will be the championship's first trip to Ireland as Mondello Park, near Dublin, will play host to two races – and plenty of Guinness-inspired hangovers the day after, no doubt.

While Nissan was the top dog in Britain, honours were shared around the rest of the touring car world. Fabrizio Giovanardi scored a nail-biting win for Alfa Romeo in the Italian Superturismo series after a gripping climax in the final round at Vallelunga against BMW's Emanuele Naspetti. The defeated Naspetti was humble about his failure, labelling his rival as 'the best touring car driver in the world'. Roberto Colciago was third in an Audi A4 Quattro, ahead of Nicola Larini (Alfa Romeo).

The German STW Cup had an even more dramatic finale and the destination of the championship changed hands at the very last corner in the most unsatisfactory fashion. Christian Abt went into the event with a 16-point lead but his battered Audi A4 Quattro, run privately by his family Abt Sportsline team, emerged from the bruising encounter with a 10-point deficit to Uwe Alzen's works Opel Vectra.

Alzen looked set for the title when he led the race in its early stages, but he was passed by Honda's Tom Kristensen. That shifted the crown back towards Abt until the last corner when Roland Asch's Opel Vectra cannoned into the back of him and sent the Audi into the gravel. Asch was being black flagged at the time for ignoring a stop–go penalty (for jumping the start) and he was fined £7,000 for his part in the apparently dark deed.

Alzen was in the wars, too, as he collided with Abt's team-mate, Kris Nissen, while attempting to lap him. Alzen crossed the finish line virtually on three wheels, but Abt's departure from the top three finishers was enough for Opel's man to be crowned as champion. The Abt team, however, has called for the race to be annulled and has appealed to the German governing body, the DMSB, for the result to be overturned.

One country where interest in Super Touring continues to grow is Sweden, where Audi took this year's title thanks to Mattias Ekström, who narrowly overcame Fredrik Ekblom (BMW 320i) and the Nissan Primera of former BTCC Independents Cup Champion Tommy Rustad. Volvo was a disappointing fourth and fifth on home turf and is considering its future participation.

Paul Morris won the TOCA-run Australian Super Touring Championship in his BMW 320i by the narrow margin of two points over Volvo's Jim Richards. Morris also won the prestigious but rain-spoiled Bathurst event, which was run as a 500 km race this season. This made up for his disappointment of 1997 when he was thrown out of the results after winning on the road. Morris again had to overcome the Volvo threat, which was led by Richards and Cameron McLean, who finished ahead of the second S40 of Matthew Coleman and former Ford BTCC racer Craig Baird.

In South America, Emiliano Spataro led the way as AUTOCOURSE closed for press with three rounds remaining in the popular South American Copa de las Naciones series in his Peugeot 406, ahead of EF Racing team-mate Carlos Bueno and former Fittipaldi F1 racer Ingo Hoffmann (BMW 320i). The beleaguered French championship, contested entirely by privateers, was won by William David (Peugeot 406), who pipped the BMW of three-time champion Eric Cayrolle.

The legacy of the Super Touring formula is plain for all to see. Championships across the world have taken on board its regulations and put touring car racing squarely on the map. But the boom time is over and next season will probably see its nadir before the new age of 2001 BTCC rules will once again capture the imaginations of the motor manufacturers.

The future of touring car racing hasn't quite yet begun.

THE FLYING DUTCHMAN STRIKES AGAIN

by Damien Smith

PORSCHE SUPERCUP REVIEW

Left: Three-times Porsche Supercup Champion Patrick Huismann.

Bottom far left: Huismann celebrates his victory in Barcelona.

Bottom left: Ralf Kelleners kicks up the dirt as he holds off Bernd Maylander during the A1-Ring race.

All photographs: Gavin Lawrence/LAT Photographic

RALF Kelleners won his third Porsche Supercup race of the season at Austria's A-1 Ring and the title looked his for the taking. With just four rounds to go he had a seemingly comfortable 22-point lead, but was still cautious – pessimistic, even – about his chances. 'I won't think about the championship,' he said. 'I've already lost a Le Mans win [with Toyota in 1998] in the late stages.'

He was right to be less than confident. In those final four races he never came close to winning again and slumped to fifth in the final points standings. The man who led the chase and grasped the title with both hands was a driver who has become 'Mr Supercup' in the last few years: Patrick Huisman.

This was the Dutchman's hat trick of championships in the Grand Prix-supporting series and was the sweetest by far. 'I was racing against some big names this year,' he said. 'I had to fight all the way to the last race to win this title which was very satisfying. Now I have done everything I can to prove myself.'

In 1997 he won the title through default, and then dominated the following season when his Eschmann-Manthey Racing team got the jump on their rivals. This year, not only did Huisman fight back from a slower start to the year, he also had to battle against a painful injury.

The Supercup kicked off in Australia in 1999, the first time Porsche's flagship one-make series had ventured outside of Europe. Kelleners got off to a cracking start to win the first race with the new GT3 model, while Huisman languished towards the back of the field.

Patrick was on the pace at Imola though, following team-mate Bernd Maylander home for a one-two. He failed to score at Monaco when oil on the circuit caught him out, but bounced back to win in Spain. It was between this race and the next at Silverstone when Huisman's season was almost ruined.

Like many drivers in the Supercup, he had found a ride for the Le Mans 24 Hours in June, driving a Porsche 911 GT2. As the quickest driver in his car, Huisman was expected to do the majority of the stints in the enduro, but it became a painful experience.

Not for the first time, his towering height became a handicap in the confines of a racing car. 'The seating position was very uncomfortable,' he explained. 'I lost all strength in my right side.'

The injury hit him hard when he returned to the Supercup at the British Grand Prix. A trapped nerve in his shoulder was the problem, and it was increased by doctors giving him the wrong treatment. The fact that he finished fifth at Silverstone says everything for his tenacity. 'My arm was so weak, changing gear was like cooking soup,' he remembered.

With hindsight, the Austrian race was the key point of the season. Kelleners won comfortably but still harboured reservations, while Huisman battled through to finish second despite his pain.

So why was Kelleners so unsure of his position? 'Because I didn't know [why] I was winning,' he explained. 'I could never give an answer. That meant I was not surprised we lost the championship. We were lucky to lead it for so long.'

His confidence in the Rhein-Oberberg/Jurgen Alzen Motorsport team appears to have taken a dive after Austria. 'They changed the rear ride height,' he said. 'We might have won, but I knew we would struggle at other circuits.'

He was right. He and the team lost their way as Huisman's momentum grew. Both were off the pace at Hockenheim, but in Hungary the Dutchman won. Kelleners could do no better than fifth. Now with two rounds to go Huisman was in range of Kelleners' points lead.

If Austria was the key race, then Belgium's Spa-Francorchamps round was where the killer blow was struck. Huisman was dominant and won easily. Kelleners qualified badly, hit another car at La Source after the start and retired with a damaged radiator. After the race, a bitter Ralf hid himself away, knowing his chance of the title had all but gone. Meanwhile, Huisman punched the air and played to the crowd. He had won the race, taken the championship lead and had the added bonus of seeing his brother Duncan join him on the podium.

At the Nürburgring finale, Patrick took no chances and took a steady third to make sure of the Supercup crown.

With Kelleners' demise, Porsche regular Oliver Mathai came through to take the runner-up place in the championship. This was his reward for consistency: he may not have won a race, but Oliver finished in the top six in eight of the 10 rounds. Second place at the Nürburgring was his best result of the season and was the result he needed to push Stephane Ortelli down to third.

Ortelli won at Le Mans with Porsche in 1998 and is renowned as a quick driver in sports car circles. But he failed to put together the consistent results he needed to be a true championship contender. A win at Silverstone was his high point, but for the most part he played second fiddle to his Manthey team-mate Huisman.

Other race winners included Bernd Maylander who won at Imola and the Nürburgring, and Roland Asch who conquered Hockenheim. Asch is a Porsche veteran who is known as something of a Hockenheim specialist and he never came near a win anywhere else. Still, such an out-of-the-blue result is always refreshing, as witnessed by Johnny Herbert's win this year in the Formula 1 Nürburgring Grand Prix.

But what of the British challenge? For the first time, a team from the United Kingdom entered the Supercup and great things were expected. Parabolica Motorsport made its name in the FIA GT Championship during 1997, doing a very respectable job with a private McLaren F1-GTR. Now, renamed Parabolica-McCulloch, the team were at least expecting race wins.

The squad started the year with a very strong driver line-up. Johnny Mowlem had impressed with his pace in his rookie Supercup year and was fired up to win in his sophomore season. His team mate was ex-British Formula 3 Champion Oliver Gavin who was attempting to revive his flagging career.

After just one race Gavin was gone, lured by the temptation of a proper crack at the Formula 3000 International Championship. Formula 1 was still on his mind. He was replaced by Parabolica favourite Gary Ayles who was treated as a stop-gap before a full-time replacement could be signed. The team found its man in time for Barcelona and touring car refugee Tim Harvey stepped on board.

Given his lack of time in the car, Harvey did a respectable job, but he was dropped for the last race in favour of F3000 race winner Jason Watt who had some fun in a car with a roof for a change.

Thus, Mowlem had four team-mates in 1999. Hardly a great advert for the team which must do better next year. Mowlem himself again promised much but was left disappointed. His season started well in Australia with a fourth place, but bad luck and mechanical failures proved to be the story of his season. He will hope to stay on for a third crack at this championship in 2000.

As the Supercup moves into the new millennium, Patrick Huisman will finally be hoping to move on from the championship that has served him so well. He wants and needs a chance in a top-line sports car or touring car. His height of 193 cm has always been a hindrance, but he refuses to give in. As 1999 showed, even through pain, this man can deliver the goods.

IF the success of Goodyear's 1999 CART season were judged solely on the number of wins posted by the race tire manufacturer, it would appear to a casual observer to be a disappointing season indeed. However, despite posting only one win in the 20-race 1999 season, Goodyear's race-tire engineers made significant progress in their development and performance efforts, even though the tiremaker was hampered by having only four CART teams running on Goodyear tires.

'At the conclusion of the 1998 CART season, we realized that while our tire performance on the oval tracks was competitive, our tire performance on the road and street courses had room for improvement,' said Stu Grant, Goodyear's general manager for global race tires. 'As a result, one of our goals going into this season was to improve significantly on our CART road and street course performance.'

Goodyear's CART engineering team worked throughout the winter and made extensive changes to its CART operations from last season in order to strengthen Goodyear's race-tire performance. The biggest, and most exciting change, was the tire technology gained from the company's Formula One successes. By transferring that knowledge and experience to its CART operations following the company's withdrawal from F1 competition in 1998, they were able to develop a more competitive product.

'What we learned over the years in F1 transferred very well to CART's road and street courses,' Grant added. 'The results posted by Goodyear-equipped teams on these types of courses speak for themselves.'

The highlight of Goodyear's road and street course performances was undoubtedly the Budweiser/G.I. Joe 500 at Portland International Raceway's permanent road course. It was here that Walker Racing's Gil de Ferran, driving on Goodyear Eagles, posted the tiremaker's CART win after an impressive third-place qualifying effort. Two weeks earlier at the Miller Lite 225 at Wisconsin's Milwaukee

Mile, de Ferran posted another podium finish by grabbing third place.

De Ferran's hot streak away from the ovals didn't stop with his Portland win. At the Medic Drug Grand Prix of Cleveland, he drove the Goodyear-equipped Honda/Reynard to a second-place qualifying and finishing position, followed closely by Marlboro Team Penske's Al Unser Jr. finishing in fifth position. Unser's Goodyear Eagle wet tires were credited with helping him drive from a starting position of 14th on the grid to a top-five finish in what can only be described as a wet and wild race.

Goodyear's good fortune continued when de Ferran grabbed the pole at Toronto's Molson Indy and then posted impressive performances by qualifying third at both the Texaco/Havoline 200 and the Detroit Grand Prix.

By the season's end, Goodyear-equipped drivers had claimed one pole, five top-three qualifying positions and two podium finishes on CART's road and street courses.

Goodyear's performance on the CART ovals was equally balanced, with de Ferran's pole and second-place finish at Motegi and a third-place finish at Milwaukee.

'Racing is, among other things, a numbers game,' Grant said. 'We made the best of a challenging situation, having only four or five Goodyear-equipped cars in a field of approximately 25 cars on race day. Couple those odds with a few crashes and mechanical problems, and the odds of a Goodyear-equipped car crossing the finish line first are reduced significantly.

'A lot of credit goes out to our team partners – Marlboro Team Penske, Walker Racing, Bettenhausen Motorsports and All American Racers – for their efforts, feedback and co-operation they provided us this season during the CART races and tire tests,' Grant added. 'The technological advances we made would certainly not have been possible without them.'

An exciting CART season was not without tragedy, however, following the deaths of CART drivers Gonzalo Rodriguez and Greg Moore in separate race accidents occurring barely a month and a half apart. 'The racing community lost two very promising young drivers,' Grant said. 'They will, undoubtedly, always be missed and remembered by the racing community,

their friends and family.'

Near the conclusion of the 1999 CART season, Goodyear announced it was taking a sabbatical from open-wheel racing in North America and would not return as a tire supplier to both the CART and Indy Racing League series, choosing instead to concentrate its efforts on the other forms of racing with which the company is involved.

'The company has enjoyed a long and successful history in motorsports competition around the world,' Grant said. 'Our long-standing commitment to racing has made this an agonizing decision. We are firmly committed to our successful supplier and marketing partnership with NASCAR, as well as our commitment to many other racing series to which Goodyear is a tire supplier.'

Despite its exit from both CART and IRL, Goodyear has left the door open for an eventual return to open-wheel racing in North America, as well as a return to F1 competition, at some point in the future. Until then, look for the Goodyear Racing Eagles to continue to fly high at racetracks around the country as able competitors in a variety of racing series.

Above: A change of Eagles for Valvoline Walker Racing's Gil de Ferran.

Over the years, Goodyear has been fortunate to have long-enduring partnerships with great racing teams such as Dan Gurney's AAR Eagle *(centre left)* and Roger Penske's Team Penske *(bottom left).*

Al Unser jr *(top left)* retires from CART competition as two-time champion, whilst 1999 Portland winner Gil de Ferran *(near left)* takes over his ride at Penske.

Paul-Henri Cahier

INSOLUBLE PROBLEMS?

by Gordon Kirby

IT was a tough year for American open-wheel racing with politics and tragedy dominating the headlines. After four years, the political split between CART and the IRL resulted in increasing commercial problems for both series. TV ratings continued to decline and crowd counts were down for races on both sides of the fence. On the CART side, all the street races and most road circuits remained strong, but there was increasing trouble drawing crowds at most oval races, whether CART or IRL.

Outside the Indy 500, every IRL race – all on ovals, of course – struggled to draw much of a crowd but some CART oval races, most notably the U.S. 500, also began to fail at the gate. All 20 CART races remain on the calendar next year, but the IRL dates at Charlotte and Dover Downs have been dropped after two years because of poor attendance, so the IRL is down to just eight races in 2000.

Through most of the summer talks dragged on between CART and the IRL about getting together but in September, Indianapolis Motor Speedway president and IRL founder Tony George failed to attend a key meeting with NASCAR president Bill France, CART chairman Andrew Craig and three top General Motors executives. A few days later George announced there would be no unification with CART, stating his commitment to two separate series and to the IRL's new rules package through to 2004.

George took pains to point out that all of CART's team were invited to compete at Indianapolis or any IRL race. 'Once again,' George said in a lengthy statement, 'I reiterate that CART teams are welcome to compete in any IRL event, including the Indianapolis 500, under the same rules that apply to everybody. We will be happy to extend invitations to any and all CART teams that wish to compete.'

Outside the IRL's true believers, the world was stunned and saddened by George's decision to spurn CART. On its editorial page *The Indianapolis Star* made exactly this point, pleading unsuccessfully with George to reopen talks with CART. 'All of Indiana, racing fans or not, should be saddened by [the] news,' the Star's editorialist wrote. 'The 500 will not set the pace

for racing until all of the best are back. A compromise is needed. Gentlemen, start your talks again!'

Of the many frustrated responses perhaps the most defining came from Roger Penske. 'All sponsors are interested in seeing Indianapolis be a key part of the total racing programme,' Penske said. 'CART made a business decision to not have any racing next May on qualifying and race weekend, trying to accommodate Indianapolis. We all know we have to be in one series, so what I want to know is, where's Tony going with this?'

With hopes for reunification behind them, it looks as if the CART teams will buy IRL chassis and engines this winter to race at Indianapolis in May 2000. As Penske says, CART has left a gap in its calendar to allow its teams to go to the Indy 500 and CART chairman Craig announced a few days after the end of the season that all his teams will race at Indianapolis next May.

Said Craig in a statement: 'The management of the Indianapolis Motor Speedway has repeatedly stated that the Indy 500 is an event fully and completely open to any race teams, including those in CART, and that teams from anywhere are welcome to run. Our teams have decided it is in their best interest, as well as that of the sport, to return to the Speedway to compete for the title of Indianapolis 500 champion.'

The CART teams will therefore have to buy, build, develop and race two different types of chassis and engines in 2000. That will obviously drive up the cost of doing business, but it will get them back to Indianapolis after four years *in absentia*. After this year's failed talks there appears little or no chance that CART and the IRL can agree on a common formula, let alone an organisation, and CART's four engine manufacturers have declared their preference for building engines to CART's formula rather than the IRL formula, so the split remains.

Both series face commercial problems, but the IRL's are dire – just look at the lack of brand name sponsors as well as the empty grandstands – and seems to be losing races and fans. George may believe that F1 at Indianapolis could give him breathing space while the IRL–CART issue is resolved.

TRAGEDY APLENTY

In addition to the continuing political war, the last year of the century saw tragedy aplenty in both CART and the IRL. Many accidents, injuries and deaths have blighted American open-wheel racing in the past four years from the infamous accident at the start of the 1996 U.S. 500 to last year's U.S. 500, one of the most exciting races of the decade, which turned deeply sour when three fans sitting in the grandstands were killed by a flying wheel from Adrian Fernandez's car.

The IRL has also had more than its share of tragedies with plenty of ragged races, driver injuries and this year's spectator deaths at Charlotte. An IRL night race at Charlotte in May resulted in the deaths of three more spectators from flying wheels and debris.

Toward the end of the year things turned grim when highly-rated F3000 graduate Gonzalo Rodriguez was killed at Laguna Seca, and then Greg Moore was killed in the early laps of the season-closing 500-mile race at the California Speedway. Rodriguez was getting ready for his second start for Team Penske, only to crash during practice at the Corkscrew when his foot apparently caught both the throttle and brake pedal.

Rodriguez's neck was broken when his car took off after hitting a tyre barrier, flipping over the safety fence and landing upside-down in a non-spectator area but well out of the ballpark. The accident set the drivers to thinking hard about the layout of run-off area and barriers at the Corkscrew, and more deeply about the whole matter of safety. When Moore was killed after he apparently lost it in the turbulence while working his way through from the back of the field on the tenth lap of the California 500, the safety issue was even more sharply defined.

Since the 1960s, the pursuit for improved safety has been a common thread through the sport. For many years CART and Indy or Champ car racing as a whole was proud to be in the forefront of the eternal search for safer cars and tracks. The cars in particular are immeasurably safer today than they were 20 years ago and we took growing confidence from the fact that not a single driver was killed in a CART race between Jim Hickman's death at Milwaukee in June 1982, and

Jeff Krosnoff's dire crash at Toronto in July 1996.

The last few years have brought us back to earth however. One has to wonder whether amid all the CART–IRL–NASCAR political rhetoric of the past few years and the boom of superspeedway building, track safety has taken a back seat. The sport as a whole needs to work together for higher, more rigorous standards.

By nature, big superspeedways are the most dangerous environment of all and for some time not only some writers but also no less an authority than Mario Andretti have warned against building high-banked superspeedways. Mario is also a proponent of energy-absorbing walls.

'These walls must be totally reliable,' Andretti says, 'so as not to cause any problems with the car digging into the barrier or the wall itself coming apart. I propose that all the major operators of oval tracks in this country band together and commission three or four engineering firms to produce a viable and durable solution.'

It's possible a tyre barrier or energy-absorbing wall of some description might have saved Greg Moore's life. Surely the time has now come for America's two giant superspeedway building combines, ISC and SMI, to invest in this much-needed technology.

Another factor in Moore's fatal accident was his car getting airborne as it slewed across an access road through the grassy infield inside the backstretch. A similar thing happened to Richie Hearn's car with far less drastic results just a few laps before Greg's crash and many observers believe the areas inside the exits onto the front- and back-stretches at most superspeedways should be paved over into one smooth, continuous piece.

A series of accidents 15 years ago coming off the fourth turn at Daytona resulted in Bill France deciding to extend the track's apron inside the fourth turn all the way to the pit lane, and that change has proved a Godsend many times over. In the wake of Moore's fatal accident, the California Speedway and other tracks like it should take a hard look at these areas. And the sport needs to extricate itself from the black hole of political squabbling and start working together as one group to create state-of-the-art safety standards for the 21st century.

CART teams battle it out at the Fontana
Speedway, the final round of an
exhausting 20-race season.
Indianapolis, however, was still
conspicuous by its absence on the
schedule due to Tony George *(top left)*
maintaining his steadfast opposition to
uniting the IRL with CART.

Far left: Juan Montoya gave Target Chip Ganassi their fourth consecutive CART championship. The Colombian 'rookie' was the season's best driver winning seven rounds, and it could so easily have been more...

Below far left and below left: Dario Franchitti came so close for team KOOL Green matching Montoya's points tally, but losing out through scoring fewer wins.

Below left (bottom): Paul Tracy added maturity to his blinding speed.

All photographs: Michael C. Brown

FIERCE BUT FRIENDLY RIVALS

It really was a sharp contrast to Formula One. Two men, fierce rivals, but respectful of each other, friends in fact, partying together on a regular basis with their peers in the grand tradition of Indy or Champ car racing.

Young as they may be at 24 and 25 years old respectively, Juan Pablo Montoya and Dario Franchitti acted like gentlemen throughout their tense, down-to-the-wire battle for CART's 1999 FedEx Championship. Incredibly, after 20 races covering more than 4,600 miles, they finished the year tied with 212 points, the championship going to Montoya because he won seven races against Franchitti's three.

Impressive as he had been in winning the 1998 FIA F3000 championship, Montoya was unknown to the wider world. He surprised everyone in CART with his immediate speed and poise under pressure and put his name on the map by scoring his first victory at Long Beach in April in only his third Champ car start.

Montoya followed that up by winning the next two races at Nazareth and Rio, and putting together another three-in-a-row string later in the season. He stumbled by crashing at both Houston and Surfers Paradise in September and October, but prevailed to become the youngest champion in Champ car racing's 90-year history and the only rookie other than Nigel Mansell in 1993 to win the CART title.

Of course, Montoya enjoyed the support of the best team in the business, taking over double champion Alex Zanardi's seat, and bringing team boss Chip Ganassi his fourth consecutive championship. Ganassi's run of four championships in a row is unprecedented in CART, breaking a tie with Penske who won three successive titles in 1981–1983.

The fact that Ganassi's four titles have come with three different drivers – Jimmy Vasser in 1996, Zanardi in 1997 and 1998, and now Montoya – demonstrates the team's depth. Ganassi's team is well-managed by Tom Anderson and Mike Hull, the cars are well-engineered, competitive on all types of tracks, and extremely reliable with an unmatched finishing record over the past four years, a salute to Rob Hill and his outstanding crew of mechanics.

Yet as Ganassi said: 'Let's not underestimate the charge Team Green made in the second half of the season. Our team had a great year. We certainly tried to throw it away the last couple of races. We tried to lose it.'

After his second run of triple wins at Mid-Ohio, Chicago and Vancouver, Montoya looked a shoo-in for the championship, particularly when Franchitti crashed while trying to pass Montoya in Vancouver and crashed again the following weekend at Laguna Seca while trying to get by his great friend Greg Moore.

People were saying that Dario was cracking under the pressure but at Houston and Surfers Paradise the worm turned. Franchitti drove masterfully in both races, finishing second to team-mate Paul Tracy in Texas and scoring his third win of the year in Australia. Meanwhile Montoya crashed into Helio Castro-Neves's already crashed car while leading in Houston and crashed again near the end in Surfers while running fourth, chasing Adrian Fernandez.

Montoya's accidents allowed Dario to surge ahead, leading 209–200 going into the season finale – 500 miles at the high-banked California Speedway. Montoya ran near the front all the way while Franchitti lost three laps because of two, separate pit stop gaffes. Montoya finished fourth, Franchitti tenth, the pair emerging in a tie. With four more wins, the championship therefore went to Montoya.

Franchitti's championship loss paled into insignificance for him when the drivers were told on the cool-down lap or, as they stopped at the pits, that Greg Moore had been killed in a violent collision with the wall early in the race. Moore and Franchitti had become very close friends and the Canadian's death brought a very sad end to a long, tough season for Dario.

NO WORRIES

Morris 'Mo' Nunn has been Ganassi's chief engineer the past four years. Nunn has been in the racing business for 35 years, as a driver, car builder, F1 team owner, and for the past 14 years, one of the most recognised engineers in Champ car racing, and he has the highest regard for Montoya's ability. Nunn says Montoya has an extreme level of physical or athletic talent.

'He's not a technical driver,' Nunn says. 'He just tells you why he can't go quicker. He says it pushes, or it's loose, or has no grip, and he expects you to fix it. He doesn't get involved in any part of the technical side. It doesn't bother him.

'He's very easy to work with. If the car is bad he'll just tell you why he can't go quicker and expect you to fix it, and he'll go quicker. He gets everything that's possible to get out of the car.'

263

Far left: Gil de Ferran scored a solitary win for Goodyear in their final season in CART.

Left: Greg Moore. A great driver and a fine young man. His loss cast a shadow not only over the CART community, but in motor racing worldwide.

Bottom far left: Adrian Fernandez produced a number of outstanding performances for Patrick Racing.

Below left: Christian Fittipaldi *(above)* and Michael Andretti *(below)* took a win each for Newman-Haas.

All photographs: Michael C. Brown

Nunn believes Montoya has an old head on young shoulders, and is capable of racing wheel-to-wheel with any driver, Michael Schumacher included. 'He doesn't show any nerves,' Nunn marvels. 'I don't see any problems at the start of races. Some drivers get nervous in different ways. Some don't want to eat anything. Some talk a lot. But he has no problems. It's just like he's 35 years old, and it doesn't bother him.

'At the moment, other than his lack of patience and his frustration when he's not at the front, I don't see any faults,' Nunn declares. 'I really don't think it would bother him a second if you told him Michael Schumacher was coming to drive in the other car. He'd say, "Good! Bring him on".'

For my part I have to say Montoya is as great a natural talent as any I've ever seen, Gilles Villeneuve included. Watching closely from the right vantage points on road or street circuits you can see Juan Pablo react to and correct a slide before the car moves! He really can be uncanny to watch.

Juan is also a very uncomplicated fellow with complete faith in his abilities. He doesn't appear to have to pump himself up or work on focusing himself. It all comes very naturally to him.

He's a young man of few words, a true man of action with little interest in reflection or pondering the past. He answers most questions with two or three short sentences, a shrug, and a flash of his brilliant grin. 'That's it!' Montoya likes to conclude his brief summations.

Team-mate Jimmy Vasser, champion in 1996, runner-up to Zanardi in 1998, enjoyed only a handful of good races in 1999. Vasser was entirely eclipsed by Montoya, making the podium just once and finishing ninth in the championship.

Franchitti and Paul Tracy produced the best team effort, finishing second and third in the championship for Barry Green's team. Both drivers showed increasing maturity and Franchitti demonstrated a toughness and strength of character that some people questioned. Champions with Jacques Villeneuve in 1995, Green's team should be very hard to beat next year.

At the heart of the success of both Ganassi and Green teams was the correct combination or package of Reynard chassis, Honda engines and Firestone tyres. The Reynard-Honda-Firestone package has won 26 CART races the past two years, 13 each year. Reynard has now won CART's constructors' championship for five straight years, and Honda has won three of the last four Manufacturer's

titles. And Firestone thrashed Goodyear 19-1 for the second year in a row, driving Goodyear out of Champ cars after 35 years.

The third most successful team was Newman-Haas Racing's pair of Swift-Fords driven to two wins by Michael Andretti and Christian Fittipaldi with Roberto Moreno substituting very effectively for the injured Fittipaldi in five races.

CART's impressive depth of field was emphasised by the fact that five other drivers won races. Adrian Fernandez won twice aboard a Patrick Reynard-Ford; Greg Moore scored Mercedes-Benz's only CART win in the season-opener; Gil de Ferran recorded Goodyear's lone victory in Derrick Walker's Reynard-Honda; rookie Tony Kanaan won the U.S. 500 in Steve Horne's Reynard-Honda; and Bryan Herta won at Laguna Seca in his last year aboard a Team Rahal Reynard-Ford. Most impressive non-winner was Max Papis who led the most laps in both of CART's 500-mile races and came within an ounce of fuel of winning July's U.S. 500, running dry in the third turn on the last lap.

And of course, seven-time champions Team Penske hit rock bottom, failing to win a race for the second year in a row. Al Unser Jr. left the team after six years for the IRL and Penske has changed everything – drivers, chassis, engines, and tyres – for 2000, joining the Reynard-Honda-Firestone trend as four-time champion Ganassi jumps to Toyota engines.

RAY IS IRL CHAMPION

The ten-race 1999 IRL series was won by Texan Greg Ray who raced Toyota-Atlantic and Indy Lights cars with some success in 1995 and 1996 before moving up to the IRL in 1997. Ray ran his own operation in 1997 and 1998 but caught the eye of John Menard, the IRL's richest team owner, who hired the Texan for 2000. Ray rewarded Menard by winning three races and beating 1997 champion Kenny Brack and Mark Dismore to the title.

Brack won the Indy 500, beating Jeff Ward and Billy Boat after Robby Gordon, the only CART driver to do the race, ran out of fuel while leading the penultimate lap. Near the end of the year Brack signed with Bobby Rahal's CART team for 2000, replacing Bryan Herta. Other drivers to win IRL races were veterans Eddie Cheever, Scott Goodyear, who won twice in 1999, Dismore, and Scott Sharp and newcomer Sam Schmidt who badly injured his right foot in the last race of the year.

DJ's FIRST TITLE

It took him 14 years of racing in NASCAR's top league to get there but 43-year old Dale Jarrett dominated NASCAR's Winston Cup championship in 1999, easily taking his first title. In his fifth year with Robert Yates's powerful Ford team, Jarrett ran away from his more youthful competitors through consistency. He won only four of 34 races and didn't score his first win until the year's eleventh round but was so utterly consistent, finishing in the first three 13 times and in the top five much more regularly than anyone else. His big win of the year came in the Brickyard 400 at Indianapolis in August.

The son of two-time NASCAR champion and contemporary TV analyst Ned Jarrett, Dale is at his best on the big tracks where experience and guile play a large role. 19 of Jarrett's 22 career victories — three of this year's four — have come on superspeedways. He's come into his own since joining Yates's two-car operation in 1995 and has been in the championship chase the past four years. In 1997, Jarrett won seven races and was beaten by Jeff Gordon to the title by only 14 points.

After winning three of the last four championships, Gordon was expected to produce a fourth title in 1999. He won the season-opening Daytona 500 for the second time in three years and won more races and led more laps than anyone else, but some bad luck and too many mechanical problems kept him from making a championship run. Gordon, 28, wound-up battling with rookie Tony Stewart for fourth in points, his weakest year since 1994.

Toward the end of the season it became clear to many Gordon wasn't as strong in 1999 as he had been the previous four years. Crew chief Ray Evernham has always been considered a key component in Gordon's success and in September Evernham announced he was leaving Rick Hendrick's state-of-the-art three-car Chevrolet superteam to lead Daimler-Chrysler's new NASCAR initiative to bring the Dodge brand back into stock car racing.

Runner-up to Jarrett in the 199 Winston Cup championship was Bobby Labonte, the 35-year old younger brother of two-time NAS-CAR champion Terry Labonte. Driving for Joe Gibbs's Pontiac team, Labonte has been a regular race-winner the five years, but this was

266

Right: Jeff Burton, one of the best racers in NASCAR, won six races in the Exide Batteries Ford.
Nigel Kinrade

the first time he pulled together a championship challenge. He won four races, made the top three just as many times as Jarrett, and was the only man to keep the champion-to-be in sight over the closing months of the long season.

Third in the championship was the ever-resolute Mark Martin who's never won the NASCAR title but has finished second or third seven times in the last 11 years. The 40-year old Martin has driven for Jack Roush's Ford team through all this time and had a comparatively poor year in 1999 winning only two races but hanging in there among the point leaders all season in typically relentless style.

One of the year's most successful drivers was Martin's team-mate Jeff Burton who won six races and finished sixth in the championship. The 32-year old Burton has been teamed with Martin at Roush for four years and has established himself as one of NASCAR's best drivers. Roush this year became the biggest operation in NASCAR, running no fewer than five cars in all 34 races!

Runaway rookie of the year was Tony Stewart who came into NASCAR via midgets, sprint cars and the IRL. Stewart won the IRL title with John Menard's team in 1997 and ran five of NASCAR's second division Busch Grand National races in 1998 to prepare for a serious run at the Winston Cup rookie title in 1999. Teamed with Bobby Labonte in Joe Gibbs's team the 28-year old Stewart was in a class of his own among the rookies, scoring his first Winston Cup win at Richmond in September and finishing fifth in the championship between Gordon and Burton.

Former champions Dale Earnhardt, Rusty Wallace, Terry Labonte, Bill Elliott and Darrell Waltrip hung in there in 1999, but none of them, 40-somethings all, save Waltrip who's 52, could claim to be in their prime. At least Earnhardt, Wallace and Labonte proved they were still capable of winning races with seven-time champion Earnhardt the most successful of this group of near-wrinklies with no fewer than three wins in 1999, finishing seventh in points.

Elliott and Waltrip however, were little more than backmarkers. Elliott hasn't won in five years while Waltrip, a three-time champion from the 1980s who is the most successful active NASCAR driver with 84 wins, hasn't won in seven years. Good ol' DW, bless his heart, has announced that 2000 will be his retirement year.

TEAM KOOL GREEN

BUILDS TOWARDS A CHAMPIONSHIP THROUGH TEAMWORK

Above: Team owner Barry Green and his brother Kim (general manager) survey the situation from Team KOOL Green's position in the pit lane.

TEAM KOOL GREEN ran on a championship pace throughout much of the 1999 CART FedEx Championship Series. Everybody was pulling in the same direction, from Team Owner Barry Green and his brother, General Manager Kim Green, their drivers Dario Franchitti and Paul Tracy, the engineering staff and to every single crew member.

"We had a fantastic season, but I guess you can say we didn't quite put the icing on the cake when we had the opportunity," said Barry Green. "But I'm thrilled about the manner in which we showed what the strength of a team is all about. We had two great drivers and two great teams working as one – using each other to go faster."

N any other year the tenacity of Franchitti and Tracy, who finished 2–3 in the series and who were dominant in three 1–2 victories, would certainly be an achievement envied by the competition.

Franchitti's 11 podiums were the most by any driver in the series, and he won poles at Mid-Ohio and Australia. Usually the fastest on the street circuits, Franchitti won at Toronto, Detroit and Australia, and finished second at Long Beach and Houston.

Franchitti and his fierce rookie rival Juan Montoya were the class of the field on every type of circuit in 1999. Their final showdown though came down to a 500-mile crapshoot on the large 2-mile oval at California Speedway. When it was over, Franchitti had brought the CART championship down to its closest finish ever, a 212–212 tie with Montoya. By virtue of Montoya's seven wins to Franchitti's three, the rookie from Colombia won the PPG Cup and its million-dollar bonus.

Tracy's third-place finish in the championship was all the more remarkable considering he began the season in the penalty box, serving a one-race suspension for alleged blocking tactics at Australia in October 1998. (Veteran driver Raul Boesel filled in for Tracy at Homestead.) Wins at

Milwaukee and Houston coupled with runner-up finishes at Toronto, Detroit and Mid-Ohio allowed Tracy to reestablish himself as a full-time front-runner. Besides finishing third, tying his highest finish in the series (1993 and 1994), he and his crew earned a pair of season-end awards. Tracy's pit crew won the season-long $50,000 Craftsman Pit Crew Challenge and for the second time in his nine years in the CART series, Tracy was selected by his fellow drivers as the STP Most Improved Driver.

"They must have really thought I stunk last year," said Tracy. On reflection, Tracy ceased being flippant. "We worked really hard over the winter with a lot of testing that helped me better understand the car. That really has been the biggest difference, along with working with [engineer] Tony Cicale."

Tracy's career totals at season-end included 15 victories and 12 pole positions in 132 starts. To say he understands the value of teamwork in his job and in winning would be an understatement. Most sports fans don't really see auto racing as a team sport like baseball or football. According to Tracy, they really need to open their eyes. He says that just like the stick-and-ball sports, the star, or driver in this case, must have a strong supporting cast.

"I'm just the monkey they put in the car," laughs Tracy, making reference to early unmanned space missions. Tracy's car is no rocket, but it's as close as you can get on land when you consider the speeds he reaches with a powerful Honda engine and a fresh set of Firestones. His type of car has been clocked at more than 245 mph, higher than the speed needed for Boeing 747 jumbo jets to take off. So, he must have absolute faith in the car and in his crew that works on it.

"I cannot do what I do without having complete confidence in the people around me," he explains. "These guys are my teammates. Nobody can have a bad day on a Sunday if we are going to win races. It's not just me or the guy with the heaviest foot that comes out on top. It's the best team that wins. We have to have flawless work from the pit crew over the wall and an excellent race strategy from our engineering staff. A lot of teamwork goes into taking the checkered flag."

While the drivers get the credit – or sometimes take the blame – their race engineers like Don Halliday (Franchitti) and Tony Cicale (Tracy) provided the set-ups that are the key to success.

Tracy's season began with John Dick returning for a second year to engineer the #26 KOOL car. But Dick left the team

three races into the season (after Long Beach). Some teams would have fallen apart under similar circumstances. Barry Green, however, was able to rally the troops and turn Tracy's season around. Green persuaded Tony Cicale to step-up his involvement with the team and assume full engineering duties on the race weekends. Green also coerced the team's aerodynamicist (and former race engineer) Tino Belli to assume Tracy's engineering responsibilities at tests and assist at many races.

According to Halliday, this was the point the #26 and #27 teams started to work as one. That may have been just the right ingredient, missing from the previous season to get both Tracy and Franchitti consistently at the front in their Honda/ Reynard/Firestone package.

"At that point we really had to funnel the thought process of all concerned for the good of both drivers. Because of that we were then able to use both drivers' performance to reference better improvements... of the whole team. So after that point I think you saw the team on average grow in qualifying and races," explained Halliday.

Cicale put aside his other plans to remain with the team. He said, "Paul says that I've helped him a lot and certainly he's helped me a lot. It's always a two-way street. When you give something

Below far left: Paul Tracy and his crew chief Tony Cicale. The pairing of the hard-charging racer and the seasoned professional paid dividends as the season progressed.

Left: Paul celebrates on the podium after his victory at the Milwaukee Mile.

Below left: Tucked into the cockpit and ready for business.

Below: Relaxing in the motorhome with wife Liisa.

you get something in return. I decided to stay on because I thought we were successful. Though I was helping him, he was helping the team."

Cicale's calm insight helped harness the raw energy that surged in Tracy. The driver is quick to credit his engineer. "When Tony came on board I knew what his credentials were, everybody does. He instantly gives you confidence."

They started a dialogue that not only helped Tracy but also helped the whole team take on the positive attitude that makes champions.

"I feel very comfortable criticizing him because I think that he realizes that I'm doing it not to criticize or praise him but to help make sure that he doesn't make that mistake down the road," added Cicale.

Halliday, who had a full season with Franchitti in 1998, was more than ready to take up the task of a championship battle. They were on the same wavelength.

"Over time you build up a rapport; I liken it to a sixth sense. I can sense what he's going to say. You see very little of the driver through the helmet, but you get a sense – from the eyes, the way the head is held and the way the hands move – of what he's trying to say. Not that he says very much, but it's enough typically to be able to do something to help him."

Green, the team owner, like his engineers has a strong track record of being able to get the most out of people around him, whether from a driver or a crew member. As a team manager beginning back in 1979, Green enjoyed a lot of success helping guide the careers of big name drivers like Danny Sullivan, Michael Andretti, Bobby Rahal, and Al Unser Jr. Making the jump to the ownership level in 1994, Green partnered with Gerry Forsythe to nurture a talented and brash rookie by the name of Jacques Villeneuve. One year later, Green parted ways with Forsythe and carried Villeneuve to an Indy 500 victory, as well as a CART PPG Cup championship.

"Keeping the chemistry right is a key factor in the success of any race team. Without it, it doesn't matter how good your drivers, engineers, crew or race car is," says the man who should know. Green has been involved in 30 CART victories as a manager or team owner. "Our type of racing is a highly competitive environment and we've got two of the best drivers and crews at Team KOOL Green. Naturally there will be an internal rivalry between Paul and Dario, as well as between their crews. That's good for the team. But the philosophy on my team is that it is a single team. We always work together."

Team chemistry has been put to the test a few times at Team KOOL Green. At Houston in 1998, Franchitti was leading the race and being chased by Tracy in second. The teammates bumped tires,

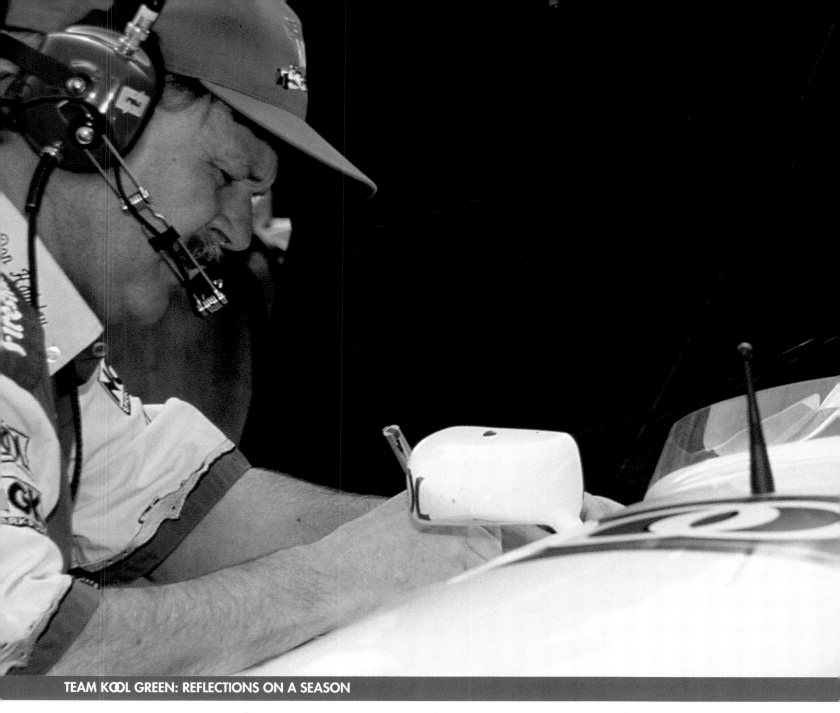

sending Tracy's car against a concrete wall. Tracy limped back into the pits and Franchitti was able to continue and win.

This past season, they tangled on the Memorial Day weekend race at Gateway International Raceway near St. Louis. This time, Tracy was running second and Franchitti was third when the two came together on lap 148 (of 236). Tracy's car hit the wall and he was unable to continue. Franchitti's car went into a slide, but he punched the throttle and saved his car from spinning. It was the kind of incident that can turn one team with two cars into two one-car teams, with everyone taking sides. Green would have none of it.

"After that one [in May], we had some very, very serious meetings," Green admitted. "Mistakes are OK, but you need to learn from them. I sat both drivers down and reminded them that the object of the game is to beat the other guys. I laid it out for both of them that we are a team and that they are teammates."

Franchitti added; "There was never any problem between Paul and myself.

The fact is we have equally fast cars and we are both capable of winning. It's only natural that at some point in a race, we'll find ourselves trying to pass each other. We just need to use our heads and consider all of the consequences in doing it."

Barry Green wasn't worried and it would turn out that things did get sorted out. Franchitti was able to continue, finishing third behind race-winner Michael Andretti and runner-up Helio Castro-Neves. It was his fourth podium and he closed to within four points of Montoya (69–65). But it might have been the low point of Tracy's season.

At the next race in Milwaukee, Tracy answered his critics and ended a two-year winless drought with his 14th career victory. And to do it, Tracy stretched his final 35 gallons of fuel over 101 laps. Green and his engineering staff had gambled with a two-stop pit strategy in the 225-lap race and needed to survive just five more laps.

"We took a big gamble and as soon as I went on the restart, the fuel-pressure warning light came on, and I said, 'Oh, #@#!$#@, we're going to

be out of fuel in a lap'," Tracy recalls. "We did the five laps and it was still running at the end. We were definitely running on fumes. It was a great call by Barry and Tony [Cicale]."

Teamwork paid off again in Toronto a few weeks later, as Green was able to enjoy the team's first of three 1–2 finishes by Franchitti and Tracy. Franchitti started second, but took the lead from Gil de Ferran at Turn 3 and led all 95 laps, jumping back into second in the point standings, just seven points behind Montoya (113–96).

In winning his first race of the season and fourth of his CART career, Franchitti chased away the jinxes that prevented him from finishing his earlier two appearances in Toronto. In 1998, he was leading with less than 8 laps to go when he spun out of the race due to a brake problem. He was on the pole in his rookie year of 1997 for Hogan Racing, but got taken out in the first corner.

"It's about time I finished a race in Toronto," said Franchitti. "I've made it difficult on myself the last couple of years and it was a great way to do it

for the team with a 1–2 finish."

Three weeks later in Detroit, Team KOOL Green did it again. Franchitti led Tracy home to another 1–2 finish, taking the championship lead (136– 131) from Montoya who crashed out and failed to score any points.

Over the next five races, Montoya stretched out to a comfortable lead in the standings with a 28-point advantage over Franchitti (199–171). At Round 18 in Houston however, Montoya was snake-bitten and the Team KOOL Green completed the hat trick with yet another 1–2 result. This time, Tracy led the way en route to his 15th career win. He led 85 laps, after pole-sitter Montoya made an unforced error, crashing into Helio Castro-Neves' stranded car on lap 13.

Once again it proved Barry Green's confidence in Tracy. And after the race, Tracy described his race in this colorful way: "I hate to say that any place owed me one, but I definitely stuck that boot [race winner's trophy] right in my ass last year. It's better to have the gold boot in my hand than in my butt. I got it right this year."

Skeptics were ready to hand Montoya the PPG Cup prior to Houston and as it turned out they were extremely premature. The next race in Australia was pure Team KOOL Green steamroller with Franchitti behind the wheel.

In the team's short but storied history, one of the few things that has eluded it is a win in Surfers Paradise, Australia – the Green family's native land. That changed in 1999 with a large part of the family in attendance.

As it turned out it was a perfect weekend for Franchitti, earning all 22 points for the pole (1), most laps led (1) and the victory (20) at the seaside street circuit. He regained the points lead (209–200) from Montoya who had another unforced error and scored no points.

"What can you say about that?" Dario asked rhetorically. "We came to Australia, hoping for a 22-point weekend. We were just working towards that and it happened. It's pretty amazing. I heard on the radio that there was a local yellow in Turn 9. When I found out Juan was out of the race, it was a big relief because of the points situation. It's never nice when something like that happens to a competitor, but we needed it."

The final weekend of the season at California Speedway in Fontana was billed as a title fight between Montoya and Franchitti. However, the race and championship became secondary with the tragic loss of Greg Moore.

Franchitti and Tracy were the best of friends with Moore, sharing a lot of good times together. They competed hard together on track and put racing behind them to have fun while away from the track. As hard as it is to concede a title, the loss of a friend and respected rival overrode the day.

In the race, Franchitti and his crew experienced problems changing a right rear tire on lap 72 that required a stop under green and he lost two laps to the leaders. In the closing laps, Franchitti was told to drive it hard and he was charging through the field. He had made up one lap, but came up just a little short. He was running ninth when he needed to pit for a splash-and-go, which cost him one position and the championship to the tiebreaker. He finished 10th, while his teammate Tracy retired much earlier (lap 141) with an electrical problem. Montoya finished fourth to become 1999 PPG Cup champion.

About the missed opportunity of winning the championship, Green said, "We had a little mistake. During a stop, for whatever reason, a wheel wasn't put on right and Dario had to come back in the next lap. He was as fast as anyone and was running fifth at the time. I promise you, without that mistake, we would have won the championship.

"Remember this though, the same crew that made the mistake in the pits was the same team that got us to second in the championship. It was a mistake by one of the pit crew guys – probably the one that I would consider our best. You can be sure that even after the mistake, I wouldn't trade him for anyone."

Green added, "I think that the secret of Team KOOL Green is to make sure everyone understands that no one's bigger than the team, and that team is absolutely everything. We win or lose as a team and everybody here understands that."

Above left: Don Halliday and Dario in deep discussion during a practice session.

Above: The trappings of success. Dario enjoys a ride in his Ferrari.

Left: Another win for Franchitti and Team KOOL Green at Surfers Paradise.

Below: Jonny Kane listens to Dario Franchitti's advice on aspects of racecraft.

Bottom: The four Team KOOL Green drivers for 1999. Jonny Kane, Alex Gurney, Paul Tracy and Dario Franchitti.

CHAMPIONSHIP contenders can't rest on their laurels. In order to keep at the front, Team KOOL Green has its own farm system much like professional baseball teams.

Team owner Barry Green said, "It's been very important, not only trying to find future drivers of tomorrow for the Champ car program, but also to find personnel, mechanics, engineers and truck drivers."

The responsibility for overseeing the driver development program lies with Kim Green, general manager of Team KOOL Green. "When Barry and I are scouting drivers, we're looking for someone with the potential to be very successful in a Champ car. Dario Franchitti and Paul Tracy sit in our Champ cars now, but I'm sure that in a couple of seasons you'll see some young guys nipping at their heels."

The 1999 season saw Team KOOL Green working with two drivers with the sort of potential the "Greens" are looking for. Jonny Kane, who has been a champion at every level he has contested in his racing career, drove the Team KOOL Green's Indy Lights car. Kane was joined in the driver development program by Alex Gurney, who drove for TKG in the 1998 Barber Dodge Pro Series before stepping up to his Team KOOL Green ride in the 1999 KOOL/Toyota Atlantic Championship.

Kane, a native of Northern Ireland, came to America to further his racing career. From his early beginnings in karting to the British Formula 3 Championship, the wiry Kane has fought hard to win races and ultimately championships. In 1994, he displayed considerable skill to capture both British and European Formula Ford

TEAM KOOL GREEN: DRIVER DEVELOPMENT PROGRAM

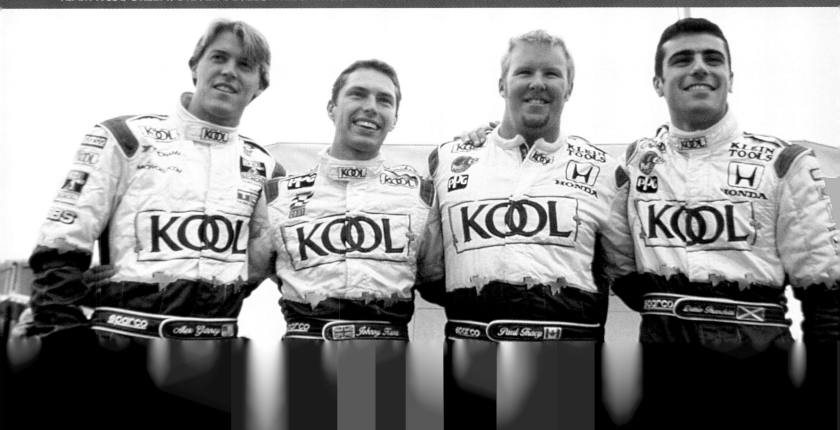

TEAM KOOL GREEN'S FARM SYSTEM

Left: Dan Gurney, a legend in racing, chats with Kim Green. Dan's son, Alex *(center)*, is currently working his way up the motorsport ladder.

thinking about a racing career.

O.K., but why the University of Colorado?

"Number One, I got in!" laughs Alex. "Seriously, I was looking to get out of California and live away from home for a while. I had a few friends who were already going to the University of Colorado. I visited the campus and fell in love with the place.

"Boulder's a couple of thousand miles away from Southern California, but the lifestyles are very similar: laid-back, with lots of things to do out of doors," he says. "But the weather was a real shock. I learned real fast I don't like the cold."

Although the cold weather and presence of the nearby ski resorts enabled Alex to trade his surfboard for a snowboard, it wasn't long before his racing heritage surfaced.

"I spent most of my free time at a go-kart track near Boulder," he says. "It's out in the middle of nowhere, a mile long and it's the most awesome go-kart track I've ever seen."

His passion for karting was just the tip of the iceberg. By his senior year Alex had convinced his parents to let him try his hand at racing, and he promptly earned rookie of the year honors in the 1997 Skip Barber Midwestern Dodge Series. After graduating with a bachelor's degree in business administration, Gurney began his "post-graduate" work as a professional driver.

"I'm glad I went to college," he says. "It's an experience that a lot of people in racing don't have. Besides, in racing you can't get by anymore on just driving fast. With the importance of commercial sponsorship you've got to be on top of things business-wise as well."

In 1997, Gurney won 10 of 14 races in the Skip Barber Midwestern Dodge Series. For his efforts, he collected Rookie of the Year honors. More importantly, however, he thoroughly impressed the management of Team KOOL Green. He spent the 1998 season, running for Team KOOL Green by learning the ins-and-outs of the Barber Dodge Pro Series. He finished 10th in the series championship in a season highlighted by four top-10 finishes, including two top-fives and the first pole of his professional career at Homestead. He felt ready for the next step.

"Driving for Team KOOL Green in the Atlantic series last season was an awesome experience," said Gurney. "I showed my rookie colors at times, but that's part of the learning curve and I felt I improved every time I got in the car."

Gurney qualified in the top-10 eight times and posted five top-10 finishes, including a season-high fifth-place result at the Canadian Grand Prix in Montreal.

Gurney and Kane certainly appear to be on top of things as a part of Team KOOL Green's ongoing driver development program. It's clear that they are on the path for future success. Now all they have to do is keep working hard, be determined, learn and oh yeah... win races. They both know that winning and patience will lead to their next opportunity.

championships. Around this time, he caught the eye of his racing mentor and former Formula One champion Jackie Stewart. In 1995, Kane led Stewart's Formula Vauxhall team to the championship as a rookie. Like his friend Franchitti and F1 star David Coulthard before him, Kane won the BRDC/McLaren Autosport Young Driver of the Year Award for his efforts that season. Two years later, he won the 1997 British Formula 3 Championship.

"Winning races is a great feeling, but being consistent enough to win a championship is the ultimate reward," says Kane. "Having the opportunity to run in the Indy Lights Championship – as a development series for Champ Car – is very exciting. I think I acquitted myself well in my first season and I look forward to posting better results and making a serious run for the championship in 2000."

While the first half of his rookie season was frustrating for Kane as he struggled to come to grips with his new Indy Lights car, new team, new country and new tracks (including his first ever oval races), the second half of the season was most impressive.

In the last five races, Kane earned two poles and finished on the podium three times, including his first win at the season-finale at the California Speedway. His stretch run, which also included 3rd place finishes at Detroit and Laguna Seca, vaulted him from 12th to fourth in the final point standings and clinched the Rookie of the Year honors.

Although Kane showed promise during the year, however, that elusive first win was frustrating.

"I think it had been too long in coming," said his race engineer Eddie Jones. "Jonny deserved more than one win this year. I know that he showed us his speed at most places. We let him down at one or two of the ovals when the car wasn't great. It's really rewarding for the whole team because every one had a hand in our car being quick on these superspeedways. Jonny got the pole position at both of them [Michigan Speedway in July and California Speedway in October] and he finished off the season with a truly professional drive."

"I'm so happy for the boys because they worked so hard all year long," added Kim Green. "They've been so close so many times. I think we'll see some really good races from Jonny next year. This was his first year and it's a tough little series."

Gurney, like Kane, is an easy-going, fun guy looking to make good on his dreams. To fulfil his dreams, however, Alex will have to follow in the footsteps of his father, Dan Gurney. Alex recognizes full well the racing legacy of his father, who was a top road racing star in America, as well as one of the most popular Formula One drivers ever.

"Without question my father is my racing hero and my mentor," explains Alex. "I have my own dreams and goals for what I want to accomplish in racing. If I can even come close to achieving what he did, I'd count myself lucky.

"Right now, I'm just stoked to be doing what I'm doing. I've got a fantastic job in the family business. I'm grateful for all the support I've been given, especially from my parents."

Alex praises his parents, but they did not want their son to become a race car driver... at first. You'd think the career path of the son of one of the most famous figures in American motorsports would lead straight to the race track. However, Dan and Evi Gurney (who worked for Porsche motorsports when she and Dan met) insisted Alex attend college before even

#26 PIT CREW FOR TEAM KOOL GREEN IS THE BEST IN BUSINESS

TEAM KOOL GREEN: CRAFTSMAN PIT STOP CHAMPIONS

DESPITE his reputation as a hard charger on the track, Paul Tracy knows that good finishes depend on good pit work.

Tracy's crew, led by Tony Cotman, got a chance to show off the right stuff when they won the inaugural $50,000 Craftsman Pit Crew Challenge preceding the series finale in Fontana, California.

The season-long competition (determined by a points system in the 19 previous events based on total time spent in the pits) culminated in a contest for four finalists in a 10-minute session requiring each driver to make a minimum of two pit stops and change all four tires. No fuel was added.

The winner was declared following calculation of the total pit times accumulated by each team, divided by the number of pit stops made. Teams were permitted to make more than one stop in an effort to lower the average time spent on each stop.

"Our plan was to do two stops and evaluate," said Cotman, but two nearly perfect stops were all that was needed.

Being in synch with the crew means a driver gains track position rather than losing it, as was seen by the close finish in the season points race. Every place counts.

"It makes my job a lot easier," Tracy said. "It takes some of the anxiety out when it comes time to stop. Rather than thinking I may lose places, I know we're going to gain a spot or two every time."

Members of the winning crew were left front tire changer Steve Price; crew chief and right front tire changer Cotman; left rear tire changer Chuck Miller; right rear tire changer Eric Haverson; fueller Jeff Simon and vent man Jeff Stafford.

Top: Paul Tracy blasts away from another pitstop by the #26 Team KOOL Green crew.

Above: Paul's crew members jump for joy at yet another win by Team KOOL Green.

HUGHES'S GAMBLE PAYS OFF

by Paul Lawrence

FRENETIC race action, bumper grids and bags of promotion. The second year of the MGF Cup mirrored the success of the inaugural season of the one-make championship for 1800 cc Fs in racing trim. Having won the 1998 title with James Rhodes, Team Firstair retained the crown, albeit with a different driver aboard its Chelsea Football Club-supported racer.

Warren Hughes faced rather a dilemma heading towards the 1999 racing season. Having consistently proven himself as a front runner in international categories like Formula 3 and touring cars, the Geordie was determined to keep his career moving. Warren had always earned drives on merit alone, but few options were now available as touring cars grids shrank for 1999. For a career driver, a year on the sidelines can be disastrous.

Then, in stepped Team Firstair's Ian Barnwell with the offer of a full MGF Cup campaign. Some drivers with touring car experience and advanced self-opinions might have considered the MGF Cup below them. But Hughes reasoned that it was better to be racing and winning than not racing at all. The real danger for his reputation would be if he raced and didn't win.

However, Hughes was prepared to take that chance and proved the wisdom of his decision by winning the opening race of the season at Silverstone in late March. Hughes was never headed in the championship after that opening race and finally settled the matter at Croft in early September, with two races still to run. At the same time, the Epsom Motor Group clinched the MG Dealer Award having supported Hughes' campaign.

His tally for the season was six wins from 14 races and with five of those wins in the opening seven races, his rivals were left gasping as they battled to keep up. But for a first-lap clash with Alastair Lyall at Thruxton and soaking conditions at Silverstone in June, Hughes could have taken even more wins. It was not until Knockhill in July that Hughes failed to finish a race. In the first of the double-header races at Scotland's only race track, Hughes didn't get as far as the first corner after a typical start line scrum sent him into the tyre wall. Undeterred, Hughes then turned in one of his best drives of the season when he started from the tail of the pack at a circuit where overtaking is notoriously difficult. His charge through the pack to sixth bore the hallmark of a champion-elect.

Six more top-six finishes, including victory at Castle Combe, wrapped up Warren's title campaign and left him

Top: Warren Hughes took the championship honours in the MGF Cup.

Above (inset): The ex-F3 star, Hughes, with his Team Firstair machine.

Above left: Thrills and spills at the back whilst David Mason (18) heads this group.

Above: Door-to-door dicing by Ray Ames and Mark Hazell.

Right: **Close racing right through the field is a feature of the MGF Cup.**

Bottom: Matt Kelly (6) leads, with Barry Benham (33) in close attendance, while behind, Alastair Lyall is involved in a spin.

champion by over 70 points. It was a case of mission accomplished for the personable Geordie and the risk had been worth taking. It remains to be seen if this title can help Warren take his career forward once more, but his speed in a one-off Formula 3 outing at the end of the season was another reminder of a fine British talent looking for an opening.

The pace of Hughes in that Thruxton Formula 3 race, where he finished on the podium, was a real boost to the rest of the MGF racers. Having spent the season battling with, and often chasing after, Hughes, it was a real indicator that the front of the MGF field was populated by some strong racers.

Like Hughes, Jamie Hunter had bigger ambitions for the 1999 season and got some way towards setting up a touring car opportunity after being a front runner in both Formula Renault and Renault Spiders. But when the touring car plans faltered, Hunter had to make very late plans and switched to the MGF Cup. He only got into the car at the pre-season test day a couple of weeks before the first race and was inevitably playing catch-up in the early races.

While Hughes racked up 71 points from the opening three races, Hunter netted just 18 points and that was really where the Chesterfield racer lost the title. By the time of the wet double-header during the MG Car Club 75th anniversary meeting at Silverstone in early June, Hunter was bang on the

pace and took a win and a second to catapult himself into contention.

Like Hughes, Jamie had one non-finish at Knockhill when a driveshaft failed but it was a retirement at Croft in early September that helped ensure Hughes clinched the title. Just to prove a point, Hunter bounced back to win the final two races at Brands and Silverstone to make certain of the runner-up position. Should he continue in the Cup in 2000, this hard-charging racer will be tough to beat. The whole Hunter operation was a real family affair, for while his father Fred managed the team, Jamie's wife Judit Forro-Hunter drove the second car. Having switched from single-seaters, the Hungarian lady was easily the best of three women racing regularly in the series.

The only other driver to win more than once was Nick Carr, a veteran of Rover-based one-make championships. His first season in the MGF Cup had been wrecked by injury, illness and

business commitments, but Nick more than made up for that in 1999. As part of the five-strong Techspeed Motorsport squad, Carr was a contender just about everywhere. His first victory came in a barn-stormer of a race at Thruxton in April when he fended off Piers Johnson and Matt Kelly in a fierce slip-streaming contest.

Carr added another victory at Knockhill and was usually up in the top six in the other races. However, a blown engine in the Silverstone double-header and being punted into the gravel at Brands later in June were the low points of his campaign and left him too far behind Hunter to challenge for second. Nonetheless, it was a cracking season for Carr and his performances ensured second place in the dealer award for Edwards of Stratford.

For Matt Kelly, 1999 turned into a character-building season. Going into the year, the Clive Sutton Group-backed racer had every reason to expect great things and was widely regarded as one of the candidates to

take the fight to Hughes. Eight podiums were more than sufficient proof of Matt's pace and he was harshly rewarded to score only one victory. Niggling qualifying problems twice left him fighting up the order in early season races, but his committed style always netted results.

The Grand Prix meeting at Silverstone was the ultimate test of character. He quit the MGF race having been on the receiving end of some robust driving and then had his National Saloon Cup BMW destroyed in a first lap shunt in the same meeting. Matt and his team dug deep to regroup and an MGF victory at Knockhill two weeks later was the perfect result, even though he was not fully recovered from the BMW accident. Had he not been docked for a false start in the second race, he would have completed a double at Knockhill.

Fourth in the final points table was slim reward for Kelly's Project Motorsport team that tended as many as four MGFs during the season. If he decides to give the MGF Cup another shot in 2000, Kelly must surely join Hunter as a pre-season favourite.

This was a strange season for Alastair Lyall. One of the elder statesmen of one-make racing, Alastair continued his association with Trinity Motors of Hinckley and Techspeed Motorsport in a bid to add the MGF title to his long list of championship titles. The fact that he took pole five times proved that Lyall had the pace, but that just didn't always translate into race results.

The clash with Hughes at Thruxton, one of Lyall's favourite tracks, was an early season blow and troubled times in the double-header meetings at Silverstone and Knockhill really hurt. Terminal engine disasters in Scotland really ended any outside title hopes but Alastair was finally able to take the top step of the podium at Croft. When race leader Hughes thought the race was over and slowed prematurely, Lyall gratefully nipped ahead to claim his only victory of the season. Just where the qualifying pace went come the race is still something

1st   Warren Hughes

2nd   Jamie Hunter

3rd   Nick Carr

4th   Matt Kelly

5th   Alastair Lyall

6th   Mark Hazell

7th   David Mason

8th   Dave Loudoun

9th   Mark Humphrey

10th   Barry Benham

Left: Warren Hughes, worthy winner of the MGF Cup in 1999.

SPECIAL FEATURE: MGF CUP

of a mystery, but fifth in the final standings was uncharacteristically poor for the Loughborough ace.

Like team-mate Carr, Mark Hazell is another veteran of Rover's one-make categories and flew the flag for Edwards of Stratford with a good season. Invariably found battling in the lower reaches of the top six, Hazell topped his season by taking a fighting fourth at Thruxton in April. That became third when Piers Johnson was excluded over a technical infringement. Elsewhere, Hazell was seldom far away from the action and was another strong player for Techspeed.

Completing the five-strong Techspeed outfit were Mark Humphrey and Ray Armes. Having stepped up from Caterhams, Humphrey supported Lyall in a second Trinity Motors-backed entry while Armes ran in the colours of Trident Garages. Humphrey had a rather thin time in the early part of the season but got stronger as the year developed. Second behind Carr at

Knockhill was a highlight result in a decent debut season in MGFs.

Armes, meanwhile, had good days and bad days. Business commitments kept him from testing several times and that surely hurt his pace at certain events. However, a strong second to the dominant Hughes in a boisterous Brands GP race in June and third at Croft were reminders that Armes can run with the best of them.

Had he not been thrown out of a debut victory at Knockhill, young David Mason would have ended the season far higher than seventh. The Kerridges (Needham Market)-supported racer turned in a fine drive to take third in the opening Scottish race but went even better in the second to fend off all challengers and win. But his joy was short-lived for a protest from a rival team resulted in the car being excluded over suspension issues. It is questionable if any performance advantage had been gained, for Mason finished a total of nine other races in

the top six as he really started to make his mark in circuit racing.

The third car in the colours of Edwards of Stratford was that of Dave Loudoun, who has probably won more one-make races than any other driver. By his own high standards, this was not a vintage season for Loudoun and a solitary visit to the podium at Oulton in May was his best result. The final top-ten finisher was former Rover GTi racer Barry Benham in the Tanswell of Towcester entry. Although his results fell away in the second half of the year, Benham had done enough in the first half to ensure a place in the top 10.

As the flag fell on the second race of the season, Piers Johnson provisionally led the championship. But it was to be a brief moment of glory for he would soon be excluded from that race for a suspension irregularity. Differing interpretations of the rules gave the Meltune Motorsport team grounds to appeal, but it was eventually

rejected and the points were lost. It was a body blow that knocked the heart out of Piers's campaign with Priests of Chesham, and a season that started with such promise was wrecked.

Shaun King and Rob Mears were regularly found in the top 10 while newcomer Marc Nordon mixed it with the best of them and topped a learning season with a podium finish at Knockhill once Kelly and Mason were penalised.

Now, the MGF Cup has earned a place on the BRDC's exciting new PowerTour venture for 2000 as it heads into its third season. Alongside other key BRDC championships, the MGF Cup will be at the forefront of a new initiative to give British motor racing mass spectator appeal. Hughes will be gone, hopefully on up the sports car racing ladder, and the way will be open for a new champion. There are plenty of pretenders to the crown.

OVERALL CHAMPIONSHIP POSITIONS

Drivers' championship

#	Driver	Pts	#	Driver	Pts	#	Driver	Pts	#	Driver	Pts
1	Warren Hughes	321	8	Dave Loudoun	119	15	Piers Johnson	71	22	Judit Forro-Hunter	10
2	Jamie Hunter	249	9	Mark Humphrey	101	16	Vince Martin	60	23	Robert Huff	7
3	Nick Carr	207	10	Barry Benham	99	17	Henry Kangas	58	24	Kevan Wells	5
4	Matt Kelly	197	11	Ray Armes	93	18	Ian Gibbons	36	25	Bill Stilwell	5
5	Alastair Lyall	184	12	Shaun King	93	19	Mick Mercer	27	26	Clinton Ogbourne	3
6	Mark Hazell	151	13	Rob Mears	85	20	Paul O'Neill	18	27	Nigel Orange	2
7	David Mason	130	14	Marc Nordon	74	21	Brian Heerey	16	28	Gerard Nieuwenhuys	2

Dealers' championship (top ten)

#	Dealer	Pts	#	Dealer	Pts
1	Epsom Motor Group	328	6	Kerridges (Needham Market)	149
2	Edwards of Stratford	221	7	Edwards of Stratford	133
3	Clive Sutton Group	216	8	Tanswell of Towcester	118
4	Trinity Motors of Hinckley	202	9	Trinity Motors of Hinckley	117
5	Edwards of Stratford	168	10	Seward	114

OTHER MAJOR RESULTS

Compiled by David Hayhoe

International Formula 3000 Championship

All cars are Lola B99/50-Zytek V8.

FIA INTERNATIONAL FORMULA 3000 CHAMPIONSHIP, Autodromo Enzo e Dino Ferrari, Imola, Italy, 1 May. Round 1. 42 laps of the 3.063-mile/4.930-km circuit, 128.517 miles/206.828 km.
1 Nick Heidfeld, D, 1h 11m 29.942s, 107.848 mph/173.564 km/h.
2 Kevin McGarrity, GB, 1h 11m 51.922s; **3** Fabrice Walfisch, F, 1h 11m 53.346s; **4** Stéphane Sarrazin, F, 1h 12m 04.542s; **5** Gonzalo Rodriguez, U, 1h 12m 13.382s; **6** Justin Wilson, GB, 1h 12m 20.596s; **7** Jamie Davies, GB, 1h 12m 28.433s; **8** Brian Smith, RA, 1h 12m 33.526s; **9** Enrique Bernoldi, BR, 1h 12m 34.359s; **10** Franck Montagny, F, 1h 12m 34.950s; **11** Marcelo Battistuzzi, BR, 1h 12m 35.739s; **12** Oliver Gavin, GB, 1h 12m 36.800s; **13** Nicolas Minassian, F, 1h 12m 38.642s; **14** Paolo Ruberti, I, 1h 12m 54.884s; **15** Ricardo Mauricio, BR, 41 laps; **16** Andrea Piccini, I, 30 (DNF – electrics); **17** Boris Derichebourg, F, 23 (DNF – spin); **18** Max Wilson, BR, 20 (DNF – accident); **19** Soheil Ayari, F, 18 (DNF – accident); **20** Norberto Fontana, RA, 1 (DNF – accident); **21** Jason Watt, DK, 1 (DNF – accident); **22** Bruno Junqueira, BR, 0 (DNF – accident); **23** André Couto, MAC, 0 (DNF – accident); **24** Jeffrey van Hooydonk, B, 0 (DNF – accident); **25** Wolf Henzler, D, 0 (DNF – accident); **26** Norman Simon, D, 0 (DNF – accident).
Fastest race lap: Heidfeld, 1m 40.199s, 110.062 mph/ 177.128 km/h.
Fastest qualifying lap: Wilson (Max), 1m 39.092s, 111.291 mph/179.106 km/h.
Did not qualify: Fabrizio Gollin, I; David Saelens, B; Tomas Enge, CZ; Bas Leinders, B; Giovanni Montanari, I; David Terrien, F; Leopoldo 'Polo' Perez de Villaamil, E; Thomas Biagi, I; Oliver Martini, I; Mario Haberfeld, BR; Marc Goossens, B; Grégoire de Galzain, F; Viktor Maslov, RUS; Sascha Bert, D; Markus Freisacher, A; Andrej Pavicevic, AUS.
Championship points: 1 Heidfeld, 10; **2** McGarrity, 6; **3** Walfisch, 4; **4** Sarrazin, 3; **5** Rodriguez, 2; **6** Wilson (Max), 1.

FIA INTERNATIONAL FORMULA 3000 CHAMPIONSHIP, Monte Carlo Street Circuit, Monaco, 15 May. Round 2. 50 laps of the 2.092-mile/3.367-km circuit, 104.608 miles/ 168.350 km.
1 Gonzalo Rodriguez, U, 1h 18m 22.018s, 80.091 mph/ 128.894 km/h.
2 Jason Watt, DK, 1h 19m 02.112s; **3** Max Wilson, BR, 1h 19m 05.281s; **4** Oliver Gavin, GB, 1h 19m 10.529s; **5** Norberto Fontana, RA, 1h 19m 16.191s; **6** Bruno Junqueira, BR, 1h 19m 17.433s; **7** Nick Heidfeld, D, 1h 19m 18.178s; **8** David Terrien, F, 1h 19m 44.860s; **9** Franck Montagny, F, 1h 19m 45.011s; **10** Jeffrey van Hooydonk, B, 1h 19m 45.761s; **11** Fabrizio Gollin, I, 1h 19m 47.121s; **12** Marcelo Battistuzzi, BR, 1h 19m 48.086s; **13** Jamie Davies, GB, 1h 19m 48.493s; **14** Stéphane Sarrazin, F, 49 laps; **15** Enrique Bernoldi, BR, 49; **16** Nicolas Minassian, F, 45 (DNF – electrics); **17** Soheil Ayari, F, 43 (DNF – spin); **18** Oliver Martini, I, 40 (DNF – accident); **19** Paolo Ruberti, I, 38 (DNF – accident); **20** Boris Derichebourg, F, 29 (DNF – accident); **21** Justin Wilson, GB, 12 (DNF – accident); **22** Ricardo Mauricio, BR, 12 (DNF – accident); **23** André Couto, MAC, 0 (DNF – accident); **24** Brian Smith, RA, 0 (DNF – accident); **25** Andrea Piccini, I, 0 (DNF – accident).
Fastest race lap: Sarrazin, 1m 30.640s, 83.095 mph/133.729 km/h.
Fastest qualifying lap: Heidfeld, 1m 30.087s, 83.605 mph/ 134.550 km/h.
Did not qualify: Bas Leinders, B; David Saelens, B; Leopoldo 'Polo' Perez de Villaamil, E; Kevin McGarrity, GB; Tomas Enge, CZ; Wolf Henzler, D; Fabrice Walfisch, F; Norman Simon, D; Thomas Biagi, I; Grégoire de Galzain, F; Viktor Maslov, RUS; Andrej Pavicevic, AUS; Marc Goossens, B; Markus Freisacher, A; Mario Haberfeld, BR.
Championship points: 1 Rodriguez, 12; **2** Heidfeld, 10; **3=** McGarrity, 6; **3=** Watt, 6; **5=** Wilson (Max), 4; **5=** Walfisch, 4.

FIA INTERNATIONAL FORMULA 3000 CHAMPIONSHIP, Circuit de Catalunya, Montmeló, Barcelona, Spain, 29 May. Round 3. 44 laps of the 2.938-mile/4.728-km circuit, 129.188 miles/207.908 km.
1 Nick Heidfeld, D, 1h 13m 16.982s, 105.772 mph/170.223 km/h.
2 Gonzalo Rodriguez, U, 1h 13m 19.984s; **3** André Couto, MAC, 1h 14m 12.504s; **4** Bruno Junqueira, BR, 1h 14m 13.742s; **5** Stéphane Sarrazin, F, 1h 14m 15.965s; **6** Justin Wilson, GB, 1h 14m 21.452s; **7** Jamie Davies, GB, 1h 14m 31.610s; **8** Nicolas Minassian, F, 1h 14m 32.632s; **9** Kevin McGarrity, GB, 1h 14m 33.308s; **10** Soheil Ayari, F, 1h 14m 34.724s; **11** Jeffrey van Hooydonk, B, 1h 14m 35.208s; **12** Fabrizio Gollin, I, 1h 14m 54.150s; **13** Max Wilson, BR, 43 laps (DNF – accident); **14** Tomas Enge, CZ, 43; **15** Norberto Fontana, RA, 42 (DNF – accident damage); **16** Enrique Bernoldi, BR, 39 (DNF – accident); **17** Fabrice Walfisch, F, 39 (DNF – spin); **18** Norman Simon, D, 32; **19** Jason Watt, DK, 9 (DNF – driveshaft); **20** Mario Haberfeld, BR, 4 (DNF – spin); **21** Franck Montagny, F, 0 (DNF – accident); **22** Paolo Ruberti, I, 0 (DNF – accident); **23** David Terrien, F, 0 (DNF – accident); **24** Ricardo Mauricio, BR, 0 (DNF – accident); **25** Marc Goossens, B, 0 (DNF – accident); **26** Bas Leinders, B, 0 (DNF – accident).
Fastest race lap: Heidfeld, 1m 35.731s, 110.479 mph/ 177.798 km/h.
Fastest qualifying lap: Heidfeld, 1m 32.491s, 114.349 mph/ 184.027 km/h.
Did not qualify: Leopoldo 'Polo' Perez de Villaamil, E; Marcelo Battistuzzi, BR; Oliver Gavin, GB; Andrea Piccini, I; David Saelens, B; Grégoire de Galzain, F; Wolf Henzler, D; Boris Derichebourg, F; Oliver Martini, I; Giovanni Montanari, I; Thomas Biagi, I; Andrej Pavicevic, AUS; Brian Smith, RA; Sascha Bert, D; Viktor Maslov, RUS; Markus Freisacher, A.
Championship points: 1 Heidfeld, 20; **2** Rodriguez, 18; **3=** McGarrity, 6; **3=** Watt, 6; **5** Sarrazin, 5; **6=** Wilson (Max), 4; **6=** Walfisch, 4; **6=** Junqueira, 4; **6=** Couto, 4.

FIA INTERNATIONAL FORMULA 3000 CHAMPIONSHIP, Circuit de Nevers, Magny-Cours, France, 26 June. Round 4. 49 laps of the 2.641-mile/4.250-km circuit, 129.284 miles/208.064 km.
1 Nick Heidfeld, D, 1h 25m 56.738s, 90.256 mph/145.253 km/h.
2 Tomas Enge, CZ, 1h 26m 09.261s; **3** David Saelens, B, 1h 26m 45.335s; **4** Jeffrey van Hooydonk, B, 1h 26m 45.894s; **5** Stéphane Sarrazin, F, 1h 26m 54.486s; **6** Bas Leinders, B, 1h 26m 55.077s; **7** Franck Montagny, F, 1h 26m 55.899s; **8** Soheil Ayari, F, 1h 26m 58.630s; **9** David Terrien, F, 1h 27m 10.638s; **10** Justin Wilson, GB, 1h 27m 19.953s; **11** Fabrizio Gollin, I, 1h 27m 20.546s; **12** Enrique Bernoldi, BR, 1h 27m 21.310s; **13** Andrea Piccini, I, 48 laps; **14** Nicolas Minassian, F, 48; **15** Paolo Ruberti, I, 48; **16** Marc Goossens, B, 47 (DNF – spin); **17** André Couto, MAC, 45 (DNF – spin); **18** Gonzalo Rodriguez, U, 43 (DNF – spin); **19** Norberto Fontana, RA, 41 (DNF – spin); **20** Mario Haberfeld, BR, 34 (DNF – accident); **21** Max Wilson, BR, 32 (DNF – spin); **22** Fabrice Walfisch, F, 31 (DNF – spin); **23** Kevin McGarrity, GB, 22 (DNF – spin); **24** Wolf Henzler, D, 17 (DNF – spin); **25** Bruno Junqueira, BR, 3 (DNF – accident); **26** Jason Watt, DK, 2 (DNF – accident).
Fastest race lap: Ayari, 1m 29.555s, 106.158 mph/170.845 km/h.
Fastest qualifying lap: Junqueira, 1m 27.112s, 109.135 mph/175.636 km/h.
Did not qualify: Oliver Martini, I; Norman Simon, D; Andrej Pavicevic, AUS; Oliver Gavin, GB; Ricardo Mauricio, BR; Grégoire de Galzain, F; Brian Smith, RA; Leopoldo 'Polo' Perez de Villaamil, E; Jamie Davies, GB.
Championship points: 1 Heidfeld, 30; **2** Rodriguez, 18; **3** Sarrazin, 7; **4=** McGarrity, 6; **4=** Watt, 6; **4=** Enge, 6.

AUTOSPORT INTERNATIONAL TROPHY, Silverstone Grand Prix Circuit, Towcester, Northamptonshire, Great Britain, 10 July. Round 5. 40 laps of the 3.194-mile/5.140-km circuit, 127.689 miles/205.496 km.
1 Nicolas Minassian, F, 1h 07m 48.722s, 112.979 mph/ 181.823 km/h.
2 Bruno Junqueira, BR, 1h 07m 51.437s; **3** Nick Heidfeld, D, 1h 07m 52.998s; **4** Soheil Ayari, F, 1h 08m 06.193s; **5** Norberto Fontana, RA, 1h 08m 07.455s; **6** Franck Montagny, F, 1h 08m 17.085s; **7** Stéphane Sarrazin, F, 1h 08m 18.830s; **8** Andrea Piccini, I, 1h 08m 20.539s; **9** David Saelens, B, 1h 08m 21.374s; **10** Jason Watt, DK, 1h 08m 35.262s; **11** David Terrien, F, 1h 08m 35.438s; **12** Jamie Davies, GB, 1h 08m 39.842s; **13** Fabrice Walfisch, F, 1h 08m 43.513s; **14** Oliver Gavin, GB, 1h 08m 44.310s; **15** Gonzalo Rodriguez, U, 1h 08m 44.759s; **16** Bas Leinders, B, 1h 08m 44.828s; **17** Tomas Enge, CZ, 1h 08m 52.370s; **18** Mario Haberfeld, BR, 1h 08m 52.825s; **19** Jeffrey van Hooydonk, B, 1h 08m 57.330s; **20** Enrique Bernoldi, BR, 1h 08m 59.064s; **21** Andrej Pavicevic, AUS, 1h 08m 01.712s; **22** Norman Simon, D, 39 laps; **23** Kevin McGarrity, GB, 39; **24** Paolo Ruberti, I, 29 (DNF – spin); **25** Max Wilson, BR, 25 (DNF – gearbox); **26** Justin Wilson, GB, 23.
Fastest race lap: Heidfeld, 1m 40.929s, 113.920 mph/ 183.337 km/h.
Fastest qualifying lap: Minassian, 1m 37.711s, 117.672 mph/189.375 km/h.
Did not qualify: Arnd Meier, D; Fabrizio Gollin, I; Alexander Müller, D; Gaston Mazzacane, I; Marc Goossens, B; Wolf Henzler, D; André Couto, MAC; Ricardo Mauricio, BR; Thomas Biagi, I; Oliver Martini, I; Leopoldo 'Polo' Perez de Villaamil, E; Andrea Boldrini, I; Viktor Maslov, RUS; Cyrille Sauvage, F.
Championship points: 1 Heidfeld, 34; **2** Rodriguez, 18; **3=** Junqueira, 10; **3=** Minassian, 10; **5** Sarrazin, 7; **6=** McGarrity, 6; **6 =** Watt, 6; **6=** Enge, 6.

FIA INTERNATIONAL FORMULA 3000 CHAMPIONSHIP, A1-Ring, Knittelfeld, Austria, 24 July. Round 6. 48 laps of the 2.684-mile/4.319-km circuit, 128.818 miles/207.312 km.
1 Nick Heidfeld, D, 1h 07m 50.994s, 113.914 mph/183.327 km/h.
2 Soheil Ayari, F, 1h 07m 59.051s; **3** Nicolas Minassian, F, 1h 08m 08.199s; **4** Jason Watt, DK, 1h 08m 30.758s; **5** Andrea Piccini, I, 1h 08m 32.011s; **6** Stéphane Sarrazin, F, 1h 08m 32.475s; **7** André Couto, MAC, 1h 08m 33.196s; **8** Norberto Fontana, RA, 1h 08m 44.842s; **9** Leopoldo 'Polo' Perez de Villaamil, E, 1h 08m 49.251s; **10** Norman Simon, D, 1h 08m 54.932s; **11** Tomas Enge, CZ, 1h 08m 55.514s; **12** Franck Montagny, F, 1h 08m 59.128s; **13** Wolf Henzler, D, 47 laps; **14** Cyrille Sauvage, F, 47; **15** Ricardo Mauricio, BR, 47; **16** Oliver Martini, I, 47; **17** Justin Wilson, GB, 46 (DNF – spin); **18** Max Wilson, BR, 33 (DNF – spin); **19** Fabrizio Gollin, I, 21 (DNF – accident damage); **20** Mario Haberfeld, BR, 18 (DNF – accident damage); **21** Enrique Bernoldi, BR, 5 (DNF – throttle linkage); **22** David Saelens, B, 1 (DNF – accident damage); **23** Andrea Boldrini, I, 1 (DNF – accident damage); **24** Bas Leinders, B, 0 (DNF – accident); **25** Marc Goossens, B, 0 (DNF – accident); **26** Fabrice Walfisch, F, 0 (DNF – accident).
Fastest race lap: Heidfeld, 1m 23.243s, 116.062 mph/ 186.783 km/h.
Fastest qualifying lap: Heidfeld, 1m 23.206s, 116.113 mph/ 186.866 km/h.
Did not qualify: Oliver Gavin, GB; Paolo Ruberti, I; Alexander Müller, D; Arnd Meier, D; Viktor Maslov, RUS; Alex Yoong, MAL; Laurent Delahaye, F; David Terrien, F; Gonzalo Rodriguez, U; Andrej Pavicevic, AUS; Kevin McGarrity, GB; Jeffrey van Hooydonk, B; Bruno Junqueira, BR; Jamie Davies, GB.
Championship points: 1 Heidfeld, 44; **2** Rodriguez, 18; **3** Minassian, 14; **4** Junqueira, 10; **5=** Watt, 9; **5=** Ayari, 9.

FIA INTERNATIONAL FORMULA 3000 CHAMPIONSHIP, Hockenheimring, Heidelberg, Germany, 31 July. Round 7. 30 laps of the 4.240-mile/6.823-km circuit, 127.188 miles/ 204.690 km.
1 Bruno Junqueira, BR, 1h 01m 17.627s, 124.504 mph/ 200.369 km/h.
2 Max Wilson, BR, 1h 01m 18.631s; **3** Stéphane Sarrazin, F, 1h 01m 22.063s; **4** Gonzalo Rodriguez, U, 1h 01m 25.536s; **5** Enrique Bernoldi, BR, 1h 01m 42.449s; **6** Franck Montagny, F, 1h 01m 52.361s; **7** Jason Watt, DK, 1h 01m 53.525s; **8** David Saelens, B, 1h 02m 00.891s; **9** Jamie Davies, GB, 1h 02m 02.181s; **10** Oliver Martini, I, 1h 02m 03.123s; **11** Cyrille Sauvage, F, 1h 02m 05.781s; **12** Soheil Ayari, F, 1h 02m 29.868s; **13** Andrej Pavicevic, AUS, 1h 02m 31.135s; **14** Mario Haberfeld, BR, 1h 02m 51.966s; **15** Kevin McGarrity, GB, 29 laps; **16** Norberto Fontana, RA, 27 (DNF – gear linkage); **17** André Couto, MAC, 11 (DNF – accident); **18** Tomas Enge, CZ, 11 (DNF – accident); **19** Bas Leinders, B, 11 (DNF – accident); **20** Paolo Ruberti, I, 6 (DNF – spin); **21** Fabrizio Gollin, I, 5 (DNF – spin); **22** Nicolas Minassian, F, 5 (DNF – water leak); **23** Nick Heidfeld, D, 3 (DNF – spin); **24** Fabrice Walfisch, F, 0 (DNF – accident); **25** Marc Goossens, B, 0 (DNF – accident); **26** Justin Wilson, GB, 0 (DNF – transmission).
Fastest race lap: Rodriguez, 2m 01.472s, 125.647 mph/ 202.210 km/h.
Fastest qualifying lap: Wilson (Max), 1m 59.828s, 127.371 mph/204.984 km/h.
Did not qualify: Andrea Piccini, I; Wolf Henzler, D; Jeffrey van Hooydonk, B; David Terrien, F; Oliver Gavin, GB; Norman Simon, D; Leopoldo 'Polo' Perez de Villaamil, E; Andrea Boldrini, I; Ricardo Mauricio, BR; Alexander Müller, D; Arnd Meier, D; Alex Yoong, MAL; Laurent Delahaye, F; Viktor Maslov, RUS.
Championship points: 1 Heidfeld, 44; **2** Rodriguez, 21; **3** Junqueira, 20; **4** Minassian, 14; **5** Sarrazin, 12; **6** Wilson (Max), 10.

FIA INTERNATIONAL FORMULA 3000 CHAMPIONSHIP, Hungaroring, Mogyorod, Budapest, Hungary, 14 August. Round 8. 52 laps of the 2.469-mile/3.973-km circuit, 128.373 miles/206.596 km.
1 Stéphane Sarrazin, F, 1h 19m 43.676s, 96.608 mph/ 155.476 km/h.
2 Nick Heidfeld, D, 1h 19m 44.468s; **3** Franck Montagny, F, 1h 19m 56.489s; **4** Soheil Ayari, F, 1h 19m 57.994s; **5** Nicolas Minassian, F, 1h 19m 59.342s; **6** Jason Watt, DK, 1h 20m 01.049s; **7** Justin Wilson, GB, 1h 20m 01.486s; **8** Enrique Bernoldi, BR, 1h 20m 27.246s; **9** Ricardo Mauricio, BR, 1h 20m 39.777s; **10** Kevin McGarrity, GB, 1h 20m 57.064s; **11** Fabrizio Gollin, I, 1h 20m 57.813s; **12** Jamie Davies, GB 1h 20m 58.329s; **13** Marcelo Battistuzzi, BR, 1h 21m 00.000s; **14** Tomas Enge, CZ, 1h 21m 00.442s; **15** Bruno Junqueira, BR, 51 laps; **16** Jeffrey van Hooydonk, B, 47 (DNF – spin); **17** Paolo Ruberti, I, 36 (DNF – accident); **18** Norberto Fontana, RA, 34 (DNF – accident); **19** Max Wilson, BR, 34 (DNF – accident); **20** Leopoldo 'Polo' Perez de Villaamil, E, 32 (DNF – accident); **21** Bas Leinders, B, 32 (DNF – driveshaft); **22** André Couto, MAC, 24 (DNF – suspension); **23** Fabrice Walfisch, F, 22 (DNF – throttle); **24** Andrea Piccini, I, 21 (DNF – accident); **25** Gonzalo Rodriguez, U, 6 (DNF – spin). Marc Goossens, B, finished 3rd in 1h 19m 56.123s but was disqualified due to an illegal suspension damper.
Fastest race lap: Heidfeld, 1m 30.801s, 97.877 mph/157.518 km/h.
Fastest qualifying lap: Walfisch, 1m 29.261s, 99.566 mph/ 160.236 km/h.
Did not qualify: Oliver Gavin, GB; David Saelens, B; Alexander Müller, D; Cyrille Sauvage, F; David Terrien, F; Laurent Delahaye, F; Viktor Maslov, RUS; Oliver Martini, I; Andrea Boldrini, I; Arnd Meier, D; Mario Haberfeld, BR; Alex Yoong, MAL; Nicolas Filiberti, RA; Andrej Pavicevic, AUS.
Championship points: 1 Heidfeld, 50; **2** Sarrazin, 22; **3** Rodriguez, 21; **4** Junqueira, 20; **5** Minassian, 16; **6** Ayari, 12.

FIA INTERNATIONAL FORMULA 3000 CHAMPIONSHIP, Circuit de Spa-Francorchamps, Stavelot, Belgium, 28 August. Round 9. 30 laps of the 4.330-mile/6.968-km circuit, 129.882 miles/209.025 km.
1 Jason Watt, DK, 1h 13m 57.599s, 105.367 mph/169.571 km/h.
2 Gonzalo Rodriguez, U, 1h 14m 00.462s; **3** Nicolas Minassian, F, 1h 14m 01.237s; **4** Nick Heidfeld, D, 1h 14m 04.095s; **5** David Saelens, B, 1h 14m 10.020s; **6** Ricardo Mauricio, BR, 1h 14m 14.468s; **7** André Couto, MAC, 1h 14m 16.413s; **8** David Terrien, F, 1h 14m 24.012s; **9** Oliver Gavin, GB, 1h 14m 24.960s; **10** Dino Morelli, GB, 1h 14m 26.488s; **11** Tomas Enge, CZ, 1h 14m 27.487s; **12** Jamie Davies, GB, 1h 14m 28.355s; **13** Fabrizio Gollin, I, 1h 14m 29.363s; **14** Norberto Fontana, RA, 1h 14m 31.325s; **15** Andrej Pavicevic, AUS, 1h 14m 47.329s; **16** Fabrice Walfisch, F, 1h 14m 47.958s; **17** Marcelo Battistuzzi, BR, 1h 14m 48.633s; **18** Marc Goossens, B, 20 laps (DNF – brakes); **19** Alex Yoong, MAL, 4 (DNF – accident); **20** Justin Wilson, GB, 4 (DNF – accident); **21** Franck Montagny, F, 3 (DNF – accident); **22** Soheil Ayari, F, 2 (DNF – accident); **23** Bruno Junqueira, BR, 2 (DNF – accident); **24** Stéphane Sarrazin, F, 1 (DNF – accident damage); **25** Kevin McGarrity, GB, 0 (DNF – accident).
Fastest race lap: Rodriguez, 2m 08.993s, 120.836 mph/ 194.466 km/h.
Fastest qualifying lap: Watt, 2m 08.829s, 120.990 mph/ 194.714 km/h.
Did not start: Laurent Delahaye, F (transmission failure during warm up).
Did not qualify: Andrea Piccini, I; Norman Simon, D; Oliver Martini, I; Mario Haberfeld, BR; Jeffrey van Hooydonk, B; Giovanni Montanari, I; Marco Apicella, I; Enrique Bernoldi, BR; Viktor Maslov, RUS; Leopoldo 'Polo' Perez de Villaamil, E; Bas Leinders, B; Paolo Ruberti, I; Steve Hiesse, F; Arnd Meier, D.
Championship points: 1 Heidfeld, 53; **2** Rodriguez, 27; **3** Sarrazin, 22; **4=** Junqueira, 20; **4=** Watt, 20; **4=** Minassian, 20.

FIA INTERNATIONAL FORMULA 3000 CHAMPIONSHIP, Nürburgring, Nürburg/Eifel, Germany, 25 September. Round 10. 45 laps of the 2.831-mile/4.556-km circuit, 127.383 miles/205.003 km.
1 Jason Watt, DK, 1h 09m 35.500s, 109.826 mph/176.748 km/h.
2 Nick Heidfeld, D, 1h 09m 36.002s; **3** Max Wilson, BR, 1h 09m 49.464s; **4** Soheil Ayari, F, 1h 09m 51.679s; **5** David Saelens, B, 1h 10m 23.870s; **6** Jamie Davies, GB 1h 10m 25.108s; **7** Kevin McGarrity, GB, 1h 10m 29.533s; **8** Oliver Gavin, GB, 1h 10m 30.024s; **9** Franck Montagny, F, 1h 10m 30.375s; **10** Norberto Fontana, RA, 1h 10m 37.233s; **11** David Terrien, F, 1h 10m 39.658s; **12** Jeffrey van Hooydonk, B, 1h 10m 40.768s; **13** Andrej Pavicevic, AUS, 1h 10m 42.358s; **14** Cyrille Sauvage, F, 1h 10m 43.096s; **15** Norman Simon, D, 1h 10m 45.602s; **16** Bruno Junqueira, BR 1h 10m 46.041s; **17** Stéphane Sarrazin, F, 1h 10m 57.155s; **18** Fabrizio Gollin, I, 44 laps; **19** Paolo Ruberti, I, 44; **20** Ricardo Mauricio, BR, 41 (DNF – accident); **21** Justin Wilson, GB, 20 (DNF – handling); **22** Tomas Enge, CZ, 11 (DNF – suspension damage/spin); **23** Fabrice Walfisch, F, 9 (DNF – suspension damage/spin); **24** Bas Leinders, B, 4 (DNF – gearbox); **25** Nicolas Minassian, F, 3 (DNF – suspension damage/spin); **26** Alex Yoong, MAL, 0 (DNF – accident damage).
Fastest race lap: Heidfeld, 1m 31.876s, 110.926 mph/ 178.519 km/h.
Fastest qualifying lap: Heidfeld, 1m 30.925s, 112.087 mph/ 180.386 km/h.
Did not start: André Couto, MAC (car underweight).
Did not qualify: Dino Morelli, IRL; Marc Goossens, B; Mario Haberfeld, BR; Andrea Piccini, I; Giovanni Montanari, I; Leopoldo 'Polo' Perez de Villaamil, E; Marcelo Battistuzzi, BR; Arnd Meier, D; Laurent Delahaye, F; Raimon Duras, F; Viktor Maslov, RUS; Enrique Bernoldi, BR.

Final championship points
1 Nick Heidfeld, D, 59; **2** Jason Watt, DK, 30; **3** Gonzalo Rodriguez †, U, 27; **4** Stéphane Sarrazin, F, 22; **5=** Bruno

Junqueira, BR, 20; 5= Nicolas Minassian, F, 20; 7 Soheil Ayari, F, 15; 8 Max Wilson, BR, 14; 9 David Saelens, B, 8; 10= Kevin McGarrity, GB, 6; 10= Tomas Enge, CZ, 6; 10= Franck Montagny, F, 6; 13= Fabrice Walfisch, F, 4; 13= André Couto, MAC, 4; 13= Norberto Fontana, RA, 4; 16= Oliver Gavin, GB, 3; 16= Jeffrey van Hooydonk, B, 3; 18= Andrea Piccini, I, 2; 18= Enrique Bernoldi, BR, 2; 18= Justin Wilson, GB, 2; 21= Bas Leinders, B, 1; 21= Ricardo Mauricio, BR, 1; 21= Jamie Davies, GB, 1.

Formula 3000 Italia

All cars are Lola-Zytek V8.

ITALIAN FORMULA 3000 CHAMPIONSHIP, Autodromo di Vallelunga, Campagnano di Roma, Italy, 6 June. Round 1. 32 laps of the 1.988-mile/ 3.200-km circuit, 63.628 miles/ 102.400 km.
1 Marco Apicella, I, 35m 42.203s, 106.928 mph/172.085 km/h.
2 Paolo Montin, I, 35m 46.249s; 3 Leopoldo 'Polo' Perez de Villaamil, E, 35m 51.226s; 4 Giorgio Vinella, I, 35m 52.125s; 5 Ananda Mikola, I, 35m 58.492s; 6 Werner Lupberger, ZA, 35m 59.868s; 7 Mark Shaw, GB, 36m 00.528s; 8 Darren Turner, GB, 36m 02.020s; 9 Gabriele Lancieri, I, 36m 12.120s; 10 Riccardo Moscatelli, I, 36m 13.454s.
Fastest race lap: Apicella, 1m 06.330s, 107.918 mph/ 173.677 km/h.
Fastest qualifying lap: Villaamil, 1m 05.750s, 108.870 mph/ 175.209 km/h.

ITALIAN FORMULA 3000 CHAMPIONSHIP, Autodromo Nazionale di Monza, Milan, Italy, 27 June. Round 2. 25 laps of the 3.585-mile/5.770-km circuit, 89.633 miles/ 144.250 km.
1 Marcelo Battistuzzi, BR, 44m 17.382s, 121.427 mph/ 195.418 km/h.
2 Giorgio Vinella, I, 44m 18.055s; 3 Werner Lupberger, ZA, 44m 19.428s; 4 Mark Shaw, GB, 44m 20.636s; 5 Cesare Manfredini, I, 44m 22.612s; 6 Riccardo Moscatelli, I, 44m 23.287s; 7 Giandomenico Brusatin, I, 44m 24.264s; 8 Ananda Mikola, I, 22 laps; 9 Gabriele Lancieri, I, 22; 10 Paolo Montin, I (DNF).
Fastest race lap: Battistuzzi, 1m 40.849s, 127.985 mph/ 205.971 km/h.
Fastest qualifying lap: Battistuzzi, 1m 38.910s, 130.494 mph/210.009 km/h.

ITALIAN FORMULA 3000 CHAMPIONSHIP, Ente Autodromo di Pergusa, Enna-Pergusa, Sicily, 18 July. Round 3. 25 laps of the 3.076-mile/4.950-km circuit, 76.895 miles/ 123.750 km.
1 Giorgio Vinella, I, 39m 22.365s, 117.180 mph/188.582 km/h.
2 Mark Shaw, GB, 39m 28.081s; 3 Gabriele Lancieri, I, 39m 32.943s; 4 Oliver Martini, I, 39m 37.132s; 5 Alex Yoong, MAL, 39m 50.956s; 6 Werner Lupberger, ZA, 24 laps; 7 Giandomenico Brusatin, I, 24; 8 Paolo Montin, I, 24; 9 Leopoldo 'Polo' Perez de Villaamil, E, 24; 10 Cesare Manfredini, I, 24. Ananda Mikola, I, finished 1st but was disqualified.
Fastest race lap: Martini, 1m 33.413s, 118.536 mph/190.766 km/h.
Fastest qualifying lap: Martini, 1m 31.986s, 120.375 mph/ 193.725 km/h.

ITALIAN FORMULA 3000 CHAMPIONSHIP, Donington Park Circuit, Derbyshire, Great Britain, 1 August. Round 4. 34 laps of the 1.946-mile/3.132-km circuit, 66.169 miles/ 106.488 km.
1 Werner Lupberger, ZA, 46m 59.700s, 84.480 mph/135.957 km/h.
2 Alex Yoong, MAL, 47m 00.917s; 3 Gabriele Lancieri, I, 47m 47.171s; 4 Marcelo Battistuzzi, BR, 47m 48.398s; 5 Giandomenico Brusatin, I, 47m 49.058s; 6 Viktor Maslov, RUS, 48m 09.035s; 7 Jaroslaw Wierczuk, PL, 48m 13.042s; 8 Marco Apicella, I, 48m 13.748s; 9 Rafael Sarandeses, E, 33 laps; 10 Riccardo Moscatelli, I (DNF).
Fastest race lap: Leopoldo 'Polo' Perez de Villaamil, E, 1m 15.010s, 93.402 mph/150.316 km/h.
Fastest qualifying lap: Mark Shaw, GB, 1m 02.327s, 112.408 mph/180.904 km/h.

ITALIAN FORMULA 3000 CHAMPIONSHIP, Autodromo Santamonica, Misano Adriatico, Rimini, Italy, 12 September. Round 5. 24 laps of the 2.523-mile/4.060-km circuit, 60.546 miles/97.440 km.
1 Marco Apicella, I, 34m 16.140s, 106.008 mph/170.603 km/h.
2 Thomas Biagi, I, 34m 18.636s; 3 Werner Lupberger, ZA, 34m 28.004s; 4 Paolo Montin, I, 34m 32.984s; 5 Giorgio Vinella, I, 34m 40.787s; 6 Ananda Mikola, I, 34m 42.651s; 7 Oliver Martini, I, 34m 46.236s; 8 Nicolas Filiberti, RA, 34m 48.177s; 9 Alex Yoong, MAL, 34m 54.018s; 10 Gabriele Lancieri, I, 34m 54.133s.
Fastest race lap: Apicella, 1m 24.971s, 106.883 mph/ 172.012 km/h.
Fastest qualifying lap: Biagi, 1m 24.623s, 107.323 mph/ 172.719 km/h.

ITALIAN FORMULA 3000 CHAMPIONSHIP, Autodromo Santamonica, Misano Adriatico, Rimini, Italy, 3 October. Round 6. 25 laps of the 2.523-mile/4.060-km circuit, 63.069 miles/101.500 km.
1 Giorgio Vinella, I, 35m 57.109s, 99.709 mph/160.467 km/h.
2 Werner Lupberger, ZA, 35m 58.911s; 3 Thomas Biagi, I, 38m 59.647s; 4 Dino Morelli, IRL, 36m 08.163s; 5 Gabriele Lancieri, I, 36m 08.799s; 6 Ananda Mikola, I, 36m 09.932s; 7 Fabrizio Gollin, I, 36m 11.724s; 8 Nicolas Filiberti, RA, 36m 19.706s; 9 Jaroslaw Wierczuk, PL; 10 Nikolaos Stremmenos, GR.
Fastest race lap: Marco Apicella, I, 1m 25.484s, 106.242 mph/170.979 km/h.
Fastest qualifying lap: Apicella, 1m 23.899s, 108.249 mph/ 174.209 km/h.

ITALIAN FORMULA 3000 CHAMPIONSHIP, Autodromo Enzo e Dino Ferrari, Imola, Italy, 24 October. Round 7. 21 laps of the 3.063-mile/4.930-km circuit, 64.331 miles/ 103.530 km.
1 Dino Morelli, IRL, 41m 25.182s, 93.188 mph/149.972 km/h.
2 Thomas Biagi, I, 41m 25.720s; 3 Paolo Ruberti, I, 42m 07.671s; 4 Gabriele Lancieri, I, 42m 13.037s; 5 Kristian Kolby, D, 42m 21.532s; 6 Werner Lupberger, ZA, 42m 34.475s; 7 Fabrizio Gollin, I, 43m 00.780s; 8 Viktor Maslov, RUS, 43m 05.748s; 9 Giorgio Vinella, I, 20 laps; 10 Paolo Montin, I, 20.
Fastest race lap: Gollin, 1m 54.889s, 95.989 mph/154.480 km/h.
Fastest qualifying lap: Morelli, 2m 07.651s, 86.393 mph/ 139.035 km/h.

Final championship points
1 Giorgio Vinella, I, 31; 2 Werner Lupberger, ZA, 27; 3 Marco Apicella, I, 20; 4 Thomas Biagi, I, 16; 5= Marcelo Battistuzzi, BR, 13; 5= Gabriele Lancieri, I, 13; 5= Dino Morelli, IRL, 13; 8= Paolo Montin, I, 9; 8= Mark Shaw, GB, 9; 10 Alex Yoong, MAL, 8; 11= Ananda Mikola, I, 4; 11= Leopoldo 'Polo' Perez de Villaamil, E, 4; 11= Paolo Ruberti, I, 4; 14 Oliver Martini, I, 3; 15= Giandomenico Brusatin, I, 2; 15= Kristian Kolby, DK, 2; 15= Cesare Manfredini, I, 2; 18= Viktor Maslov, RUS, 1; 18= Riccardo Moscatelli, I, 1.

British Formula 3 Championship

AUTOSPORT BRITISH FORMULA 3 CHAMPIONSHIP, Donington Park Grand Prix Circuit, Derbyshire, Great Britain, 21 March. Round 1. 20 laps of the 2.500-mile/ 4.023-km circuit, 50.000 miles/80.467 km.
1 Marc Hynes, GB (Dallara F399-Mugen Honda), 29m 58.171s, 100.102 mph/161.098 km/h.
2 Jenson Button, GB (Dallara F399-Renault), 30m 02.049s; 3 Luciano Burti, BR (Dallara F399-Mugen Honda), 30m 04.056s; 4 Narain Karthikeyan, IND (Dallara F399-Mugen Honda), 30m 07.566s; 5 Kristian Kolby, DK (Dallara F399-Mugen Honda), 30m 09.831s; 6 Doug Bell, GB (Dallara F399-Opel), 30m 15.334s; 7 Michael Bentwood, GB (Dallara F399-Mugen Honda), 30m 16.829s; 8 Aluizio Coelho, BR (Dallara F399-Renault), 30m 17.442s; 9 Andrew Kirkcaldy, GB (Dallara F399-Mugen Honda), 30m 20.868s; 10 Timothy Spouge, GB (Dallara F399-Opel), 30m 41.842s.
Fastest race lap: Hynes, 1m 28.993s, 101.132 mph/162.755 km/h.
National Class winner: Jeremy Smith, GB (Dallara F398-Opel), 31m 07.607s (13th).
Fastest qualifying lap: Button, 1m 38.076s, 91.766 mph/ 147.683 km/h.
Championship points: 1 Hynes, 21; 2 Button, 15; 3 Burti, 12; 4 Karthikeyan, 10; 5 Kolby, 8; 6 Bell, 6.
National Class: 1 Smith, 20; 2 O'Connell, 1.

AUTOSPORT BRITISH FORMULA 3 CHAMPIONSHIP, Silverstone International Circuit, Towcester, Northamptonshire, Great Britain, 28 March. Round 2. 22 laps of the 2.249-mile/3.619-km circuit, 49.478 miles/79.627 km.
1 Marc Hynes, GB (Dallara F399-Mugen Honda), 28m 12.036s, 105.270 mph/169.416 km/h.
2 Kristian Kolby, DK (Dallara F399-Mugen Honda), 28m 12.253s; 3 Luciano Burti, BR (Dallara F399-Mugen Honda), 28m 27.553s; 4 Martin O'Connell, GB (Dallara F398-TOM'S Toyota), 28m 30.085s (1st National class); 5 Matthew Davies, GB (Dallara F399-Mugen Honda), 28m 35.698s; 6 Jenson Button, GB (Dallara F399-Renault), 28m 36.637s; 7 Andrew Kirkcaldy, GB (Dallara F399-Mugen Honda), 28m 41.771s; 8 Doug Bell, GB (Dallara F399-Opel), 28m 43.249s; 9 Yudai Igarashi, J (Dallara F399-Mugen Honda), 28m 47.454s; 10 Toby Scheckter, ZA (Dallara F399-Mugen Honda), 28m 51.968s.
Fastest race lap: Kolby, 1m 16.111s, 106.376 mph/171.196 km/h.
Fastest qualifying lap: Kolby, 1m 15.466s, 107.285 mph/ 172.659 km/h.
Championship points: 1 Hynes, 41; 2= Burti, 24; 2= Kolby, 24; 4 Button, 23; 5= Bell, 10; 5= Davies, 10; 5= Karthikeyan, 10.
National Class: 1 Smith, 35; 2 O'Connell, 22.

AUTOSPORT BRITISH FORMULA 3 CHAMPIONSHIP, Thruxton Circuit, Andover, Hampshire, Great Britain, 11 April. Round 3. 20 laps of the 2.356-mile/3.792-km circuit, 47.120 miles/75.832 km.
1 Jenson Button, GB (Dallara F399-Renault), 23m 42.508s, 119.249 mph/191.912 km/h.
2 Andrew Kirkcaldy, GB (Dallara F399-Mugen Honda), 23m 44.369s; 3 Marc Hynes, GB (Dallara F399-Mugen Honda), 23m 44.808s; 4 Kristian Kolby, DK (Dallara F399-Mugen Honda), 23m 51.052s; 5 Matthew Davies, GB (Dallara F399-Mugen Honda), 23m 53.041s; 6 Alex Yoong, MAL (Dallara F399-Mugen Honda), 23m 53.960s; 7 Martin O'Connell, GB (Dallara F398-TOM'S Toyota), 23m 54.354s (1st National class); 8 Michael Bentwood, GB (Dallara F399-Mugen Honda), 23m 55.860s; 9 Aluizio Coelho, BR (Dallara F399-Renault), 23m 58.745s; 10 Timothy Spouge, GB (Dallara F399-Opel), 23m 59.110s.
Fastest race lap: Luciano Burti, BR (Dallara F399-Mugen Honda), 1m 09.978s, 121.204 mph/195.059 km/h.
Fastest qualifying lap: Kirkcaldy, 1m 08.747s, 123.374 mph/ 198.551 km/h.
Championship points: 1 Hynes, 53; 2 Button, 43; 3 Kolby, 34; 4 Burti, 25; 5 Kirkcaldy, 25; 6 Davies, 18.
National Class: 1 Smith, 50; 2 O'Connell, 43.

AUTOSPORT BRITISH FORMULA 3 CHAMPIONSHIP, Brands Hatch Short Circuit, Dartford, Kent, Great Britain, 25 April. 2 x 25 laps of the 1.226-mile/1.973-km circuit. Round 4 (30.650 miles/49.326 km).
1 Luciano Burti, BR (Dallara F399-Mugen Honda), 18m 18.430s, 100.452 mph/ 161.663 km/h.
2 Narain Karthikeyan, IND (Dallara F399-Mugen Honda), 18m 18.667s; 3 Marc Hynes, GB (Dallara F399-Mugen Honda), 18m 19.158s; 4 Martin O'Connell, GB (Dallara F398-TOM'S Toyota), 18m 19.487s (1st National class); 5 Alex Yoong, MAL (Dallara F399-Mugen Honda), 18m 20.724s; 6 Michael Bentwood, GB (Dallara F399-Mugen Honda), 18m 21.000s; 7 Kristian Kolby, DK (Dallara F399-Mugen Honda), 18m 21.868s; 8 Jenson Button, GB (Dallara F399-Renault), 18m 25.788s; 9 Toby Scheckter, ZA (Dallara F399-Mugen Honda), 18m 28.004s; 10 Yudai Igarashi, J (Dallara F399-Mugen Honda), 18m 28.515s.
Fastest race lap: Karthikeyan, 42.901s, 102.879 mph/ 165.567 km/h.
Fastest qualifying lap: Karthikeyan, 42.253s, 104.456 mph/ 168.106 km/h.

Round 5 (30.650 miles/49.326 km)
1 Narain Karthikeyan, IND (Dallara F399-Mugen Honda), 18m 00.604s, 102.110 mph/164.329 km/h.
2 Alex Yoong, MAL (Dallara F399-Mugen Honda), 18m 07.881s; 3 Luciano Burti, BR (Dallara F399-Mugen Honda), 18m 09.414s; 4 Matthew Davies, GB (Dallara F399-Mugen Honda), 18m 09.525s; 5 Martin O'Connell, GB (Dallara F398-TOM'S Toyota), 18m 11.225s (1st National class); 6 Marc Hynes, GB (Dallara F399-Mugen Honda), 18m 12.168s; 7 Jenson Button, GB (Dallara F399-Renault), 18m 12.841s; 8 Michael Bentwood, GB (Dallara F399-Mugen Honda), 18m 14.929s; 9 Yudai Igarashi, J (Dallara F399-Mugen Honda), 18m 19.426s; 10 Aluizio Coelho, BR (Dallara F399-Renault), 18m 19.924s.
Fastest race lap: Karthikeyan, 42.617s, 103.564 mph/ 166.671 km/h.
Fastest qualifying lap: Karthikeyan, 42.325s, 104.279 mph/ 167.820 km/h.
Championship points: 1 Hynes, 73; 2 Burti, 57; 3 Button, 53; 4 Karthikeyan, 47; 5 Kolby, 40; 6 Yoong, 31.
National Class: 1 O'Connell, 85; 2 Smith, 74; 3 John Bender, USA, 30.

AUTOSPORT BRITISH FORMULA 3 CHAMPIONSHIP, Oulton Park International Circuit, Tarporley, Cheshire, Great Britain, 3 May. Round 6. 18 laps of the 2.775-mile/4.466-km circuit, 49.950 miles/80.387 km.
1 Luciano Burti, BR (Dallara F399-Mugen Honda), 27m 34.347s, 108.695 mph/174.928 km/h.
2 Kristian Kolby, DK (Dallara F399-Mugen Honda), 27m 36.520s; 3 Matthew Davies, GB (Dallara F399-Mugen Honda), 27m 37.522s; 4 Andrew Kirkcaldy, GB (Dallara F399-Mugen Honda), 27m 38.895s; 5 Jenson Button, GB (Dallara F399-Renault), 27m 39.242s; 6 Alex Yoong, MAL (Dallara F399-Mugen Honda), 27m 43.833s; 7 Aluizio Coelho, BR (Dallara F399-Renault), 27m 49.106s. 8 Michael Bentwood, GB (Dallara F399-Mugen Honda), 27m 55.559s; 9 Timothy Spouge, GB (Dallara F399-Opel), 27m 56.058s; 10 Marc Hynes, GB (Dallara F399-Mugen Honda), 27m 56.909s.
Fastest race lap: Burti, 1m 31.177s, 109.567 mph/176.331 km/h.
National Class winner: Martin O'Connell, GB (Dallara F398-TOM'S Toyota), 27m 58.651s (11th).
Fastest qualifying lap: Burti, 1m 30.101s, 110.876 mph/ 178.437 km/h.
Championship points: 1 Burti, 78; 2 Hynes, 74; 3 Button, 61; 4 Kolby, 55; 5 Karthikeyan, 47; 6 Davies, 40.
National Class: 1 O'Connell, 106; 2 Smith, 86; 3 Bender, 30.

AUTOSPORT BRITISH FORMULA 3 CHAMPIONSHIP, Croft Circuit, Croft-on-Tees, North Yorkshire, Great Britain, 6 June. Round 7. 25 laps of the 2.127-mile/3.423-km circuit, 53.175 miles/85.577 km.
1 Marc Hynes, GB (Dallara F399-Mugen Honda), 33m 52.909s, 94.166 mph/151.545 km/h.
2 Luciano Burti, BR (Dallara F399-Mugen Honda), 33m 53.982s; 3 Narain Karthikeyan, IND (Dallara F399-Mugen Honda), 34m 10.663s; 4 Timothy Spouge, GB (Dallara F399-Opel), 34m 12.741s; 5 Aluizio Coelho, BR (Dallara F399-Renault), 34m 16.426s; 6 Tor Sriachavanon, TH (Dallara F399-Mugen Honda), 34m 26.701s; 7 Michael Bentwood, GB (Dallara F399-Mugen Honda), 34m 27.550s; 8 Yudai Igarashi, J (Dallara F399-Mugen Honda), 34m 27.854s; 9 Doug Bell, GB (Dallara F399-Mugen Honda), 34m 29.333s; 10 Martin O'Connell, GB (Dallara F398-TOM'S Toyota), 34m 29.794s (1st National class).
Fastest race lap: Burti, 1m 14.551s, 102.711 mph/165.297 km/h.
Fastest qualifying lap: Hynes, 1m 14.626s, 102.608 mph/ 165.131 km/h.
Championship points: 1= Burti, 94; 1= Hynes, 94; 3 Button, 61; 4 Karthikeyan, 59; 5 Kolby, 55; 6 Davies, 40.
National Class: 1 O'Connell, 127; 2 Smith, 101; 3 Bender, 30.

AUTOSPORT BRITISH FORMULA 3 CHAMPIONSHIP, Brands Hatch Grand Prix Circuit, Dartford, Kent, Great Britain, 20 June. Round 8. 18 laps of the 2.623-mile/4.221-km circuit, 47.214 miles/75.984 km.
1 Narain Karthikeyan, IND (Dallara F399-Mugen Honda), 29m 00.707s, 97.644 mph/157.144 km/h.
2 Luciano Burti, BR (Dallara F399-Mugen Honda), 29m 06.555s; 3 Andrew Kirkcaldy, GB (Dallara F399-Mugen Honda), 29m 07.488s; 4 Marc Hynes, GB (Dallara F399-Mugen Honda), 29m 07.896s; 5 Matthew Davies, GB (Dallara F399-Mugen Honda), 29m 08.339s; 6 Jenson Button, GB (Dallara F399-Renault), 29m 08.746s; 7 Kristian Kolby, DK (Dallara F399-Mugen Honda), 29m 11.106s; 8 Aluizio Coelho, BR (Dallara F399-Renault), 29m 19.311s; 9 Tor Sriachavanon, TH (Dallara F399-Mugen Honda), 29m 22.545s; 10 Michael Bentwood, GB (Dallara F399-Mugen Honda), 29m 22.908s.
Fastest race lap: Karthikeyan, 1m 19.859s, 118.243 mph/ 190.294 km/h. National Class winner: John Bender, USA (Dallara F398-Mugen Honda), 29m 49.524s (13th).
Fastest qualifying lap: Burti, 1m 18.637s, 120.081 mph/ 193.251 km/h.
Championship points: 1 Burti, 109; 2 Hynes, 104; 3 Karthikeyan, 80; 4 Button, 67; 5 Kolby, 59; 6 Davies, 48.
National Class: 1 O'Connell, 127; 2 Smith, 111; 3 Bender, 51.

AUTOSPORT BRITISH FORMULA 3 CHAMPIONSHIP, Silverstone Grand Prix Circuit, Towcester, Northamptonshire, Great Britain, 10 July. Round 9. 15 laps of the 3.194-mile/5.140-km circuit, 47.955 miles/77.176 km.
1 Marc Hynes, GB (Dallara F399-Mugen Honda), 26m 24.564s, 108.950 mph/175.338 km/h.
2 Jenson Button, GB (Dallara F399-Renault), 26m 24.947s; 3 Luciano Burti, BR (Dallara F399-Mugen Honda), 26m 29.348s; 4 Kristian Kolby, DK (Dallara F399-Mugen Honda), 26m 30.569s; 5 Narain Karthikeyan, IND (Dallara F399-Mugen Honda), 26m 39.942s; 6 Matthew Davies, GB (Dallara F399-Mugen Honda), 26m 46.931s; 7 Toby Scheckter, ZA (Dallara F399-Mugen Honda), 26m 47.160s; 8 Timothy Spouge, GB (Dallara F399-Opel), 26m 49.523s; 9 Michael Bentwood, GB (Dallara F399-Mugen Honda), 26m 54.847s; 10 Doug Bell, GB (Dallara F399-Mugen Honda), 26m 54.943s.
Fastest race lap: Button, 1m 44.630s, 109.896 mph/176.860 km/h. National Class winner: Takuma Sato, J (Dallara F398-Mugen Honda), 27m 23.549s (16th).
Fastest qualifying lap: Hynes, 1m 43.506s, 111.089 mph/ 178.781 km/h.
Championship points: 1 Hynes, 124; 2 Burti, 121; 3 Karthikeyan, 88; 4 Button, 83; 5 Kolby, 69; 6 Davies, 54.
National Class: 1 O'Connell, 127; 2 Smith, 111; 3 Bender, 64.

AUTOSPORT BRITISH FORMULA 3 CHAMPIONSHIP, Snetterton Circuit, Norfolk, Great Britain, 25 July. Round 10. 21 laps of the 1.952-mile/3.141-km circuit, 40.992 miles/65.970 km.
1 Luciano Burti, BR (Dallara F399-Mugen Honda), 24m 26.067s, 100.658 mph/161.993 km/h.
2 Marc Hynes, GB (Dallara F399-Mugen Honda), 24m 26.515s; 3 Matthew Davies, GB (Dallara F399-Mugen Honda), 24m 27.345s; 4 Kristian Kolby, DK (Dallara F399-Mugen Honda), 24m 28.255s; 5 Martin O'Connell, GB (Dallara F398-TOM'S Toyota), 24m 32.250s (1st National class); 6 Doug Bell, GB (Dallara F399-Mugen Honda), 24m 33.058s; 7 Narain Karthikeyan, IND (Dallara F399-Mugen Honda), 24m 37.583s; 8 Timothy Spouge, GB (Dallara F399-Opel), 24m 40.666s; 9 Warren Carway, IRL (Dallara F399-Mugen Honda), 24m 44.526s; 10 Takuma Sato, J (Dallara F398-Mugen Honda), 24m 48.019s.
Fastest race lap: Burti, 1m 02.588s, 112.277 mph/180.692 km/h.
Fastest qualifying lap: Burti, 1m 02.461s, 112.505 mph/ 181.060 km/h.
Championship points: 1 Burti, 142; 2 Hynes, 139; 3 Karthikeyan, 94; 4 Button, 85; 5 Kolby, 79; 6 Davies, 66.
National Class: 1 O'Connell, 148; 2 Smith, 111; 3 Bender, 64.

AUTOSPORT BRITISH FORMULA 3 CHAMPIONSHIP, Pembrey Circuit, Llanelli, Dyfed, Great Britain, 15 August. 2 x 20 laps of the 1.456-mile/2.343-km circuit. Round 11 (29.120 miles/46.864 km)
1 Kristian Kolby, DK (Dallara F399-Mugen Honda), 17m 19.874s, 100.812 mph/162.242 km/h.
2 Jenson Button, GB (Dallara F399-Renault), 17m 27.524s; 3 Luciano Burti, BR (Dallara F399-Mugen Honda), 17m 29.083s; 4 Michael Bentwood, GB (Dallara F399-Mugen Honda), 17m 34.091s; 5 Matthew Davies, GB (Dallara F399-Mugen Honda), 17m 34.835s; 6 Marc Hynes, GB (Dallara F399-Mugen Honda), 17m 35.894s; 7 Tor Sriachavanon, TH (Dallara F399-Mugen Honda), 17m 39.066s; 8 Andrew Kirkcaldy, GB (Dallara F399-Mugen Honda), 17m 41.702s; 9 Martin O'Connell, GB (Dallara F398-TOM'S Toyota), 17m 42.827s (1st National class); 10 Toby Scheckter, ZA (Dallara F399-Mugen Honda), 17m 43.245s.
Fastest race lap: Button, 50.971s, 102.835 mph/165.497 km/h.
Fastest qualifying lap: Kolby, 50.586s, 103.618 mph/ 166.756 km/h.

Round 12 (29.120 miles/46.864 km)
1 Jenson Button, GB (Dallara F399-Renault), 19m 52.321s, 87.923 mph/141.498 km/h.
2 Matthew Davies, GB (Dallara F399-Mugen Honda), 19m 54.534s; 3 Kristian Kolby, DK (Dallara F399-Mugen Honda), 19m 54.976s; 4 Marc Hynes, GB (Dallara F399-Mugen Honda), 19m 58.753s; 5 Michael Bentwood, GB (Dallara F399-Mugen Honda), 20m 01.121s; 6 Timothy Spouge, GB (Dallara F399-Opel), 20m 01.368s; 7 Narain Karthikeyan, IND (Dallara F399-Mugen Honda), 20m 02.628s; 8 Luciano Burti, BR (Dallara F399-Mugen Honda), 20m 04.931s; 9 Tor Sriachavanon, TH (Dallara F399-Mugen Honda), 20m 08.443s; 10 Martin O'Connell, GB (Dallara F398-TOM'S Toyota), 20m 09.785s (1st National class).
Fastest race lap: Button, 51.579s, 101.623 mph/163.546 km/h.
Fastest qualifying lap: Button, 51.207s, 102.361 mph/ 164.734 km/h.
Championship points: 1 Burti, 157; 2 Hynes, 155; 3 Button, 122; 4 Kolby, 111; 5 Karthikeyan, 98; 6 Davies, 89.
National Class: 1 O'Connell, 190; 2 Smith, 111; 3 Bender, 91.

AUTOSPORT BRITISH FORMULA 3 CHAMPIONSHIP, Donington Park Grand Prix Circuit, Derbyshire, Great Britain, 5 September. Round 13. 20 laps of the 2.500-mile/ 4.023-km circuit, 50.000 miles/80.467 km.
1 Marc Hynes, GB (Dallara F399-Mugen Honda), 29m 55.180s, 100.268 mph/161.367 km/h.
2 Jenson Button, GB (Dallara F399-Renault), 29m 59.466s; 3 Luciano Burti, BR (Dallara F399-Mugen Honda), 30m 00.213s; 4 Toby Scheckter, ZA (Dallara F399-Mugen Honda), 30m 16.556s; 5 Andrew Kirkcaldy, GB (Dallara F399-Mugen Honda), 30m 23.307s; 6 Kristian Kolby, DK (Dallara F399-Mugen Honda), 30m 23.678s; 7 Timothy Spouge, GB (Dallara F399-Opel), 30m 24.815s; 8 Matthew Davies, GB (Dallara F399-Mugen Honda), 30m 25.187s; 9 Michael Bentwood, GB (Dallara F399-Mugen Honda), 30m 32.513s; 10 Doug Bell, GB (Dallara F399-Mugen Honda), 30m 32.997s.
Fastest race lap: Hynes, 1m 29.083s, 101.029 mph/162.591 km/h.
National Class winner: John Bender, USA (Dallara F398-Mugen Honda), 30m 52.340s (12th).
Fastest qualifying lap: Hynes, 1m 28.413s, 101.795 mph/ 163.823 km/h.
Championship points: 1 Hynes, 176; 2 Burti, 169; 3 Button, 137; 4 Kolby, 117; 5 Karthikeyan, 98; 6 Davies, 92.
National Class: 1 O'Connell, 190; 2= Bender, 112; 2= Smith, 111.

FINA F3 MASTERS, Circuit de Spa-Francorchamps, Stavelot, Belgium, 26 September. Round 14. 14 laps of the 4.330-mile/6.968-km circuit, 60.616 miles/97.552 km.
1 Luciano Burti, BR (Dallara F399-Mugen Honda), 37m 50.948s, 96.09 mph/154.643 km/h.
2 Marc Hynes, GB (Dallara F399-Mugen Honda), 37m 51.847s; 3 Kristian Kolby, DK (Dallara F399-Mugen Honda), 37m 55.688s; 4 Jenson Button, GB (Dallara F399-Renault), 37m 56.299s; 5 Aluizio Coelho, BR (Dallara F399-Renault), 37m 59.781s; 6 Yves Olivier, B (Dallara F399-Opel), 38m 02.703s; 7 Tiago Monteiro, P (Dallara F399-Renault), 38m 03.240s; 8 Julien Beltoise, F (Dallara F399-Renault), 38m 04.344s; 9 Andrew Kirkcaldy, GB (Dallara F399-Mugen Honda), 38m 05.861s; 10 Toby Scheckter, ZA (Dallara F399-Mugen Honda), 38m 06.308s.
Fastest race lap: Christijan Albers, NL (Dallara F399-Opel), 2m 17.333s, 113.498 mph/182.657 km/h.
National Class winner: Takuma Sato, J (Dallara F398-Mugen Honda), 38m 29.210s (18th).
Fastest qualifying lap: Button, 2m 16.173s, 114.464 mph/ 184.213 km/h.
Championship points: 1 Hynes, 191; 2 Burti, 189; 3 Button, 147; 4 Kolby, 129; 5 Karthikeyan, 98; 6 Davies, 92.
National Class: 1 O'Connell, 205; 2 Bender, 112; 3 Smith, 111.

AUTUMN GOLD CUP, Silverstone International Circuit, Towcester, Northamptonshire, Great Britain, 10 October. Round 15. 22 laps of the 2.249-mile/3.619-km circuit, 49.478 miles/79.627 km.
1 Jenson Button, GB (Dallara F399-Renault), 28m 15.956s, 105.027 mph/169.024 km/h.
2 Matthew Davies, GB (Dallara F399-Mugen Honda), 28m 21.700s; **3** Marc Hynes, GB (Dallara F399-Mugen Honda), 28m 23.137s; **4** Aluizio Coelho, BR (Dallara F399-Renault), 28m 24.647s; **5** Kristian Kolby, DK (Dallara F399-Mugen Honda), 28m 25.450s; **6** Narain Karthikeyan, IND (Dallara F399-Mugen Honda), 28m 33.863s; **7** Andrew Kirkcaldy, GB (Dallara F399-Mugen Honda), 28m 44.160s; **8** Takuma Sato, J (Dallara F398-Mugen Honda), 28m 45.280s (1st National class); **9** Martin O'Connell, GB (Dallara F398-TOM'S Toyota), 28m 45.752s; **10** Yudai Igarashi, J (Dallara F399-Mugen Honda), 28m 58.951s. Luciano Burti,BR (Dallara F399-Mugen Honda) finished 3rd in 28m 22.936s, but was disqualified for driving into Hynes on the first lap.
Fastest race lap: Button, 1m 16.160s, 106.308 mph/171.086 km/h.
Fastest qualifying lap: Burti, 1m 15.052s, 107.877 mph/173.612 km/h.
Championship points: 1 Hynes, 203; **2** Burti, 189; **3** Button, 168; **4** Kolby, 137; **5** Davies, 107; **6** Karthikeyan, 104.
National Class: 1 O'Connell, 221; **2** Bender, 124; **3** Smith, 111.

AUTOSPORT BRITISH FORMULA 3 CHAMPIONSHIP, Thruxton Circuit, Andover, Hampshire, Great Britain, 17 October. Round 16. 20 laps of the 2.356-mile/3.792-km circuit, 47.120 miles/75.832 km.
1 Luciano Burti, BR (Dallara F399-Mugen Honda), 23m 23.183s, 120.891 mph/194.555 km/h.
2 Kristian Kolby, DK (Dallara F399-Mugen Honda), 23m 34.502s; **3** Warren Hughes, GB (Dallara F399-Mugen Honda), 23m 37.114s; **4** Marc Hynes, GB (Dallara F399-Mugen Honda), 23m 41.576s; **5** Timothy Spouge, GB (Dallara F399-Opel), 23m 44.037s; **6** Matthew Davies, GB (Dallara F399-Mugen Honda), 23m 46.189s; **7** Toby Scheckter, ZA (Dallara F399-Mugen Honda), 23m 46.475s; **8** Martin O'Connell, GB (Dallara F398-TOM'S Toyota), 23m 47.244s (1st National class); **9** Aluizio Coelho, BR (Dallara F399-Renault), 23m 47.923s; **10** John Bender, USA (Dallara F398-TOM'S Toyota), 23m 54.997s.
Fastest race lap: Kolby, 1m 09.104s, 122.737 mph/197.526 km/h.
Fastest qualifying lap: Burti, 1m 07.955s, 124.812 mph/200.865 km/h.

Final championship points
1 Marc Hynes, GB, 213; **2** Luciano Burti, BR, 209; **3** Jenson Button, GB, 168; **4** Kristian Kolby, DK, 153; **5** Matt Davies, GB, 113; **6** Narain Karthikeyan, IND, 104; **7** Andrew Kirkcaldy, GB, 64; **8** Michael Bentwood, GB, 50; **9** Aluizio Coelho, BR, 45; **10** Tim Spouge, GB, 42; **11** Alex Yoong, MAL, 37; **12** Toby Scheckter, ZA, 27; **13** Doug Bell GB, 22; **14** Tor Sriachavanon, TH, 17; **15** Yudai Igarashi, J, 14; **16** Warren Hughes, GB, 12; **17** Warren Carway, IRL, 7; **18** Yves Olivier, B, 6; **19** Tiago Monteiro, P, 4; **20** Julien Beltoise, F, 3; **21** Christijan Albers, NL, 1.

National Class
1 Martin O'Connell, GB, 241; **2** John Bender, USA, 140; **3** Jeremy Smith, GB, 111; **4** Takuma Sato, J, 103; **5** Gavin Jones, GB, 45; **6** Nick Eliades, GR, 35; **7** Steven Shanly, GB, 22; **8** Charles Hall, GB, 12; **9** John Ingram, GB, 8.

French Formula 3 Championship

COUPES DE PAQUES DE NOGARO, Circuit Automobile Paul Armagnac, Nogaro, France, 5 April. Round 1. 2 x 11 laps of the 2.259-mile/3.636-km circuit.
Race 1 (24.852 miles/39.996 km)
1 Sébastien Bourdais, F (Martini MK79-Opel), 15m 25.012s, 96.721 mph/155.658 km/h.
2 Benoit Tréluyer, F (Dallara F399-Renault), 15m 26.970s; **3** Bruno Besson, F (Dallara F399-Renault), 15m 28.803s; **4** Jonathan Cochet, F (Dallara F399-Renault), 15m 31.173s; **5** Sébastien Dumez, F (Dallara F399-Renault), 15m 32.681s; **6** Julien Beltoise, F (Dallara F399-Renault), 15m 32.993s; **7** Tiago Monteiro, P (Dallara F399-Renault), 15m 34.763s; **8** Ryo Fukuda, J (Martini MK79-Opel), 15m 38.795s; **9** Yann Goudy, F (Dallara F399-Renault), 15m 39.267s; **10** Yannick Schroeder, F (Martini MK79-Opel), 15m 40.863s.
Fastest race lap: Tréluyer, 1m 47.442s, 75.701 mph/121.829 km/h.
Fastest qualifying lap: Bourdais, 1m 21.770s, 99.468 mph/160.078 km/h.

Race 2 (24.852 miles/39.996 km)
1 Sébastien Bourdais, F (Martini MK79-Opel), 15m 22.847s, 96.948 mph/156.023 km/h.
2 Benoit Tréluyer, F (Dallara F399-Renault), 15m 26.345s; **3** Bruno Besson, F (Dallara F399-Renault), 15m 28.444s; **4** Jonathan Cochet, F (Dallara F399-Renault), 15m 33.592s; **5** Tiago Monteiro, P (Dallara F399-Renault), 15m 39.140s; **6** Ryo Fukuda, J (Martini MK79-Opel), 15m 39.478s; **7** Yannick Schroeder, F (Martini MK79-Opel), 15m 39.944s; **8** Alexander Müller, D (Dallara F399-Opel), 15m 40.233s; **9** Julien Beltoise, F (Dallara F399-Renault), 15m 44.732s; **10** Jean-Christophe Ravier, F (Dallara F396-Opel), 15m 48.231s.
Fastest race lap: Bourdais.

TROPHÉE MOBIL 1 DE PRINTEMPS, Circuit de Nevers, Magny-Cours, France, 2 May. Round 2. 2 x 12 laps of the 2.641-mile/4.250-km circuit.
Race 1 (31.690 miles/51.000 km)
1 Benoit Tréluyer, F (Dallara F399-Renault), 18m 36.820s, 102.151 mph/164.395 km/h.
2 Jonathan Cochet, F (Dallara F399-Renault), 18m 37.932s; **3** Bruno Besson, F (Dallara F399-Renault), 18m 41.179s; **4** Tiago Monteiro, P (Dallara F399-Renault), 18m 41.482s; **5** Sébastien Dumez, F (Dallara F399-Renault), 18m 46.692s; **6** Alexander Müller, D (Dallara F399-Opel), 18m 47.553s; **7** David Loger, F (Dallara F399-Renault), 18m 49.560s; **8** Yannick Schroeder, F (Martini MK79-Opel), 18m 50.647s; **9** Yann Goudy, F (Dallara F399-Renault), 18m 56.146s; **10** Ryo Fukuda, J (Martini MK79-Opel), 18m 56.549s.
Fastest race lap: Sébastien Bourdais, F (Martini MK79-Opel), 1m 32.586s, 102.683 mph/165.252 km/h.
Fastest qualifying lap: Tréluyer, 1m 32.128s, 103.193 mph/166.073 km/h.

Race 2 (31.690 miles/51.000 km)
1 Benoit Tréluyer, F (Dallara F399-Renault), 18m 42.570s, 101.627 mph/163.553 km/h.
2 Jonathan Cochet, F (Dallara F399-Renault), 18m 44.336s; **3** Bruno Besson, F (Dallara F399-Renault), 18m 47.104s; **4** Alexander Müller, D (Dallara F399-Opel), 18m 48.058s; **5** Sébastien Dumez, F (Dallara F399-Renault), 18m 52.659s; **6** Julien Beltoise, F (Dallara F399-Renault), 18m 53.189s; **7** Ryo Fukuda, J (Martini MK79-Opel), 18m 53.446s; **8** Sébastien Bourdais, F (Martini MK79-Opel), 18m 53.799s; **9** Yannick Schroeder, F (Martini MK79-Opel), 18m 57.428s; **10** Marcel Costa, E (Martini MK73-Opel), 19m 01.610s.
Fastest race lap: Tréluyer, 1m 32.972s, 102.256 mph/164.566 km/h.

GRAND PRIX DE DIJON BOURGOGNE, Circuit de Dijon-Prenois, Fontaine-les-Dijon, France, 6 June. Round 3. 2 x 11 laps of the 2.361-mile/3.800-km circuit.
Race 1 (25.973 miles/41.800 km)
1 Sébastien Bourdais, F (Martini MK79-Opel), 13m 26.829s, 115.891 mph/186.508 km/h.
2 Alexander Müller, D (Martini MK79-Opel), 13m 30.429s; **3** Bruno Besson, F (Dallara F399-Renault), 13m 31.293s; **4** Tiago Monteiro, P (Dallara F399-Renault), 13m 32.589s; **5** Sébastien Dumez, F (Dallara F399-Renault), 13m 34.580s; **6** Jonathan Cochet, F (Dallara F399-Renault), 13m 39.557s; **7** David Loger, F (Dallara F399-Renault), 13m 40.626s; **8** Ryo Fukuda, J (Martini MK79-Opel), 13m 48.938s; **9** Jean-Christophe Ravier, F (Dallara F396-Opel), 13m 53.245s; **10** Alban Gauthier, F (Dallara F396-Fiat), 13m 54.515s.
Fastest race lap: Bourdais, 1m 13.021s, 116.410 mph/187.343 km/h.
Fastest qualifying lap: Müller, 1m 30.186s, 94.254 mph/151.687 km/h.

Race 2 (25.973 miles/41.800 km)
1 Sébastien Bourdais, F (Martini MK79-Opel), 13m 33.885s, 114.886 mph/184.891 km/h.
2 Alexander Müller, D (Martini MK79-Opel), 13m 37.561s; **3** Tiago Monteiro, P (Dallara F399-Renault), 13m 40.938s; **4** Sébastien Dumez, F (Dallara F399-Renault), 13m 41.316s; **5** Bruno Besson, F (Dallara F399-Renault), 13m 42.543s; **6** Jonathan Cochet, F (Dallara F399-Renault), 13m 42.575s; **7** David Loger, F (Dallara F399-Renault), 13m 53.736s; **8** Jean-Christophe Ravier, F (Dallara F396-Opel), 13m 57.803s; **9** James Andanson, F (Martini MK73-Opel), 13m 58.024s; **10** Marcel Costa, E (Martini MK73-Opel), 14m 01.458s.
Fastest race lap: Bourdais, 1m 13.379s, 115.842 mph/186.429 km/h.

39th TROPHÉES D'AUVERGNE, Circuit de Charade, Clermont-Ferrand, France, 20 June. Round 4. 2 x 11 laps of the 2.470-mile/3.975-km circuit.
Race 1 (27.169 miles/43.725 km)
1 Sébastien Bourdais, F (Martini MK79-Opel), 19m 09.724s, 85.073 mph/136.911 km/h.
2 Benoit Tréluyer, F (Dallara F399-Renault), 19m 11.799s; **3** Jonathan Cochet, F (Dallara F399-Renault), 19m 21.882s; **4** Ryo Fukuda, J (Martini MK79-Opel), 19m 23.436s; **5** Julien Beltoise, F (Dallara F399-Renault), 19m 28.169s; **6** Sébastien Dumez, F (Dallara F399-Renault), 19m 28.638s; **7** Tiago Monteiro, P (Dallara F399-Renault), 19m 29.089s; **8** Bruno Besson, F (Dallara F399-Renault), 19m 32.983s; **9** Yann Goudy, F (Dallara F399-Renault), 19m 35.201s; **10** Jean-Christophe Ravier, F (Dallara F396-Opel), 19m 35.476s.
Fastest race lap: Bourdais, 1m 43.827s, 85.641 mph/137.825 km/h.
Fastest qualifying lap: Bourdais, 1m 42.732s, 86.554 mph/139.294 km/h.

Race 2 (27.169 miles/43.725 km)
1 Sébastien Bourdais, F (Martini MK79-Opel), 19m 16.304s, 84.589 mph/136.132 km/h.
2 Benoit Tréluyer, F (Dallara F399-Renault), 19m 17.717s; **3** Jonathan Cochet, F (Dallara F399-Renault), 19m 18.643s; **4** Ryo Fukuda, J (Martini MK79-Opel), 19m 22.729s; **5** Tiago Monteiro, P (Dallara F399-Renault), 19m 41.574s; **6** Bruno Besson, F (Dallara F399-Renault), 19m 43.563s; **7** Sébastien Dumez, F (Dallara F399-Renault), 19m 44.460s; **8** Yann Goudy, F (Dallara F399-Renault), 19m 45.751s; **9** Yannick Schroeder, F (Martini MK79-Opel), 19m 46.226s; **10** David Loger, F (Dallara F399-Renault), 19m 46.616s.
Fastest race lap: Tréluyer, 1m 44.437s, 85.141 mph/137.020 km/h.

57th GRAND PRIX D'ALBI, Circuit d'Albi, France, 5 September. Round 5. 11 and 13 laps of the 2.206-mile/3.551-km circuit.
Race 1 (24.271 miles/39.061 km)
1 Sébastien Bourdais, F (Martini MK79-Opel), 13m 07.229s, 110.993 mph/178.626 km/h.
2 Tiago Monteiro, P (Dallara F399-Renault), 13m 10.329s; **3** Jonathan Cochet, F (Dallara F399-Renault), 13m 11.679s; **4** Benoit Tréluyer, F (Dallara F399-Renault), 13m 12.405s; **5** Julien Beltoise, F (Dallara F399-Renault), 13m 14.503s; **6** Ryo Fukuda, J (Martini MK79-Opel), 13m 15.652s; **7** Yannick Schroeder, F (Martini MK79-Opel), 13m 19.547s; **8** David Loger, F (Dallara F399-Renault), 13m 23.607s; **9** Jean-Christophe Ravier, F (Dallara F396-Opel), 13m 26.868s; **10** Patrick Freisacher, A (Martini MK73-Opel), 13m 28.420s.
Fastest race lap: Bourdais, 1m 10.588s, 112.531 mph/181.102 km/h.
Fastest qualifying lap: Monteiro, 1m 09.177s, 114.827 mph/184.796 km/h.

Race 2 (28.684 miles/46.163 km)
1 Tiago Monteiro, P (Dallara F399-Renault), 15m 27.593s, 111.324 mph/179.159 km/h.
2 Jonathan Cochet, F (Dallara F399-Renault), 15m 28.684s; **3** Benoit Tréluyer, F (Dallara F399-Renault), 15m 30.138s; **4** Sébastien Bourdais, F (Martini MK79-Opel), 15m 32.433s; **5** Julien Beltoise, F (Dallara F399-Renault), 15m 34.359s; **6** David Loger, F (Dallara F399-Renault), 15m 42.523s; **7** Jean-Christophe Ravier, F (Dallara F396-Opel), 15m 45.543s; **8** Yann Goudy, F (Dallara F399-Renault), 15m 47.736s; **9** Patrick Freisacher, A (Martini MK73-Opel), 15m 53.527s; **10** Westley Barber, GB (Martini MK73-Opel), 15m 54.361s.
Fastest race lap: Monteiro, 1m 10.541s, 112.606 mph/181.222 km/h.

ÉPREUVE DU MANS, Circuit Le Mans-Bugatti, France, 19 September. Round 6. 9 and 10 laps of the 2.675-mile/4.305-km circuit.
Race 1 (24.075 miles/38.745 km)
1 Sébastien Bourdais, F (Martini MK79-Opel), 18m 09.322s, 79.563 mph/128.045 km/h.
2 Alexander Müller, D (Martini MK79-Opel), 18m 11.565s; **3** Jérôme dalla Lana, F (Dallara F399-Opel), 18m 12.277s; **4** Jean-Christophe Ravier, F (Dallara F396-Opel), 18m 19.822s; **5** Ryo Fukuda, J (Martini MK79-Opel), 18m 21.377s; **6** Sébastien Dumez, F (Dallara F399-Renault), 18m 21.980s; **7** Benoit Tréluyer, F (Dallara F399-Renault), 18m 26.550s; **8** Bruno Besson, F (Dallara F399-Renault), 18m 34.713s; **9** Patrick Freisacher, A (Martini MK73-Opel), 18m 36.677s; **10** Julien Beltoise, F (Dallara F399-Renault), 18m 39.307s.
Fastest race lap: dalla Lana, 1m 59.310s, 80.714 mph/129.897 km/h.
Fastest qualifying lap: Bourdais, 1m 36.189s, 100.116 mph/161.120 km/h.

Race 2 (26.750 miles/43.050 km)
1 Alexander Müller, D (Martini MK79-Opel), 19m 55.580s, 80.547 mph/129.627 km/h.
2 Sébastien Bourdais, F (Martini MK79-Opel), 20m 02.365s; **3** Jérôme dalla Lana, F (Dallara F399-Opel), 20m 03.770s; **4** Sébastien Dumez, F (Dallara F399-Renault), 20m 06.138s; **5** Jean-Christophe Ravier, F (Dallara F396-Opel), 20m 15.128s; **6** Bruno Besson, F (Dallara F399-Renault), 20m 20.075s; **7** Patrick Freisacher, A (Martini MK73-Opel), 20m 22.133s; **8** Julien Beltoise, F (Dallara F399-Renault), 20m 23.187s; **9** James Andanson, F (Martini MK73-Opel), 20m 33.075s; **10** Westley Barber, GB (Martini MK73-Opel), 20m 49.177s.
Fastest race lap: Müller, 1m 58.123s, 81.525 mph/131.202 km/h.

GRAND PRIX DE LA VILLE DE NÎMES, Circuit de Lédenon, Remoulins, Nîmes, France, 10 October. Round 7. 2 x 16 laps of the 1.957-mile/3.150-km circuit.
Race 1 (31.317 miles/50.400 km)
1 Bruno Besson, F (Dallara F399-Renault), 21m 39.673s, 86.746 mph/139.604 km/h.
2 Benoit Tréluyer, F (Dallara F399-Renault), 21m 40.279s; **3** Jonathan Cochet, F (Dallara F399-Renault), 21m 40.882s; **4** Sébastien Dumez, F (Dallara F399-Renault), 21m 43.190s; **5** Yannick Schroeder, F (Martini MK79-Opel), 21m 43.640s; **6** Alexander Müller, D (Martini MK79-Opel), 21m 48.640s; **7** Julien Beltoise, F (Dallara F399-Renault), 21m 49.263s; **8** David Loger, F (Dallara F399-Renault), 21m 50.074s; **9** Ryo Fukuda, J (Martini MK79-Opel), 21m 50.579s; **10** Damien Bianchi, F (Dallara F399-Renault), 21m 51.196s.
Fastest race lap: Tiago Monteiro, P (Dallara F399-Renault), 1m 20.304s, 87.746 mph/141.213 km/h.
Fastest qualifying lap: Tréluyer, 1m 18.141s, 90.175 mph/145.122 km/h.

Race 2 (31.317 miles/50.400 km)
1 Bruno Besson, F (Dallara F399-Renault), 21m 52.852s, 85.875 mph/138.203 km/h.
2 Benoit Tréluyer, F (Dallara F399-Renault), 21m 53.169s; **3** Jonathan Cochet, F (Dallara F399-Renault), 21m 53.941s; **4** Sébastien Dumez, F (Dallara F399-Renault), 21m 58.169s; **5** Yannick Schroeder, F (Martini MK79-Opel), 21m 59.785s; **6** Julien Beltoise, F (Dallara F399-Renault), 22m 04.178s; **7** Damien Bianchi, F (Dallara F399-Renault), 22m 05.471s; **8** David Loger, F (Dallara F399-Renault), 22m 06.584s; **9** James Andanson, F (Martini MK73-Opel), 22m 09.229s; **10** Patrick Freisacher, A (Martini MK73-Opel), 22m 11.449s.
Fastest race lap: Sébastien Bourdais, F (Martini MK79-Opel), 1m 20.092s, 87.978 mph/141.587 km/h.

FRENCH FORMULA 3 CHAMPIONSHIP, Circuit de Nevers, Magny-Cours, France, 17 October. Round 8. 2 x 12 laps of the 2.641-mile/4.250-km circuit.
Race 1 (31.690 miles/51.000 km)
1 Jonathan Cochet, F (Dallara F399-Renault), 18m 42.153s, 101.665 mph/163.614 km/h.
2 Sébastien Bourdais, F (Martini MK79-Opel), 18m 46.218s; **3** Tiago Monteiro, P (Dallara F399-Renault), 18m 47.036s; **4** Alexander Müller, D (Martini MK79-Opel), 18m 47.429s; **5** Benoit Tréluyer, F (Dallara F399-Renault), 18m 48.818s; **6** Ryo Fukuda, J (Martini MK79-Opel), 18m 53.636s; **7** Sébastien Dumez, F (Dallara F399-Renault), 18m 56.544s; **8** Julien Beltoise, F (Dallara F399-Renault), 18m 57.031s; **9** Bruno Besson, F (Dallara F399-Renault), 18m 57.912s; **10** James Andanson, F (Martini MK73-Opel), 19m 02.866s.
Fastest race lap: Tréluyer, 1m 33.057s, 102.163 mph/164.415 km/h.
Fastest qualifying lap: Cochet, 1m 31.068s, 104.394 mph/168.006 km/h.

Race 2 (31.690 miles/51.000 km)
1 Jonathan Cochet, F (Dallara F399-Renault), 18m 28.487s, 102.918 mph/165.631 km/h.
2 Sébastien Bourdais, F (Martini MK79-Opel), 18m 32.118s; **3** Benoit Tréluyer, F (Dallara F399-Renault), 18m 35.518s; **4** Tiago Monteiro, P (Dallara F399-Renault), 18m 37.330s; **5** Ryo Fukuda, J (Martini MK79-Opel), 18m 37.826s; **6** Sébastien Dumez, F (Dallara F399-Renault), 18m 40.199s; **7** Julien Beltoise, F (Dallara F399-Renault), 18m 40.881s; **8** Bruno Besson, F (Dallara F399-Renault), 18m 42.922s; **9** Patrick Freisacher, A (Martini MK73-Opel), 18m 50.476s; **10** Jérôme dalla Lana, F (Dallara F399-Opel), 18m 54.440s.
Fastest race lap: Tréluyer, 1m 32.726s, 102.528 mph/165.002 km/h.

8th COUPE DU VAL DE VIENNE, Circuit du Val de Vienne, Le Vigeant, France, 31 October. Round 9. 2 x 12 laps of the 2.334-mile/3.757-km circuit.
Race 1 (28.014 miles/45.084 km)
1 Sébastien Dumez, F (Dallara F399-Renault), 19m 05.954s, 88.005 mph/141.631 km/h.
2 Jonathan Cochet, F (Dallara F399-Renault), 19m 06.643s; **3** Bruno Besson, F (Dallara F399-Renault), 19m 08.134s; **4** Julien Beltoise, F (Dallara F399-Renault), 19m 08.726s; **5** Benoit Tréluyer, F (Dallara F399-Renault), 19m 09.439s; **6** Sébastien Bourdais, F (Martini MK79-Opel), 19m 09.659s; **7** Sébastien Philippe, F (Dallara F399-Renault), 19m 09.838s; **8** Yannick Schroeder, F (Martini MK79-Opel), 19m 10.931s; **9** Jean-Christophe Ravier, F (Dallara F396-Opel), 19m 11.313s; **10** Ryo Fukuda, J (Martini MK79-Opel), 19m 15.544s.
Fastest race lap: Philippe, 1m 34.502s, 88.931 mph/143.121 km/h.
Fastest qualifying lap: Cochet, 1m 32.563s, 90.794 mph/146.119 km/h.

Race 2 (28.014 miles/45.084 km)
1 Sébastien Dumez, F (Dallara F399-Renault), 19m 16.414s, 87.209 mph/140.350 km/h.
2 Jonathan Cochet, F (Dallara F399-Renault), 19m 18.150s; **3** Bruno Besson, F (Dallara F399-Renault), 19m 20.287s; **4** Sébastien Bourdais, F (Martini MK79-Opel), 19m 20.566s; **5** Julien Beltoise, F (Dallara F399-Renault), 19m 21.146s; **6** Jean-Christophe Ravier, F (Dallara F396-Opel), 19m 21.701s; **7** Yannick Schroeder, F (Martini MK79-Opel), 19m 23.109s; **8** Ryo Fukuda, J (Martini MK79-Opel), 19m 23.925s; **9** David Loger, F (Dallara F399-Renault), 19m 28.603s; **10** Alexander Müller, D (Martini MK79-Opel), 19m 30.185s.
Fastest race lap: Cochet, 1m 34.900s, 88.558 mph/142.521 km/h.

Final championship points
Class A
1 Sébastien Bourdais, F, 246; **2** Jonathan Cochet, F, 215; **3** Benoit Tréluyer, F, 210; **4** Bruno Besson, F, 182; **5** Sébastien Dumez, F, 164; **6** Tiago Monteiro, P, 149; **7** Alexander Müller, D, 128; **8** Julien Beltoise, F, 124; **9** Ryo Fukuda, J, 123; **10** Yannick Schroeder, F, 91; **11** David Loger, F, 84; **12** Yann Goudy, F, 56; **13** Jérôme dalla Lana, F, 0; **14** Jean-Christophe Ravier, F, 15; **15** Damien Bianchi, F, 13; **16** Sébastien Philippe, F, 9.

'Challenge Michelin' (Class B)
1 Jean-Christophe Ravier, F, 289; **2** James Andanson, F, 256; **3** Patrick Freisacher, A, 244; **4** Westley Barber, GB, 185; **5** Xavier Armat, F, 183; **6** Alban Gauthier, F, 176; **7** Nicolas Poulain, F, 131; **8** Ying Kin Lee, RC, 118; **9** Nassim Sidi Said, DZ, 104; **10** Marcel Costa, E, 91.

Trophée Sébastien Enjolras
(Best rookie of the year)
Sébastien Bourdais, F.

German Formula 3 Championship

INT. ADAC-SPARKASSENPREIS, Saschenring, Germany, 9 May. Round 1. 2 x 24 laps of the 2.139-km/3.442-mile circuit.
Race 1 (51.330 miles/82.608 km)
1 Marcel Fässler, CH (Dallara F399-Opel), 38m 43.747s, 79.522 mph/127.978 km/h.
2 Timo Scheider, D (Dallara F399-Opel), 38m 55.976s; **3** Thomas Jäger, D (Dallara F399-Opel), 38m 56.210s; **4** Stefan Mücke, D (Dallara F399-Opel), 39m 12.899s; **5** Timo Rumpfkeil, D (Martini MK79-Opel), 39m 23.260s; **6** Yves Olivier, B (Dallara F399-Opel), 39m 35.784s; **7** Gabriele Gardel, CH (Dallara F399-Opel), 39m 49.728s; **8** Roland Rehfeld, D (Dallara F397-Opel), 39m 54.914s; **9** Herbert Jerich, A (Dallara F399-Opel), 40m 20.276s; **10** Etienne van der Linde, ZA (Dallara F399-Opel), 40m 20.905s.
Fastest race lap: Scheider, 1m 33.494s, 82.353 mph/132.535 km/h.
Fastest qualifying lap: Pierre Kaffer, D (Dallara F399-Renault), 1m 32.115s, 83.586 mph/134.519 km/h.

Race 2 (51.330 miles/82.608 km)
1 Timo Scheider, D (Dallara F399-Opel), 32m 22.696s, 95.120 mph/153.080 km/h.
2 Marcel Fässler, CH (Dallara F399-Opel), 32m 24.608s; **3** Pierre Kaffer, D (Dallara F399-Renault), 32m 36.056s; **4** Thomas Jäger, D (Dallara F399-Opel), 32m 36.940s; **5** Robert Lechner, A (Dallara F399-Opel), 32m 37.470s; **6** Thomas Mutsch, D (Dallara F399-Opel), 32m 38.007s; **7** Christijan Albers, NL (Dallara F399-Opel), 32m 48.504s; **8** Gabriele Gardel, CH (Dallara F399-Opel), 32m 55.168s; **9** Walter van Lent, NL (Dallara F399-Opel), 32m 55.683s; **10** Stefan Mücke, D (Dallara F399-Opel), 32m 56.360s.
Fastest race lap: Scheider, 1m 20.337s, 95.840 mph/154.240 km/h.
Fastest qualifying lap: Kaffer, 1m 24.733s, 90.868 mph/146.238 km/h.

INT. ADAC-PREIS ZWEIBRÖCKEN, Zweibrücken (Flugplatz) Circuit, Germany, 24 May. Round 2. 2 x 29 laps of the 1.734-mile/2.790-km circuit.
Race 1 (50.275 miles/80.910 km)
1 Thomas Jäger, D (Dallara F399-Opel), 30m 10.533s, 99.965 mph/160.879 km/h.
2 Timo Scheider, D (Dallara F399-Opel), 30m 11.678s; **3** Thomas Mutsch, D (Dallara F399-Opel), 30m 16.410s; **4** Pierre Kaffer, D (Dallara F399-Renault), 30m 23.064s; **5** Andreas Feichtner, D (Dallara F398-Opel), 30m 29.238s; **6** Etienne van der Linde, ZA (Dallara F399-Opel), 30m 29.874s; **7** Christijan Albers, NL (Dallara F399-Opel), 30m 36.237s; **8** Walter van Lent, NL (Dallara F399-Opel), 30m 37.526s; **9** Herbert Jerich, A (Dallara F399-Opel), 30m 42.385s; **10** Stefan Mücke, D (Dallara F399-Opel), 30m 48.253s.
Fastest race lap: Jäger, 1m 01.654s, 101.227 mph/162.909 km/h.
Fastest qualifying lap: Robert Lechner, A (Dallara F399-Opel), 1m 08.792s, 90.724 mph/146.005 km/h.

Race 2 (50.275 miles/80.910 km)
1 Thomas Jäger, D (Dallara F399-Opel), 30m 01.177s, 100.485 mph/161.714 km/h.
2 Timo Scheider, D (Dallara F399-Opel), 30m 01.941s; **3** Christijan Albers, NL (Dallara F399-Opel), 30m 13.904s; **4** Walter van Lent, NL (Dallara F399-Opel), 30m 18.834s; **5** Yves Olivier, B (Dallara F399-Opel), 30m 24.229s; **6** Sven Heidfeld, D (Dallara F399-Opel), 30m 31.769s; **7** Herbert Jerich, A (Dallara F399-Opel), 30m 33.885s; **8** Thomas Mutsch, D (Dallara F399-Opel), 30m 39.809s; **9** Timo Rumpfkeil, D (Martini MK79-Opel), 30m 43.110s; **10** Robert Lechner, A (Dallara F399-Opel), 30m 43.596s.
Fastest race lap: Lechner, 1m 01.438s, 101.583 mph/163.482 km/h.
Fastest qualifying lap: Olivier, 1m 02.846s, 99.307 mph/159.819 km/h.

INT. ADAC-PREIS VON 'SACHSEN-ANHALT', Oschersleben Motopark, Germany, 20 June. Round 3. 2 x 22 laps of the 2.279-mile/3.667-km circuit.
Race 1 (50.128 miles/80.674 km)
1 Christijan Albers, NL (Dallara F399-Opel), 30m 02.642s, 100.110 mph/161.112 km/h.
2 Thomas Jäger, D (Dallara F399-Opel), 30m 06.330s; **3** Marcel Fässler, CH (Dallara F399-Opel), 30m 06.670s; **4** Yves Olivier, B (Dallara F399-Opel), 30m 12.089s; **5** Thomas Mutsch, D (Dallara F399-Opel), 30m 13.789s; **6** Robert Lechner, A (Dallara F399-Opel), 30m 16.847s; **7** Walter van Lent, NL (Dallara F399-Opel), 30m 23.858s; **8** Gabriele Gardel, CH (Dallara F399-Opel), 30m 31.848s; **9** Timo Scheider, D (Dallara F399-Opel), 30m 31.712s; **10** Elran Nijenhuis, NL (Dallara F399-Opel), 30m 37.917s.
Fastest race lap: Albers, 1m 20.649s, 101.710 mph/163.687 km/h.
Fastest qualifying lap: Jäger, 1m 20.469s, 101.938 mph/164.053 km/h.

Race 2 (50.128 miles/80.674 km)
1 Marcel Fässler, CH (Dallara F399-Opel), 30m 20.269s, 99.141 mph/159.551 km/h.
2 Thomas Jäger, D (Dallara F399-Opel), 30m 22.544s; **3** Christijan Albers, NL (Dallara F399-Opel), 30m 24.779s; **4** Walter van Lent, NL (Dallara F399-Opel), 30m 30.112s; **5** Robert Lechner, A (Dallara F399-Opel), 30m 32.040s; **6** Etienne van der Linde, ZA (Dallara F399-Opel), 30m 32.700s; **7** Yves Olivier, B (Dallara F399-Opel), 30m 37.997s; **8** Timo Scheider, D (Dallara F399-Opel), 30m 38.556s; **9** Sven Heidfeld, D (Dallara F399-Opel), 30m 35.450s; **10** Stefan Mücke, D (Dallara F399-Opel), 30m 45.555s.
Fastest race lap: Fässler, 1m 21.546s, 100.592 mph/161.887 km/h.
Fastest qualifying lap: Mutsch, 1m 20.215s, 102.261 mph/164.573 km/h.

INT. ADAC NORISRINGRENNEN, Norisring, Nürnberg, Germany, 4 July. Round 4. 2 x 35 laps of the 1.429-mile/2.300-km circuit.
Race 1 (50.020 miles/80.500 km)
1 Christijan Albers, NL (Dallara F399-Opel), 30m 01.339s, 99.966 mph/160.880 km/h.
2 Yves Olivier, B (Dallara F399-Opel), 30m 08.273s; **3** Thomas Jäger, D (Dallara F399-Opel), 30m 12.522s; **4** Thomas Mutsch, D (Dallara F399-Opel), 30m 12.723s; **5** Stefan Mücke, D (Dallara F399-Opel), 30m 17.192s; **6** Marcel Fässler, CH (Dallara F399-Opel), 30m 18.681s; **7** Pierre Kaffer, D (Dallara F399-Renault), 30m 20.105s; **8** Sven Heidfeld, D (Dallara F399-Opel), 30m 21.813s; **9** Andreas Feichtner, D (Dallara F398-Opel), 30m 25.482s; **10** Ken Grandon, IRL (Dallara F397-Opel), 30m 32.925s.
Fastest race lap: Mutsch, 50.697s, 101.484 mph/163.323 km/h.
Fastest qualifying lap: Olivier, 50.623s, 101.633 mph/163.562 km/h.

Race 2 (50.020 miles/80.500 km)
1 Robert Lechner, A (Dallara F399-Opel), 29m 48.590s, 100.679 mph/162.027 km/h.
2 Christijan Albers, NL (Dallara F399-Opel), 29m 58.654s; **3** Yves Olivier, B (Dallara F399-Opel), 29m 59.340s; **4** Thomas Mutsch, D (Dallara F399-Opel), 29m 59.737s; **5** Marcel Fässler, CH (Dallara F399-Opel), 30m 06.103s; **6** Herbert Jerich, A (Dallara F399-Opel), 30m 11.672s; **7** Etienne van der Linde, ZA (Dallara F399-Opel), 30m 11.745s; **8** Ken Grandon, IRL (Dallara F397-Opel), 30m 18.626s; **9** Andreas Feichtner, D (Dallara F398-Opel), 30m 21.489s; **10** Walter van Lent, NL (Dallara F399-Opel), 30m 25.068s.
Fastest race lap: Mutsch, 50.399s, 102.084 mph/164.289 km/h.
Fastest qualifying lap: Lechner, 50.443s, 101.995 mph/164.146 km/h.

INT. ADAC GROSSER PREIS DER TOURENWAGEN, Nürburgring, Nürburg/Eifel, Germany, 22 August. Round 5. 18 and 9 laps of the 2.828-mile/4.551-km circuit.
Race 1 (50.901 miles/81.918 km)
1 Christijan Albers, NL (Dallara F399-Opel), 28m 34.584s, 106.875 mph/171.998 km/h.
2 Marcel Fässler, CH (Dallara F399-Opel), 28m 41.211s; **3** Thomas Jäger, D (Dallara F399-Opel), 28m 42.170s; **4** Robert Lechner, A (Dallara F399-Opel), 28m 43.930s; **5** Etienne van der Linde, ZA (Dallara F399-Opel), 28m 44.748s; **6** Walter van Lent, NL (Dallara F399-Opel), 28m 49.917s; **7** Yves Olivier, B (Dallara F399-Opel), 28m 50.295s; **8** Sven Heidfeld, D (Dallara F399-Opel), 28m 52.533s; **9** Pierre Kaffer, D (Dallara F399-Renault), 28m 52.979s; **10** Roland Rehfeld, D (Dallara F397-Opel), 29m 04.374s.
Fastest race lap: Albers, 1m 34.57s, 107.648 mph/173.243 km/h.
Fastest qualifying lap: Albers, 1m 34.079s, 108.210 mph/174.147 km/h.

Race 2 (25.451 miles/40.959 km)
1 Christijan Albers, NL (Dallara F399-Opel), 14m 17.263s, 106.878 mph/172.004 km/h.
2 Robert Lechner, A (Dallara F399-Opel), 14m 20.649s; **3** Marcel Fässler, CH (Dallara F399-Opel), 14m 22.900s; **4** Timo Scheider, D (Dallara F399-Opel), 14m 23.460s; **5** Yves Olivier, B (Dallara F399-Opel), 14m 24.712s; **6** Walter van Lent, NL (Dallara F399-Opel), 14m 26.070s; **7** Thomas Mutsch, D (Dallara F399-Opel), 14m 31.217s; **8** Pierre Kaffer, D (Dallara F399-Renault), 14m 31.528s; **9** Ken Grandon, IRL (Dallara F397-Opel), 14m 37.766s; **10** Sven Heidfeld, D (Dallara F399-Opel), 14m 38.621s.
Fastest race lap: Thomas Jäger, D (Dallara F399-Opel), 1m 34.120s, 108.163 mph/174.071 km/h.
Fastest qualifying lap: Albers, 1m 33.801s, 108.531 mph/174.663 km/h.

INT. ADAC ALPENTROPHÉE, Salzburgring, Salzburg, Austria, 5 September. Round 6. 2 x 19 laps of the 2.644-mile/4.255-km circuit.
Race 1 (50.235 miles/80.845 km)
1 Christijan Albers, NL (Dallara F399-Opel), 25m 38.494s, 117.547 mph/189.173 km/h.
2 Yves Olivier, B (Dallara F399-Opel), 25m 41.785s; **3** Robert Lechner, A (Dallara F399-Opel), 25m 44.000s; **4** Stefan Mücke, D (Dallara F399-Opel), 25m 45.245s; **5** Thomas Jäger, D (Dallara F399-Opel), 25m 48.060s; **6** Gabriele Gardel, CH (Dallara F399-Opel), 25m 53.046s; **7** Roland Rehfeld, D (Dallara F397-Opel), 25m 53.458s; **8** Thomas Mutsch, D (Dallara F399-Opel), 25m 56.185s; **9** Elran Nijenhuis, NL (Dallara F399-Opel), 25m 56.781s; **10** Timo Scheider, D (Dallara F399-Opel), 25m 57.742s.
Fastest race lap: Jäger, 1m 19.833s, 119.226 mph/191.876 km/h.
Fastest qualifying lap: Albers, 1m 18.936s, 120.581 mph/194.056 km/h.

Race 2 (50.235 miles/80.845 km)
1 Yves Olivier, B (Dallara F399-Opel), 25m 27.726s, 118.375 mph/190.507 km/h.
2 Robert Lechner, A (Dallara F399-Opel), 25m 29.312s; **3** Marcel Fässler, CH (Dallara F399-Opel), 25m 29.813s; **4** Walter van Lent, NL (Dallara F399-Opel), 25m 42.542s; **5** Pierre Kaffer, D (Dallara F399-Renault), 25m 50.465s; **6** Jacky van der Ende, NL (Dallara F399-Opel), 25m 51.304s; **7** Christijan Albers, NL (Dallara F399-Opel), 25m 54.432s; **8** Sven Heidfeld, D (Dallara F399-Opel), 25m 55.165s; **9** Andreas Feichtner, D (Dallara F398-Opel), 26m 00.319s; **10** Ken Grandon, IRL (Dallara F397-Opel), 26m 00.885s.
Fastest race lap: Albers, 1m 19.153s, 120.250 mph/193.524 km/h.
Fastest qualifying lap: Oliver, 1m 19.160s, 120.240 mph/193.507 km/h.

INT. ADAC-PREIS VON NIEDERSACHSEN, Oschersleben Motopark, Germany, 19 September. Round 7. 2 x 22 laps of the 2.279-mile/3.667-km circuit.
Race 1 (50.128 miles/80.674 km)
1 Marcel Fässler, CH (Dallara F399-Opel), 30m 19.212s, 99.198 mph/159.644 km/h.
2 Yves Olivier, B (Dallara F399-Opel), 30m 24.027s; **3** Christijan Albers, NL (Dallara F399-Opel), 30m 24.472s; **4** Sven Heidfeld, D (Dallara F399-Opel), 30m 33.711s; **5** Thomas Mutsch, D (Dallara F399-Opel), 30m 40.086s; **6** Robert Lechner, A (Dallara F399-Opel), 30m 40.479s; **7** Pierre Kaffer, D (Dallara F399-Renault), 30m 42.320s; **8** Thomas Jäger, D (Dallara F399-Opel), 30m 49.943s; **9** Gabriele Gardel, CH (Dallara F399-Opel), 30m 50.555s; **10** Stefan Mücke, D (Dallara F399-Opel), 30m 50.962s.
Fastest race lap: Albers, 1m 21.875s, 100.187 mph/161.236 km/h.
Fastest qualifying lap: Albers, 1m 21.132s, 101.105 mph/162.713 km/h.

Race 2 (50.128 miles/80.674 km)
1 Thomas Jäger, D (Dallara F399-Opel), 30m 22.053s, 99.044 mph/159.395 km/h.
2 Pierre Kaffer, D (Dallara F399-Renault), 30m 22.903s; **3** Marcel Fässler, CH (Dallara F399-Opel), 30m 28.856s; **4** Yves Olivier, B (Dallara F399-Opel), 30m 32.419s; **5** Timo Scheider, D (Dallara F399-Opel), 30m 33.429s; **6** Thomas Mutsch, D (Dallara F399-Opel), 30m 44.311s; **7** Jacky van der Ende, NL (Dallara F399-Opel), 30m 46.991s; **8** Walter van Lent, NL (Dallara F399-Opel), 30m 48.125s; **9** Stefan Mücke, D (Dallara F399-Opel), 30m 53.709s; **10** Ken Grandon, IRL (Dallara F397-Opel), 30m 58.814s.
Fastest race lap: Kaffer, 1m 22.024s, 100.005 mph/160.943 km/h.
Fastest qualifying lap: Jäger, 1m 20.649s, 101.710 mph/163.687 km/h.

INT. ADAC-PREIS VON HOCKENHEIM, Hockenheimring short circuit, Heidelberg, Germany, 3 October. Round 8. 2 x 32 laps of the 1.639-mile/2.638-km circuit.
Race 1 (52.454 miles/84.416 km)
1 Christijan Albers, NL (Dallara F399-Opel), 31m 57.605s, 98.473 mph/158.478 km/h.
2 Robert Lechner, A (Dallara F399-Opel), 32m 07.115s; **3** Thomas Jäger, D (Dallara F399-Opel), 32m 08.919s; **4** Marcel Fässler, CH (Dallara F399-Opel), 32m 10.225s; **5** Thomas Mutsch, D (Dallara F399-Opel), 32m 22.749s; **6** Jacky van der Ende, NL (Dallara F399-Opel), 32m 23.335s; **7** Timo Scheider, D (Dallara F399-Opel), 32m 23.628s; **8** Yves Olivier, B (Dallara F399-Opel), 32m 24.938s; **9** Pierre Kaffer, D (Dallara F399-Renault), 32m 25.552s; **10** Elran Nijenhuis, NL (Dallara F399-Opel), 32m 30.743s.
Fastest race lap: Albers, 59.304s, 99.505 mph/160.138 km/h.
Fastest qualifying lap: Albers, 58.641s, 100.630 mph/161.948 km/h.

Race 2 (52.454 miles/84.416 km)
1 Marcel Fässler, CH (Dallara F399-Opel), 33m 52.294s, 92.916 mph/149.534 km/h.
2 Stefan Mücke, D (Dallara F399-Opel), 33m 54.762s; **3** Yves Olivier, B (Dallara F399-Opel), 34m 02.756s; **4** Walter van Lent, NL (Dallara F399-Opel), 34m 34.437s; **5** Christijan Albers, NL (Dallara F399-Opel), 34m 44.196s; **6** Robert Lechner, A (Dallara F399-Opel), 34m 51.086s; **7** Thomas Jäger, D (Dallara F399-Opel), 34m 56.248s; **8** Pierre Kaffer, D (Dallara F399-Renault), 31 laps; **9** Ken Grandon, IRL (Dallara F397-Opel), 31; **10** Andreas Feichtner, D (Dallara F398-Opel), 31.
Fastest race lap: Mutsch, 1m 00.400s, 97.699 mph/157.232 km/h.
Fastest qualifying lap: Albers, 58.435s, Kaffer, 100.985 mph/162.519 km/h.

INT. ADAC-BILSTEIN-SUPERSPRINT, Nürburgring (Sprint course), Nürburg/Eifel, Germany, 17 October. Round 9. 2 x 27 laps of the 1.891-mile/3.043-km circuit.
Race 1 (51.052 miles/82.161 km)
1 Robert Lechner, A (Dallara F399-Opel), 30m 01.893s, 101.998 mph/164.149 km/h.
2 Christijan Albers, NL (Dallara F399-Opel), 30m 02.597s; **3** Thomas Mutsch, D (Dallara F399-Opel), 30m 12.548s; **4** Thomas Jäger, D (Dallara F399-Opel), 30m 16.661s; **5** Marcel Fässler, CH (Dallara F399-Opel), 30m 17.312s; **6** Stefan Mücke, D (Dallara F399-Opel), 30m 22.137s; **7** Sven Heidfeld, D (Dallara F399-Opel), 30m 32.989s; **8** Gabriele Gardel, CH (Dallara F399-Opel), 30m 38.129s; **9** Yves Olivier, B (Dallara F399-Opel), 30m 38.508s; **10** Elran Nijenhuis, NL (Dallara F399-Opel), 30m 41.500s.
Fastest race lap: Albers, 1m 06.057s, 103.047 mph/165.839 km/h.
Fastest qualifying lap: Lechner, 1m 05.848s, 103.374 mph/166.365 km/h.

Race 2 (51.052 miles/82.161 km)
1 Robert Lechner, A (Dallara F399-Opel), 30m 18.578s, 101.062 mph/162.643 km/h.
2 Christijan Albers, NL (Dallara F399-Opel), 30m 18.831s; **3** Timo Scheider, D (Dallara F399-Opel), 30m 20.707s; **4** Yves Olivier, B (Dallara F399-Opel), 30m 24.404s; **5** Stefan Mücke, D (Dallara F399-Opel), 30m 40.242s; **6** Jacky van der Ende, NL (Dallara F399-Opel), 30m 56.792s; **7** Pierre Kaffer, D (Dallara F399-Renault), 31m 14.206s; **8** Thomas Mutsch, D (Dallara F399-Opel), 31m 32.046s; **9** Kari Mäenpää, NL (Dallara F399-Renault), 31m 55.931s; **10** Ken Grandon, IRL (Dallara F397-Opel), 32m 20.458s.
Fastest race lap: Albers, 1m 06.092s, 102.993 mph/165.751 km/h.
Fastest qualifying lap: Mutsch, 1m 05.684s, 103.633 mph/166.780 km/h.

Final championship points
1 Christijan Albers, NL, 229; **2** Marcel Fässler, CH, 184; **3** Thomas Jäger, D, 179; **4** Robert Lechner, A, 163.5; **5** Yves Olivier, B, 159; **6** Timo Scheider, D, 100; **7** Thomas Mutsch, D, 97; **8** Pierre Kaffer, D, 71.5; **9** Stefan Mücke, D, 63; **10** Walter van Lent, NL, 62; **11** Sven Heidfeld, D, 31.5; **12** Etienne van der Linde, ZA, 25; **13** Jacky van der Ende, NL, 22; **14** Gabriele Gardel, CH, 21; **15** Andreas Feichtner, D, 15; **16** Herbert Jerich, A, 14; **17** Timo Rumpfkeil, D, 10; **18** Ken Grandon, IRL, 9; **19** Roland Rehfeld, D, 8; **20** Elran Nijenhuis, NL, 5; **21** Kari Mäenpää, NL, 2.

Other German Formula 3 race

ZOLDER FORMULA 3 RACE, Omloop van Zolder, Hasselt, Belgium, 18 April, 20 laps of the 2.600-mile/4.184-km circuit, 51.996 miles/83.680 km.
1 Robert Lechner, A (Dallara F399-Opel), 30m 28.990s, 102.344 mph/164.707 km/h.
2 Christijan Albers, NL (Dallara F399-Opel), 30m 29.665s; **3** Thomas Mutsch, D (Dallara F399-Opel), 30m 41.299s; **4** Stefan Mucke, D (Dallara F399-Opel), 30m 47.945s; **5** Yves Olivier, B (Dallara F399-Opel), 39m 49.617s; **6** Elran Nijenhuis, NL (Dallara F399-Opel), 30m 56.163s.
Fastest race lap: Albers, 1m 29.750s, 104.282 mph/167.826 km/h.

Italian Formula 3 Championship

GRAN PREMIO CAMPAGNANO-TROFEO IGNAZIO GIUNTI, Autodromo di Vallelunga, Campagnano di Roma, Italy, 29 March. 2 x 25 laps of the 1.988-mile/3.200-km circuit. Round 1 (49.710 miles/80.000 km)
1 Juan Manuel Lopez, RA (Dallara F399-Opel), 30m 38.535s, 97.336 mph/156.646 km/h.
2 Michele Spoldi, I (Dallara F399-BMW), 30m 39.556s; **3** Peter Sundberg, S (Dallara F399-Opel), 30m 52.043s; **4** Davide Uboldi, I (Dallara F399-Fiat), 30m 52.97s; **5** Gabriele Varano, CH (Dallara F399-Opel); **6** Filippo Zadotti, I (Dallara F399-Fiat).
Fastest race lap: Gianluca Calcagni, I (Dallara F399-Opel), 1m 09.528s, 102.954 mph/165.689 km/h.

Round 2 (49.710 miles/80.000 km)
1 Gianluca Calcagni, I (Dallara F399-Opel), 29m 21.828s, 101.573 mph/163.467 km/h.
2 Juan Manuel Lopez, RA (Dallara F399-Opel), 29m 22.465s; **3** Peter Sundberg, S (Dallara F399-Opel), 29m 23.028s; **4** Michele Spoldi, I (Dallara F399-BMW), 29m 24.110s; **5** Filippo Zadotti, I (Dallara F399-Fiat); **6** Gabriele Varano, CH (Dallara F399-Opel).
Fastest race lap: Lopez, 1m 08.917s, 103.867 mph/167.158 km/h.

ITALIAN FORMULA 3 CHAMPIONSHIP, Autodromo Internazionale del Mugello, Scarperia, Firenze (Florence), Italy, 11 April. 2 x 15 laps of the 3.259-mile/5.245-km circuit. Round 3 (48.886 miles/78.675 km)
1 Peter Sundberg, S (Dallara F399-Opel), 26m 27.182s, 110.883 mph/178.448 km/h.
2 Gianluca Calcagni, I (Dallara F399-Opel), 26m 28.411s; **3** Enrico Toccacelo, I (Dallara F399-Fiat), 26m 30.083s; **4** Michele Spoldi, I (Dallara F399-BMW), 26m 34.919s; **5** Davide Uboldi, I (Dallara F399-Fiat); **6** Filippo Zadotti, I (Dallara F399-Fiat).
Fastest race lap: Sundberg, 1m 44.745s, 112.012 mph/180.266 km/h.

Round 4 (48.886 miles/78.675 km)
1 Enrico Toccacelo, I (Dallara F399-Fiat), 26m 31.637s, 110.572 mph/177.949 km/h.
2 Peter Sundberg, S (Dallara F399-Opel), 26m 39.123s; **3** Gianluca Calcagni, I (Dallara F399-Opel), 26m 43.618s; **4** Michele Spoldi, I (Dallara F399-BMW), 26m 44.119s; **5** Juan Manuel Lopez, RA (Dallara-Opel); **6** Davide Uboldi, I (Dallara F399-Fiat).
Fastest race lap: Toccacelo, 1m 44.620s, 112.146 mph/180.482 km/h.

ITALIAN FORMULA 3 CHAMPIONSHIP, Autodromo di Magione, Perugia, Italy, 9 May. 2 x 31 laps of the 1.616-mile/2.600-km circuit. Round 5 (50.083 miles/80.600 km)
1 Enrico Toccacelo, I (Dallara F399-Fiat), 35m 02.184s, 85.767 mph/138.028 km/h.
2 Michele Spoldi, I (Dallara F399-BMW), 35m 10.294s; **3** Peter Sundberg, S (Dallara F399-Opel), 35m 13.826s; **4** Gianluca Calcagni, I (Dallara F399-Opel), 35m 17.135s; **5** Juan Manuel Lopez, RA (Dallara F399-Opel), 35m 22.662s; **6** Filippo Zadotti, I (Dallara F399-Fiat), 35m 32.210s.

Round 6 (50.083 miles/80.600 km)
1 Gianluca Calcagni, I (Dallara F399-Opel), 35m 29.245s, 84.677 mph/136.274 km/h.
2 Michele Spoldi, I (Dallara F399-BMW), 35m 30.455s; **3** Davide Uboldi, I (Dallara F399-Fiat), 35m 46.154s; **4** Peter Sundberg, S (Dallara F399-Opel), 35m 47.899s; **5** Stanislas d'Oultremont, F (Dallara F399-Opel), 36m 08.772s; **6** Filippo Zadotti, I (Dallara F399-Fiat), 36m 09.497s.

38th TROFEO AUTOMOBILE CLUB PARMA, Autodromo Riccardo Paletti, Varano, Parma, Italy, 13 June. Round 7. 56 laps of the 1.118-mile/1.800-km circuit, 62.634 miles/100.800 km.
1 Gianluca Calcagni, I (Dallara F399-Opel), 41m 48.89s, 89.874 mph/144.638 km/h.
2 Enrico Toccacelo, I (Dallara F399-BMW), 41m 49.44s; **3** Michele Spoldi, I (Dallara F399-BMW), 41m 57.09s; **4** Peter Sundberg, S (Dallara F399-Opel), 42m 04.15s; **5** Davide Uboldi, I (Dallara F399-Fiat), 42m 04.72s; **6** Gabriele Varano, CH (Dallara F399-Opel), 42m 08.80s; **7** Fulvio Cavicchi, I (Dallara F399-Opel), 42m 10.41s; **8** Juan Manuel Lopez, RA (Dallara F399-Opel), 42m 20.44s; **9** Stanislas d'Oultremont, F (Dallara F399-Opel), 55 laps; **10** Filippo Zadotti, I (Dallara F399-Fiat), 55.
Fastest race lap: Toccacelo, 44.228s, 91.039 mph/146.514 km/h.

40th GRAN PREMIO LOTTERIA DI MONZA, Autodromo Nazionale di Monza, Milan, Italy, 27 June. 2 x 14 laps of the 3.585-mile/5.770-km circuit, Round 8 (50.194 miles/80.780 km)
1 Peter Sundberg, S (Dallara F399-Opel), 24m 51.820s, 121.127 mph/194.935 km/h.
2 Gabriele Varano, CH (Dallara F399-Opel), 24m 58.539s; **3** Davide Uboldi, I (Dallara F399-Fiat), 25m 00.754s; **4** Enrico Toccacelo, I (Dallara F399-BMW), 25m 01.101s; **5** Michele Spoldi, I (Dallara F399-BMW), 25m 06.024s; **6** Fulvio Cavicchi, I (Dallara F399-Opel), 25m 06.729s; **7** Filippo Zadotti, I (Dallara F399-Fiat), 25m 15.645s; **8** Stanislas d'Oultremont, F (Dallara F399-Opel), 25m 20.219s; **9** Ettore Lagazio, I (Dallara F398-Fiat), 25m 48.265s; **10** Silvio Alberti, I (Dallara F398-Fiat), 25m 48.717s.
Fastest race lap: Sundberg, 1m 45.393s, 122.467 mph/197.091 km/h.

Round 9 (50.194 miles/80.780 km)
1 Peter Sundberg, S (Dallara F399-Opel), 24m 57.251s, 120.688 mph/194.228 km/h.
2 Gabriele Varano, CH (Dallara F399-Opel), 24m 58.978s; **3** Juan Manuel Lopez, RA (Dallara F399-Opel), 25m 01.121s; **4** Enrico Toccacelo, I (Dallara F399-BMW), 25m 01.495s; **5** Fulvio Cavicchi, I (Dallara F399-Opel), 25m 04.535s; **6** Filippo Zadotti, I (Dallara F399-Fiat), 25m 22.343s; **7** Stanislas d'Oultremont, F (Dallara F399-Opel), 25m 22.495s; **8** Silvio Alberti, I (Dallara F398-Fiat), 25m 52.706s; **9** Ettore Lagazio, I (Dallara F398-Fiat), 25m 53.617s; **10** Angelo Valentino, I (Dallara F399-Fiat), 26m 19.243s.
Fastest race lap: Gianluca Calcagni, I (Dallara F399-Opel), 1m 45.598s, 122.229 mph/196.708 km/h.

43nd GRAN PREMIO PERGUSA, Ente Autodromo di Pergusa, Enna-Pergusa, Sicily, 18 July. 2 x 16 laps of the 3.013-mile/4.849-km circuit. Round 10 (48.208 miles/77.584 km)
1 Peter Sundberg, S (Dallara F399-Opel), 26m 31.363s, 109.058 mph/175.511 km/h.
2 Gianluca Calcagni, I (Dallara F399-Opel), 26m 31.813s; **3** Gabriele Varano, CH (Dallara F399-Opel), 26m 38.557s; **4** Enrico Toccacelo, I (Dallara F399-BMW), 26m 40.951s; **5** Juan Manuel Lopez, RA (Dallara F399-Opel), 26m 44.156s; **6** Michele Spoldi, I (Dallara F399-BMW), 26m 44.428s; **7** Filippo Zadotti, I (Dallara F399-Fiat), 26m 53.056s; **8** Stanislas d'Oultremont, F (Dallara F399-Opel), 27m 10.437s; **9** Davide Uboldi, I (Dallara F399-Fiat), 27m 11.268s; **10** Fulvio Cavicchi, I (Dallara F399-Opel), 27m 14.991s.
Fastest race lap: Calcagni, 1m 36.121s, 112.846 mph/181.609 km/h.

Round 11 (48.208 miles/77.584 km)
1 Gabriele Varano, CH (Dallara F399-Opel), 26m 32.520, 108.979 mph/175.384 km/h.
2 Enrico Toccacelo, I (Dallara F399-BMW), 26m 34.328s; **3** Michele Spoldi, I (Dallara F399-BMW), 26m 38.574; **4** Davide Uboldi, I (Dallara F399-Fiat), 26m 53.361s; **5** Filippo Zadotti, I (Dallara F399-Fiat), 27m 11.696s; **6** Peter Sundberg, S (Dallara F399-Opel), 15 laps; **7** Fulvio Cavicchi, I (Dallara F399-Opel), 15.
Fastest race lap: Calcagni, 1m 36.086s, 112.887 mph/181.675 km/h.

10th GRAN PREMIO DEL LEVANTE, Autodromo del Levante, Binetto, Italy, 19 September. Round 12. 63 laps of the 0.980-mile/1.577-km circuit, 61.734 miles/99.351 km.
1 Gianluca Calcagni, I (Dallara F399-Opel), 46m 44.687s, 79.239 mph/127.524 km/h.
2 Gabriele Varano, CH (Dallara F399-Opel), 47m 05.447s; **3** Michele Spoldi, I (Dallara F399-Mugen Honda), 47m 05.447s; **4** Peter Sundberg, S (Dallara F399-Opel), 47m 07.607s; **5** Fulvio Cavicchi, I (Dallara F399-Opel), 47m 09.274s; **6** Stanislas d'Oultremont, F (Dallara F399-Opel), 62 laps; **7** Davide Uboldi, I (Dallara F399-Fiat), 61; **8** Juan Manuel Lopez, RA (Dallara F399-Opel), 61; **9** Enrico Toccacelo, I (Dallara F399-Fiat), 59.
Fastest race lap: Toccacelo, 43.266s, 81.534 mph/131.216 km/h.

ITALIAN FORMULA 3 CHAMPIONSHIP, Autodromo Santamonica, Misano Adriatico, Rimini, Italy, 3 October. 2 x 20 laps of the 2.523-mile/4.060-km circuit. Round 13 (50.455 miles/81.200 km)
1 Michele Spoldi, I (Dallara F399-Mugen Honda), 29m 18.264s, 103.306 mph/166.255 km/h.
2 Gianluca Calcagni, I (Dallara F399-Opel), 29m 19.411s; **3** Gabriele Varano, CH (Dallara F399-BMW), 29m 31.192s; **4** Enrico Toccacelo, I (Dallara F399-Fiat), 29m 31.654s; **5** Peter Sundberg, S (Dallara F399-Opel), 29m 46.345s; **6** Davide Uboldi, I (Dallara F399-Fiat); **7** Lorenzo del Gallo, I (Dallara F398-Fiat); **8** Fulvio Cavicchi, I (Dallara F399-Opel); **9** Stanislas d'Oultremont, F (Dallara F399-Opel); **10** Ettore Lagazio, I (Dallara F398-Fiat).
Fastest race lap: Spoldi, 1m 27.224s, 104.122 mph/167.569 km/h.

Round 14 (50.455 mph/81.200 km/h)
1 Gianluca Calcagni, I (Dallara F399-Opel), 29m 33.097s, 102.442 mph/164.864 km/h.
2 Juan Manuel Lopez, RA (Dallara F399-Opel), 29m 36.562s; **3** Gabriele Varano, CH (Dallara F399-Opel), 29m 39.923s; **4** Peter Sundberg, S (Dallara F399-Opel), 29m 42.016s; **5** Michele Spoldi, I (Dallara F399-Mugen Honda), 29m 42.363s; **6** Lorenzo del Gallo, I (Dallara F398-Fiat); **7** Stanislas d'Oultremont, F (Dallara F399-Opel); **8** Fulvio Cavicchi, I (Dallara F399-Opel); **9** Silvio Alberti, I (Dallara F398-Fiat); **10** Ettore Lagazio, I (Dallara F398-Fiat).
Fastest race lap: Spoldi, 1m 27.933s, 103.283 mph/166.217 km/h.

ITALIAN FORMULA 3 CHAMPIONSHIP, Autodromo di Magione, Perugia, Italy, 17 October. 2 x 31 laps of the 1.616-mile/2.600-km circuit. Round 15 (50.083 miles/80.600 km)
1 Enrico Toccacelo, I (Dallara F399-Fiat), 35m 01.574s, 85.791 mph/138.068 km/h.
2 Peter Sundberg, S (Dallara F399-Opel), 35m 15.766s; **3** Juan Manuel Lopez, RA (Dallara F399-Opel), 35m 18.526s; **4** Gianluca Calcagni, I (Dallara F399-Opel), 35m 20.698s; **5** Gabriele Varano, CH (Dallara F399-Opel), 35m 29.346s; **6** Fulvio Cavicchi, I (Dallara F399-Opel), 35m 34.240s; **7** Stanislas d'Oultremont, F (Dallara F399-Opel), 35m 37.723s; **8** Lorenzo del Gallo, I (Dallara F398-Fiat), 35m 53.706s; **9** Alberto Morelli, I (Dallara F399-Fiat), 30 laps; **10** Ettore Lagazio, I (Dallara F398-Fiat), 30.
Fastest race lap: Toccacelo, 1m 07.215s, 86.529 mph/139.255 km/h.

Round 16 (50.083 miles/80.600 km)
1 Enrico Toccacelo, I (Dallara F399-Fiat), 34m 55.746s, 86.030 mph/138.452 km/h.
2 Gianluca Calcagni, I (Dallara F399-Opel), 35m 17.866s; **3** Peter Sundberg, S (Dallara F399-Opel), 35m 26.721s; **4** Juan Manuel Lopez, RA (Dallara F399-Opel), 35m 28.027s; **5** Michele Spoldi, I (Dallara F399-Mugen Honda), 35m 28.508s; **6** Davide Uboldi, I (Dallara F399-Fiat), 35m 29.930s; **7** Stanislas d'Oultremont, F (Dallara F399-Opel), 35m 37.009s; **8** Fulvio Cavicchi, I (Dallara F399-Opel), 35m 38.973s; **9** Lorenzo del Gallo, I (Dallara F398-Fiat), 30 laps; **10** Alberto Morelli, I (Dallara F399-Fiat), 30.
Fastest race lap: Toccacelo, 1m 07.092s, 86.687 mph/139.510 km/h.

ITALIAN FORMULA 3 CHAMPIONSHIP, Autodromo Enzo e Dino Ferrari, Imola, Italy, 24 October. 2 x 16 laps of the 3.063-mile/4.930-km circuit. Round 17 (49.014 miles/78.880 km)
1 Michele Spoldi, I (Dallara F399-Mugen Honda), 35m 05.842s, 83.790 mph/134.848 km/h.
2 Tony Schmidt, D (Dallara F399-Opel), 33m 06.314s **3** Davide Uboldi, I (Dallara F399-Fiat), 33m 20.936s; **4** Robert Lechner, A (Dalara F399-Opel), 33m 38.757s; **5** Gianluca Calcagni, I (Dallara F399-Opel), 33m 57.401s; **6** Gabriele Varano, CH (Dallara F399-Opel), 34m 01.633s; **7** Peter Sundberg, S (Dallara F399-Opel), 34m 02.072s; **8** Juan Manuel Lopez, RA (Dallara F399-Opel), 34m 13.435s; **9** Ettore Lagazio, I (Dallara F398-Fiat), 34m 16.867s; **10** Stanislas d'Oultremont, F (Dallara F399-Opel), 34m 50.733s.
Fastest race lap: Schmidt, 2m 02.299s, 90.173 mph/145.120 km/h.

Round 18 (49.014 miles/78.880 km)
1 Enrico Toccacelo, I (Dallara F399-Fiat), 31m 00.460s, 94.842 mph/152.633 km/h.
2 Gabriele Varano, CH (Dallara F399-Opel), 31m 03.551s; **3** Juan Manuel Lopez, RA (Dallara F399-Opel), 31m 03.853s; **4** Fulvio Cavicchi, I (Dallara F399-Opel), 31m 04.986s; **5** Davide Uboldi, I (Dallara F399-Fiat), 31m 42.778s; **6** Tony Schmidt, D (Dallara F399-Opel), 31m 46.095s; **7** Michele Spoldi, I (Dallara F399-Mugen Honda), 31m 50.828s; **8** Stanislas d'Oultremont, F (Dallara F399-Opel), 31m 51.580s; **9** Lorenzo del Gallo, I (Dallara F398-Fiat), 32m 26.254s; **10** Ettore Lagazio, I (Dallara F398-Fiat), 33m 01.308s.
Fastest race lap: Lopez, 1m 54.146s, 96.614 mph/155.485 km/h.

Final championship points
1 Peter Sundberg, S, 224; **2** Gianluca Calcagni, I, 221; **3** Enrico Toccacelo, I, 207; **4** Michele Spoldi, I, 196; **5** Gabriele Varano, CH, 160; **6** Juan Manuel Lopez, RA, 140.

Major Non-Championship Formula 3 Results

1998 Result

The Macau Formula 3 race was run after AUTOCOURSE 1998/99 went to press.

FIA F3 WORLD CUP, 45th MACAU GP, Circuito Da Guia, Macau, 22 November. 2 x 15 laps of the 3.801-mile/6.117-km circuit, 114.028 miles/183.510 km.
Aggregated results from two races.
1 Peter Dumbreck, GB (Dallara F398-Toyota), 1h 12m 49.588s, 93.945 mph/151.190 km/h.
2 Ricardo Mauricio, BR (Dallara F398-Mugen Honda), 1h 12m 49.591s; **3** Enrique Bernoldi, BR (Dallara F398-Renault), 1h 12m 51.492s; **4** Robert Lechner, A (Dallara F398-Opel), 1h 13m 01.429s; **5** Darren Manning, GB (Dallara F398-Mugen Honda), 1h 13m 04.435s; **6** Hiroki Kato, J (Dallara F398-Mugen Honda), 1h 13m 10.849s; **7** Andre Couto, MAC (Dallara F398-Opel), 1h 13m 28.136s; **8** Bas Leinders, B (Dallara F398-Opel), 1h 13m 54.569s; **9** Alex Yoong, MAL (Dallara F398-Mugen Honda), 1h 13m 56.185s; **10** Paolo Martini, I (Dallara F398-Fiat), 1h 13m 59.043s.
Fastest race lap: Leinders, 2m 14.491s, 101.742 mph/163.737 km/h.
Fastest qualifying lap: Lechner, 2m 15.932s, 100.663 mph/162.002 km/h.

1999 Results

FIA FORMULA 3 EUROPEAN CUP, Circuit de Pau Ville, France, 24 May. 2 x 25 laps of the 1.715-mile/2.760-km circuit, 85.749 miles/138.000 km.
Overall result.
1 Benoit Tréluyer, F (Dallara F399-Renault), 1h 01m 42.537s, 83.375 mph/134.178 km/h.
2 Sébastien Dumez, F (Dallara F399-Renault), 1h 01m 57.202s; **3** Gianluca Calcagni, I (Dallara F399-Opel), 1h 02m 02.224s; **4** Peter Sundberg, S (Dallara F399-Opel), 1h 02m 06.253s; **5** Jonathan Cochet, F (Dallara F399-Renault), 1h 02m 10.983s; **6** Bruno Besson, F (Dallara F399-Renault), 1h 02m 17.604s; **7** Juan Manuel Lopez, RA (Dallara F399-Opel), 1h 02m 31.097s; **8** Michele Spoldi, I (Dallara F399-BMW), 1h 02m 32.705s; **9** Jérémie Dufour, F (Dallara F399-Opel), 1h 02m 45.431s; **10** Enrico Toccacelo, I (Dallara F399-BMW), 1h 02m 45.467s.
Fastest race lap: Tréluyer, 1m 12.990s, 84.586 mph/136.128 km/h.

9th MARLBORO MASTERS OF FORMULA 3, Circuit Park Zandvoort (Grand Prix Circuit), Holland, 8 August. 31 laps of the 1.724-mile/2.774-km circuit, 53.434 miles/85.994 km.
1 Marc Hynes, GB (Dallara F399-Mugen Honda), 32m 11.979s, 99.568 mph/160.239 km/h.
2 Thomas Mutsch, D (Dallara F399-Opel), 32m 13.786s; **3** Etienne van der Linde, ZA (Dallara F399-Opel), 32m 14.419s; **4** Christijan Albers, NL (Dallara F399-Opel), 32m 15.298s; **5** Jenson Button, GB (Dallara F399-Renault), 32m 16.160s; **6** Walter van Lent, NL (Dallara F399-Opel), 32m 25.329s; **7** Kristian Kolby, DK (Dallara F399-Mugen Honda), 32m 26.368s; **8** Michele Spoldi, I (Dallara F399-Mugen Honda), 32m 30.342s; **9** Toby Scheckter, ZA (Dallara F399-Mugen Honda), 32m 30.711s; **10** Sébastien Bourdais, F (Dallara F399-Opel), 32m 32.779s.
Fastest race lap: Hynes, 1m 35.452s, 65.009 mph/104.622 km/h.
Fastest qualifying lap: Mutsch, 1m 34.301s, 65.803 mph/105.899 km/h.

Result of Macau Formula 3 race will be given in AUTOCOURSE 2000/2001.

Sports Racing World Cup

1000 KM DI MONZA, Autodromo Nazionale di Monza, Milan, Italy, 11 April. Round 1. 86 laps of the 3.585-mile/5.770-km circuit, 308.337 miles/496.220 km.
1 Karl Wendlinger/Olivier Beretta, A/MC (Chrysler Viper GTS-R), 2h 40m 19.880s, 115.387 mph/185.698 km/h.
2 Jean-Philippe Belloc/David Donohue, F/USA (Chrysler Viper GTS-R), 2h 40m 20.110s; **3** Wolfgang Kaufmann/Michel Ligonnet, D/F (Porsche 911 GT2), 85 laps; **4** Christian Vann/Christian Gläsel, GB/D (Chrysler Viper GTS-R), 85; **5** Vincent Vosse/Didier Defourny, B/B (Chrysler Viper GTS-R), 85; **6** Paul Belmondo/Claude-Yves Gosselin, F/F (Chrysler Viper GTS-R), 84; **7** Luca Capellari/Michel Neugarten/Filippo Salvarini, I/B/I (Porsche 911 GT2), 83; **8** Claudia Hurtgen/Stéphane Ortelli, D/F (Porsche 911 GT2), 83; **9** Marco Spinelli/Gabriele Sabatini/Fabio Villa, I/I/I (Porsche 911 GT2), 83; **10** Robert Nearn/Ernst Palmberger/Nigel Smith, GB/D/GB (Porsche 911 GT2), 82.
Fastest race lap: Beretta, 1m 46.281s, 121.443 mph/195.444 km/h.
Fastest qualifying lap: Beretta, 1m 45.344s, 122.524 mph/197.183 km/h.

SILVERSTONE 500, Silverstone Grand Prix Circuit, Towcester, Northamptonshire, Great Britain, 9 May. Round 2. 157 laps of the 3.194-mile/5.140-km circuit, 501.434 miles/806.980 km.
1 Karl Wendlinger/Olivier Beretta, A/MC (Chrysler Viper GTS-R), 5h 12m 24.959s, 96.301 mph/154.982 km/h.
2 David Donohue/Jean-Philippe Belloc/Justin Bell, USA/F/GB (Chrysler Viper GTS-R), 5h 13m 35.330s; **3** Marc Duez/Vincent Vosse/Didier Defourny, B/B/B (Chrysler Viper GTS-R), 155 laps; **4** Christian Vann/Christian Gläsel/Hans Hugenholtz, GB/D/NL (Chrysler Viper GTS-R), 154; **5** Claudia Hurtgen/Stéphane Ortelli, D/F (Porsche 911 GT2), 154; **6** Wolfgang Kaufmann/Michel Ligonnet, D/F (Porsche 911 GT2), 152; **7** Paul Belmondo/Claude-Yves Gosselin/Marc Rostan, F/F/F (Chrysler Viper GTS-R), 151; **8** Geoff Lister/Maxwell Beaverbrook, GB/GB (Porsche 911 GT2), 150; **9** Robert Nearn/Ernst Palmberger/Nigel Smith, GB/D/GB (Porsche 911 GT2), 149; **10** Patrick Vuillaume/Gerold Ried/Christian Ried, F/D/D (Porsche 911 GT2), 147.
Fastest race lap: Belloc, 1m 50.763s, 103.806 mph/167.059 km/h.
Fastest qualifying lap: Wendlinger, 1m 49.266s, 105.228 mph/169.348 km/h.

INT. DMV-BADEN-POKAL 'HOCKENHEIM 500', Hockenheimring, Heidelberg, Germany, 27 June. Round 3. 161 laps of the 1.639-mile/2.638-km circuit, 263.908 miles/424.718 km.
1 Jean-Philippe Belloc/Dominique Dupuy, F/F (Chrysler Viper GTS-R), 3h 00m 30.894s, 87.718 mph/141.169 km/h.
2 Justin Bell/Luca Drudi, GB/I (Chrysler Viper GTS-R), 3h 00m 34.213s; **3** Bob Wollek/Franz Konrad, F/A (Porsche 911 GT2), 159 laps; **4** Julian Bailey/Tim Sugden/Jamie Campbell-Walter, GB/GB/GB (Lister Storm), 159; **5** Wolfgang Kaufmann/Michel Ligonnet, D/F (Porsche 911 GT2), 158; **6** Hubert Haupt/André Ahrlé, D/CH (Porsche 911 GT2), 156; **7** Paul Belmondo/Claude-Yves Gosselin, F/F (Chrysler Viper GTS-R), 156; **8** Luca Capellari/Michel Neugarten/Patrice Goueslard, I/B/F (Porsche 911 GT2), 155; **9** Sascha Maassen/Michael Eschmann/Paul Hulverscheid, D/D/D (Porsche 911 GT2), 155; **10** Cor Euser/Herman Buurmann, NL/NL (Marcos Mantara LM600), 155.
Fastest race lap: Belloc, 1m 03.505s, 92.922 mph/149.544 km/h.
Fastest qualifying lap: Belloc, 1m 01.532s, 95.902 mph/154.339 km/h.

HUNGARORING 500, Hungaroring, Mogyorod, Budapest, Hungary, 4 July. Round 4. 104 laps of the 2.468-mile/3.972-km circuit, 256.681 miles/413.088 km.
1 Jean-Philippe Belloc/Dominique Dupuy, F/F (Chrysler Viper GTS-R), 3h 01m 46.020s, 84.729 mph/136.357 km/h.
2 Karl Wendlinger/Olivier Beretta, A/MC (Chrysler Viper GTS-R), 3h 01m 57.462s; **3** Bob Wollek/Franz Konrad, F/A (Porsche 911 GT2), 103 laps; **4** Toni Seiler/Ni Amorim, CH/P (Chrysler Viper GTS-R), 103; **5** Sascha Maassen/Michael Eschmann/Paul Hulverscheid, D/D/D (Porsche 911 GT2), 103; **6** Wolfgang Kaufmann/Michel Ligonnet, D/F (Porsche 911 GT2), 103; **7** Hubert Haupt/André Ahrlé, D/CH (Porsche 911 GT2), 103; **8** Christian Vann/Christian Gläsel, GB/D (Chrysler Viper GTS-R), 102; **9** Mike Hezemans/Steffen Widmann, NL/D (Chrysler Viper GTS-R), 102; **10** Paul Belmondo/Claude-Yves Gosselin/Emmanuel Clérico, F/F/F (Chrysler Viper GTS-R), 102.
Fastest race lap: Claudia Hurtgen/Stéphane Ortelli, D/F (Porsche 911 GT2), 1m 39.634s, 89.177 mph/143.517 km/h.
Fastest qualifying lap: Beretta, 1m 38.862s, 89.874 mph/144.638 km/h.

ZOLDER 500KM, Omloop van Zolder, Hasselt, Belgium, 18 July. Round 5. 106 laps of the 2.600-mile/4.184-km circuit, 275.581 miles/443.504 km.
1 Karl Wendlinger/Olivier Beretta, A/MC (Chrysler Viper GTS-R), 3h 00m 17.215s, 91.714 mph/147.599 km/h.
2 Toni Seiler/Ni Amorim, CH/P (Chrysler Viper GTS-R), 3h 01m 23.073s; **3** Mike Hezemans/David Hart, NL/NL (Lister Storm), 105 laps; **4** Wolfgang Kaufmann/Michel Ligonnet, D/F (Porsche 911 GT2), 105; **5** Paul Belmondo/Claude-Yves Gosselin, F/F/F (Chrysler Viper GTS-R), 104; **6** Altfrid Heger/Franz Konrad, D/A (Porsche 911 GT2), 101; **7** Manfred Jurasz/Yukihiro Hane, A/J (Porsche 911 GT2), 100; **8** Gerold Ried/Christian Ried, D/D (Porsche 911 GT2), 99; **9** Mauro Casadei/Patrick Vuillaume/Raffaele Sangiuolo, I/F/I (Porsche 911 GT2), 97; **10** Ben Lievens/Michel Meers, B/B (Porsche 996), 97.
Fastest race lap: Bailey, 1m 35.636s, 97.864 mph/157.497 km/h.
Fastest qualifying lap: Bailey/Wallace/Campbell-Walter, 1m 34.314s, 99.236 mph/159.705 km/h.

MOTOPARK OSCHERSLEBEN 500, Oschersleben Motopark, Germany, 8 August. Round 6. 117 laps of the 2.279/3.667-km circuit, 266.592 miles/429.039 km.
1 Karl Wendlinger/Olivier Beretta, A/MC (Chrysler Viper GTS-R), 3h 00m 07.613s, 88.802 mph/142.912 km/h.
2 Jean-Philippe Belloc/Marc Duez, F/B (Chrysler Viper GTS-R), 3h 00m 58.823s; **3** Toni Seiler/Ni Amorim, CH/P (Chrysler Viper GTS-R), 3h 01m 31.636s; **4** Christian Vann/Christian Gläsel, GB/D (Chrysler Viper GTS-R), 3h 01m 34.024s; **5** Wolfgang Kaufmann/Michel Ligonnet, D/F (Porsche 911 GT2), 116 laps; **6** Claude-Yves Gosselin/Emmanuel Clérico, F/F/F (Chrysler Viper GTS-R), 115; **7** Patrick Vuillaume/Luca Capellari/Axel Rohr, F/I/D (Porsche 911 GT2), 112; **8** Bob Wollek/Franz Konrad, F/A (Porsche 911 GT2), 112; **9** Ernst Palmberger/Robert Nearn/Nigel Smith, D/GB/GB (Porsche 911 GT2), 112; **10** Manfred Jurasz/Yukihiro Hane, A/J (Porsche 911 GT2), 112.
Fastest race lap: Beretta/Wendlinger, 1m 28.243s, 92.957 mph/149.601 km/h.
Fastest qualifying lap: Ortelli, 1m 26.457s, 94.878 mph/152.691 km/h.

DONINGTON PARK 500 KM, Donington Park Grand Prix Circuit, Derbyshire, Great Britain, 5 September. Round 7. 111 laps of the 2.500-mile/4.023-km circuit, 277.500 miles/446.593 km.
1 Karl Wendlinger/Olivier Beretta, A/MC (Chrysler Viper GTS-R), 3h 01m 02.389s, 91.969 mph/148.009 km/h.
2 Julian Bailey/Andy Wallace/William Hewland, GB/GB/GB (Lister Storm), 3h 01m 28.210s; **3** Sascha Maassen/Franz Konrad, D/A (Porsche 911 GT2), 3h 02m 30.491s; **4** Vincent Vosse/Didier Defourny, B/B (Chrysler Viper GTS-R), 110 laps; **5** Christian Vann/Christian Gläsel, GB/D (Chrysler Viper GTS-R), 110; **6** Toni Seiler/Ni Amorim, CH/P (Chrysler Viper GTS-R), 110; **7** Claude-Yves Gosselin/Paul Belmondo, F/F (Chrysler Viper GTS-R), 108; **8** Martin Stretton/Maxwell Beaverbrook, GB/GB (Porsche 911 GT2), 108; **9** Manfred Jurasz/Yukihiro Hane, A/J (Porsche 911 GT2), 106; **10** Gerold Ried/Christian Ried, D/D (Porsche 911 GT2), 106.
Fastest race lap: Beretta, 1m 33.338s, 96.424 mph/155.179 km/h.
Fastest qualifying lap: Bailey/Wallace/Hewland, 1m 31.716s, 98.129 mph/157.923 km/h.

MIAMI 500 KM, Miami-Dade Homestead Motorsports Complex, Florida, USA, 26 September. Round 8. 122 laps of the 2.210-mile/3.557-km circuit, 269.620 miles/433.911 km.
1 Emmanuel Clérico/Paul Belmondo, F/F (Chrysler Viper GTS-R), 3h 01m 31.143s, 89.121 mph/143.427 km/h.
2 Karl Wendlinger/Olivier Beretta, A/MC (Chrysler Viper GTS-R), 3h 02m 28.463s; **3** Vincent Vosse/Xavier Pompidou/Hans Hugenholtz, B/F/NL (Chrysler Viper GTS-R), 121 laps; **4** Jean-Philippe Belloc/David Donohue, F/USA (Chrysler Viper GTS-R), 120; **5** Wolfgang Kaufmann/Bob Wollek, D/F (Porsche 911 GT2), 119; **6** Lance Stewart/Manfred Jurasz, USA/A (Porsche 911 GT2), 116; **7** Larry Schumacher/John O'Steen/Cort Wagner, USA/USA/USA (Porsche 911 GT2), 116; **8** Christian Vann/Christian Gläsel, GB/D (Chrysler Viper GTS-R), 116; **9** Patrick Vuillaume/Luca Capellari/Paolo Rapetti, F/I/I (Porsche 911 GT2), 113; **10** Charles Slater/Ugo Colombo, USA/USA (Porsche 911 GT2), 113.
Fastest race lap: Wendlinger, 1m 22.597s, 96.323 mph/155.017 km/h.
Fastest qualifying lap: Wendlinger, 1m 34.442s, 84.242 mph/135.575 km/h.

WATKINS GLEN 500 KM, Watkins Glen International, New York, USA, 3 October. Round 9. 93 laps of the 3.400-mile/5.472-km circuit, 316.200 miles/508.875 km. 1 Jean-Philippe Belloc/David Donohue, F/USA (Chrysler Viper GTS-R), 2h 54m 56.456s, 108.448 mph/174.530 km/h.
2 Karl Wendlinger/Olivier Beretta, A/MC (Chrysler Viper GTS-R), 2h 55m 07.056s; **3** Christian Vann/Christian Gläsel, GB/D (Chrysler Viper GTS-R), 92 laps; **4** Wolfgang Kaufmann/Bob Wollek, D/F (Porsche 911 GT2), 91; **5** Luca Drudi/Paul Belmondo, I/F (Chrysler Viper GTS-R), 91; **6** Vincent Vosse/Xavier Pompidou/Michel Ligonnet, B/F/F (Chrysler Viper GTS-R), 91; **7** Larry Schumacher/John O'Steen, USA/USA (Porsche 911 GT2), 90; **8** Rael/Steven Pfeffer, CDN/USA (Chrysler Viper GTS-R), 90; **9** Yukihiro Hane, Manfred Jurasz, J/A (Porsche 911 GT2), 86; **10** David Murry/Joel Reiser, USA/USA (Porsche 911 GT3), 86.
Fastest race lap: Belloc, 1m 47.717s, 113.631 mph/182.872 km/h.
Fastest qualifying lap: Belloc, 1m 47.576s, 113.780 mph/183.111 km/h.

Provisional championship points
Drivers
1= Olivier Beretta, MC, 68; **1=** Karl Wendlinger, A, 68; **3** Jean-Philippe Belloc, F, 51; **4** David Donohue, USA, 25; **5** Dominique Dupuy, F, 20; **6** Wolfgang Kaufmann, D, 18; **7=** Paul Belmondo, F, 15; **7=** Christian Gläsel, D, 15; **7=** Christian Vann, GB, 15; **10=** Ni Amorim, P, 14; **10=** Toni Seiler, CH, 14; 10= Michel Ligonnet, F, 14; **10=** Vincent Vosse, B, 14; **14=** Franz Konrad, A, 13; **14=** Bob Wollek, F, 13; **16** Justin Bell, GB, 12; **17** Emmanuel Clérico, F, 11; **18=** Marc Duez, B, 10; **18=** Ron Atapattu, USA, 10; **20=** Didier Defourny, B, 9; **20=** Julian Bailey, GB, 9; **22** Luca Drudi, I, 8; **23** Hans Hugenholtz, NL, 7; **24** Sascha Maassen, D, 6; **25** Xavier Pompidou, F, 5; **26=** Mike Hezemans, NL, 4; **26=** David Hart, NL, 4; **26=** Claude-Yves Gosselin, F, 4; **29=** Tim Sugden, GB, 3; **29=** Jamie Campbell-Walter, GB, 3.

Teams
1 Chrysler Viper Team ORECA, 125; **2** Chamberlain Motorsport, 34; **3** Freisinger Motorsport, 19; **4** Paul Belmondo Racing, 16; **5=** Konrad Motorsport, 13; **5=** Lister Storm Racing, 13; **7** GL PK Racing, 9; **8** Roock Racing, 3; **9** Roock Sportsystem 2.

Result of the Zhuhai race will be given in AUTOCOURSE 2000/2001.

Other Sports Car Race

67th 24 HEURES DU MANS, Circuit International Du Mans, Les Raineries, Le Mans, France, 12-13 June. 365 laps of the 8.454-mile/13.605-km circuit, 3085.621 miles/4965.825 km.
1 Yannick Dalmas/Joachim Winkelhock/Pierluigi Martini, F/D/I (BMW V12 LMR), 24h 00m 00s, 128.568 mph/206.909 km/h (1st Class 1).
2 Ukyo Katayama/Keiichi Tsuchiya/Toshio Suzuki, J/J/J (Toyota GT-One), 364 laps; **3** Emanuele Pirro/Frank Biela/Didier Theys, I/D/B (Audi R8R), 360; **4** Michele Alboreto/Rinaldo Capello/Laurent Aïello, I/I/F (Audi R8R), 346; **5** Steve Soper/Thomas Bscher/Bill Auberlen, GB/D/USA (BMW V12 LM98), 345; **6** Alex Caffi/Andrea Montermini/Domenico 'Mimmo' Schiattarella, I/I/I (Courage C52-Nissan), 342; **7** David Brabham/Eric Bernard/Butch Leitzinger, AUS/F/USA (Panoz LMP Spyder-Ford), 336; **8** Marc Goossens/Didier Cottaz/Fredrik Ekblom, B/F/S (Courage C52-Nissan), 334; **9** Michel Ferté/Henri Pescarolo/Patrice Gay, F/F/F (Courage C50-Porsche), 327; **10** Olivier Beretta/Karl Wendlinger/Dominique Dupuy, MC/A/F (Chrysler Viper GTS-R), 325 (1st Class 2); **11** Johnny O'Connell/Jan Magnussen/Max Angelelli, USA/DK/I (Porsche LMP Spyder-Ford), 323; **12** Marc Duez/Tommy Archer/Justin Bell, B/USA/GB (Chrysler Viper GTS-R), 318; **13** Luca Riccitelli/Uwe Alzen/Patrick Huisman, I/D/NL (Porsche 996 GT3), 317 (1st Class 3); **14** Ni Amorim/John Hugenholtz/Toni Seiler, P/NL/CH (Chrysler Viper GTS-R), 314; **15** Manuel Breyner/Tomaz Breyner/Pedro Breyner, P/P/P (Chrysler Viper GTS-R), 312; **16** Emmanuel Clérico/Jean-Claude Lagniez/Guy Martinolle, F/F/F (Chrysler Viper GTS-R), 309; **17** Paul Belmondo/Tiago Monteiro/Marc Rostan, F/P/F (Chrysler Viper GTS-R), 299; **18** Franz Konrad/Peter Kitchak/Charles Slater, A/USA/USA (Porsche 911 GT2), 293; **19** Dirk Müller/Bob Wollek/Bernd Mayländer, D/F/D (Porsche 996 GT3), 292; **20** Claudia Hurtgen/André Ahrlé/Vincent Vosse, D/CH/D (Porsche 993 GT2), 290; **21** Thierry Perrier/Jean-Louis Ricci/Michel Nourry, F/F/F (Porsche 993 RSR), 288; **22** Tommy Erdos/Christian Vann/Christian Gläsel, BR/GB/D (Chrysler Viper GTS-R), 270; **23** Jean-Luc Chereau/Patrice Goueslard/Pierre Yver, F/F/F (Porsche 911 GT2), 240; **24** Tom Kristensen/JJ Lehto/Jörg Müller, DK/FIN/D (BMW V12 LMR), 304 (DNF – accident damage); **25** David Donohue/Jean-Philippe Belloc/Soheil Ayari, USA/F/F (Chrysler Viper GTS-R), 271 (DNF – engine); **26** Hubert Haupt/John Robinson/Hugh Price, D/GB/GB (Porsche 993 GT2), 232 (DNF – engine); **27** Hiroki Kato/Hiro Matsushita/Akihiko Nakaya, J/J/J (BMW V12 LM98), 223 (DNF – transmission); **28** Jan Lammers/Peter Kox/Tom Coronel, NL/NL/NL (Lola B98/10-Ford), 213 (DNF – gearbox); **29** Andy Wallace/James Weaver/Perry McCarthy, GB/GB/GB (Audi R8C), 198 (DNF – gearbox); **30** Thierry Boutsen/Ralf Kelleners/Allan McNish, B/D/GB (Toyota GT-One), 173 (DNF – accident); **31** Wolfgang Kaufmann/Ernst Palmberger/Michel Ligonnet, D/D/F (Porsche 911 GT2), 157 (DNF – engine); **32** Didier de Radigues/Tomas Saldana/Grat Orbell, B/E/ZA (Kremer Lola B98/10-Ford), 146 (DNF – gearbox); **33** Pierre de Thoisy/Jean-Pierre Jarier/Sébastien Bourdais, F/F/F (Porsche 911 GT2), 134 (DNF – engine); **34** Michel Maisonneuve/Manuel Monteiro/Michel Monteiro, F/F/F (Porsche 911 GT2), 123 (DNF – accident damage); **35** Erik Comas/Satoshi Motoyama/Michel Krumm, F/J/D (Nissan R391), 110 (DNF – engine); **36** Martin Brundle/Emmanuel Collard/Vincenzo Sospiri, GB/F/I (Toyota GT-One), 90 (DNF – accident damage); **37** Christophe Tinseau/Franck Montagny/Didier Terrien, F/F/F (Lola T98/10-Judd), 77 (DNF – engine); **38** Bernd Schneider/Pedro Lamy/Franck Lagorce, D/P/F (Mercedes CLR), 76 (DNF – withdrawn due to Dumbreck's accident); **39** Christophe Bouchut/Nick Heidfeld/Peter Dumbreck, F/D/GB (Mercedes CLR), 75 (DNF – accident); **40** Yorijo Terada/Franck Fréon/Robin Donovan, J/F/GB (Autexe LMP99-Ford), 74 (DNF – engine); **41** Mauro Baldi/Jérime Policand/Christian Pescatori, I/F/I (Ferrari 333SP), 71 (DNF – engine); **42** Carl Rosenblad/Marco Apicella/Shane Lewis, S/I/USA (Riley & Scott MkIII-Ford), 67 (DNF – engine); **43** Stéphane Ortelli/Stefan Johansson/Christian Abt, F/S/D (Audi R8C), 55 (DNF – differential); **44** Phillipe Gache/Gary Formato/Olivier Thévenin, F/ZA/F (Riley & Scott MkIII-Ford), 25 (DNF – engine); **45** Katsunori Iketani/Ray Lintott/Manfred Jurasz, J/A/A (Porsche 911 GT2), 24 (DNF – accident).
Fastest race lap: Katayama/Tsuchiya, 3m 35.032s, 141.530 mph/227.771 km/h.
Fastest qualifying lap: Brundle, 3m 29.930s, 144.970 mph/233.306 km/h.

FedEx CART Championship Series

MARLBORO GRAND PRIX OF MIAMI PRESENTED BY TOYOTA, Miami-Dade Homestead Motorsports Complex, Florida, USA, 21 March. Round 1. 150 laps of the 1.502-mile/2.417-km circuit, 225.300 miles/362.585 km.
1 Greg Moore, CDN (Reynard 99I-Mercedes Benz E3), 1h 38m 54.535s, 136.671 mph/219.951 km/h.
2 Michael Andretti, USA (Swift 010.c-Ford Cosworth XD), 1h 38m 55.645s; **3** Dario Franchitti, GB (Reynard 99I-Honda Turbo V8), 1h 38m 56.681s; **4** Jimmy Vasser, USA (Reynard 99-Honda Turbo V8), 1h 39m 03.713s; **5** Massimiliano 'Max' Papis, I (Reynard 99I-Ford Cosworth XD), 1h 39m 15.946s; **6** Gil de Ferran, BR (Reynard 99I-Honda Turbo V8), 1h 39m 16.235s; **7** Patrick Carpentier, CDN (Reynard 99I-Mercedes Benz E3), 1h 39m 16.573s; **8** Mark Blundell, GB (Reynard 99I-Mercedes Benz E3), 1h 39m 19.397s; **9** Christian Fittipaldi, BR (Swift 010.c-Ford Cosworth XD), 1h 39m 20.022s; **10** Juan Pablo Montoya, CO (Reynard 99I-Honda Turbo V8), 149 laps.
Most laps led: Moore, 96.
Fastest qualifying lap: Moore, 24.886s, 217.279 mph/349.676 km/h.
Championship points: **1** Moore, 22; **2** Andretti, 16; **3** Franchitti, 14; **4** Vasser, 12; **5** Papis, 10; **6** de Ferran, 8.

FIRESTONE FIREHAWK 500, Twin Ring Motegi, Haga gun, Japan, 10 April. Round 2. 201 laps of the 1.549-mile/ 2.493-km circuit, 311.349 miles/501.068 km.
1 Adrian Fernandez, MEX (Reynard 98I-Ford Cosworth XD), 1h 46m 01.463s, 176.195 mph/283.558 km/h.
2 Gil de Ferran, BR (Reynard 99I-Honda Turbo V8), 1h 46m 07.810s; **3** Christian Fittipaldi, BR (Swift 010.c-Ford Cosworth XD), 1h 46m 09.132s; **4** Greg Moore, CDN (Reynard 99I-Mercedes Benz E3), 1h 46m 39.490s; **5** Michael Andretti, USA (Swift 010.c-Ford Cosworth XD), 200 laps; **6** Tony Kanaan, BR (Reynard 99I-Honda Turbo V8), 200; **7** Mauricio Gugelmin, BR (Reynard 99I-Mercedes Benz E3), 200; **8** Robby Gordon, USA (Reynard 98I-Toyota), 200; **9** Helio Castro-Neves, BR (Lola B99/00-Mercedes Benz E3), 199; **10** Richie Hearn, USA (Swift 010.c-Toyota), 198.
Most laps led: Fernandez, 153.
Pole Position: de Ferran, 25.463s, 219.000 mph/352.447 km/h.
Championship points: 1 Moore, 34; **2** Andretti, 26; **3** de Ferran, 25; **4** Fernandez, 21; **5** Fittipaldi, 18; **6** Franchitti, 14.

TOYOTA GRAND PRIX OF LONG BEACH, Long Beach Street Circuit, California, USA, 18 April. Round 3. 85 laps of the 1.824-mile/2.935-km circuit, 155.040 miles/249.513 km.
1 Juan Pablo Montoya, CO (Reynard 99I-Honda Turbo V8), 1h 45m 48.688s, 87.915 mph/141.485 km/h.
2 Dario Franchitti, GB (Reynard 99I-Honda Turbo V8), 1h 45m 51.493s; **3** Bryan Herta, USA (Reynard 99I-Ford Cosworth XD), 1h 45m 55.691s; **4** Adrian Fernandez, MEX (Reynard 99I-Ford Cosworth XD), 1h 45m 57.298s; **5** Christian Fittipaldi, BR (Swift 010.c-Ford Cosworth XD), 1h 45m 57.519s; **6** Gil de Ferran, BR (Reynard 99I-Honda Turbo V8), 1h 46m 02.254s; **7** Michael Andretti, USA (Swift 010.c-Ford Cosworth XD), 1h 46m 04.282s; **8** Greg Moore, CDN (Reynard 99I-Mercedes Benz E3), 1h 46m 06.087s; **9** Massimiliano 'Max' Papis, I (Reynard 99I-Ford Cosworth XD), 1h 46m 06.406s; **10** Jimmy Vasser, USA (Reynard 99I-Honda Turbo V8), 1h 46m 10.816s.
Most laps led: Tony Kanaan, BR (Reynard 99I-Honda Turbo V8), 44.
Fastest qualifying lap: Kanaan, 1m 01.109s, 107.454 mph/ 172.930 km/h.
Championship points: 1 Moore, 39; **2=** de Ferran, 33; **2=** Fernandez, 33; **4** Andretti, 32; **5** Franchitti, 30; **6** Fittipaldi, 28.

BOSCH SPARK PLUG GRAND PRIX PRESENTED BY TOYOTA, Nazareth Speedway, Pennsylvania, USA, 2 May. Round 4. 225 laps of the 0.946-mile/1.522-km circuit, 212.850 miles/342.549 km.
1 Juan Pablo Montoya, CO (Reynard 99I-Honda Turbo V8), 1h 46m 13.527s, 120.225 mph/193.484 km/h.
2 PJ Jones, USA (Swift 010.c-Ford Cosworth XD), 1h 46m 18.630s; **3** Paul Tracy, USA (Reynard 99I-Honda Turbo V8), 1h 46m 19.407s; **4** Cristiano da Matta, BR (Reynard 99I-Toyota), 1h 46m 19.832s; **5** Adrian Fernandez, MEX (Reynard 99I-Ford Cosworth XD), 1h 46m 29.928s; **6** Michael Andretti, USA (Swift 010.c-Ford Cosworth XD), 1h 46m 30.246s; **7** Christian Fittipaldi, BR (Swift 010.c-Ford Cosworth XD), 1h 46m 34.151s; **8** Dario Franchitti, GB (Reynard 99I-Honda Turbo V8), 1h 46m 35.363s; **9** Alex Barron, USA (Eagle 997-Toyota), 224 laps; **10** Scott Pruett, USA (Reynard 99I-Toyota), 224.
Most laps led: Montoya, 210.
Fastest qualifying lap: Montoya, 19.600s, 173.755 mph/ 279.632 km/h.
Championship points: 1 Montoya, 45; **2** Fernandez, 43; **3=** Andretti, 40; **3=** Moore, 40; **5** Franchitti, 35; **6** Fittipaldi, 34.

GP TELEMAR RIO 200, Emerson Fittipaldi Speedway at Nelson Piquet International Raceway, Jacarepagua, Rio de Janeiro, Brazil, 15 May. Round 5. 108 laps of the 1.864-mile/3.000-km circuit, 201.312 miles/323.980 km.
1 Juan Pablo Montoya, CO (Reynard 99I-Honda Turbo V8), 1h 36m 32.233s, 125.120 mph/201.361 km/h.
2 Dario Franchitti, GB (Reynard 99I-Honda Turbo V8), 1h 36m 33.969s; **3** Christian Fittipaldi, BR (Swift 010.c-Ford Cosworth XD), 1h 36m 36.187s; **4** Massimiliano 'Max' Papis, I (Reynard 99I-Ford Cosworth XD), 1h 36m 37.163s; **5** Tony Kanaan, BR (Reynard 99I-Honda Turbo V8), 1h 36m 39.269s; **6** Patrick Carpentier, CDN (Reynard 99I-Mercedes Benz E3), 1h 36m 39.851s; **7** PJ Jones, USA (Swift 010.c-Ford Cosworth XD), 1h 36m 40.290s; **8** Greg Moore, CDN (Reynard 99I-Mercedes Benz E3), 1h 36m 40.537s; **9** Tarso Marques, BR (Penske PC27B-Mercedes Benz E3), 1h 36m 42.921s; **10** Gil de Ferran, BR (Reynard 99I-Honda Turbo V8), 1h 36m 43.474s.
Most laps led: Montoya, 93.
Fastest qualifying lap: Fittipaldi, 38.565s, 174.002 mph/ 280.030 km/h.
Championship points: 1 Montoya, 66; **2** Franchitti, 51; **3** Fittipaldi, 49; **4** Moore, 45; **5** Fernandez, 43; **6** Andretti, 40.

MOTOROLA 300, Gateway International Raceway, Madison, Illinois, USA, 29 May. Round 6. 236 laps of the 1.270-mile/2.044-km circuit, 299.720 miles/482.353 km.
1 Michael Andretti, USA (Swift 010.c-Ford Cosworth XD), 2h 25m 35.829s, 123.513 mph/198.776 km/h.
2 Helio Castro-Neves, BR (Lola B99/00-Mercedes Benz E3), 2h 25m 36.158s; **3** Dario Franchitti, GB (Reynard 99I-Honda Turbo V8), 2h 25m 36.876s; **4** Roberto Moreno, BR (Reynard 99I-Mercedes Benz E3), 2h 25m 41.564s; **5** Massimiliano 'Max' Papis, I (Reynard 99I-Ford Cosworth XD), 2h 25m 46.806s; **6** Greg Moore, CDN (Reynard 99I-Mercedes Benz E3), 2h 25m 47.032s; **7** Tony Kanaan, BR (Reynard 99I-Honda Turbo V8), 2h 25m 52.680s; **8** PJ Jones, USA (Swift 010.c-Ford Cosworth XD), 2h 26m 01.598s; **9** Christian Fittipaldi, BR (Swift 010.c-Ford Cosworth XD), 2h 26m 01.810s; **10** Jimmy Vasser, USA (Reynard 99I-Honda Turbo V8), 2h 26m 02.360s.
Most laps led: Andretti, 91.
Fastest qualifying lap: Juan Pablo Montoya, CO (Reynard 99I-Honda Turbo V8), 25.014s, 182.778 mph/294.152 km/h.
Championship points: 1 Montoya, 69; **2** Franchitti, 65; **3** Andretti, 61; **4=** Fittipaldi, 53; **4=** Moore, 53; **6** Fernandez, 43.

MILLER LITE 225, The Milwaukee Mile, Wisconsin State Fair Park, West Allis, Milwaukee, Wisconsin, USA, 6 June. Round 7. 225 laps of the 1.032-mile/1.661-km circuit, 232.200 miles/373.690 km.
1 Paul Tracy, USA (Reynard 99I-Honda Turbo V8), 1h 48m 49.169s, 128.029 mph/206.042 km/h.
2 Greg Moore, CDN (Reynard 99I-Mercedes Benz E3), 1h 48m 55.049s; **3** Gil de Ferran, BR (Reynard 99I-Honda Turbo V8), 1h 48m 55.625s; **4** Jimmy Vasser, USA (Reynard 99I-Honda Turbo V8), 1h 48m 57.106s; **5** Adrian Fernandez, MEX (Reynard 99I-Ford Cosworth XD), 1h 48m 59.098s; **6** Christian Fittipaldi, BR (Swift 010.c-Ford Cosworth XD), 1h 49m 00.420s; **7** Dario Franchitti, GB (Reynard 99I-Honda Turbo V8), 1h 49m 01.747s; **8** Mauricio Gugelmin, BR (Reynard 99I-Mercedes Benz E3), 1h 49m 04.392s; **9** Patrick Carpentier, CDN (Reynard 99I-Mercedes Benz E3), 224 laps; **10** Juan Pablo Montoya, CO (Reynard 99I-Honda Turbo V8), 224.
Most laps led: Montoya, 84.
Fastest qualifying lap: Helio Castro Neves, BR (Lola B99/00-Mercedes Benz E3), 21.931s, 169.404 mph/272.629 km/h.
Championship points: 1 Montoya, 73; **2** Franchitti, 71; **3** Moore, 69; **4=** Andretti, 61; **4=** Fittipaldi, 61; **6** Fernandez, 53.

BUDWEISER/G.I. JOE'S 200 PRESENTED BY TEXACO/ HAVOLINE, Portland International Raceway, Oregon, USA, 20 June. Round 8. 98 laps of the 1.969-mile/3.169-km circuit, 192.962 miles/310.542 km.
1 Gil de Ferran, BR (Reynard 99I-Honda Turbo V8), 1h 47m 44.560s, 107.457 mph/172.936 km/h.
2 Juan Pablo Montoya, CO (Reynard 99I-Honda Turbo V8), 1h 47m 48.953s; **3** Dario Franchitti, GB (Reynard 99I-Honda Turbo V8), 1h 47m 49.556s; **4** Adrian Fernandez, MEX (Reynard 99I-Ford Cosworth XD), 1h 47m 58.128s; **5** Paul Tracy, USA (Reynard 99I-Honda Turbo V8), 1h 48m 04.853s; **6** Bryan Herta, USA (Reynard 99I-Ford Cosworth XD), 1h 48m 12.491s; **7** Roberto Moreno, BR (Reynard 99I-Mercedes Benz E3), 1h 48m 13.010s; **8** Massimiliano 'Max' Papis, I (Reynard 99I-Ford Cosworth XD), 1h 48m 14.628s; **9** Patrick Carpentier, CDN (Reynard 99I-Mercedes Benz E3), 1h 48m 20.948s; **10** Michael Andretti, USA (Swift 010.c-Ford Cosworth XD), 1h 48m 26.471s.
Most laps led: de Ferran, 39.
Fastest qualifying lap: Montoya, 58.193s, 121.808 mph/ 196.032 km/h.
Championship points: 1 Montoya, 90; **2** Franchitti, 85; **3** de Ferran, 71; **4** Moore, 65; **5** Fernandez, 65; **6** Andretti, 64.

MEDIC DRUG GRAND PRIX OF CLEVELAND PRESENTED BY FIRSTAIR, Burke Lakefront Airport Circuit, Cleveland, Ohio, USA, 27 June. Round 9. 90 laps of the 2.106-mile/3.389-km circuit, 189.540 miles/305.035 km.
1 Juan Pablo Montoya, CO (Reynard 99I-Honda Turbo V8), 2h 01m 04.277s, 93.931 mph/151.168 km/h.
2 Gil de Ferran, BR (Reynard 99I-Honda Turbo V8), 2h 01m 14.881s; **3** Michael Andretti, USA (Swift 010.c-Ford Cosworth XD), 2h 01m 16.974s; **4** Paul Tracy, USA (Reynard 99I-Honda Turbo V8), 2h 01m 22.126s; **5** Al Unser Jr., USA (Lola B99/00-Mercedes Benz E3), 2h 01m 23.486s; **6** Bryan Herta, USA (Reynard 99I-Ford Cosworth XD), 2h 01m 24.031s; **7** Patrick Carpentier, CDN (Reynard 99I-Mercedes Benz E3), 2h 01m 24.873s; **8** Roberto Moreno, BR (Reynard 99I-Mercedes Benz E3), 2h 01m 27.979s; **9** Robby Gordon, USA (Swift 010.c-Toyota), 89 laps; **10** Richie Hearn, USA (Reynard 99I-Toyota), 88.
Most laps led: Montoya, 76.
Fastest qualifying lap: Montoya, 56.813s, 133.448 mph/ 214.764 km/h.
Championship points: 1 Montoya, 112; **2** de Ferran, 87; **3** Franchitti, 85; **4** Andretti, 78; **5** Moore, 69; **6** Fernadez, 65.

TEXACO/HAVOLINE 200, Road America Circuit, Elkhart Lake, Wisconsin, USA, 11 July. Round 10. 55 laps of the 4.048-mile/6.515-km circuit, 222.640 miles/358.304 km.
1 Christian Fittipaldi, BR (Swift 010.c-Ford Cosworth XD), 1h 37m 00.799s, 137.697 mph/221.601 km/h.
2 Michael Andretti, USA (Swift 010.c-Ford Cosworth XD), 1h 37m 01.859s; **3** Adrian Fernandez, MEX (Reynard 99I-Ford Cosworth XD), 1h 37m 18.226s; **4** Greg Moore, CDN (Reynard 99I-Mercedes Benz E3), 1h 37m 20.196s; **5** Massimiliano 'Max' Papis, I (Reynard 99I-Ford Cosworth XD), 1h 37m 35.292s; **6** Tony Kanaan, BR (Reynard 99I-Honda Turbo V8), 1h 37m 59.233s; **7** Michel Jourdain Jr., MEX (Lola B99/00-Ford Cosworth XD), 54 laps; **8** Robby Gordon, USA (Swift 010.c-Toyota), 54; **9** Al Unser Jr., USA (Lola B99/00-Mercedes Benz E3), 54; **10** Richie Hearn, USA (Reynard 99I-Toyota), 54.
Most laps led: Montoya, 46.
Fastest qualifying lap: Andretti, 1m 40.206s, 145.428 mph/ 234.044 km/h.
Championship points: 1 Montoya, 113; **2** Andretti, 95; **3** de Ferran, 87; **4** Franchitti, 85; **5** Fittipaldi, 82; **6** Moore, 81.

MOLSON INDY, Exhibition Place Circuit, Toronto, Ontario, Canada, 18 July. Round 11. 95 laps of the 1.755-mile/2.824-km circuit, 166.725 miles/268.318 km.
1 Dario Franchitti, GB (Reynard 99I-Honda Turbo V8), 1h 56m 27.550s, 85.897 mph/138.238 km/h.
2 Paul Tracy, USA (Reynard 99I-Honda Turbo V8), 1h 56m 30.174s; **3** Christian Fittipaldi, BR (Swift 010.c-Ford Cosworth XD), 1h 56m 34.537s; **4** Roberto Moreno, BR (Reynard 99I-Mercedes Benz E3), 1h 56m 38.285s; **5** Massimiliano 'Max' Papis, I (Reynard 99I-Ford Cosworth XD), 1h 56m 43.030s; **6** Adrian Fernandez, MEX (Reynard 99I-Ford Cosworth XD), 1h 56m 50.453s; **7** Scott Pruett, USA (Reynard 99I-Toyota), 1h 56m 51.806s; **8** Jimmy Vasser, USA (Reynard 99I-Honda Turbo V8), 1h 57m 00.944s; **9** Al Unser Jr., USA (Lola B99/00-Mercedes Benz E3), 1h 57m 02.659s; **10** PJ Jones, USA (Swift 010.c-Ford Cosworth XD), 1h 57m 03.565s.
Most laps led: Franchitti, 95.
Fastest qualifying lap: Gil de Ferran, BR (Reynard 99I-Honda Turbo V8), 57.143s, 110.565 mph/177.937 km/h.
Championship points: 1 Montoya, 113; **2** Franchitti, 106; **3** Fittipaldi, 96; **4** Andretti, 95; **5** de Ferran, 88; **6** Fernandez, 87.

U.S. 500 PRESENTED BY TOYOTA, Michigan Speedway, Brooklyn, Michigan, USA, 25 July. Round 12. 250 laps of the 2.000-mile/3.219-km circuit, 500.000 miles/804.672 km.
1 Tony Kanaan, BR (Reynard 99I-Honda Turbo V8), 2h 41m 12.362s, 186.097 mph/299.494 km/h.
2 Juan Pablo Montoya, CO (Reynard 99I-Honda Turbo V8), 2h 41m 12.394s; **3** Paul Tracy, USA (Reynard 99I-Honda Turbo V8), 2h 41m 20.815s; **4** Michael Andretti, USA (Swift 010.c-Ford Cosworth XD), 2h 41m 20.868s; **5** Dario Franchitti, GB (Reynard 99I-Honda Turbo V8), 2h 41m 21.499s; **6** Adrian Fernandez, MEX (Reynard 99I-Ford Cosworth XD), 2h 41m 21.883s; **7** Massimiliano 'Max' Papis, I (Reynard 99I-Ford Cosworth XD), 2h 41m 22.705s; **8** Christian Fittipaldi, BR (Swift 010.c-Ford Cosworth XD), 2h 41m 27.772s; **9** Jimmy Vasser, USA (Reynard 99I-Honda Turbo V8), 249 laps; **10** Patrick Carpentier, CDN (Reynard 99I-Mercedes Benz E3), 248.
Most laps led: Papis, 143.
Fastest qualifying lap: Vasser, 31.358s, 229.606 mph/ 369.516 km/h.
Championship points: 1 Montoya, 129; **2** Franchitti, 116; **3** Andretti, 107; **4** Fittipaldi, 101; **5** Fernandez, 95; **6** Tracy, 90.

TENNECO AUTOMOTIVE GRAND PRIX OF DETROIT, The Raceway on Belle Isle, Detroit, Michigan, USA, 8 August. Round 13. 71 laps of the 2.346-mile/3.776-km circuit, 166.566 miles/268.062 km.
1 Dario Franchitti, GB (Reynard 99I-Honda Turbo V8), 2h 02m 24.662s, 81.643 mph/131.391 km/h.
2 Paul Tracy, USA (Reynard 99I-Honda Turbo V8), 2h 02m 24.797s; **3** Greg Moore, CDN (Reynard 99I-Mercedes Benz E3), 2h 02m 25.192s; **4** Michael Andretti, USA (Swift 010.c-Ford Cosworth XD), 2h 02m 26.133s; **5** Jimmy Vasser, USA (Reynard 99I-Honda Turbo V8), 2h 02m 27.256s; **6** Tony Kanaan, BR (Reynard 99I-Honda Turbo V8), 2h 02m 28.314s; **7** Helio Castro-Neves, BR (Lola B99/00-Mercedes Benz E3), 2h 02m 29.464s; **8** Scott Pruett, USA (Reynard 99I-Toyota), 2h 02m 31.412s; **9** Bryan Herta, USA (Reynard 99I-Ford Cosworth XD), 2h 02m 31.873s; **10** Mark Blundell, GB (Reynard 99I-Mercedes Benz E3), 2h 02m 32.892s;
Most laps led: Juan Pablo Montoya, CO (Reynard 99I-Honda Turbo V8), 58.
Fastest qualifying lap: Montoya, 1m 13.585s, 114.773 mph/ 184.710 km/h.
Championship points: 1 Franchitti, 136; **2** Montoya, 131; **3** Andretti, 119; **4** Tracy, 106; **5** Fittipaldi, 101; **6=** Moore, 95; **6=** Fernandez, 95.

MILLER LITE 200, Mid-Ohio Sports Car Course, Lexington, Ohio, USA, 15 August. Round 14. 83 laps of the 2.258-mile/3.634-km circuit, 186.446 miles/300.056 km.
1 Juan Pablo Montoya, CO (Reynard 99I-Honda Turbo V8), 1h 42m 03.808s, 109.606 mph/176.394 km/h.
2 Paul Tracy, USA (Reynard 99I-Honda Turbo V8), 1h 42m 14.735s; **3** Dario Franchitti, GB (Reynard 99I-Honda Turbo V8), 1h 42m 16.121s; **4** Jimmy Vasser, USA (Reynard 99I-Honda Turbo V8), 1h 42m 18.536s; **5** Massimiliano 'Max' Papis, I (Reynard 99I-Ford Cosworth XD), 1h 42m 23.507s; **6** Gil de Ferran, BR (Reynard 99I-Honda Turbo V8), 1h 42m 27.490s; **7** Helio Castro-Neves, BR (Lola B99/00-Mercedes Benz E3), 1h 42m 28.905s; **8** Michael Andretti, USA (Swift 010.c-Ford Cosworth XD), 1h 42m 35.107s; **9** Cristiano da Matta, BR (Reynard 99I-Toyota), 1h 42m 35.680s; **10** Robby Gordon, USA (Swift 010.c-Toyota), 1h 42m 36.630s.
Most laps led: Franchitti, 54.
Fastest qualifying lap: Franchitti, 1m 05.347s, 124.394 mph/ 200.193 km/h.
Championship points: 1 Franchitti, 152; **2** Montoya, 151; **3** Andretti, 124; **4** Tracy, 122; **5** Fittipaldi, 101; **6** Moore, 97.

TARGET GRAND PRIX PRESENTED BY SHELL, Chicago Motor Speedway, Cicero, Illinois, USA, 22 August. Round 15. 225 laps of the 1.029-miles/1.656-km circuit, 231.525 miles/372.603 km.
1 Juan Pablo Montoya, CO (Reynard 99I-Honda Turbo V8), 1h 53m 38.704s, 122.236 mph/196.720 km/h.
2 Dario Franchitti, GB (Reynard 99I-Honda Turbo V8), 1h 53m 39.487s; **3** Jimmy Vasser, USA (Reynard 99I-Honda Turbo V8), 1h 53m 54.483s; **4** Massimiliano 'Max' Papis, I (Reynard 99I-Ford Cosworth XD), 1h 53m 54.659s; **5** Helio Castro-Neves, BR (Lola B99/00-Mercedes Benz E3), 1h 53m 55.039s; **6** Patrick Carpentier, CDN (Reynard 99I-Mercedes Benz E3), 1h 54m 00.055s; **7** PJ Jones, USA (Reynard 99I-Ford Cosworth XD), 1h 54m 03.237s; **8** Bryan Herta, USA (Reynard 99I-Ford Cosworth XD), 224 laps; **9** Roberto Moreno, BR (Swift 010.c-Ford Cosworth XD), 223; **10** Robby Gordon, USA (Eagle 997-Toyota), 223.
Most laps led: Montoya, 132.
Fastest qualifying lap: Papis, 22.788s, 162.559 mph/ 261.614 km/h.
Championship points: 1 Montoya, 172; **2** Franchitti, 168; **3** Andretti, 124; **4** Tracy, 122; **5** Fittipaldi, 101; **6** Moore, 97.

MOLSON INDY VANCOUVER, Vancouver Street Circuit, Concord Pacific Place, Vancouver, British Columbia, Canada, 5 September. Round 16. 74 laps of the 1.781 mile/2.866-km circuit, 131.794 miles/212.102 km.
1 Juan Pablo Montoya, CO (Reynard 99I-Honda Turbo V8), 2h 01m 08.183s, 65.279 mph/105.056 km/h.
2 Patrick Carpentier, CDN (Reynard 99I-Mercedes Benz E3), 2h 01m 15.768s; **3** Jimmy Vasser, USA (Reynard 99I-Honda Turbo V8), 2h 01m 16.147s; **4** Mauricio Gugelmin, BR (Reynard 99I-Mercedes Benz E3), 2h 01m 21.226s; **5** Cristiano da Matta, BR (Reynard 99I-Toyota), 2h 01m 22.184s; **6** Richie Hearn, USA (Reynard 99I-Toyota), 2h 01m 22.475s; **7** Jan Magnussen, DK (Reynard 99I-Ford Cosworth XD), 2h 01m 23.426s; **8** Helio Castro-Neves, BR (Lola B99/00-Mercedes Benz E3), 2h 01m 23.500s; **9** Tony Kanaan, BR (Reynard 99I-Honda Turbo V8), 2h 01m 24.848s; **10** Dario Franchitti, GB (Reynard 99I-Honda Turbo V8), 2h 01m 27.200s.
Most laps led: Montoya, 38.
Fastest qualifying lap: Montoya, 1m 00.641s, 105.730 mph/ 170.157 km/h.
Championship points: 1 Montoya, 194; **2** Franchitti, 171; **3** Andretti, 124; **4** Tracy, 122; **5** Fittipaldi, 101; **6** Moore, 97.

HONDA GRAND PRIX OF MONTEREY FEATURING THE SHELL 300, Laguna Seca Raceway, Monterey, California, USA, 12 September. Round 17. 83 laps of the 2.238-mile/ 3.602-km circuit, 185.754 miles/298.942 km.
1 Bryan Herta, USA (Reynard 99I-Ford Cosworth XD), 1h 49m 20.898s, 101.924 mph/164.031 km/h.
2 Roberto Moreno, BR (Swift 010.c-Ford Cosworth XD), 1h 49m 22.723s; **3** Massimiliano 'Max' Papis, I (Reynard 99I-Ford Cosworth XD), 1h 49m 24.516s; **4** Paul Tracy, USA (Reynard 99I-Honda Turbo V8), 1h 49m 28.942s; **5** Adrian Fernandez, MEX (Reynard 99I-Ford Cosworth XD), 1h 49m 36.639s; **6** Gil de Ferran, BR (Reynard 99I-Honda Turbo V8), 1h 49m 37.387s; **7** Scott Pruett, USA (Reynard 99I-Toyota), 1h 49m 38.203s; **8** Juan Pablo Montoya, CO (Reynard 99I-Honda Turbo V8), 1h 49m 38.763s; **9** Patrick Carpentier, CDN (Reynard 99I-Mercedes Benz E3), 1h 49m 39.244s; **10** Michael Andretti, USA (Swift 010.c-Ford Cosworth XD), 1h 49m 39.744s.
Most laps led: Herta, 83.
Fastest qualifying lap: Herta, 1m 08.334s, 117.903 mph/ 189.747 km/h.
Championship points: 1 Montoya, 199; **2** Franchitti, 171; **3** Tracy, 134; **4** Andretti, 127; **5=** Fernandez, 105; **5=** Papis, 105.

TEXACO GRAND PRIX OF HOUSTON, Houston Street Circuit, Texas, USA, 26 September. Round 18. 100 laps of the 1.527-mile/2.457-km circuit, 152.026 miles/244.662 km.
1 Paul Tracy, USA (Reynard 99I-Honda Turbo V8), 1h 55m 31.263s, 78.960 mph/127.074 km/h.
2 Dario Franchitti, GB (Reynard 99I-Honda Turbo V8), 1h 55m 44.996s; **3** Michael Andretti, USA (Swift 010.c-Ford Cosworth XD), 1h 55m 57.124s; **4** Massimiliano 'Max' Papis, I (Reynard 99I-Ford Cosworth XD), 1h 55m 58.795s; **5** Bryan Herta, USA (Reynard 99I-Ford Cosworth XD), 1h 56m 12.201s; **6** Mauricio Gugelmin, BR (Reynard 99I-Mercedes Benz E3), 1h 56m 15.426s; **7** Christian Fittipaldi, BR (Swift 010.c-Ford Cosworth XD), 1h 56m 15.873s; **8** Richie Hearn, USA (Reynard 99I-Toyota), 1h 56m 20.125s; **9** Tony Kanaan, BR (Reynard 99I-Honda Turbo V8), 99 laps; **10** Scott Pruett, USA (Reynard 99I-Toyota), 99.
Most laps led: Tracy, 85.
Fastest qualifying lap: Montoya, 58.699s, 93.651 mph/ 150.716 km/h.
Championship points: 1 Montoya, 200; **2** Franchitti, 187; **3** Tracy, 155; **4** Andretti, 141; **5** Papis, 117; **6** Fittipaldi, 107.

HONDA INDY 300, Surfers Paradise Street Circuit, Gold Coast, Queensland, Australia, 17 October. Round 19. 65 laps of the 2.795-mile/4.498-km circuit, 181.675 miles/ 292.378 km.
1 Dario Franchitti, GB (Reynard 99I-Honda Turbo V8), 1h 58m 40.726s, 91.849 mph/147.816 km/h.
2 Massimiliano 'Max' Papis, I (Reynard 99I-Ford Cosworth XD), 1h 58m 43.335s; **3** Adrian Fernandez, MEX (Reynard 99I-Ford Cosworth XD), 1h 58m 48.171s; **4** Bryan Herta, USA (Reynard 99I-Ford Cosworth XD), 1h 58m 51.119s; **5** Michael Andretti, USA (Swift 010.c-Ford Cosworth XD), 1h 58m 51.911s; **6** Tony Kanaan, BR (Reynard 99I-Honda Turbo V8), 1h 58m 52.085s; **7** Paul Tracy, USA (Reynard 99I-Honda Turbo V8), 1h 58m 52.456s; **8** Robby Gordon, USA (Eagle 997-Toyota), 1h 59m 00.616s; **9** Scott Pruett, USA (Reynard 99I-Toyota), 1h 59m 02.054s; **10** Gualter Salles, BR (Reynard 99I-Mercedes Benz E3), 1h 59m 08.820s.
Most laps led: Franchitti, 49.
Fastest qualifying lap: Franchitti, 1m 31.703s, 109.724 mph/ 176.583 km/h.
Championship points: 1 Franchitti, 209; **2** Montoya, 200; **3** Tracy, 161; **4** Andretti, 151; **5** Papis, 133; **6** Fernandez, 120.

MARLBORO 500 PRESENTED BY TOYOTA, California Speedway, Fontana, California, USA, 31 October. Round 20. 250 laps of the 2.029-mile/3.265-km circuit, 507.250 miles/816.340 km.
1 Adrian Fernandez, MEX (Reynard 99I-Ford Cosworth XD), 2h 57m 17.542s, 171.666 mph/276.269 km/h.
2 Massimiliano 'Max' Papis, I (Reynard 99I-Ford Cosworth XD), 2h 57m 25.176s; **3** Christian Fittipaldi, BR (Swift 010.c-Ford Cosworth XD), 2h 57m 26.385s; **4** Juan Pablo Montoya, CO (Reynard 99I-Honda Turbo V8), 2h 57m 31.858s; **5** Jimmy Vasser, USA (Reynard 99I-Honda Turbo V8), 2h 57m 38.248s; **6** Mauricio Gugelmin, BR (Reynard 99I-Mercedes Benz E3), 2h 58m 01.738s; **7** Al Unser Jr., USA (Penske PC27B-Mercedes Benz E3), 249 laps; **8** Tony Kanaan, BR (Reynard 99I-Honda Turbo V8), 249; **9** Gil de Ferran, BR (Reynard 99I-Honda Turbo V8), 249; **10** Dario Franchitti, GB (Reynard 99I-Honda Turbo V8), 248.
Most laps led: Papis, 111.
Fastest qualifying lap: Scott Pruett, USA (Reynard 99I-Toyota), 31.030s, 235.398 mph/378.836 km/h.

Final championship points
1 Juan Pablo Montoya, CO, 212; **2** Dario Franchitti, GB, 212; **3** Paul Tracy, CDN, 161; **4** Michael Andretti, USA, 151; **5** Massimiliano 'Max' Papis, I, 150; **6** Adrian Fernandez, MEX, 140; **7** Christian Fittipaldi, BR, 121; **8** Gil de Ferran, BR, 108; **9** Jimmy Vasser, USA, 104; **10** Greg Moore ≈, CDN, 97; **11** Tony Kanaan, BR, 85; **12** Bryan Herta, USA, 84; **13** Patrick Carpentier, CDN, 61; **14** Roberto Moreno, BR, 58; **15** Helio Castro-Neves, BR, 48; **16** Mauricio Gugelmin, BR, 44; **17** PJ Jones, USA, 38; **18** Cristiano da Matta, BR, 32; **19** Scott Pruett, USA, 28; **20** Robby Gordon, USA, 27; **21=** Al Unser Jr., USA, 26; **21=** Richie Hearn, USA, 26; **23** Mark Blundell, GB, 9; **24** Jan Magnussen, DK, 8; **25** Michel Jourdain Jr., MEX, 7; **26** Gualter Salles, BR, 5; **27=** Alex Barron, USA, 4; **27=** Tarso Marques, BR, 4; **27=** Memo Gidley, USA, 4; **30=** Dennis Vitolo, USA, 2; **30=** Andrea Montermini, I, 2; **32=** Raul Boesel, BR, 1; **32=** Gonzalo Rodriguez †, 1.

Nations' Cup
1 Brazil, 271; **2** United States, 264; **3** Canada, 248; **4=** Colombia, 212; **4=** Scotland, 212; **6** Italy, 152; **7** Mexico, 140; **8** England, 9; **9** Denmark, 8; **10** Uruguay, 1.

Manufacturers' Championship (engines)
1 Honda, 383; **2** Ford Cosworth, 301; **3** Mercedes Benz, 193; **4** Toyota, 80.

Constructors' Championship
1 Reynard, 424; **2** Swift, 241; **3** Lola, 69; **4** Eagle, 13; **5** Penske, 10.

Rookie of the Year
1 Juan Pablo Montoya.

Marlboro Pole Award
1 Juan Pablo Montoya; 2= Dario Franchitti; 2= Gil de Ferran.

Indy Car race

83rd INDIANAPOLIS 500, Indianapolis Motor Speedway, Speedway, Indiana, USA, 30 May. 200 laps of the 2.500-mile/4.023-km circuit, 500.000 miles/804.672 km.
1 Kenny Bräck, S (Dallara-Aurora), 3h 15m 51.182s, 153.176 mph/246.513 km/h.
2 Jeff Ward, USA (Dallara-Aurora), 3h 15m 57.744s; **3** Billy Boat, USA (Dallara-Aurora), 200 laps; **4** Robby Gordon, USA (Dallara-Aurora), 200; **5** Robby McGehee, USA (Dallara-Aurora), 199; **6** Robbie Buhl, USA (Dallara-Aurora), 199; **7** Buddy Lazier, USA (Dallara-Aurora), 198; **8** Robby Unser, USA (Dallara-Aurora), 197; **9** Tony Stewart, USA (Dallara-Aurora), 196; **10** Hideshi Matsuda, J (Dallara-Aurora), 196; **11** Davey Hamilton, USA (Dallara-Aurora), 196; **12** Raul Boesel, BR (Riley &

Scott-Aurora), 195; **13** John Hollinsworth Jr., USA (Dallara-Aurora), 192; **14** Tyce Carlson, USA (Dallara-Aurora), 190; **15** Jeret Schroeder, USA (G-Force-Infiniti), 175 (DNF – engine); **16** Mark Dismore, USA (Dallara-Aurora), 168 (DNF – accident); **17** Stan Wattles, USA (Dallara-Aurora), 147; **18** Eddie Cheever, Jr., USA (Dallara-Infiniti), 139 (DNF – engine); **19** Buzz Calkins, USA (G-Force-Aurora), 133; **20** Roberto Moreno, BR (G-Force-Aurora), 122 (DNF – transmission); **21** Greg Ray, USA (Dallara-Aurora), 120 (DNF – accident); **22** Arie Luyendyk, NL (G-Force-Aurora), 117 (DNF – accident); **23** Wim Eyckmans, B (Dallara-Aurora), 113 (DNF – timing chain); **24** Jimmy Kite, USA (G-Force-Aurora), 111 (DNF – engine); **25** Roberto Guerrero, USA (G-Force-Infiniti), 105 (DNF – engine); **26** Steve Knapp, USA (G-Force-Aurora), 104 (DNF – handling); **27** Scott Goodyear, CDN (G-Force-Aurora), 101 (DNF – engine); **28** Scott Sharp, USA (Dallara-Aurora), 83 (DNF – transmission); **29** Donnie Beechler, USA (Dallara-Aurora), 74 (DNF – engine); **30** Sam Schmidt, USA (G-Force-Aurora), 62 (DNF – accident); **31** Dr. Jack Miller, USA (Dallara-Aurora), 29 (DNF – clutch); **32** Johnny Unser, USA (Dallara-Aurora), 10 (DNF – brakes); **33** Eliseo Salazar, RCH (G-Force-Aurora), 7 (DNF – accident). (Engines: Aurora = Oldsmobile; Infinity = Nissan).
Most laps led: Bräck, 66.
Fastest race lap: Ray, 41.118s, 218.882 mph/352.257 km/h.
Fastest leading lap: Luyendyk, 41.242s, 218.224 mph/351.198 km/h.
Fastest qualifying lap: Luyendyk, 2m 39.873s, 225.179 mph/362.390 km/h (over four laps).

NASCAR Winston Cup

DAYTONA 500, Daytona International Speedway, Daytona Beach, Florida, USA, 14 February. Round 1. 200 laps of the 2.500-mile/4.023-km circuit, 500.000 miles/804.672 km.
1 Jeff Gordon, USA (Chevrolet Monte Carlo), 3h 05m 42.0s, 161.551 mph/259.991 km/h.
2 Dale Earnhardt, USA (Chevrolet Monte Carlo), 3h 05m 42.128s; **3** Kenny Irwin Jr., USA (Ford Taurus), 200 laps; **4** Mike Skinner, USA (Chevrolet Monte Carlo), 200; **5** Michael Waltrip, USA (Chevrolet Monte Carlo), 200; **6** Ken Schrader, USA (Chevrolet Monte Carlo), 200; **7** Kyle Petty, USA (Pontiac Grand Prix), 200; **8** Rusty Wallace, USA (Ford Taurus), 200; **9** Chad Little, USA (Ford Taurus), 200; **10** Rick Mast, USA (Ford Taurus), 200.
Fastest qualifying lap: Gordon, 46.138s, 195.067 mph/313.930 km/h.
Drivers' championship points: **1** Gordon, 180; **2** Earnhardt, 170; **3=** Irwin Jr., 165; **3=** Skinner, 165; **5** Waltrip (Michael), 155; **6** Wallace (Rusty), 152.

DURA LUBE/BIG KMART 400, North Carolina Motor Speedway, Rockingham, North Carolina, USA, 21 February. Round 2. 393 laps of the 1.017-mile/1.637-km circuit, 399.681 miles/643.224 km.
1 Mark Martin, USA (Ford Taurus), 3h 18m 36.0s, 120.750 mph/194.328 km/h.
2 Dale Jarrett, USA (Ford Taurus), 3h 18m 37.397s; **3** Bobby Labonte, USA (Pontiac Grand Prix), 393 laps; **4** Jeff Burton, USA (Ford Taurus), 393; **5** Jeremy Mayfield, USA (Ford Taurus), 393; **6** Mike Skinner, USA (Chevrolet Monte Carlo), 393; **7** Terry Labonte, USA (Chevrolet Monte Carlo), 393; **8** Geoff Bodine, USA (Chevrolet Monte Carlo), 393; **9** Bobby Hamilton, USA (Chevrolet Monte Carlo), 393; **10** Rusty Wallace, USA (Ford Taurus), 393.
Fastest qualifying lap: Ricky Rudd, USA (Ford Taurus), 23.284s, 157.241 mph/253.055 km/h.
Drivers' championship points: **1** Skinner, 315; **2** Wallace (Rusty), 286; **3** Schrader, 280; **4=** Labonte (Bobby), 263; **4=** Mayfield, 263; **6** Irwin Jr., 259.

LAS VEGAS 400, Las Vegas Motor Speedway, Nevada, USA, 7 March. Round 3. 267 laps of the 1.500-mile/2.414-km circuit, 400.500 miles/644.542 km.
1 Jeff Burton, USA (Ford Taurus), 2h 54m 43.0s, 137.537 mph/221.344 km/h.
2 Ward Burton, USA (Pontiac Grand Prix), 2h 54m 44.074s; **3** Jeff Gordon, USA (Chevrolet Monte Carlo), 267 laps; **4** Mike Skinner, USA (Chevrolet Monte Carlo), 267; **5** Bobby Labonte, USA (Pontiac Grand Prix), 267; **6** Ernie Irvan, USA (Pontiac Grand Prix), 267; **7** Dale Earnhardt, USA (Chevrolet Monte Carlo), 267; **8** Terry Labonte, USA (Chevrolet Monte Carlo), 267; **9** Rusty Wallace, USA (Ford Taurus), 267; **10** Mark Martin, USA (Ford Taurus), 267.
Fastest qualifying lap: Labonte (Bobby), 31.645s, 170.643 mph/274.623 km/h.
Drivers' championship points: **1** Skinner, 475; **2** Wallace (Rusty), 424; **3** Labonte (Bobby), 423; **4** Burton (Jeff), 413; **5** Gordon, 401; **6=** Martin, 389; **6=** Schrader, 389.

CRACKER BARREL 500, Atlanta Motor Speedway, Hampton, Georgia, USA, 14 March. Round 4. 325 laps of the 1.540-mile/2.478-km circuit, 500.500 miles/805.477 km.
1 Jeff Gordon, USA (Chevrolet Monte Carlo), 3h 29m 35.0s, 143.284 mph/230.594 km/h.
2 Bobby Labonte, USA (Pontiac Grand Prix), 3h 29m 37.537s; **3** Mark Martin, USA (Ford Taurus), 325 laps; **4** Jeff Burton, USA (Ford Taurus), 325; **5** Dale Jarrett, USA (Ford Taurus), 325; **6** Mike Skinner, USA (Chevrolet Monte Carlo), 325; **7** Ernie Irvan, USA (Pontiac Grand Prix), 325; **8** Ward Burton, USA (Pontiac Grand Prix), 325; **9** Chad Little, USA (Ford Taurus), 325; **10** Michael Waltrip, USA (Chevrolet Monte Carlo), 325.
Fastest qualifying lap: Labonte (Bobby), 28.437s, 194.957 mph/313.753 km/h.
Drivers' championship points: **1** Skinner, 630; **2** Labonte (Bobby), 598; **3** Gordon, 586; **4** Burton (Jeff), 578; **5** Martin, 554; **6** Jarrett, 512.

TRANSOUTH FINANCIAL 400, Darlington Raceway, South Carolina, USA, 21 March. Round 5. 164 laps of the 1.366-mile/2.198-km circuit, 224.024 miles/360.532 km. Scheduled for 293 laps, but stopped early, due to an accident.
1 Jeff Burton, USA (Ford Taurus), 1h 50m 49.0s, 121.294 mph/195.204 km/h.
2 Jeremy Mayfield, USA (Ford Taurus), 164 laps (under caution); **3** Jeff Gordon, USA (Chevrolet Monte Carlo), 164; **4** Dale Jarrett, USA (Ford Taurus), 164; **5** Mark Martin, USA (Ford Taurus), 164; **6** Tony Stewart, USA (Pontiac Grand Prix), 164; **7** Bobby Hamilton, USA (Chevrolet Monte Carlo), 164; **8** Ward Burton, USA (Pontiac Grand Prix), 164; **9** John Andretti, USA (Pontiac Grand Prix), 164; **10** Bobby Labonte, USA (Pontiac Grand Prix), 164.
Fastest qualifying lap: Gordon, 28.396s, 173.179 mph/278.705 km/h.
Drivers' championship points: **1** Burton (Jeff), 763; **2** Gordon, 756; **3** Labonte (Bobby), 737; **4** Martin, 714; **5** Skinner, 697; **6** Jarrett, 672.

PRIMESTAR 500, Texas Motor Speedway, Fort Worth, Texas, USA, 28 March. Round 6. 334 laps of the 1.500-mile/2.414-km circuit, 501.000 miles/806.281 km.
1 Terry Labonte, USA (Chevrolet Monte Carlo), 3h 28m 21.0s, 144.276 mph/232.190 km/h.
2 Dale Jarrett, USA (Ford Taurus), 334 laps (under caution); **3** Bobby Labonte, USA (Pontiac Grand Prix), 334; **4** Rusty Wallace, USA (Ford Taurus), 334; **5** Jeremy Mayfield, USA (Ford Taurus), 334; **6** Tony Stewart, USA (Pontiac Grand Prix), 334; **7** Jeff Burton, USA (Ford Taurus), 334; **8** Dale Earnhardt, USA (Chevrolet Monte Carlo), 334; **9** Sterling Marlin, USA (Chevrolet Monte Carlo), 334; **10** Elliott Sadler, USA (Ford Taurus), 334.
Fastest qualifying lap: Kenny Irwin Jr., USA (Ford Taurus), 28.398s, 190.154/306.024 km/h.
Drivers' championship points: **1** Burton (Jeff), 909; **2** Labonte (Bobby), 907; **3** Jarrett, 847; **4** Gordon, 790; **5** Labonte (Terry), 786; **6** Martin, 780.

FOOD CITY 500, Bristol Motor Speedway, Tennessee, USA, 11 April. Round 7. 500 laps of the 0.533-mile/0.858-km circuit, 266.500 miles/428.890 km.
1 Rusty Wallace, USA (Ford Taurus), 2h 51m 16.0s, 93.363 mph/150.253 km/h.
2 Mark Martin, USA (Ford Taurus), 2h 51m 16.223s; **3** Dale Jarrett, USA (Ford Taurus), 500 laps; **4** John Andretti, USA (Pontiac Grand Prix), 500; **5** Jeff Burton, USA (Ford Taurus), 500; **6** Jeff Gordon, USA (Chevrolet Monte Carlo), 500; **7** Ted Musgrave, USA (Ford Taurus), 500; **8** Kyle Petty, USA (Pontiac Grand Prix), 500; **9** Ward Burton, USA (Pontiac Grand Prix), 500; **10** Dale Earnhardt, USA (Chevrolet Monte Carlo), 500.
Fastest qualifying lap: Wallace (Rusty), 15.333s, 125.142 mph/201.396 km/h.
Drivers' championship points: **1** Burton (Jeff), 1064; **2** Jarrett, 1012; **3** Labonte (Bobby), 959; **4** Martin, 955; **5** Gordon, 940; **6** Labonte (Terry), 910.

GOODY'S BODY PAIN 500, Martinsville Speedway, Virginia, USA, 18 April. Round 8. 500 laps of the 0.526-mile/0.847-km circuit, 263.000 miles/423.257 km.
1 John Andretti, USA (Pontiac Grand Prix), 3h 28m 35.0s, 75.653 mph/121.752 km/h.
2 Jeff Burton, USA (Ford Taurus), 3h 28m 36.066s; **3** Jeff Gordon, USA (Chevrolet Monte Carlo), 500 laps; **4** Mike Skinner, USA (Chevrolet Monte Carlo), 500; **5** Mark Martin, USA (Ford Taurus), 500; **6** Kenny Wallace, USA (Chevrolet Monte Carlo), 500; **7** Rusty Wallace, USA (Ford Taurus), 500; **8** Dale Jarrett, USA (Ford Taurus), 500; **9** Ken Schrader, USA (Chevrolet Monte Carlo), 500; **10** Kyle Petty, USA (Pontiac Grand Prix), 500.
Fastest qualifying lap: Tony Stewart, USA (Pontiac Grand Prix), 19.875s, 95.275 mph/153.331 km/h.
Drivers' championship points: **1** Burton (Jeff), 1239; **2** Jarrett, 1154; **3** Martin, 1115; **4** Gordon, 1110; **5** Labonte (Bobby), 1055; **6** Wallace (Rusty), 1047.

DIEHARD 500, Talladega Superspeedway, Alabama, USA, 25 April. Round 9. 188 laps of the 2.660-mile/4.281-km circuit, 500.080 miles/804.801 km.
1 Dale Earnhardt, USA (Chevrolet Monte Carlo), 3h 03m 38.0s, 163.395 mph/262.959 km/h.
2 Dale Jarrett, USA (Ford Taurus), 3h 03m 38.137s; **3** Mark Martin, USA (Ford Taurus), 188 laps; **4** Bobby Labonte, USA (Pontiac Grand Prix), 188; **5** Tony Stewart, USA (Pontiac Grand Prix), 188; **6** Ken Schrader, USA (Chevrolet Monte Carlo), 188; **7** Kenny Wallace, USA (Chevrolet Monte Carlo), 188; **8** Jerry Nadeau, USA (Ford Taurus), 188; **9** John Andretti, USA (Pontiac Grand Prix), 188; **10** Bill Elliott, USA (Ford Taurus), 188.
Fastest qualifying lap: Schrader, 48.421s, 197.765 mph/318.273 km/h.
Drivers' championship points: **1** Burton (Jeff), 1369; **2** Jarrett, 1329; **3** Martin, 1285; **4** Labonte (Bobby), 1220; **5** Gordon, 1159; **6** Wallace (Rusty), 1087.

CALIFORNIA 500 PRESENTED BY NAPA, California Speedway, Fontana, California, USA, 2 May. Round 10. 250 laps of the 2.000-mile/3.219-km circuit, 500.000 miles/804.672 km.
1 Jeff Gordon, USA (Chevrolet Monte Carlo), 3h 10m 38.0s, 153.370 mph/253.263 km/h.
2 Jeff Burton, USA (Ford Taurus), 3h 10m 42.492s; **3** Bobby Labonte, USA (Pontiac Grand Prix), 250 laps; **4** Tony Stewart, USA (Pontiac Grand Prix), 250; **5** Dale Jarrett, USA (Ford Taurus), 250; **6** Ward Burton, USA (Pontiac Grand Prix), 250; **7** Jeremy Mayfield, USA (Ford Taurus), 250; **8** Wally Dallenbach, USA (Chevrolet Monte Carlo), 250; **9** Terry Labonte, USA (Chevrolet Monte Carlo), 250; **10** Mike Skinner, USA (Chevrolet Monte Carlo), 249.
Fastest qualifying lap: none due to inclement weather.
Drivers' championship points: **1** Burton (Jeff), 1544; **2** Jarrett, 1489; **3** Labonte (Bobby), 1390; **4** Gordon, 1344; **5** Martin, 1339; **6** Stewart, 1247.

PONTIAC EXCITEMENT 400, Richmond International Raceway, Virginia, USA, 15 May. Round 11. 400 laps of the 0.750-mile/1.207-km circuit, 300.000 miles/482.803 km.
1 Dale Jarrett, USA (Ford Taurus), 2h 59m 49.0s, 100.102 mph/161.098 km/h.
2 Mark Martin, USA (Ford Taurus), 2h 59m 49.616s; **3** Bobby Labonte, USA (Pontiac Grand Prix), 400 laps; **4** Bobby Hamilton, USA (Chevrolet Monte Carlo), 400; **5** Rusty Wallace, USA (Ford Taurus), 400; **6** Joe Nemechek, USA (Chevrolet Monte Carlo), 400; **7** Kyle Petty, USA (Pontiac Grand Prix), 400; **8** Dale Earnhardt, USA (Chevrolet Monte Carlo), 400; **9** Ward Burton, USA (Pontiac Grand Prix), 400; **10** Rich Bickle, USA (Pontiac Grand Prix), 400.
Fastest qualifying lap: Jeff Gordon, USA (Chevrolet Monte Carlo), 21.344s, 126.499 mph/203.581 km/h.
Drivers' championship points: **1** Jarrett, 1669; **2** Burton (Jeff), 1606; **3** Labonte (Bobby), 1560; **4** Martin, 1514; **5** Gordon, 1419; **6** Wallace (Rusty), 1372.

COCA-COLA 600, Lowe's Motor Speedway, Concord, North Carolina, USA, 30 May. Round 12. 400 laps of the 1.500-mile/2.414-km circuit, 600.000 miles/965.606 km.
1 Jeff Burton, USA (Ford Taurus), 3h 57m 50.0s, 151.367 mph/243.601 km/h.
2 Bobby Labonte, USA (Pontiac Grand Prix), 3h 57m 50.574s; **3** Mark Martin, USA (Ford Taurus), 400 laps; **4** Tony Stewart, USA (Pontiac Grand Prix), 400; **5** Dale Jarrett, USA (Ford Taurus), 400; **6** Dale Earnhardt, USA (Chevrolet Monte Carlo), 400; **7** Ken Schrader, USA (Chevrolet Monte Carlo), 400; **8** Ward Burton, USA (Pontiac Grand Prix), 399 laps; **9** Mike Skinner, USA (Chevrolet Monte Carlo), 399; **10** Jeremy Mayfield, USA (Ford Taurus), 399.
Fastest qualifying lap: Labonte (Bobby), 29.153s, 185.230 mph/298.098 km/h.
Drivers' championship points: **1** Jarrett, 1824; **2** Burton (Jeff), 1791; **3** Labonte (Bobby), 1735; **4** Martin, 1684; **5** Stewart, 1530; **6** Burton (Ward), 1481.

MBNA PLATINUM 400, Dover Downs International Speedway, Dover, Delaware, USA, 6 June. Round 13. 400 laps of the 1.000-mile/1.609-km circuit, 400.000 miles/643.738 km.
1 Bobby Labonte, USA (Pontiac Grand Prix), 3h 19m 00.0s, 120.603 mph/194.092 km/h.
2 Jeff Gordon, USA (Chevrolet Monte Carlo), 3h 19m 22.071s; **3** Mark Martin, USA (Ford Taurus), 399 laps; **4** Tony Stewart, USA (Pontiac Grand Prix), 399; **5** Dale Jarrett, USA (Ford Taurus), 399; **6** Rusty Wallace, USA (Ford Taurus), 399; **7** Johnny Benson Jr., USA (Ford Taurus), 399; **8** Jeff Burton, USA (Ford Taurus), 399; **9** Jeremy Mayfield, USA (Ford Taurus), 398; **10** Ernie Irvan, USA (Ford Taurus), 398.
Fastest qualifying lap: Labonte (Bobby), 22.596s, 159.320 mph/256.401 km/h.
Drivers' championship points: **1** Jarrett, 1984; **2** Burton (Jeff), 1933; **3** Labonte (Bobby), 1915; **4** Martin, 1854; **5** Stewart, 1700; **6** Gordon, 1645.

KMART 400, Michigan Speedway, Brooklyn, Michigan, USA, 13 June. Round 14. 200 laps of the 2.000-mile/3.219-km circuit, 400.000 miles/643.738 km.
1 Dale Jarrett, USA (Ford Taurus), 2h 17m 56.0s, 173.997 mph/280.021 km/h.
2 Jeff Gordon, USA (Chevrolet Monte Carlo), 2h 17m 56.505s; **3** Jeff Burton, USA (Ford Taurus), 200 laps; **4** Ward Burton, USA (Pontiac Grand Prix), 200; **5** Bobby Labonte, USA (Pontiac Grand Prix), 200; **6** Steve Park, USA (Chevrolet Monte Carlo), 199; **7** Ernie Irvan, USA (Pontiac Grand Prix), 199; **8** John Andretti, USA (Pontiac Grand Prix), 199; **9** Tony Stewart, USA (Pontiac Grand Prix), 198; **10** Mark Martin, USA (Ford Taurus), 198.
Fastest qualifying lap: Gordon, 38.514s, 186.945 mph/300.859 km/h.
Drivers' championship points: **1** Jarrett, 2169; **2** Burton (Jeff), 2103; **3** Labonte (Bobby), 2075; **4** Martin, 1993; **5** Stewart, 1838; **6** Gordon, 1820.

POCONO 500, Pocono Raceway, Long Pond, Pennsylvania, USA, 20 June. Round 15. 200 laps of the 2.500-mile/4.023-km circuit, 500.000 miles/804.672 km.
1 Bobby Labonte, USA (Pontiac Grand Prix), 4h 12m 19.0s, 118.898 mph/191.348 km/h.
2 Jeff Gordon, USA (Chevrolet Monte Carlo), 4h 12m 19.340s; **3** Dale Jarrett, USA (Ford Taurus), 200 laps; **4** Sterling Marlin, USA (Chevrolet Monte Carlo), 200; **5** Mark Martin, USA (Ford Taurus), 200; **6** Tony Stewart, USA (Pontiac Grand Prix), 200; **7** Dale Earnhardt, USA (Chevrolet Monte Carlo), 200; **8** Ernie Irvan, USA (Pontiac Grand Prix), 200; **9** Jeremy Mayfield, USA (Ford Taurus), 200; **10** Bobby Hamilton, USA (Chevrolet Monte Carlo), 200.
Fastest qualifying lap: Marlin, 52.784s, 170.506 mph/274.403 km/h.
Drivers' championship points: **1** Jarrett, 2344; **2** Labonte (Bobby), 2255; **3** Burton (Jeff), 2158; **4** Martin, 2153; **5** Gordon, 1995; **6** Stewart, 1993.

SAVE MART/KRAGEN 350, Sears Point Raceway, Sonoma, California, USA, 27 June. Round 16. 112 laps of the 1.949-mile/3.137-km circuit, 218.288 miles/351.300 km.
1 Jeff Gordon, USA (Chevrolet Monte Carlo), 3h 06m 06.0s, 70.378 mph/113.262 km/h.
2 Mark Martin, USA (Ford Taurus), 3h 06m 06.197s; **3** John Andretti, USA (Pontiac Grand Prix), 112 laps; **4** Rusty Wallace, USA (Ford Taurus), 112; **5** Jimmy Spencer, USA (Ford Taurus), 112; **6** Dale Jarrett, USA (Ford Taurus), 112; **7** Jeremy Mayfield, USA (Ford Taurus), 112; **8** Kyle Petty, USA (Pontiac Grand Prix), 112; **9** Dale Earnhardt, USA (Chevrolet Monte Carlo), 112; **10** Michael Waltrip, USA (Chevrolet Monte Carlo), 112.
Fastest qualifying lap: Gordon, 1m 11.219s, 98.519 mph/158.550 km/h.
Drivers' championship points: **1** Jarrett, 2494; **2** Labonte (Bobby), 2337; **3** Martin, 2328; **4** Burton (Jeff), 2254; **5** Gordon, 2180; **6** Stewart, 2111.

PEPSI 400, Daytona International Speedway, Daytona Beach, Florida, USA, 3 July. Round 17. 160 laps of the 2.500-mile/4.023-km circuit, 400.000 miles/643.738 km.
1 Dale Jarrett, USA (Ford Taurus), 2h 21m 50.0s, 169.213 mph/272.321 km/h.
2 Dale Earnhardt, USA (Chevrolet Monte Carlo), 160 laps (under caution); **3** Jeff Burton, USA (Ford Taurus), 160; **4** Mike Skinner, USA (Chevrolet Monte Carlo), 160; **5** Bobby Labonte, USA (Pontiac Grand Prix), 160; **6** Tony Stewart, USA (Pontiac Grand Prix), 160; **7** Ward Burton, USA (Pontiac Grand Prix), 160; **8** Bobby Hamilton, USA (Chevrolet Monte Carlo), 160; **9** Ernie Irvan, USA (Pontiac Grand Prix), 160; **10** Terry Labonte, USA (Chevrolet Monte Carlo), 160.
Fastest qualifying lap: Joe Nemechek, USA (Chevrolet Monte Carlo), 46.187s, 194.860 mph/313.597 km/h.
Drivers' championship points: **1** Jarrett, 2674; **2** Labonte (Bobby), 2497; **3** Martin, 2440; **4** Burton (Jeff), 2419; **5** Gordon, 2280; **6** Stewart, 2261.

JIFFY LUBE 300, New Hampshire International Speedway, Loudon, New Hampshire, USA, 11 July. Round 18. 300 laps of the 1.058-mile/1.703-km circuit, 317.400 miles/510.806 km.
1 Jeff Burton, USA (Ford Taurus), 3h 06m 56.0s, 101.876 mph/163.953 km/h.
2 Kenny Wallace, USA (Chevrolet Monte Carlo), 3h 06m 57.347s; **3** Jeff Gordon, USA (Chevrolet Monte Carlo), 300 laps; **4** Dale Jarrett, USA (Ford Taurus), 300; **5** Bill Elliott, USA (Ford Taurus), 300; **6** Mark Martin, USA (Ford Taurus), 300; **7** Wally Dallenbach, USA (Chevrolet Monte Carlo), 300; **8** Dale Earnhardt, USA (Chevrolet Monte Carlo), 300; **9** Jimmy Spencer, USA (Ford Taurus), 300; **10** Tony Stewart, USA (Pontiac Grand Prix), 300.
Fastest qualifying lap: Gordon, 29.037s, 131.171 mph/211.099 km/h.
Drivers' championship points: **1** Jarrett, 2839; **2** Burton (Jeff), 2599; **3** Martin, 2590; **4** Labonte (Bobby), 2551; **5** Gordon, 2450; **6** Stewart, 2405.

PENNSYLVANIA 500, Pocono Raceway, Long Pond, Pennsylvania, USA, 25 July. Round 19. 200 laps of the 2.500-mile/4.023-km circuit, 500.000 miles/804.672 km.
1 Bobby Labonte, USA (Pontiac Grand Prix), 4h 16m 27.0s, 116.982 mph/188.264 km/h.
2 Dale Jarrett, USA (Ford Taurus), 4h 16m 35.653s; **3** Mark Martin, USA (Ford Taurus), 200 laps; **4** Tony Stewart, USA (Pontiac Grand Prix), 200; **5** Wally Dallenbach, USA (Chevrolet Monte Carlo), 200; **6** Terry Labonte, USA (Chevrolet Monte Carlo), 200; **7** Rich Bickle, USA (Pontiac Grand Prix), 200; **8** Steve Park, USA (Chevrolet Monte Carlo), 200; **9** Dale Earnhardt, USA (Chevrolet Monte Carlo), 200; **10** Mike Skinner, USA (Chevrolet Monte Carlo), 200.
Fastest qualifying lap: Skinner, 52.801s, 170.451 mph/274.315 km/h.
Drivers' championship points: **1** Jarrett, 3014; **2** Martin, 2760; **3** Labonte (Bobby), 2731; **4** Burton (Jeff), 2659; **5** Stewart, 2565; **6** Gordon, 2522.

BRICKYARD 400, Indianapolis Motor Speedway, Speedway, Indiana, USA, 7 August. Round 20. 160 laps of the 2.500-mile/4.023-km circuit, 400.000 miles/643.738 km.
1 Dale Jarrett, USA (Ford Taurus), 2h 41m 57.0s, 148.194 mph/238.495 km/h.
2 Bobby Labonte, USA (Pontiac Grand Prix), 2h 42m 00.351s; **3** Jeff Gordon, USA (Chevrolet Monte Carlo), 160 laps; **4** Mark Martin, USA (Ford Taurus), 160; **5** Jeff Burton, USA (Ford Taurus), 160; **6** Ward Burton, USA (Pontiac Grand Prix), 160; **7** Tony Stewart, USA (Pontiac Grand Prix), 160; **8** Rusty Wallace, USA (Ford Taurus), 160; **9** Ricky Rudd, USA (Ford Taurus), 160; **10** Dale Earnhardt, USA (Chevrolet Monte Carlo), 160.
Fastest qualifying lap: Gordon, 50.108s, 179.612 mph/289.058 km/h.
Drivers' championship points: **1** Jarrett, 3199; **2** Martin, 2925; **3** Labonte (Bobby), 2906; **4** Burton (Jeff), 2819; **5** Stewart, 2711; **6** Gordon, 2692.

FRONTIER AT THE GLEN, Watkins Glen International, New York, USA, 15 August. Round 21. 90 laps of the 2.450-mile/3.943-km circuit, 220.500 miles/354.860 km.
1 Jeff Gordon, USA (Chevrolet Monte Carlo), 2h 30m 49.0s, 87.722 mph/141.176 km/h.
2 Ron Fellows, USA (Chevrolet Monte Carlo), 2h 30m 49.763s; **3** Rusty Wallace, USA (Ford Taurus), 90 laps; **4** Dale Jarrett, USA (Ford Taurus), 90; **5** Jerry Nadeau, USA (Ford Taurus), 90; **6** Tony Stewart, USA (Pontiac Grand Prix), 90; **7** Wally Dallenbach, USA (Chevrolet Monte Carlo), 90; **8** Kyle Petty, USA (Pontiac Grand Prix), 90; **9** Mike Skinner, USA (Chevrolet Monte Carlo), 90; **10** Mark Martin, USA (Ford Taurus), 90.
Fastest qualifying lap: Wallace (Rusty), 1m 12.752s, 121.234 mph/195.107 km/h.
Drivers' championship points: **1** Jarrett, 3359; **2** Martin, 3059; **3** Labonte (Bobby), 2997; **4** Burton (Jeff), 2943; **5** Gordon, 2877; **6** Stewart, 2861.

PEPSI 400 PRESENTED BY MEIJER, Michigan Speedway, Brooklyn, Michigan, USA, 22 August. Round 22. 200 laps of the 2.000-mile/3.219-km circuit, 400.000 miles/643.738 km.
1 Bobby Labonte, USA (Pontiac Grand Prix), 2h 46m 17.0s, 144.332 mph/232.280 km/h.
2 Jeff Gordon, USA (Chevrolet Monte Carlo), 2h 46m 17.865s; **3** Tony Stewart, USA (Pontiac Grand Prix), 200 laps; **4** Dale Jarrett, USA (Ford Taurus), 200; **5** Dale Earnhardt, USA (Chevrolet Monte Carlo), 200; **6** Chad Little, USA (Ford Taurus), 200; **7** Mark Martin, USA (Ford Taurus), 200; **8** Jimmy Spencer, USA (Ford Taurus), 200; **9** Hut Stricklin, USA (Ford Taurus), 200; **10** John Andretti, USA (Pontiac Grand Prix), 200.
Fastest qualifying lap: Burton (Ward), 38.127s, 188.843 mph/303.913 km/h.
Drivers' championship points: **1** Jarrett, 3524; **2** Martin, 3210; **3** Labonte (Bobby), 3177; **4** Gordon, 3057; **5** Stewart, 3031; **6** Burton (Jeff), 2995.

GOODY'S HEADACHE POWDER 500, Bristol Motor Speedway, Tennessee, USA, 28 August. Round 23. 500 laps of the 0.533-mile/0.858-km circuit, 266.500 miles/428.890 km.
1 Dale Earnhardt, USA (Chevrolet Monte Carlo), 2h 55m 11.0s, 91.276 mph/146.894 km/h.
2 Jimmy Spencer, USA (Ford Taurus), 2h 55m 11.189s; **3** Ricky Rudd, USA (Ford Taurus), 500 laps; **4** Jeff Gordon, USA (Chevrolet Monte Carlo), 500; **5** Tony Stewart, USA (Pontiac Grand Prix), 500; **6** Mark Martin, USA (Ford Taurus), 500; **7** Sterling Marlin, USA (Chevrolet Monte Carlo), 500; **8** Terry Labonte, USA (Chevrolet Monte Carlo), 499; **9** Ward Burton, USA (Pontiac Grand Prix), 499; **10** Ken Schrader, USA (Chevrolet Monte Carlo), 499.
Fastest qualifying lap: Stewart, 15.401s, 124.589 mph/200.507 km/h.
Drivers' championship points: **1** Jarrett, 3573; **2** Martin, 3360; **3** Labonte (Bobby), 3262; **4** Gordon, 3222; **5** Stewart, 3196; **6** Burton (Jeff), 3107.

PEPSI SOUTHERN 500, Darlington Raceway, South Carolina, USA, 5 September. Round 24. 270 laps of the 1.366-mile/2.198-km circuit, 368.820 miles/593.558 km. Scheduled for 367 laps, but stopped early, due to rain.
1 Jeff Burton, USA (Ford Taurus), 3h 25m 15.0s, 107.816 mph/173.513 km/h.
2 Ward Burton, USA (Pontiac Grand Prix), 270 laps (under caution); **3** Jeremy Mayfield, USA (Ford Taurus), 270; **4** Mark Martin, USA (Ford Taurus), 270; **5** Kevin Lepage, USA (Frd Taurus), 270; **6** Joe Nemechek, USA (Chevrolet Monte Carlo), 270; **7** Bobby Hamilton, USA (Chevrolet Monte Carlo), 270; **8** Rusty Wallace, USA (Ford Taurus), 270; **9** Ken Schrader, USA (Chevrolet Monte Carlo), 270; **10** Steve Park, USA (Chevrolet Monte Carlo), 270.

Fastest qualifying lap: Kenny Irwin Jr., USA (Ford Taurus), 28.763s, 170.970 mph/275.149 km/h.
Drivers' championship points: **1** Jarrett, 3693; **2** Martin, 3525; **3** Labonte (Bobby), 3373; **4** Gordon, 3351; **5** Stewart, 3323; **6** Burton (Jeff), 3292.

EXIDE NASCAR SELECT BATTERIES 400, Richmond International Raceway, Virginia, USA, 11 September. Round 25. 400 laps of the 0.750-mile/1.207-km circuit, 300.000 miles/482.803 km.
1 Tony Stewart, USA (Pontiac Grand Prix), 2h 53m 04.0s, 104.006 mph/167.382 km/h.
2 Bobby Labonte, USA (Pontiac Grand Prix), 2h 53m 05.115s; **3** Dale Jarrett, USA (Ford Taurus), 400 laps; **4** Sterling Marlin, USA (Chevrolet Monte Carlo), 400; **5** Kenny Irwin Jr., USA (Ford Taurus), 400; **6** Dale Earnhardt, USA (Chevrolet Monte Carlo), 400; **7** Bobby Hamilton, USA (Chevrolet Monte Carlo), 400; **8** Ted Musgrave, USA (Ford Taurus), 400; **9** John Andretti, USA (Pontiac Grand Prix), 399; **10** Dale Earnhardt Jr., USA (Chevrolet Monte Carlo), 399.
Fastest qualifying lap: Skinner, 21.520s, 125.465 mph/201.916 km/h.
Drivers' championship points: **1** Jarrett, 3858; **2** Martin, 3588; **3** Labonte (Bobby), 3548; **4** Stewart, 3508; **5** Burton (Jeff), 3416; **6** Gordon, 3399.

DURA-LUBE/KMART 300, New Hampshire International Speedway, Loudon, New Hampshire, USA, 19 September. Round 26. 300 laps of the 1.058-mile/1.703-km circuit, 317.400 miles/510.806 km.
1 Joe Nemechek, USA (Chevrolet Monte Carlo), 3h 09m 10.0s, 100.673 mph/162.018 km/h.
2 Tony Stewart, USA (Pontiac Grand Prix), 300 laps (under caution); **3** Bobby Labonte, USA (Pontiac Grand Prix), 300 laps; **4** Jeff Burton, USA (Ford Taurus), 300; **5** Jeff Gordon, USA (Chevrolet Monte Carlo), 300; **6** Rusty Wallace, USA (Ford Taurus), 300; **7** Johnny Benson Jr., USA (Ford Taurus), 300; **8** Ward Burton, USA (Pontiac Grand Prix), 300; **9** Rick Mast, USA (Ford Taurus), 300; **10** Kenny Irwin Jr., USA (Ford Taurus), 300.
Fastest qualifying lap: Wallace (Rusty), 29.339s, 129.820 mph/208.926 km/h.
Drivers' championship points: **1** Jarrett, 3972; **2** Labonte (Bobby), 3718; **3** Martin, 3700; **4** Stewart, 3683; **5** Burton (Jeff), 3576; **6** Gordon, 3554.

MBNA GOLD 400, Dover Downs International Speedway, Dover, Delaware, USA, 26 September. Round 27. 400 laps of the 1.000-mile/1.609-km circuit, 400.000 miles/643.738 km.
1 Mark Martin, USA (Ford Taurus), 3h 08m 20.0s, 127.434 mph/205.085 km/h.
2 Tony Stewart, USA (Pontiac Grand Prix), 3h 08m 21.145s; **3** Dale Jarrett, USA (Ford Taurus), 400 laps; **4** Matt Kenseth, USA (Ford Taurus), 400; **5** Bobby Labonte, USA (Pontiac Grand Prix), 400; **6** Jeff Burton, USA (Ford Taurus), 400; **7** Chad Little, USA (Ford Taurus), 399; **8** Dale Earnhardt, USA (Chevrolet Monte Carlo), 399; **9** Steve Park, USA (Chevrolet Monte Carlo), 399; **10** Kenny Irwin Jr., USA (Ford Taurus), 399.
Fastest qualifying lap: Wallace (Rusty), 22.505s, 159.964 mph/257.438 km/h.
Drivers' championship points: **1** Jarrett, 4142; **2** Martin, 3885; **3** Labonte (Bobby), 3878; **4** Stewart, 3858; **5** Burton (Jeff), 3731; **6** Gordon, 3671.

NAPA AUTOCARE 500, Martinsville Speedway, Virginia, USA, 3 October. Round 28. 500 laps of the 0.526-mile/0.847-km circuit, 263.000 miles/423.257 km.
1 Jeff Gordon, USA (Chevrolet Monte Carlo), 3h 38m 07.0s, 72.347 mph/116.431 km/h.
2 Dale Earnhardt, USA (Chevrolet Monte Carlo), 3h 38m 07.198s; **3** Geoff Bodine, USA (Chevrolet Monte Carlo), 500 laps; **4** Rusty Wallace, USA (Ford Taurus), 500; **5** Kenny Wallace, USA (Chevrolet Monte Carlo), 500; **6** Mike Skinner, USA (Chevrolet Monte Carlo), 500; **7** Kyle Petty, USA (Pontiac Grand Prix), 500; **8** Bobby Labonte, USA (Pontiac Grand Prix), 500; **9** Jeff Burton, USA (Ford Taurus), 499; **10** Dale Jarrett, USA (Ford Taurus), 499.
Fastest qualifying lap: Joe Nemechek, USA (Chevrolet Monte Carlo), 19.886s, 95.223 mph/153.246 km/h.
Drivers' championship points: **1** Jarrett, 4276; **2** Labonte (Bobby), 4025; **3** Martin, 4000; **4** Stewart, 3898; **5** Burton (Jeff), 3869; **6** Gordon, 3851.

UAW-GM QUALITY 500, Charlotte Motor Speedway, Concord, North Carolina, USA, 10 October. Round 29. 334 laps of the 1.500-mile/2.414-km circuit, 501.000 miles/806.281 km.
1 Jeff Gordon, USA (Chevrolet Monte Carlo), 3h 07m 31.0s, 160.306 mph/257.987 km/h.
2 Bobby Labonte, USA (Pontiac Grand Prix), 3h 07m 31.851s; **3** Mike Skinner, USA (Chevrolet Monte Carlo), 334 laps; **4** Mark Martin, USA (Ford Taurus), 334; **5** Ward Burton, USA (Pontiac Grand Prix), 334; **6** Jeremy Mayfield, USA (Ford Taurus), 334; **7** Dale Jarrett, USA (Ford Taurus), 334; **8** Rusty Wallace, USA (Ford Taurus), 333; **9** Kevin Lepage, USA (Ford Taurus), 333; **10** Steve Park, USA (Chevrolet Monte Carlo), 333.
Fastest qualifying lap: Labonte (Bobby), 29.082s, 185.682 mph/298.826 km/h.
Drivers' championship points: **1** Jarrett, 4427; **2** Labonte (Bobby), 4205; **3** Martin, 4165; **4** Gordon, 4031; **5** Stewart, 4004; **6** Burton (Jeff), 3921.

WINSTON 500, Talladega Superspeedway, Alabama, USA, 17 October. Round 30. 188 laps of the 2.660-mile/4.281-km circuit, 500.080 miles/804.801 km.
1 Dale Earnhardt, USA (Chevrolet Monte Carlo), 3h 00m 04.0s, 166.632 mph/268.168 km/h.
2 Dale Jarrett, USA (Ford Taurus), 3h 00m 04.114s; **3** Ricky Rudd, USA (Ford Taurus), 188 laps; **4** Ward Burton, USA (Pontiac Grand Prix), 188; **5** Kenny Wallace, USA (Chevrolet Monte Carlo), 188; **6** Tony Stewart, USA (Pontiac Grand Prix), 188; **7** Bobby Labonte, USA (Pontiac Grand Prix), 188; **8** Jeff Burton, USA (Ford Taurus), 188; **9** Bobby Hamilton, USA (Chevrolet Monte Carlo), 188; **10** Kenny Irwin Jr., USA (Ford Taurus), 188.
Fastest qualifying lap: Joe Nemechek, USA (Chevrolet Monte Carlo), 48.283s, 198.331 mph/319.182 km/h.
Drivers' championship points: **1** Jarrett, 4602; **2** Labonte (Bobby), 4356; **3** Martin, 4283; **4** Gordon, 4168; **5** Stewart, 4159; **6** Burton (Jeff), 4063.

POP SECRET MICROWAVE POPCORN 400, North Carolina Motor Speedway, Rockingham, North Carolina, USA, 24 October. Round 31. 393 laps of the 1.017-mile/1.637-km circuit, 399.681 miles/643.224 km.
1 Jeff Burton, USA (Ford Taurus), 3h 02m 55.0s, 131.103 mph/210.989 km/h.
2 Ward Burton, USA (Pontiac Grand Prix), 3h 02m 55.337s; **3** Bobby Labonte, USA (Pontiac Grand Prix), 393 laps; **4** Dale Jarrett, USA (Ford Taurus), 393; **5** Rusty Wallace, USA (Ford Taurus), 393; **6** Mark Martin, USA (Ford Taurus), 393; **7** John Andretti, USA (Pontiac Grand Prix), 393; **8** Sterling Marlin, USA (Chevrolet Monte Carlo), 393; **9** Jeremy Mayfield, USA (Ford Taurus), 392; **10** Bobby Hamilton, USA (Chevrolet Monte Carlo), 392.
Fastest qualifying lap: Martin, 23.263s, 157.383 mph/253.283 km/h.
Drivers' championship points: **1** Jarrett, 4772; **2** Labonte (Bobby), 4526; **3** Martin, 4438; **4** Gordon, 4298; **5** Stewart, 4286; **6** Burton (Jeff), 4243.

CHECKER AUTO PARTS/DURA LUBE 500, Phoenix International Raceway, Arizona, USA, 7 November. Round 32. 312 laps of the 1.000-mile/1.609-km circuit, 312.000 miles/502.115 km.
1 Tony Stewart, USA (Pontiac Grand Prix), 2h 38m 28.0s, 118.132 mph/190.115 km/h.
2 Mark Martin, USA (Ford Taurus), 2h 38m 30.081s; **3** Bobby Labonte, USA (Pontiac Grand Prix), 312 laps; **4** Jeff Burton, USA (Ford Taurus), 312; **5** Ricky Rudd, USA (Ford Taurus), 312; **6** Dale Jarrett, USA (Ford Taurus), 312; **7** Kyle Petty, USA (Pontiac Grand Prix), 312; **8** John Andretti, USA (Pontiac Grand Prix), 312; **9** Wally Dallenbach, USA (Chevrolet Monte Carlo), 312; **10** Jeff Gordon, USA (Chevrolet Monte Carlo), 312.
Fastest qualifying lap: Andretti, 27.126s, 132.714 mph/213.582 km/h.

Provisional championship points
Drivers
1 Dale Jarrett, USA, 4927; **2** Bobby Labonte, USA, 4696; **3** Mark Martin, USA, 4613; **4** Tony Stewart, 4471; **5** Jeff Gordon, USA, 4432; **6** Jeff Burton, USA, 4403; **7** Dale Earnhardt, USA, 4212; **8** Rusty Wallace, USA, 3904; **9** Ward Burton, USA, 3806; **10** Mike Skinner, USA, 3706; **11** Terry Labonte, USA, 3467; **12** Jeremy Mayfield, USA, 3449; **13** Bobby Hamilton, USA, 3342; **14** Ken Schrader, USA, 3297; **15** Steve Park, USA, 3243; **16=** Sterling Marlin, USA, 3210; **16=** John Andretti, USA, 3210; **18** Kenny Irwin Jr., USA, 3198; **19** Jimmy Spencer, USA, 3172; **20** Wally Dallenbach, USA, 3135; **21** Bill Elliott, USA, 3058; **22** Kenny Wallace, USA, 3031; **23** Chad Little, USA, 2997; **24** Kevin Lepage, USA, 2983; **25** Elliott Sadler, USA, 2962; **26** Johnny Benson Jr., USA, 2903; **27** Kyle Petty, USA, 2861; **28** Michael Waltrip, USA, 2859; **29** Geoff Bodine, USA, 2814; **30** Joe Nemechek, USA, 2789.

Raybestos Rookie of the Year: Tony Stewart.
Bud Pole Award Winner: Jeff Gordon.
MCI Worldcom Fast Pace Award (fastest lap): Bobby Labonte.

Manufacturers
1 Ford, 213; **2** Chevrolet, 198; **3** Pontiac, 178.

Results of the Homestead and Atlanta races will be given in AUTOCOURSE 2000/2001.

Other NASCAR races

1998 Result

The Motegi race was run after AUTOCOURSE 1998/99 went to press.

NASCAR THUNDER SPECIAL COCA-COLA 500, Twin Ring Motegi, Haga gun, Japan, 22 November. 201 laps of the 1.549-mile/2.493-km circuit, 311.349 miles/501.068 km.
1 Mike Skinner, USA (Chevrolet Monte Carlo), 2h 45m 58.0s, 112.558 mph/181.145 km/h.
2 Jeff Gordon, USA (Chevrolet Monte Carlo), 201 laps; **3** Jeremy Mayfield, USA (Ford Taurus), 201; **4** Jeff Burton, USA (Ford Taurus), 201; **5** Rusty Wallace, USA (Chevrolet Monte Carlo), 201; **6** Dale Earnhardt Jr., USA (Chevrolet Monte Carlo), 201; **7** Bill Elliott, USA (Ford Taurus), 201; **8** Dale Earnhardt, USA (Chevrolet Monte Carlo), 201; **9** Sterling Marlin, USA (Chevrolet Monte Carlo), 201; **10** Michael Waltrip, USA (Ford Taurus), 199.

1999 Results

THE BUD SHOOTOUT AT DAYTONA, Daytona International Speedway, Daytona Beach, Florida, USA, 7 February, 25 laps of the 2.500-mile/4.023-km circuit, 62.500 miles/100.584 km.
1 Mark Martin, USA (Ford Taurus), 20m 37.964s, 181.750 mph/292.498 km/h.
2 Ken Schrader, USA (Chevrolet Monte Carlo), 20m 38.179s; **3** Bobby Labonte, USA (Pontiac Grand Prix); **4** Mike Skinner, USA (Chevrolet Monte Carlo); **5** Jeremy Mayfield, USA (Ford Taurus); **6** Ward Burton, USA (Pontiac Grand Prix); **7** Rusty Wallace, USA (Ford Taurus); **8** Dale Jarrett, USA (Ford Taurus); **9** Rick Mast, USA (Ford Taurus); **10** Kenny Irwin Jr., USA (Ford Taurus).
Pole Position: Wallace (Rusty).

THE WINSTON, Charlotte Motor Speedway, Concord, North Carolina, USA, 22 May. 70 laps of the 1.500-mile/2.414-km circuit, 105.000 miles/168.981 km. Run over three segments (30, 30 and 10 laps). Aggregate results given.
1 Terry Labonte, USA (Chevrolet Monte Carlo), 34m 20.0s, 183.495 mph/295.307 km/h.
2 Tony Stewart, USA (Pontiac Grand Prix), 34m 21.229s; **3** Jeff Gordon, USA (Chevrolet Monte Carlo), 70 laps; **4** Dale Earnhardt, USA (Chevrolet Monte Carlo), 70; **5** Jeremy Mayfield, USA (Ford Taurus), 70; **6** Geoff Bodine, USA (Chevrolet Monte Carlo), 70; **7** Sterling Marlin, USA (Chevrolet Monte Carlo), 70; **8** Michael Waltrip, USA (Chevrolet Monte Carlo), 70; **9** Bill Elliott, USA (Ford Taurus), 70; **10** John Andretti, USA (Pontiac Grand Prix), 70.
Fastest qualifying lap: Bobby Labonte, USA (Pontiac Grand Prix), 36.777s, 146.831 mph/236.301 km/h.

Result of the Japanese race will be given in AUTOCOURSE 2000/2001.

PPG-Dayton Indy Lights Championship

All cars are Lola T97/20 GS-Buick.

DAYTONA TIRE CHALLENGE, Metro-Dade Homestead Motorsports Complex, Florida, USA, 21 March. Round 1. 67 laps of the 1.502-mile/2.417-km circuit, 100.634 miles/161.955 km.
1 Mario Dominguez, MEX, 36m 56.920s, 163.417 mph/262.994 km/h.
2 Airton Dare, BR, 36m 57.675s; **3** Scott Dixon, AUS, 37m 10.528s; **4** Andy Boss, USA, 37m 17.734s; **5** Casey Mears, USA, 37m 22.130s; **6** Oriol Servia, E, 37m 28.309s; **7** Jonny Kane, GB, 37m 28.726s; **8** Geoff Boss, USA, 37m 29.019s; **9** Chris Menninga, USA, 66 laps; **10** Ben Collins, GB, 66.
Most laps led: Dominguez, 66.
Fastest qualifying lap: Dominguez, 30.103s, 179.623 mph/289.076 km/h.

LONG BEACH INDY LIGHTS RACE, Long Beach Street Circuit, California, USA, 18 April. Round 2. 41 laps of the 1.824-mile/2.935-km circuit, 74.784 miles/120.353 km.
1 Philipp Peter, A, 51m 22.270s, 87.345 mph/140.569 km/h.
2 Scott Dixon, AUS, 51m 23.629s; **3** Geoff Boss, USA, 51m 33.283s; **4** Didier Andre, F, 51m 35.215s; **5** Casey Mears, USA, 51m 35.668s; **6** Mario Dominguez, MEX, 51m 36.213s; **7** Oswaldo Negri Jr., BR, 51m 59.573s; **8** Chris Menninga, USA, 40 laps; **9** Rodolfo Lavin Jr., MEX, 39; **10** Felipe Giaffone, BR, 38.
Most laps led: Giaffone, 38
Fastest qualifying lap: Giaffone, 1m 07.668s, 97.038 mph/156.168 km/h.

NAZARETH INDY LIGHTS RACE, Nazareth Speedway, Pennsylvania, USA, 2 May. Round 3. 100 laps of the 0.946-mile/1.522-km circuit, 94.600 miles/152.244 km.
1 Airton Dare, BR, 46m 29.029s, 122.107 mph/196.512 km/h.
2 Oriol Servia, E, 46m 29.466s; **3** Casey Mears, USA, 46m 30.105s; **4** Scott Dixon, AUS, 46m 46.012s; **5** Ben Collins, GB, 46m 48.462s; **6** Chris Menninga, USA, 46m 48.684s; **7** David Pook, USA, 46m 48.976s; **8** Philipp Peter, A, 46m 53.984s; **9** Rodolfo Lavin Jr., MEX, 99 laps; **10** Guy Smith, GB, 98.
Most laps led: Dare, 87.
Fastest qualifying lap: Servia, 22.225s, 153.233 mph/246.604 km/h.

MILWAUKEE INDY LIGHTS RACE, The Milwaukee Mile, Wisconsin State Fair Park, West Allis, Milwaukee, Wisconsin, USA, 6 June. Round 4. 97 laps of the 1.032-mile/1.661-km circuit, 100.104 miles/161.102 km.
1 Derek Higgins, IRL, 59m 48.353s, 100.429 mph/161.625 km/h.
2 Casey Mears, USA, 59m 48.879s; **3** Tony Renna, USA, 59m 50.257s; **4** Felipe Giaffone, BR, 59m 50.804s; **5** Oriol Servia, E, 59m 51.765s; **6** David Pook, USA, 59m 52.839s; **7** Airton Dare, BR, 59m 55.779s; **8** Guy Smith, GB, 59m 56.135s; **9** Jonny Kane, GB, 59m 56.691s; **10** Andy Boss, USA, 59m 57.393s.
Most laps led: Higgins, 59.
Fastest qualifying lap: Giaffone, 24.918s, 149.097 mph/239.948 km/h.

PORTLAND INDY LIGHTS RACE, Portland International Raceway, Oregon, USA, 20 June. Round 5. 38 laps of the 1.969-mile/3.169-km circuit, 74.822 miles/120.414 km.
1 Philipp Peter, A, 55m 42.214s, 80.593 mph/129.702 km/h.
2 Oriol Servia, E, 55m 42.996s; **3** Guy Smith, GB, 55m 43.645s; **4** Casey Mears, USA, 55m 44.216s; **5** Airton Dare, BR, 55m 44.559s; **6** Jonny Kane, GB, 55m 44.666s; **7** Chris Menninga, USA, 55m 48.745s; **8** Andy Boss, USA, 56m 00.380s; **9** Ben Collins, GB, 37 laps; **10** Felipe Giaffone, BR, 32.
Most laps led: Peter, 38.
Fastest qualifying lap: Servia, 1m 06.112s, 107.218 mph/172.551 km/h.

CLEVELAND INDY LIGHTS RACE, Burke Lakefront Airport Circuit, Cleveland, Ohio, USA, 27 June. Round 6. 36 laps of the 2.106-mile/3.389-km circuit, 75.816 miles/122.014 km.
1 Derek Higgins, IRL, 45m 03.045s, 100.974 mph/162.502 km/h.
2 Oriol Servia, E, 45m 07.411s; **3** Felipe Giaffone, BR, 45m 07.897s; **4** Philipp Peter, A, 45m 08.192s; **5** Airton Dare, BR, 45m 08.491s; **6** Ben Collins, GB, 45m 11.046s; **7** Andy Boss, USA, 45m 12.152s; **8** Casey Mears, USA, 45m 14.926s; **9** Mario Dominguez, MEX, 45m 15.23s; **10** Chris Menninga, USA, 45m 15.196s.
Most laps led: Higgins, 31.
Fastest qualifying lap: Didier Andre, 1m 05.594s, 115.584 mph/186.014 km/h.

TORONTO INDY LIGHTS RACE, Exhibition Place Circuit, Toronto, Ontario, Canada, 18 July. Round 7. 43 laps of the 1.755-mile/2.824-km circuit, 75.465 miles/121.449 km.
1 Geoff Boss, USA, 59m 14.033s, 76.441 mph/123.020 km/h.
2 Oriol Servia, E, 59m 15.338s; **3** Didier Andre, F, 59m 19.598s; **4** Felipe Giaffone, BR, 59m 22.932s; **5** Jonny Kane, GB, 59m 24.192s; **6** Guy Smith, GB, 59m 25.029s; **7** Philipp Peter, A, 59m 25.568s; **8** Casey Mears, USA, 59m 35.309s; **9** Kenny Wilden, USA, 59m 37.009s; **10** Chris Menninga, USA, 59m 50.493s.
Most laps led: Boss, 43.
Fastest qualifying lap: Boss, 1m 04.437s, 98.049 mph/157.795 km/h.

THE DETROIT NEWS 100, Michigan Speedway, Brooklyn, Michigan, USA, 24 July. Round 8. 50 laps of the 2.000-mile/3.219-km circuit, 100.000 miles/160.934 km.
1 Philipp Peter, A, 37m 52.586s, 158.410 mph/254.936 km/h.
2 Casey Mears, USA, 37m 52.588s; **3** Felipe Giaffone, BR, 37m 52.812s; **4** Mario Dominguez, MEX, 37m 52.939s; **5** Oriol Servia, E, 37m 53.013s; **6** Guy Smith, GB, 37m 53.078s; **7** Jonny Kane, GB, 37m 53.092s; **8** Rodolfo Lavin Jr., MEX, 37m 53.232s; **9** Geoff Boss, USA, 37m 53.247s; **10** Andy Boss, USA, 37m 53.676s.
Most laps led: Peter, 49.
Fastest qualifying lap: Kane, 39.486, 182.343 mph/293.453 km/h.

THE DETROIT NEWS CHALLENGE, The Raceway at Belle Isle Park, Detroit, Michigan, USA, 8 August. Round 9. 32 laps of the 2.346-mile/3.776-km circuit, 75.072 miles/120.817 km.
1 Derek Higgins, IRL, 56m 58.424s, 79.060 mph/127.234 km/h.
2 Oriol Servia, E, 56m 59.226s; **3** Jonny Kane, GB, 57m 00.023s; **4** Felipe Giaffone, BR, 57m 06.115s; **5** Didier Andre, F, 57m 06.476s; **6** Geoff Boss, USA, 57m 07.154s; **7** Scott Dixon, AUS, 57m 08.146s; **8** Philipp Peter, A, 57m 08.784s; **9** Casey Mears, USA, 57m 09.501s; **10** Andy Boss, USA, 57m 09.707s.
Most laps led: Higgins, 17.
Fastest qualifying lap: Servia, 1m 22.353s, 102.554 mph/165.044 km/h.

THE MI-JACK 100 OF CHICAGO, Chicago Motor Speedway, Cicero, Illinois, USA, 22 August. Round 10. 97 laps of the 1.029-mile/1.656-km circuit, 99.813 miles/160.633 km.
1 Scott Dixon, AUS, 50m 46.736s, 117.938 mph/189.803 km/h.
2 Guy Smith, GB, 50m 47.098s; **3** Casey Mears, USA, 50m 57.217s; **4** Oriol Servia, E, 50m 57.657s; **5** Mario Dominguez, MEX, 50m 58.200s; **6** Derek Higgins, IRL, 50m 58.868s; **7** Ben Collins, GB, 51m 02.083s; **8** Felipe Giaffone, BR, 51m 02.197s; **9** Jonny Kane, GB, 51m 02.921s; **10** Chris Menninga, USA, 51m 03.431s.
Most laps led: Dixon, 97.
Fastest qualifying lap: Dixon, 25.919s, 142.922 mph/230.011 km/h.

LAGUNA SECA INDY LIGHTS RACE, Laguna Seca Raceway, Monterey, California, USA, 12 September. Round 11. 34 laps of the 2.238-mile/3.602-km circuit, 76.092 miles/122.458 km.
1 Didier Andre, F, 49m 46.824, 91.713 mph/147.598 km/h.
2 Scott Dixon, AUS, 49m 47.395s; **3** Jonny Kane, GB, 49m 51.467s; **4** Guy Smith, GB, 49m 55.271s; **5** Casey Mears, USA, 49m 57.071s; **6** Chris Menninga, USA, 50m 04.044s; **7** Oriol Servia, E, 50m 05.035s; **8** Philipp Peter, A, 50m 08.650s; **9** Boris Derichebourg, F, 50m 22.850s; **10** Luis Miguel Diaz, MEX, 50m 39.755s.
Most laps led: Andre, 33.
Fastest qualifying lap: Smith, 1m 17.425s, 104.059 mph/167.467 km/h.

THE LOS ANGELES TIMES INDY LIGHTS RACE, California Speedway, Fontana, California, USA, 31 October. Round 12. 50 laps of the 2.029-mile/3.265-km circuit, 101.450 miles/163.268 km.
1 Jonny Kane, GB, 46m 51.509s, 129.902 mph/209.057 km/h.
2 Ben Collins, GB, 46m 51.558s; **3** Didier Andre, F, 46m 51.684s; **4** Cory Witherill, USA, 46m 51.863s; **5** Mario Dominguez, MEX, 46m 53.081s; **6** Tony Renna, USA, 46m 53.093s; **7** Chris Menninga, USA, 46m 53.122s; **8** Airton Dare, BR, 46m 53.490s; **9** Rodolfo Lavin Jr., MEX, 46m 53.525s; **10** Philipp Peter, A, 46m 53.811s.
Most laps led: Andre, 23.
Fastest qualifying lap: Kane, 39.198s, 186.346 mph/299.895 km/h.

Final championship points
1 Oriol Servia, E, 130; **2** Casey Mears, USA, 116; **3** Philipp Peter, A, 101; **4** Jonny Kane, GB, 89; **5** Scott Dixon, AUS, 88; **6** Felipe Giaffone, BR, 78; **7** Derek Higgins, IRL, 76; **8** Didier Andre, F, 74; **9** Guy Smith, GB, 71; **10** Airton Dare, BR, 69; **11** Mario Dominguez, MEX, 66; **12** Geoff Boss, USA, 58; **13** Ben Collins, GB, 50; **14** Chris Menninga, USA, 47; **15** Andy Boss, USA, 32; **16** Tony Renna, USA, 22; **17** Rodolfo Lavin Jr., MEX, 19; **18** Cory Witherill, USA, 17; **19** David Pook, USA, 16; **20** Oswaldo Negri Jr., BR, 6; **21=** Boris Derichebourg, F, 4; **21=** Kenny Wilden, USA, 4; **23** Luis Miguel Diaz, MEX, 3.

Nation's Cup
1 United States, 156; **2** Ireland, 139; **3** Brazil, 131; **4** Spain, 130; **5** England, 103; **6** Austria, 101; **7** New Zealand, 88; **8** Mexico, 75; **9** France, 74; **10** Canada, 4.

Rookie of the year
1 Jonny Kane; **2** Scott Dixon; **3** Mario Dominguez; **4** Ben Collins; **5** Chris Menninga; **6** Cory Witherill; **7** Boris Derichebourg; **8** Kenny Wilden; **9** Luis Miguel Diaz; **10** Rolando Quintanilla.